Enhancing Client, Family, and Community Health Management:

Self, Society, State, Systems, and Spirituality

Minhaj A. Qidwai
American Institute of Healthcare Quality, Pakistan & Unet Consultants, Canada

IGI Global
Scientific Publishing
Publishing Tomorrow's Research Today

Vice President of Editorial — Melissa Wagner
Director of Acquisitions — Mikaela Felty
Director of Book Development — Jocelynn Hessler
Production Manager — Mike Brehm
Cover Design — Jose Rosado

Published in the United States of America by
IGI Global Scientific Publishing
701 East Chocolate Avenue
Hershey, PA, 17033, USA
Tel: 717-533-8845
Fax: 717-533-7115
Website: https://www.igi-global.com E-mail: cust@igi-global.com

Library of Congress Cataloging-in-Publication Data

Names: Qidwai, Minhaj editor
Title: Enhancing client, family, and community health management : self, society, state, systems, and spirituality / edited by Minhaj Qidwai.
Description: Hershey, PA : IGI Global Scientific Publishing, [2026] | Includes bibliographical references and index. | Summary: "This book introduces a transformative framework that integrates the concepts of Self, Society, State, and Systems in the realm of healthcare management"-- Provided by publisher.
Identifiers: LCCN 2024055631 (print) | LCCN 2024055632 (ebook) | ISBN 9798369390924 hardcover | ISBN 9798369390931 paperback | ISBN 9798369390948 ebook
Subjects: LCSH: Community health services | Holistic medicine | Social medicine | Health services administration
Classification: LCC RA427 .E564 2025 (print) | LCC RA427 (ebook) | DDC 362.12--dc23/eng/20250409
LC record available at https://lccn.loc.gov/2024055631
LC ebook record available at https://lccn.loc.gov/2024055632

British Cataloguing in Publication Data
A Cataloguing in Publication record for this book is available from the British Library.

This book is dedicated to my parents and family. Their unwavering support and love have been the foundation of my journey in life, playing an instrumental role in shaping the path I walk today. This book is dedicated to my wife Dr. Rubeena Qidwai. Her constant encouragement, insightful guidance and unconditional support at every step, has given me the strength to pursue my professional and academic career. This book is also dedicated to late Prof. Dr. John H. Bryant and Prof. Dr. Ruth Harner, who laid the foundation of Community Health in Pakistan, at the Department of Community Health Sciences-Aga Khan University, where the seeds for Community Health were sown and an insight was fostered among the Healthcare Professionals for managing client beyond clinical management. This book is also dedicated to my classmate, friend and colleague late Dr. Asif Aslam Farrukhi who was an institution himself in community health. To Prof. Dr. Al Assaf of American Institute for Healthcare Quality, as my mentor in pursuing the professional career in Health Management. I would also like to dedicate this book to my beloved children, Dr. Sarah Qidwai, who inspired me in undertaking this scholarly task and to my sons Saad Qidwai and Asad Qidwai.

Editorial Advisory Board

Table of Contents

Detailed Table of Contents

Understanding the central distinctions and connections between the roles of leadership and management and their impact on the context of health service delivery is crucial. Self-awareness, cultural competencies, emotional intelligence, and ethical behavior are key traits at the heart of a good leader, regardless of their favored leadership style. Moreover, three key strategies are necessary for leadership development to occur: an education pathway, mentorship or coaching, and a publication or research appraisal, if deemed appropriate by the individual. With age, experience, and also the learning from mistakes of mismatched attitudes, leadership styles, and behaviors, some of these traits evolve in both senior managers and leaders in pursuit of greater effectiveness for the organization and the employees. Education, workshops, more mentorship, and continuous professional growth among senior management would promote authentic and effective healthcare leadership.

This chapter, "The Role of Self in Health Management," explores the crucial role of individual effort in maintaining and improving health. It focuses on self-management, highlighting how individuals actively engage in their health care, make informed decisions, and adopt behaviors that enhance well-being. The chapter emphasizes self-awareness, motivation, and personal responsibility in managing both physical and mental health. It examines how attitudes, beliefs, and knowledge shape health behaviors, stressing the link between self-confidence and overcoming health challenges. Furthermore, it covers self-care practices, preventive measures, stress reduction, and healthy lifestyle choices as essential for sustaining long-term health. By integrating theoretical insights and research findings, the chapter provides strategies for developing a proactive health mindset, resilience, and adaptability. Additionally, it discusses the empowering impact of digital tools in self-management, urging readers to take an active role in shaping their health for lasting well-being.

In this chapter, the authors provide a basic understanding of the health system and its components. It explores philosophical dimensions of health and how individuals, populations, and health systems are interconnected. The chapter also describes various elements of healthcare systems, including service delivery, healthcare workforce, financing, medical technology, and governance. Furthermore, it discusses the dynamics of the healthcare delivery system, the importance of healthcare planning, and the role of health insurance in providing financial protection. Moreover, the chapter highlights the challenges of healthcare systems, particularly in low- and middle-income countries, and underpins the need for effective management and strategic planning to improve health outcomes. In addition, the chapter introduces the "4S" model—Self, Society, State, and Systems— to highlight how they interact to promote health and well-being. In a nutshell, it provides a foundational understanding of health systems and prepares health professionals to contribute to effective healthcare management.

A quality management system (QMS) integrates planning, assurance, control, and improvement to effectively meet customer needs. In healthcare, where complex interactions involve human patients, advanced technology, and critical infrastructure, the challenges are significant, especially as patients seek care when most vulnerable. Accreditations and certifications provide structured frameworks to assess elements like infrastructure and human resources, using audits based on documentation, observations, and interviews. Though resource-intensive, these methods are the gold standard for healthcare evaluation. However, these processes have limitations. Clinicians often lack evidence of their impact on outcomes, and the focus on accreditation may detract from care quality. In high-income countries (HICs), focusing on quality improvement initiatives is key, while low- and middle-income countries (LMICs) must address all QMS components, given greater systemic challenges. A holistic approach to QMS is essential for meaningful progress, especially in LMICs.

Sensors and wearables are making digital healthcare management a reality by allowing for round the clock health monitoring and individualized care. These gadgets are capable of monitoring the data on vital signs, activities of health and mind as well thereby making us proactive towards healthcare. New technologies facilitate remote diagnostics and treatments through smart implants or AI-driven wearables, leading to better patient outcomes with fewer hospital visits. Increasing amounts of patient engagement thanks to wearable technologies allow individuals greater control over their health and give healthcare providers access more accurate, real-time information for better decision-making. In addition, these advancements enable remote patient monitoring on a larger scale for chronic disease management and provide care to rural or underserved populations. The deployment of these technologies mark a pivot to proactive, patient-specific care and improve health outcomes more broadly at scale.

Early detection of disease is important in healthcare not only for the hope that the patient might get cured, but also due to the low risk factor for conducting an operation. The current chapter will discuss some newly defined techniques and technologies that are changing the way early disease detection is done-from machine learning and wearable health monitoring devices to advanced medical imaging. Right application of newly given medical technology is making the concept of good patient recovery possible by coordinating machine learning with the medical field. Considering predictive algorithm in the identification of diseases with the use of large datasets for identifying the diseases through the help of machine learning and, with an upper hand of AI, finding proper cure along with experience from the doctors is allowing a patient to live more i.e. Better, faster recovery.

All schools of nursing in Pakistan offer community health nursing as a core course. Unfortunately, there aren't enough avenues open for them to practice CHN due to lack of deployment plan. Despite this there are multiple roles that CHNs are performing and can perform at local and national levels. The need is to duly acknowledge this role within the health care delivery model and there is a need for evidenced based studies to explore the impact of these roles on the health of population at local and national levels. This chapter would serve as a guiding tool to make health care delivery system more responsive to health and developmental needs of the country. Moreover, the chapter gives an insight into how the CHNs are actively engaged in various settings and provide population based services with focus on sustainability.

Family Constellations is a therapeutic approach used to reveal and resolve family dynamics that may influence individual health. This chapter explores its application within healthcare, examining both its potential benefits and the ethical challenges it presents. Specifically, it focuses on issues related to patient consent, privacy, the role of cultural sensitivity, and the need for professional boundaries in clinical practice. Drawing on case studies and evidence-based practice, the chapter outlines best practices for incorporating Family Constellations responsibly and effectively into patient care. Strategies for practitioner training, safeguarding vulnerable populations, and aligning therapeutic goals with patient-centred care are discussed. The chapter concludes by proposing guidelines for ethical implementation, emphasising collaborative care models and continued professional reflection.

This chapter explores the application of Family Constellations within community health, emphasising its role in promoting population wellness through systemic healing. By examining the interconnectedness of individual and collective health dynamics, the chapter outlines how unresolved familial patterns impact community well-being. It discusses Family Constellations' potential contributions to addressing key challenges in the care of older people, including loneliness, chronic illness, and social exclusion, while supporting Sustainable Development Goals (SDGs) such as good health and well-being, reduced inequalities, and sustainable communities. Drawing on case studies, theoretical frameworks, and practical applications, the chapter presents evidence-based strategies for integrating this approach into public health initiatives, fostering resilience, social cohesion, and preventive care.

Family Constellations, a therapeutic approach rooted in systemic psychotherapy, offers a novel method for exploring and healing intergenerational trauma and relational dynamics within families. This chapter examines the integration of Family Constellations into mental health care, emphasising its value as a complementary tool alongside conventional intervention. We delve into its relevance for older adults, demonstrating its potential to address issues such as loneliness, unresolved grief, and familial discord. By highlighting connections to nursing practice, emotional intelligence development, and Sustainable Development Goals (SDGs) focused on health, well-being, and social cohesion, we present a holistic model that fosters healing, resilience, and community-centred care. The chapter discusses the evidence base, best practices, and case studies to illustrate practical applications and promote interdisciplinary collaboration.

This chapter explores the profound impact of societal dynamics on health, focusing on Family Constellations as a framework for systemic healing. Rooted in transgenerational psychology, this approach identifies patterns within family systems that contribute to

Considering the limitations of current treatment plans and the rising need for a more holistic approach to health, mixing spirituality into the medical curriculum is indispensable. Standardizing the integration of Energy or Spiritual Diagnostics with Therapeutic Programs Like Guided Consciousness Liberation Program (GCLP) can meaningfully improve health outcomes. By including Spiritual Healing Techniques, Future Healthcare Providers can better address the root causes of illnesses, promote comprehensive healing, and improve the quality of life for their patients.

This chapter explores the principles and implementation of humanistic medicine as a spiritual driver for improving the quality of work life of healthcare providers and managing improved health outcomes. The focus is on integrating the specific attributes of spirituality, like mindfulness, introspection, gratitude, and appreciation, with humanistic medicine's emphasis on its features of empathy, compassion, and holistic care. The goal is to explore how this strategy can improve the quality of work life of healthcare providers, helping them to rediscover their passion and enabling them to provide care that is humanistic and person-centered to improve patient experiences and outcomes. This approach also acts as a spiritual and emotional driver for addressing physician burnout and job satisfaction. The chapter also discusses implementation strategies for humanistic medicine. While discussing the challenges of such an approach to health management, the chapter also advocates policies prioritizing and balancing person-centered care and healthcare provider well-being.

Foreword

It gives me great pleasure to write this foreword on the subject book titled "Enhancing Client, Family, and Community Health Management: Self, Society, State, Systems, and Spirituality". A. Alassaf

Dr. Qidwai introduces the 5S Approach—Self, Society, State, Systems, and Spirituality—rooted in the philosophy of holistic health management. By examining healthcare through these interconnected dimensions, this book equips professionals with the tools to address both the tangible and intangible factors affecting individual and community wellness.

This book is geared towards a diverse audience, including: Healthcare Professionals: Physicians, nurses, and allied health practitioners who seek to enhance their understanding of comprehensive health management. Healthcare Undergraduates: Students in medical and health-related fields who will benefit from a curriculum that includes the 5Ss approach.

Academicians and Researchers: Educators and scholars interested in innovative teaching methods and research in healthcare management. Policy Makers: Individuals involved in health policy development who need insights into the broader implications of health management.

Community Health Managers: Professionals focused on improving community health outcomes through integrated approaches.

The 5Ss' philosophy gives a new dimension to the medical undergraduate and graduate in dealing the patient as a client for managing health of the individual, his family and the community. The expected impact of the book is to:

- Transform the medical curriculum from pure clinical management by HCP to a holistic management of a client.
- Enlighten the healthcare professional for the importance of health management of a client, family and community by adding the concepts of State, Systems, Society, and Self related matters under Spiritual guidelines outlined in the 5S Approach.

- Improve quality of service delivery and patient safety by the HCPs' practice. Thus, improving personal, family and community health.
- Have an overall impact on the healthcare indicators and transformation in the approach towards community health management.

I am honored to contribute this forward to a work that I believe will become a cornerstone for healthcare professionals worldwide. I commend Dr. Minhaj Qidwai for giving a new dimension to the medical curriculum, enabling the healthcare professional to amicably manage health of a client, family and community.

A. Al-Assaf
American Institute for Healthcare Quality, USA

Preface

Considering my experience of more than four decades in healthcare profession, one thing was strongly felt that the undergraduate curriculum is focused mainly on clinical management, dealing with the symptomatic management of patient. So, when these students graduate, they are not familiar with the ground realities in terms of the new environment they have to face in the community. The Healthcare Professionals (HCPs'), who choose for post-graduation lead to a path to be the consultants in their area of specialization; while the others set up their healthcare establishment (HCE). Whatever pathway is chosen the fresh medical graduate is unaware of the family and the community dynamics. There is lacking in the areas of communication skills, coaching and counselling, health administration and management etc., which are imperative in dealing with a client, family and community. Furthermore, he is exposed to a new set of problems and issues apart from patient management. Understanding of Societal aspects, the State policies, laws, rules, regulations and quality standards for patient management. The Health Systems aspects on how to deal with governance and leadership, financial and human resources management, medical products, technology; and service delivery. In addition, as the Health Management aspect is not taught to HCP, there is lack of aspects for Governance-Clinical, Societal, Corporate, Self and Spiritual. The lack of stringent practice of governance leads to the development of unethical practices and quackery.

Being the pioneer of MBA in health management program in Pakistan, and the founder CEO for Sindh Healthcare Commission-a regulatory body for quality improvement of HCEs', I felt the need to write a book for the healthcare professionals to enable them to customize themselves with the eco system out of medical colleges. However, structuring the book was important for understanding wellness management of a client, family and community. Wellness management revolves around that of body, mind and spirit. Physical body is influenced by the Society (local and global environment), the State laws, rules and regulations and the Systems that we need to work within. While the Mind Management is through the Self-dealing with the Physical aspects of body, intellect, emotions, vocational and financial dimensions of an individual. The Spirit deals with the Spiritual aspect of an individual, to find his meaning for Self-existence. Therefore, wellness management revolves around managing and dealing with 5Ss'-Self, Society, State, Systems and Spirituality.

Considering the 5Ss' for wellness management and teachings to healthcare professionals in dealing with client, family and community health management their significance need to be understood. Role of Self is foremost important, so that a medical graduate is able to develop personal skills for client, family and community health management. He needs to understand Systems other than body Systems, like Human Resource, Finance, Quality Management, Communication, Information Management etc. The medical professional has to practice within a community, so needs to understand the Societal norms, the local and global environment for working. State laws, rules and regulations need compliance, so he needs to know them for practice. Compassionate Care is the epic of client care. The healthcare professional needs to dive deep into the aspects of Spirituality, to be able to find his own meaning for survival. Therefore, the healthcare curriculum need to be redesigned, considering the 5Ss'-Self, Society, Systems, State and Spirituality. Thus, the need to follow the 5Ss' approach for Managing Health of Patient, Family and Community.

Healthcare undergraduates' curriculum is mostly based on clinical assessment and management of the patients. Consideration to the client, family, and community aspect is negligible. Health Management of a client requires a holistic approach encompassing the role of quality of services, communications skills, managing family and community; with ethical practices abiding the rules and regulations etc.

The World Health Organization (WHO) defines health (World Health Organization, 1948) as a dynamic state of complete physical, mental, spiritual, and social well-being and not merely the absence of disease or infirmity" Considering the WHO's definition, there are four basic parameters in this definition which are highlighted-physical, mental, social, and spiritual well-being. Although WHO has defined health in an ideal manner, a health care provider (HCP) considers managing the physical and mental health of a client or an individual (Self). Thus, the physical and spiritual health are left to be managed by the individual or self. However, for managing even the physical and mental health, the HCP needs complete engagement of the Self. Therefore, managing health becomes completely dependent on Self. The Self comprises of taking care of his physical body outside and inside at the cellular level. The physical health is usually apparent and visible, however, the cellular health is gauged through estimation of the biomarkers through laboratory diagnostics. Therefore, cell (Varda, 2011) and the biomarkers within the cell, become the focus of research, diagnosis, and management of an individual in primary care. Human body has life through Spirit, which is inside the body and reflected through our behavior. The spirit keeps us alive and provide quest to survive and to find meaning of our life and existence or the Spirituality. Thus, we maintain our physical health through keeping the body healthy and mental health through shaping our behavior and spiritual health. While the physical health is dependent on our diet, nutrition and daily activities; the spiritual health is enriched through gaining knowledge, and the intellectual virtues;-arts, science, wisdom, understanding and prudence. The physical, mental and spiritual health also enables the Self to connect with the environment and the Society to maintain social health and well-being. While living in society one has to follow the State policies, the existing Systems and norms of Society for ethical practices. Thus, the cohesion of the 5SsÂ'-Self, Society, State, Systems and Spirituality; are imperative for health, healthy living and for the success of all projects.

The current undergraduate curriculum of healthcare professionals teaches and prepares a HCP for clinical management of a client, which is symptomatic management. Therefore, the focus of a clinician is mostly on the physical and mental well-being of an individual and managing disease. The inner Spirit and will to survive is essential for an individual in coping with disease. This is particularly pertinent for managing chronic disease of Self (individual). The HCP needs to consider beyond cell and physical body, as the majority of illnesses are linked to behavior and lifestyle with an impact from Society. Society, is comprised of a group of people living together. The Societal elements (Sharma & Singh, n.d.) include likeness or hate for each other, reciprocal awareness, differences in caste, creed, values, status, and interdependence, which make us cooperate or conflict with each other. However, a HCP has hardly any education in the areas of health education and behavior change to integrate biological, behavioral, and social determinants of health in consideration of the dynamics of society. Health is managed through the Systems comprising of: People (delivering the services for the System as individuals, within the State and within the Society); Institutions (comprising of Self or the individuals, Society served by the institution, and following State laws and policies), Resources (from Self, State, and Society for the functioning of the System). People in the System are key with their capacity to serve. Institutions provide the necessary capacity building for the manpower, research, innovation, and production for economic development through the engagement of Self, Society and State; and Resources provided mainly by the State, additionally by individuals or Self and Society through philanthropy, corporate social responsibility, and public-private partnerships to run the System. The Systems function around and ensure the implementation of State policies, rules, regulations and the laws warrantying the functioning of State. The healthcare undergraduate curriculum mainly covers the clinical management of physical and mental health, and some aspects of society through public health or community medicine. However, the spiritual part is lacking. Therefore, for managing client, family and community health and well-being, the WHOs definition need to be viewed considering the lens of five pillars of "5Ss"- (Self, Society, System, State and Spirituality). The wheel of System (Varda, 2011) provides integration at the State, Society and Self levels and is responsible for maintaining ease of functioning. The biological immune System is responsible at the level of the cell. The body and behavior are responsible at the level of the Self. The Society builds a social system with moral factors determining right and wrong; our beliefs, values, and behavior towards using the means to achieve the end of what we value. Thus, the System impacts an individual's or Self behavior for personal ease towards physical, mental, spiritual and social well-being. The overall functioning ease is provided through the System administrators, healthcare workers, and the leadership of the State. However, communication lapses are the main source of dysfunctional system having an impact on healthcare such as: medical procedure error, long waiting time, wrong, delayed, or expensive treatment, uninformed recommendations etc. In addition, conflicts may also occur with the patients and their families. Further, the medication errors (Kohn et al., 2000) account for one out of 131 outpatient deaths and one out of 854 inpatient deaths. These sentinel events cost lives as the health management and quality aspect is missing from the HCP curriculum. This highlights that a HCP considers managing health at the cellular or biological level through laboratory investigations, diagnosis and clinical management for physical and mental health; needs additional tools. The above para needs to be made more coherent. Seems like a comparison is drawn between the Societal System– that shapes the behavior of an individual; entailing the political, social, ethical value system and state policies, and the human system based on cellular and sub-cellular level. However, the author needs to create a symphonic relationship between the two attributions for the reader to understand and construct a clearer paradigm. Similarly, the idea of sub-cellular level as the Spiritual level needs to be more firmly established. Medical undergraduate curriculum-5Ss and WHO definition The medical undergraduate curriculum not only lacks teachings on the social aspects of health but also about health systems, state policies, rules, regulations, and laws relevant to healthcare (Sanaii et al., 2016). So, if we consider the WHO's definition of health, the HCP is mainly capable of managing physical and mental health, leaving a void for social and spiritual well-being. Thus, a HCP needs to understand the philosophy of health for managing client, family, and community health, considering the lens of the five basic pillars of Â“5Ss (self, society, spirituality, system, and state).

The HCP's current focus, as per his their undergraduate teaching, is only on clinical management at the level of the physical and mental health of a client (Peavey & Cai, 2020). Therefore, additional teachings (courses/trainings) are needed (required) in terms of health systems and state policies for making the HCP aware of managing health with a health systems approach and knowledge of relevant policies, laws, rules, and regulations to remain within state boundaries for quality service delivery (how does this address the Spiritual aspect discussed above?). Subjects on society will assist the HCP in understanding societal morals and values for community management (community management has not be mentioned in this paper before Â– this is a new concept, how does it align with the self (individual) mental/physical health management?), and subjects on behavior management will assist in influencing the behavior of clients and managing their own behavior. Similarly, the nurses are also taught somewhat similar clinical oriented curriculum. However, the teachings of community health nurses are focused on

> 1-Managing clients and families to take an active role in their well-being by promoting self-care practices and healthy lifestyle choices;
> 2- Collaboration with community groups, non-profit organizations, and public health initiatives to address social determinants of health like education; and
> 3- Contributing to public health advocacy by voicing the needs of the community to policymakers and supporting.

The above role assists them in playing an important role in community health management. Additional support is provided by community health workers, psychologists, and social workers to ensure health in the social system. However, the HCP in most of the academic institutions are not exposed to Public/Community Health in an extensive manner and mostly to the clinical management of clients. Whereas, for managing health of the client, family, and community, a HCP needs to adopt a community health management systems approach, ensuring the health of the people, understanding the role of state systems (policies, rules, regulations, engagement with institutions, and resource allocation for projects), and the implications of Self acts towards the client and family on the community and overall society management (Fredrick, 2016). Thus, client management is not merely clinical management and it is evident that the clinical-oriented curriculum leaves a void in client, family, and community health management (Bloom et al., 2018).

The 5th S-Spirituality As previously stated, WHO defines health as the combination of physical, mental, social, and spiritual well-being. The above-mentioned 4Ss lack a spiritual context. The interior part of the cell represents the individual's spirit. Spirituality is complex; at one extreme, it deals with religious expression, seeking the sacred or divine in order to ensure reciprocity. On the other end, it prepares Self for problem solving and decision making. The inner self is equipped with knowledge through intellectual virtues and systems, which include arts, science, wisdom, insight, and prudence. The spiritual section also discusses the growth of morality and ethics in dealing with society and relationships. The state laws and regulations will be followed with an insight of Spirituality while deciding in reaching the ends by the adopted means. The spiritual part of medical education is left to the discretion of the HCP, with little focus in the undergraduate curriculum. However, the notion of health is insufficient unless Spirituality is included. Spiritual health influences the body, mind, and overall well-being. While it is important to train healthcare personnel to provide clients, families, and communities with physical, mental, emotional, social, and vocational well-being, it is quintessential important to include spiritual aspects in the curriculum alongside. Spiritual health is a dynamic state (Fisher 2011) that includes the quality of connections in four dimensions of spiritual well-being. A person's personal domain is where they interact with themselves. Communal sphere, with deep interpersonal interactions; Environmental domain, connecting with nature. Transcendental realm refers to something or someone beyond the human level. The Four Domains Model of Spiritual Health and Well-Being encompasses all current worldviews, from the fervently religious to the atheistic rationalist (Fisher, 2011). Dovetailing Health and the 5Ss Model For managing health, all the pieces of the puzzle (5Ss') need to work together in a systematic manner. This warrants that the WHO definition of health needs to be revisited to understand the concept of what influences body equilibrium to convert ease to "disease." Furthermore, the definition covers only the self or an individual aspect and misses other factors like the System, Society, and state impacting the Self. For example, if a client is ill, his investigations will be evaluated in accordance with the management's expectations. If the results do not meet expectations, corrective actions are implemented to reassess the therapeutic approaches for client management. These measures affect the cellular level of the self or individual being handled. Thus, the initial level of therapeutic intervention targets an individual's cell. Dietary conditions and human behavior cause changes at the cellular level. Maintaining health is under a person's control, regardless of their genetics. Individuals' harmful actions, such as smoking, impact the basic functioning of cells in lung tissue. Continuous smoking brings complications, expanding to other body organs. It further creates an impact on social functioning of an individual through economic, social, and disease burden affecting the family. Passive smoking affects those in the surroundings within the community. The disease burden not only individuals and Society, but also the System as more individuals need to be managed. This highlights the role of State in developing a System with rules and regulations in general and at the level of healthcare establishments, ensuring that cigarettes are not marketed or limiting marketing with cautionary remarks on the packet and healthcare services are available to provide quality care. The role of Society in reducing exposure to smoking can also be important in restricting smoking. Thus, the health behaviors (Varda, 2011) of individuals have an impact on the health of their own Self (which may deteriorate), Society (creation of burden on the family), System (may need health promotion and disease prevention approaches at community-based health facilities such as primary/family health centers, etc. to alter the eco-system), and State (financial burden for the State to manage). The addition of Spiritual aspect to the curriculum will assist healthcare workers in supplementing the clinical management aspect of teaching with a holistic approach to managing clients. At the same time, the healthcare professional himself will seek from himself the self-reflection and Self-regulation aspects. Thus, he uses his intellectual virtues in tandem with the spiritual aspect of managing the body and mind for the wellness of himself, his clients, his family, and the community. Thus, validating the revision to be made in the curriculum for teaching healthcare workers. Thus, the therapeutic importance of the "5Ss" approach towards managing Client, Family and Community Health. 5Ss model for various target groups The unique concept of the 5Ss approach, encompassing of Self, Society, State, Systems' and Spirituality; will enlighten all the cadres of healthcare, enabling them to understand the role of the 5Ss' in managing client, family, and community health. The concept endorses that traditional teaching of medical undergraduate curriculum is mostly based on using diagnostic and clinical approaches for client management and has lacunae that need to be covered through the 5Ss approach. It also provides an insight for academicians and researchers, opening doors and concepts other than the traditional teaching of clinical aspects, where the health of a client is usually managed clinically based on pathological identification and diagnosis of a disease. Summary The current medical curriculum leaves a gap in the management of health and well-being, as defined by the World Health Organization. While healthcare professionals (HCPs) are being prepared for physical and mental well-being, they are not being equipped with the necessary skills for managing health, dealing with family, societal, and spiritual issues, and promoting the well-being of clients, families, and communities. The 5Ss approach, which includes Self, Society, System, State, and Spirituality, offers a holistic philosophy for managing health that dovetails clinical management with client, family, and community health management. This approach considers not only the presence of disease but also the ease of life as a reality and health as a universal value for all. Therefore, to align with the true spirit of the WHO definition, it is necessary to revise the HCPs' curriculum to adopt the 5Ss approach, which takes into account Selfhood as a valued possession, societal well-being ensured by the eco-system, a spiritual lens for wellness management, and the State securing health as an asset for all.

To summarize, the current medical curriculum leaves a gap in the management of health and well-being, as defined by the World Health Organization. While healthcare professionals (HCPs) are being prepared for physical and mental well-being, they are not being equipped with the necessary skills for managing health, dealing with family, societal, and spiritual issues, and promoting the well-being of clients, families, and communities. The 5Ss approach, which includes Self, Society, System, State, and Spirituality, offers a holistic philosophy for managing health that dovetails clinical management with client, family, and community health management. This approach considers not only the presence of disease but also the ease of life as a reality and health as a universal value for all. Therefore, to align with the true spirit of the WHO definition, it is necessary to revise the HCPs' curriculum to adopt the 5Ss approach, which takes into account Selfhood as a valued possession, societal well-being ensured by the eco-system, a spiritual lens for wellness management, and the State securing health as an asset for all.

This book compiles insights from global experts in healthcare, including community health doctors and nurses, unified under the innovative 5Ss framework—Self, Society, State, System, and Spirituality. By integrating these themes, the following chapters offer a comprehensive guide for healthcare professionals and policymakers to enhance patient, family, and community health management. The numbered overview below outlines the key topics explored in each chapter:

Chapter 1 examines the distinctions and connections between leadership and management in health service delivery, emphasizing self-awareness, cultural competencies, emotional intelligence, and ethical behavior as key leadership traits. It outlines three strategies for leadership development—education, mentorship, and research appraisal—and discusses how these traits evolve with experience to enhance organizational effectiveness.

Chapter 2 focuses on individual effort in health management, highlighting self-awareness, motivation, and personal responsibility. It explores how attitudes, beliefs, and knowledge shape health behaviors, emphasizing self-care practices, preventive measures, and digital tools to foster a proactive health mindset and long-term well-being.

Chapter 3 provides an overview of health system components, including service delivery, workforce, financing, technology, and governance. It introduces the "4S" model (Self, Society, State, Systems) to illustrate their interaction in promoting health, addressing challenges in low- and middle-income countries, and emphasizing strategic planning for improved health outcomes.

Chapter 4 discusses quality management systems (QMS) in healthcare, integrating planning, assurance, control, and improvement. It highlights the role of accreditations, challenges in resource-intensive evaluations, and the need for a holistic QMS approach, particularly in low- and middle-income countries.

Chapter 5 explores how sensors and wearables enable continuous health monitoring and personalized care. It discusses their role in remote diagnostics, chronic disease management, and improving patient engagement, marking a shift toward proactive, patient-specific care.

Chapter 6 examines advanced techniques for early disease detection, including machine learning, wearable devices, and medical imaging. It highlights how predictive algorithms and AI integration with medical expertise enhance patient recovery and survival rates.

Chapter 7 discusses the roles of community health nurses (CHNs) in Pakistan, despite limited deployment opportunities. It emphasizes the need for evidence-based studies to assess their impact and integrate their contributions into the healthcare delivery model for sustainability.

Chapter 8 explores the use of Family Constellations to address family dynamics affecting health, focusing on ethical challenges like consent, privacy, and cultural sensitivity. It provides best practices for responsible integration into patient care.

Chapter 9 examines Family Constellations' role in community health, addressing familial patterns impacting well-being. It discusses its contributions to tackling loneliness, chronic illness, and social exclusion, supporting Sustainable Development Goals for health and social cohesion.

Chapter 10 investigates Family Constellations as a complementary mental health tool, particularly for older adults, addressing loneliness and grief. It highlights its integration with nursing practice and emotional intelligence to foster holistic healing.

Chapter 11 explores societal influences on health through Family Constellations, identifying transgenerational patterns contributing to illness. It advocates for systemic healing using therapeutic techniques to address health challenges.

Chapter 12 analyzes TB patients' perceptions of the 5Ss approach (Self, Society, State, System, Spirituality) in community engagement, using a survey of 75 patients to assess its role in reducing stigma and improving treatment outcomes.

Chapter 13 examines the state's role in health policy, resource allocation, and international collaboration, using the 5S framework to highlight the interplay of personal, societal, and systemic factors in achieving equitable and resilient public health.

Chapter 14 discusses the role of community health nurses in promoting empowerment and sustainability through community participation, health promotion, and capacity building, emphasizing the need for training in theory and practice.

Chapter 15 explores the development of community health nursing education, its inclusion in undergraduate curricula, and its role in preparing nurses to deliver culturally sensitive, accessible care at the grassroots level.

Chapter 16 advocates for integrating spirituality into medical curricula, using techniques like Spiritual Diagnostics and Guided Consciousness Liberation to address illness root causes and improve patient outcomes.

Chapter 17 explores humanistic medicine's integration of spirituality, empathy, and holistic care to enhance healthcare providers' work-life quality and patient outcomes, addressing burnout and advocating for person-centered care policies.

I am confident that the book focusing the 5Ss' approach for Managing Health of Patient, Family and Community will be useful and handy for all the healthcare professionals and policy makers.

References:

8. Bloom, D. E., Cafiero, E. T., Jané-Llopis, E., Abrahams-Gessel, S., Bloom, L. R., Fathima, S., Feigl, A. B., & Weiss, J. (2018). The promise and peril of universal health care. *Science, 361*(6404), eaat9644. Advance online publication. DOI: 10.1126/science.aat9644 PMID: 30139847

4. Fisher, J. (2011). The four domains model: Connecting spirituality, health and wellbeing. *Religions*, *2*(1), 17–28. DOI: 10.3390/rel2010017

7. Fredrick, N. B. (2016). Exploring health systems within the context of social determinants of health: A global health case study. *MedEdPORTAL: the Journal of Teaching and Learning Resources*, *12*, 10457. DOI: 10.15766/mep_2374-8265.10457 PMID: 31008235

9. Kohn, L. T., Corrigan, J. M., & Donaldson, M. S. (2000). Errors in health care: a leading cause of death and injury. In *To err is human: Building a safer health system*. National Academies Press.

6. Peavey, E., & Cai, H. (2020). A systems framework for understanding the environment's relation to clinical teamwork: A systematic literature review of empirical studies. *Environment and Behavior*, *52*(7), 726–760. DOI: 10.1177/0013916518815535

5. Sanaii, M., Mosalanejad, L., Rahmanian, S., Sahraieyan, A., & Dehghani, A. (2016). Reflection on the future of medical care: Challenges of social accountability from the viewpoints of care providers and patients. *Journal of Advances in Medical Education & Professionalism*, *4*(4), 188–194. PMID: 27795969

3. Sharma, S., & Singh, A. (n.d.). Society: 6 basic elements or characteristics which constitutes society. Your Article Library. https://www.yourarticlelibrary.com/society/6-basic-elements-or-characteristics-which-constitutes-society-927-words/8506

2. Varda, D. M. (2011). A network perspective on state-society synergy to increase community-level social capital. *Nonprofit and Voluntary Sector Quarterly*, *40*(5), 896–923. DOI: 10.1177/0899764010378171

1. World Health Organization. (1948). Preamble to the Constitution of the World Health Organization as adopted by the International Health Conference, New York, 19–22 June 1946; signed on 22 July 1946 by the representatives of 61 states (Official Records of the World Health Organization, No. 2, p. 100) and entered into force on 7 April 1948.

Acknowledgement

First and foremost, I extend my heartfelt gratitude to the Almighty, whose guidance and grace have been my strength throughout this journey of writing this book-"Enhancing Client, Family, and Community Health Management: Self, Society, State, Systems, and Spirituality"; which may bring a paradigm shift in academia towards teaching in healthcare.

I would like to express my sincere appreciation to IGI Global Publications for giving me the opportunity and platform to bring this book to life. Their support in facilitating this project has been invaluable.

My deepest thanks goes to Dr. Saleema Gulzar, who nurtured the idea of 5Ss for the book, in bringing this to a reality. Initially started with the concept of 4Ss' (Self, Society, State and Systems), however, I was deeply impressed by Dr. Christina M. Puchalsi's use of Spirituality for compassionate care in academic teachings especially for history taking. This led to the addition of the 5th S of Spirituality in the existing 4Ss'. Endorsement of the Spirituality factor and the 5Ss' philosophy also received acknowledgement from Prof. Dr. Asif Ahmad and Prof. Dr. Kashif Ikram, whose use of Spirituality teachings in healthcare were instrumental, in adding the "5th S" of Spirituality in my philosophy. The 5Ss' (Self, Society, State, System and Spirituality) now represented a unique, innovative and comprehensive model for managing human well-being with dignity. Thus, the basis of this book "Enhancing Client, Family, and Community Health Management: Self, Society, State, Systems, and Spirituality".

This book required a project director and Dr. Noor-ul-Huda Shah's role was instrumental. Her dedication, and passion for this project helped turning a vision into a reality. My special thanks to Ms. Alina Arshad whose tireless efforts navigated the incorporation of reviewers' responses with the authors, facilitating the timelines; and her commitment was pivotal in completion of this book. I am equally indebted to my contributors for adding value through their insight, intellect and academic rigor has enriched the content of this book.

This book could not have been completed without the time dedicated by our authors and the Editorial Advisory Board (EAB). With the valuable input of EAB, the authors were guided in polishing their contributions. Furthermore, I must acknowledge the valuable contribution of Ms. Hira Salim, whose diligent efforts and collaboration was essential to the project's successful completion.

Finally, a special thanks to my mentor, Prof. Dr. Al Assaf, for graciously accepting to write the foreword. His support and wisdom have been guiding lights in my academic and professional career.

To everyone involved, directly or indirectly, in the creation of this book—thank you. Your support has been the cornerstone of this achievement, and this book stands as a testament to the power of teamwork and shared vision.

Chapter 1
Exploring Connections Between Leadership and Management in the Health Sector:
Identifying True Leaders and Factors Contributing to their Development: Basics of Leadership

Muhammad Farooq Umer
https://orcid.org/0000-0001-7779-1929
King Faisal University, Hofuf, Saudi Arabia

ABSTRACT

Understanding the central distinctions and connections between the roles of leadership and management and their impact on the context of health service delivery is crucial. Self-awareness, cultural competencies, emotional intelligence, and ethical behavior are key traits at the heart of a good leader, regardless of their favored leadership style. Moreover, three key strategies are necessary for leadership development to occur: an education pathway, mentorship or coaching, and a publication or research appraisal, if deemed appropriate by the individual. With age, experience, and also the learning from mistakes of mismatched attitudes, leadership styles, and behaviors, some of these traits evolve in both senior managers and leaders in pursuit of greater effectiveness for the organization and the employees. Education, workshops, more mentorship, and continuous professional growth among senior management would promote authentic and effective healthcare leadership.

DOI: 10.4018/979-8-3693-9092-4.ch001

1. INTRODUCTION AND BACKGROUND

It can be difficult to define leadership without referencing a level of responsibility for directing and ensuring the efficient operation of an organization, system, or service, as in the most widely used definition of leaders who influence, motivate, and enable others to contribute towards the effectiveness and success of the organizations of which they are members. Therefore, it can also be challenging to distinguish the roles of leadership from those of management in the service sector, where essential functions include working with staff to ensure service deliverables meet established standards of quality, effectiveness, and efficiency.

The characteristics of those individuals are referred to as the true leaders within this essay; they have the opportunity to shape the healthcare system through these multidisciplinary contributions. However, currently, there are no detailed job descriptions for such posts; no country in the world has codified the true leader in health. This essay addresses the need to provide a more systematic account of the functions and characteristics of those taking on roles that might be considered as system leaders. (Ince 2023).

When considering the distinctions and similarities between management and leadership within the health sector, we need to reflect on their origins and what they have come to mean in our contemporary context. Many perspectives suggest that the role of those in charge of the fledgling health care services in the UK and USA before the beginning of the 19th century was to organize, control, and coordinate the many functions of their institutions. As this century developed, the nature and style of organizations changed and reached new levels of complexity. From this point on, mistakes and errors in the name of management were punished with dismissals, while those individuals who proved themselves by achieving targets were rewarded with promotions. Management became distinct from leadership due to a restructuring within society, where structures and leadership became synonymous. From the middle of the century though until the modern day, the role of leaders has been defined and redefined in response to a series of important social policy changes which have transformed what is expected within health care more generally. The changes increasing the distinctions between management and leadership have led to a range of imperatives on the expectation of the successful healthcare leader. (Chatzipanagiotou & Katsarou, 2023) (Vuorivirta-Vuoti et al., 2024)(Darling-Hammond et al.2021)

The recognition of a leader-manager dichotomy presents everyone with an imperative to move forward, as at the most simple level individuals sometimes purporting to be one or another can receive criticism not just from research and theory, but also from those they are expected to manage and lead. Indirectly, this paper argues that this separate 'mission' is crucial; it is the place where the interplay of traits, behaviors, and results become manifest, and can facilitate an approach to determining why some people are better leaders when there seems to be little difference in their experience, education, or training. The healthcare industry has long been regarded as too complex and distinct in terms of culture, context, and task to use the leadership simplifications perpetrated in business or traditional public organizations. The aforementioned high levels of turnover in leadership roles, rising public expectations and concerns, and leadership effectiveness perhaps are indications of how different a world the health sector actually represents. Certainly, the public and the workforce have caused the search for healthcare leaders to focus on those competent in both leadership and modern public management. Understanding this paradox will deepen our understanding and ensure leaders are ideally identified, trained, and supported. (Falko and Zhukov, 2023)

This essay is about leadership and will make distinctions between leadership and management as they relate to both the private and public service provision. This will provide clear guidelines and understanding of both management and the essence of leadership, which is the emphasis for this essay. Management can be defined as a conduit to the health and well-being of the body and mind, despite personal intelligence and other special capacities. This essay starts with the distinctions and connections because, in order for one to see who a true leader is, one has to take a close look at all the above according to the intent and ambitions that each role brings. Therefore, the objective of this essay is to analyze the characteristics of true leaders and to identify the factors that contribute to leadership development. By doing so, a significant disambiguation is to be made in leadership and management paradigms so that one can call a true leader either a bureaucratic manager or an entrepreneur. For example, no matter how hard the bureaucratic manager tries to be effective as an entrepreneur and jump on the leadership bandwagon, he can never become one because he lacks creativity, initiative, and many more aspects that are included in the description of a true leader. Practical implications are vitally important for current and aspiring healthcare managers. (Falko and Zhukov, 2023)

2. UNDERSTANDING LEADERSHIP AND MANAGEMENT: KEY DEFINITIONS, CONCEPTS AND THEIR IMPORTANCE

In this section, we begin our exploration of understanding leadership and management in the health sector and distinguishing between the two, the context within which these roles are engaged and the way they are practiced. This is necessary as, in many areas, confusion exists in the understanding and application of the two. Also, this paper reflects an exploration of both leadership and management. We will describe leadership and management and their core concepts, principles, and approaches and their contributions to organizational effectiveness and the delivery of appropriate healthcare in the health sector. This includes a review of the diversity in perspective in defining leadership and management, their differentiation, and the extent of their complementarity.

Leadership and management continue to receive substantial attention. Regrettably, the understanding and application of these two complex terms are usually used interchangeably despite the body of knowledge that highlights their distinctiveness. Management as a concept in health is derived from medicine, and the purest form of management in the health sector is clinical management. However, this pure form of management is not well understood because of the predilection of the senior medical practitioner to observe management with a clinical perspective rather than a managerial one. The absence of formal managerial education, inappropriate medical education, and absence of personal awareness of the need for formal management concepts often compounds the issue. Establishing a management process to satisfy both clinical and non-clinical individuals is always a challenge for the health professional personifying pure management. (Batko & Ślęzak, 2022)

2.1. Defining Leadership and Management

In addressing issues of leadership and management, the most basic question concerns distinguishing between these two approaches. The terms are frequently used interchangeably; some use the term 'manager' and 'leader' synonymously, while others recognize distinctions, claiming that managers look after day-to-day activities, while leaders look ahead and think long-term. Wide differences in perception and definitions reflect the many and varied factors involved but clearly build on theories, research, and a practical knowledge base to suggest or advise about what individuals should do to effectively lead or manage.

Leadership theories and research reflect an overall direction, an understood importance mostly against a background of less favored management practice. Definitions of leadership index a range of themes and concepts that establish a wide field of leadership studies. These include effective leadership practice, relevant to context and content, including the identification of leaders and the development of future leaders; charisma and emotional elements; features of leadership at different levels, including boards and teams; leadership in relation to service delivery, community welfare, and government; the need for leaders to support employees, boost morale and well-being, and for their interaction with staff to support practice and safety, and in a number of associated areas such as job satisfaction or burnout. (Kamel Boulos & Zhang, 2021)

2.2. Key Differences and Overlaps and Theoretical Frameworks

Despite the distinctions and overlaps a number of suggestions can be made that draw out the leadership–administration/management debate and identify more specific attributes that may help define 'true' leaders. In the first instance, there is a reason that the terms are often linked in text and used interchangeably. The connection between the two terms is grounded in an understanding of the need to manage and lead in every organization. Both management and leadership behavior is needed within every organization, regardless of the degree of change that may be required.

Both sets of activities are important to commit, motivate, encourage, and guide, which together facilitate the quest for delivering health services. To deliver health services, both the form of management and guiding/leading behavior may differ in degree and specific nuanced activities, but the need for both remains necessary. The health sector is therefore not different from providing either of these actions. The proposition for healthcare leaders, therefore, is the challenge of embracing both behavior sets and then operationalizing the appropriate activities to produce the desired outcomes against a recognized set of healthcare-focused and specific individual, organizational, and societal responsibilities. (Benmira & Agboola, 2021) (Roberson & Perry, 2022)

We will now explain how the concept of leadership has evolved through the years into various theories and frameworks, and the distinction made between the leader and leadership. Furthermore, we will describe some recognized models of leadership in the health sector. In addition, we will provide a brief overview of the patient safety issues related to leadership constructs and the impact of leaders on patient care and safety in healthcare settings. In essence, the leadership framework should clarify why certain individuals become recognized and accepted leaders, or why others are not accepted as leaders, as well as determine the influence that leaders have on their followers, the performance of their followers, and the overall effectiveness of the organization.

Leadership Concepts and Theories The term "leadership" has been defined in many ways, and the definitions are replete with implicit and explicit assumptions about what leadership is and how it operates. The definitions range from the self-evident to the diffuse. In a comprehensive review of leadership theories, leadership concepts are summarized as varied and disparate, producing a muddle, which is a sign of this muddled practical attempts to make sense of it. But since the late 20th century, there has been increasing support for recognizing the distinction between "leader" and "leadership", particularly with respect to theory and models, to better understand the role of leadership. Leadership can still be inspiring through its ability to make a difference at all levels of an organization, but the distinction between leadership and leader implies that everybody has the potential to make that difference. (Kilag and Sasan2023)(Steffens et al.2021)

3. LEADERSHIP IN THE HEALTH SECTOR

The role of leadership in shaping health care delivery and outcomes is increasingly recognized as key to effectively working with health systems. Quality health care is delivered by engaged, motivated employees working in high-functioning organizations where effective leadership is apparent at all levels. Effective leadership increases organizational resilience and addresses clinical and regulatory risks. Research shows that individual organization performance increases with the effectiveness of its leadership and that leadership capability at all levels of an organization can lead to improved patient care. Leadership in the health sector has its own challenges and opportunities. Health care leaders can contribute to the health and economic base of the communities they serve, providing opportunities for partnerships in research and service delivery.

Few organizations, however, appear able to develop leaders who can respond successfully to the challenges. Leaders often are recruited based on their technical and interpersonal skills and not their capabilities to set a vision, create strategy and implement change. A study of North American health care leaders showed significant gaps in leaders' capabilities. Weaknesses were seen in developing partnerships and collaborations, ability to navigate the complexity of both the organization and the external environment, application of regulatory expertise to meet the need for transparency and oversight, and the ability to work in teams. In a distributed leadership culture, one expects leaders at all levels to manage conversations related to the foundations of health, ethics and practice. Management and leadership are not the same thing. Leadership requires a vision; an ability to set the future direction with others and to create a context in which people can be responsible and innovative. There are no value-neutral choices in health care; the work of health is fraught with ethical risk. Effective leaders are expected to demonstrate the ability to draw on ethical practice to improve health. Ethical leadership is not only important, it is essential. (Singh et al.2022 (Karatas et al.2022)(Vuong et al.2022)

3.1. Importance of Leadership in Healthcare

Healthcare is a constantly evolving and ever-expanding field, wherein new advances in treatments, care processes, information systems, and technology are being developed and adopted. Effective leaders have been identified as the necessary catalysts to drive the constructive culture necessary for rapid change surrounding these healthcare advancements. In a team, an effective leader can improve communication networks, ultimately increasing team performance. Strong organizational leaders strategize with other strong organizational leaders about the most fiscally responsible ways to continue to enhance patient safety, quality of care, outcomes, and efficiency. A leader with a vision of the future and a plan for exactly how to merge current systems with future systems in order to enhance care processes is essential to the entire system surviving and evolving. Additionally, visionary leaders can inspire the clinical and business components of healthcare to harmoniously innovate medical practices on a scale much larger than would be possible using any motivation scheme. Fostering effective leadership helps individuals and organizations hit the mark in many of the core competencies necessary to provide top-quality care. From an individual standpoint, leaders are able to encourage the establishment of a team culture in which leadership is encouraged from any position, and the necessity of patient safety reporting is well understood. Additionally, it encourages the exercising of evidence-based thinking and best practices, and it reinforces the focus on continuous quality improvement. It also has implications for the center overall by ensuring adherence to the goals for effective communication and organizational information management, and creating an environment with clear priorities where roles and accountabilities are well defined and understood. Empirical studies have shown a linkage between leadership practices and organizational outcomes. Adult learning theory holds that leaders can be developed, not just born, from any position in the organization. Achieving the above leadership goals in turn uses some best practices. Some work at the individual or dyad level. The emergence of a strategic objective for developing leadership has been found to be among the predictors of present and future organizational culture. Such a situation harmonizes with the transcendence theory that posits that leaders are an essential factor in organizations to achieve high performance. Leadership development is an investment in building rather than attracting these leaders. (Hashimy et al.2023)(Radu, 2023)(Haddad2024) (Groenewald et al.2023)

3.2 Management in the Health Sector

Management plays a crucial role in the effective functioning of the health sector. Planning, organization, leading, and controlling, integrated with different phases of the management cycle, ensure efficient internal operations and foster administrative and operational processes. The strategic level of planning, or strategic management, defines the direction and mission of the organization or facility. The ultimate goal of any healthcare institution is to provide the best possible care to patients. In this regard, various programs and guidelines on patient safety and the implementation of processes to evaluate the quality of the services provided have been elaborated and implemented. The practical implementation of these statements creates an essential space for managers who are both good doctors and talented organizers.

Healthcare organizations are, in many respects, the same as non-healthcare organizations and face similar management problems and issues. However, some distinctions in management systems could be observed. First, health sector reform occurred at later periods compared to the business sector. Second, the existence of high levels of risk and uncertainty, and occasionally life-threatening consequences for individuals, organizations, and entire health systems presents some significant differences. Further arguments differ in terms of operating features of services, goods, and patients. The perspectives match the expectations that specify the competencies and expertise required by individuals to become successful managers in the healthcare sector. A new approach to health services management, based on a new set of management functions, is needed. Safe and effective performance of the system requires a coherent, thoughtful approach to the development and implementation of healthcare management strategies. (Bryce et al., 2022)(Juvet et al.2021)

3.3. Functions of Management in Healthcare

The functions performed by management, as designated by the description of the work of managers, are largely the same across a range of industries. They include strategic planning and management, human resource management, financial management, time management, and systems management. Management within healthcare, then, includes the management of healthcare systems. The healthcare managerial functions identified as necessary to achieve optimal patient care in difficult environments, including those with poor resources, are the following: (a) Human resource management, which includes both the management of organizational culture and individuals; (b) Financial management, which includes the transformation of organizational inputs into system efficiencies while watching the business of the medical involvement zone.

Healthcare systems management includes the use of healthcare information systems and data research management of the operational flow of resources, including activities such as bed management, theatre and other procedural scheduling, human resource rostering, patient referral flow, resource allocation and utilization, outcome-focused services, and cost utilization. Healthcare management is contingent on the degree of market orientation and decentralization within the system. Current literature frequently refers to the importance of a good fit and a common strategy or culture between or within an organization and its manager. Default co-alignment also includes the importance of an obvious and articulable strategy, an easy-to-understand vision, a comfortable culture, and clearly documented patient care professional standards. Given a co-alignment framework, having a manager in charge whose actions complement the standard care activity produces more standardized and effective operations. Healthcare management also includes the use of computer decision support systems by medical and nursing staff, as well as management through the use of advanced planning systems and across-the-board operational data.

Management is the attainment of specific process and social ends to achieve predetermined standards of care. Management and leadership differ from each other. Managers plan, budget, organize, command, control, and problem-solve to achieve clinical, human, and environmental outcome efficiency and effectiveness. High-performance leadership acts as a force multiplier, inspiring and guiding employees to heightened ambition and empowerment so that individual and team effort is systematically directed towards focused performance outcomes. The alternative is a less than ideal performance when management and clinical effort is spread broadly. (Jerab & Mabrouk, 2023)(Toendepi, 2021)

3.4. Comparative Analysis of Leadership and Management Roles

Leadership and management research has explored the conceptions of roles and responsibilities for each as distinct disciplines. Some researchers argue that leadership is different from management, as leaders focus on change while managers focus on delivering the work and supporting subordinates. Leadership is more about the process of decision-making and getting subordinates to buy into change, while managers are more concerned with the delivery of the work program, building and managing teams, and managing performance. Other researchers contend that management is the same as leadership but has a different focus, seeing leaders as developing and inspiring people towards a vision, while managers deal with complexity and the day-to-day issues faced by the service. Subsequently, the term 'managing' becomes virtually synonymous with 'leading' in the way it is embodied through each individual, irrespective of the level of seniority.

Leadership is associated with powerful social expectations of service. In stark contrast, the rise of workforce management in the health sector tends to occur against a backdrop of social critique and distrust. The leader is one who abdicates his or her ego and social position in favor of actively following the lead of willing and inspired followers. Also, working with 'the new reality' of a modern business environment, leaders must envision a better way and ensure that all employees and staff move toward that goal. This involves building the healthcare organization on distinctive competencies as well as leveraging the opportunities presented by employees and partners. (Kaluza et al.2021)(Bolden et al., 2023)(Koehrsen, 2021)

4. INNOVATIVE LEADERSHIP PRACTICES IN HEALTH

Many forces shape innovative leadership in the health sector today. These include a rapid pace of change, raised consumer expectations, increased service integration, the need to attract, retain, and refresh our workforces, public policy reforms beyond the health sector, and international and social reform. Many see that new management forms are being debated publicly. Human resources, information technologies, new managerial practices, decentralization, and other service delivery instruments are becoming prioritized out of some initiatives. They are divergent, less bureaucratically centered, more innovative, and have as a common theme the release of the creative power of individuals and organizations to "make a difference." "Making a difference" represents a vividness, relevance, and energy in health systems leadership that is its hope and mandate. To support the requisite level of innovation and creative enterprise will need specific leadership and organizational strategies and systematic approaches, potent enough to counter risk and democratic enough to deal with a deeper malaise that can erode public support for good leaders and expedite their isolation. (Flessa and Huebner2021)(Cortes and Herrmann2021)(Scher & Schett, 2021)(Liu et al.2022)

The new health landscapes are making things such as lifelong learning, transformational leadership, change management, and freedom to operate at the clinical level a priority. Low-income countries are getting back to the future, paring away wasteful and overly extravagant management systems and replacing them with low-technology, manageable protocols. But the leadership challenge in terms of devising and driving through innovative delivery organizations to practice best international practice will face similar contexts and dilemmas. Can managers play the more proactive role they advocate given the levels of resistance on the part of consumers, politicians, and workforces to significant departures in organizational form? Certainly, successful strategies are available; examples already exist, while challenges such as building sustainable leadership and linked capabilities remain to be addressed.

5. HEALTH POLICY AND ADVOCACY LEADERSHIP

Being in a leadership position within health provides opportunities to influence health policy and advocacy. While policy provides a mechanism to fulfill health goals, health relates to every aspect of our lives and our well-being. The policies that affect our health outcomes are diverse and not just associated with health services or universal health coverage. When leaders are involved and have their views heard in the policy formulation and implementation process, there are greater opportunities to influence the direction and implementation of resulting policy, as well as support others in the health system to act. Translating policy into practice can directly impact the individuals who need health care, so it is important to understand the effects on access, delivery, responsiveness, quality, and safety of this care. The way that health policy translates into health care is known as the determinants of health, the factors that influence whole populations and health access for individuals. Adverse policies may provide more benefit to the population than any potential issues arising from those adverse effects.

The capacity for these decisions to privilege one group over another, or to fail to act for the most disadvantaged, contributes to health inequity across the globe. Health leaders active in health policy, working with a range of government agencies, can have a real positive outcome on population health. However, it's not always easy to succeed. To influence legislative agendas and prioritize the development or implementation of disadvantage-reducing and equitable policies, health leaders need to develop their advocacy skills. The same skills will also assist in embedding and operationalizing those policies within the health system for those they serve.

Effective advocacy of evidence-based policy principles can lead to better-informed policy processes and decisions with direct health entitlements. At an international level, aligning these evidence-based principles to the health of the public is important when motivating state parties to progress the current international declarations, agreements, and statements. Aid in driving the agendas of major health issues such as antimicrobial resistance, non-communicable diseases, and planetary health, particularly within the sustainable development goals. Incredible progress with tested positive outcomes for health is thus possible via health leaders' impact on policy both nationally and internationally, successfully creating enabling environments supportive of equitable health for all. A sound appreciation and understanding of health leadership within political contexts are important for improved individual, community, and population health. Understanding of the policy environment, the values underpinning the documentation, and the focus of the policy need to be examined, including the impact of aligned or conflicting policies from other sectors. For political leaders and policy writers, appreciating the determinants of health policy and providing the best political solutions is equally critical. (Mousa et al.2021)

6. GLOBAL HEALTH LEADERSHIP

The concept of global health leadership includes efforts to define and respond to health concerns that affect people across the world. A global health leader has a responsibility to promote equity and fairness with a focus on health outcomes achieved through sustainable practices. Global health leaders must be aware of current trends in order to reach out and harness global leadership in a time of widespread health concerns. Global health leadership works to intentionally integrate ethical, moral, ideological, and technological leadership frameworks into praxis for a collective approach to addressing extraordinary global challenges that have local implications. Public health concerns are increasingly borderless, taking into consideration that poor health outcomes in one country or region can have a profound effect on the health of other countries.

Globalization may also permit the spread of interventions and efforts to improve populations' health, allowing countries and regions to benefit from the experiences and knowledge of others. Public health is everyone's business and has become an increasingly global enterprise. A framework that emerged from research conducted by a team of healthcare leaders in global health effectiveness indicates that leaders' potential impacts exist between the poles of managing and leadership. Leaders emphasize inspiration over supervision, creating change rather than maintaining order while managing conduct and systems. Effectiveness in leadership must be developed via experience. The leadership that is shared leaves more opportunities for followers to build and embrace a strategy, creating the conditions for change. Leaders either shift from checking items and evaluating performance to linking others in working on bringing life to action. (Shanafelt et al.2021)(Alderwick et al., 2021)(Broome, 2025)

7. GENDER AND DIVERSITY IN HEALTH LEADERSHIP

Gender and Diversity in Health Leadership While women constitute a significant percentage of the health workforce, they are only marginally (and slowly) represented in health leadership, governance, and health policy setting at all levels and in all countries. Women, for example, generally account for fewer of leading roles – i.e., those requiring policy negotiation and decision-making – within governance structures, leadership, and health ministries globally. Among the private sector, data suggests women hold only 25% of healthcare CEO positions. In a recent study, 86% of hospital executive boards and 74% of hospital senior management teams had less than gender parity. Similar underrepresentation of minorities in leadership roles exists. Leadership that is devoid of diversity comes at a cost. Leadership teams where different diversities are represented have been shown to perform better and create more innovative practices. (Bulmer et al., 2021)(Curado & Santos, 2022)

Progress is slow. Why this is so reflects complex societal norms and the slow-consuming nature of culture change. Leadership positions are subject to a cultural fitness test. A key barrier is systemic unconscious bias evident in recruitment. Both power and leadership in health are perceived to be male. Norms also exist surrounding the leadership of the ways in which we understand health and health care, and one of the barriers to cultural change comes from the sanctity of the clinical – with only a small subset of health professionals lent the imprimatur of leadership. There is also denialism, elite reproduction, and inordinate resource. Norms, thinking the unthinkable, and political will are combined essentials in the discussion moving forward.

Leadership programs in health, therefore, need to engage in strategies in order to recruit, develop, and support an inclusive health leadership cohort. Investment is needed in identification, promotion, and support of mentorship and sponsorship for female clinicians and allied health professionals for large system-level leadership positions. Both leadership and emerging leaders need opportunities for gender-focused and culturally safe reflections on leadership. Gender-focused leadership programs have the ability to engage in shared discussion around joint mentoring and learning. Diverse leadership in health is a priority. Uneven health outcomes demonstrate an impoverished response. In reality, leadership appointments do little to reflect that, except on occasion, unwittingly. For that to happen, political willpower is requisite.

8. TECHNOLOGY AND INNOVATION IN HEALTH LEADERSHIP

Technology and innovation have become part and parcel of health. Digital tools and technologies not only ensure quality care for patients but radically transform health professional practices. Health is quickly becoming consumer-centric, with many providers investing in health technology and innovation. As naturally follows, leaders in health are making enormous investments in the best ways to adopt and integrate digital and other technologies for maximum patient outcomes, as well as maximum operational efficiency. Questions/Issues To ask ourselves, then, could it be that those in health leadership are in fact ahead of the curve, doing their own work in leading others as well as their organizations through complex technological innovation and adaptability? Equally, what do we need to watch out for, support, critique, and caution around in this adoption and advent of sophisticated and omnipresent health technologies? What could it mean to those interested in technology, in leadership, and in healthcare? Discussion The use of digital technology is a powerful enabler for innovation in health. An example such as involving patients in innovation investment is a future possibility. Cloud computing has changed emergency, chronic, and planned healthcare forever, from patient triage to outcomes analysis. It can equilibrate first and third world hospitals. Social media and mobile apps directly and indirectly saved huge numbers of lives across the globe in various calamities like earthquakes and other disasters. Smarter data and information can presage and create better business outcomes for healthcare organizations. Meeting the technology health leaders of tomorrow involves dialoguing about innovation. The ethical dilemmas that come with any technology interface are already being preempted by good training, collegial discussion, and the development of healthcare trust guidelines for our future generations of health leaders. The best and most effective leaders will foster a culture that is creative, willing, and able to apply technology innovation to the provision of the best patient care. (Sheikh et al.2021)(Wang et al.2021)(Chandra et al.2022)

9. MEASURING AND EVALUATING LEADERSHIP EFFECTIVENESS IN HEALTH

A key feature of well-functioning systems is feedback. How does an organization or industry know if the right people are identified for leadership roles, and if leadership practice is effective in a rapidly changing health sector? Frameworks for evaluation help in refining practices, both in terms of identifying and defining leadership practices that are effective, and for developing leaders

There are several indicators of leadership. One is the impact of leaders' decisions and actions on patient outcomes such as mortality, morbidity, patient satisfaction, and patient safety. A second indicator is the satisfaction and engagement of the workforce with their work, which are related to the leadership practices within a health organization. There are several measures of a health professional's readiness for a leadership appointment. In addition, performance, which might include data on the management of wait lists, time taken to transfer patients, human resource management, financial management of clinical skills, technical skills in addition to non-technical skills, would be an indicator of leadership. One recent development is the work on developing leadership metrics in terms of how effective the health sector is at developing leadership. There have also been initiatives to define leadership as distinct from management for the purposes of the healthcare sector. One of the primary foci is the development of leadership capacity, and the identification of whether organizations have systems in place to develop leadership. Such activities include appointing a senior leader to the team, support for team learning, performance management and development, and having regular team meetings that include time for problem-solving. Given the pace of change in the healthcare sector and the lack of an evidence base, a broad brush approach to the identification of leadership practices is adopted. (Franklin, 2021)(Lazzara et al.2022)

10. IDENTIFYING TRUE LEADERS

True leaders are those possessing values such as headship, impressive character, compassion, integrity, and leadership competence. Leaders possess clearly recognizable traits and behaviors that can be measured using standardized tools. A modern leader also has to be emotionally intelligent in order to be successful in the healthcare environment, which is socially oriented and growth-oriented, and who uses empathy with their clients and staff to broker a successful outcome. Furthermore, the psychologically informed leaders have been measured in the mental health field and showed significant effects with positive development of their staff in the form of lower absenteeism, lower sickness, earlier return to work, better timekeeping, absence of theft, and an increased success in employment rates. Emotional intelligence is not enough on its own. The job of a leader involves making decisions about the direction that the organization and clients should follow and maintaining a firm hold on that while leading the organization through the hard times of structural change, managing staff attention to coincide with the organizations need for change.

Leadership styles need neither to be similar to each other nor to be consistent across the years and different employees. Expert followers may value things such as vision, direction, conviction, inspiration, innovative thinking, the ability to create winning strategies, valuing results compared to effort, and good decision-making. Some young people may view the dependence of the professional on its followers to provide information and solutions as a flawed expression of the leader's need to act from an individual point of political caution. A good leader in healthcare will be required to use a variety of power strategies to make sure they reach the maximum number of employees at any given point in time, who may possess different personalities, cultural differences, and who may present with various attitudes and values. They may not want to give too much power to certain employees due to their perceived lack of work commitment. Good leadership contributes to a better functioning team, greater patient satisfaction, and better clinical outcomes when the patient is accessing medical, surgical, dental, and psychiatric treatment. (Di et al.2021)(Hung et al.2021)

10.1. Characteristics of Effective Leaders

Thus far, this chapter has provided evidence of the strategic aspects of leadership by examining the difference between leadership and management, the importance of leadership for effective organizational functioning, and the theoretical underpinnings surrounding different styles of leadership. It has been proposed that leadership requires an adaptive response to the world as it is and the world as it is becoming, a quality that is necessary for a healthcare system steeped in complexity, ambiguity, and uncertainty. However, knowing the difference between leadership and management and understanding the constructive use of strategic leadership does not provide the answer to distinguishing between a true leader and an imposter; rather, it gives a theoretical context to explore the answer.

Despite the noted importance of defining appropriate behaviors and characteristics, the idea of a deliberate set of characteristics and/or roles that define a leader and distinguish him or her from other managers and supervisors is also examined in the organizational literature more broadly. In healthcare settings, it is suggested that the setting adds additional challenges, and that such investigations need to account for the context in which healthcare leaders operate. Using social psychology and sociology, a number of authors have argued that we recognize who leaders are according to how they come to develop self-concepts. Leadership is imbued with meaning not through the leader's traits, abilities, or behaviors, but rather through the mindset of followers.

When you survey the list of qualities and characteristics of several effective leaders around the world, and within healthcare specifically, it is not sunny dispositions or relentlessly cheerful attitudes that appear in every laundry list of strong leadership characteristics. It is not even the number of qualifications that these leaders have, or their intellect, though some have those in spades. For these individuals, real leaders in healthcare generally serve the purpose of a force multiplier, bringing together teams comprised of intelligent, skilled staff so that the organization can deepen and broaden their power to perform. This is the uncommon quality and energy that actual leaders bring to their teams and how you can easily tell the difference between leaders and everyone else (after a highly competitive recruitment process, of course). Many would argue that the six characteristics mentioned above are innate and not indeed a result of education or developmental experience. We would argue instead that they can be developed and influenced, as many leaders have demonstrated this, often citing early life experiences as significant contributing factors. The concept of 'resilience'—having faced and triumphed over challenging events or experiences in the past—is cited by scholars in the 21st century as being central to an exploration of effective leadership. It is argued, in fact, that those who would be effective leaders must now 'come from the school of hard knocks.' In other words, they must have demonstrated an ability to be resilient in the face of a crucial defining crisis in their personal and professional experience. (Chang et al., 2022)(Cappelli et al.2024) (Moodley et al.2024)

10.2. Leadership Styles in Healthcare

Healthcare organizations face their own unique challenges, which require unique behavior from their leaders. The most prevalent leadership behaviors fall into one of the following styles:

- **Transformational leader:** The transformational leader is focused on change. It is believed that transformational leaders possess characteristics that their followers find inspiring, which lifts motivation. In healthcare, transformational leadership is often found to have a positive impact on performance outcomes.
- **Transactional leader:** Transactional leaders are concerned with the day-to-day running of a team. They work effectively with a team that needs certain things, such as clear structure, discipline, and encouragement. As such, it is believed that transactional leadership is likely to be effective in a healthcare environment.
- **Servant leader:** The servant leader leads by putting the needs of their team first. Just as a healthcare professional might put the patient needs above their own, the servant leader does the same. Research in health agency environments has found that teams led by the servant leader were more likely to display extra effort, cooperation, or engagement, all factors linked to improved health outcomes.
- **Democratic leader:** The definition of a democratic leader is one who involves employees in organizational decisions. In healthcare, research has found that employees feel more authentic and committed to their work when leaders have this style.

The style of leadership that is adopted depends on the situation. In healthcare, this is of relevance to turnover and absentee rates, teamwork, and patient satisfaction. Research has shown that teams led by individuals who display the leadership style that best matches the situation perform better. Furthermore, followers tend to derive greater job satisfaction when their organization's leaders adopt a style that is congruent with the organization's dominant values. The conclusion, therefore, is that different styles are required in different situations and that in healthcare, the most effective and positively received style is one that is collaboratively focused and patient centered. (Ince, F. 2023)

11. FACTORS CONTRIBUTING TO LEADERSHIP DEVELOPMENT

In a sector focused on research and evidence-based functioning, identifying true leadership abilities is of paramount importance. In the field of healthcare, the development of these skills could help safeguard higher levels of patient experience and welfare, possibly leading to a stronger and more clinically attuned health service. The role of an effective leader within healthcare bears as great an importance as any other industry. The aforementioned organizational requirements dictate that healthcare focuses on leadership, not management, as a basis for operation and success.

Various factors may contribute to the development of effective leadership. Many hold the notion that formal education can only take learners so far. However, in the field of leadership, there are numerous education and training programs to enhance clinically trained people. This is a description of what should be in order for learners to grow as clinical leaders.

Certain themes have been agreed upon in the literature, alongside the previous convictions about self-assessment, but have been questioned and reasoned with extensively. These include how to evaluate if someone is, in reality, a true leader beyond learning how to develop corporate leadership. It is determined that formal education is essential in equipping clinicians with a leg into the leadership forum as it offers leadership language, the contribution of specialists, and an understanding of how managers work. It is considered important in the developed leadership context that formal university qualifications require a Master's course in Organizational Change as well as ongoing professional updates. The specialism or context varies for each person, as this is what they aim to lead, but others who come onto the course without any management qualifications are thought by experienced leaders to struggle as they get stuck on the language of leadership and management, figuring out if they are truly managers or chiefs of something.

11.1. Education and Training

Educating Potential Healthcare Leaders

Increasing numbers of individualized educational pathways are becoming available to those considering leadership roles in the health field. Undergraduate and graduate degree programs in healthcare management or administration are available through many colleges, universities, and professional schools. Certification in health management is offered by several organizations that include a supervised practicum experience before eligibility for examination. Many professional and trade organizations sponsor management courses, workshops, or seminars focused on healthcare.

These experiences increase the range of topics learned, exposure to current leader-practitioners in the field, and exploration of the different environments of the health field that members come from. Structured learning situations emphasize improved management practices based on successful models, trends, critical thinking, and new, emerging philosophy and strategic management in healthcare.

The health field is rich with different experiences and management models. These can range from small, isolated, and self-contained facilities which employ one person in an office of three at the top, to multi-facility operations employing hundreds. Most healthcare management employees have four to seven years of experience in some supervisory role. Many of the job opportunities in the health field prefer and/or require baccalaureate preparation. Experiential education may often be an "internship" that exposes the learner-participant to the field through work on individual projects and assignments. The healthcare system allows students to get needed experience through volunteerism at hospitals and skilled facilities, shadowing professionals in the field of interest, working as nursing assistants in long-term care facilities, and the like. But the learner also often needs familiarity with issues such as aging components of micro and macroeconomics, cause and societal budgeting and access services, technological innovation altering both the cure and prevention paradigm, the changing social values of privacy, ethics, equity, and genetics, and the at-risk behaviors of society. Experiential learning does not necessarily reinforce ethical, conceptual, or functional knowledge without also having the learner experience some systematic knowledge building. Staying current with today's technology and systems, rules, regulations, and new accreditation and certification is imperative in the health management field. This is often indicated as involvement in continuing education programs and networking within the healthcare councils. Some potential healthcare leaders are academically prepared as medical doctors, public health specialists, psychologists, pharmacists, and allied healthcare professionals. These individuals have some critical, frontline non-nursing experience that can effectively lead direct care. Some of these professionals also understand healthcare's grant funding, are conversant in interdisciplinary thought, and can competitively move in and out of leadership roles such as doctor to nurse practitioner or physician's assistant.

11.2. Mentorship and Coaching

In tandem with formal leadership development initiatives, high-quality mentorship has been acknowledged as a central method of leadership development within the healthcare sector. Given the paucity of leadership-specific academic avenues, mentorship relationships are commonly established. The one-on-one relationship established through mentorship allows for shared wisdom, insights, and best practices. Beyond this dyadic relationship, mentorship assists with several aspects of professional development, such as career choice, promotion, and habilitation. Personal insight, increased confidence, leadership skills, and ongoing career advancement have all been linked to mentorship. Because of its benefits, the mentorship of up-and-coming leaders is frequently considered one of the primary responsibilities of a good leader. Modeling of the formal mentorship relationship in healthcare-specific models has been promoted, which delineates appropriate reading, best practices, the underpinning theory, and potential barriers to mentorship. Examples of formal nursing mentorship programs have been illustrated, along with their effects on nurse leadership skills and professional commitment. However, mentorship is not without its barriers. Perhaps the largest is the need for time, a valuable and finite resource for all individuals involved. Time, leadership, and the compatibility of the mentorship relationship between mentor and mentee are three of the most common barriers.

Coaching has also been considered a leadership development tool. It assists in the continuous improvement of leadership abilities and fosters professionally accountable roles. Many coach-led mentorship models might be applied to those involved in executive leadership and professional development both in general and specifically. For those developing into future healthcare leaders, the benefits of one-on-one coach-led mentorship have yet to be fully elucidated. Feedback from a coach fosters leadership abilities, observes behaviors, strengthens efficient interactions, and tasks both the coach and the leader to set, check on, develop, and reach personal targets. The translation of coaching to healthcare encourages individual leader development and helps the entire institution. Coaching also reflects the organization's dedication to developing talents and offers a clear method for evaluating leader development after a mentoring program.

12. FUTURE TRENDS AND CHALLENGES IN HEALTH LEADERSHIP

The years to come promise to be marked by significant changes. Among some of the issues that will massively impact health systems and, hence, the focus of health leadership are: the digital or technological revolution; the aging population; the increasing gap between high- and low-income countries; the growing number of chronic diseases; the preventive role of strengthened primary care services; and the transformation from volume to value. These changes will influence health professionals, their future numbers and their values, and thereby the way of collaboration and personnel management; all issues that are relevant to health leadership. In addition, a possible shortage in the workforce due to pandemics will also complicate the leadership role. The rapid development of new technical procedures and learning experiences may influence the way health care will eventually be delivered, thereby putting a new perspective on academic advances - a new sort of popularism. On the other hand, health care leaders must be able to steer through this continuous state of flux, lacking the ability to provide a solid landmark to follow, where the implemented decisions can autonomously pave the path to the underpinning strategies. Paradoxically, today's health care leaders are now forced to become leaders for tomorrow. These leaders should be able to foster in their followers a search for or movement towards mental agility and continuous learning. This implies that innovative behavior, combining creativity with sharp pacing methods, could lead to those often sought-after situations, which are so desperately needed to become change masters themselves. Leaders emerge through crisis and challenge and learn their main, let alone enduring, functions and tasks from events that life throws at them. The concentration on shaping events into their required form of potential change is among the most significant differentiation patterns in the leaders/manager-as-leaders debate, shaping the change context of which change leaders as leaders and managers are part. Cognitive paradigms are democratizing, guided by learning and sharing between individuals. (Imamov & Semenikhina, 2021)(Dal Mas et al., 2023)

Healthcare is a moving target; changes in regulations, technology, or patient and community partnerships, priorities, and preferences are continuous. Effective healthcare talent and organizational management must change as well. The health landscape often feels particularly rapid and turbulent, at least in comparison to other sectors, in part because healthcare data and issues are reported in the lay media literally every day. A reasonable argument can be made that these dynamics also add an element of appeal and reward to healthcare leadership as a career choice. There is, for example, the need to improve financial performance and deliver better care to more people at the same time. How to manage technological change should be an important part of our presentation. There are many facets to resilience and the career required in health, some of them are lush and sensual, while others are not. It's complicated, as usual. All of these also affect the quality of care and efficiency of the system in which it is provided. Building a better quality, value, and access to the healthcare system with the help of leadership research is paramount.

13. CONCLUSION

In conclusion, this chapter explored the management and leadership distinctions in healthcare and highlighted a general agreement that good management is essential to overcome the current challenges in healthcare. The key themes explored in this essay were the meaning and significance of leadership in healthcare. At the individual level, there is an increasing focus on identifying a true leader. A number of characteristics were identified as essential leadership qualities, in particular, the ability to set a vision for the future and galvanize a team towards it. Education, mentorship, the values and technical skills, as one gains experience, organizational loyalty, and the development of the ability to lead successfully in varied contexts.

For effective and quality healthcare delivery and positively influencing health outcomes, leadership is a critical reflection of any health system. This chapter investigates the themes of leadership preparation towards delivering health change, the diverse roles and practices of health leadership, and enhancing the practice of leadership in health. In conclusion, we reiterate the importance of developing leadership in health. As we prepare future generations of healthcare providers for whole system change, there is a growing need for clinical leadership development with a focus on the clinical context and preparedness for whole system change. In this rapidly changing context with new and increasingly complex challenges, a focus on the system-leadership capability of understanding the interprofessional, interdisciplinary, and interorganizational context and the ability to lead in this space is strongly recommended.

Given the rapid rate of change in health, the lack of a clear understanding of the best leadership approaches to match the need, and calls for such leadership, we recommend a strategy of continuous learning and the development of a sonar capability where leaders can listen to or observe data from the environment which will prompt either a speed shift in the plans or a completely new direction. We also see a need for a combined business and leadership program to ensure that future health leaders are equally skilled in leadership and in ensuring their organizations are delivering outcomes to ever higher standards. We need to take that task seriously—going beyond good intentions to carefully prepare and skillfully influence people.

13.1. Implications for Practice and Future Research

Current leadership behavior and effectiveness are reflective of current patient safety measures and are predictive of future safety scores. This has significant implications for healthcare practitioners and leaders as it shows the benefits of focused pro-leadership approaches. Training in leadership effectiveness has already been shown to improve levels of safety. Healthcare organizations that wish to invest in leadership effectiveness will expend resources in leadership development, including action learning sets and peer coaching, and will offer career structures that support leadership development. In addition, these organizations should work on developing effective mentorship programs that help successful leaders replicate their authenticity and work at all levels in healthcare organizations in order to identify and sponsor or facilitate future leadership.

The analyses presented suggest several avenues for future research. For example, improvements in technology mean that increasing amounts of healthcare can be moved into the community, and to date, most leadership theory is based on face-to-face situations. Because patients will automatically flow into hospitals more and more 'naked' by managing technology that masks previous pre-existing illnesses, the role of leadership in managing this technological component in patients in urgent and unplanned care settings would be an area for research. We hypothesize that in these resource-constrained situations, transformational leadership behaviors might be less relevant, and efficiencies and permissive additional leadership styles become increasingly important. A second research avenue may be to investigate certain leadership profiles in other healthcare contexts, for example, leadership behaviors in crises such as may be seen with the increasing imposition of pandemics. The nature of these crises can change suddenly, perhaps requiring changes to a more directive, larger volume leadership approach, while at the same time, certain strategic behaviors that support longer-term resilience become fundamentally important. Headline crises that reveal systemic or leadership management failure may also reveal areas where the capabilities requirements have changed.

ACKNOWLEDGMENT

This chapter was written with the assistance from Dr. Minhaj A. Qidwai, who is the editor of the book "Enhancing Client, Family and Community Health" and his 5Ss approach of Self, Society, State, Systems and Spirituality".

REFERENCES

Alderwick, H., Hutchings, A., Briggs, A., & Mays, N. (2021). The impacts of collaboration between local health care and non-health care organizations and factors shaping how they work: A systematic review of reviews. *BMC Public Health*. Retrieved from springer.com

Batko, K., & Ślęzak, A. (2022). The use of Big Data Analytics in healthcare. *Journal of Big Data*. Retrieved from springer.com

Benmira, S., & Agboola, M. (2021). Evolution of leadership theory. *BMJ Leader*. Retrieved from bmj.com

Bolden, R., Gosling, J., & Hawkins, B. (2023). Exploring leadership: Individual, organizational, and societal perspectives. Retrieved from academia.edu

Broome, M. E. (2025). *Transformational leadership in nursing: From expert clinician to influential leader*. Retrieved from. [HTML]

Bryce, C., Ring, P., Ashby, S., & Wardman, J. K. (2022). Resilience in the face of uncertainty: Early lessons from the COVID-19 pandemic. *COVID*, *19*, •••. city.ac.uk

Cappelli, E., Zaghini, F., Fiorini, J., & Sili, A. (2024). Healthcare-associated infections and nursing leadership: A systematic review. *Journal of Infection Prevention*. Advance online publication. DOI: 10.1177/17571774241287467 PMID: 39544633

Chandra, M., Kumar, K., Thakur, P., Chattopadhyaya, S., Alam, F., & Kumar, S. (2022). Digital technologies, healthcare and COVID-19: Insights from developing and emerging nations. [Retrieved from springer.com]. *Health and Technology*, *12*(2), 547–568. DOI: 10.1007/s12553-022-00650-1 PMID: 35284203

Chang, D., Chang, X., He, Y., & Tan, K. J. K. (2022). The determinants of COVID-19 morbidity and mortality across countries. *Scientific Reports*. Retrieved from nature.com

Chatzipanagiotou, P., & Katsarou, E. (2023). Crisis management, school leadership in disruptive times, and the recovery of schools in the post-COVID-19 era: A systematic literature review. *Education Sciences*. Retrieved from mdpi.com

Darling-Hammond, L., Cobb, V., & Bullmaster, M. (2021). Professional Development Schools as Contexts for Teacher Learning and Leadership. In *Organizational Learning in Schools* (pp. 149–175). Taylor & Francis. DOI: 10.1201/9781003077459-9

Di Trani, M., Mariani, R., Ferri, R., De Berardinis, D., & Frigo, M. G. (2021). From resilience to burnout in healthcare workers during the COVID-19 emergency: The role of the ability to tolerate uncertainty. [Retrieved from frontiersin.org]. *Frontiers in Psychology*, *12*, 646435. DOI: 10.3389/fpsyg.2021.646435 PMID: 33935905

Falko, N., & Zhukov, O. (2023). Transition from hierarchy to adhocratic organizational culture in a Ukrainian university: From survival to successful development in the conditions of war. [Retrieved from]. *Problems and Perspectives in Management*, *21*(2), 15–22. DOI: 10.21511/ppm.21(2-si).2023.03

Franklin, K. (2021). Strategies healthcare leaders use to improve patient satisfaction. Retrieved from waldenu.edu

Groenewald, E., Kilag, O. K., Cabuenas, M. C., Camangyan, J., Abapo, J. M., & Abendan, C. F. (2023). The influence of principals' instructional leadership on the professional performance of teachers. *Excellencia: International Multi-disciplinary* [Retrieved from multijournals.org]. *Journal of Education*, *1*(6), 433–443.

Haddad, E. (2024). Leveraging social media, big data, and smart technologies for intercultural communication and effective leadership: Empirical study at the Ministry of Digital Economy and Entrepreneurship. [Retrieved from growingscience.com]. *International Journal of Data and Network Science*, *8*(2), 857–870. DOI: 10.5267/j.ijdns.2023.12.019

Hung, M., Licari, F. W., Hon, E. S., Lauren, E., Su, S., Birmingham, W. C., Wadsworth, L. L., Lassetter, J. H., Graff, T. C., Harman, W., Carroll, W. B., & Lipsky, M. S. (2021). In an era of uncertainty: Impact of COVID-19 on dental education. [Retrieved from wiley.com]. *Journal of Dental Education*, *85*(2), 148–156. DOI: 10.1002/jdd.12404 PMID: 32920890

Imamov, M., & Semenikhina, N. (2021). The impact of the digital revolution on the global economy. *Linguistics and Culture Review*. Retrieved from lingcure.org

Ince, F. (2023). Transformational leadership in a diverse and inclusive organizational culture. In *Handbook of Research on Promoting an Inclusive Organizational Culture for Entrepreneurial Sustainability* (pp. 188–201). Retrieved from. [HTML]

Jerab, D., & Mabrouk, T. (2023). The role of leadership in changing organizational culture. Available at *SSRN* 4574324. Retrieved from *ssrn*.com DOI: 10.2139/ssrn.4574324

Juvet, T. M., Corbaz-Kurth, S., Roos, P., Benzakour, L., Cereghetti, S., Moullec, G., Suard, J.-C., Vieux, L., Wozniak, H., Pralong, J. A., & Weissbrodt, R. (2021). Adapting to the unexpected: Problematic work situations and resilience strategies in healthcare institutions during the COVID-19 pandemic's first wave. [Retrieved from sciencedirect.com]. *Safety Science*, *139*, 105277. DOI: 10.1016/j.ssci.2021.105277 PMID: 34720426

Kaluza, A. J., Weber, F., van Dick, R., & Junker, N. M. (2021). When and how health-oriented leadership relates to employee well-being—The role of expectations, self-care, and LMX. [Retrieved from wiley.com]. *Journal of Applied Social Psychology*, *51*(4), 404–424. DOI: 10.1111/jasp.12744

Kamel Boulos, M. N., & Zhang, P. (2021). Digital twins: From personalised medicine to precision public health. *Journal of Personalized Medicine*. Retrieved from mdpi.com

Karatas, M., Eriskin, L., Deveci, M., Pamucar, D., & Garg, H. (2022). Big Data for Healthcare Industry 4.0: Applications, challenges, and future perspectives. [Retrieved from]. *Expert Systems with Applications*, *200*, 116912. DOI: 10.1016/j.eswa.2022.116912

Kilag, O. K. T., & Sasan, J. M. (2023). Unpacking the role of instructional leadership in teacher professional development. [Retrieved from researchsynergypress.com]. *Advanced Qualitative Research*, *1*(1), 63–73. DOI: 10.31098/aqr.v1i1.1380

Koehrsen, J. (2021). Muslims and climate change: How Islam, Muslim organizations, and religious leaders influence climate change perceptions and mitigation activities. *Wiley Interdisciplinary Reviews: Climate Change*. Retrieved from wiley.com

Lazzara, E. H., Salisbury, M., Hughes, A. M., Rogers, J. E., King, H. B., & Salas, E. (2022). The morbidity and mortality conference: Opportunities for enhancing patient safety. [Retrieved from rice.edu]. *Journal of Patient Safety*, *18*(1), e275–e281. DOI: 10.1097/PTS.0000000000000765 PMID: 34951610

Moodley, N., Weidler, E. M., Ochoa, B., Eldredge, R. S., Rakkar, M., Boles, K., & van Leeuwen, K. (2024). Satisfaction with multidisciplinary team structure and function in a pediatric outpatient clinic. [Retrieved from]. *Journal of Pediatric Surgery*, •••, 162103. PMID: 39733606

Mousa, M., Boyle, J., Skouteris, H., Mullins, A. K., Currie, G., Riach, K., & Teede, H. J. (2021). Advancing women in healthcare leadership: A systematic review and meta-synthesis of multi-sector evidence on organisational interventions. [Retrieved from thelancet.com]. *EClinicalMedicine, 39*, 39. DOI: 10.1016/j.eclinm.2021.101084 PMID: 34430838

Radu, C. (2023). Fostering a positive workplace culture: Impacts on performance and agility. *Human Resource Management—An Update*. Retrieved from intechopen.com

Roberson, Q., & Perry, J. L. (2022). Inclusive leadership in thought and action: A thematic analysis. *Group & Organization Management*. Retrieved from umich.edu

Shanafelt, T., Trockel, M., Rodriguez, A., & Logan, D. (2021). Wellness-centered leadership: Equipping healthcare leaders to cultivate physician well-being and professional fulfillment. [Retrieved from lww.com]. *Academic Medicine, 96*(5), 641–651. DOI: 10.1097/ACM.0000000000003907 PMID: 33394666

Sheikh, A., Anderson, M., Albala, S., Casadei, B., Franklin, B. D., Richards, M., Taylor, D., Tibble, H., & Mossialos, E. (2021). Health information technology and digital innovation for national learning health and care systems. [Retrieved from thelancet.com]. *The Lancet. Digital Health, 3*(6), e383–e396. DOI: 10.1016/S2589-7500(21)00005-4 PMID: 33967002

Singh, N., Ogunseitan, O. A., & Tang, Y. (2022). Medical waste: Current challenges and future opportunities for sustainable management. [Retrieved from escholarship.org]. *Critical Reviews in Environmental Science and Technology, 52*(11), 2000–2022. DOI: 10.1080/10643389.2021.1885325

Steffens, N. K., Munt, K. A., van Knippenberg, D., Platow, M. J., & Haslam, S. A. (2021). Advancing the social identity theory of leadership: A meta-analytic review of leader group prototypicality. [Retrieved from sagepub.com]. *Organizational Psychology Review, 11*(1), 35–72. DOI: 10.1177/2041386620962569

Toendepi, J. (2021). The catalytic role of authentic leadership in raising collective consciousness in the South African social systems. *Journal of Contemporary Management*. Retrieved from journals.co.za

Vuong, Q. H., Le, T. T., La, V. P., Nguyen, H. T. T., Ho, M. T., Van Khuc, Q., & Nguyen, M. H. (2022). COVID-19 vaccines production and societal immunization under the serendipity-mindsponge-3D knowledge management theory and conceptual framework. *Humanities and Social Sciences Communications, 9*(1). Retrieved from nature.com

Vuorivirta-Vuoti, E., Kuha, S., & Kanste, O. (2024). Nurse leaders' perceptions of future leadership in hospital settings in the post-pandemic era: A qualitative descriptive study. *Leadership in Health Services*, *37*(5), 33–48. DOI: 10.1108/LHS-05-2023-0032 PMID: 37750849

Chapter 2

The Role of Self in Health Management

Awesh Khati
https://orcid.org/0009-0009-9090-1593
Lakshmibai National Institute of Physical Education, Gwalior, India

Anindita Das
https://orcid.org/0000-0002-6502-9619
Lakshmibai National Institute of Physical Education, Gwalior, India

Debajit Karmakar
https://orcid.org/0000-0001-9272-0627
Lakshmibai National Institute of Physical Education, Gwalior, India

ABSTRACT

This chapter, "The Role of Self in Health Management," explores the crucial role of individual effort in maintaining and improving health. It focuses on self-management, highlighting how individuals actively engage in their health care, make informed decisions, and adopt behaviors that enhance well-being. The chapter emphasizes self-awareness, motivation, and personal responsibility in managing both physical and mental health. It examines how attitudes, beliefs, and knowledge shape health behaviors, stressing the link between self-confidence and overcoming health challenges. Furthermore, it covers self-care practices, preventive measures, stress reduction, and healthy lifestyle choices as essential for sustaining long-term health. By integrating theoretical insights and research findings, the chapter provides strategies for developing a proactive health mindset, resilience, and adaptability. Additionally, it discusses the empowering impact of digital tools in self-management, urging readers to take an active role in shaping their health for lasting well-being.

DOI: 10.4018/979-8-3693-9092-4.ch002

UNDERSTANDING SELF-AWARENESS IN HEALTH

Self-awareness in health refers to the ability to deliberately observe and assess one's physical, emotional, and mental conditions (Vago & Silbersweig, 2012). It provides individuals with the power to manage their health by recognizing signs of potential health issues, acknowledging the connection between emotions and physical responses, and making knowledgeable decisions to enhance their overall well-being. This concept can be categorized into three main areas: physical self-awareness, emotional self-awareness, and mental self-awareness. Each plays a vital role in maintaining a healthy lifestyle (Urdang, 2010).

Definition and Importance

Self-awareness in the context of health refers to the ability to recognize and comprehend one's own physical, emotional, and psychological health states. It involves being consciously aware of one's health conditions, behaviors, and their impact on overall well-being (Carden et al., 2022). Being self-aware plays a vital role in maintaining and improving one's health, as it allows individuals to gain a more comprehensive understanding of their physical and mental state. This awareness enables better decision-making regarding their health. By paying attention to subtle changes in the body or recognizing ongoing symptoms, individuals can detect potential health issues early, leading to quicker intervention and treatment. For instance, noticing persistent headaches, fatigue, or unexpected weight changes could prompt someone to seek medical advice before the problem worsens, helping to prevent more serious health concerns. Therefore, self-awareness acts as a preventative measure, aiding individuals in addressing health risks early and minimizing the chances of developing more significant health problems(Alpay et al., 2011) .

In addition to early detection, self-awareness is essential for initiating positive behavioral changes that contribute to better health. By recognizing harmful habits, such as unhealthy eating, a lack of physical activity, or high levels of stress, individuals can take action to modify these behaviors. For example, if someone becomes aware that a sedentary lifestyle is contributing to weight gain or decreased energy, they may choose to increase their physical activity. Awareness of how their actions impact their health allows individuals to make informed decisions that can improve their overall well-being. Self-awareness also boosts motivation to maintain healthy habits. When individuals understand the benefits of healthy behaviors, such as how a balanced diet can improve energy levels or how regular exercise positively impacts both physical and mental health, they are more likely to stick to these habits (Goldman & Smith, 2002). Recognizing the connection between their actions and their health outcomes strengthens their commitment to following health guidelines and sustaining long-term practices that promote well-being. This not only supports behavior modification but also reinforces the drive to maintain these improvements over time. Moreover, self-awareness enhances communication with healthcare providers, which is critical for effective treatment. Individuals who can clearly articulate their symptoms, medical history, and concerns are more likely to receive accurate diagnoses and appropriate treatment plans. Clear communication between patients and healthcare professionals enables better understanding of the patient's condition, resulting in more personalized care. For instance, a person who can effectively describe their symptoms and health patterns provides valuable information that helps healthcare providers make more informed decisions (K. R. Lorig et al., 2001). In this way, self-awareness not only empowers individuals to take control of their health but also fosters better collaboration with healthcare professionals, ultimately leading to improved health outcomes.

How Self-Reflection Impacts Health Choices

Self-reflection is crucial for guiding health decisions as it allows individuals to analyze and comprehend their behaviors, emotions, and health experiences. By regularly evaluating their health patterns and results, people can uncover important insights that guide their choices and actions. This reflective process helps in recognizing persistent issues, establishing achievable health goals, and making necessary adjustments for enhanced well-being (K. Lorig, 1996). Through self-reflection, individuals gain a clearer understanding of how their emotions and behaviors impact their health, leading to more thoughtful and effective health management approaches.

- **Identifying Patterns:** Self-reflection helps individuals observe recurring behaviors and their impact on health. For instance, recognizing that emotional stress leads to unhealthy eating habits can highlight the need for stress management strategies. Identifying these patterns allows for more targeted and effective interventions.
- **Setting Goals:** Reflecting on previous health behaviors and outcomes helps in setting realistic and achievable health goals. For example, if someone has previously succeeded in improving their diet, they can set new goals related to increasing physical activity or enhancing sleep quality based on those past experiences.
- **Evaluating Outcomes:** Self-reflection enables individuals to assess the effectiveness of their current health strategies. By reviewing what has and hasn't worked, they can make informed adjustments. For instance, if a particular exercise regimen hasn't improved fitness, exploring alternative workouts might be beneficial (Xie et al., 2020).

- **Emotional Awareness:** Understanding how emotions affect health choices is critical. For example, reflecting on how anxiety leads to emotional eating can prompt the development of healthier coping strategies, such as mindfulness practices or seeking support from a therapist. This awareness helps in making more balanced health decisions.

BUILDING MINDFULNESS FOR BETTER HEALTH MANAGEMENT

Cultivating mindfulness for effective health management involves integrating practices that enhance awareness of the present moment and regulate emotions. Techniques like meditation and mindful eating play a crucial role in improving overall health by alleviating stress, promoting healthier eating habits, and supporting better sleep quality (Camerini et al., 2012). By staying present and gaining a deeper understanding of one's thoughts and feelings, individuals can make more informed health choices and manage their well-being more effectively. This mindful approach fosters a proactive and balanced lifestyle, leading to better physical and mental health outcomes.

- **Stress Reduction:** Mindfulness practices, such as meditation, are effective in reducing stress by promoting relaxation and present-moment awareness. Lower stress levels are linked to various health benefits, including a decreased risk of chronic diseases like hypertension and enhanced immune system function. Mindfulness assists individuals in managing stress more effectively, contributing to overall health improvement (Liu & Willoughby, 2018).
- **Improved Eating Habits:** Mindful eating encourages attention to the sensory experience of eating and the recognition of hunger and fullness cues. This approach promotes healthier eating habits by encouraging slow eating and mindful enjoyment of food, which can prevent overeating and support better nutritional choices.
- **Enhanced Emotional Regulation:** Mindfulness helps individuals recognize and manage their emotions without being overwhelmed. For instance, it can aid in handling anger or frustration more constructively, reducing the risk of emotional eating or other negative health behaviors.
- **Better Sleep:** Engaging in mindfulness practices can improve sleep quality by alleviating anxiety and calming racing thoughts that often disrupt restful sleep. Techniques such as mindfulness meditation or deep breathing exercises before bed can help soothe the mind and promote better sleep, which is crucial for health and recovery.

- **Increased Self-Awareness:** Regular mindfulness practice enhances self-awareness by encouraging individuals to observe their thoughts, feelings, and bodily sensations in a non-judgmental manner. This heightened self-awareness allows individuals to make more informed health decisions and respond more effectively to their health needs (Bronikowski et al., 2016).

SELF-CARE PRACTICES FOR PHYSICAL HEALTH

Physical health, developing mental acuity, and preserving one's general well-being fall under the broader scope of self-care. Regular exercise, wholesome nutrition, adequate rest, and frequent recovery help prevent ailing conditions of the body from arising, restore energy to promote feelings of elation and well-being, and foster lifelong health (Du & Yuan, 2010). Besides building resilience against all forms of physical and mental stressors, self-care activities also encourage sustainable lifestyle changes that can lead to a good quality of life.

Importance of Regular Exercise and Nutrition

Exercise is one of the best self-care practices undertaken. It helps strengthen the cardiovascular system, improve muscle tone and flexibility, and enhance endurance. Among aerobic exercises-running, swimming, and cycling help maintain heart health and prevent the onset of diseases such as diabetes, hypertension, or obesity. Meanwhile, strength training builds muscle mass that improves metabolism, supports joint health, and lessens the chances of sustaining a serious injury. Besides the physical benefits, exercise also releases endorphins and dopamine-related neurochemicals, which reduce stress and improve mood, making exercise an essential element, not only for the health of the body but also for mental health (Heijmans et al., 2015).

Nutrition: Nutrition is just as important because it gives the body the quality nutrients needed for growth, repair, and maximum performance. A balanced diet requires proteins, carbohydrates, fats, vitamins, and minerals in appropriate proportions. Proteins repair the muscles and boost immunity. Carbohydrates give one energy while healthy fats provide brain functions with a sufficient amount of it. The vitamins and minerals coming from fruits, vegetables, whole grains, and lean proteins all add up to cellular health, bone density, and energy metabolism. Lastly, hydration is very important because water is used in almost every bodily function-from digestion to temperature regulation. The foundation of physical health is a robust, energized body that can be relied on in everyday life, achieved through exercise and nutrition (Dineen-Griffin et al., 2019).

Developing Sustainable Health Routines

Sustainable health routines translate to making daily habits realistic and effective in the long run. Routines may range from simple, manageable practices like regular walks, involvement in stretching or yoga, and creating a pattern for consistent meal times with healthy options. The crux of the matter lies in setting goals that are realistic because radical changes are often very hard to sustain (Normand, 2008). For example, one might begin with 20 minutes of daily exercise and, as one's body builds up tolerance, gradually increase the duration or intensity for a more sustainable routine. Accountability tools such as a fitness tracker, an app, or workout buddy can help to stay to new habits. Meal prep and planning would be very helpful in keeping a balance with food choices and avoiding falling into the trap of unhealthy processed food. Sustainable routines include developing a balanced approach that will work specifically for that schedule, preference, and physiological capacity to ensure self-care is consistent and enjoyable in life.

Understanding the Role of Sleep and Recovery

- **Sleep:** They need to keep up good sleep to recover their body, cognitive function, and well-being. These periods of deep sleep repair tissues and also assist in the consolidation of memories which lets the growth hormones repair muscles and maintain the immune system. Recommended for 7-9 hours every night; poor sleep or not resting well enough makes people fall behind with decreased alertness, reduced immunity, and more susceptibility to stress factors, affecting health in general and productivity.
- **Recovery:** Again, recovery is more than just sleeping; it's activities to enable recovery and adaptation of the body to exertion. For example, there are days of active recovery where low-level activity will be used to walk or stretch; regular stretching enhances flexibility, and some days resting so as not to burn out or injure someone. Recovery also affects the mental plane: because of the downtime, stress levels can decrease, the focus may increase, and motivation is enhanced. For instance, one may integrate sleep hygiene practices such as having regular bedtime hours, limiting screen time before bed, and establishing a restful sleep environment. Also, planned recovery days and relaxation methods, such as meditation or breathing exercises, can contribute to a balanced approach to maintaining physical and mental well-being (Sadler et al., 2014).

MENTAL AND EMOTIONAL HEALTH MANAGEMENT

Mental and emotional health management is a basic aspect of human life that is critical to the needs of people in this fast-paced, highly interconnected world characterized by constant, pressing stresses emanating from the multiple life spheres. Mental health is more subtle than physical health, whereby people can visibly be suffering from either illness or injury, while mental health highly controls how people think, feel, and act in their daily lives. An integrated approach to effective management takes into account both emotional needs, implementing techniques of stress control and emotional regulation, and fostering emotional intelligence. An all-around approach to managing mental and emotional health, people can stand up well to the stresses of life, stay in healthy relationships, and gain personal and professional success with resilience and confidence. This holistic care of one's mental state is the beginning principle for leading a balanced and fulfilling life.

Recognizing Mental Health Needs

Recognition of mental health needs is one of the first steps toward effective mental health management. Mental health includes our emotional, psychological, and social well-being and impacts every part of our lives, including the way we cope with stress, respond to other people, and make decisions. A recognition of mental health needs is understanding that everyone is bound to have problems at some point in time and that these problems need to be tackled for overall wellness (Holman & Lorig, 2014). This awareness demands alertness for signs of mental health disorders which could be from persistent melancholy, nervousness, and restlessness to even physical manifestations such as headache, tiredness, or a sleep pattern that might have resulted from emotional stress. Early recognition may therefore prevent this situation from becoming worse and allow for a better opportunity for positive intervention. Apart from self-awareness, society is now progressively coming to understand the relevance of mental health issues and the stigma attached to it, and people can open up freely about their challenges. People will be more likely to seek avenues of support through counseling, therapy, or wellness programs if they feel they will not be judged when asking for help. This thereby encompasses both personal awareness and social culture which nurtures the encouragement of getting help. This lays a foundation for individuals to seek leading mental management strategies that can make society better health-wise and supportive.

Techniques for Stress Management and Emotional Regulation

Stress management and emotional regulation are necessary skills for maintaining mental wellness, as they provide tools to overcome life's challenges. Stress is an integral part of life, but uncontrolled stress causes several negative impacts on mental and physical health, which can lead to anxiety, depression, high blood pressure, and weakened immunity, among others (Saunders et al., 2007). Hence, learning and practicing stress management techniques is necessary and should be done constantly. Typical practices include the use of time management and boundary-setting, which enable individuals to best apply their time and energy, thus reducing feelings of overwhelm. Physical activities, such as exercise, yoga, and taking walks around outside, reduce stress by releasing endorphins, which promotes a good mood.

Mindfulness-based practices, such as meditation and deep breathing, have commonly been popularly practiced in relation to benefits with regard to stress management and emotional regulation. Meditation is the practice of focus on the present and letting go of judgment (Kendall et al., 2007). This calms the mind and opens the mind to a new perspective for stressful situations. Deep breathing and progressive muscle relaxation help decrease physical tension, commonly associated with stress, while bringing a sense of calm that may be used in both preventive and responsive ways to stressors. Another helpful approach is cognitive reframing, through which there is conscious changing of one's perspective regarding a stressful situation. Through shifting the thoughts from negative to more constructive perspectives, people can reduce the emotional impact of given situations and therefore live a healthier mental state and improved adaptability. Emotional regulation involves the process by which people manage their emotions, how they feel, and how they express them in various situations. The key techniques that inculcate emotional regulation include identification of triggers or what pushes one to become upset, self-soothing methods, and proper healthy ways of coping, like writing or talking to a supportive friend. Emotional regulation also fosters the acceptance and feeling of emotions without being drenched by them (Dobie, 2007). Such inner strength has been often termed as emotional resilience which enables people to bounce back from trying phases of life with a balance of inner well-being. Therefore, both stress management and emotional regulation merge towards better mental health since it helps the individuals maintain a calm existence, face the problems in life with more composed approach, and develops inner peace to enhance the quality of life .

The Role of Emotional Intelligence in Health

Increasingly accepted as an integral part of mental and emotional health, emotional intelligence (EI) involves the capacity to identify, understand, control, and utilize emotions effectively in oneself and in others. Having a direct bearing on the relationship, communication, and stress-coping mechanism of any individual, high EI facilitates one in decoding accurately one's own emotional state and those connected to others, thereby providing a boost to empathy and social bonding. This emotional intelligence empowers people to respond appropriately in most social and professional settings, handling conflicts, misunderstandings, and collaborative efforts with relative ease (Mohebi et al., 2013).

Self-awareness, an important element of emotional intelligence, is a major component of mental health management. It enables one to identify his or her emotional triggers and stressors. Understanding what makes them feel a certain way will allow people to be proactive and so control those emotions in a manner that will not compromise their well-being. For instance, high EI may make an individual realize they get anxious about a specific work environment; this means they can prepare themselves psychologically and avoid stress at an overwhelming level. The second key EI capability is self-regulation - the control of impulses by thoughtful responses to situations rather than overreacting - which helps to prevent oversensitivities and ensuing stress and perhaps conflict.

Social awareness and relationship management are two more key capabilities of EI contributing to appropriate mental health. Social awareness; it's the feeling of what one is experiencing. Empathy in human beings leads to understanding and sharing the same feelings thus creating a stronger network. Social support, one of the key dimensions for mental health resilience, is likely to be higher among emotionally intelligent individuals who tend to hold positive relationship and avoid social complexities which result in reduced stress and greater overall satisfaction with their interactions (Richards et al., 2010). Emotional intelligence develops appropriate relationship management skills to enable constructive and collective communication management of conflict, hence reducing interpersonal tensions that might otherwise lead to emotional strain. Apart from contributing to personal well-being, EI has a striking contribution to physical health through the reduction of stress responses that later develop to chronic health issues. It has been proven that high EI leads to low levels of cortisol levels; it is the stress hormone that leads to all illnesses through responses to stress. In addition, emotionally intelligent people are more likely to have healthier lifestyles because they are more aware of their general wellbeing and often prioritize self-care practices- regular exercise, balanced nutrition, and adequate sleep-all of which support mental health. In sum, EI is an incredibly valuable resource for the management of mental and emotional health: not only about individual resilience but also about healthier, more harmonious interactions and a better sense of well-being in everyday life.

THE INFLUENCE OF PERSONAL BELIEFS ON HEALTH

Personal beliefs are also influential to health choices and behaviors; through them, an individual defines his approach both in preventive and reactive health care. Health beliefs are not only personal but are mainly intertwined with the social, cultural, and environmental environments with which changes occur all throughout life. Health-related beliefs are initially obtained from parents, peers, and community members by people who learned it at a very young age and would fixate into personal convictions. Such beliefs can be liberating and encourage healthy behavior, or they can be restrictive and bring about poor health outcomes as a result of avoidable neglect or resistance to medical advice. Personal health beliefs influence not only the decision to participate in behaviors such as regular exercise, a healthy diet, and regular checks but also decisions about risks, such as smoking or overconsumption of alcohol (Bell et al., 2016). Understanding these beliefs might, therefore, help to consider the depth of them and why they make a particular health choice and how, from here, they might be supported to make different decisions in the future.

How Health Beliefs Shape Behavior

Heath beliefs form the kind of prism that follows through in people's perception of risks to their health, the seriousness of a possible health problem, and the advantages and disadvantages of acting. Health beliefs are a concept in many theories, such as the Health Belief Model (HBM), which proposes that behaviors are influenced by several basic factors, among which are: perceived susceptibility, perceived severity, perceived benefits, and perceived barriers (K. R. Lorig & Holman, 2003). For example, a person is more vulnerable to an ailment like diabetes or heart-related disease; they feel that such diseases hamper them drastically, and hence, there are greater chances of adopting prevention measures like healthy diet and exercise. However, if they perceive high barriers-for instance, the cost or hassle of routine medical check-ups-they may be less likely to act even if they know or believe the risks. For instance, an ardent believer in natural remedies will avoid certain types of medication, even if it has been proven and regarded scientifically to be the best. It will help in the management of chronic illness or seeking early intervention in mostly preventable diseases. Therefore, health beliefs are both motivators and inhibitors, as perceived pros and cons associate with each action. These beliefs form a base from which interventions can be attuned to be sensitive toward the point of view of each individual, but simultaneously enhance behavior for better health.

Overcoming Limiting Beliefs in Health Management

These are beliefs that limit an individual's engagement in a healthy way of life or even to seek necessary medical care. It is deep-rooted, and it may be owing to past history, cultural narratives, or misinformation. For example, the idea that physical fitness is not needed or indiscernible may make a person who has grown up in such an environment avoid physical activity. Similarly, one raised to believe that mental health issues indicate weakness may avoid mental health care even after they become mentally ill.

The process of elimination of such beliefs needs to be active at times with education, healthy model exposure, and psychological support. For instance, limiting exercise-related beliefs can be reframed so that people embrace the idea of 'happiness' and incremental progresses in adopting an active lifestyle instead of living in fear of fitness. Similarly, if one believes that some diseases are indeed inevitable due to a hereditary predisposition, he or she might not even try lifestyle changes to handle such potential risks. Educating these people about how diet, exercise, and managing stress can reduce certain risks for diseases may even lead this limiting belief to something motivating. Professionals in the health and wellness community are just as crucial in helping to raise these beliefs and leading them towards empowering, evidence-based perspectives on health and self-care (Udlis, 2011).

The Impact of Cultural and Social Factors on Personal Health

Cultural and social factors greatly affect individual beliefs and practices surrounding health, from the type of food that we prefer to eat to the kind of exercise that we like, and from attitudes toward medical intervention to healthy or unhealthy practices. An important influence on health practices are those cultural norms about what is "healthy" or "unhealthy," and such norms are based upon a concept of identity and tradition. For instance, in some cultures, preference will be to herbal and home remedies as opposed to pharmaceutical solutions, which will heighten reluctance to seek modern medical treatment when needed. Secondly, cultural belief systems regarding the human body and weight seem to impact diet and exercise behavior tremendously; for example, there are cultures where a fuller body is an indicator of good health and prosperity, therefore seemingly engaging in various health practices as opposed to those other cultures where thin bodies are the ideal.

Social factors also play a significant role in formulating health beliefs. Health-related behaviors and attitudes are closely linked with family, community, socio-economic status, and availability of health care resources. For instance, individuals belonging to better socio-economic status background have greater access towards information, medical services, and options for preventive care that enhance their health beliefs and practice. People in underserved communities may perceive healthcare as an emergency service rather than preventive service because they do not have much to begin with, thereby creating a health belief system centered around crisis management rather than health maintenance. Social support networks of friends and family will often reinforce or discourage certain health practices (K. Lorig, 1993). Behavior is more likely to occur if social networks share the commitment to and promote behaviors like regular physical activity and healthy eating. Health education and intervention programs that factor in the cultural and social elements need a culturally responsive approach that will take into account the uniqueness of the participants' backgrounds, while focusing them on the positive aspects of health behavior. For example, service providers within the targeted cultural groups can easily earn the trusts of the patients by assimilating local beliefs and practices in treatment recommendations where applicable, which might lead to high compliance with medical advice. This understanding creates channels for effective communication that bridge the gap between modern health care delivery techniques and beliefs in traditional health, leading to supporting persons into taking culturally relevant healthy choices in order to make informed health choices that resonate with cultural values.

GOAL-SETTING AND SELF-MONITORING IN HEALTH AND FITNESS

For long-term health and fitness, then, it seems the salient approaches will include not only goal-setting but also self-monitoring. Together, they construct a planned, dynamic set of actions that both facilitate movement toward desired goals-but equally accommodate improvement and flexibility. Well-designed goal-setting brings meaning, direction, and fundamentally breaks grand, often intimidating or very complex objectives into manageable, attainable moves. By contrast, self-monitoring provides the foundation for accountability-an immediate view of one's journey and a guide for making adjustments as needed (Grady & Gough, 2014). Putting these together enables people to build healthier lifestyles and to achieve sustainable, personalized fitness outcomes.

Setting SMART Health Goals

Out of the many approaches devised for setting health and fitness goals, one which has proved to be very effective is the SMART goal setting. SMART is an acronym that stands for Specific, Measurable, Achievable, Relevant, and Time-bound. Each of these components makes a unique contribution to goal-setting. For example, the "Specific" component requires that the goals be clearly defined, thus removing ambiguity. Instead of simply saying "I want to lose weight," a specific goal would be "I want to lose five pounds in one month." That type of accuracy gives a clear objective, and the individual will know exactly what he or she is working for.

The "Measurable" component of SMART goals introduces an objective standard of measurement to define the level of progress attained in the area of health and fitness (McDonald, 2012). Measurable goals allow the possibility of some kind of track record being kept about the progress being made. This might be pounds lost, steps taken, time spent on exercise, and so forth. This would be motivating and one would literally know how well things are improving due to his or her efforts. The "Achievable" part is as important because it must be realistic considering one's current health status, lifestyle, and given resources. The setting of achievable goals gives the confidence not to get into burnout or discouragement. "Relevant" goals make it sure that the work done by the individual has to be in tune with that person's motivation and preference (Mackey et al., 2016). For example, when an individual wants to exercise based on family history for heart disease, the related goal may be daily brisk walks or running. Finally, time-bound goals contain a specific time-frame, leading to creating the need for constant effort and thereby circumventing procrastination. For instance, time-bound goals might be to run 5k in three months of time, which gives an individual a specific amount of time to strive for.

Tracking Progress: Tools and Techniques

The importance of tracking progress in health and fitness is that it yields evidence for the measurement of how far one has come, in addition to pointing out areas that might need extra attention. Tools and techniques are now available to make tracking easier and more efficient than ever. Examples of popular devices are Fitbits, Garmin watches, or even Apple Watches. Users get real data about health with such devices, including steps and calories burned, heart rate, and sleep patterns. Such devices also sync with apps on mobile phones, allowing a view of progress as well as trends over time. It is this kind of mechanism that creates positive consistent feedback, which is often more motivating because it shows immediate conditions and habits.

Nutrition and weight management people can log food intake, followed by tracking macronutrient ratios, monitoring what one has consumed and showing whether one is in balance or not when using food tracking apps such as MyFitness-Pal or Lose It. Such applications greatly help in identifying patterns in choice of food, understanding the size of portions, and keeping within a target calorie range. Besides digital technology, maintaining a health journal can prove to be a very effective method for those who prefer a more hands-on approach. Writing routines of exercise, food choices, mood, and energy levels creates a personal record, which supplies an all-round view of one's journey to be reflected upon in order to comment on the progress made or identify patterns in behavior (Zimmerman & Kitsantas, 1996). Other tracking methods may include fitness tests or regular check-in with health professionals. For example, the individual can conduct routine tests of fitness-something like running timed intervals, maxes on weights lifted, or flexibility tests to determine improvement over time. Regular weigh-ins, body measurements, or blood tests, if medically encouraged, can give other dimensions of feedback on their physical well-being. These metrics create a more holistic view of improvements and point out what works and what might not work.

Adjusting Goals Based on Self-Monitoring and Feedback

Based on self-monitoring and feedback, the aim should be adjusted because such practice helps a health or fitness goal remain relevant, realistic, and possible over time. It usually involves periodic assessment of the progress attained and any other potential barriers that hinder more progress in the task at hand. For example, if one intent to run 5 miles daily, then after a short period discovers the distance is too far or even causes pain and considerable fatigue on the joints, the distance may be cut down, or rest days may be included to avoid injury. This flexibility of compromising a couple of goals can easily be taken to a more feasible practice, not to mention the reduction of frustration and burnout as a result of attempting to accomplish unrealistic expectations. Self-monitoring feedback is also very useful in knowing when it is time to set higher goals (Rasheed et al., 2019). Once the goal has become too easy or even redundant, lifting the challenge may continue the interest and motivation moving onward. For example, a person sets a goal to do a given number of repetitions with a certain weight and achieves it without strain consecutively for several repetitions in a row, they might raise the weight or increase the repetitions. This process, often called "progressive overload" in the gym, ensures that goals are constantly being upgraded with the individual's developing capabilities and that there will be no plateaus in their development process and constant improvement.

Feedback should not only arise from personal tools for monitoring but also from professionals, such as personal trainers, nutritionists, or coaches. A coach might analyze running form to identify chances for improving efficiency, while a nutritionist might advise changes to the diet in an effort to boost energy levels. Such type of external feedback keeps individuals from repeating their mistakes ever and provides some objective ideas to modify one's plan while enhancing the overall effectiveness of that very plan. Change goals on such feedback keeping a balance between challenge and achievability, as well as making effective engagement with the progress made.

The Role of Goal-Setting and Self-Monitoring in Developing Self-Discipline and Motivation

Incorporation of goal setting and self-monitoring not only provides the capability of improving health but also self-control and intrinsic motivation. Once they can envision concrete progress toward achieving a goal, such as losing the intended weight or attaining strength, it encourages positive behavior and enhances their belief in their achievement potential. This result acts as a good motivator for the accomplishment, keeping them on the same track. This eventually becomes self-discipline as health and fitness activities simply become accustomed parts of their lifestyle rather than isolated attempts. The process of changing goals and tracking of progress also assists students in acquiring other significant life skills, such as resilience and adaptability. The common experience during health and fitness is that improvement stalls at one juncture or another, whether due to illness, injury, or just general lack of motivation, and the process of continually modifying goals based on feedback helps students develop a flexible mentality. They view setbacks as possibly the only opportunities to review their strategic approach and redirect efforts toward realistic and achievable goals rather than just failing if they do not get immediate positive results. Resilience then benefits other areas of life because it tries to instill a proactive or solution-oriented approach to challenges rather than the passively reactive approach of mere health and fitness (McDonald & Trost, 2015).

Goal-Setting and Self-Monitoring as Cornerstones of Long-Term Health Success

Together, goal setting and selfmonitoring become a sustainable route to health and fitness wherein one guides the other. Thus, using SMART goals gives an individual a clear vision of objectives to be realized that would match his capabilities and aspiration. Self-monitoring provides insight through means of tools, techniques, and feedback in order to remain responsible and accountable toward changes over time. This cycle of establishing, tracking, adjusting, and attaining fosters a sense of personal ownership over one's health journey. This kind of application over time can help to develop habits as long-lasting as fitness, mental outlook, and the quality of life. Progressing individuals' goals usually change periodically as their needs and circumstances do. This flexibility- augmented by discipline and motivation from self-monitoring ensures that health and fitness do not become fads but are instead integral components of a meaningful life. Of course, goal-setting and self-monitoring should transcend narrower goals to make it so that health and fitness are no longer the same as short-term goals but long-term concerns as well.

DEVELOPING A POSITIVE HEALTH IDENTITY

A positive health identity takes a while, and its influence is phenomenal when it comes to engagement with the own well-being. In this sense, an integral perspective of physical and mental health influences how a person perceives and values as well as actively manages global well-being. Unlike the transitory nature of health goals, a good health identity becomes a stable aspect of the self. It simply reiterated the belief that health cannot be only the absence of disease but a dynamic pursuit of strength, vitality, and emotional balance. A positive health identity reflects a person seeing health as an important aspect of life. They perceive themselves as being assisted in the pursuit and maintenance of relationships and goals by that health (Furler et al., 2008). It essentially translates to wellness and the practice of living in a way that will nourish the body, mind, and emotions. This is an identity assumed conscientiously through self-observation and the intent to set up a healthy environment and lifestyle. Health-oriented thought processes and activities become so internalized with time that well-being becomes a nucleus of one's self-configuration.

Building a Positive Relationship with One's Body

Most fundamental to a positive health identity is building a good relationship with one's body. This relationship with the body impacts attitudes toward appearance, strength, and actual physical capabilities. Instead of regarding their body purely in terms of aesthetics or performance, a person with positive health identity honors and respects his or her body for all that it lets him or her do. The change in mind set toward supporting people to view the body as a companion through the journey to wellness. Positive body relation is often undertaken with some self-affirmation activities such as regards of body achievements, self-compassion, and appreciating the qualities of strength and flexibility of the body (Vassilev et al., 2014). For example, it may be as simple as taking a few minutes a day to reflect on how strong the body is, the flexibility of the body, and even the recuperation from being ill. Also, aware practices like yoga or stretching or even meditation promote body awareness and sense of knowing one's body. In addition, a body-loving relationship entails accepting one's body as it ages or suffering from any medical condition. Changing life from age, pregnancy, health condition, or otherwise would impact the physical capacity and, therefore the look which is sometimes hard to accept for most people in a society celebrating only the young who are free from physical flaws. However, tolerance of the body in all stages of development helps the individuals build resilience and encourages them to keep geared and committed to the care of their bodies since health comes first and not the looks. This way of balancing body positivity becomes less about fulfilling societal expectations and much more about having the motivation to live in a healthy way which honors the special, changing nature of one's physicality.

Overcoming Negative Health Perceptions

Overcoming negative health perceptions is incredibly important because such perceptions shape how people view their bodies, health potential, and the ability to engage in wellness activities (Ownsworth et al., 2002). Negative health perceptions often arise from either the experience of illness or injury or from pressure from others to conform to certain body types. If a person is carrying some negative health beliefs, then this makes the person resistive to exercise and a healthy diet or any type of medical check-up due to fear or insecurity or feeling that everything they do would be a waste of time. So, in this case, it becomes extremely necessary to change this perception for being healthy and for betterment. Awareness and reflection of the self, then reframing thought patterns into being more constructive and optimistic is a requirement for changing unhealthy beliefs with more healthy ones (Strecher et al., 1986). Through this means, distorted or over-critical thinking can be identified and challenged. Instead of dwelling on perceived weaknesses, one can now focus on his strengths as well as areas for improvement. Instead of dwelling on actual physical weakness, for instance, a person may focus on the advantage of taking small, consistent steps toward greater health. More so, education can be mainly directed towards disproof of the prevalent health myths and the enlightening of individuals based on correct information about what their body is capable of if well-taken care of. The more an individual is exposed to credible health information, be it from books, consultations, or any known resource, the more they are bound to change their outlook based on realistic expectations of health. A good support system, including a friendly family or a health community, can aid in the creation of a positive perspective that encourages the pursuit of health.

Cultivating a Health-Promoting Identity

A health-promoting identity involves the integration of wellness as part of a sense of self, where health-promoting behaviors become natural and rewarding. A health-promoting identity is a perception that one is someone who puts health first, values self-care, and fits decisions with that value (Chen et al., 2018). It is not an identity based on short-term health goals but a long-term orientation towards well-being. A health-promoting identity is self-sustaining; they do not require rewards or pressure from the outside in order to sustain it because wellness habits have become part of who they are. For example, while someone else may consider it a chore to move their body, somebody with a health-promoting identity would have fun with exercise, trying new ways of engaging their fitnesseque, and seeing fitness as a way of rejoicing in the power and energy inside of them. In order to create that identity, one can set realistic, meaningful health objectives in line with his or her values and lifestyle. For example, such objectives can be about developing the habits of daily life like the intake of water, exercising, meditation against stress, or sleep. The success at those objectives further reinforces a positive self-image as someone who cares about health, and success after success makes him/her more intertwined with health in one's identity. The development of this identity involves encouraging and fostering an atmosphere that promotes wellness. The readying of a kitchen to stand before one with health-positive foods or the creation of a comfortable setting for meditation and relaxation makes it easier to behave positively in terms of health (Cramm et al., 2013).

A health-positive identity is also elastic and flexible, bending to changes of life stages, bodily conditions, and emotional needs. Those with the health-promoting identity understand that health is fluid, so they align their activities and changes with the natural flow of their lives, yet still prioritize health. For example, at times of great stress or frailty, an individual with the health-promoting identity will redirect his or her attention to less strenuous forms of exercise or emphasize mental wellness practices; after all, he or she has learned to shift his or her practices sometimes as a function of maintaining long-term health. Ultimately, a healthy identity puts personal values into lifestyle choices and actually allows people to live purposefully, proactively, and in a meaningful way that is nourishing for both body and mind (Page et al., 2020).

CONCLUSION

This chapter has underlined some very important roles of self-awareness, self-reflection, and mindfulness regarding effective proactive health management. Developing self-awareness helps one observe physical, emotional, and mental states properly and can thereby identify the potential health issues early and make proper decision that helps the overall well-being. Developing self-awareness enables people to notice even slight changes in their physical and mental well-being, possibly a developing health issue. For instance, pattern recognition for tiredness, mood changes, or changes in health status may send out the individual to look for professional help early or to make lifestyle changes that would reduce risk. The concept of self-awareness is divided into three: the physical, emotional, and mental planes showing how each uniquely contributes to balanced and healthy life. Also, closely linked to self-awareness is the activity of self-reflection, where there is an appraisal of one's past behaviors, emotions, and health outcomes that can guide future choices regarding health. Analyzing past experiences, making patterns out, provides individuals with greater awareness of how behaviors and emotions impact their wellness. For example, reflection helps people identify sources of stress or bad habits, like emotional eating, a sedentary way of life, and change behavior in ways that might enhance well-being. Reflection is also helpful in goal setting because it enables one to set personal health goals that may be suited to one's experience and level of need. Having set realistic, concrete objectives diet, exercise, or mental well-being clients can stay motivated and develop habits that may create long-term health.

Another referenced tool in effective management of health is mindfulness. In the execution of exercises, such as meditation, attention while eating, or concentration on the present moment, the person cultivates more elevated control over themselves and their emotions. It leads to reduced stress because it encourages relaxation and, therefore, positively affects mental and physical health. Studies have shown that an individual who regularly practices mindfulness tends to reduce stress hormone levels and shows emotional stability and improved sleep quality. All these are keys to well-being. A person who happens to be aware and present with sensations in the body, thoughts, and emotions without judgment can better understand the health needs and therefore make more appropriate decisions. Acceptance and compassion through mindfulness-based practice help a lot in dealing with health journeys rather than criticisms. It is important in that it discusses the self-care subject, which bases a healthy regime of sustainability on regular exercise, proper nutrition, sleep, and recovery. For instance, exercises favoring cardiovascular health strengthen the muscles, and with the released endorphins, they contribute to strength both in body and mind. Conversely, well-balanced nutrition provides the body with essential nutrients, fuels cellular functions, and gives immune health, thereby lowering the risk of chronic diseases. All of these ensure proper replenishment of the body and mind and are the source foundation of physical vitality, mental clarity, and emotional resilience. Thus, they are indispensable elements in an overall health management approach.

The mental and emotional health management goes further into techniques that help people negotiate stress, regulate emotions, and cultivate emotional intelligence. Stress management techniques such as time management, establishing boundaries, and engaging in physical activity would help offset the adverse implications of chronic stress, which may have effects like anxiety, depression, and physical complaints. Use of skills related to emotional regulation, such as deep breathing and cognitive reframing, allows the person to do constructive processing rather than acting impulsively. It suggests that the development of emotional intelligence-that is, the ability to understand and manage emotions appropriately and use them effectively-is particularly important for enhancing not only one's own well-being but also harmonious relations with others. High emotional intelligence reveals facilities such as empathy, social bonding, and resilience, which in turn fortify stability of mind and generally enhance the quality of life.

The chapter also underlines the influences of personal beliefs, cultural norms, and social factors on health behaviors and serves to demonstrate the way in which these influences shape the way one approaches health. Health beliefs often derive from early experiences with family and culture and dictate decision-making about diet, exercise, and preventive care. In this respect, the underlying cultural belief that natural remedies work better will limit the amount people will go to for medical care. Apart from medical factors, other social determinants of socioeconomic status, among many others, may facilitate or limit health-promoting behaviors. Becoming knowledgeable about the cultural and social dimensions of health can overcome wrong beliefs, hence following the scientifically proven health practice path. The chapter discusses this further in building a positive health identity as part of overcoming negative health perceptions, and that having a supportive relationship with the body is also discussed in the chapter. Developing a positive health identity requires embracing the construct of health as dynamic and more deeply intertwined with self-concept than as nothing less than the absence of illness. Such an identity leads to urge towards well-being, ability to be healthy conscious, and it involves health behaviors that are better congruent with respect for the body. Positive relationship with body develops through having self-compassion and welcoming change within one's body, but even more so, through focusing on functionality rather than on appearance. Breaking down negative perceptions of health, such as those that include body dissatisfaction or fatalistic beliefs regarding illness, is important in keeping health on a proactive attitude.

REFERENCES

Alpay, L., Van Der Boog, P., & Dumaij, A. (2011). An empowerment-based approach to developing innovative e-health tools for self-management. *Health Informatics Journal*, *17*(4), 247–255. DOI: 10.1177/1460458211420089 PMID: 22193825

Bell, J., Dziekan, G., Pollack, C., & Mahachai, V. (2016). Self-Care in the Twenty First Century: A Vital Role for the Pharmacist. *Advances in Therapy*, *33*(10), 1691–1703. DOI: 10.1007/s12325-016-0395-5 PMID: 27535290

Bronikowski, M., Bronikowska, M., & Glapa, A. (2016). Do they need goals or support? A report from a goal-setting intervention using physical activity monitors in youth. *International Journal of Environmental Research and Public Health*, *13*(9), 914. DOI: 10.3390/ijerph13090914 PMID: 27649219

Camerini, L., Schulz, P. J., & Nakamoto, K. (2012). Differential effects of health knowledge and health empowerment over patients' self-management and health outcomes: A cross-sectional evaluation. *Patient Education and Counseling*, *89*(2), 337–344. DOI: 10.1016/j.pec.2012.08.005 PMID: 22959333

Carden, J., Jones, R. J., & Passmore, J. (2022). Defining Self-Awareness in the Context of Adult Development: A Systematic Literature Review. *Journal of Management Education*, *46*(1), 140–177. DOI: 10.1177/1052562921990065

Chen, Y., Chang, L., Liu, C., Ho, Y., Weng, S., & Tsai, T. (2018). The Roles of Social Support and Health Literacy in Self-Management Among Patients With Chronic Kidney Disease. *Journal of Nursing Scholarship*, *50*(3), 265–275. DOI: 10.1111/jnu.12377 PMID: 29569423

Cramm, J. M., Hartgerink, J. M., Steyerberg, E. W., Bakker, T. J., Mackenbach, J. P., & Nieboer, A. P. (2013). Understanding older patients' self-management abilities: Functional loss, self-management, and well-being. *Quality of Life Research: An International Journal of Quality of Life Aspects of Treatment, Care and Rehabilitation*, *22*(1), 85–92. DOI: 10.1007/s11136-012-0131-9 PMID: 22350532

Dineen-Griffin, S., Garcia-Cardenas, V., Williams, K., & Benrimoj, S. I. (2019). Helping patients help themselves: A systematic review of self-management support strategies in primary health care practice. *PLoS One*, *14*(8), e0220116. DOI: 10.1371/journal.pone.0220116 PMID: 31369582

Dobie, S. (2007). Reflections on a well-traveled path: Self-awareness, mindful practice, and relationship-centered care as foundations for medical education. *Academic Medicine*, *82*(4), 422–427. DOI: 10.1097/01.ACM.0000259374.52323.62 PMID: 17414201

Du, S., & Yuan, C. (2010). Evaluation of patient self-management outcomes in health care: A systematic review. *International Nursing Review*, *57*(2), 159–167. DOI: 10.1111/j.1466-7657.2009.00794.x PMID: 20579149

Furler, J., Walker, C., Blackberry, I., Dunning, T., Sulaiman, N., Dunbar, J., Best, J., & Young, D. (2008). The emotional context of self-management in chronic illness: A qualitative study of the role of health professional support in the self-management of type 2 diabetes. *BMC Health Services Research*, *8*(1), 214. DOI: 10.1186/1472-6963-8-214 PMID: 18928555

Goldman, D. P., & Smith, J. P. (2002). Can patient self-management help explain the SES health gradient? *Proceedings of the National Academy of Sciences of the United States of America*, *99*(16), 10929–10934. DOI: 10.1073/pnas.162086599 PMID: 12140364

Grady, P. A., & Gough, L. L. (2014). Self-Management: A Comprehensive Approach to Management of Chronic Conditions. *American Journal of Public Health*, *104*(8), e25–e31. DOI: 10.2105/AJPH.2014.302041 PMID: 24922170

Heijmans, M., Waverijn, G., Rademakers, J., van der Vaart, R., & Rijken, M. (2015). Functional, communicative and critical health literacy of chronic disease patients and their importance for self-management. *Patient Education and Counseling*, *98*(1), 41–48. DOI: 10.1016/j.pec.2014.10.006 PMID: 25455794

Holman, H., & Lorig, K. (2014). Perceived self-efficacy in self-management of chronic disease. *Self-Efficacy*, 305–324.

Kendall, E., Catalano, T., Kuipers, P., Posner, N., Buys, N., & Charker, J. (2007). Recovery following stroke: The role of self-management education. *Social Science & Medicine*, *64*(3), 735–746. DOI: 10.1016/j.socscimed.2006.09.012 PMID: 17079060

Liu, S., & Willoughby, J. F. (2018). Do Fitness Apps Need Text Reminders? An Experiment Testing Goal-Setting Text Message Reminders to Promote Self-Monitoring. *Journal of Health Communication*, *23*(4), 379–386. DOI: 10.1080/10810730.2018.1455768 PMID: 29601270

Lorig, K. (1993). Self-management of chronic illness: A model for the future. *Generations: Journal of the American Society on Aging*, *17*(3), 11–14.

Lorig, K. (1996). Chronic Disease Self-Management: A Model for Tertiary Prevention. *The American Behavioral Scientist*, *39*(6), 676–683. DOI: 10.1177/0002764296039006005

Lorig, K. R., & Holman, H. R. (2003). Self-management education: History, definition, outcomes, and mechanisms. *Annals of Behavioral Medicine*, *26*(1), 1–7. DOI: 10.1207/S15324796ABM2601_01 PMID: 12867348

Lorig, K. R., Ritter, P., Stewart, A. L., Sobel, D. S., Brown, B. W.Jr, Bandura, A., Gonzalez, V. M., Laurent, D. D., & Holman, H. R. (2001). Chronic disease self-management program: 2-year health status and health care utilization outcomes. *Medical Care*, *39*(11), 1217–1223. DOI: 10.1097/00005650-200111000-00008 PMID: 11606875

Mackey, L. M., Doody, C., Werner, E. L., & Fullen, B. (2016). Self-Management Skills in Chronic Disease Management: What Role Does Health Literacy Have? *Medical Decision Making*, *36*(6), 741–759. DOI: 10.1177/0272989X16638330 PMID: 27053527

McDonald, S. M. (2012). *The effects of a SMART goal setting and self-monitoring intervention on physical activity and fitness in middle school students.* https://ir.library.oregonstate.edu/concern/graduate_thesis_or_dissertations/xd07gw96b

McDonald, S. M., & Trost, S. G. (2015). The effects of a goal setting intervention on aerobic fitness in middle school students. *Journal of Teaching in Physical Education*, *34*(4), 576–587. DOI: 10.1123/jtpe.2014-0138

Mohebi, S., Azadbakht, L., Feizi, A., Sharifirad, G., & Kargar, M. (2013). Review the key role of self-efficacy in diabetes care. *Journal of Education and Health Promotion*, *2*(1), 36. DOI: 10.4103/2277-9531.115827 PMID: 24083286

Normand, M. P. (2008). Increasing physical activity through self-monitoring, goal setting, and feedback. *Behavioral Interventions*, *23*(4), 227–236. DOI: 10.1002/bin.267

Ownsworth, T. L., McFarland, K., & Young, R. McD. (2002). The investigation of factors underlying deficits in self-awareness and self-regulation. *Brain Injury : [BI]*, *16*(4), 291–309. DOI: 10.1080/02699050110103986 PMID: 11953001

Page, E. J., Massey, A. S., Prado-Romero, P. N., & Albadawi, S. (2020). The Use of Self-Monitoring and Technology to Increase Physical Activity: A Review of the Literature. *Perspectives on Behavior Science*, *43*(3), 501–514. DOI: 10.1007/s40614-020-00260-0 PMID: 33029577

Rasheed, S. P., Younas, A., & Sundus, A. (2019). Self-awareness in nursing: A scoping review. *Journal of Clinical Nursing*, *28*(5–6), 762–774. DOI: 10.1111/jocn.14708 PMID: 30362645

Richards, K. C., Campenni, C. E., & Muse-Burke, J. L. (2010). Self-care and well-being in mental health professionals: The mediating effects of self-awareness and mindfulness. *Journal of Mental Health Counseling*, *32*(3), 247–264. DOI: 10.17744/mehc.32.3.0n31v88304423806

Sadler, E., Wolfe, C. D., & McKevitt, C. (2014). Lay and health care professional understandings of self-management: A systematic review and narrative synthesis. *SAGE Open Medicine*, *2*, 2050312114544493. DOI: 10.1177/2050312114544493 PMID: 26770733

Saunders, P. A., Tractenberg, R. E., Chaterji, R., Amri, H., Harazduk, N., Gordon, J. S., Lumpkin, M., & Haramati, A. (2007). Promoting self-awareness and reflection through an experiential Mind-Body Skills course for first year medical students. *Medical Teacher*, *29*(8), 778–784. DOI: 10.1080/01421590701509647 PMID: 17852720

Strecher, V. J., McEvoy DeVellis, B., Becker, M. H., & Rosenstock, I. M. (1986). The Role of Self-Efficacy in Achieving Health Behavior Change. *Health Education Quarterly*, *13*(1), 73–92. DOI: 10.1177/109019818601300108 PMID: 3957687

Udlis, K. A. (2011). Self-management in chronic illness: Concept and dimensional analysis: Self-management in chronic illness: concept and dimensional analysis. *Journal of Nursing and Healthcare of Chronic Illness*, *3*(2), 130–139. DOI: 10.1111/j.1752-9824.2011.01085.x

Urdang, E. (2010). Awareness of Self—A Critical Tool. *Social Work Education*, *29*(5), 523–538. DOI: 10.1080/02615470903164950

Vago, D. R., & Silbersweig, D. A. (2012). Self-awareness, self-regulation, and self-transcendence (S-ART): A framework for understanding the neurobiological mechanisms of mindfulness. *Frontiers in Human Neuroscience*, *6*, 296. DOI: 10.3389/fnhum.2012.00296 PMID: 23112770

Vassilev, I., Rogers, A., Kennedy, A., & Koetsenruijter, J. (2014). The influence of social networks on self-management support: A metasynthesis. *BMC Public Health*, *14*(1), 719. DOI: 10.1186/1471-2458-14-719 PMID: 25023948

Xie, Z., Liu, K., Or, C., Chen, J., Yan, M., & Wang, H. (2020). An examination of the socio-demographic correlates of patient adherence to self-management behaviors and the mediating roles of health attitudes and self-efficacy among patients with coexisting type 2 diabetes and hypertension. *BMC Public Health*, *20*(1), 1227. DOI: 10.1186/s12889-020-09274-4 PMID: 32787809

Zimmerman, B. J., & Kitsantas, A. (1996). Self-regulated learning of a motoric skill: The role of goal setting and self-monitoring. *Journal of Applied Sport Psychology*, *8*(1), 60–75. DOI: 10.1080/10413209608406308

Chapter 3
Health Systems

Minhaj Ahmed Qidwai
https://orcid.org/0009-0003-0770-481X
Al-Kawthar University, Karachi, Pakistan & American Institute of Healthcare Quality, Pakistan & Unet Consultants, Canada

Mohammad Kabir Gawhari
https://orcid.org/0009-0008-3936-9530
French Medical Institute for Mothers and Children (FMIC), Kabul, Afghanistan

ABSTRACT

In this chapter, the authors provide a basic understanding of the health system and its components. It explores philosophical dimensions of health and how individuals, populations, and health systems are interconnected. The chapter also describes various elements of healthcare systems, including service delivery, healthcare workforce, financing, medical technology, and governance. Furthermore, it discusses the dynamics of the healthcare delivery system, the importance of healthcare planning, and the role of health insurance in providing financial protection. Moreover, the chapter highlights the challenges of healthcare systems, particularly in low- and middle-income countries, and underpins the need for effective management and strategic planning to improve health outcomes. In addition, the chapter introduces the "4S" model—Self, Society, State, and Systems— to highlight how they interact to promote health and well-being. In a nutshell, it provides a foundational understanding of health systems and prepares health professionals to contribute to effective healthcare management.

DOI: 10.4018/979-8-3693-9092-4.ch003

A. INTRODUCTION TO HEALTH SYSTEMS

From a Philosophical perspective, health investigates three levels of health: cell, self, and society (Saad & Prochaska, 2020). The level of the cell accounts for biological functioning within human beings. The level of the self. accounts for the first-person functioning of each human being. The level of society accounts for the group functioning of human beings.

Figure 1.

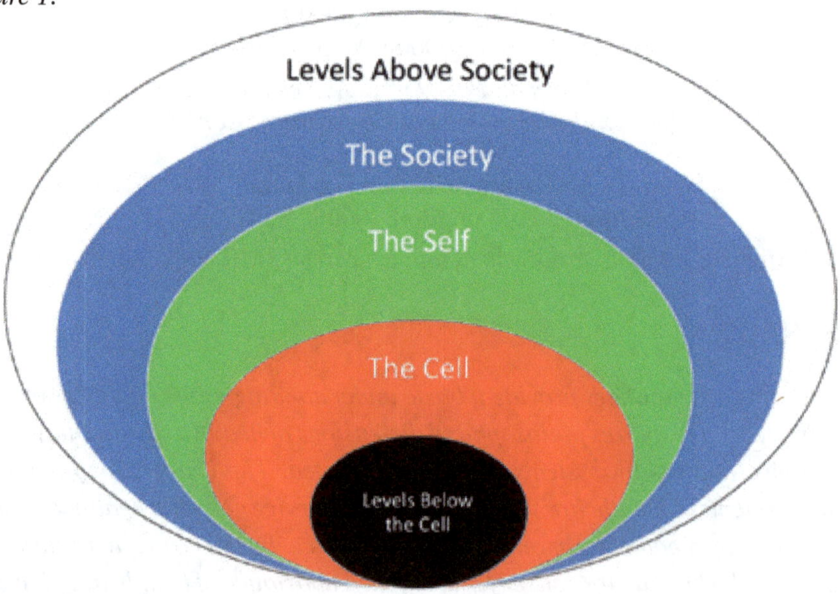

Each System develops its own managing mechanisms. While the State develops its own System, the Society develops its own to manage the Society based on morals and values, while the Self or the individual has two different sets of Systems, one based on his paradigm, believes, and values, while the body System has its own System at the cellular level to manage the biological and immune System.

Figure 2.

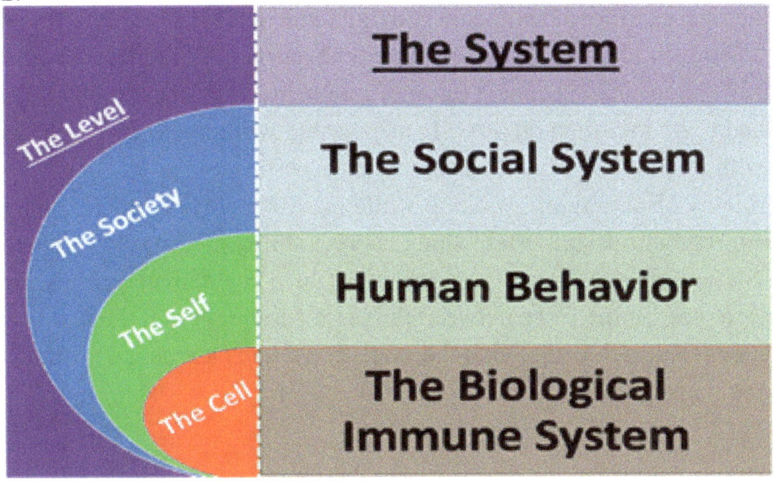

Each system (World Health Organization, 2000) is responsible for generating a maintainable ease of functioning at a level. The biological immune system is responsible at the level of the cell. A human's system of health behaviors is responsible at the level of the self. The social system is responsible at the level of the society. However, the overall System is run by the administrators, healthcare workers, and the leadership of the State.

Figure 3.

The State is responsible for catering to the rights of individuals and developing a System. Considering the Healthcare Management System within the State will depend upon the State policies, regulations, allocation of funds, service delivery quality standards at the institutions, and the people involved in healthcare service delivery. However, if the Public System is inadequate and unable to play its due role, the Private sector or the Society bridges the gap. Thus, the people in Society are responsible for developing a System to serve the needs of the Society. However, Private sector involvement also brings the business aspect in healthcare and the focus is on revenue generation. Therefore, the lack of an adequate healthcare System will bring economic pressure on Self and his health-seeking behaviors. The System offered by the State is essential to provide the needed service to the individual and thus plays a therapeutic role in healthcare management. The biological immune system within the body is involved in the therapeutic measures through the appearance of early warning signs in lung cancer through cough, breathlessness, or bloody sputum which need to be investigated as early as possible while the therapeutic measures in the health system will play their role when accessed. Society also plays its therapeutic role by discouraging smoking while the State plays its therapeutic role by developing regulations and establishing accountability. So, all the "Quad S"-Self, Society, State, and Systems play a therapeutic role in health management. However, Systems are the binding force between the people to be served, the institution, and the resources required to establish the system. Systems are usually established by the State to manage its affairs.

Figure 4.

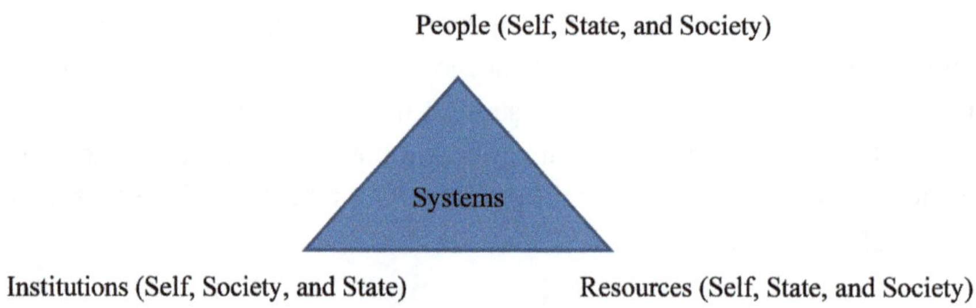

The above explains that Systems are made to manage the Self, Society, and the State and produce the desired impact. Therefore, to run and manage an organization or a project, proper systems basics need to be understood and developed for the organization. Thus, it is essential to understand the basics of "Systems".

Systems comprise the inputs consisting of all resources, which are processed or taken through or throughput for the results or output for an expected result or the intended outcome to achieve the impact or the goals set for the systems. If the outcome is not as per expectations, feedback is given for the reassessment of the inputs.

Figure 5.

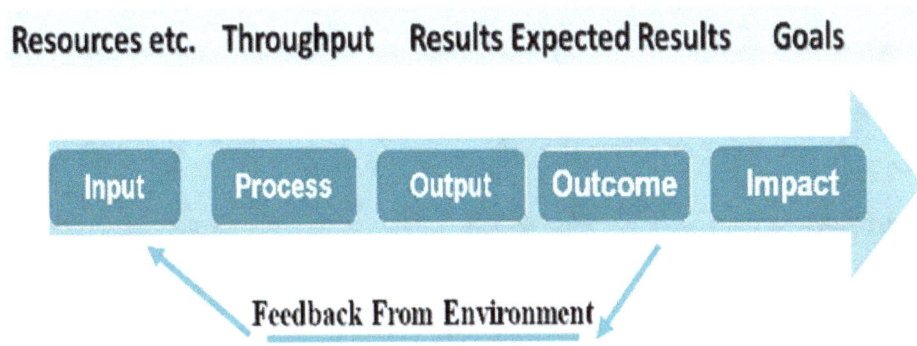

Considering the systems in healthcare, first, we need to understand the definition of health. WHO (World Health Organization, 2000) defines health for an individual, as a "State of Physical, Mental, and Social Well Being and not merely the absence of disease or infirmity". However, Thus, health systems are complex comprising several elements to be handled at the same time to be healthy. WHO defines Health Systems to comprise Service Delivery, Healthcare Workforce, Medical Products and Technology, Finance, Information, Leadership, and Governance.

Figure 6.

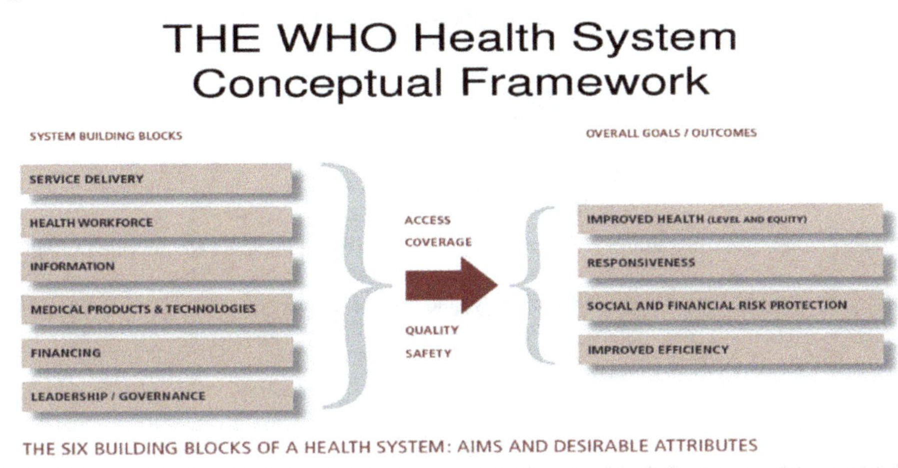

Source: WHO Health System Strengthening Strategy 2007

As per the above framework, the following are the factors that may be the administration and management issues for these components:

Figure 7.

Components	Administration and Management Issues
Leadership and Governance	Accountability, Resources, Health Transition, Bio-terrorism Pandemic, Strategic Planning....
Service Delivery	Purchasing of services, Quality, Diversity and Community Behavior, Effective and Efficient, Equitable and Fair, Social Morbidity-HIV.....
Health Work Force	Motivation/Rewards, Accountability, Capacity Building.....
Information	Management Information System, Patient Centered.....
Healthcare Products and Technology	Social Morbidity-HIV, Drugs, Digital Health......
Financing	Pooling of Resources, Risk Pooling, Purchasing

These factors can be organized under three parameters of Systems-People (Healthcare Workers, Leadership, and Governance), Institutions (involved in providing information, using medical products and technology and service delivery); and providing the necessary resources (towards ensuring the Financing of healthcare and Service Delivery through workforce).

Figure 8.

People (Healthcare Workers, Leadership, and Governance)

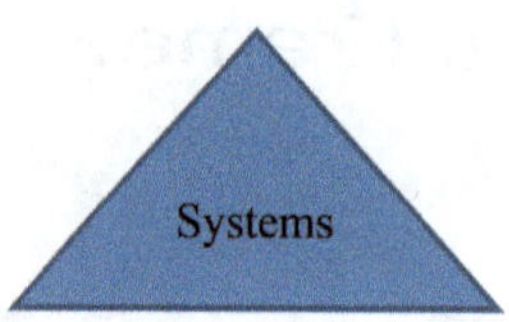

Institutions

Resources (Financing for Service Delivery).

(information, medical products and technology, and service delivery)

B. DEFINING HEALTHCARE SYSTEMS

In healthcare administration, the principal concern is healthcare systems. This is composed of human beings, money, materials, methods, equipment, and so on, which are related to the accomplishment of some goal, or goals. Healthcare systems are essentially social systems (in the attitudes, perceptions, motivations, and expectations of human beings). The goals of the health systems can revolve around prolonging life with quality and preventing premature death; minimizing departures from physiological or function norms by focusing attention on precursors of illness; minimizing discomfort and disability, promoting high-level "wellness" or satisfaction with the environment; extending resistance to ill health by building immunity, and increasing opportunities for consumers to participate in health matters. Therefore, the Health System should deal with health in the context of complete wellbeing! Thus, it can be defined as:

- The totality of socio-cultural beliefs and practices, policies, programs, structural arrangements, and institutions involved in the production and distribution of goods and services meant to promote health, prevent illness, and treat disease.
- A set of sociocultural beliefs about health and illness that form the basis for health-seeking and promotion behavior.
- Institutional arrangements (family, community, health care services) within which that behavior occurs; and
- The socio-economic, political, and physical context for those beliefs and institutions.

To maintain this state of wellbeing, resources are required and Systems are to be managed by People, which include the Self (individuals), Society, and State; and institutions responsible for service delivery.

C. COMPONENTS OF HEALTHCARE SYSTEMS

The components of healthcare systems consist of several interrelated subsystems. Each of these subsystems has a purpose which, if attained, aids the larger system in reaching its overall goals.

If the goal is set to ensure patient safety, then the actors within the system will be the patient and the family members; while the subsystem will include: the patient, nurse, physician, healthcare delivery system, allied healthcare professionals, insurance agency, and the hospital.

Figure 9.

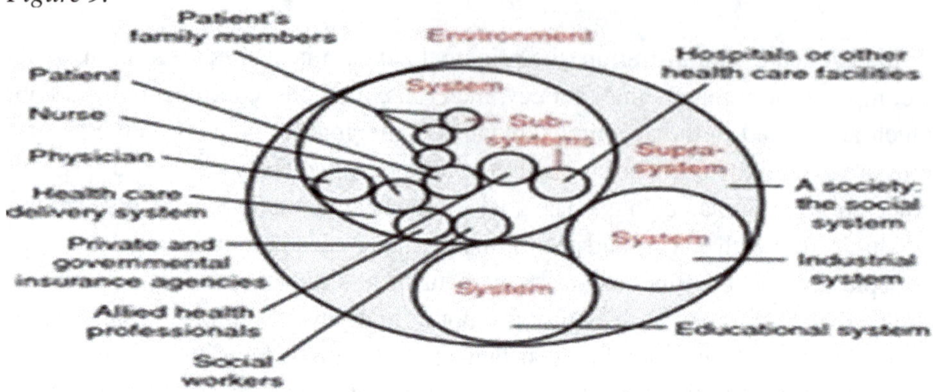

The other systems affecting the system will be the industrial system and the educational system; while the society and the social system will be the supra system surrounded by the environment surrounding them. To consider the environment adequately, an organization must operate as an open system.

D. THE HEALTH CARE DELIVERY SYSTEM

It functions through complex interaction among different sets of people (individuals, healthcare professionals etc.), institutions (public, private, public-private mixed, society, insurance, etc.); and the services rendered to run the system. Over the years, healthcare service delivery has gone through a transition. Following is a comparison between the old and new views:

Figure 10.

Transformation of Healthcare Service Delivery

Old View	New View
• Emphasis on Acute Inpatient	• Continuum of Care
• Emphasis on treating illness	• Maintaining and Promoting Wellness
• Responsible for Individual Pt.	• Defined Population
• Emphasis on Tangible Assets	• Intangible-Knowledge/Relationship
• All Providers are similar	• Sub-Specialty/Adding Value
• Success by Mkt Share/In-Pt.	• Keeping People Well
• Care Provided by Individuals	• By Team
• Info-Record for Health Proff.	• Dynamic to be used for Pt. interest
• Managers run organizations	• Manager/Leadership in charge.
• Managers coordinate services	• Managers pursue for quality improvement.

The service delivery systems use competition, standards, a regulations to pursue a balance in their respective healthcare goals of access, quality, and affordability. As per WHO conceptual framework, it consists of six basic elements- Workforce, Finances, Products/Technologies, Information System, Leadership, and Services. All these are geared to provide accessibility, affordability, and quality ensuring patient safety. However, from a health management perspective, there are challenges which need to be understood and managed.

There could be nine external forces that may have implications for the management:

- Financial Incentives: These are important for the workforce. These need to be linked with the performance indicators of the employees. Stakeholders need to be engaged for business development. If need be the organization may be redesigned to increase the financial gains.
- Performance Accountability: Without accountability in place systems are doomed to failure. The performance of all individuals needs to be monitored and reported through Health Management Information System, Guidelines and Standard Operating Procedures may be developed and Total Quality Improvement Philosophy may be implemented throughout the organization.
- Technology Advances: The health staff need to keep themselves with the latest information in terms of therapies and patient management and cognizance of the ethical issues in patient management.
- Aging and Chronic Illness: Health Promotion and Disease Prevention activities need to be planned at all levels of care. Special Geriatric Care and Home Healthcare also need consideration.

- Ethnic & Cultural Diversity: For the health planners establishing systems, ethnic and cultural diversity must be considered with universal policies for the community.
- Supply & Education Of Professionals: Human resources in managing healthcare are usually scarce and always in demand. The challenge is their retention and keeping them motivated to perform.
- Social Morbidity (AIDS, Drugs…): Society-related behavioral issues harming the health of an individual results in Social Morbidity. AIDS, Drug Addiction, and stressors of life are common factors for Social Morbidity. Strategies need to be adopted in coping with them.
- Information Communication Technology (ICT): With the advent of Social Media, this is the key advancement at the moment. However, ensuring privacy has become challenging. Strict rules need to be implemented to ensure confidentiality. Capacity building in technology and retaining the workforce is a challenge that needs to be addressed.
- Globalization and Economy: With the global village shrinking due to social media, it has brought organizations closer to interaction. Keeping pace with the globalization and economy new alliances, networking, and strong marketing need to be undertaken for survival.

Figure 11.

NINE FORCES INFLUENCING HEALTH SERVICE DELIVERY-IMPLICATIONS FOR MANAGEMENT

EXTERNAL FORCES	MANAGEMENT IMPLICATIONS
• FINANCIAL INCENTIVES	• KPIS', STAKE HOLDER, REDESIGN
• PERFORMANCE ACCOUNTABILITY	• HMIS, GUIDELINES, CQI, TQM
• TECHNOLOGY ADVANCES	• NEW RX, MANAGED CARE, ETHICS
• AGING AND CHRONIC ILLNESS	• PHC, HPDP, GERIATRIC CARE
• ETHNIC & CULTURAL DIVERSITY	• DIFFICULTY IN HANDLING PTS.
• SUPPLY & EDUCATION OF PROFFS.	• PROFF. DEV., RETENTION ....
• SOCIAL MORBIDITY (AIDS, DRUGS...)	• COPE WITH DEMAND/PREPAREDNESS
• ICT	• TRAINING, CONFIDENTIALITY
• GLOBALIZATION AND ECONOMY	• MANAGING ALLIANCES, MARKETING

So, the development of Systems is just like doing groundwork to build the foundations of the Healthcare Establishment (HCE). However, to develop this system, one needs to undertake a planning exercise.

E. PLANNING FOR A HEALTHCARE ESTABLISHMENT

Medical graduates are taught clinical management of patients, therefore, they are somewhat exposed to some sort of management skills. However, they lack professional management skills and planning. To plan for the development of the clinic one needs to understand the planning process. Processes are a part of a System. Any change in one part may affect the other part and the system. Systems lead us to structured thinking and a focused approach to achieve the desired results. For planning, it is essential to understand the basics of the System, and its intricacies and to elucidate principles (such as purpose, measure, methods, tools, etc.) that can be discerned and applied to other systems at every level in the system. A better understanding of the system will also assist in developing proactive measures to prevent any future accidents.

In a systemic approach planning has three Components-Planning, Implementation, and Evaluation or P.I.E.

i. Planning

Introduction

Planning is essential for initiating any project. Plans fail, if we fail to plan. For planning purposes, Deming Cycle is used. This has four Components-Plan, Do, Check, and Act or PDCA cycle. The concept of planning, doing, and checking to evaluate the outputs based on the expected outcome is also a part of the quality improvement cycle.

Figure 12.

To improve quality, certain indicators are set up for monitoring and evaluation of the process or the outcome from the outputs. If we take an example of a patient suffering from an illness, his investigations will be gauged as per the expected outcome of the management. If the results are not as expected corrective measures are taken for the reassessment of the therapeutic measures for patient management. These measures act at the cellular level of the Self or the individual being managed. Thus, the first level of therapeutic measure acts on the cell of an individual. The dietary conditions and individual behavior bring changes at the cellular level of the individual. Barring the genes that a person receives, maintaining a health-cautious behavior is within the control of an individual. The health risk behaviors are unique determinants of health as they alter biological functioning (e.g. chronic smoking alters cells in lung tissue), behavioral functioning (e.g. chronic smoking alters decision-making and daily habits), and social functioning (e.g. chronic smoking creates an economic, social, and healthcare burden) of the population. Here the role of the State in ensuring that cigarettes are not marketed or limit marketing with caution remarks on the packet. The role of Society in reducing exposure to smoking can also be important in restricting smoking. Thus, the health behaviors (Saad & Prochaska, 2020) of individuals have an impact on the health of his own Self (which may deteriorate), Society (creation of burden on the family), System (may need hospitalization and alteration in the eco System), and State (financial burden for the State to manage). This shows the therapeutic importance of "QUAD S". One single factor the Self has a limited but important role in exercising self-restraint from Smoking, however, Society or the company he keeps has an influence and encourages him to smoke. Similarly, once the body System is affected at the cellular level, lung cancer may eventually appear. So, managing the body system becomes one's own responsibility.

What Planning Will Entail?

For initiating the process of establishing a healthcare establishment, we need to pose ourselves with the following questions:

a. Why Develop a Practice Plan?

Creating a practice plan is one of the most important steps towards owning a successful practice that not only thrives but helps you achieve your personal and professional goals.

If you are seeking a loan from a financial organization or investor(s), they will want to see your practice plan so they know you have completed the necessary financial analysis and long-term planning.

b. *What Does a Good Practice Plan Contain?*

Your practice plan needs to:

- articulate your goals and vision for your practice
- analyses your practice environment and market
- identify potential risks and how to mitigate them
- describe your current and planned financial position, along with your practice structure and financial control
- set out what you will be accountable for
- describe how you will measure your practice's success
- identify aspects of your practice you want to give high priority to so that you increase the likelihood of your practice being successful.

c. *What is My Business Plan?*

The first step in establishing an HCE is writing a business plan. One of the best ways to learn about writing a business plan is to study the plans of established businesses. Sustainability is the key dimension of any planning process. It has been praised as an important new planning paradigm. The focus of any business planning or goal is the planning process involved in achieving long-term sustainability. Key areas that can be considered, include focus group discussions, key informant interviews, or a research methodology like surveys and studies to outline the data and key parameters of panning. Setting indicators for evaluation, at the same time should also be considered as a key to success and sustainability.

Elements of Planning for Healthcare Establishment Systems

Inputs (human resources, material, technology, information, capital, ……. Are processed for the Outputs (patient care, acceptable costs, training, and other objectives). If the expected outcomes are achieved they will create an impact. If the Outcomes (improvement in infant mortality rate, life expectancy at birth, improvement in patient's condition…….); are not as expected, Feedback is given for the revision in the inputs, and the entire process is redone till the expected Outcomes are not achieved.

Figure 13.

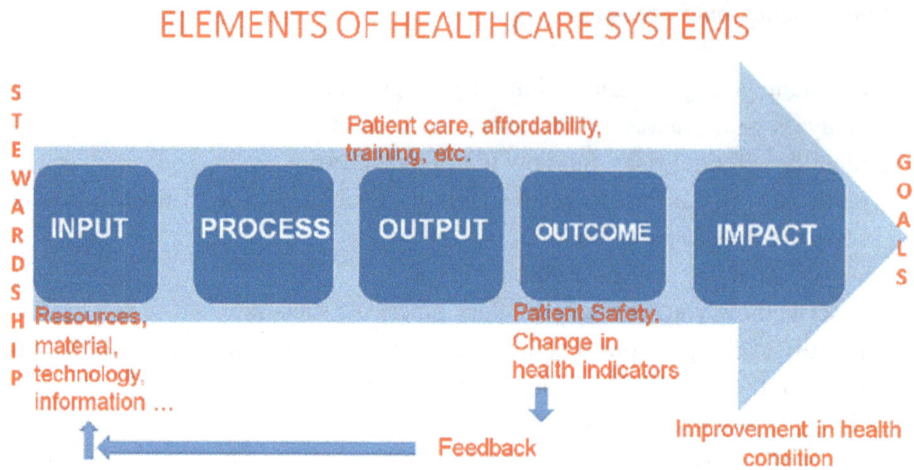

To summarize, the planning of establishing a HCE is a crucial step, and writing a business plan is key.

Implementation

Implementation is putting the plan into action. Considering the PDCA cycle Planning starts first followed by Doing and Checking the activity and Acting accordingly.

In the case, of setting up of HCE, it will mean to start planning the practice at a small scale with minimum staff and focusing on the main problems of the community in the catchment area. This will be followed by evaluating the indicators for the stage of the activity. If the outcomes are achieved, then the impact can also be expected. However, if the outcomes are not achieved feedback is given for the revision of the inputs to be processed again for the desired outputs and outcomes to be achieved.

Evaluation

For evaluation, the five major components are: INPUT, PROCESS, OUTPUT, OUTCOME, and IMPACT. However, indicators need to be established from the outset of the planning process to guide us through the implementation process. While evaluation is being planned as a part of the planning process, we need to consider:

a. Why do we want to evaluate?
   - Effectiveness of plans/results
   - Implementation/Performance of activities

- Efficiency (use of resources/control)

b. What can be evaluated?
   - The plan
   - The people

c. What to evaluate?
   - Achievements
   - Comparison with past
   - Analysis-causes/failure

d. Pre-action evaluation
   - o -Activities in the initiation of a project,
   - o -Exploration and planning phases.

e. Post-action evaluation
   - Activities to measure the progress of plans, and programs and to measure the achievements of the plans and the programs.
   - Evaluating work progress
   - -Evaluating the Management-Strategic business evaluation Evaluating use of resources

All the indicators for the evaluation process need to be identified in the planning process. Thus, where do we stand? For example, we can set our timeline for any activity and measure its achievement as per timelines.

F. HEALTH INSURANCE

i. Introduction

Modern economies are built on skilled labor. Health directly affects labor productivity but indirectly education, personality traits, and skill development are all affected by health. According to the *Lancet Commission on Investing in Health*, health investments in low and middle-income countries like Pakistan can produce economic benefits that would exceed the costs of investment between 9 and 20 times. This will also effect poverty eradication in Pakistan. One hopes that the next budget will re-prioritize health spending. By investing in health through a health-sensitive budget, Pakistan would not only be saving lives and promoting human rights, but it can also further its economic interests strategically for a safer, healthier, and wealthier Pakistan.

For operating an HCE, an HCP needs to understand the basics of health insurance. Health Insurance is defined as "coverage that provides for the payments of benefits as a result of sickness or injury. It includes insurance for losses from accident, medical expense, disability, or accidental death and dismemberment.

When we see the bigger picture, we are often taken aback by the fact that the Pakistani healthcare system is divided into two major categories. The first category includes low-cost government systems that offer basic medical services, mostly catering to those in lower economic strata. Parallel to that is the system that relies on private-sector medical hospitals-cum-educational institutions.

Although health insurance is not an unknown concept to the Pakistani urban population, there are not many people who take the initiative and buy a coverage policy on their own. In fact, most people who do have health insurance in our country are usually provided the facility as part of their work contract. Although healthcare insurance is a wise investment since a person can never predict when he/she might need financial assistance for medical reasons. While there might be conflicting views on the benefits and practicality of health insurance, there is no denying the peace of mind one can acquire with the knowledge of having something to fall back upon during times of health crises. However, due to low per capita income, high inflation, and increasing cost of living, the trend of buying health insurance policy for individuals and family is quite rare. Paying the monthly premium for one's health insurance is virtually unimaginable for someone who can hardly provide two meals to the family.

Even though access to health facilities should be the basic right of a citizen, successive Pakistani governments have failed to provide it. Moreover, after the 18th amendment, it has become a provincial rather federal issue. Few schemes were initiated, however, political and funding factors became the main impediment to implementation. In such a scenario, private insurance companies have to strive hard to create mass awareness regarding the significance of health insurance but have not been able to bring about any strategic changes in governmental policies.

The dream of universal health coverage cannot be attained if the health systems are not appropriately placed. The **elements** of a **System (S1)** include people, institutions, and resources.

Figure 14.

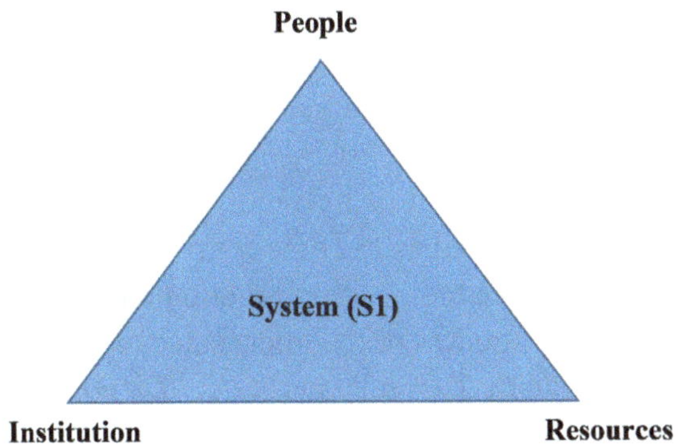

People need universal health coverage. Pakistan ranks 136th on the Legatum Prosperity Index, 122/191 countries on overall efficiency in the index of best healthcare in 2020 among all WHO member states. Due to a lack of transparency in data sharing for budgets Pakistan ranked 28/100 in the Open Budget Index in 2019 (Majid, 2020). Therefore, it is estimated that Public health expenditure in Pakistan is 0.7% of GDP and National public expenditure on health is $4 per capita, while total expenditure on health is $18 per capita. This makes State contribution to healthcare around 20% and out-of-pocket expenses 80%. Thus, adequate resources are not provisioned for healthcare from the government sector and as it is mostly the private sector that offers healthcare services, it puts a burden on the individuals and their resources. Furthermore, lack of planning for any health catastrophe at an individual level, with meager health promotion and disease prevention efforts (Primary Healthcare), the health of an individual is compromised. This puts an additional burden on the secondary and tertiary care institutions; where an individual ends up in such institutions at a late stage of the disease. Thus, the goals of an ideal healthcare **System** will be for the people to receive financial protection for universal health coverage (health insurance/assurance), quality of healthcare service delivery through the institutions, and use of efficient and effective resources for Health gain.

ii. S4 and Health Insurance

Considering the S4 (Society, State, Systems, and Self) therapy, a few models are being proposed for general debate and discussion for testing and developing a unique model that is suitable for ensuring universal coverage.

To start any project a prototype needs to be developed for its further study and replication. Let us consider the 4"S" model in this regard.

Systems (S1): This project needs to have elements of the system; with the role of people, institutions, and resources. The goal of the system would be to provide financial protection to the people, institutions geared towards quality service delivery focusing on health gain; and resources to be available for the functioning of the system.

Self (S2): An individual should be made responsible for his health and that of his/her family. Behavior change has to come from within the Self. Change in behavior towards life style related to health promotion and taking measures towards disease prevention. Self-awareness of the importance of health is also emphasized by the Holy Quran and Hadith at several places e.g. *"Do not kill yourselves, for God is merciful to you .... [Surah An-Nisa, (4:29–30)] or* Preventive medicine, *tibb wiqa'i*, is a series of pro-active measures under the Islamic concept of prevention, *wiqayat*[4]. For Personal Hygiene: *"Believers, when you are about to pray, wash .... [Surah Al-Ma'idahh, (5:6)]";* and Respect for Body: *"Do not with your own hands throw yourselves to ruin. [Surah Al-Baqarah, (2:195)]"*. Therefore, campaigns be designed to raise awareness about "Self" care for health and to be a role model for Society. Thus, an individual becomes an agent of Social change in the Society (S3).

Society (S3): Islam promotes brotherhood. Muslims contribute their share to the development of Society through Zakat, Sadaqah, and Infaq. There are different forms of Zakat. These include:

- Zakat Al-Mal: The Muslims' wealth tax for the poor.
- Zakatul Huboob: Zakat of grain/corn.
- Zakatul Ma'dan: Zakat of minerals.
- Zakatur Rikaaz: Zakat of treasure/precious stones.

Thus Islam encourages fellow Muslims to support their Islamic brothers. In Corporate sector the community is supported through Corporate Social Responsibility. Thus, both aspects could be nurtured for the contribution of society towards resource generation for financial protection in the system. The Self role for health promotion and disease prevention can be expanded to society and the environment thus created can in turn effect the individuals at large. Focusing on improving Community Mental Health can also in turn influence the overall society and individuals. From an Islamic perspective following need to be considered:

- **Parents Responsibility**-To provide good nutrition to children: *Mothers shall breast-feed their babies for two years .... [Surah Al-Baqarah, (2:233)]*
- **Protection from Infection**-*"In the black seed is healing for every disease except death." (Sahih Bukhari)*

- **Healthy Environment**-Prophet (PBUH) says: *"Faith is made up of over seventy items ... the simplest of which is to remove any source of harm from the road". Tirmizi*
- **Role of Community**-In the Quran, God commands every Muslim: *"Be kind to the neighbor who is related to you and the neighbor who is a stranger, and the friend by your side ... [Surah An-Nisa, (4:36)]"*

Therefore, Society(S3) influencing Self (S2), plays an important role in achieving the goals set by the System (S1) focusing on the health gains of the community. However, it all depends on the policies of the State (S4), towards the health of the citizens.

State (S4): As mentioned earlier, the State supports around only 20% of the healthcare provision. Therefore, there is a severe financial burden on the individuals who are mostly dependent on seeking healthcare from the private sector. From an Islamic perspective: Perfection', or Ihsan in Arabic-denotes 'goodness'. The Prophet (PBUH) says: *"Ihsan, or perfection, is to worship God as if you see Him"*. Hazrat Umar (RA) "As he passed through Al-Jabiyah in Damascus, through a group of Christians suffering from leprosy and ordered they be given a portion of zakat and food allowance-" Sick people had the right to medical care by the state".

G. SUMMARY

To summarize the 4"S" model, the State needs to take steps towards ensuring health to be made a part of the constitution. Providing financial protection to the people for their health is a fundamental right of the citizens of Pakistan. Thus, the State needs to develop a System for ensuring universal coverage of health. The individuals (Self) need to be made conscious of health promotion and disease prevention aspect of their health, while the Society also need to play its role in contributing towards supporting universal health coverage and creating an environment focusing on bringing behavioral change among the individuals. Leveraging Islamic guidelines towards health can assist in bringing a change in the Self and Society; while utilizing the Takaful model, can be a unique attempt to utilize this insurance/ assurance model for universal health coverage.

REFERENCES

Majid, M. F. (2020, June 7). *Rethinking health spending. The News (Pakistan).* https://www.thenews.com.pk/tns/detail/668387-rethinking-health-spending

Saad, J. M., & Prochaska, J. O. (2020). A philosophy of health: Life as reality, health as a universal value. *Palgrave Communications*, *6*(1), 1–11. DOI: 10.1057/s41599-020-0420-9 PMID: 32226633

World Health Organization. (2000). *Measuring overall health system performance for 191 countries* (GPE Discussion Paper No. 30). https://www.who.int/healthinfo/paper30.pdf

Chapter 4
Quality Management System and Practice

Fozia Asif
https://orcid.org/0000-0003-0319-9329
Aga Khan University, Karachi, Pakistan

Minhaj Ahmed Qidwai
https://orcid.org/0009-0003-0770-481X
Al-Kawthar University, Karachi, Pakistan & American Institute of Healthcare Quality, Pakistan & Unet Consultants, Canada

ABSTRACT

A quality management system (QMS) integrates planning, assurance, control, and improvement to effectively meet customer needs. In healthcare, where complex interactions involve human patients, advanced technology, and critical infrastructure, the challenges are significant, especially as patients seek care when most vulnerable. Accreditations and certifications provide structured frameworks to assess elements like infrastructure and human resources, using audits based on documentation, observations, and interviews. Though resource-intensive, these methods are the gold standard for healthcare evaluation. However, these processes have limitations. Clinicians often lack evidence of their impact on outcomes, and the focus on accreditation may detract from care quality. In high-income countries (HICs), focusing on quality improvement initiatives is key, while low- and middle-income countries (LMICs) must address all QMS components, given greater systemic challenges. A holistic approach to QMS is essential for meaningful progress, especially in LMICs.

DOI: 10.4018/979-8-3693-9092-4.ch004

1. INTRODUCTION

The healthcare sector is globally recognized for its complexity and high stakes due to the nature of its services. Humans interact with humans in vulnerable conditions to deliver the service. Maintaining quality in healthcare services requires a structured quality management system to achieve optimal patient outcomes. A QMS consists of planning, assurance, control, and improvement, and it is a framework that healthcare organizations adopt to meet quality and safety standards. Accreditations are assessments of quality measures according to set benchmarks. Accreditations provide a framework to establish a QMS system but have some limitations.

Two of the most prominent global standards in QMS for healthcare are those set by the International Organization for Standardization (ISO) and the Joint Commission of International Accreditation (JCIA). These organizations provide a structured foundation for healthcare facilities worldwide to maintain high standards of patient care, safety, and operational efficiency. These accreditation systems can be implemented in high-income countries and lower-income countries. Few high-income countries with centralized healthcare systems, like the United Kingdom (UK), Canada, and Australia, have their local accreditation system, which is more specific to local systems. However, accreditations have limitations regarding patient safety, patient engagement, and patient roles in quality management systems.

2. THE DEMAND FOR QMS AND THE COMPLEXITY OF HEALTHCARE

The healthcare industry operates as a highly complex ecosystem involving patients, healthcare providers, technology, infrastructure, and stringent regulations. Patients seek treatment at vulnerable moments, increasing the need for compassionate, efficient, and safe healthcare (WHO, 2021). As healthcare systems worldwide adopt QMS frameworks, they face the challenges of adapting these systems to specific national and cultural contexts. Integrating QMS in healthcare helps streamline processes, manage risks, and set clear standards for quality care (Accreditation Canada, 2021).

The demand for QMS has escalated in recent years due to the digital transformation of healthcare, with technologies like electronic health records (EHRs), telemedicine, and artificial intelligence (AI) becoming integral (Kruk et al., 2018). While these tools have improved diagnosis and patient engagement, they require additional quality controls related to data privacy, interoperability, and cybersecurity, highlighting the growing importance of QMS frameworks.

3. COMPONENTS OF QUALITY MANAGEMENT SYSTEMS IN HEALTHCARE

Each component of QMS—planning, assurance, control, and improvement—plays a critical role in ensuring healthcare quality:

- **Planning**: Setting goals and defining quality standards help facilities align resources with patient care requirements (Meara et al., 2015).
- **Assurance**: Continuous assessment through audits and monitoring ensures that healthcare providers meet established standards (Joint Commission International, 2022).
- **Control**: Standardized protocols allow organizations to minimize errors and inconsistencies.
- **Improvement**: Ongoing improvement, driven by data and evidence-based practices, helps facilities address gaps in care quality.

In LMICs, the application of these components varies, with planning and control often prioritized due to resource limitations. At the same time, continuous improvement remains challenging due to limited access to data and training resources.

4. IMPACT OF QUALITY MANAGEMENT SYSTEMS IN HEALTHCARE

The quality management system impacts institutions, providers, and patients. QMS benefits institutions by allowing them to achieve accreditation/certification, legal coverage, and competitive advantage. QMS benefits providers by enabling them to achieve optimal clinical outcomes, job satisfaction, and a safe culture. QMS benefits patients by allowing them to achieve satisfaction, empowerment, and value for their resources. QMS improves quality and safety for institutions, providers, and patients (Figure 01).

Figure 1.

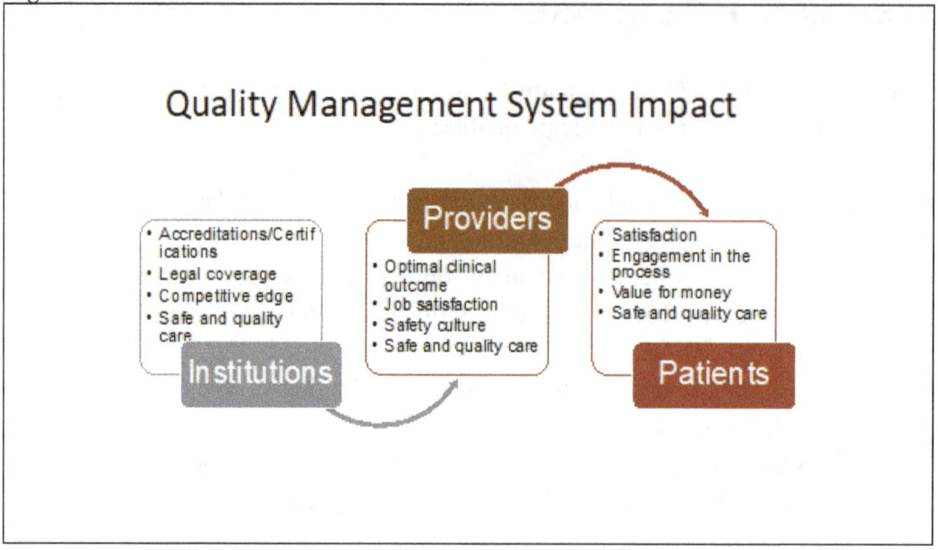

5. THE PLACE OF CERTIFICATIONS AND ACCREDITATIONS

Certifications and accreditations are critical for establishing benchmarks in healthcare quality. Global standards such as JCI and ISO provide structured frameworks for ensuring compliance with safety protocols, clinical governance, and quality management. While these certifications signal a commitment to excellence, achieving them is resource-intensive, posing challenges for LMICs like Pakistan. Nevertheless, a few high-profile healthcare institutions in LMICs have pursued JCI and ISO certifications to demonstrate quality assurance, setting an example for others (Joint Commission International, 2022; ISO, 2022). However, this is a novel practice in overall healthcare infrastructure and fails to create an impact in LMICs.

5.1 International Organization for Standardization (ISO)

The **International Organization for Standardization (ISO)** is an independent, non-governmental international organization with over 160 member countries. Established in 1947, ISO develops voluntary, consensus-based standards for various industries, including healthcare. ISO standards are highly regarded globally and serve as quality, safety, and efficiency benchmarks across multiple sectors.

In healthcare, the **ISO 9001:2015** standard is widely adopted. ISO 9001 is part of the ISO 9000 family, which focuses on quality management systems and principles that enable organizations to ensure customer satisfaction, improve operational efficiency, and foster continuous improvement. **ISO 9001:2015** emphasizes several core principles:

- **Customer Focus:** Ensuring that healthcare services meet or exceed patient expectations.
- **Leadership Commitment:** Engaging leadership to drive quality objectives and create a quality-focused culture.
- **Engagement of People:** Involving employees at all levels in maintaining quality and fostering a shared responsibility for patient care.
- **Process Approach:** Using a systematic approach to manage processes improves efficiency and reduces variability in service delivery.
- **Improvement:** Emphasizing continual improvement to enhance patient outcomes and organizational performance.
- **Evidence-Based Decision Making:** Making informed decisions based on data analysis and evaluation.
- **Relationship Management:** Building and maintaining good relationships with stakeholders, including patients, suppliers, and regulatory authorities.

ISO 9001 in healthcare provides a structured framework for hospitals and clinics to streamline their processes, improve patient safety, and enhance operational efficiency. Adhering to ISO standards helps healthcare providers ensure that their services are consistently delivered with quality and safety in mind. Facilities certified with ISO 9001 are recognized for their commitment to quality, which enhances patient trust and organizational credibility. Although ISO certification is voluntary, many healthcare organizations pursue it to demonstrate their dedication to high standards, efficiency, and patient-centered care.

5.2 Joint Commission International Accreditation (JCIA)

Joint Commission International (JCI) is a division of the Joint Commission, a U.S.-based organization that accredits and certifies healthcare organizations in the United States. Established in 1994, JCI provides a global accreditation framework for healthcare facilities outside the United States. **Joint Commission International Accreditation (JCIA)** is widely recognized as one of the most comprehensive and stringent healthcare accreditation programs globally. JCI's standards and accreditation processes focus on patient safety, clinical quality, and operational excellence, providing healthcare organizations with a roadmap to achieving high standards of care.

JCIA's accreditation process involves a detailed assessment of healthcare organizations across several domains:

- **Patient-centered standards** include patient safety goals, rights, and infection control protocols. JCI's patient-centered standards ensure that healthcare facilities focus on patients' well-being, rights, and safety throughout their care journey.
- **Healthcare Organization Management Standards:** JCI assesses leadership, facility management, and human resources to ensure that healthcare providers have a stable infrastructure and trained personnel to deliver quality care.
- **Quality Improvement and Patient Safety (QPS):** This is a core area in JCIA standards. It encourages healthcare organizations to adopt a culture of continuous improvement and safety. Quality Improvement and Patient Safety goals include implementing risk management strategies, reducing errors, and promoting a blame-free culture where staff can report issues without fear of punishment.
- **Access to Care and Continuity of Care:** JCI ensures that healthcare facilities have protocols to provide timely and accessible patient care, with structured plans for transitions between care settings.
- **Medication Management and Use:** JCI has detailed standards for safe medication practices, emphasizing the importance of accurate prescribing, dispensing, and administration to minimize errors.
- **Facility and Environment Management:** This standard focuses on ensuring that the physical environment of healthcare facilities supports patient safety and is in compliance with health regulations.

The JCIA accreditation process is rigorous, often involving extensive pre-assessment, on-site evaluations, and continuous monitoring. Hospitals seeking JCI accreditation must demonstrate adherence to over 300 standards and 1,200 measurable elements across the spectrum of patient care and management practices. Accreditation is granted for a limited period, requiring healthcare organizations to re-evaluate every three years to maintain their accredited status.

The impact of JCIA on healthcare quality is well-documented. Accredited facilities often report improved clinical outcomes, reduced infection rates, and enhanced patient satisfaction. Furthermore, JCIA helps organizations build a culture of patient safety and accountability, emphasizing the importance of continuous quality improvement and adherence to best practices. JCIA accreditation is highly valued in the healthcare industry, as it signals a commitment to international quality standards and gives patients confidence in the safety and quality of care they receive

5.3 Global Standards and Their Effectiveness

Global accreditation bodies, including JCI and ISO, have developed standards emphasizing patient safety, risk management, and continuous improvement. JCI, for instance, offers a rigorous framework covering various healthcare aspects, from infection control to clinical governance, thus fostering a quality-oriented culture (Accreditation Canada, 2021). ISO 9001:2015, a widely adopted quality management standard, provides principles for risk-based thinking, leadership engagement, and operational efficiency.

These certifications have shown tangible benefits in high-income countries, where adherence to these standards has reduced adverse events, improved patient satisfaction, and ensured regulatory compliance. However, their implementation in LMICs remains limited due to resource constraints. Hospitals with these certifications report better organizational structure, enhanced patient trust, and improved care outcomes.

6. ADVANTAGES OF CERTIFICATIONS AND ACCREDITATIONS

Certifications and accreditations provide several advantages, particularly in standardizing healthcare practices and ensuring quality:

- **Standardized Practices**: Adherence to accreditation standards minimizes variability, ensuring consistency in clinical practices and operational protocols.
- **Enhanced Patient Safety**: Safety protocols reduce the likelihood of adverse events and ensure patients receive appropriate care.
- **Improved Accountability**: Accreditation encourages transparency and holds healthcare organizations accountable for quality assurance.
- **Staff Development**: Certification often mandates regular training, which keeps healthcare staff updated on best practices and recent advancements.

7. CHALLENGES OF CERTIFICATIONS AND ACCREDITATIONS

Despite the benefits, certifications and accreditations pose unique challenges, especially in resource-limited settings:

- **Resource Constraints**: High costs and limited funding make it difficult for many facilities to meet certification standards (ISO, 2022).
- **Staff Burnout**: The effort required to maintain compliance can strain healthcare staff, leading to burnout. Understaffed and overworked facilities fail to motivate employees' efforts for accreditations and certifications (Kruk et al., 2018).
- **Sustainability Issues**: Efforts toward accreditation often peak around inspection times, leading to gaps in quality maintenance between evaluations (Accreditation Canada, 2021).
- **Lack of Evidence on Outcomes**: There is limited research on the direct impact of accreditation on patient outcomes, making it difficult for many healthcare providers to justify the investment (Donabedian, 1988).

These challenges highlight the need for flexible and scalable QMS models tailored to the specific constraints of LMICs.

8. WHY HIGH-INCOME COUNTRIES DON'T ALWAYS ACHIEVE OPTIMAL OUTCOMES

Even with advanced resources and established QMS frameworks, high-income countries (HICs) often struggle to achieve optimal healthcare outcomes for several reasons:

1. **Fragmented Healthcare Systems**: In countries like the United States, the healthcare system is highly fragmented, with numerous providers, insurers, and payers operating independently. This fragmentation can lead to inefficiencies, duplication of services, and gaps in care, affecting patient outcomes (Berwick, 2009).
2. **Overemphasis on Compliance**: HICs often focus heavily on compliance with accreditation standards. While compliance is crucial, it can sometimes overshadow patient-centered care, with healthcare providers concentrating on meeting requirements rather than improving care quality (Donabedian, 1988).
3. **Resource Utilization and Waste**: HICs have access to advanced technologies and treatments, which, while beneficial, can lead to overuse and unnecessary interventions. This phenomenon, sometimes called "over-medicalization," can result in higher costs without proportionate improvements in patient health outcomes (Kruk et al., 2018).

4. **Chronic Disease Burden and Lifestyle Factors**: Despite advanced healthcare systems, HICs face a high burden of chronic diseases like obesity, diabetes, and heart disease. Lifestyle factors, such as poor diet and lack of exercise, contribute significantly to these diseases, making it challenging to achieve optimal health outcomes even with superior medical infrastructure (WHO, 2021).
5. **Staff Burnout and Turnover**: The high demands placed on healthcare providers in HICs can lead to burnout, reducing staff morale and impacting the quality of patient care. High turnover rates in healthcare professions add to the challenges, leading to staff shortages and inconsistent care (Institute for Healthcare Improvement, 2022).

These factors underscore the need for HICs to look beyond resources and infrastructure and focus on holistic healthcare approaches that prioritize patient well-being, prevention, and sustainable practices.

9. INTERNATIONAL PERSPECTIVES ON QMS IMPLEMENTATION

Case Study: United States

The Joint Commission (TJC) sets stringent quality standards for hospitals to achieve accreditation in the United States. US hospitals that comply with TJC standards benefit from a structured framework that improves patient outcomes and operational efficiency. These standards cover patient safety, medication management, infection control, and emergency preparedness, creating a comprehensive, quality-focused environment (Berwick, 2009). However, evidence has shown that healthcare benefits to the patients are similar in hospitals that TJC does not accredit (Lam et al., 2018).

Case Study: Canada

Canada's Accreditation Canada operates a QMS program known as Qmentum. Accreditation Canada's (AC) Qmentum Global accreditation programs enable organizations to improve quality and provide a framework for relevant standards, assessment methods, and quality improvement models. AC program assesses organizations against standards developed by the Health Standards Organization (HSO) and International Standards Organization (ISO). HSO standards are used for research, education, or policy work assessments. Clients of AC assessment programs such as

Qmentum accreditation and clients of AC Diagnostic and medical lab accreditation use ISO standards use AC standards. (Accreditation Canada, 2021).

Case Study: UK

In the UK, the Care Quality Commission (CQC) assesses facilities based on safety, effectiveness, patient experience, and care quality, ensuring that healthcare providers meet the high standards of the National Health Services (NHS). Through regular inspections and feedback, CQC-accredited facilities have seen improvements in patient safety, infection control, and staff satisfaction (Care Quality Commission, 2023). In a centralized healthcare system, the NHS has the added advantage of centralized quality improvement data, which helps to develop evidence-based health strategies compared to fragmented healthcare systems.

Case Study: South Africa

South Africa's public healthcare system, which serves the majority of the population, faces challenges related to overcrowding, resource shortages, and high rates of patient safety incidents. To address these issues, the South African National Department of Health launched the Ideal Clinic Realization and Maintenance Program (ICRM) in 2013, which aimed to create a standardized QMS framework to improve the quality of care in public clinics.

Case Study: Pakistan

In Pakistan, provincial healthcare commissions like the Punjab Health Care Commission and Sindh Health Care Commission have introduced standards for essential healthcare quality, known as Minimum Service Delivery Standards (MSDS). While these standards are less comprehensive than JCI or ISO, they represent a step toward formalizing healthcare quality requirements within a national context (Punjab Healthcare Commission, 2021).

11. PATIENT SAFETY SCIENCE AND QMS

Patient safety science plays a crucial role in strengthening and enhancing the Quality Management System (QMS) in healthcare by providing a framework that focuses on identifying, mitigating, and preventing risks that could harm patients. In the current world, most quality management systems are inclined to infrastructure, compliance, and monitoring of processes with minimal focus on patient safety . By incorporating patient safety science, QMS becomes more proactive, shifting from a purely compliance-driven approach to one that prioritizes the detection and prevention of adverse events before they occur. Patient safety science promotes a culture of transparency and learning, encouraging healthcare providers to report errors without fear of punishment. This enables the organization to identify patterns and underlying causes of failures. Techniques such as root cause analysis (RCA), failure mode and effects analysis (FMEA), and safety audits are instrumental in understanding how errors occur and developing targeted strategies to address them. This continuous loop of assessment, feedback, and improvement aligns with QMS's goals of maintaining high standards of care through ongoing refinement of processes. Furthermore, patient safety science emphasizes the importance of involving patients and their families in safety practices, which can provide valuable insights and foster trust. This patient-centered approach in QMS aligns with regulatory and accreditation standards and reinforces a safety culture crucial for sustainable healthcare quality improvement.

12. CONCLUSION

A well-implemented QMS integrates planning, assurance, control, and improvement to deliver safe, patient-centered healthcare. While certifications like JCI and ISO set high standards, the unique challenges of LMICs require adaptable QMS models. By investing in a strong QMS framework, healthcare providers can make meaningful improvements in care quality, patient safety, and service delivery, ensuring better health outcomes for all.

ACKNOWLEDGMENT

This chapter was written with the assistance from Dr. Minhaj A. Qidwai, who is the editor of the book "Enhancing Client, Family and Community Health" and his 5Ss approach of Self, Society, State, Systems and Spirituality".

REFERENCES

Accreditation Canada. (2021). Overview of healthcare accreditation.

Berwick, D. M. (2009). What 'patient-centered' ought to mean—Confessions of an extremist. *Health Affairs*, *28*(4, Supplement 1), w555–w565. DOI: 10.1377/hlthaff.28.4.w555 PMID: 19454528

Care Quality Commission. (2023). Safety and quality norms.

Donabedian, A. (1988). The standard of treatment: How might one measure it? *Journal of Medicine*, *260*(12), 1743–1748.

Institute for Healthcare Improvement. (2022). Applied science for healthcare improvement.

ISO. (2022). Quality management systems ISO 9001:2015.

Joint Commission International. (2022). Hospital JCI accreditation guidelines.

Kruk, M. E., Gage, A. D., Arsenault, C., Jordan, K., Leslie, H. H., Roder-DeWan, S., Adeyi, O., Barker, P., Daelmans, B., Doubova, S. V., English, M., García-Elorrio, E., Guanais, F., Gureje, O., Hirschhorn, L. R., Jiang, L., Kelley, E., Lemango, E. T., Liljestrand, J., & Pate, M. (2018). High-quality health systems in the Sustainable Development Goals era: Time for a revolution. *The Lancet. Global Health*, *6*(11), e1196–e1252. DOI: 10.1016/S2214-109X(18)30386-3 PMID: 30196093

Lam, M. B., Figueroa, J. F., Feyman, Y., Reimold, K. E., Orav, E. J., & Jha, A. K. (2018). Association between patient outcomes and accreditation in US hospitals: Observational study. *BMJ (Clinical Research Ed.)*, *363*, k4011. DOI: 10.1136/bmj.k4011 PMID: 30337294

Meara, J. G., Leather, A. J., Hagander, L., Alkire, B. C., Alonso, N., Ameh, E. A., Bickler, S. W., Conteh, L., Dare, A. J., Davies, J., Mérisier, E. D., El-Halabi, S., Farmer, P. E., Gawande, A., Gillies, R., Greenberg, S. L. M., Grimes, C. E., Gruen, R. L., Ismail, E. A., & Yip, W. (2015). Global Surgery 2030: Evidence and solutions for achieving health, welfare, and economic development. *Lancet*, *386*(9993), 569–624. DOI: 10.1016/S0140-6736(15)60160-X PMID: 25924834

Punjab Healthcare Commission. (2021). Minimum service delivery standards.

WHO. (2021). Quality of treatment in LMICs.

Chapter 5
Empowering Sensors and Wearable Technologies in Fostering Digital Healthcare Management:
Innovation and Enactments in Human Augmentation

Saurabh Chandra
https://orcid.org/0000-0003-4172-9968
Bennett University, Greater Noida, India

Bhupinder Singh
https://orcid.org/0009-0006-4779-2553
Sharda University, India

ABSTRACT

Sensors and wearables are making digital healthcare management a reality by allowing for round the clock health monitoring and individualized care. These gadgets are capable of monitoring the data on vital signs, activities of health and mind as well thereby making us proactive towards healthcare. New technologies facilitate remote diagnostics and treatments through smart implants or AI-driven wearables, leading to better patient outcomes with fewer hospital visits. Increasing amounts of patient engagement thanks to wearable technologies allow individuals greater control over their health and give healthcare providers access more accurate, real-time information for better decision-making. In addition, these advancements enable remote patient monitoring on a larger scale for chronic disease management and provide care to rural or underserved populations. The deployment of these

DOI: 10.4018/979-8-3693-9092-4.ch005

technologies mark a pivot to proactive, patient-specific care and improve health outcomes more broadly at scale.

1. INTRODUCTION

The recent proliferation of sensors and wearable technologies has triggered a novel paradigm in digital healthcare management that enables the development of breakthrough health monitoring, diagnostic, and patient care tools. These are critical innovations that allow for a healthcare system proactive, tailored and personalized according to the needs of patients (Khan et al., 2020). Wearable sensors, which communicate health data to the internet in real-time, are changing interactions between patients and clinicians through collection of personal health status information combined with electronic medical records (Rani, 2022). In this changing scenario, human augmentation technologies that leverage artificial intelligence (AI), the Internet of Things (IoT) and machine learning technology are improving natural capabilities within the body to facilitate optimal health outcomes.

Wearable devices and smart sensors are inarguably marking a major shift from reactive to preventive care conditions that can be monitored long before they require critical attentions. They provide a full monitoring environment for physiological data which can be recorded, monitored and outliers detected in such systems to deliver an intervention. For example, wearables can supervise heart rates, blood oxygen levels, and glucose to let both patient and doctor know if abnormalities are detected ahead of time in order prevent the complications. Also, when wearables are connected in digital healthcare platforms it ensures that continuous data is captured and analyzed which eventually results into customized care driven by patient health specific knowledge.

Wearable technologies are fueling this era of patient empowerment, where people take a proactive role in managing their health. Mobile applications based on which the users can monitor their vital signs, keep track of fitness goals and avail insights about health have made managing your well-being easier than ever- especially for sufferers from chronic diseases. Concurrently, these technologies have huge relevance to healthcare systems in terms of remote patient monitoring and control such that leads advance care delivery efficiency with a decrease on hospital admissions among others. This chapter reflects the importance of sensor and wearable technologies becoming empowering tools in a digital health ecosystem, as well their new alternative applications; what we mean by human augmentation from these integrations into people's daily lifestyle practices to improve our overall health care (Ahirwar & Khan, 2022).

Figure 1. Shows the dimensions of introduction section

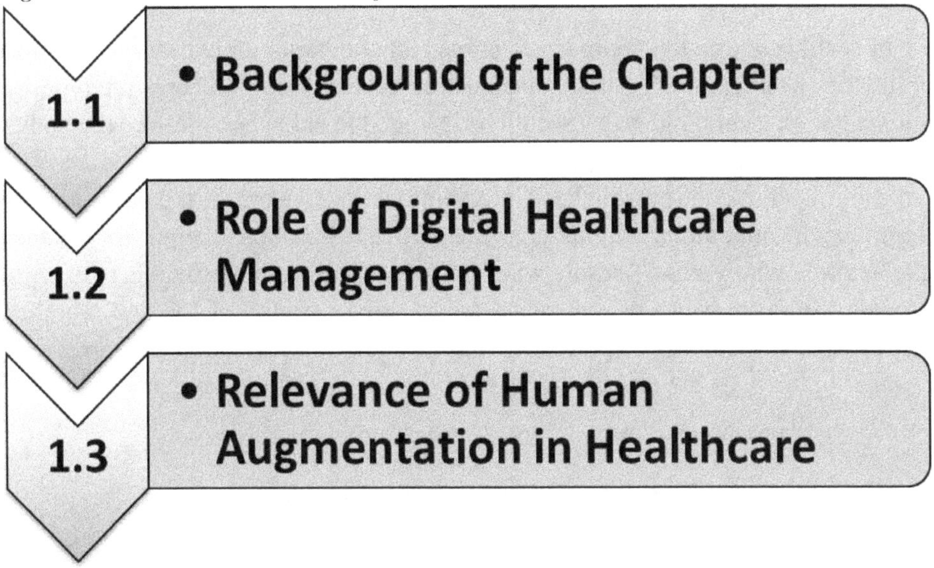

(Source- Self Prepared- Original)

1.1 Background of the Chapter

This advancement in the healthcare sensors and wearable technologies can be linked with many technological breakthroughs over the last few decades. Consumers first picked up wearable devices for fitness trackers and smartwatches, which monitored physical activity, sleep quality levels and heart rate (Han et al., 2020). Over the years, these devices have been utilized more widely in medical and clinical usage as technology progressed. Now, wearables and sensors can monitor health metrics such as glucose levels for a person with diabetes to an electrocardiogram (ECG) if heart health is on the line (Pramanik et al., 2022).

The key technology in the wearable devices is sensors that can collect real-time physiological data. Optical sensors, chemical sensors and mechanical sensor are some of the most common types used to detect these health indicators (Nazari, 2020). Optical sensors can be found in smartwatch bands to measure your heart rate by spotting shifts in blood flow, and chemical sensors able to monitor everything from glucose levels, vital for many diabetics or carbon dioxide output that gives a direct indicator of aerobic metabolism. Combined with wearable devices, this has provided a leap in capability to continuous health monitoring that will help us catch diseases early and manage chronic conditions better (Sahil & Kaushik, 2022).

1.2 Role of Digital Healthcare Management

In healthcare, too the approach of human augmentation or expanding a human ability has been gaining traction. Implantable devices and prostheses are types of augmentation technologies that would be intended to enhance or restore the body's natural capabilities. When coupled with wearable sensors, the technologies can offer real-time feedback and personalized interventions which have great possibilities for improving health outcomes (Oukhatar et al., 2021). Smart prosthetics, for instance can be fitted with various sensors which ensure movement adjustments in order to provide natural movements enhancing an amputee's quality of life and mobility. Implantable devices to monitor vital signs or deliver medication in response to changes in the body are also changing how chronic conditions are managed (He & Eastburn, 2022).

1.3 Relevance of Human Augmentation in Healthcare

Advances in AI, IoT and ML further actualize human augmentation technologies by enabling these devices to digest huge data sets making decisions based on information that is up-to-the-minute. Algorithms powered by AI can measure data recorded with wearable sensors over time to better understand when subtle changes and movements could point towards the beginning stages of a disease. Connectivity with IoT means that data from wearables could be relayed through those same devices back to healthcare providers in real time, helping support remote monitoring and telemedicine solutions. As these techs continue to mature new opportunities are being created for personalized medical treatment and general improving the yield of healthcare systems (Mujawar et al., 2020).

2. EVOLUTION OF SENSORS AND WEARABLE DEVICES: TECHNOLOGIES IN FOSTERING DIGITAL HEALTHCARE MANAGEMENT

From bulky, mostly impractical wrist-type computers to the now stylish and fashionable smartwatches we wear on a daily basis these are all incredible milestones in wearable technology. The history of wearables have evolved monumentally over the past century and started as simple early gadgets to today's AI-Powered sophisticated health monitors that allow you to monitor your environment, interact with technology in an entirely new way even help manage chronic medical conditions. Just as is true of innovation in general, wearable device development has incorporated trends toward smaller size and enhanced communications powered by improved sensor technology. Both of these devices, at one time thought to be luxuries of the future, are now also crucial fitness aides - as well as accurate medical diagnostic tools (Udoh et al., 2023).

From the earliest wristwatches and hearing aids for targeted single functions (to display time, to amplify sound. These were simple tools and not much functionality can be implemented on them. The late 20th century has also seen the introduction of digital technologies in wearables such as digital watches and, more recently fitness trackers that can measure basic health information like steps taken or heartbeats (Chelliah et al., 2021). The first breakthroughs were pedometers and heart rate monitors, which enabled athletes or fitness advocates to monitor their physical exercise instantly. They were mostly standalone during this time, not connected to external systems as is now the case with most of them. They were good at providing data but it found them to be too closed systems and unable integrate with the health or fitness ecosystem. Microprocessors, smaller batteries and more efficient sensors provided a foundation for the next wave of innovation.

Arguably, the real shift in wearable technology began with the smartphone age of consumer electronics gaining traction by about 2000. Wearables began to incorporate wireless connectivity and started syncing with smartphones as well as other gadgets. This was a boon to their diversity in functions. The release of smartwatches like the Pebble and later on with Apple Watch, it combined fitness tracking/communication/app ecosystem all in one device which changed everything. Not only did these wearables function as data collection gadgets, but they also allowed users to interact with direct notifications in apps or make phone calls using very simple user interfaces (Materon et al., 2021).

Bluetooth and Wi-Fi enabled wearables connected to cloud-based platforms where data could be live streamed for better health/fitness monitoring. Now applications in things like personalized health monitoring and disease management were opened. For example, smartwatches and fitness bands started tracking heart beats per second (BPM), sleeping hours in a night or oxygen levels making the user aware about ones health trends. Wearable devices evolved more around healthcare as they continued to change shape and size. Current health-centric wearables, such as continuous glucose monitors (CGMs) and electrocardiogram sensors can monitor vital signs constantly and are able to notify users of potential medical problems. Today, these devices are monitoring us for chronic conditions such as diabetes, heart disease and hypertension giving both patients with health care professionals the continuous information they need to manage this better ways (Kumar & Kumari, 2021). Besides this, existing wearable devices are even more improved with AI and machine learning integration which facilitate for analysis of data in real-time so that insights can be predicted. AI can identify patterns in wearable data, even recognize early warning signs of health problems like irregular heartbeats or sleep apnea. That means these wearables can move beyond tracking, alerting and reminding to providing actionable recommendations that could potentially counter serious health events

These capabilities will only become more robust as wearables advance and their use cases widen, applying to remote patient monitoring, mental health management support for human augmentation in the future. Wearable Technology is the future of personalized healthcare and these devices are incomplete without AI, IoT, advanced sensors that will be an inevitable part of this modern life (Vivejananthan et al., 2022). More integration with the human body and a higher level of health related features is where we will eventually see wearable devices go. I know that inventions like smart clothes, devices with biohacking capabilities and sensors to be implanted, have expanded the limits of such technologies. Such increases herald a future where the capacity of humans gets amplified with real-time health proofing and data collection, which might redefine medical care as well personal wellness.

3. IMPORTANCE OF EMPOWER HEALTH MANAGEMENT WITH WEARABLE SENSORS

This could significantly change the way in which healthcare consultation and management are conducted by enabling uninterrupted, non-invasive phone sharing of patient status and hence early diagnosis. This provides both the patients and their care providers an opportunity to track real-time health information, thus enabling a shift towards proactive healthcare (Pradhan et al., 2023).

Enhancing Preventive Care: The single largest contribution of sensors and wearables was in enabling a new paradigm for preventative care. Through a more traditional healthcare model, patients would only turn to medical assistance after being symptomatic; which is frequently the case of when disease appear too late with an advanced stage and treatment. This non-invasive way of monitoring health, worn by the user allows for early detection of a potential issue before it escalates (Manogaran et al., 2021). For example, wearables that track heart rate variability could be used to identify the first signs of future cardiovascular problems and turn them into preventive measures such as increased physical exercise or medication.

Continuous monitoring of health factors like heart rate, blood pressure, oxygen saturation and glucose data gives patients an insight on their own well-being to help them lead healthier lives. This type of proactive approach is able to catch diseases much earlier which not only realize the ease and importance of this potentially life-saving service but also bring down hospital visits, thus reducing healthcare costs. This integration allows the accumulation and storage of this biological data, so wearables can give you personalized health suggestions from your decisions or report to help improve your real-time life care as well assist on possible future complications.

Remote Patient Monitoring: Remote patient monitoring (RPM) has held an uptrend over the past years particularly with COVID-19 revealing limitations in standard healthcare methodologies and a surge of needs for remote-based health services (Suma, 2021). RPM heavily relies on Sensors and wearable technologies, which allow Healthcare Providers to monitor the health conditions of patients from a remote location. This is especially valuable for patients with chronic conditions like diabetes, hypertension or heart failure that need ongoing monitoring and control.

Getting data on the real-time health situation of a patient, healthcare providers can make an insight-driven solution for treatment and care plans which remove an in-person visit. This not just enhances the value of care but helps early interventions and least chances for hospitalizations & complications. The use of wearables for RPM, especially if locally available in rural or underserved areas with limited access to healthcare services can also add significant value powered by the data (Jenkins, 2022). Using wearables, health can be pushed to these communities so that no one is too far away from the care they need.

Increased Patient Engagement and Adherence: Wearable technologies have also helped in increasing patient engagement and treatment adherence. Wearables give users instant access to their health inputs, fostering a closer relationship with your own body and ideally increasing compliance in proper management of said metrics. Fitness trackers that measure physical activity and deliver daily goals, for example, can encourage users to be more physically active (boosting heart rate), get better sleep quality for enhancing recovery or reduce stress levels.

The use of wearables can remind patients to take their medications and track if they follow treatment plans, as well as provide insights into how healthy life choices affect health outcomes. The degree of engagement also helps patients to realise the value that following prescribed treatments can help them achieve, as well a better health outcomes. In this way, wearables can be an enabling technology that allows healthcare providers to monitor patient adherence from afar and intervene when required while offering additional support to ensure patients remain compliant with their treatment regimes (Malik & Kumar, 2022).

Transforming Chronic Disease Management: Diabetes, hypertension and cardiovascular diseases are the topusitas that affect human health for a long time. This puts patients as well the health care system for a tough ride with continued surveillance, follow up visits and lifestyle changes to be done on both sides. Continuous, real-time information with wearable technologies and sensors can perhaps be the most valuable asset in chronic disease care as it allows for a more personalized and effective management (Kumar et al., 2022). Today, Type 1 diabetes can be managed with continuous glucose monitors (CGMs) which are built into wearables and track blood sugar levels around the clock so patients know when their sugars get too high or fall. This empowers patients to take immediate actions, like change in diet or insulin variation, for balancing glucose levels. Similarly, blood pressure-monitoring wearables can also be an effective health tracker for hypertensive patients who will want to monitor their condition to reduce the risk of stroke or heart attack by making lifestyle changes.

The data, collected in real time by those devices can then be automatically integrated into digital health platforms to enable ongoing monitoring and treatment adjustments for healthcare providers. And, as clinicians provide feedback on medication and care plans built for the patient in real-time during his or her daily life. This continuous loop of information gives patients insight into appropriate interventions to improve their health outside of hospitals delivered both at right time removing their load towards chronic disease management improving long term clinical outcomes (Han, 2023).

Figure 2. Illuminates importance of empower health management with wearable sensors

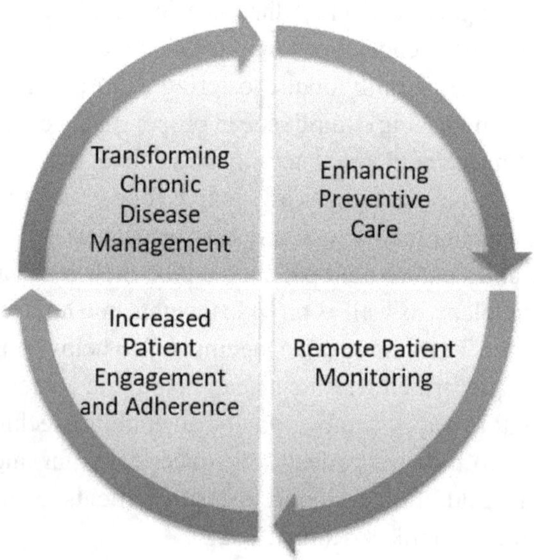

(Source- Self Prepared- Original)

4. INTEGRATION OF AI, IOT AND ML IN WEARABLE HEALTH TECHNOLOGIES

Introduction of Artificial Intelligence (AI), Internet of Things(IoT) and Machine Learning(ML) into the field wearable health technology arena has changed the conventional paradigms of healthcare by providing advanced insights on medical care,for patient management with algorithms based pro-active predication analysis, data driven continuous monitoring. The evolution of wearable devices Wearable sensing has moved beyond basic tracking to complex systems that provide real-time measurement and analysis of data over every walk-of-life, be it daily routines or specialized medical observation. With the combination of AI, IoT and ML into these technologies have opened a new dimension for intelligent and individualized healthcare solutions which benefit both patients as well as health-managers.

4.1 Artificial Intelligence in Wearables: Smarter Data Interpretation

Wearable health technologies use sensors to capture health data, and then AI is used as a tool in the analysis of these complex results. Using AI algorithms, this data can be crunched and various patterns or trends could emerge that both the healthcare providers as well its users are able to act upon. For example, AI feature in a wearable can identify when heart rate is out of range or sleep patterns maybe off and alert users about possible arrhythmias, sleep apnea issues or stress levels going beyond normal. Real-time the algorithm will run in real time and can provide feedback that may help you heads-off emergencies, or to adjust your lifestyle habits.

Personalization of care is one of the biggest benefits AI can bring to wearable health tech. AI uses population health data to provide personalized wellness plans from the specific physiological measurements and medical record of an individual Such a personalized level of care results in better management and timely treatment delivery for chronic diseases like diabetes, hypertension, or heart disease.

4.2 Wearable Devices and IoT in Healthcare: Better Health Management With Connectivity

The Internet of Things (IoT) is another key component that brings wearable devices together in a wider healthcare environment. Connected to other healthcare tools such as electronic health records (EHRs), telemedicine platforms and remote monitoring systems, wearables can communicate through IoT. With the internet of things (IoT), wearables can connect to relay data directly and in real-time to healthcare professionals, allowing for round-the-clock remote patient monitoring.

IoT-enabled wearables can offer this network for more efficient chronic disease management. This includes anticipating the state of an ailment like diabetes in which patients who have continuous glucose (CGMs) monitors can receive data on their blood sugar levels directly through to a smartphone or medical device (Raghav et al., 2024). This information can in turn be passed onto their physician, allowing for interventions at a much earlier time. It also makes it possible to unite and integrate several wearable devices, allowing data from heart rate monitors with the activity trackers or sleep-monitor information into a broader picture of patient health.

The power that IoT has to offer is seen significantly in telemedicine, from diagnosis to consultation and all the way back as patients can have remote check-ups where from their wearables they share real-time health data as opposed to them having multiple visits in a month (Banerjee et al., 2020). This IoT and wearables integration enables greater tele-healthcare access to save time, travel cost for patients especially in rural or underserved markets whilst reducing the number of on-site visits/consultations/hospital re-admissions.

4.3 Proactive Healthcare using Machine Learning: Predictive Analytics

ML works in the capacities of predictive analytics, and it as an added layer makes wearables even smarter for Health. They not only read the historical health data coming from wearables but also predict future outcomes using Machine Learning algorithms. Patients and providers can be proactive rather than reactive when it comes to health. ML algorithms may be able to predict a heart attack or stroke based on range of vital signs and lifestyle factors along with a record of past data. Basically, a healthcare provider can even get to know in advance by using the plotted data and act before any medical crisis. ML can also forecast exacerbations or deteriorations in conditions like asthma and COPD (Chronic Obstructive Pulmonary Disease) in the case of chronic diseases, which allow doctors to make treatment adjustments ahead.

This ability to learn also ensures that a wearable becomes more accurate and effective the longer it is worn. However, wearables embedded with ML algorithms can develop deeper levels of analyses by processing new user data and adapting the predictions it provides for each individual in a smarter way over time. This continuous learning is what makes ML the most essential technology in any wearables to achieve long term disease management (Barnes & Zvarikova, 2021).

Although this trio offers enormous opportunities to wearable health technologies, there are a plethora of challenges that should be smoothened so as to realise its full potential. Wearable devices share health data that is critically sensitive and needs to therefore be well protected which has become more important as remote work became the norm because it often increases current threats of identity theft, unauthorized access etc. (Desai & Shende, 2021). Secure transport and encryption of data, across IoT networks is vital for patient confidence as well a mandatory obligation under regulations including HIPAA (Health Insurance Portability and Accountability Act) it can also have implications related to GDPR (General Data Protection Regulation).

The digital divide and accessibility are also serious considerations at play here. Many patients, especially those in low-income or rural areas, do not have access to a wearable technology. These are all positive prospects, but for AI and the IoT in wearable health devices more fully realised there will need be an effort levied towards these innovations being both viable and affordable across a wide range of populations. Apart from this, a difficulty is experienced in the precision of wearables (Hurley & Popescu, 2021). Even as AI and ML algorithms are getting better by the day, wearable devices may not always produce accurate data resulting in false alarms or wrong diagnosis. Validity of wearable sensors and AI models trained on more diverse data holds tremendous promise for bolstering the reliability of these tools.

However, with all of these challenges to solving them by implementing AI, IoT and ML in Wearable Health Tech there are also large opportunities for revolutionizing healthcare. Continuous health monitoring, tailored care plans and long-term predictions all could dramatically change patient treatment and outcomes. With further developments in these new technologies, resulting integration will increasingly be necessary for prevention treatment and management of chronic disease as well as remote patient monitoring that enable a future unified smart health eco-system (Goel et al., 2021).

5. INNOVATIONS IN HUMAN AUGMENTATION FOR HEALTHCARE

Human augmentation the development and application devices that extend human capability is becoming more relevant in medicine. The Assemblage of Wearable's embedded with artificial intelligence, internet-of-things enabled and sensing features can lead to a significantly advanced form human beings that will enhance health and well-being (Kumar et al., 2022). In healthcare, human augmentation can support a variety of applications which range from prosthetics and exoskeletons that facilitate body movement to implantables capable of monitoring or delivering medication. One great example is smart prosthetics which contain built-in sensors and can accommodate for the fineness of a user's actions, making them more natural and responsive. They have the potential to dramatically improve the quality of lives lived by disabled men and women, allowing these people greater mobility without assistance.

Beyond physical augmentation, we are learning to augment cognitive and mental functions with wearable technologies. Neurofeedback devices are capable of tracking brain activity and providing feedback to the users this can help in enhancing focus, relieve stress or boost cognitive performance (Huang et al., 2021). In the same vein, some new wearables cater to improving cognitive function and overall well-being by tracking data on sleep patterns in order for you to use this information from day-to-day.

The healthcare industry has seen the most growth in human augmentation, when it comes to integrating technology with humans. Using advances such as wearables, prosthetics, neuroprosthetics and AI-powered solutions to enhance physical functioning also sensory or cognitive function this can be incredibly helpful for people experiencing disabilities yes even chronic conditions/age-related impairments. Human augmentation is changing the face of healthcare from robotic limbs powered by neural impulses to exoskeletons aiding biomechanics, advancing capabilities for rehabilitation, bio-medical applications and general life quality.

5.1 Prosthetics and Neuroprosthesis

Advances in prosthetics, most notably neuroprosthetics that can be controlled by the nervous system are some of the most remarkable developments. These instruments use sensors and neural connections, which permit sufferers to command artificial limbs using their brain signals. A new generation of robotic arms can now be controlled by people whose limbs have been amputated, responding to the electrical signals from their brains in ways that allow them surprisingly natural movement and dexterity. This technological jump results in a quantum shift of life enhancement for inhabitants who have misplaced limbs giving back autonomy as well making it even functional (Malik et al., 2021).

The term neuroprosthetics means more than just a device augmenting limbs. Another way in which human augmentation is enhancing sensory capabilities is with cochlear implants for hearing and retinal implants, to restore vision to the visually impaired (Kumar et al., 2021). The integration of human biology and technology in these devices has made it possible for patients to partake with more varied sensory experiences than previous.

5.2 Mobility and Rehabilitation Exoskeletons

Wearable exoskeletons are another major advance in human augmentation, especially for those affected by mobility impairments. These power suits for disabled were created to help people with spinal cord injuries, stroke or muscular disorders be on foot and sum of movement. These exoskeletons are designed to emulate the natural movements of the human body, while offering explosive support for a variety of tasks.

An exoskeleton in rehabilitation lets you support or resist patients to help them regain motor skills after injuries (Kaushik et al., 2024). A device stroke patients can wear to walk that gradually remembers muscle strength and coordination. Rehabilitation with exoskeletons achieves this and in addition, lessens the physical burden of therapists helping patients manually. Additionally, the use of exoskeletons with sensors and AI can provide real-time feedback that enable therapy to be adjusted more accurately than traditional approaches which can lead better patient outcomes.

5.3 Brain-Computer Interfaces (BCIs)

Brain-computer interfaces (BCIs) belong to a new type of emerging technology in the field of human augmentation with promise for healthcare. BCIs provide for direct communication between the brain and external devices, letting individuals operate machines or even prosthetic limbs, or computer applications in some cases with their thoughts. BCIs enable patients with severe neurological disorders such as amyotrophic lateral sclerosis (ALS) or locked-in syndrome to communicate and interact with the environment. In addition to the treatment of patients with neurological impairments, BCI have potential use in cognitive enhancement. Scientists even hope to involve BCIs in amping up memory and learning capabilities or problem-solving skills a possibility that could prove high-seas change when it comes to tackling cognitive decline of conditions such as Alzheimer's disease.

5.4 Sensory Augmentation

These technologies that have been initially designed to augment or restore the functions of a sensory modality (vision, hearing and touch). Sensory aids, a mainstay of sensory aid technology until today for example like eyeglasses or hearing aids Less than certain recently developed technologies have aimed to add new functionality. For example, haptic feedback systems that provide a sense of touch can enable users to “touch” objects in virtual reality environment and increase the potential for telemedicine and remote surgery. Also, sensors embedded in wearable devices can supplement balance and spatial awareness for individuals suffering from vestibular disorders as well.

5.5 Ethical Reflections and Dilemmas

These changes have huge potential for healthcare, but they also pose significant ethical dilemmas. Ensuring that critical questions about who benefits from, and in what ways these technologies are implemented advance enough to be considered a variety of ethical implications will also lend themselves as areas for future study. This begin to progressively incorporate these technologies and safeguarding their safety, confidentiality, privacy as well establishing a-stakeholder empowered oversight are essential.

The human augmentation and enhancement technologies remain at core of transformational healthcare by boosting our physical, sensory as well cognitive capabilities to levels unimagined! These are the technologies which address disabilities or impairments among patients and have a transformative, adaptive potential of pushing our human capabilities beyond what is natural. Into the future, human augmentation will increasingly improve patient care and rehabilitation, among other things (Arora et al., 2024).

Figure 3. Innovations in human augmentation for healthcare

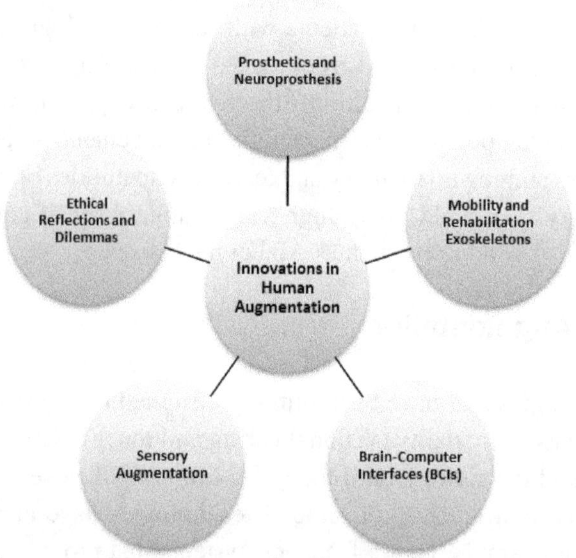

(Source- Self Prepared- Original)

6. ETHICAL ISSUES AND CHALLENGES

That is, when it comes to using wearable technologies in healthcare, a number of ethical considerations and challenges need to be overcome. Data privacy and security is one of the most important ones. Wearable devices capture enormous amounts of sensitive biometric data that could be prone to hacking or unauthorized access if measures are not taken to shield these vulnerable sources. The security of this data is critically important from a patient trust perspective and to prevent potential misuse (Kaushik et al., 2024). The other issue has to be that we do not over-promise technology. Wearable devices can give an excellent idea of your health metrics, but are by no means a substitute for professional medical advice. However, using this data should not replace the need for medical consultation when someone is chronically unwell. Furthermore, wearables can be inaccurate to a varying degree which may lead to false positives or negatives that cause unneeded anxiety or missed diagnoses.

An additional challenge of wearable technology concerns their accessibility. While the cost of these devices is going down annually, there remains a digital divide that can prevent some populations often in low-income areas or rural locations from accessing cell phones. It is important to aim towards the broad scale adoption of wearables, as with healthcare disparities in this country and differences based on socioeconomic status are certainly culprits for unjust health outcomes (Raghav et al., 2024).

7. CONCLUSION AND FUTURE SCOPE

Wearable technology and sensors are the core of a healthcare revolution that is delivering continuous monitoring, personalized care and proactive health management. These technologies could materially improve patient care outcomes, especially in managing chronic disease and offering preventative services. Human augmentation, then opens up a new realm of possibilities for physical and cognitive health. With the increasing uses of wearable devices, it is important to answer problems related with using them such as privacy issues or whether device provides reliable result and broadly available. In this way, the healthcare system could fully benefit from sensors & wearables to create an even more efficient, equal and personalized main care. Where the future of healthcare is headed, however, will be in providing individuals with resources and tools to become masters over their health and senses & wearable devices are central enablers on this path.

Sensors and wearables are among the major enabling technologies for digital healthcare management that can bring disruptive change to monitor patients around-the-clock, provide individualised care programs and actively control chronic diseases. The convergence of AI, IoT and human augmentation can extend the promise through evolutionary capabilities in physical as well as cognitive health. In order to work at full capacity, ethical issues like data privacy, availability and accuracy of the wearables need proper handling. The most proactive ideal for the future of healthcare is to give people tools and technologies that help them take control of their health, making wearables one of the key enablers. The healthcare industry must continue to work towards equity, safety and ethics as innovation carries on so that the potential of wearable technologies can be realised for all.

REFERENCES

Ahirwar, R., & Khan, N. (2022). *Smart Wireless Nanosensor Systems for Human Healthcare*. CRC Press. DOI: 10.1201/9781003093534-15

Arora, M. K., Lal, S., Singh, B., & Olyaee, M. (2024). Through an Energy Lens: Examining SDGs From a Policy Perspective. In Riswandi, B., Singh, B., Kaunert, C., & Vig, K. (Eds.), *AI Applications for Clean Energy and Sustainability* (pp. 320–343). IGI Global., DOI: 10.4018/979-8-3693-6567-0.ch016

Banerjee, A., Chakraborty, C., & Rathi, M.Sr. (2020). Medical imaging, artificial intelligence, internet of things, wearable devices in terahertz healthcare technologies. In *Terahertz biomedical and healthcare technologies* (pp. 145–165). Elsevier. DOI: 10.1016/B978-0-12-818556-8.00008-2

Barnes, R., & Zvarikova, K. (2021). Artificial intelligence-enabled wearable medical devices, clinical and diagnostic decision support systems, and Internet of Things-based healthcare applications in COVID-19 prevention, screening, and treatment. *American Journal of Medical Research (New York, N.Y.)*, *8*(2), 9–22. DOI: 10.22381/ajmr8220211

Chelliah, R., Wei, S., Daliri, E. B. M., Rubab, M., Elahi, F., Yeon, S. J., Jo, K., Yan, P., Liu, S., & Oh, D. H. (2021). Development of nanosensors based intelligent packaging systems: Food quality and medicine. *Nanomaterials (Basel, Switzerland)*, *11*(6), 1515. DOI: 10.3390/nano11061515 PMID: 34201071

Desai, D., & Shende, P. (2021). Integration of Internet of Things with Quantum Dots: A State-of-the-art of Medicine. *Current Pharmaceutical Design*, *27*(17), 2068–2075. DOI: 10.2174/1381612827666210222113740 PMID: 33618640

Gaobotse, G., Mbunge, E., Batani, J., & Muchemwa, B. (2022). Non-invasive smart implants in healthcare: Redefining healthcare services delivery through sensors and emerging digital health technologies. *Sensors International*, *3*, 100156. DOI: 10.1016/j.sintl.2022.100156

Goel, S. S., Goel, A., Kumar, M., & Moltó, G. (2021). A review of Internet of Things: Qualifying technologies and boundless horizon. *Journal of Reliable Intelligent Environments*, *7*(1), 23–33. DOI: 10.1007/s40860-020-00127-w

Han, B., Tomer, V., Nguyen, T. A., Farmani, A., & Singh, P. K. (Eds.). (2020). *Nanosensors for smart cities*. Elsevier.

Han, X. (2023). A novel assimilated navigation model based on advanced optical systems (AOS), internet of things (IoT) and artificial intelligence (AI). *Optical and Quantum Electronics*, *55*(7), 655. DOI: 10.1007/s11082-023-04947-x

He, L., & Eastburn, M. (2022, August). Smart nanosensor networks for body injury detection. In 2022 IEEE International Conference on Smart Internet of Things (SmartIoT) (pp. 15-19). IEEE. DOI: 10.1109/SmartIoT55134.2022.00012

Huang, J., Wu, X., Huang, W., Wu, X., & Wang, S. (2021). Internet of things in health management systems: A review. *International Journal of Communication Systems*, *34*(4), e4683. DOI: 10.1002/dac.4683

Hurley, D., & Popescu, G. H. (2021). Medical big data and wearable internet of things healthcare systems in remotely monitoring and caring for confirmed or suspected COVID-19 patients. *American Journal of Medical Research (New York, N.Y.)*, *8*(2), 78–90. DOI: 10.22381/ajmr8220216

Jenkins, T. (2022). Wearable medical sensor devices, machine and deep learning algorithms, and internet of things-based healthcare systems in COVID-19 patient screening, diagnosis, monitoring, and treatment. *American Journal of Medical Research (New York, N.Y.)*, *9*(1), 49–64. DOI: 10.22381/ajmr9120224

Khan, T., Civas, M., Cetinkaya, O., Abbasi, N. A., & Akan, O. B. (2020). Nanosensor networks for smart health care. In *Nanosensors for Smart Cities* (pp. 387–403). Elsevier. DOI: 10.1016/B978-0-12-819870-4.00022-0

Kumar, P. M., Hong, C. S., Afghah, F., Manogaran, G., Yu, K., Hua, Q., & Gao, J. (2021). Clouds proportionate medical data stream analytics for internet of things-based healthcare systems. *IEEE Journal of Biomedical and Health Informatics*, *26*(3), 973–982. DOI: 10.1109/JBHI.2021.3106387 PMID: 34415841

Kumar, P. M., Khan, L. U., & Hong, C. S. (2022). Affirmative fusion process for improving wearable sensor data availability in artificial intelligence of medical things. *IEEE Sensors Journal.*

Kumar, P. M., Khan, L. U., & Hong, C. S. (2022). Notice of Violation of IEEE Publication Principles: Affirmative Fusion Process for Improving Wearable Sensor Data Availability in Artificial Intelligence of Medical Things. IEEE Sensors Journal.

Kumar, S., & Kumari, P. (2021). Flexible Nano Smart sensors. Nanosensors for Smart Manufacturing, 199.

Lal, S., Arora, M. K., Riswandi, B. A., Singh, N., & Singh, B. (2024). Melding Artificial Intelligence and Remote Sensing Data for Real-Time Monitoring of Marine Biodiversity. In Riswandi, B., Singh, B., Kaunert, C., & Vig, K. (Eds.), *AI Applications for Clean Energy and Sustainability* (pp. 299–319). IGI Global., DOI: 10.4018/979-8-3693-6567-0.ch015

Malik, A., & Kumar, A. (2022). assimilation of blockchain with Internet of Things (IoT) with possible issues and solutions for better connectivity and proper security. In New Trends and Applications in Internet of Things (IoT) and Big Data Analytics (pp. 187-207). Cham: Springer International Publishing.

Malik, P. K., Sharma, R., Singh, R., Gehlot, A., Satapathy, S. C., Alnumay, W. S., Pelusi, D., Ghosh, U., & Nayak, J. (2021). Industrial Internet of Things and its applications in industry 4.0: State of the art. *Computer Communications*, *166*, 125–139. DOI: 10.1016/j.comcom.2020.11.016

Manogaran, G., Alazab, M., Song, H., & Kumar, N. (2021). CDP-UA: Cognitive data processing method wearable sensor data uncertainty analysis in the internet of things assisted smart medical healthcare systems. *IEEE Journal of Biomedical and Health Informatics*, *25*(10), 3691–3699. DOI: 10.1109/JBHI.2021.3051288 PMID: 33439849

Materon, E. M., Gómez, F. R., Joshi, N., Dalmaschio, C. J., Carrilho, E., & Oliveira Jr, O. N. (2021). Smart materials for electrochemical flexible nanosensors: advances and applications. Nanosensors for smart manufacturing, 347-371.

Mujawar, M. A., Gohel, H., Bhardwaj, S. K., Srinivasan, S., Hickman, N., & Kaushik, A. (2020). Nano-enabled biosensing systems for intelligent healthcare: Towards COVID-19 management. *Materials Today. Chemistry*, *17*, 100306. DOI: 10.1016/j.mtchem.2020.100306 PMID: 32835155

Nazari, A. (2020). Nanosensors for smart cities: an introduction. In *Nanosensors for smart cities* (pp. 3–8). Elsevier. DOI: 10.1016/B978-0-12-819870-4.00001-3

Oukhatar, A., Bakhouya, M., & El Ouadghiri, D. (2021). Electromagnetic-Based Wireless Nano-Sensors Network: Architectures and Applications. *Journal of Communication*, *16*(1), 8–19. DOI: 10.12720/jcm.16.1.8-19

Pradhan, M. R., Mago, B., & Ateeq, K. (2023). A classification-based sensor data processing method for the internet of things assimilated wearable sensor technology. *Cluster Computing*, *26*(1), 807–822. DOI: 10.1007/s10586-022-03605-3

Pramanik, P. K. D., Solanki, A., Debnath, A., Nayyar, A., El-Sappagh, S., & Kwak, K. S. (2020). Advancing modern healthcare with nanotechnology, nanobiosensors, and internet of nano things: Taxonomies, applications, architecture, and challenges. *IEEE Access : Practical Innovations, Open Solutions*, *8*, 65230–65266. DOI: 10.1109/ACCESS.2020.2984269

Raghav, A., Singh, B., & Jermsittiparsert, K. (2024). Role of Artificial Intelligence and Machine Learning in Clean and Blue Energy for Enhancing Efficiency and Sustainability. In Riswandi, B., Singh, B., Kaunert, C., & Vig, K. (Eds.), *AI Applications for Clean Energy and Sustainability* (pp. 366–386). IGI Global., DOI: 10.4018/979-8-3693-6567-0.ch018

Rani, P. (2022). Nanosensors and their Potential Role in Internet of Medical Things. In *Nanosensors for Futuristic Smart and Intelligent Healthcare Systems* (pp. 293–317). CRC Press. DOI: 10.1201/9781003093534-16

Sahi, K. S. S., & Kaushik, S. (2022). Smart Nanosensors for Healthcare Monitoring and Disease Detection using AIoT Framework. In *Nanosensors for Futuristic Smart and Intelligent Healthcare Systems* (pp. 387–400). CRC Press. DOI: 10.1201/9781003093534-19

Suma, D. V. (2021). Wearable IoT based distributed framework for ubiquitous computing. *Journal of Ubiquitous Computing and Communication Technologies*, *3*(1), 23–32. DOI: 10.36548/jucct.2021.1.003

Udoh, E. E., Hermel, M., Bharmal, M. I., Nayak, A., Patel, S., Butlin, M., & Bhavnani, S. P. (2023). Nanosensor technologies and the digital transformation of healthcare. *Personalized Medicine*, *20*(3), 251–269. DOI: 10.2217/pme-2022-0065 PMID: 37403731

Vivekananthan, V., Khandelwal, G., Alluri, N. R., & Kim, S. J. (2022). E-Skin for Futuristic Nanosensor Technology for the Healthcare System. In Nanosensors for Futuristic Smart and Intelligent Healthcare Systems (pp. 133-157). CRC Press.

Chapter 6
Cancer Intercept – Early Detection Strategies for Enhanced Survival Rates

Anshika Tyagi
https://orcid.org/0009-0004-6199-3074
Sharda University, Greater Noida, India

Vishal Jain
https://orcid.org/0000-0003-1126-7424
Sharda University, Greater Noida, India

ABSTRACT

Early detection of disease is important in healthcare not only for the hope that the patient might get cured, but also due to the low risk factor for conducting an operation. The current chapter will discuss some newly defined techniques and technologies that are changing the way early disease detection is done-from machine learning and wearable health monitoring devices to advanced medical imaging. Right application of newly given medical technology is making the concept of good patient recovery possible by coordinating machine learning with the medical field. Considering predictive algorithm in the identification of diseases with the use of large datasets for identifying the diseases through the help of machine learning and, with an upper hand of AI, finding proper cure along with experience from the doctors is allowing a patient to live more i.e. Better, faster recovery.

DOI: 10.4018/979-8-3693-9092-4.ch006

1. INTRODUCTION

An important aspect of current health care is catching diseases in their earliest stages. Finding cancer, heart disease, diabetes, and brain disorders at their onset often-even before the patient realizes anything-puts patients on the road to recovery much more easily, because treatments can be administered at the time they will do the best, when the disease is least bad. For diseases such as cancer, catching it early will greatly advance a better prognosis, possibly lowering the burden of tough treatment, which is hard on the patient's body and spirit. The sooner the disease is detected, the greater the options for less intense or even more benign treatments that most of the time yield better results and, above all, a better quality of life.

Advances in the development of early-detection methods have been influenced by the introduction of new technologies. Traditional screening methods such as mammograms, Pap smears, and colonoscopies have long been able to detect diseases before they reach an advanced stage. The pace of innovation, however has relatively recently led us to improve upon early detection diagnostics using biomarkers, advanced imaging techniques, and artificial intelligence. Biomarkers give information about disease at the molecular level. They often depict problems in genes or proteins that can indicate a disease even before the symptoms surface. These molecular signs can be found in blood, tissue, or any other body fluid and especially prove helpful when finding cancers and other serious health issues early. (Bannasch, P., & Van Kaick, G., 1992).

New imaging technologies have really improved the early detection of diseases by showing very clear pictures of what is inside the body. Techniques like MRI, PET, and molecular imaging allow healthcare providers to find tiny changes in tissues and organs that may indicate the beginning of a disease. The imaging techniques can identify tumors, lesions, or other abnormalities at minute levels, and doctors have a far clearer view of the patient's health considerably earlier than when a person manifests diseases. Combining molecular imaging with standard techniques helps doctors identify problems such as cancers, heart disease, and brain disorders earlier when they can be treated more effectively. (Patriotis & Srivastava, 2023)

It becomes an even more important tool for early detection. It can look at large amounts of data and find patterns that human doctors might not see right away. AI algorithms can quickly and accurately identify early signs of disease from medical images, genetic data, and electronic health records. Such AI techniques have been helpful where, in terms of radiology and pathology, they prove to be very useful in spotting problems like tumors or lesions that might typically appear in medical images than in traditional methods. AI can collect information from sources such as images, biomarkers, and genetic data. This provides a wider view of a patient's condition and helps in giving a more accurate diagnosis. It enhances the speed of identification and reduces the risk of human error, which, in turn, increases the accuracy of diagnostic results. (Newsham et al., 2024)

Even though early discovery of diseases offers many benefits, there are problems that need to be solved:

One major problem is the likelihood of false positives. This is when tests mistakenly claim that someone is suffering from a disease, thereby subjecting him/her to undue stress and further tests. False negatives are also unsettling; this is when a disease cannot be detected, which may lead to late treatment and even worse results for patients. Again, not all people have easy access to advanced diagnostic technologies; their availability seems to vary based on the difference between rich and poor areas. Many new technologies for diagnosis, such as liquid biopsies or AI-based tests, are expensive and inaccessible in all healthcare systems. Therefore, their potential to benefit global health is limited. The high cost of these technologies reaches far beyond the reach of patients in underdeveloped areas, which is another indication for better access and more affordable prices.

Looking forward, further progress in early disease detection would help to alleviate some of these limitations. Some of the popular and promising non-invasive techniques include liquid biopsies, where tumor DNA is found in the blood, and wearable health monitoring devices, which are increasingly popular. These technologies allow constant observation and can detect alterations in health with minimal distress for the patient. AI will also be very important in making early detection methods better. It will help reduce biases in diagnostic models, improve accuracy, and bring together data from different sources to create a more precise and personalized way of providing healthcare. As these technologies become easier to get and cheaper, they are likely to change healthcare from reacting to diseases to preventing them, which will greatly enhance global health results. (Rhmann & Pandey, 2021).

In essence, the discovery of diseases early has several advantages because one is bound to find illnesses when they just begin, which calls for quick and better treatments. New technology in biomarkers, advanced imaging, and artificial intelligence has made it much easier to detect diseases early and correctly. Despite this, issues such as false positives, accessibility, and cost still make it difficult to use these tools broadly. As research continues and these technologies become easier to use, the future of early detection may change healthcare more from a focus on prevention and help millions of patients across the globe have better outcomes. (Patel, H. N., Ghodgaonkar, D. K., & Suri, J. S. (2022)).

1.1 Importance of Early Detection

Early detection is important because, knowing a disease early can really change the picture for the better in terms of health results, with a reduced burden from chronic illness and increased quality of life for individuals. The term “early detection” refers to establishing the presence of a disease at an early or initial stage that may often be before the development of apparent clinical signs. Early diagnosis of diseases enhances the chances of treatment and lessens the necessity of aggressive treatment protocols. Such preventive healthcare practices preserve lives but also reduce chronic physical, psychological, and financial burdens that diseases create both for patients and healthcare systems.

The most significant advantage of early detection is the decrease in the rate of mortality. It is at this point that the stage of diagnosis of such diseases as cancer, heart disease, and diabetes turns out to be the predictor of survival. For instance, in cancer, if it's at the stage I, then there is a much bigger survival rate compared to an advanced stage whereby the cancer has spread to some parts of the body. A similar thing applies to cardiovascular diseases. Risk factors or minor abnormalities may be intervened on very early, thereby preventing a heart attack or stroke and maybe saving the patient from grave complication and eventual loss of life. (Rhmann & Pandey, 2021).

Early detection also preserves quality of life. For diseases caught early, less intensive treatment results in fewer side effects and even less disruption of the patient's daily life. Early-stage cancer might require a patient to be administered minor surgery or localized radiation, whereas late-stage cancer might include more invasive surgeries, chemotherapies, and sometimes the combination of severe treatments that could severely impact the whole health and well-being of the patient. Chronic diseases like diabetes need to be diagnosed at an early stage to make lifestyle changes and drug management in order to avoid undesirable complications like nerve damage, kidney failure, and vision loss. (Newsham et al., 2024)

Early disease detection benefits people at the level of health outcome but has much wider impacts in public health and, for that matter, on healthcare services. Treatment of diseases at their early stages is less costly than treatment of advanced conditions. The cost of early interventions, such as screening tests and prevention efforts, generally outweighs the expense of late-stage illness care, often involving long periods of hospitalization, costly pharmaceuticals, and much more involved care. All these price effectiveness only help patients to reduce their medical bills, but it also reduces the financial burden on the healthcare system, and therefore early detection can be a strategic approach in order to manage health care resources efficiently.

In addition, early detection reduces the spread of infectious diseases and minimizes its outbreak. This kind of disease includes tuberculosis, HIV, and COVID-19, which, if diagnosed early, enables proper isolation and treatment of the individuals affected, thereby minimizing further spread in the community. For example, this is an important consideration in the control of epidemics and pandemics in public health efforts, where diagnosis and intervention have to be accomplished early to minimize the spread of infectious diseases among people. (Patel, H. N., Ghodgaonkar, D. K., & Suri, J. S. (2022)).

The other thing that makes early detection important is that it would allow the offering of a treatment optimized to the characteristics of the specific condition in an individual. That would be possible only when there exists a diagnosis at the earliest molecular or genetic levels of the diseases. For example, biomarker-based tests can indicate genetically mutated mutations or expressions of proteins unique to a patient's tumor, thus allowing the utilization of targeted therapies, which are far more effective and have fewer side effects than the general prescriptions applied. Such a system could offer a better treatment outcome and is rather a big step forward in modern medicine away from the one-size-fits-all kind of system towards a more detailed and specific care for an individual.

However, early disease detection depends entirely on available and accessible diagnostic tools and screening programs. Equal access to health care also deprives many people of low resource settings from accessing the benefits of early detection. Resolution of such inequalities and making screening and diagnostic technologies more affordable and accessible will be a key tool in realizing the full scope offered by early detection. It also raises public awareness and education, encouraging people to take routine screenings and go in for medical attentions on early signs of disease.

Conclusion Early detection of disease is the bedrock for a proper health care delivery system, reaping multiple benefits in terms of increased survival rates, better quality of life, cost- effectiveness, and further public health. An early detection shift in perspective shifts the focus away from reactive treatment of the disease and toward proactive prevention and management, changing healthcare outcomes for people as well as for society at large. As research and technology continue to advance, reach, and accuracy in methods of early detection expand, the role it plays in disease prevention and health optimization will only increase, paving a healthier future. (Patel, H. N., Ghodgaonkar, D. K., & Suri, J. S. (2022b)).

1.2 Types of Early Detection Methods

Nowadays, early disease detection is conducted through different methods, each one of which is prepared to detect a particular disease at the earliest possible stage. This ranges from simple traditional screening tests up to the most recent molecular and artificial intelligence-driven technologies.

1. **Screening Tests:** Most patients diagnosed with diseases are detected early using screening tests. These tests are not invasive or least invasive. The diseases screened include cancers and other diseases, depending on age or high risk. (*Screening for Early Detection | AACR Cancer Progress Report 2023*, 2024).

   Common screening tests include:

   - **Mammograms:** A breast tissue imaging technique that is employed for the early diagnosis of breast cancer. ("Mammography and Beyond," 2001).
   - **Pap Smears and HPV Testing:** They are done to detect cervical cancer. Cells from the cervix are utilized for the diagnosis of this test.
   - **Colonoscopy:** This is the procedure in which interior parts of colon are screened for abnormal growth or polyps for the diagnosis of colorectal cancer.
   - **Low-Dose CT scans:** They are conducted for lung cancer screening. People who smoke regularly are more susceptible to this type of cancer.
   - **Blood Pressure and Cholesterol Tests:** They are pretty common tests for the early detection of cardiovascular diseases. (Bannasch & Van Kaick, 1992)

   Advantages:

   - Easy to administer and widely available
   - Good for detecting the presence of certain cancers or chronic condition before its chronic stage
   - Non-invasive or minimally invasive.

   Disadvantages:

   - Not all cancers or diseases have screening tests that have proved to be effective. There are gaps in the early detection of certain conditions.
   - Some of the screening tests can give false positives thus leading to unnecessary anxiety and additional tests.

- Screening tests may sometimes miss diseases if performed at inappropriate intervals or if the disease is not at a detectable stage yet.

Figure 1. Types of cancer

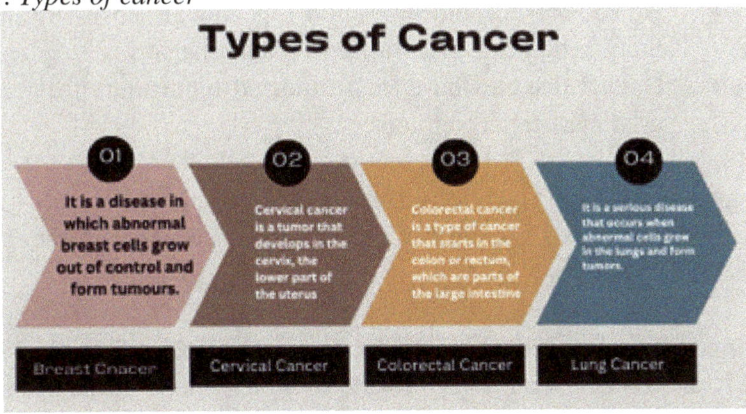

2. **Biomarkers:** Biomarkers are biological molecules found in blood, tissues, or other body fluids that provide indications of disease. Biomarker-based testing is increasingly being used to detect cancers, cardiovascular diseases, and neurological disorders.

   Examples of biomarkers include:

   - **Genetic Markers:** Mutations in the BRCA1 and BRCA2 genes are associated with an increased risk of developing breast and ovarian cancer.
   - **Protein Biomarkers:** A PSA (Prostate-Specific Antigen) test is a commonly used screening method for prostate cancer.
   - **Liquid Biopsies:** This term applies to blood or fluid tests that contain circulating tumor DNA, allowing for the detection of cancer at the earliest moments possible, without the need for a tissue biopsy. (Connal et al., 2023)

   Advantages:

   - Disease detection at the molecular level often even before symptoms may show up, which enables early diagnosis
   - It gives insight into whether it is a matter of genetics or a problem with proteins thus leading to targeted treatments.

- Many of the biomarker tests are non-invasive, and hence the liquid biopsies can be administered easily and are more acceptable to the patients.

Disadvantages:

- No Biomarkers sometimes may lack enough sensitivity and specificity, producing false positives or false negatives.
- Not all diseases have well-validated biomarkers that cannot be used in certain conditions.

Biomarker-based testing is still an emerging field, and much more research needs to be done to make these tests reliable and in easy reach. (Tenchov et al., 2024), (Pepe et al., 2001).

3. **Advanced Imaging Technologies:** Imaging technologies form the backbone of early disease detection; They provide very clear views of the inner organs, tissues, and even molecular activities.

   Some advanced imaging techniques include:

   - **MRI (Magnetic Resonance Imaging):** This technique involves magnetic fields and radio waves to provide detailed images of the body's organs and tissues, and it is mainly applied for diseases like tumors, brain disorders, and musculoskeletal disorders.

Figure 2. Image Processing in MRI ([23]

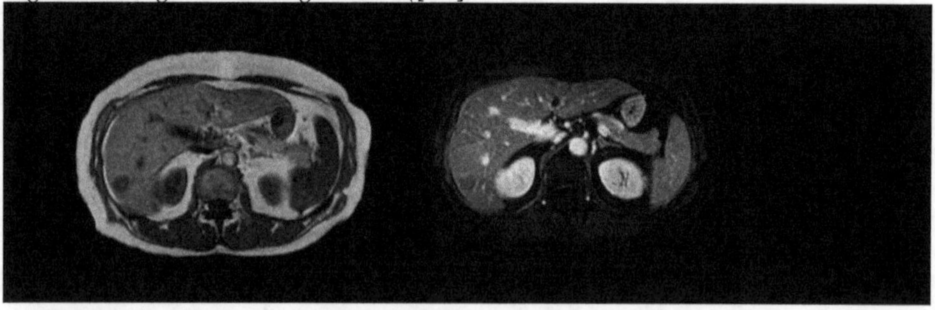

(CT Scans | Cancer Imaging Program (CIP), n.d.) - Google Search, n.d.)

- **PET-CT (Positron Emission Tomography-Computed Tomography):** PET-CT combines two imaging techniques that provide rich information regarding both structure and function in tissues; therefore, it is very commonly applied in cancer diagnosis and staging.

- **Molecular Imaging:** It can be used to visualize the real-time cellular and molecular processes, early insights into disease development, especially in cancer and cardiovascular diseases.

Advantages:

- Advanced techniques in imaging produce images that are so detailed and accurate such small tumors or abnormalities can be detected early.
- These technologies help in accurate staging of the cancer; this aids in ascertaining the choice of treatment
- Imaging aids in guiding biopsies and surgeries hence making them more accurate.

Disadvantages:

- This technology is expensive and may only be available in few places, especially where resources are scarce.
- Some diagnostic imaging modalities expose patients to the harmful effects of radiation (e.g., CT scans).
- The possibility of overdiagnosis is there, especially with techniques that identify cancers that are very slow growing or even benign and thus may not require intervention. (Ahmad & Alqurashi, 2024).

Figure 3. CT scan of breast cancer

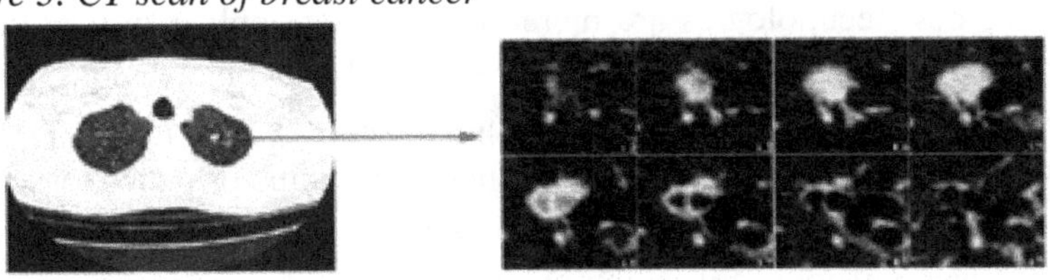

(CT Scans | Cancer Imaging Program (CIP), n.d.) - Google Search, n.d.)

4. **Machine Learning and Artificial Intelligence:** AI and ML are fast turning out to be an integral part of early disease detection. The technologies can evaluate massive amount of data sourced from a patient's medical records, genetic tests, and imaging scans to establish norms and discover possible indicators of disease much before what traditional methods would have done.

Advantages:

- Difference in disease detection can be made by dealing with large datasets much faster than before; so, accuracy while detecting in its early stages is much higher.
- Machine learning models can integrate information from various sources, including biomarkers, imaging, and genetic tests, allowing for a holistic and individualized diagnosis.
- Reducing chances of human error in test interpretation, thereby enhancing the accuracy of results.

Disadvantages:

- AI models may present biased opinions if the base dataset used is unrepresentative and hence may come up with false diagnoses.
- Such AI-based diagnoses will succeed only in hospitals that are equipped with high-level technology, which may not be the case in many places.
- With AI aiding in medical diagnosis, there comes a question regarding the privacy of the patient's data and how much can be trusted through it. (Milner & Lennerz, 2024b), (Thaker et al., 2024).

2. LITERATURE SURVEY

Advances of new technologies are increasingly being applied in new cancer detection, thus being a new hope for the disease's early finding. Amongst many promising fields of research, one of the most interesting is found in what's called "biomarkers". These are things in the body, such as proteins or genes, or special molecules, which can indicate the presence of cancer, even sometimes before the individual perceives any noticeable symptoms of the disease. These markers can be detected in blood, urine, or tissue samples and are considered markers of early growth within a disease. Indeed, some of them were found to correlate well with cancers diagnosed early on, whereby there is, therefore, a basis to start treatment earlier; something very much appreciated in the progression of improving patients' results.

Techniques in machine learning and artificial intelligence are some of the great technologies for the early diagnosis of cancers. Such tools are pretty good at scanning large volumes of medical data- test results, images, patient histories. This can be achieved with AI and ML, which can detect patterns in such data that might be opaque even to the brightest doctors; thus, preclinical signs of cancer may be caught that otherwise would have escaped notice. It is the ability to look at things very deeply-a capability already quite useful in identifying small changes that betoken the beginning of a disease, long before physical symptoms arise. (Patel, H. N., Ghodgaonkar, D. K., & Suri, J. S. (2022)).

In addition, computed tomography (CT) and magnetic resonance imaging (MRI) and other advanced imaging techniques took tremendous strides. These technologies could now identify much smaller tumors, even the earliest forms of body physiological changes. To reduce their patients' radiation exposure while not sacrificing crisp images, low-dose CT scans were designed. Among the improvements in MRI technologies under development, these better detect early signs of cancer. To illustrate, these include high-definition images of soft tissues and organs. This means that doctors can detect and address the onset of cancer when they start to develop. At this point, it's where treatment is usually most effective.

Well, taking the different methods together has made real progress in the detection of early cancer. Researchers found that using a mix of biomarkers, smart data analysis with machine learning, and very precise imaging techniques helps in finding cancer much better than only one method alone. For example, a patient may have undergone a biomarker test and appeared to show some possible risk of cancer. Then it becomes easy for AI tools to analyze this result and find more patterns of the patient's medical history or test results. Such a confirmation or finding of any tumors can be done through advanced imaging methods. This provides the greatest chances for catching cancer at an early stage, where treatment is effective. In general terms, it appears that the body has reached such an evolutionary stage concerning early detection and treatment for cancer through biomarkers, machine learning, and advanced imaging combined. Thus, the use of such tools by researchers and health service providers improves diagnoses, makes interventions possible at an earlier stage than before, treatments become effective, survival chances are increased, and ensures long-term recovery for patients or families afflicted or affected, which is a tremendous step forward in the fight against the disease. (Patel, H. N., Ghodgaonkar, D. K., & Suri, J. S. (2022)).

3. METHODOLOGY

Early cancer detection has a very multifaceted methodology where numerous advanced technologies and research techniques are allowed to come into play. Biomarker identification is the most important because researchers collect samples of blood, urine, or tissue from patients with the objective of analyzing these to detect specific proteins, genes, or other molecular markers that may indicate early cancer presence. These biomarkers are compared across differing populations of patients, such as healthy subjects versus early-stage cancer cases, to validate their effectiveness in early detection. (Newsham et al., 2024b)

Then, mass data analysis is done using machine learning and artificial intelligence. Large datasets comprising huge medical records, test reports, and imaging data are fed into the ML algorithms to identify the various patterns and correlations that may serve as early warning signs of cancer. AI models learn to recognize these kinds of patterns and improve their accuracy over time through supervised and unsupervised learning processes. (Rhmann & Pandey, 2021).

Through such processes, it tends to help automate the complex analysis on datasets that provide insights that may go a long way in helping clinicians make quicker and more accurate diagnoses.

Components must also be imaging techniques, such as low-dose CT scans and advanced MRI methods. Patients agreeing to screenings are subjected to the non-invasive procedures of generating an image of their body from within. Researchers and clinicians study these images to detect minuscule tumors, or other potentially very early indications of cancer. Imaging procedures are typically conducted over time to track how the changes are made. It enhances the possibility that cancerous growths are sought better at an earlier stage.

The methodologies are finally integrated into a hybrid approach. Biomarker analysis is a precursor before AI-driven data analysis and imaging to validate the findings. This multi-step process ensures proper and accurate assessment of potential risks of cancer for early intervention. The integrated method between biomarkers, AI, and imaging provides a more comprehensive diagnostic method for more effective early detection of cancer. (*Promoting Cancer Early Diagnosis*, 2024).

3.1. Preliminary Data

Early indications for the studies on the early detection of cancer with an integrated method, using biomarkers and ML, AI, and high imaging technologies, are also very promising. Early explorations into the role played by biomarkers in cancer detection have been encouraging; some proteins, genes, and molecular markers seem promising enough to give reliable signals that cancer is present during its earliest stages. Some biomarkers in the blood, urine, and tissue samples have been observed to be elevated among apparently asymptomatic people with occult early cancers. Even before the patients appear to have any clinical abnormality, the biomarkers are specific to cancers of the lung, prostate, and breast. This may modify the process of screening by non-invasive testing based on a biomarker for detection of cancer.

This is because it entails a simple and low- risk form of patient monitoring. (Milner & Lennerz, 2024)

Biomarker research aside, ML and AI have radically altered the landscape in medical data analysis. Thus, so far, trials have included massive datasets compiled from patient history, genetic information, test results, and images upon which high powered ML algorithms have been trained. The models have shown very impressive accuracy in finding early patterns of cancer. This represents how these models can illustrate efficiency in analyzing medical data. AI systems would scan through complex data much faster than human experts and therefore unveil correlations and trends that might otherwise not be noticed. For example, even small changes in cellular structure or tissue composition detected by imaging studies or biopsy by an AI tool could indicate the preliminary stages of tumor development. It has, in some instances identified cancer-prone patients using predictive models developed by AI, that were not clinically diagnosed at the time and were not reported by other screening methods. Such early detection may lead to interventions that delay the progression of the cancer. Preliminary data of imaging technique indicate better detection of cancers at earlier stages. Low-dose CT scans are capable of identifying lesions as small as 1 mm and sometimes even smaller, difficult to locate, without much exposition to radiation. This makes them safer for repeated application. Other improved MRI techniques optimized mainly for an enhancement of soft tissue contrast are also very sensitive to early abnormalities in organs such as the liver, pancreas, and even the brain. The imaging technology allows health care providers to observe early alterations within the body that might otherwise go unnoticed until the disease progresses. For cancers that are hard to detect with more conventional imaging, such as ovarian and pancreatic cancer, detection of even very subtle changes is much more important. (Bast & Srivastava, 2020).

One impressive characteristic of the research conducted here is the accumulated new technologies and techniques with their applications. Preliminary results from studies, which include biomarkers, machine learning, artificial intelligence, and imaging techniques, show promising improvement in cancer detection accuracy and timing with an integrated approach. For instance, blood-based biomarker tests integrated with AI-driven data analysis and advanced imaging increase the chances of being cured before cancer becomes lethal. There is a reported pilot study for this combination therapy in diagnosing patients even before those who have only been on regular screening using either mammograms or colonoscopies only. This hybrid approach increases the sensitivity of detection of cancer and does not allow for unnecessary follow-ups, thus having a reduced false positive, making the whole process more efficient and less stressing on the patient.

Early data also bring much promise concerning the potential impacts on survival rates and results of treatment. In most cases of cancer diagnosis, early detection becomes the key: these cancers also happen to be more responsive to treatment when it is early. Patients whose cancers were discovered early will benefit from less aggressive treatments that will enhance quality of life and reduce long-term effects. Moreover, early detection of cancer before it can spread to other parts of the body greatly improves the prospect that the cancer can be curatively treated and reduces the general burden caused by cancer. It is in the context of the preliminary data presented here that scientists are optimistic that the widespread use of these integrated detection approaches will lead to remarkably increased cancer survival rates for many neoplasms diagnosed at a very late stage.

Conclusion In a nutshell, the preliminary information that these technologies may offer in terms of integration with biomarkers, machine learning, AI, and advanced imaging techniques seems to offer a promising pathway toward early detection of cancers. Better treatment outcomes and survival rates will help researchers along with healthcare providers detect cancer accurately at much earlier stages. This has given more opportunities to promote the science of cancer diagnosis, a possibility of better customized and more accurate treatment strategies, along with a better experience for patients. (Amor et al., 2019).

3.2. Discussions

It really opens up the doors to revolutionary potential with the discussion of preliminary data from early cancer detection studies based on biomarkers, ML, AI, and advanced imaging techniques. Most importantly, one could know from this study that early detection is the most important factor in improving the outcome of cancer. Therefore, if the patient is diagnosed with cancer at an early stage, he or she would have a better chance to be treated with a treatment that may lead to a much higher survival rate. Biomarkers introduced combined with AI analysis and imagery techniques have provided a more efficient approach to screening compared to the general approaches that sometimes appear to fail by not realizing slight cancer symptoms early enough.

One of the great challenges to early detection of cancers has been the reliance on imaging or invasive biopsy procedures for confirmation purposes, representing a great technological advance over the last centuries. While these have been good approaches to some forms of cancer, they generally tend to identify the disease at a later stage when treatment options are constrained. Biomarkers on the other hand provide a highly effortless non-invasive method of detecting molecular changes due to cancer. Preliminary findings indicate that some biomarkers can act as reasonably good tumor-specific markers for certain cancers, such as ovarian or pancreatic cancer.

However, much work remains to be done before the specificity and sensitivity of the biomarkers are confirmed and hence the likelihood of false positives or failure to identify specific cancers. Much still needs to be done by research scientists to improve these cancer markers.

It has been an innovative answer to this problem by taking a machine learning and artificial intelligence-based approach. AI systems process enormous quantities of data and indicate trends that human observation cannot reach. Preliminary data are promising in complex datasets which rely on patient medical histories, genetic profiles, and imaging results - otherwise a daunting task for which AI models show predictable trends. This function not only enhances the chances of correctness but also time-effectiveness. It enables practitioners to make decisions within a set time-frame; hence, it is much more efficient than its counterparts. However, the debate regarding limitations in terms of AI cannot be ignored. The quality of data that the AI model has been trained on is as powerful as the AI model itself. Holes or biases in data may result in inaccuracies with the predictions. Hence, AI models need to be trained on diverse and wide-ranging datasets to bring down the possibilities of wrong predictions. (Anisman & Kusnecov, 2022).

Image techniques also generally help in early-stage cancer detection. Low-dose CT scans and even more advanced MRI methods have provided for much clearer detection of tumors. Such imaging technologies indicate much less invasiveness and accuracy in viewing the inner structures of the human body. Although promising, such imaging advances have brought along new challenges: they are costly and inaccessible for substantial parts of health services; high-quality imaging equipment and expert skills to interpret the scans are far from universal availability, especially in resource-poor settings. This raises questions of how such access to these new technologies should be covered to increase reach to more patients, which is key to wide improvements in early detection.

A very important topic of discussion will thus be combining these methodologies together. At this stage, though each of these has its strength in the form of biomarkers, AI, and imaging, it is only through their integration that they will shine. Preliminary studies did demonstrate a marked increase in the rate of detection of early cancers when applying all the methodologies together, but certainly much more work is needed to identify the best and most efficient ways to combine them for integration into routine clinical practice. With biomarkers and AI analysis and imaging, false positives were avoided, yet with more personalized approach towards cancer screening, accuracy of diagnoses improved. Yet, integration of technology into clinical workflows will impose new protocols and proper education and training for service providers-not to mention infrastructure investments. (Amor et al., 2019).

In brief, it is an early detection of cancer for the management of cancer with an integrated approach combining biomarkers, AI, and advanced imaging, though there remain a lot of issues of accuracy, accessibility, and effective implementation. One thing that should be continued on these technologies is refinement through studies to ensure effective application in real-world clinical settings. If these difficulties can be overcome, then the various potential gains of earlier detection, better diagnoses, and tailored treatment approaches could have the potential to transform cancer outcomes for patients around the globe. (Milner & Lennerz, 2024)

Figure 4. Workflow of patient under treatment

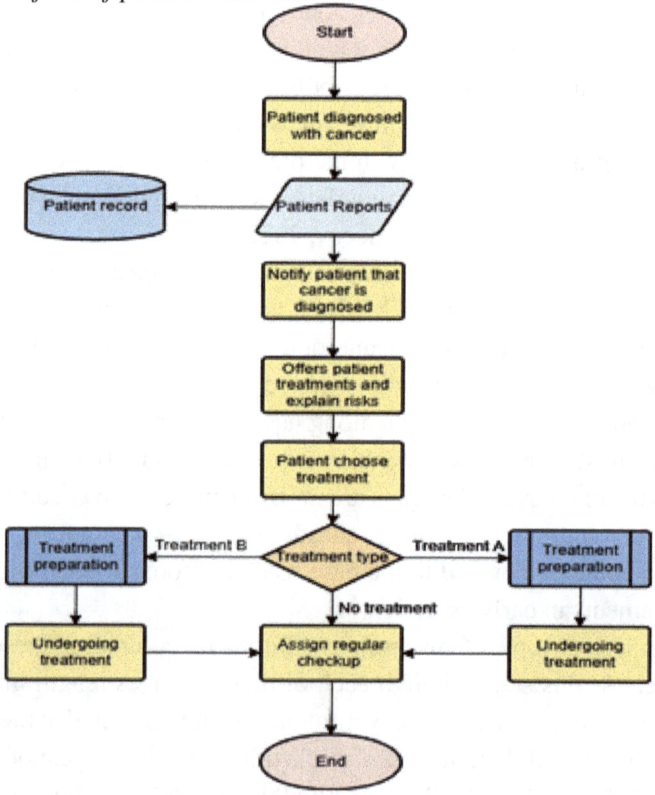

(Cancer Therapy Process | Flowchart Template, n.d.)

4. LIMITATIONS

Preliminary results in early cancer detection by use of biomarkers, ML, AI, and advanced imaging techniques point towards a few promising directions, but there are several limitations that cannot be ignored. Biomarkers sensitivity and specificity are as yet to be sorted out. A few biomarkers state the presence of the disease. Their result may lead to false positives or negatives in distinguishing the cancerous from the noncancerous conditions. It thus creates anxiety, more investigations, or even missed diagnoses.

Another limitation has to do with the state of machine learning and AI models. The models are only as good as the data on which they have been trained, and large, high-quality, and diverse datasets remain critical. All biases in training data-that is, an overrepresentation of certain populations-would bring about skewed predictions that don't generalize well to other demographics. Yet another aspect of some AI algorithms is the "black box," and decision-making is obscure. This might have the effect of further hindering further adoption and trust in clinical settings of AI-driven diagnostics.

Although the imaging technologies are more sensitive, they are challenging in accessibility and cost. The costly, high end imaging equipment like low dose CT scans, and highly advanced MRI systems, are not only cost prohibitive but not available in many places; this has been specially so in the low resource health setup. The cost of frequent imagining, mainly for the purpose of prevention, could also be cost effective; the concern here would be about equity in access.

Therefore, the development of biomarkers in conjunction with AI and imaging is at a very nascent stage and the amalgamation of these technologies requires new protocols and infrastructures along with broad training by health providers. This practical hurdle might confine the broad-scale implementation of integrated early detection systems into mainstream healthcare: ensuring that practitioners possess the skill to interpret biomarker tests, findings acquired through AI, and imaging output in an integrative, overarching context.

To date, such technologies have yet to be validated on large scales to prove their long-term efficacy. Preliminary data appear promising; however, large-scale clinical trials and longitudinal studies have yet to establish accuracy, reliability, and their impact on patient outcomes over time. Given that long-term data are not yet available in sufficient detail, it is difficult to predict how the technologies would perform in diverse patient populations or types of cancer.

Some of the major failures with the currently implemented early cancer detection methods include the shortcomings of varied biomarkers for accuracy, prospects of biasing in AI models developed, advanced imaging with a very high cost and limited availability, clinical integration problems, and a requirement of further validation in long-term studies. Resolution of these failures would be a critical necessity for the realization of all the potential effects from such innovative technologies.

5. CONCLUSION

The landscape of cancer diagnosis and care is undergoing a profound transformation, driven by the integration of biomarkers, advanced imaging technologies, machine learning (ML), and artificial intelligence (AI). These cutting-edge innovations are gradually shifting the paradigm from conventional diagnostic methods to a more refined, precise, and early detection system, one that offers the potential for enhanced patient outcomes. The synergy between these technologies not only improves the accuracy of diagnosis but also tailors it to the unique needs of each patient, allowing for a more personalized approach to cancer care.

Biomarkers, which are biological molecules that indicate the presence of disease, are providing deep molecular insights into cancer. These markers are increasingly enabling clinicians to detect cancers at a much earlier stage, long before symptoms become apparent. Biomarkers can reveal specific genetic mutations, protein expressions, or other molecular changes that are associated with different types of cancers. The ability to detect these subtle changes in the body's biological systems is revolutionizing the way we understand the onset and progression of cancer, offering opportunities for earlier intervention, more targeted treatments, and improved patient prognoses. (Milner & Lennerz, 2024)

Meanwhile, advanced imaging techniques such as functional MRI, PET-CT scans, and molecular imaging are significantly enhancing the visualization of tumors, especially in their early stages. These technologies allow clinicians to see the intricate details of cancerous tissues, including their size, shape, and metabolic activity. More importantly, they provide information about the tumor's exact location and how it interacts with surrounding tissues. This is crucial for accurate diagnosis, determining the stage of the cancer, and developing the most effective treatment plans. These imaging methods, when combined with AI and biomarkers, create a comprehensive, multi-faceted view of the cancer, allowing for more informed decision-making.

Machine learning (ML) and artificial intelligence (AI) play a pivotal role in accelerating the processing of the enormous amounts of data generated by biomarker testing and imaging. Traditional methods of analyzing such data are often time-consuming and prone to human error, but AI-driven algorithms are changing the game by significantly enhancing the speed and accuracy of data analysis. AI can quickly sift through vast amounts of complex information, identify patterns, and detect anomalies that may indicate cancer. Moreover, it can integrate data from multiple sources—biomarkers, imaging, genetic information, and even patient history—to provide a more comprehensive and personalized diagnostic report. In doing so, AI not only streamlines the diagnostic process but also helps reduce the likelihood of missed diagnoses and false positives, ultimately improving patient care.

The combined use of these technologies is pushing the boundaries of personalized medicine in cancer diagnosis and treatment. By leveraging the strengths of biomarkers, imaging, and AI,clinicians can create individualized diagnostic and treatment plans tailored to the specific characteristics of each patient's cancer. This personalized approach not only enhances the accuracy of the diagnosis but also increases the likelihood of successful treatment outcomes. Patients can receive targeted therapies based on their unique cancer profiles, reducing unnecessary treatments and improving overall survival rates.

However, despite the significant advancements, several challenges still hinder the widespread implementation of these technologies. One of the primary concerns is the specificity and sensitivity of biomarkers. While biomarkers hold great promise, not all of them are reliable indicators of cancer. Some may fail to detect cancer at an early stage, while others may yield false positives, leading to unnecessary interventions. Therefore, more research is needed to identify and validate biomarkers that are both highly specific and sensitive to different types of cancer.

Another challenge lies in the biases present in AI models. AI systems are only as good as the data they are trained on, and if the training data is not representative of diverse populations, the resulting AI models may produce biased outcomes. This could lead to disparities in cancer diagnosis and treatment, particularly for underrepresented groups. Ensuring that AI models are trained on diverse datasets is crucial for creating equitable diagnostic tools that benefit all patients, regardless of their background.

In addition, the accessibility of advanced imaging technologies remains a significant hurdle. Many of the cutting-edge imaging techniques, such as molecular imaging and advanced MRI, are expensive and not readily available in all healthcare settings, particularly in low-resource regions. Without widespread access to these technologies, many patients may not benefit from early and accurate cancer detection, exacerbating existing disparities in cancer care. Efforts to make these technologies more affordable and accessible are essential to realizing their full potential.

The future of cancer diagnosis and care is likely to see continued progress in these areas, driven by several key trends. Biomarker discovery will advance, leading to the identification of more reliable and diverse biomarkers for a wider range of cancers. This will increase the accuracy of early detection and enable the development of more effective, tailored therapies. Additionally, AI and machine learning models will continue to improve, becoming more powerful and sophisticated in their ability to analyze complex data sets, integrate diverse sources of information, and provide accurate and personalized diagnostic insights.

Non-invasive diagnostic tools, such as liquid biopsies, are expected to play a more prominent role in cancer care. Liquid biopsies involve analyzing small samples of blood or other bodily fluids to detect cancer-related genetic mutations or other molecular markers. These tests offer a less invasive alternative to traditional tissue biopsies, making cancer detection easier and less risky for patients. Additionally, wearable monitoring devices may offer real-time insights into patients' health, allowing for continuous monitoring of cancer markers and early intervention if any concerning changes are detected. In the years to come, these advancements have the potential to revolutionize cancer care, making early detection and personalized treatment more widely accessible. As technologies like AI, biomarkers, and advanced imaging continue to evolve, the future holds the promise of earlier, more accurate diagnoses, more effective treatments, and ultimately, better survival rates for cancer patients. If these innovations can be made affordable and accessible to all, they could fundamentally change the way cancer is treated, shifting the focus from reactive treatment to proactive prevention and early intervention. This could bring new hope to millions of cancer patients and their families worldwide, turning the tide in the battle against cancer. (Anisman & Kusnecov, 2022).

6. FUTURE SCOPE

The scope is humongous for early detection of cancer through integrated approaches using biomarkers, machine learning, artificial intelligence, and advanced techniques of imaging; it has a lot of scope for breakthroughs. Most of these items are still waiting in the wings and promise a new change in approach toward cancer diagnostics that will benefit patients toward better outcomes, given the research and technology.

6.1. Better Discovery and Validation of Biomarkers

The last area of future research will be the discovery and validation of even more specific and reliable biomarkers. The further advancement in genomics, proteomics, and metabolomics will make it easy to discover a wide range of cancer-specific biomarkers for various types and stages. Much of this work may one day be translated to panels of a few biomarkers, which would better highlight risk or the progression of a disease in a patient. For instance, it could be possible to integrate genetic mutations with epigenetic alteration, circulating tumor cells, microRNAs, and other molecular signals for high-precision, personalized diagnostics. Future research can then target more infrequent biomarkers for less common forms of cancer, as well as those that are naturally difficult to diagnose at an early stage, such as ovarian or pancreatic cancers. (Pepe et al., 2001).

6.2. AI and ML in the Precision Medicine Age

The future for cancer diagnosis is bright indeed, for AI and ML will only have evolved and become even stronger in the precision medicine era. With improved computation power and access to large, heterogenous datasets, AI can analyze really complex patterns in medical data. AI may predict, for instance, the tendency of a patient who will be prone to cancer, based on their respective genetic predispositions, lifestyle factors, and conditions exposed to. It will suggest ideal screens for cancer in each individual. Further development will eventually help real-time diagnosis support in suggesting data-driven recommendations in real-time to the clinician on options for treatment that are intended to impact, more profoundly, timeliness and accuracy of care.Widespread adoption of explainable AI models might herald another landmark moment, since such models attempt to explain the decision-making process of AI in a manner that will make clinicians have higher trust in AI-driven diagnostics and so adopt them in clinical practice. Furthermore, with their burgeoning capacities on steroids, the AI models will then be able to do more than identify the presence of cancer; they may also give a clue regarding the type, stage, or aggressiveness of the disease, thus allowing far more nuanced decision-making with perhaps much more individualized treatment plans at the very time of diagnosis. (Foser et al., 2024).

6.3. Next-Generation Imaging Techniques

For the patient, technology for imaging is likely to become more refined-higher resolution and precision of diagnosis and reduced doses of radiation. Hybrid imaging techniques-the strengths of multiple modalities, such as PET with MRI-are likely to provide detailed information in both metabolic and anatomical information in one modality at a time, allowing the detection of early cancers, even some of the smallest and hardest to see cancers with current technologies.

With the emergence of molecular imaging, it is now possible to track cancer cells in real-time live at the molecular level; thus, the tracking of tumor activity can now become dynamic and more responsive to drug therapy. Next-generation innovations for imaging include nanoparticle-based contrast agents with much greater specificity to target specific cancer cells, thus fewer false positives and much greater accuracy in imaging. (Foser et al., 2024).

6.4. Liquid Biopsy and Non-Invasive Testing

It has immense potential in the future of non-invasive cancer detection through technology- analyzing circulating tumor DNA, exosomes, or CTCs from an ordinary blood sample. With this field of research, liquid biopsies are likely to become more routine additions to annual health check-ups for easy and simple monitoring of patients' progression in catching early signs of cancer or recurrence without the invasive procedures like tissue biopsies. Of course, sensitivity for liquid biopsies will increase. Perhaps it can get to the level of an amount in blood equivalent to the pinhead quantities to draw distinguishable even the earliest phases of cancer.

Liquid biopsies will also be important in the follow-up of whether the patient is responding to the treatment or not. It will provide real-time assessment if the tumor has begun shrinking, or the progression of the disease has formed resistance to the therapy. This will allow oncologists to fine- tune their therapeutic treatment much more quickly and efficiently. (Foser et al., 2024), Ahmad, I., & Alqurashi, F. (2024).

6.5 Data Harmonization at Multi-Omics Levels

In the future, integration of multi-omics data, which would include genomic, transcriptomic, proteomic, and metabolomic information, might be applicable for cancer detection. This approach may prove to give a more holistic view of the biology behind cancer, which would thus aid the

identification of such complex molecular signatures that may hint towards the presence of cancer at an early stage, thereby improving the sensitivity and specificity of the detection methods, thereby reducing the chances of false positives and false negatives.

The integration and analysis of multi-omics data will have a particularly critical role to play with regard to AI and ML in facilitating discoveries of underlying patterns and relationships. With such rich datasets, clinicians will be much better positioned to counsel patients more appropriately and sensitively concerning their risk for cancer and adapt measures of prevention accordingly.

6.6 Wider Deployment of Wearable and Remote Monitoring Technologies

Other technologies that could exist in the near future of cancer detection are wearable technologies and remote monitoring devices. For instance, such devices may monitor physiological changes like temperature, heart rates, or blood biomarkers, which will be continuously monitored for signs of developing cancers. For example, future wearables may contain sensors that will detect changes in cancer-like phenomena; that is, from the appearance of specific proteins or rate of metabolism, thus providing real-time information on early warning signs towards these patients and their physicians.

This form of continuous monitoring would be profoundly useful to the most vulnerable patients, so interventions could start taking place even before cancer becomes symptomatic. The data generated by wearable devices may be assimilated into electronic health records; AI systems could continuously review the risk of a patient contracting cancer and make recommendations for screening or other preventive measures. (Connal et al., 2023).

6.7 Universality and Equity of Cancer Detection

Some of the fields that in the future should be developed include the advanced technologies that can be reached for the detection of cancers. Technology is highly beneficial to individuals living in low-resource settings as with others such as making the detection technologies available and not too expensive for their reach. Eventually, ensuring that countries with high income provide equal opportunities to the early mechanisms of cancer detection should be prioritized so that equality can be provided to all mankind over time. The future work should be that the developed imaging machine, AI tools, and biomarker test versions will be economical enough to be easily deployed in different healthcare environments.

Telemedicine and cloud-based AI platforms could thereby facilitate remote analysis of medical data. Here, the services of the best cancer centers could reach the doorsteps of the underserved. The issues described here improve access to early cancer detection technologies spread all over the world, meaning improved treatment for patients everywhere. (Chahal, 2021).

6.8 Ethical Considerations and Data Privacy

With the reliance on big data, AI, and personalized medicines for detection of cancer as the new method, ethical considerations as well as issues regarding data privacy would come to the foreground. Therefore, it has to ensure scope in the form of robust policies as well as frameworks that are able to protect patient data while these technologies have to be used responsibly. These include appropriateness and completeness of consent, use of genetic information, and data-sharing practices among healthcare providers as these technologies become more commonplace in mainstream practice. (Chahal, 2021).

REFERENCES

Ahmad, I., & Alqurashi, F. (2024, December). Early cancer detection using deep learning and medical imaging: A survey. *Critical Reviews in Oncology/Hematology*, *204*, 104528. DOI: 10.1016/j.critrevonc.2024.104528 PMID: 39413940

American Association for Cancer Research. (2023). *Screening for early detection*. In *AACR Cancer Progress Report 2023*. Retrieved November 7, 2024, from https://cancerprogressreport.aacr.org/progress/cpr23-contents/cpr23-screening-for-early-detection/

Amor, R. E., Nakhleh, M. K., Barash, O., & Haick, H. (2019, June). Breath analysis of cancer in the present and the future. *European Respiratory Review : an Official Journal of the European Respiratory Society*, *28*(152), 190002. Advance online publication. DOI: 10.1183/16000617.0002-2019 PMID: 31243094

Anisman, H., & Kusnecov, A. W. (2022, January). Cancer therapies: Caveats, concerns, and momentum. In *Cancer* (pp. 401–430). DOI: 10.1016/B978-0-323-91904-3.00001-X

Bannasch, P., & van Kaick, G. (1992). What does 'early' stand for in cancer diagnosis? *Cancer Diagnosis*, *1–2*, 1–2. Advance online publication. DOI: 10.1007/978-3-642-76899-6_1

Bast, R. C.Jr, & Srivastava, S. (2020, December). The National Cancer Institute Early Detection Research Network: Two decades of progress. *Cancer Epidemiology, Biomarkers & Prevention*, *29*(12), 2396–2400. DOI: 10.1158/1055-9965.EPI-20-1158 PMID: 33262198

Cancer Council Australia. (n.d.). *Types of cancer*. Retrieved November 9, 2024, from https://www.cancer.org.au/cancer-information/types-of-cancer

Cancer Imaging Program. (n.d.). *CT scans*. Retrieved November 14, 2024, from https://imaging.cancer.gov/imaging_basics/cancer_imaging/ct_scans.htm

Connal, S., Cameron, J. M., Sala, A., Brennan, P. M., Palmer, D. S., Palmer, J. D., Perlow, H., & Baker, M. J. (2023, December). Liquid biopsies: The future of cancer early detection. *Journal of Translational Medicine*, *21*(1), 1–18. DOI: 10.1186/s12967-023-03960-8 PMID: 36774504

Connal, S., Cameron, J. M., Sala, A., Brennan, P. M., Palmer, D. S., Palmer, J. D., Perlow, H., & Baker, M. J. (2023, December). Liquid biopsies: The future of cancer early detection. *Journal of Translational Medicine*, *21*(1), 1–18. DOI: 10.1186/s12967-023-03960-8 PMID: 36774504

Foser, S., Maiese, K., Digumarthy, S. R., Puig-Butille, J. A., & Rebhan, C. (2024, January). Looking to the future of early detection in cancer: Liquid biopsies, imaging, and artificial intelligence. *Clinical Chemistry*, *70*(1), 27–32. DOI: 10.1093/clinchem/hvad196 PMID: 38175601

Li, C., Liu, Y., Xue, D., & Chan, C. W. H. (2020, October). Effects of nurse-led interventions on early detection of cancer: A systematic review and meta-analysis. *International Journal of Nursing Studies*, *110*, 103684. DOI: 10.1016/j.ijnurstu.2020.103684 PMID: 32702568

Milner, D. A.Jr, & Lennerz, J. K. (2024). Technology and future of multi-cancer early detection. *Life (Chicago, Ill.)*, *14*(7), 833. DOI: 10.3390/life14070833 PMID: 39063587

National Research Council. (2001, May). *Mammography and beyond*. DOI: 10.17226/10107

Newsham, I., Sendera, M., Jammula, S. G., & Samarajiwa, S. A. (2024, January). Early detection and diagnosis of cancer with interpretable machine learning to uncover cancer-specific DNA methylation patterns. *Biology Methods and Protocols*, *9*(1), bpae028. Advance online publication. DOI: 10.1093/biomethods/bpae028 PMID: 38903861

Patel, H. N., Ghodgaonkar, D. K., & Suri, J. S. (2022, December). The role of AI in diagnosis, treatment and monitoring of breast cancer during COVID-19 and ahead. In *Breast Image Reconstruction and Cancer Detection Using Microwave Imaging* (pp. 11-1–11-21). DOI: 10.1088/978-0-7503-2592-9ch11

Patriotis, C., & Srivastava, S. (2023). Early cancer detection: Challenges and opportunities. *Current Cancer Research*, (Part F1235), 619–631. DOI: 10.1007/978-3-031-22903-9_24

Pepe, M. S., Etzioni, R., Feng, Z., Potter, J. D., Thompson, M. L., Thornquist, M., Winget, M., & Yasui, Y. (2001, July). Phases of biomarker development for early detection of cancer. *Journal of the National Cancer Institute*, *93*(14), 1054–1061. DOI: 10.1093/jnci/93.14.1054 PMID: 11459866

Rhmann, W., & Pandey, B. (2021, October). Early cancer predictions using ensembles of machine learning and deep learning. In *Deep Learning for Personalized Healthcare Services* (pp. 91–114). DOI: 10.1515/9783110708127-005

Tenchov, R., Sapra, A. K., Sasso, J., Ralhan, K., Tummala, A., Azoulay, N., & Zhou, Q. A. (2024, March). Biomarkers for early cancer detection: A landscape view of recent advancements, spotlighting pancreatic and liver cancers. *ACS Pharmacology & Translational Science*, *7*(3), 586–613. DOI: 10.1021/acsptsci.3c00346 PMID: 38481702

Thaker, N. G., Dicker, A. P., Loaiza-Bonilla, A., Wallace, A., Kolman, D., Godshalk Ruggles, A., Manda, S., Frank, S. J., Orio, P., & Doria, C. (2024, April). The role of artificial intelligence in early cancer detection: Exploring early clinical applications. *Artificial Intelligence in Precision Oncology*, *1*(2), 91–105. DOI: 10.1089/aipo.2023.0011

World Health Organization. (n.d.). *Promoting cancer early diagnosis*. Retrieved November 9, 2024, from https://www.who.int/activities/promoting-cancer-early-diagnosis

World Health Organization. (n.d.). *Cancer*. Retrieved November 12, 2024, from https://www.who.int/health-topics/cancer#tab=tab_1

Chapter 7
Beyond the Clinic: Expanding Horizons for Community Health Nurses in Pakistan

Saleema Gulzar
https://orcid.org/0000-0001-7245-9214
Aga Khan University, Karachi, Pakistan

Samina Subzali Vertejee
https://orcid.org/0000-0001-9080-4560
Aga Khan University, Karachi, Pakistan

Tazeen Saeed Ali
https://orcid.org/0000-0002-8896-8766
Aga Khan University, Karachi, Pakistan

Rozina Karmaliani
https://orcid.org/0000-0002-9565-5514
Aga Khan University, Karachi, Pakistan

ABSTRACT

All schools of nursing in Pakistan offer community health nursing as a core course. Unfortunately, there aren't enough avenues open for them to practice CHN due to lack of deployment plan. Despite this there are multiple roles that CHNs are performing and can perform at local and national levels. The need is to duly acknowledge this role within the health care delivery model and there is a need for evidenced based studies to explore the impact of these roles on the health of population at local and national levels. This chapter would serve as a guiding tool to make health care

DOI: 10.4018/979-8-3693-9092-4.ch007

delivery system more responsive to health and developmental needs of the country. Moreover, the chapter gives an insight into how the CHNs are actively engaged in various settings and provide population based services with focus on sustainability.

SESSION OBJECTIVES

After reading the chapter learner will be able to:

1. Appreciate the expanded roles of CHNs to address the health care needs of population.
2. Appraise the diverse role of CHN in health care delivery system in global and local context
3. Integrate the competencies of CHN for role performance in education, practice and research

INTRODUCTION

In today's world, nurses' role has expanded from tertiary care setting to community settings. Even in Pakistan, nurses are playing critical roles in diversified settings to promote the population's health. The underlying notion is to decrease the burden of disease and increase the quality of people's life to impact on economic stability of the nation. *Thus,* nurses are not confined to hospital settings rather broaden up to the extent and performing various roles as an integral part of the health care team. This chapter aims to highlight various roles that are practiced by CHNs in Pakistan. (Refer figure 1).

CHNS IN PRIMARY HEALTH CARE

Primary Health Care (PHC) approach is used in health services organizations to serve the population; and CHNs are integral part of PHC approach. CHNs work at individual, family, and community levels, utilizing population or risk approach. For instance, CHNs works with collaborators and identifies non communicable diseases such as high blood pressure, high cholesterol levels and diabetes mellitus as priority health problems. One of the examples of CHN work is a healthy heart program which is planned to promote community health focusing on healthy lifestyle. Mostly, CHNs are well prepared to see the community as a client and Partner. Along with the team members she/he examines the health of population in consideration of health and social determinants including social, political, cultural, spiritual, and biological perspectives. Thus, the causes of death or illnesses are not seen in isolation of biological nature rather the interplay of all other factors mentioned leading to web of causation using the holistic approach.

Several case studies have determined the CHN's holistic nature of care, where she/he have played pivotal role by understanding the web of causation for occurrence of disease or death. For instance, a child who died of a diarrhea/dehydration or a woman dies of pre/post-partum hemorrhage can be due to interplay of factors such as poverty, ignorance, and lack of awareness and accessibility of health services. Thus, individual is webbed into the interplay of factors and cannot be spared; eventually ends up in disease, disability or death.

CASE STUDY: WHY DID FARIDA DIE?

Farida, 35 years old woman, lived in a village with her five children husband and mother-in-law. She had never been to school and at the age of 14, she got married fisherman called Rehmat Jan. He used to earn Rs.9000 per month, barely enough for the family's survival. Farida also supported family by household chores at the landlord's house and she used to get Rs. 1500 a month. Farida was pregnant again for the ninth time. She had two miscarriages, and her one-year-old daughter had died of diarrhea. Although she had no desire for more children and during her previous pregnancy Lady Health visitors from nearby rural health center had also advised her not to have any more children because she was too weak and was severely anemic. However, husband never supported her decision, and she was pregnant again. He believed that contraception is a sin and is an interruption against God's will. Moreover, he was a strong follower of "pir", or spiritual guru.

Farida started per-vaginal bleeding at sixth month of pregnancy and a local Traditional Birth Attendance (TBA) locally called "Dai" was asked to help Farida. TBA administered her herbal medication and inserted some herbs per-vagina for onset of labor. Unfortunately, the condition didn't improve; rather she presented signs of hypovolemic shock. Farida's mother-in-law called a local faith healer to help Farida overcome an evil eye. This also worsened her condition, at this time TBA advised to take Farida to the health center, but the decision was not made as husband was not at home. On the other hand, she also didn't have enough money to be transported to the health facility. After long waiting for husband and arrangement of money she was taken to the district hospital which was 10 Km away from home.

By the time she reached hospital she was in shock due to a hemorrhage, and unfortunately there was no doctor or nurse available to rescue Farida as doctor was on leave and the nurse had left early for home. After 10 hours of suffering Farida could not survive, and the family had to return home with Farida's dead body in hand and huge debt which they had borrowed from the landlord to transport Farida to the district hospital for the treatment.

QUESTION: WHY DID FARIDA DIE?

Acknowledgement: AKU-SONAM & CHS Department

Figure 1.

Activity: Looking at the above mentioned case study, you may draw a web of causation for Ms. Farida and suggest an action plan which may help in combating the issue. While doing that reflect what factors contributes to farida death including, social, health and organizational

In PHC setting CHN along with the team members investigate the issues in depth to strategize preventative measures in the community to reduce such maternal morbidity cases within the catchment area. One of the tools (Table 1) shown below is an example of a planning process used to address the identified health/development issues in the community.

Table 1. Action Plan

Goal and Objectives				
S. No	**Activity**	**Strategy**	**Responsibility**	**Time frame**

Figure 2. Community Health Nursing Practice Settings

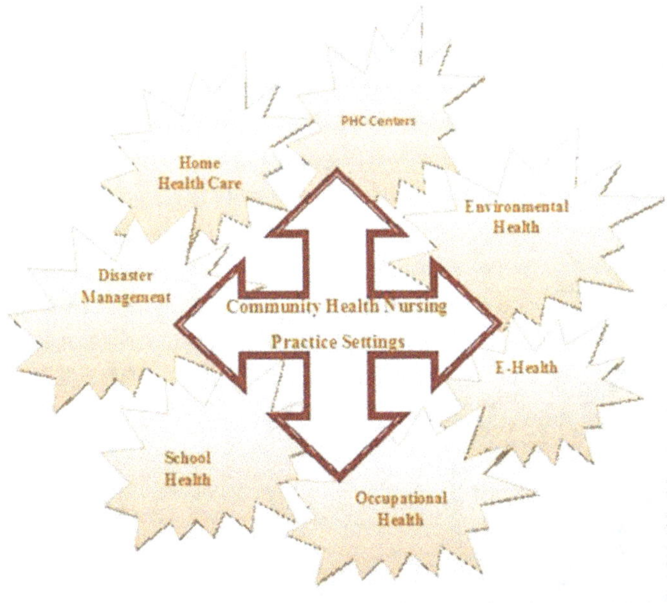

Figure 3. Web of Causation

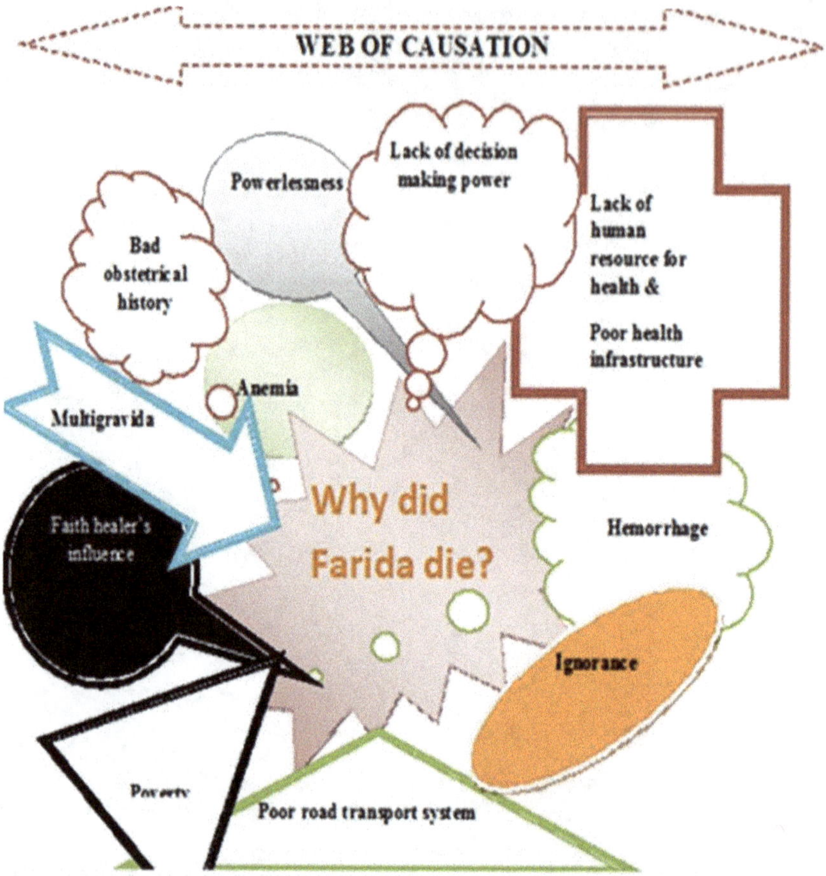

DISASTER MANAGEMENT

Internally Displaced People (IDPs) such as people from disaster situations are the group of people that require thoughtful attention especially of the CHN who plays imperative role. She/he along with other health care providers addresses the immediate health and developmental needs with long term goal of rehabilitation. In local context, a dearth of evidence available is supporting the role of nurses in disaster management. However, literature depicts the importance of the role of nurses in collaboration with other healthcare providers to address the immediate and long-term healthcare needs of the people and provide healthcare using the nursing process as a tool (Gulzar, Faheem, & Somani, 2012; Pourvakhshoori et al., 2017).

During a disaster, healthcare locations are not steady, and nurses may need to move from one place to another as the circumstances change. Scarcities of resources and problems with equipment also compel adaptability and innovations. Innovation is extemporaneous but must be grounded in sound nursing knowledge and experience to be able to act rationally and deal with the situation. Flexibility related to the variety of assigned or improvised tasks nurses perform will be needed; these tasks may range from direct patient care to leading the healthcare facility or community disaster effort (Stanhope & Lancaster, 2019; Vertejee & Karamali, 2013; Said & Chiang, 2020).

Thus, strategic and innovative approaches are used to provide care in a resource constraint situation to uplift the quality of life for IDPs.

The constraints nurses face during their work with IPDs may include a lack of electrical power, poor/no water supply and difficulties with communication systems. While doing so, nurses practice critical thinking skills, for example, a shortage of supplies may lead to improvising in sharing the limited resources between IDP dwellers. Despite multiple challenges, nurses in disaster management.

SCHOOL HEALTH PROMOTION

A considerable number of children in Pakistan have access to education through schools. In 2021, 80.7% of 6-16-year-old children in rural Pakistan were registered in governmental and non-governmental schools (ASER Pakistan Secretariat, 2022). Hence, the school is a setting where students and staff spend a great deal of their time. It is a setting where education and health programs can have their greatest impact because they influence students at an important stage in their lives: childhood and adolescence.

In Pakistan, school health promotion programs (SHPP) are still nascent; moreover, the role of a school health nurse is yet to be appreciated at the national level in improving the health of school children. In the given scenario, therefore amongst many factors one of them is a lack of understanding of the relationship between health and education. Furthermore, many schools in both the public and private sectors haven't adopted any such health programs to meet the health needs of school children. Other reasons for this gap include a lack of evidence for school health promotion and academic achievement.

Another significant aspect of SHPP is hiring nurses to act as School Health Nurses (SHN) for the promotion of the health and development of school children. A nurse contributes to school health settings with a focus to promote the health of school children involving students, teachers and parents. The systematic review of the literature reveals that school nurses are mainly involved in (a) health promotion and disease prevention, (b) triage and treatment of acute issues (e.g., injuries and infectious diseases), (c) management of chronic conditions, and (d) psychosocial support. This research study shows a strong and progressive relationship between health and learning. Students who possess good health also perform better in school. By encouraging schools that promote health, school leaders all over the world can foster health as actively as they foster learning. Thus, school nursing activities are associated with increased attendance, and cost savings (Said & Chiang, 2020; Lineberry & Ickes, 2014).

However, resource constraint society like Pakistan, hiring of SHN and provision of culturally appropriate health education material is another bottleneck in employing of SHPP at a national level. However, there are several isolated examples available to demonstrate the role of SHPP in school health promotion programs. See case study I for explanation.

On the contrary, internationally the SHN's role is well recognized and acknowledged at a wider level. Evidence proves that healthy children are successful learners. The school nurse has assorted roles within the school setting, one that supports the physical, mental, emotional, and social health of students and their success in the learning process. It is the scope of nursing activities contained within the role of the school nurse and the unique non-health care setting that differentiates school nursing from other nursing specialties (Magalnick & Mazyck, 2008).

Therefore, in Pakistan, comprehensive school health promotion programs are more important now than ever before.

OCCUPATIONAL HEALTH

According to W.H.O., occupational health services provided by nurses at the workplace to address the health care needs of working populations have been identified as a vital component of the public health strategy. These services have an impact on other government initiatives, such as; reducing health inequalities, days off at work due to ill health, and by protecting and promoting the health of the working population. Thus, occupational health services can help to reduce the overall burden of illness (World Health Organization [WHO], 2011). The role of a nurse is pivotal in occupational health services; and thereby occupational health

Nursing is another specialty role a CHN plays within the workplace settings with the mandate of enhancing employees' health and their families.

OHNs are registered nurses who independently assess the worker's health status and working conditions according to the nature of their jobs and potential workplace hazards. Using their specialized experience and education, these nurses discern and prevent health effects from hazardous exposures and treat workers' injuries/illnesses (Occupational Safety and Health Administration [OSHA], n.d.; La Torre et al., 2020).

However, in Pakistan very few nurses are designated as occupational health nurse. It seems that there is an apparent lack of obligation concerning the presence and training of occupational health nurses. Literature supports the lack of availability of data on the number of occupational health nurses working in most countries, except Luxembourg, Norway, and Finland, and specialist training is hardly available. Legal obligations within countries or directives by international organizations such as the World Health Organization, the International Labour Office, the International Commission on Occupational Health, and the European Union may help to upgrade and upsurge awareness concerning compulsory education and training for occupational health nurses (Bigaignon-Cantineau et al., 2005).

CARE OF ELDERLY PEOPLE

The life expectancy of people in Pakistan is increasing to 67.43 as of 2020, leading to growing number of aging population (Index Mundi, 2023). The given development demands for redirecting of the resources to provide specialized care for elderly population. Although the Constitution of Pakistan, article 38D and 14 both endorses provision of necessities of life, respect, and reverence for all; this includes elderly population as well. This is contradicting in the current situation where there is hardly any resource relocation to ensure quality of life for elderly in Pakistan (Vertejee & Karamali, 2013).

The vitality of nursing care for elderly is depicted in the case of a 78-year-old, Mrs. X. She lives alone and complained about decreased mobility due to frequent shortness of breath. The home health care team provided services to her from diagnosis to management of chronic obstructive pulmonary disease (COPD) without hospitalization (Lee et al., 2017). This eventually support the client to enhance her health and wellbeing.

The recent development depicts that specialized care for elderly can be integrated in all undergraduate nursing programs to address the growing needs of aging population. Hence the concept of caring for elderly clients is emerging as an important need of the country. Nonetheless, quality care and nurses' competencies in gerontology along with qualification are questionable yet they do serve in various capacities to provide care to elderly. Obviously, there are numerous challenges encountered, and literature also highlighted that nurses need resources and good leadership to be able to deliver effective care to older people. In organizations where staff feel supported and valued, visible clinical leadership is very apparent (Lomas, 2009).

CHNs can act as caregivers at the community settings to able to cater their unique health care needs. Responding to the needs a private academic institution in Karachi Pakistan in 2012, has introduced a "Care of Elderly" course to prepare human resource for health especially nurses in the field of gerontology (Todays News Paper, 2013).

Capacity building helps nurses to appraise the special health care needs of elderly and requires them to be passionate to provide the need based care. She/he needs to be equipped with prerequisite knowledge and competencies during her course of study. According to one of the study findings, specific content areas should be included in nursing curricula. These content areas address: a) social changes as well as physical changes that occur to elderly people and adaptation patterns of these individuals; b) usefulness of aged people and the contributions they can and do make to society; c) characteristics of the well elderly as opposed to total concentration on the sick elderly. The inclusion of these content in the curriculum may facilitate the nursing students in developing insight about the unique health needs about aging (Tollett & Thornby, 1982).

HOME HEALTH CARE

Home health care is a rapidly expanding practice specialty. It refers to a wide variety of holistic services provided to clients of all ages in their residences and in a non-institutional setting (2). In Pakistan, the concept of home health care has also been materialized at tertiary care level with nurses providing home based care. Nurses provide continuity of care when a patient is discharged from the hospital and needs nursing care at home. Well-equipped and trained home health care teams including nurses make scheduled visit/s to patient in their residence to provide need based care. Services such as catheterization, nasogastric tube insertion/feeding or wound dressing are some of the examples of home-based services. Since this concept is quite new in health care setup, it needs more diligent attention and refinement to fairly justify its purpose. (Lee et al., 2017; World Health Organization [WHO], n.d.)

Internationally the purpose of home nursing is to provide an individual with independence while remaining under supervised care. The nurse is accountable for the health and well-being of his/her patients. According to the Joint Commission, homebound patients are at risk of depression and feelings of isolation, but home care nurses also address the psychological needs of patients and provide companionship

(Chron.com, n.d.). Utilizing interpersonal and communication skills, she/he builds rapport with patients and thus provides culture appropriate care. Thereby enhances the client's satisfaction.

In addition, the concept of home-based palliative care provided to terminally ill patients and their families, is receiving considerable importance in health care, and so being integrated well in the system. Home based palliative care offers many benefits such as comfort and accomplishment of wish to dying at home. Literature supports that, patients with terminal illnesses shared more comfortable and dignified experience when they were asked about their experiences of living at home (Aldred, Gott, & Gariballa, 2005; Hudson, 2003)

Caring for terminally ill patients at home is a challenging task for care givers. They need structured training to provide physical and psychological support to patient at home. Unfortunately, such training facility is not available in many health care settings and due to accessibility issue though home healthcare facility is established by many healthcare organizations, but these services mostly focus on physical dimensions of health and give less priority to emotional aspects (Jarrett, Payne, & Wiles, 1999).

NON-GOVERNMENTAL ORGANIZATIONS

Alongside CHNs also practice in Non-Governmental Organizations (NGOs) and private sectors; to contribute to provision of health and development services to population. Though their role is not labeled as CHNs parse, the nature of job they indulge in is mostly related to community health practice. Anecdotal evidences demonstrates that many nurses currently are hired by NGOs and work as field health officer, an administrator, and few are recruited for leadership positions in different organizations. In the capacities of these roles, they offer PHC services to address the health and developmental needs of the population. For instance, a field health officer, in a Family Health Center, a CHN serves as leader with the aim of improving health indicators of assigned population/catchment area. Under this role, she/he provides the supportive supervision to his/her team, analyze the community data to be able to plan the further interventions in the community and disseminate and coordinate to the next level facility accordingly and ensure that the health is accessible and affordable in the vicinity.

To take this role to the subsequent level, provincial level interest group at an academic institution was established at with the mandate of providing the platform to the community health professionals to share health issues of Pakistani population, and collaboratively work for planning and improve the standard of CHN practice with collaboration of Pakistan Nursing Council (PNC). It is a forum to exchange ideas on community curriculum by keeping in mind the national needs. At this forum, nurses (CHNs) collaboratively share knowledge of teaching and clinical expertise, and research interest with each other for development of cadre.

The forum provides an opportunity for mentorship to new CHN faculty to support community nurses to effectively work at local and national level. Its long-term goal is to serve as liaison between nursing leaders, policy makers (health ministry) and then to develop an insight of creating positions for community health nurses in the health care system of Pakistan. The members for community health nursing interest group include CHNs who are practicing as teachers, School health nurses, occupational health nurses from all private, and government institutions.

CHNS IN DIGITAL HEALTH

Journey doesn't stop here for CHNs as the nurse also are well-equipped with global trends in public health; therefore she/he is also doing her/his efforts to make the health accessible and affordable in the remotest areas of Pakistan such as Gilgit Baltistan using digital health solutions (also referred as information technology in health).

Pakistan being a developing country and is struggling hard to provide even the necessities to many of its population. Miserably, access to quality health care to a critical mass of the population, particularly those living in rural and remote areas, is nearly impossible. Therefore, to address the needs of these people, the concept of Digital Health has been introduced in Pakistan. Digital Health has been defined as "the use of electronic information and communication technologies to provide and support health care when distance separates the participants" (Justin Starren, 2005 cited by Gulzar. S) (Gulzar, Khoja, & Sajwani, 2013; Gulzar, Shamim, & Khuwaja, n.d.) It is a new and emerging field in Pakistan, and it is seen as a possible route to provide health care in remote areas (Gulzar, 2012).

Evidences also reveal that nurses appreciated Digital Health for reducing their professional isolation and providing exposure to new knowledge through teleconsultation and eLearning. According to the study findings in Pakistan, Digital Health enhanced access to care for remote communities, and improved quality of health services by providing opportunities for continuing learning. Low-cost and simple Digital Health solutions have showed to benefit nurses, and the communities in the remote mountainous regions of Pakistan (Khoja, Gulzar, & Tirmizi, 2015).

In the same study nurses mentioned significant advantages of Digital Health for themselves and for the community. Nurses are the first point of contact when patients seek care at the health facilities. Patients got treated and received quality nursing care at their nearest facility. Looking at the scenario of Gilgit-Baltistan, where people must travel long distances to the next care facility for special care, and are accompanied by their attendants, the cost of travel becomes an added burden on them. Digital Health removes these inconveniences and additional costs for the patients. In addition, findings of this study also show that when patients were receiving timely care at their own vicinity, it resulted in building a good rapport between patients and nurses (Gulzar, Khoja, & Sajwani, 2013).

CONCLUSION

To conclude, all schools of nursing in Pakistan offer community health nursing as a core course. Unfortunately, there aren't enough avenues open for them to practice CHN due to lack of deployment plan. In addition to this there are other bottlenecks including poor motivation of nurses towards community nursing, lack of awareness and hesitation of families allowing their girls to work in the communities, poor incentives offered to those who are willing to fill those available positions in public and private sector which refrain nurse to practice as CHNs. Despite this there are multiple roles that CHNs are performing and can perform at local and national levels.

The need is to duly acknowledge this role within the health care delivery model and there is a need for evidenced based studies to explore the impact of these roles on the health of population at local and national levels. These impact studies would serve as a guiding tool to make health care delivery system more responsive to health and developmental needs of the country.

Moreover, the chapter gives an insight into how the CHNs are actively engaged in various settings and provide population-based serves with focus on sustainability. Unfortunately, we are far behind in breakeven to meet the demand verses supply of human resource for health especially community health nurses. Therefore, there is tremendous need to look at the health care system comprehensively to be able to recognize the roles of CHNs in diverse settings.

ACKNOWLEDGMENT

Sarah Naveed Lalani for reviewing the chapter.

REFERENCES

Aldred, H., Gott, M., & Gariballa, S. (2005). Advanced heart failure: Impact on older patients and informal carers. *Journal of Advanced Nursing*, *49*(2), 116–124. DOI: 10.1111/j.1365-2648.2004.03271.x PMID: 15641944

Bigaignon-Cantineau, J., Gonzalez, M., Broessel, N., Denu, B., Hamzaoui, H., & Cantineau, A. (2005). Occupational health nurses' contribution to health care workers' health. *Scandinavian Journal of Work, Environment & Health*, (Supplements, 1), 54–57.

Chron. (n.d.). Role & duties of a home care nurse. https://work.chron.com/role-duties-home-care-nurse-13396.html

Gulzar, S., & Khoja, S. (2012, May 27). Innovation: Health care at doorstep. Daily Dawn. http://dawn.com/2012/05/27/innovation-healthcare-at-the-doorstep/

Gulzar, S., Khoja, S., & Sajwani, A. (2013). Experience of nurses with using eHealth in Gilgit-Baltistan, Pakistan: A qualitative study in primary and secondary healthcare. *BMC Nursing*, *12*(1), 6. DOI: 10.1186/1472-6955-12-6 PMID: 23452373

Gulzar, S. A., Faheem, Z. A., & Somani, R. K. (2012). Role of community health nurse in earthquake affected areas. *JPMA. The Journal of the Pakistan Medical Association*, *62*(10), 1083. PMID: 23866452

Gulzar, S. A., Shamim, M. S., & Khuwaja, A. K. (2010). Promoting motivation towards community health care: A qualitative study from nurses in Pakistan. *JPMA. The Journal of the Pakistan Medical Association*, *60*(6), 501. PMID: 20527656

Hudson, P. (2003). Home-based support for palliative care families: Challenges and recommendations. *The Medical Journal of Australia*, *179*(6), S35. DOI: 10.5694/j.1326-5377.2003.tb05576.x PMID: 12964935

Index Mundi. (n.d.). Pakistan – Life expectancy at birth. https://www.indexmundi.com/facts/pakistan/life-expectancy-at-birth

Jarrett, N. J., Payne, S. A., & Wiles, R. A. (1999). Terminally ill patients' and lay carers' perceptions and experiences of community-based services. *Journal of Advanced Nursing*, *29*(2), 476–483. DOI: 10.1046/j.1365-2648.1999.00908.x PMID: 10197949

Khoja, S., Gulzar, S., & Tirmizi, S. (2015). Low cost telehealth network on the roof of the world: Evidences from Pakistan. *Journal of Nursing (Luton, England)*, *5*(1).

La Torre, G., D'Andreano, F., Lecce, G., Di Muzio, M., Chiarini, M., & Pulimeno, A. M. (2020). The occupational health nurse and his/her role in the prevention of work-related diseases: Results of an observational study. *Annali d'Igiene*, *32*(1).

Lee, G., Pickstone, N., Facultad, J., & Titchener, K. (2017). The future of community nursing: Hospital in the home. *British Journal of Community Nursing*, *22*(4), 174–180. DOI: 10.12968/bjcn.2017.22.4.174 PMID: 28414540

Lee, G., Pickstone, N., Facultad, J., & Titchener, K. (2017). The future of community nursing: Hospital in the home. *British Journal of Community Nursing*, *22*(4), 174–180. DOI: 10.12968/bjcn.2017.22.4.174 PMID: 28414540

Lineberry, M. J., & Ickes, M. J. (2014). The role and impact of nurses in American elementary schools: A systematic review of the research. *The Journal of School Nursing: the Official Publication of the National Association of School Nurses*. Advance online publication. DOI: 10.1177/1059840514540940 PMID: 24972802

Lomas, C. (2009). Is nursing's great challenge care of the elderly? *Nursing Times*.

Magalnick, H., & Mazyck, D. (2008). Role of the school nurse in providing school health services. *Pediatrics*, *121*(5), 1052–1056. DOI: 10.1542/peds.2008-0382 PMID: 18450912

Occupational Safety and Health Administration. (n.d.). Occupational Health Nursing. https://www.osha.gov/dts/oohn/ohn.html

Pakistan Secretariat, A. S. E. R. (2022, March). ASER-Pakistan 2021. http://aserpakistan.org/document/aser/2021/reports/national/ASER_report_National_2021.pdf

Pourvakhshoori, N., Norouzi, K., Ahmadi, F., Hosseini, M., & Khankeh, H. (2017). Nursing in disasters: A review of existing models. *International Emergency Nursing*, *31*, 58–63. DOI: 10.1016/j.ienj.2016.06.004 PMID: 27423385

Said, N. B., & Chiang, V. C. (2020). The knowledge, skill competencies, and psychological preparedness of nurses for disasters: A systematic review. *International Emergency Nursing*, *48*, 100806. DOI: 10.1016/j.ienj.2019.100806 PMID: 31685363

Stanhope, M., & Lancaster, J. (2019). *Public health nursing e-book: Population-centered health care in the community*. Elsevier Health Sciences.

Tollett, S. M., & Thornby, J. I. (1982). Geriatric and gerontology nursing curricular trends. *The Journal of Nursing Education*, *21*(6), 16–23. DOI: 10.3928/0148-4834-19820601-05 PMID: 6286577

Vertejee, S. S., & Karamali, N. N. (2013). Women's health: An achievable goal for public health nursing in Pakistan. *Women's Health.* PMID: 24397102

World Health Organization. (2011). Role of the occupational health nurse in the workplace. https://www.who.int/occupational_health/regions/en/oeheurnursing.pdf?ua=1

World Health Organization. (n.d.). Enhancing the role of community health nursing for universal health coverage.

Chapter 8
Applying Family Constellations in Healthcare:
Ethical Challenges and Best Practices

Tiago Manuel Horta Reis da Silva
https://orcid.org/0000-0001-5220-1718
King's College London, UK

ABSTRACT

Family Constellations is a therapeutic approach used to reveal and resolve family dynamics that may influence individual health. This chapter explores its application within healthcare, examining both its potential benefits and the ethical challenges it presents. Specifically, it focuses on issues related to patient consent, privacy, the role of cultural sensitivity, and the need for professional boundaries in clinical practice. Drawing on case studies and evidence-based practice, the chapter outlines best practices for incorporating Family Constellations responsibly and effectively into patient care. Strategies for practitioner training, safeguarding vulnerable populations, and aligning therapeutic goals with patient-centred care are discussed. The chapter concludes by proposing guidelines for ethical implementation, emphasising collaborative care models and continued professional reflection.

DOI: 10.4018/979-8-3693-9092-4.ch008

1. INTRODUCTION

Family Constellations, a therapeutic approach developed by Bert Hellinger in the 1990s, has gained significant traction in various therapeutic and healthcare settings. This method is predicated on the belief that individuals are often influenced by the dynamics and unresolved issues within their family systems, which can manifest as emotional and psychological distress (Stiefel et al., 2002; Cohen, 2006). The therapeutic process involves a group setting where participants represent family members, allowing for the visualisation and exploration of familial relationships and dynamics. This experiential approach aims to uncover hidden patterns and entanglements that may contribute to an individual's current struggles, thereby facilitating healing and resolution (Stiefel et al., 2002; Cohen, 2006; Thege et al., 2021).

1.1 Overview of Family Constellations as a Therapeutic Approach

Historically, the roots of Family Constellations can be traced back to systemic family therapy and phenomenological approaches, integrating elements from various psychological and philosophical traditions. The method emphasises the importance of acknowledging and addressing the roles of ancestors and familial legacies, which can profoundly impact individual behaviour and mental health (Stiefel et al., 2002; Cohen, 2006). As the practice evolved, it began to incorporate insights from various disciplines, including psychology, sociology, and anthropology, thereby enriching its theoretical underpinnings and practical applications (Mayer & Viviers, 2015; Hurley et al., 2018; Gyimesi, 2022). In contemporary healthcare settings, Family Constellations have been utilised to address a range of issues, including trauma, grief, and chronic illness, highlighting its versatility as a therapeutic tool (Thege et al., 2021; Weinhold et al., 2013; Welford, 2014).

The relevance of Family Constellations in modern healthcare cannot be overstated. With the increasing recognition of the biopsychosocial model of health, which posits that biological, psychological, and social factors are interconnected, Family Constellations offer a unique lens through which to view patient care. This approach aligns with the growing emphasis on holistic and patient-centred care, where understanding the patient's family dynamics is crucial for effective treatment (Lombana, 2021; Thege et al., 2021; Schneider et al., 2023). Moreover, the integration of Family Constellations into healthcare practices raises important ethical considerations, particularly concerning patient consent, privacy, and cultural sensitivity. As healthcare providers navigate these complexities, it becomes imperative to establish best practices that ensure the responsible and ethical application of this therapeutic approach (DeCamp et al., 2022; Breslin et al., 2005; Lillemoen & Pedersen, 2012; Panfilis et al., 2020).

The purpose of this chapter is to explore the application of Family Constellations within healthcare settings, focusing on both its potential benefits and the ethical challenges it presents. This chapter aims to provide a comprehensive overview of the ethical dilemmas that practitioners may encounter, including issues related to informed consent, confidentiality, and the need for cultural competence in therapeutic interventions (Rezaee et al., 2020; Avula et al., 2021; Molewijk et al., 2015; Woods et al., 2000). By drawing on case studies and evidence-based practices, the chapter will outline best practices for incorporating Family Constellations into patient care, emphasizing the importance of safeguarding vulnerable populations and aligning therapeutic goals with patient-centred care (Panfilis et al., 2020; Kristanti et al., 2021; Schneider et al., 2023).

In addition, the chapter will delve into the training and preparation required for practitioners to effectively implement Family Constellations in clinical settings. This includes fostering an understanding of the ethical implications of family dynamics in therapy and developing strategies for maintaining professional boundaries while engaging with patients and their families (Mohammadi, 2023; Moen et al., 2008; Zahedi et al., 2022; Hem et al., 2023). The conclusion will propose guidelines for the ethical implementation of Family Constellations, advocating for collaborative care models that prioritize ongoing professional reflection and ethical deliberation in practice (DeCamp et al., 2022; Panfilis et al., 2020; Blackler et al., 2021; Schneider et al., 2023).

2. THEORETICAL FOUNDATIONS OF FAMILY CONSTELLATIONS

Family Constellations, a therapeutic approach pioneered by Bert Hellinger, is grounded in several theoretical principles that emphasise the interconnectedness of family members and the influence of familial dynamics on individual well-being. The fundamental premise of Family Constellations is that unresolved issues within a family system can manifest as psychological distress or physical ailments in individuals. This approach operates on the belief that individuals are not isolated entities but rather part of a larger familial system, where the behaviours, traumas, and unresolved conflicts of previous generations can significantly impact current family members (Stiefel et al., 2002; Cohen, 2006; Thege et al., 2021).

2.1 Basic Principles and Mechanisms (e.g., Systemic Constellations and Their Effects)

The mechanisms of Family Constellations involve a unique experiential process where participants represent family members in a spatial arrangement, allowing for the visualisation of relationships and dynamics. This method, often conducted in group settings, enables participants to gain insights into their familial entanglements and the underlying issues that may be affecting their lives. The process is designed to reveal hidden dynamics, such as loyalty to family members, exclusion of certain individuals, or unresolved grief, which can hinder personal growth and healing (Hurley et al., 2018; Mayer & Viviers, 2015; Gyimesi, 2022). By bringing these dynamics to light, Family Constellations facilitate a reorganisation of the family system, allowing for the possibility of resolution and healing.

2.2 Relevance to Physical and Mental Health Outcomes

The relevance of Family Constellations extends beyond psychological insights; it has been linked to positive physical and mental health outcomes. Research indicates that participation in Family Constellation seminars can lead to significant improvements in psychological functioning, reductions in psychological distress, and enhanced motivation (Weinhold et al., 2013; Welford, 2014). A randomised controlled trial demonstrated that individuals who engaged in Family Constellation therapy reported better overall goal attainment and a more profound understanding of their personal social systems over time (Lombana, 2021). These findings underscore the potential of Family Constellations as a therapeutic intervention that not only addresses psychological issues but also contributes to holistic health outcomes.

2.3 Intersection with Integrative and Holistic Health Practices

Furthermore, Family Constellations intersect with integrative and holistic health practices, aligning with the growing recognition of the biopsychosocial model of health. This model posits that health is influenced by biological, psychological, and social factors, and Family Constellations provide a framework for exploring these interconnected dimensions. By addressing familial relationships and dynamics, practitioners can enhance the effectiveness of treatment plans that consider the whole person, including their social context and familial history (Schneider et al., 2023; DeCamp et al., 2022; Breslin et al., 2005). This holistic approach is particularly relevant in contemporary healthcare settings, where there is an increasing emphasis on patient-centred care that acknowledges the importance of social determinants of health.

3. APPLICATIONS IN HEALTHCARE: FAMILY CONSTELLATIONS

The application of Family Constellations in healthcare settings has emerged as a transformative approach to understanding and addressing the complex interplay of familial dynamics and individual health outcomes. This therapeutic method, which visualises family relationships and dynamics, has been employed in various clinical practices to facilitate healing and promote psychological well-being.

3.1 Case Examples of Family Constellations Used in Clinical Practice

Case examples illustrate the diverse applications of Family Constellations, highlighting its potential benefits for both patients and healthcare teams. One notable case involves the use of Family Constellations in a hospital setting to support patients dealing with chronic illness. In this scenario, a group of patients participated in a Family Constellation workshop aimed at exploring the emotional and relational factors contributing to their health challenges. Participants reported significant insights into their familial relationships, which often revealed patterns of behaviour and emotional entanglements that had previously gone unexamined. This process not only facilitated individual healing but also fostered a sense of community among participants, enhancing their emotional resilience and coping strategies (Stiefel et al., 2002; Cohen, 2006; Thege et al., 2021).

Another case example can be found in mental health clinics, where Family Constellations have been utilised to address issues such as anxiety, depression, and trauma. In one study, therapists integrated Family Constellation techniques into their therapeutic practices, allowing clients to visualise and reframe their family dynamics. The results indicated that clients experienced reduced symptoms of anxiety and depression, improved self-awareness, and a greater sense of agency in their lives (Hurley et al., 2018; Mayer & Viviers, 2015; Gyimesi, 2022).

3.2 Integration Within Multidisciplinary Care Models

These findings underscore the potential of Family Constellations to complement traditional therapeutic modalities, providing a holistic approach to mental health care. The integration of Family Constellations within multidisciplinary care models further enhances its applicability in healthcare settings. By collaborating with various healthcare professionals, including psychologists, social workers, and medical practitioners, Family Constellations can be incorporated into comprehensive treatment plans that address both psychological and physical health needs. For instance, a multidisciplinary team may use Family Constellations to explore the familial factors influencing a patient's chronic pain condition, thereby informing a more tailored and effective treatment strategy (Weinhold et al., 2013; Welford, 2014; Lombana, 2021).

This collaborative approach not only enriches the therapeutic process but also promotes a more holistic understanding of patient care.

3.3 Potential Benefits

Potential benefits of incorporating Family Constellations into healthcare practices extend beyond individual patient outcomes. Healthcare teams can benefit from enhanced communication and collaboration, as the process encourages open dialogue about familial influences on health. This shared understanding can lead to improved teamwork and a more cohesive approach to patient care (Schneider et al., 2023; DeCamp et al., 2022; Breslin et al., 2005). Additionally, the insights gained from Family Constellations can inform healthcare providers about the social determinants of health, allowing them to address broader systemic issues that may impact patient well-being. Moreover, the integration of Family Constellations into healthcare practices aligns with the growing emphasis on patient-centred care.

By recognising the importance of family dynamics in shaping health outcomes, healthcare providers can better understand the unique contexts of their patients' lives. This understanding fosters a more empathetic and responsive approach to care, ultimately leading to improved patient satisfaction and engagement (Lillemoen & Pedersen, 2012; Panfilis et al., 2020; Rezaee et al., 2020).

4. ETHICAL CHALLENGES IN APPLYING FAMILY CONSTELLATIONS

The application of Family Constellations in therapeutic settings raises several ethical challenges that must be carefully navigated to ensure the safety and well-being of participants. These challenges encompass issues related to patient autonomy, consent, confidentiality, cultural sensitivity, the risk of re-traumatisation, and the balance between professional boundaries and therapeutic engagement. Addressing these ethical considerations is crucial for the responsible implementation of Family Constellations in healthcare.

4.1 Patient Autonomy, Consent, and Informed Decision-Making

One of the primary ethical concerns in applying Family Constellations is ensuring patient autonomy and informed consent. Participants must fully understand the nature of the therapeutic process, including its potential risks and benefits, before engaging in Family Constellation sessions. This involves providing clear information about the methodology, the role of participants, and the possible emotional impacts of exploring familial dynamics (Stiefel et al., 2002; Cohen, 2006; Thege et al., 2021). Informed consent is not merely a formality; it is a fundamental ethical principle that empowers individuals to make choices about their own therapeutic journeys.

Moreover, the dynamic nature of group settings can complicate the consent process, as participants may be influenced by the experiences and reactions of others. It is essential for facilitators to create an environment that encourages open dialogue and allows participants to voice their concerns or withdraw from the process if they feel uncomfortable (Hurley et al., 2018; Mayer & Viviers, 2015). This approach not only respects individual autonomy but also fosters a sense of safety within the group, which is vital for effective therapeutic outcomes.

4.2 Confidentiality and Privacy Concerns in Group Settings

Confidentiality is another critical ethical consideration in Family Constellations, particularly in group settings where sensitive personal information is shared. Participants may disclose deeply personal experiences related to their family histories, and it is imperative that facilitators establish clear guidelines to protect the privacy of all individuals involved (Gyimesi, 2022; Weinhold et al., 2013). Breaches of confidentiality can lead to significant emotional harm and may deter individuals from participating in future therapeutic interventions.

Facilitators must emphasise the importance of confidentiality at the outset of the sessions and encourage participants to respect one another's privacy. Additionally, it may be beneficial to implement measures such as anonymising case discussions or using pseudonyms in documentation to further safeguard participants' identities (Welford, 2014; Lombana, 2021). By prioritising confidentiality, practitioners can cultivate a trusting therapeutic environment that enhances the effectiveness of Family Constellations.

4.3 Cultural Sensitivity and Respect for Diverse Belief Systems

Cultural sensitivity is paramount when applying Family Constellations, as individuals come from diverse backgrounds with varying beliefs about family dynamics, healing practices, and mental health. Practitioners must be aware of these differences and approach each participant's experiences with respect and openness (Schneider et al., 2023; DeCamp et al., 2022). This includes recognising that certain familial issues may be viewed through different cultural lenses, and what is considered a norm in one culture may not be in another.

Facilitators should engage in ongoing education about cultural competence and seek to understand the unique contexts of the families represented in their sessions. This understanding can inform the therapeutic process and ensure that interventions are culturally appropriate and relevant (Breslin et al., 2005; Lillemoen & Pedersen, 2012). By honouring diverse belief systems, practitioners can enhance the therapeutic experience and promote inclusivity within Family Constellations.

4.4 Risk of Re-Traumatization and Management of Emotional Responses

The potential for re-traumatisation is a significant concern in Family Constellations, particularly for participants who have experienced trauma related to family dynamics. Engaging in a process that brings unresolved family issues to the forefront can evoke strong emotional responses, which may lead to distress or re-experiencing of past traumas (Panfilis et al., 2020; Rezaee et al., 2020). It is essential for facilitators to be equipped with strategies to manage these emotional responses effectively.

Practitioners should conduct thorough assessments prior to participation to identify individuals who may be at higher risk for re-traumatization. Additionally, providing pre-session preparation and post-session debriefing can help participants process their experiences and mitigate the risk of emotional overwhelm (Avula et al., 2021; Molewijk et al., 2015). Creating a supportive environment where participants feel safe to express their emotions is crucial for minimising the potential for harm.

4.5 Balancing Professional Boundaries and Therapeutic Engagement

Finally, maintaining professional boundaries while fostering therapeutic engagement is a delicate balance that practitioners must navigate in Family Constellations. The intimate nature of exploring family dynamics can lead to strong emotional connections between facilitators and participants, which may blur the lines of professional conduct (Woods et al., 2000; Kristanti et al., 2021). It is vital for practitioners to establish clear boundaries to protect both themselves and their clients.

Facilitators should engage in regular supervision and reflection to assess their own emotional responses and ensure that they remain grounded in their professional roles (Mohammadi, 2023; Moen et al., 2008). Additionally, setting clear expectations regarding the facilitator's role and the limits of the therapeutic relationship can help maintain a safe and effective therapeutic environment. By prioritising professional boundaries, practitioners can enhance the integrity of the Family Constellations process and promote positive outcomes for participants.

5. BEST PRACTICES FOR ETHICAL APPLICATION OF FAMILY CONSTELLATIONS

The application of Family Constellations in therapeutic settings necessitates adherence to ethical guidelines that prioritize patient safety, informed consent, cultural competence, and accountability. Establishing best practices is essential for healthcare professionals to navigate the complexities of this therapeutic approach effectively. This section outlines key guidelines for ethical practice, training requirements, cultural sensitivity, monitoring outcomes, and case studies that illustrate ethical dilemmas and their resolutions.

5.1 Guidelines for Ethical Practice and Patient Safety

To ensure ethical practice in Family Constellations, practitioners must adhere to established guidelines that prioritise patient safety and well-being. This includes obtaining informed consent from participants, which involves providing comprehensive information about the therapeutic process, potential risks, and benefits (Stiefel et al., 2002; Cohen, 2006). Practitioners should ensure that participants understand their rights to withdraw from the process at any time without repercussions. This transparency fosters trust and empowers individuals to make informed decisions regarding their participation.

Additionally, practitioners should implement measures to safeguard confidentiality and privacy, particularly in group settings where sensitive information may be shared. Establishing ground rules regarding confidentiality at the outset of sessions can help create a safe environment for participants to explore their familial dynamics (Thege et al., 2021; Hurley et al., 2018). Furthermore, practitioners should be trained to recognise signs of emotional distress and have protocols in place to address any adverse reactions that may arise during the process.

5.2 Training and Supervision for Healthcare Professionals

Training and ongoing supervision are critical components of ethical practice in Family Constellations. Healthcare professionals should receive specialised training that encompasses not only the theoretical foundations of Family Constellations but also practical skills for facilitating sessions effectively (Mayer & Viviers, 2015; Gyimesi, 2022). This training should include strategies for managing group dynamics, addressing emotional responses, and maintaining professional boundaries.

Supervision is equally important, as it provides practitioners with opportunities for reflection and feedback on their practice. Regular supervision sessions can help practitioners navigate ethical dilemmas, enhance their skills, and ensure that they remain grounded in their professional roles (Weinhold et al., 2013; Welford, 2014). By fostering a culture of continuous learning and reflection, healthcare organizations can promote ethical practice and improve the quality of care provided to patients.

5.3 Cultural Competence and Adaptation of Methods to Different Healthcare Contexts

Cultural competence is essential when applying Family Constellations, as individuals come from diverse backgrounds with varying beliefs and values regarding family dynamics and healing practices. Practitioners must be aware of these cultural differences and adapt their methods accordingly (Lombana, 2021; Schneider et al., 2023). This may involve incorporating culturally relevant practices or engaging with community leaders to ensure that the therapeutic approach resonates with the values of the participants.

Moreover, practitioners should engage in ongoing education about cultural sensitivity and the impact of cultural factors on family dynamics. Understanding the cultural context of participants can inform the therapeutic process and enhance the effectiveness of Family Constellations (DeCamp et al., 2022; Breslin et al., 2005). By respecting and honouring diverse belief systems, practitioners can create an inclusive environment that promotes healing and growth.

5.4 Monitoring Outcomes and Ensuring Accountability

Monitoring outcomes is a vital aspect of ethical practice in Family Constellations. Practitioners should implement mechanisms to assess the effectiveness of the therapeutic process and gather feedback from participants regarding their experiences (Lillemoen & Pedersen, 2012; Panfilis et al., 2020). This feedback can inform future practice and help identify areas for improvement.

Additionally, healthcare organisations should establish accountability measures to ensure that practitioners adhere to ethical guidelines and best practices. This may involve regular audits of practice, peer reviews, and the establishment of ethical committees to address any concerns that arise (Rezaee et al., 2020; Avula et al., 2021). By fostering a culture of accountability, organizations can enhance the integrity of Family Constellations as a therapeutic approach.

5.5 Case Studies Illustrating Ethical Dilemmas and Resolutions

Case studies can provide valuable insights into the ethical dilemmas that may arise in the application of Family Constellations and the strategies employed to resolve them. For instance, in one case, a participant experienced significant emotional distress during a session, leading to concerns about the appropriateness of the therapeutic approach. The facilitator promptly recognised the signs of distress and implemented a debriefing session to address the participant's feelings and provide support (Molewijk et al., 2015; Woods et al., 2000). This proactive response not only mitigated the immediate emotional impact but also reinforced the importance of monitoring participants' well-being throughout the process.

In another case, a facilitator encountered challenges related to cultural sensitivity when working with a group from a diverse background. To address this, the facilitator engaged with community leaders to gain insights into the cultural values and beliefs of the participants, allowing for a more tailored and respectful approach to the therapeutic process (Kristanti et al., 2021; Mohammadi, 2023). This case highlights the importance of cultural competence and the need for practitioners to adapt their methods to align with the values of the communities they serve.

6. REGULATORY AND LEGAL CONSIDERATIONS IN FAMILY CONSTELLATIONS

The integration of Family Constellations into healthcare practices necessitates a thorough understanding of the regulatory and legal considerations that govern therapeutic interventions. This includes adherence to licensing and accreditation standards, alignment with healthcare laws and ethical codes, and the establishment of professional standards that ensure the safety and efficacy of the therapeutic process. This section explores these critical aspects, emphasising the importance of regulatory compliance and ethical practice in the application of Family Constellations.

6.1 Licensing, Accreditation, and Professional Standards

Licensing and accreditation are fundamental components of ensuring that healthcare professionals are qualified to practice Family Constellations. In many jurisdictions, practitioners must hold relevant licenses in mental health or counselling, which typically require completion of accredited educational programs and adherence to continuing education requirements (Stiefel et al., 2002; Cohen, 2006). Accreditation bodies often establish specific standards for training in therapeutic modalities, including Family Constellations, to ensure that practitioners possess the necessary skills and knowledge to facilitate sessions safely and effectively (Thege et al., 2021; Hurley et al., 2018).

Professional standards also play a crucial role in guiding the practice of Family Constellations. These standards are often developed by professional organizations and associations that focus on family therapy and systemic practices. They provide a framework for ethical practice, including guidelines for informed consent, confidentiality, and the management of emotional responses during sessions (Mayer & Viviers, 2015; Gyimesi, 2022). Adhering to these standards not only protects practitioners but also enhances the credibility of Family Constellations as a therapeutic approach within the healthcare system.

6.2 Alignment with Healthcare Laws and Ethical Codes

Family Constellations must align with existing healthcare laws and ethical codes to ensure compliance and protect patient rights. This includes adherence to laws governing mental health practice, such as those related to informed consent, patient confidentiality, and the duty to report any harm or risk of harm (Weinhold et al., 2013; Welford, 2014). Practitioners must be aware of the legal implications of their work, particularly in group settings where sensitive information may be shared among participants.

Ethical codes established by professional organisations also guide the practice of Family Constellations. These codes emphasise the importance of respecting patient autonomy, maintaining confidentiality, and providing culturally competent care (Lombana, 2021; Schneider et al., 2023). Practitioners should engage in ongoing education about ethical standards and legal requirements to ensure that their practice remains compliant with evolving regulations and societal expectations.

6.3 Case Studies Illustrating Regulatory and Legal Challenges

Case studies can provide valuable insights into the regulatory and legal challenges that practitioners may encounter when applying Family Constellations. For instance, one case involved a practitioner who facilitated a Family Constellation session without obtaining proper informed consent from participants. This oversight led to a complaint regarding the breach of confidentiality, as sensitive family issues were discussed openly in a group setting (DeCamp et al., 2022). The case highlighted the importance of adhering to informed consent protocols and the potential legal ramifications of neglecting this critical aspect of practice.

Another case involved a practitioner who faced scrutiny for not adequately addressing cultural sensitivity in their Family Constellation sessions. Participants from diverse backgrounds reported feeling marginalised and disrespected during the process, leading to concerns about the practitioner's adherence to ethical codes regarding cultural competence (Breslin et al., 2005). This case underscores the necessity for practitioners to engage in ongoing training and reflection on cultural issues to ensure that their practice is inclusive and respectful of diverse belief systems.

7. COLLABORATIVE CARE MODELS: INTEGRATING FAMILY CONSTELLATIONS

The integration of Family Constellations within collaborative care models represents a promising approach to enhancing therapeutic outcomes in healthcare settings. Collaborative care models emphasise teamwork among healthcare professionals, fostering communication and shared decision-making to provide comprehensive care to patients. This section discusses the integration of Family Constellations with other therapeutic approaches, the building of interdisciplinary teams, and the promotion of patient-centred care.

7.1 Integrating Family Constellations with Other Therapeutic Approaches

Family Constellations can be effectively integrated with various therapeutic modalities, enhancing the overall treatment experience for patients. For instance, combining Family Constellations with cognitive-behavioural therapy (CBT) can provide a holistic approach to addressing mental health issues. While Family Constellations focus on exploring familial dynamics and their impact on individual behaviour, CBT offers structured techniques for modifying negative thought patterns and behaviours (Stiefel et al., 2002; Cohen, 2006). This integration can lead to improved outcomes for patients dealing with complex emotional and psychological challenges.

Moreover, the collaborative care model has been shown to improve depression outcomes in primary care settings, as evidenced by studies demonstrating significant improvements in patient outcomes when collaborative care interventions are employed (Thege et al., 2021; Hurley et al., 2018). By incorporating Family Constellations into these models, healthcare providers can address the underlying familial issues that may contribute to depression, thereby enhancing the effectiveness of the overall treatment plan. For example, the IMPACT trial highlighted a 50% improvement in depression treatment outcomes when collaborative care was used, suggesting that integrating Family Constellations could further enhance these results (Mayer & Viviers, 2015).

7.2 Building Interdisciplinary Teams and Fostering Communication

The success of collaborative care models relies heavily on the establishment of interdisciplinary teams that bring together professionals from various fields, including psychology, social work, and family therapy. Building such teams allows for a more comprehensive understanding of patient needs and fosters effective communication among providers (Gyimesi, 2022; Weinhold et al., 2013). In the context of Family Constellations, interdisciplinary collaboration can facilitate a deeper exploration of family dynamics, as different professionals can contribute their expertise and perspectives.

Effective communication is essential for the successful implementation of collaborative care models. Regular team meetings and case discussions can help ensure that all team members are aligned in their approach to patient care. This collaborative environment encourages the sharing of insights and strategies, ultimately leading to more effective interventions (Welford, 2014; Lombana, 2021). Additionally, fostering open lines of communication with patients and their families is crucial for promoting shared decision-making and ensuring that treatment plans align with the values and preferences of those involved.

7.3 Promoting Patient-Centred Care and Shared Decision-Making

Patient-centred care is a core principle of collaborative care models, emphasising the importance of involving patients in their treatment decisions. Integrating Family Constellations into this framework can enhance patient engagement by encouraging individuals to explore their familial relationships and how these dynamics influence their health (Schneider et al., 2023; DeCamp et al., 2022). By facilitating discussions about family history and dynamics, healthcare providers can empower patients to take an active role in their treatment, leading to more personalized and effective care.

Shared decision-making is a critical component of patient-centred care, allowing patients to collaborate with their healthcare providers in determining the best course of action for their treatment. Family Constellations can serve as a valuable tool in this process, as they provide insights into the familial factors that may impact a patient's health and well-being. By incorporating these insights into treatment discussions, healthcare providers can help patients make informed decisions that reflect their unique circumstances and values (Breslin et al., 2005; Lillemoen & Pedersen, 2012).

8. SUSTAINABLE DEVELOPMENT GOALS AND FAMILY CONSTELLATIONS

The Sustainable Development Goals (SDGs), established by the United Nations in 2015, represent a comprehensive framework aimed at addressing global challenges such as poverty, inequality, and environmental degradation (Reis da Silva, 2024a; Reis da Silva, 2024b; da Silva and Rodrigues, 2023). Family Constellations, a therapeutic approach that explores familial dynamics and their impact on individual well-being, can play a significant role in achieving several of these goals. This section discusses the intersections between Family Constellations and the SDGs, highlighting how this therapeutic method can contribute to sustainable development.

8.1 Family Constellations and SDG 3: Good Health and Well-Being

One of the most direct connections between Family Constellations and the SDGs is with Goal 3, which aims to ensure healthy lives and promote well-being for all at all ages (da Silva and Rodrigues, 2023). Family Constellations address psychological and emotional issues rooted in family dynamics, which can significantly affect mental health outcomes (Schneider et al., 2023; DeCamp et al., 2022). By facilitating the exploration of intergenerational trauma and familial relationships, Family Constellations can help individuals achieve better mental health, thereby contributing to the overall health and well-being of communities. Research has shown that addressing familial issues can lead to improvements in mental health conditions such as anxiety and depression, which are critical components of SDG 3 (Schneider et al., 2023; DeCamp et al., 2022). Furthermore, the holistic nature of Family Constellations aligns with the SDG's emphasis on integrated approaches to health, recognising the interconnectedness of physical, mental, and social well-being (Suvarnabhumi et al., 2022).

8.2 Family Constellations and SDG 5: Gender Equality

Goal 5 focuses on achieving gender equality and empowering all women and girls. Family Constellations can be instrumental in addressing gender-related issues within family systems, such as domestic violence, gender roles, and the impact of patriarchal structures on women's mental health (Vu et al., 2023; Dariah et al., 2019). By providing a safe space for women to explore their familial relationships and the societal expectations placed upon them, Family Constellations can empower women to reclaim their narratives and foster resilience (Vu et al., 2023; Dariah et al., 2019). Moreover, the insights gained from Family Constellations can inform policies and practices aimed at promoting gender equality, as they highlight the underlying familial and societal dynamics that contribute to gender disparities (Vu et al., 2023; Dariah et al., 2019).

8.3 Family Constellations and SDG 10: Reduced Inequalities

Goal 10 aims to reduce inequality within and among countries. Family Constellations can address systemic issues of inequality by exploring how familial and societal structures contribute to individual experiences of marginalisation and disadvantage (Filho et al., 2023). By facilitating discussions around family history and social context, this therapeutic approach can help individuals understand the roots of their challenges and empower them to advocate for themselves and their communities. Additionally, Family Constellations can be particularly beneficial for marginalised populations, as they provide a culturally sensitive framework for exploring issues related to identity, belonging, and systemic oppression. This aligns with the SDG's focus on promoting social, economic, and political inclusion for all (Filho et al., 2023).

8.4 Family Constellations and SDG 16: Peace, Justice, and Strong Institutions

Goal 16 emphasises the importance of promoting peaceful and inclusive societies, providing access to justice for all, and building effective, accountable institutions (da Silva and Rodrigues, 2023). Family Constellations can contribute to this goal by addressing conflicts and unresolved issues within family systems that may lead to broader societal tensions. By fostering understanding and reconciliation within families, this therapeutic approach can promote social cohesion and reduce violence. Furthermore, the insights gained from Family Constellations can inform community-based interventions aimed at conflict resolution and restorative justice, thereby contributing to the establishment of more peaceful and just societies (Fonseca et al., 2020; Agirreazkuenaga, 2019).

9. CASE STUDIES OF INCLUSION FAMILY CONSTELLATIONS IN GERIATRIC NURSING

To provide an example, the integration of Family Constellations into geriatric nursing offers a unique approach to addressing the complex needs of older adults. By exploring familial dynamics and their impact on health, this therapeutic method can enhance the quality of care provided to elderly patients. Below are several case studies (as example) that illustrate the inclusion of Family Constellations in geriatric nursing settings, highlighting the benefits and challenges encountered.

9.1 Case Study 1: Addressing Family Dynamics in Hip Fracture Recovery

Falls and hip fractures are closely linked, as falls often lead to fractures that significantly impact mobility and overall health, necessitating careful management and rehabilitation (Reis da Silva, 2023a; Reis da Silva, 2024c).

Background: An 82-year-old female patient, Mrs. Johnson, was admitted to a geriatric ward following a hip fracture. She had a history of depression and anxiety, exacerbated by strained relationships with her adult children, who had differing opinions on her care.

Intervention: The interdisciplinary team, including a geriatrician, nursing staff, and a psychologist trained in Family Constellations, conducted a session with Mrs. Johnson and her family. The session aimed to explore the underlying familial tensions, fear of falling (Reis da Silva, 2023a) and how they affected her recovery process.

Outcome: The Family Constellation session revealed deep-seated feelings of guilt and resentment among family members. By facilitating open communication, the therapist helped the family members understand each other's perspectives, leading to improved support for Mrs. Johnson. Post-session, the patient reported reduced anxiety levels and a stronger sense of familial support, which positively impacted her recovery trajectory (Saltvedt et al., 2012).

9.2 Case Study 2: Enhancing Communication in Dementia Care

Effective communication in dementia care is crucial to reducing loneliness, preventing elder abuse, and maintaining a supportive environment (da Silva, 2022; Reis da Silva, 2023b; Reis da Silva, 2024d; Reis da Silva, 2024e).

Background: Mr. Smith, a 75-year-old man with moderate dementia, was experiencing behavioural issues that strained his relationship with his primary caregiver, his daughter. The nursing staff noted that the daughter often felt overwhelmed and unsupported.

Intervention: The geriatric nursing team organised a Family Constellation workshop that included Mr. Smith, his daughter, and other family members. The goal was to explore the family dynamics and the impact of Mr. Smith's dementia on their relationships.

Outcome: The workshop provided a platform for family members to express their feelings and concerns. It became evident that the daughter felt a lack of acknowledgment for her caregiving efforts. By addressing these issues, the family was able to develop a more collaborative approach to Mr. Smith's care. Following the intervention, the daughter reported feeling more empowered and supported, which improved her caregiving experience and Mr. Smith's overall well-being (Buhr et al., 2019).

9.3 Case Study 3: Supporting End-of-Life Decisions

End-of-life decisions often involve navigating complex family dynamics, values, and preferences, requiring sensitive approaches to care planning (Reis da Silva, 2024f; Reis da Silva, 2024g).

Background: Mrs. Thompson, a 90-year-old patient with terminal cancer, was facing end-of-life decisions. Her family was divided on her treatment preferences, causing significant stress for both the patient and her caregivers.

Intervention: The geriatric nursing team facilitated a Family Constellation session to address the family's conflicting views and emotional responses regarding Mrs. Thompson's care. The session aimed to clarify her wishes and promote understanding among family members.

Outcome: The Family Constellation process helped the family members articulate their fears and desires regarding Mrs. Thompson's care. By visualising their familial roles and responsibilities, they reached a consensus on her end-of-life care plan that honoured her wishes. This collaborative decision-making process not only reduced family conflict but also provided Mrs. Thompson with peace of mind during her final days (Powers & Eubank, 2018).

9.4 Case Study 4: Improving Transitional Care for Frail Elders

Transition care for frail elders must prioritise mobility, nutrition, and hydration to ensure safe, effective recovery and quality of life, while managing polypharmacy to minimise medication-related complications (Reis da Silva, 2023a; Reis da Silva, 2023b; Reis da Silva, 2023c; Reis da Silva, 2024h; Reis da Silva, 2024i; Reis da Silva, 2024j).

Background: A community-based geriatric program aimed to improve transitional care for frail older adults. The program included a multidisciplinary team that often faced challenges in communication and coordination of care.

Intervention: The team integrated Family Constellations into their regular meetings to explore the familial contexts of their patients. This approach aimed to enhance understanding of the patients' backgrounds and the impact of family dynamics on their health outcomes.

Outcome: Incorporating Family Constellations into team meetings fostered better communication among team members and improved their understanding of patients' needs. The team reported enhanced collaboration and more effective care planning, leading to reduced hospital readmissions and improved patient satisfaction (Akoria, 2016).

9.5 Case Study 5: Addressing Polypharmacy in Geriatric Patients

Addressing Polypharmacy and Medicine Management is a priority in Care for Older Adult (Reis da Silva, 2024j; Reis da Silva, 2024k; Reis da Silva, 2024l).

Background: A 78-year-old male patient, Mr. Lee, was on multiple medications for various chronic conditions. His family expressed concerns about his medication management and the potential for adverse effects.

Intervention: The geriatric nursing team utilised Family Constellations to explore the family's perceptions of Mr. Lee's health and medication regimen. The session aimed to identify family dynamics that contributed to medication adherence issues.

Outcome: The Family Constellation session revealed that family members had differing views on the necessity of certain medications, leading to confusion and non-adherence. By facilitating a discussion, the team helped the family reach a consensus on Mr. Lee's medication management, which improved adherence and reduced the risk of adverse drug reactions (Rocca et al., 2013).

These case studies illustrate the potential benefits of integrating Family Constellations into geriatric nursing practice. By addressing familial dynamics and enhancing communication, this therapeutic approach can significantly improve the quality of care for older adults. As the geriatric population continues to grow, incorporating innovative methods like Family Constellations will be essential for meeting the complex needs of this demographic.

10. CONCLUSION

Family Constellations represent a valuable therapeutic approach that can enhance the understanding of individual health within the context of family dynamics. However, the ethical challenges associated with its application necessitate careful consideration and the establishment of best practices to ensure that this method is utilized responsibly and effectively in healthcare settings. The theoretical foundations of Family Constellations are rooted in the understanding of family systems and their impact on individual health. The principles and mechanisms of this therapeutic approach highlight the significance of familial relationships in shaping psychological and physical well-being. As research continues to support the efficacy of Family Constellations in improving mental health outcomes, its integration into holistic health practices presents a promising avenue for enhancing patient care and fostering comprehensive healing (Reis da Silva, 2024m).

The application of Family Constellations in healthcare settings presents a promising avenue for enhancing patient care and promoting holistic health outcomes. Through case examples, the potential benefits for patients and healthcare teams are evident, highlighting the importance of integrating this therapeutic approach within multidisciplinary care models. As the field continues to evolve, further research and exploration of Family Constellations will be essential in maximising its impact on healthcare practices. The ethical challenges associated with applying Family Constellations in therapeutic settings are multifaceted and require careful consideration. By prioritising patient autonomy, confidentiality, cultural sensitivity, emotional safety, and professional boundaries, practitioners can navigate these challenges effectively. Addressing these ethical considerations is essential for fostering a safe and supportive environment that promotes healing and growth through Family Constellations.

The ethical application of Family Constellations in healthcare settings requires adherence to best practices that prioritise patient safety, informed consent, cultural competence, and accountability. By implementing guidelines for ethical practice, providing comprehensive training and supervision, and monitoring outcomes, healthcare professionals can navigate the complexities of this therapeutic approach effectively. Case studies further illustrate the importance of addressing ethical dilemmas and demonstrate the potential for positive resolutions when practitioners remain committed to ethical principles. The regulatory and legal considerations surrounding the application of Family Constellations in healthcare are multifaceted and require careful attention from practitioners. By adhering to licensing and accreditation standards, aligning with healthcare laws and ethical codes, and being mindful of the challenges illustrated through case studies, practitioners can navigate the complexities of this therapeutic approach responsibly. Establishing a solid foundation of regulatory compliance and ethical practice is essential for the successful integration of Family Constellations into healthcare settings, ultimately enhancing patient care and therapeutic outcomes.

Integrating Family Constellations within collaborative care models offers a promising approach to enhancing patient outcomes in healthcare settings. By combining Family Constellations with other therapeutic approaches, building interdisciplinary teams, and promoting patient-centred care and shared decision-making, healthcare providers can create a more holistic and effective treatment experience. As collaborative care continues to evolve, the incorporation of Family Constellations may play a vital role in addressing the complex interplay of familial dynamics and individual health.

The integration of Family Constellations into healthcare represents a promising avenue for enhancing patient-centred care and addressing the complex dynamics that influence health. By prioritising ethical practice, fostering interdisciplinary collaboration, and embracing innovative approaches, healthcare providers can leverage the transformative potential of Family Constellations to improve outcomes for individuals and families alike.

10.1 Summary

The exploration of Family Constellations as a therapeutic approach within healthcare settings has illuminated both ethical challenges and opportunities for enhancing patient care. As this method continues to gain traction, it is essential to reflect on the ethical dilemmas encountered and the potential pathways forward. The integration of Family Constellations into collaborative care models presents a unique opportunity to address the complex interplay of familial dynamics and individual health, but it also necessitates a commitment to ethical practice and ongoing professional development.

10.2. Reflection on Ethical Challenges and Opportunities Ahead

The ethical challenges associated with Family Constellations are multifaceted, encompassing issues of patient autonomy, informed consent, confidentiality, and cultural sensitivity. As practitioners navigate these complexities, it is crucial to prioritise ethical principles that safeguard patient rights and promote a therapeutic environment conducive to healing (Hem et al., 2016; Al-Wathinani, 2023). The COVID-19 pandemic has further highlighted the need for ethical vigilance in healthcare, as providers grapple with new challenges related to resource allocation, patient privacy, and the delivery of care (Shrestha et al., 2023; Mejdahl et al., 2022).

Despite these challenges, the integration of Family Constellations offers significant opportunities for enhancing therapeutic outcomes. By fostering a deeper understanding of familial influences on health, practitioners can develop more comprehensive treatment plans that address the root causes of psychological and emotional distress. This holistic approach aligns with the growing emphasis on patient-centred care, which prioritizes the unique needs and preferences of individuals (Hem et al., 2014).

10.3 Recommendations for Research, Practice, and Policy Development

To harness the full potential of Family Constellations in healthcare, several recommendations can be made for research, practice, and policy development:

1. Research: Further empirical studies are needed to evaluate the effectiveness of Family Constellations in various healthcare contexts, particularly in relation to specific mental health conditions and chronic illnesses. Longitudinal studies could provide valuable insights into the long-term benefits of this therapeutic approach (Schofield et al., 2021). Conduct empirical studies to assess the impact of Family Constellations on mental health outcomes, particularly in relation to the SDGs. This research can help establish evidence-based practices that align with global sustainability goals.
2. Practice: Healthcare professionals should receive specialised training in Family Constellations, emphasising ethical considerations, cultural competence, and effective facilitation techniques. Ongoing supervision and peer support can help practitioners navigate ethical dilemmas and enhance their skills (Mousavi et al., 2021).
3. Policy Development: Healthcare organisations should establish clear guidelines and policies regarding the ethical application of Family Constellations. This includes protocols for informed consent, confidentiality, and the management of emotional responses during sessions. Additionally, policies should promote interdisciplinary collaboration and communication among healthcare providers (Bhattarai et al., 2022).
4. Integration: Encourage the integration of Family Constellations into existing health and social programs that aim to achieve the SDGs. This can enhance the effectiveness of interventions by addressing the underlying familial dynamics that contribute to individual and community challenges.
5. Training: Provide training for healthcare professionals and social workers on the principles and practices of Family Constellations, emphasising their relevance to the SDGs. This can help build capacity within communities to use this therapeutic approach effectively.

10.4 The Evolving Role of Family Constellations in Transforming Healthcare

As the healthcare landscape continues to evolve, the role of Family Constellations in transforming patient care is becoming increasingly significant. This therapeutic approach not only addresses individual psychological needs but also recognises the importance of familial relationships in shaping health outcomes. By integrating Family Constellations into collaborative care models, healthcare providers can create a more holistic and inclusive approach to treatment that prioritizes the interconnectedness of patients' lives (Drewett et al., 2021).

Moreover, the ongoing advancements in technology and telehealth present new opportunities for the application of Family Constellations in diverse settings. Virtual platforms can facilitate access to this therapeutic approach for individuals who may otherwise face barriers to participation, such as geographical limitations or mobility issues (Cox, 2020). As the field continues to grow, it is essential for practitioners to remain adaptable and responsive to the changing needs of patients and the healthcare system as a whole.

REFERENCES

Agirreazkuenaga, L. (2019). Embedding sustainable development goals in education. teachers' perspective about education for sustainability in the Basque autonomous community. *Sustainability (Basel), 11*(5), 1496. DOI: 10.3390/su11051496

Akoria, O. (2016). Establishing in-hospital geriatrics services in Africa: Insights from the university of Benin teaching hospital geriatrics project. *Annals of African Medicine, 15*(3), 145. DOI: 10.4103/1596-3519.188896 PMID: 27549420

Al-Wathinani, A., Barten, D. G., Alsahli, H., Alhamid, A., Alghamdi, W., Alqahtani, W., Alghamdi, R., Aljuaid, M., Albaqami, N. A., & Goniewicz, K. (2023). The right to refuse: Understanding healthcare providers' perspectives on patient autonomy in emergency care. *Health Care, 11*(12), 1756. DOI: 10.3390/healthcare11121756 PMID: 37372874

Avula, H., Dittborn, M., & Brierley, J. (2021). 'who ya gonna call …?' ethical and legal dilemmas in specialist children centres and district general hospitals. *Clinical Ethics, 17*(4), 415–424. DOI: 10.1177/14777509211036649

Bhattarai, S., Adhikari, A., Rayamajhee, B., Dhungana, J., Singh, R., Koirala, S., & Shakya, D. (2022). Participatory approach to develop evidence-based clinical ethics guidelines for the care of covid-19 patients: A mixed method study from Nepal. *Frontiers in Public Health, 10*, 873881. Advance online publication. DOI: 10.3389/fpubh.2022.873881 PMID: 35832276

Blackler, L., Scharf, A., Matsoukas, K., Colletti, M., & Voigt, L. (2021). Call to action: Empowering patients and families to initiate clinical ethics consultations. *Journal of Medical Ethics, 49*(4), 240–243. DOI: 10.1136/medethics-2021-107426 PMID: 34732393

Breslin, J., MacRae, S., Bell, J., & Сингер, П. (2005). Top 10 health care ethics challenges facing the public: Views of Toronto bioethicists. *BMC Medical Ethics, 6*(1), 5. Advance online publication. DOI: 10.1186/1472-6939-6-5 PMID: 15978136

Buhr, G., Dixon, C., Dillard, J., Nickolopoulos, E., Bowlby, L., Canupp, H., Matters, L., Konrad, T., Previll, L., Heflin, M., & McConnell, E. (2019). Geriatric resource teams: Equipping primary care practices to meet the complex care needs of older adults. *Geriatrics (Basel, Switzerland), 4*(4), 59. DOI: 10.3390/geriatrics4040059 PMID: 31640232

Cohen, D. (2006). "Family constellations": An innovative systemic phenomenological group process from Germany. *The Family Journal (Alexandria, Va.), 14*(3), 226–233. DOI: 10.1177/1066480706287279

Cox, D. (2020). A guide to establishing ethics committees in behavioral health settings. *Behavior Analysis in Practice, 13*(4), 939–949. DOI: 10.1007/s40617-020-00455-6 PMID: 33269203

da Silva, T. H. R. (2022). Emotional awareness and emotional intelligence. *British Journal of Community Nursing, 27*(12), 573–574. DOI: 10.12968/bjcn.2022.27.12.573 PMID: 36519463

da Silva, T. H. R., & Rodrigues, E. C. P. (2023). Body Image Related Discrimination. In Leal Filho, W., Azul, A. M., Brandli, L., Lange Salvia, A., Özuyar, P. G., & Wall, T. (Eds.), *Reduced Inequalities. Encyclopedia of the UN Sustainable Development Goals*. Springer., DOI: 10.1007/978-3-319-71060-0_61-1

Dariah, A., Salleh, M., Yahaia, M., & Mafruhat, A. (2019). Integrating dimensions of sustainable development goals (SDGs) within Umranic framework. *Journal of Sustainable Development, 12*(6), 82. DOI: 10.5539/jsd.v12n6p82

DeCamp, M., Alasmar, A., Fischer, S., & Kutner, J. (2022). Meeting ethical challenges with authenticity when engaging patients and families in end-of-life and palliative care research: A qualitative study. *BMC Palliative Care, 21*(1), 74. Advance online publication. DOI: 10.1186/s12904-022-00964-x PMID: 35578262

Drewett, G., Gibney, G., & Ko, D. (2021). Practical ethical challenges and moral distress among staff in a hospital covid-19 screening service. *Internal Medicine Journal, 51*(9), 1513–1516. DOI: 10.1111/imj.15471 PMID: 34541765

Filho, W., Simaens, A., Diaz, P., Vasconcelos, C., Fritzens, B., & Mac-Lean, C. (2023). Integrating the sustainable development goals into the strategy of higher education institutions. *International Journal of Sustainable Development and World Ecology, 30*(5), 564–575. DOI: 10.1080/13504509.2023.2167884

Fonseca, L., Domingues, P., & Dima, A. (2020). Mapping the sustainable development goals relationships. *Sustainability (Basel), 12*(8), 3359. DOI: 10.3390/su12083359

Gyimesi, J. (2022). Family constellation therapy in the context of esotericism. *Perspectives on Psychological Science, 18*(4), 749–761. DOI: 10.1177/17456916221120424 PMID: 36301913

Hem, M., Gjerberg, E., Husum, T., & Pedersen, R. (2016). Ethical challenges when using coercion in mental healthcare: A systematic literature review. *Nursing Ethics, 25*(1), 92–110. DOI: 10.1177/0969733016629770 PMID: 26931767

Hem, M., Molewijk, B., Weimand, B., & Pedersen, R. (2023). Patients with severe mental illness and the ethical challenges related to confidentiality during family involvement: A scoping review. *Frontiers in Public Health, 10*, 960815. Advance online publication. DOI: 10.3389/fpubh.2022.960815 PMID: 36711422

Hem, M., Pedersen, R., Norvoll, R., & Molewijk, B. (2014). Evaluating clinical ethics support in mental healthcare. *Nursing Ethics, 22*(4), 452–466. DOI: 10.1177/0969733014539783 PMID: 25091004

Hurley, J., Koenning, M., & Bray, A. (2018). Responding to intergenerational psychological trauma: A literature review paper on the place of family constellation therapy. *Psychotherapy and Counselling Journal of Australia, 6*(1). Advance online publication. DOI: 10.59158/001c.71192

Kristanti, M., Kusmaryanto, K., & Effendy, C. (2021). Common ethical dilemmas of family caregivers of palliative patients in Indonesia. *Belitung Nursing Journal, 7*(3), 246–250. DOI: 10.33546/bnj.1457 PMID: 37469338

Lillemoen, L., & Pedersen, R. (2012). Ethical challenges and how to develop ethics support in primary health care. *Nursing Ethics, 20*(1), 96–108. DOI: 10.1177/0969733012452687 PMID: 22918061

Lombana, Y. (2021). Possibilities and challenges in providing psychotherapeutic interventions to meet the needs of the Latinx population in the United States. *Genealogy, 5*(1), 12. DOI: 10.3390/genealogy5010012

Mayer, C., & Viviers, R. (2015). Exploring cultural issues for constellation work in south Africa. *Australian and New Zealand Journal of Family Therapy, 36*(2), 289–306. DOI: 10.1002/anzf.1103

Mejdahl, C., Nielsen, B., Mehlsen, M., Hollesen, M., Pedersen, M., Engkjaer-Trautwein, G., Funch, L. V., & Terkildsen, M. (2022). Covid-19 as moral breakdown: Entangled ethical demands experienced by hospital-based nurses in the early onset of the pandemic. *Nursing Inquiry, 30*(1), e12508. Advance online publication. DOI: 10.1111/nin.12508 PMID: 35709227

Moen, P., Kelly, E., & Huang, R. (2008). Fit inside the work-family black box: An ecology of the life course, cycles of control reframing. *Journal of Occupational and Organizational Psychology, 81*(3), 411–433. DOI: 10.1348/096317908X315495 PMID: 19809532

Mohammadi, F., Naderi, Z., Nikrouz, L., Oshvandi, K., Masoumi, S. Z., Sabetsarvestani, P., & Bijani, M. (2023). Ethical challenges as perceived by nurses in pediatric oncology units. *Nursing Ethics*, *31*(2-3), 268–280. DOI: 10.1177/09697330231191278 PMID: 37624231

Molewijk, B., Hem, M., & Pedersen, R. (2015). Dealing with ethical challenges: A focus group study with professionals in mental health care. *BMC Medical Ethics*, *16*(1), 4. Advance online publication. DOI: 10.1186/1472-6939-16-4 PMID: 25591923

Mousavi, M., Khodayari-Zarnaq, R., & Hajizadeh, A. (2021). Main challenges in adoption of consultation services of hospital ethics committees: A systematic review of the literature. *Clinical Ethics*, *17*(1), 41–50. DOI: 10.1177/1477750921994278

Panfilis, L., Tanzi, S., Perin, M., Turola, E., & Artioli, G. (2020). "teach for ethics in palliative care": A mixed-method evaluation of a medical ethics training programme. *BMC Palliative Care*, *19*(1), 149. Advance online publication. DOI: 10.1186/s12904-020-00653-7 PMID: 32977796

Powers, J., & Eubank, K. (2018). Geriatrics evaluation and management in the veterans administration—An historical perspective. *Geriatrics (Basel, Switzerland)*, *3*(4), 84. DOI: 10.3390/geriatrics3040084 PMID: 31011119

Reis da Silva, T. H. (2023a). Falls assessment and prevention in the nursing home and community. *British Journal of Community Nursing*, *28*(2), 68–72. DOI: 10.12968/bjcn.2023.28.2.68

Reis da Silva, T. H. (2023b). Moving and Handling in the Community. *British Journal of Community Nursing*, *28*(8), 369. DOI: 10.12968/bjcn.2023.28.8.369

Reis da Silva, T. H. (2023c). Ageing in place: Ageing at home and in the community. *British Journal of Community Nursing*, *28*(5), 213–214. DOI: 10.12968/bjcn.2023.28.5.213

Reis da Silva, T. (2024a). Advancing Gender Equity In Nursing Care For Older Adults: A Pathway To Achieving The United Nations Sustainable Development Goals. *J Comm Med and Pub Health Rep*, *5*(12). Advance online publication. https://doi.org/10.38207/JCMPHR/2024/JUL051201105

Reis da Silva, T. (2024b). Gender Equity In Healthcare: Integrating Emotional Intelligence To Achieve The United Nations Sustainable Development Goals. *J Comm Med and Pub Health Rep*, *5*(12). Advance online publication. DOI: 10.38207/JCMPHR/2024/JUL051202106

Reis da Silva, T. H. (2024c). Falls prevention in older people and the role of nursing. *British Journal of Community Nursing, 29*(7), 335–339. DOI: 10.12968/bjcn.2024.0005

Reis da Silva, T. H. (2024d). Loneliness in older adults. *British Journal of Community Nursing, 29*(2), 60–66. DOI: 10.12968/bjcn.2024.29.2.60

Reis da Silva, T H (2024e). Prevalence of elder abuse: a narrative review. British journal of community nursing vol. 29,9 (2024): 442-446. doi: https://doi.org/10.12968/bjcn.2024.0004

Reis da Silva, T. H (2024f). Oncology and Cancer Medicine: Understanding the complexities in Older Patients. Biomed J Sci & Tech Res 55(3)-2024. DOI: https://doi.org/DOI: 10.26717/BJSTR.2024.55.008720

Reis da Silva. Tiago Horta (2024g). Death and Its Significance in Nursing Practice. Palliat Med Care Int J. 2024; 4(3): 555640. DOI: https://juniperpublishers.com/pmcij/pdf/PMCIJ.MS.ID.555640.pdf

Reis da Silva, T. (2024h). Can supplementing vitamin B12 improve mental health outcomes?: A literature review. *British Journal of Community Nursing, 29*(3), 137–146. DOI: 10.12968/bjcn.2024.29.3.137

Reis da Silva, T. H. (2024i). Understanding body fluid balance, dehydration and intravenous fluid therapy. *Emergency Nurse*. Advance online publication. DOI: 10.7748/en.2024.e2201

Reis da Silva, T. H. (2024j). Pharmacokinetics in older people: An overview of prescribing practice. *Journal of Prescribing Practice, 6*(9), 374–381. https://doi.org/10.12968/jprp.2024.6.9.374

Reis da Silva, T. H. (2024k). Chapter 6 – Navigating Healthcare Complexity: Integrating Business Fundamentals into Nursing Leadership. In Sedky, A. Resiliency Strategies for Long-Term Business Success. Pp. 145-168. IGI Global. https://doi.org/DOI: 10.4018/979-8-3693-9168-6.ch006

Reis da Silva, T. H. (2024l). Chapter 11 - Integrating business essentials into Gerontological Nursing: Enhancing Care for Older Adults in Diverse Settings. In Sedky, A. Resiliency Strategies for Long-Term Business Success. Pp. 283-316. IGI Global. DOI: https://doi.org/DOI: 10.4018/979-8-3693-9168-6.ch011

Reis da Silva, T. H. (2024m). Enhancing the mental health of refugees and asylum seekers through music interventions. *Mental Health Practice*. Advance online publication. DOI: 10.7748/mhp.2024.e1717

Rezaee, N., Mardani-Hamooleh, M., & Seraji, M. (2020). Nurses' perception of ethical challenges in caring for patients with covid-19: A qualitative analysis. *Journal of Medical Ethics and History of Medicine*. Advance online publication. DOI: 10.18502/jmehm.v13i23.4954 PMID: 34055239

Rocca, G., Moylan, K., Crist, B., Volgas, D., Stannard, J., & Mehr, D. (2013). Co-management of geriatric patients with hip fractures. *Geriatric Orthopaedic Surgery & Rehabilitation*, *4*(1), 10–15. DOI: 10.1177/2151458513495238 PMID: 23936734

Saltvedt, I., Prestmo, A., Einarsen, E., Johnsen, L., Helbostad, J., & Sletvold, O. (2012). Development and delivery of patient treatment in the Trondheim hip fracture trial. a new geriatric in-hospital pathway for elderly patients with hip fracture. *BMC Research Notes*, *5*(1), 355. Advance online publication. DOI: 10.1186/1756-0500-5-355 PMID: 22800378

Schneider, N., Steinberg, D., Pahl, D., Steffin, D., & Gangopadhyay, M. (2023). Ethical quandaries at end of life: Navigating real-world case examples as a pediatric psychologist. *Clinical Practice in Pediatric Psychology*, *11*(2), 244–251. DOI: 10.1037/cpp0000432

Schofield, G., Dittborn, M., Selman, L., & Huxtable, R. (2021). Defining ethical challenge(s) in healthcare research: A rapid review. *BMC Medical Ethics*, *22*(1), 135. Advance online publication. DOI: 10.1186/s12910-021-00700-9 PMID: 34587950

Shrestha, E., Pokharel, R., Rs, M., & Rai, G. (2023). Ethical challenges faced by the healthcare workers to provide health service during covid-19 pandemic. *Journal of Bp Koirala Institute of Health Sciences*, *6*(1), 14–19. DOI: 10.3126/jbpkihs.v6i1.52502

Stiefel, I., Harris, P., & Zollmann, A. (2002). Family constellation — A therapy beyond words. *Australian and New Zealand Journal of Family Therapy*, *23*(1), 38–44. DOI: 10.1002/j.1467-8438.2002.tb00484.x

Suvarnabhumi, K., Jorajit, S., Dechpichai, W., & Ativitthayaporn, J. (2022). Expert consensus on core topics of sustainable development online learning module for family physicians: A Delphi study. *BMJ Open*, *12*(12), e061407. DOI: 10.1136/bmjopen-2022-061407 PMID: 36581405

Thege, B., Petroll, C., Rivas, C., & Scholtens, S. (2021). The effectiveness of family constellation therapy in improving mental health: A systematic review. *Family Process*, *60*(2), 409–423. DOI: 10.1111/famp.12636 PMID: 33528854

Vu, M., Cruz, A., & Burton, N. (2023). Contributing to the sustainable development goals as normative and instrumental acts: The role of Buddhist religious logics in family SMES. *International Small Business Journal*, *42*(2), 246–275. DOI: 10.1177/02662426231182425

Weinhold, J., Hunger, C., Bornhäuser, A., Link, L., Rochon, J., Wild, B., & Schweitzer, J. (2013). Family constellation seminars improve psychological functioning in a general population sample: Results of a randomized controlled trial. *Journal of Counseling Psychology*, *60*(4), 601–609. DOI: 10.1037/a0033539 PMID: 23957767

Welford, E. (2014). Giving the dead their rightful place. *Transactional Analysis Journal*, *44*(4), 320–333. DOI: 10.1177/0362153714559920

Woods, S., Beaver, K., & Luker, K. (2000). Users' views of palliative care services: Ethical implications. *Nursing Ethics*, *7*(4), 314–326. DOI: 10.1177/096973300000700405 PMID: 11221408

Zahedi, F., Kadivar, M., Mojen, L., Asadabadi, M., Tajalli, S., Ilkhani, M., & Larijani, B. (2022). The ethical challenges of palliative care from the perspectives of pediatricians: A qualitative study in Iran. *Frontiers in Pediatrics*, *10*, 928476. Advance online publication. DOI: 10.3389/fped.2022.928476 PMID: 36105856

Chapter 9
Family Constellations in Community Health: A Systemic Approach to Population Wellness

Tiago Manuel Horta Reis da Silva
https://orcid.org/0000-0001-5220-1718
King's College London, UK

ABSTRACT

This chapter explores the application of Family Constellations within community health, emphasising its role in promoting population wellness through systemic healing. By examining the interconnectedness of individual and collective health dynamics, the chapter outlines how unresolved familial patterns impact community well-being. It discusses Family Constellations' potential contributions to addressing key challenges in the care of older people, including loneliness, chronic illness, and social exclusion, while supporting Sustainable Development Goals (SDGs) such as good health and well-being, reduced inequalities, and sustainable communities. Drawing on case studies, theoretical frameworks, and practical applications, the chapter presents evidence-based strategies for integrating this approach into public health initiatives, fostering resilience, social cohesion, and preventive care.

1. INTRODUCTION

In the realm of community health, the concept of Family Constellations emerges as a significant framework for understanding the intricate dynamics that influence both individual and collective well-being (Tambunan, 2024; Ho et al., 2018). Family Constellations, a therapeutic approach developed by Bert Hellinger, posits

DOI: 10.4018/979-8-3693-9092-4.ch009

that unresolved familial patterns and traumas can have profound effects on the health and wellness of individuals and communities alike (Tambunan, 2024; Ho et al., 2018). This chapter explores the application of Family Constellations within community health contexts, emphasising its role in promoting population wellness through systemic healing. By examining the interconnectedness of individual and collective health dynamics, the chapter outlines how unresolved familial patterns impact community well-being.

1.1 Overview of Family Constellations in Community Health Contexts

Family Constellations operate on the premise that individuals are deeply influenced by their family systems, including historical traumas and relational dynamics. This approach recognises that family members are interconnected, and issues faced by one member can reverberate throughout the family unit, affecting the health and well-being of all members. Research indicates that effective family communication patterns are crucial for fostering resilience and well-being within families, as they facilitate emotional support and understanding among members (Tambunan, 2024; Ho et al., 2018; Buehler et al., 2022). For instance, studies have shown that families with open communication tend to exhibit higher levels of well-being, as they can address conflicts and emotional needs more effectively (Sit et al., 2022; Gayatri & Puspitasari, 2022; Balistreri & Alvira-Hammond, 2016).

Moreover, the impact of familial relationships extends beyond the immediate family, influencing broader community dynamics. The quality of family interactions can significantly affect community health outcomes, as families often serve as the primary support systems for individuals facing health challenges (Kim et al., 2022; Shen et al., 2017). In this context, Family Constellations provide a valuable lens through which to examine the systemic issues that contribute to community health disparities, particularly among vulnerable populations, such as the elderly and those experiencing chronic illnesses (Kates et al., 2023; Erdoğan, 2020).

1.2 Purpose and Scope of the Chapter

The purpose of this chapter is to elucidate the potential contributions of Family Constellations to community health initiatives, particularly in addressing key challenges such as loneliness, chronic illness, and social exclusion among older adults. By integrating theoretical frameworks and practical applications of Family Constellations, the chapter aims to present evidence-based strategies for enhancing community health outcomes. This includes exploring how systemic healing can foster resilience, social cohesion, and preventive care within communities (Ho et al., 2016; Gaston, 2021).

Furthermore, the chapter will delve into case studies that illustrate the successful implementation of Family Constellations in various community health settings. These examples will highlight the transformative potential of this approach in promoting holistic health and well-being, thereby supporting Sustainable Development Goals (SDGs) such as good health and well-being, reduced inequalities, and sustainable communities (da Silva and Rodrigues, 2023; Abdullah & Salim, 2020; Keldal et al., 2023; Martín-Martín et al., 2021). By examining these case studies, the chapter seeks to provide a comprehensive understanding of the practical implications of Family Constellations in community health contexts.

1.3 Relevance to Population Wellness

The relevance of Family Constellations to population wellness cannot be overstated. As communities grapple with the complexities of modern health challenges, including the impacts of the COVID-19 pandemic, the need for innovative approaches to health promotion becomes increasingly urgent (Guedes et al., 2022; Cornally et al., 2022; O'Neal et al., 2018; Reis da Silva, 2024a; Reis da Silva, 2024b). Family Constellations offer a unique perspective by addressing the underlying familial and systemic issues that contribute to individual and community health outcomes.

Research has demonstrated that positive family dynamics are associated with improved mental health and overall well-being, underscoring the importance of fostering healthy family relationships as a means of enhancing community health (Fakfare & Wattanacharoensil, 2020; Anisti, 2023). For instance, interventions that promote family communication and cohesion have been shown to mitigate the effects of social isolation and enhance the psychological well-being of community members (Zhao et al., 2021; Wittenberg-Lyles et al., 2012; Johns et al., 2022). Furthermore, as communities strive to achieve the SDGs, integrating Family Constellations into public health initiatives can provide a pathway for addressing health disparities and promoting equity in health outcomes (Urban et al., 2022; Kaveh-Farsani et al., 2020; Byaello, 2023).

2. KEY CONCEPTS OF FAMILY CONSTELLATIONS

Family Constellations is a therapeutic approach developed by Bert Hellinger that focuses on understanding and resolving family dynamics and patterns (Tambunan, 2024; Ho et al., 2018). This method emphasises the systemic nature of relationships within families, highlighting how these dynamics can influence individual behaviour and emotional well-being. Below are key concepts associated with Family Constellations, supported by relevant literature.

2.1 Key Concepts of Family Constellations

1. Systemic Perspective: Family Constellations operate on the principle that individuals are part of larger family systems. Each family member's behaviour and emotional state can be influenced by the dynamics within the family unit, including unresolved issues from previous generations. This systemic perspective allows for a holistic understanding of individual problems, as noted by Gyimesi (2022), who discusses the integration of systemic thinking in therapeutic practices.
2. Representational Dynamics: In a Family Constellation session, participants represent family members or significant figures in the individual's life. This representation helps to visualise and explore the underlying dynamics and relationships within the family system. The work of Mcquillin and Welford (2013) emphasizes how group dynamics can impact individual psyche and how these representations can facilitate healing.
3. Entanglements and Exclusions: A core concept in Family Constellations is the idea of entanglements, where unresolved issues or traumas from one generation can affect subsequent generations. This can manifest as emotional burdens or patterns of behaviour that are passed down. Welford (2014) discusses how unresolved family issues can interfere with effective grieving and emotional processing, highlighting the importance of addressing these entanglements.
4. Healing Through Awareness: The process of Family Constellations aims to bring awareness to these hidden dynamics, allowing individuals to understand their roles within the family system. By recognising these patterns, individuals can begin to heal and break free from negative cycles. The systematic review by Thege et al. (2021) supports the effectiveness of Family Constellation therapy in improving mental health outcomes, demonstrating its potential for facilitating healing.
5. Intergenerational Trauma: Family Constellations also address the concept of intergenerational trauma, where the effects of trauma experienced by one generation can impact the emotional and psychological well-being of subsequent generations. Research by Hurley et al. (2018) highlights the relevance of Family Constellation therapy in addressing these traumas, suggesting that individual therapy may not be sufficient without considering the family context.
6. Family Secrets and Dynamics: The method emphasises the importance of family secrets and how they can create barriers to healthy relationships. Secrets often lead to feelings of shame, guilt, or isolation among family members. Capec et al. (2022) discuss how Family Constellation seminars can help manage family

secrets and improve interactions within the family, thereby enhancing overall well-being.

7. Cultural Context: Family Constellations are influenced by cultural contexts, which shape family dynamics and perceptions of relationships. Mayer and Viviers (2015) explore how cultural issues impact constellation work, emphasising the need for culturally sensitive approaches in therapeutic settings. This understanding is crucial for practitioners to effectively engage with diverse populations.
8. Facilitation and Group Dynamics: The role of the facilitator in Family Constellations is critical. The facilitator guides the process, ensuring a safe and supportive environment for participants. This involves managing group dynamics and fostering open communication. The work of Hunger et al. (2013) highlights the importance of skilled facilitation in achieving positive outcomes in Family Constellation seminars.
9. Therapeutic Outcomes: The therapeutic outcomes of Family Constellations can include improved emotional well-being, enhanced family relationships, and greater self-awareness. Participants often report feelings of relief and clarity after engaging in the process. Finn et al. (2022) provide evidence of the positive impact of Family Constellation therapy on psychological functioning in various populations.
10. Integration with Other Therapeutic Approaches: Family Constellations can be integrated with other therapeutic modalities, such as cognitive-behavioural therapy or psychodynamic approaches. This integration allows for a more comprehensive treatment plan that addresses both individual and systemic issues. The potential for combining Family Constellations with other therapeutic methods is discussed by Lück and Castrén (2018), who emphasise the importance of understanding diverse family structures.

3. THE SYSTEMIC NATURE OF COMMUNITY HEALTH

Applying Family Constellations to community health challenges presents a unique opportunity to address chronic illness, mental health issues, and social exclusion through a systemic lens (Budhthoki, 2013). Family Constellations, a therapeutic approach developed by Bert Hellinger, emphasises the importance of familial relationships and their impact on individual and collective well-being. This approach can be particularly beneficial in community health settings where social dynamics and collective histories significantly influence health outcomes. By understanding the systemic nature of these relationships, health practitioners can develop interventions that not only address individual health concerns but also foster community cohesion and resilience.

Chronic illnesses often have multifaceted origins, including genetic, environmental, and social factors (Reis da Silva, 2024c; Reis da Silva, 2024d; Reis da Silva, 2024e). The systemic perspective offered by Family Constellations allows for a deeper exploration of these factors, particularly how family histories and dynamics contribute to health outcomes. For instance, Budhthoki (2013) discusses how socioeconomic inequality and social exclusion can lead to adverse health outcomes, particularly among marginalised groups. By applying Family Constellations, health practitioners can identify and address the underlying familial patterns that may perpetuate these inequalities, thereby improving health outcomes for individuals suffering from chronic illnesses.

Mental health issues are similarly influenced by familial and social dynamics. Research highlights the struggles faced by individuals experiencing social exclusion, which can exacerbate mental health problems (Watson et al., 2016; Reis da Silva, 2024f; Reis da Silva, 2024g). Family Constellations can facilitate discussions around these issues, allowing individuals to explore their familial relationships and the impact of these dynamics on their mental health. This therapeutic approach can help individuals understand their place within their family system and how this influences their mental health, ultimately leading to more effective interventions that address both individual and collective needs (Pagorek-Eshel et al., 2022).

Social exclusion is a critical factor that affects health outcomes across various populations (Reis da Silva, 2024h). Pagorek-Eshel et al. (2022) found that social exclusion was a strong predictor of depression and anxiety among marginalised groups. By using Family Constellations, community health initiatives can address the root causes of social exclusion, fostering a sense of belonging and connection among community members. This approach not only helps individuals feel more included but also promotes collective healing and resilience within the community.

Case examples demonstrating community-level interventions highlight the effectiveness of applying Family Constellations in addressing health challenges. For instance, community-based support groups that utilise Family Constellations principles have been shown to improve mental health outcomes among participants (Quinn et al., 2016). These groups provide a safe space for individuals to share their experiences and explore the familial patterns that may contribute to their mental health struggles. By fostering open communication and understanding, these interventions can lead to significant improvements in mental health and well-being (Pagorek-Eshel et al., 2022).

Moreover, the integration of Family Constellations into public health frameworks can enhance the effectiveness of community health initiatives. By recognising the systemic nature of health challenges, public health practitioners can develop more holistic approaches that address the interconnected factors influencing health outcomes. For example, Quinn et al. (2016) discuss the barriers faced by women with disabilities in accessing healthcare, emphasising the need for inclusive practices that consider the broader social context. By incorporating Family Constellations into public health strategies, practitioners can create more inclusive and effective interventions that address the unique needs of marginalized populations (Pagorek-Eshel et al., 2022). The integration of Family Constellations into public health frameworks also aligns with the principles of community-based participatory research (CBPR), which emphasises collaboration between researchers and community members. This approach fosters a sense of ownership and agency among community members, empowering them to take an active role in addressing their health challenges. By using Family Constellations, health practitioners can facilitate discussions that allow community members to explore their familial and social dynamics, ultimately leading to more effective and sustainable health interventions (Pagorek-Eshel et al., 2022).

4. CARE OF OLDER PEOPLE AND FAMILY CONSTELLATIONS

The care of older people is increasingly recognised as a complex interplay of intergenerational dynamics, social inclusion, and systemic approaches to health and well-being (Reis da Silva, 2024i; Reis da Silva, 2024j; Reis da Silva, 2024k). Family Constellations, a therapeutic approach that emphasises the importance of familial relationships and their impact on individual and collective well-being, can be effectively applied to address the challenges faced by older adults. This approach not only enhances the understanding of elder care but also promotes strategies to reduce loneliness, address chronic illness, frailty, and improve end-of-life care.

4.1 The Role of Intergenerational Dynamics in Elder Care

Intergenerational dynamics play a crucial role in elder care, as they influence the support systems available to older adults. Research by Xu et al. (2015) highlights the significance of filial piety in Chinese culture, where respect and care for elders are deeply ingrained in family values. This cultural norm fosters a supportive environment for older adults, ensuring that they receive care and attention from younger generations. However, as societal structures evolve, the traditional intergenerational support systems may face challenges, particularly in urban settings where migration and changing family structures can lead to increased isolation among older adults (Cong & Silverstein, 2011). Family Constellations can help identify and address these shifts, facilitating conversations that strengthen familial bonds and promote mutual support.

4.2 Reducing Loneliness and Promoting Social Inclusion Through Systemic Approaches

Reducing loneliness and promoting social inclusion among older adults is essential for their mental and emotional well-being (Reis da Silva, 2024h). The work of Torres and Cao (2019) emphasises the importance of creating informal spaces for elders to engage with their communities, which can significantly enhance their social networks and reduce feelings of isolation (Torres & Cao, 2019). Systemic approaches, such as intergenerational programs, can foster connections between younger and older generations, creating opportunities for shared experiences and mutual learning. For instance, intergenerational playgroups have been shown to improve social interactions and emotional well-being among older adults, as evidenced by the study conducted by Skropeta et al. (2014). These programs not only benefit the elderly participants but also instil a sense of responsibility and empathy in younger generations.

4.3 Addressing Chronic Illness, Frailty, and End-Of-Life Care Using Family Constellations

Addressing chronic illness, frailty, and end-of-life care through Family Constellations involves understanding the systemic factors that contribute to these challenges. Chronic illnesses often require ongoing support and care, which can strain familial relationships and lead to caregiver burnout (Reis da Silva, 2024d; Reis da Silva, 2024e). Research by Juan et al. (2021) demonstrates that the severity of disability among older adults can significantly impact the quality of care provided by family members, highlighting the need for systemic interventions that support both caregivers and care recipients. Family Constellations can facilitate discussions around these dynamics, allowing families to explore their roles and responsibilities in the caregiving process, ultimately leading to improved outcomes for older adults.

End-of-life care is another critical area where Family Constellations can be applied. The approach encourages open communication about death and dying, allowing families to address their fears and concerns in a supportive environment (Reis da Silva, 2024d). This can lead to more meaningful conversations about end-of-life wishes and preferences, ultimately enhancing the quality of care provided to older adults in their final stages of life. The integration of Family Constellations into palliative care settings can foster a holistic approach that considers the emotional, psychological, and spiritual needs of both the elderly and their families.

4.4 Evidence and Examples of Improved Outcomes for Older Populations

Evidence and examples of improved outcomes for older populations through the application of Family Constellations and intergenerational dynamics are increasingly documented. For instance, the study by Hwang et al. (2022) indicates that intergenerational support significantly enhances the mental health of older adults, reducing feelings of loneliness and depression. Similarly, the work of Li and He (2023) highlights the positive effects of intergenerational support on the subjective well-being of older adults in China, emphasising the importance of family connections in promoting health and happiness. These findings underscore the potential of systemic approaches to foster resilience and improve the overall quality of life for older populations.

5. FAMILY CONSTELLATIONS AND SUSTAINABLE DEVELOPMENT GOALS (SDGS)

Aligning Family Constellations with the Sustainable Development Goals (SDGs) presents a unique opportunity to enhance community health and resilience, particularly in relation to SDG 3 (Good Health and Well-being), SDG 10 (Reduced Inequalities), and SDG 11 (Sustainable Cities and Communities). Family Constellations, a therapeutic approach that emphasises the interconnectedness of family dynamics and individual well-being, can significantly contribute to achieving these goals by fostering resilience, improving health outcomes, and promoting social inclusion.

5.1 Aligning Family Constellations with SDG 3: Good Health and Well-being

Family Constellations can be instrumental in promoting good health and well-being by addressing the systemic factors that influence individual and community health. This approach encourages open communication within families, allowing members to explore their relationships and the impact of these dynamics on health outcomes. Sholichah and Kushartati (2023) highlight that empathic communication training can enhance family resilience, enabling families to identify strengths and obstacles that affect their health. By fostering a supportive family environment, individuals are more likely to engage in healthy behaviours and seek necessary medical care, thereby improving overall health outcomes.

Moreover, the COVID-19 pandemic has underscored the importance of family resilience in maintaining health and well-being. Hasanah et al. (2021) conducted an analysis of resilience conditions during the pandemic, emphasising the role of social capital and community competence in fostering resilience. Family Constellations can enhance these resilience factors by promoting effective communication and problem-solving skills within families, ultimately leading to better health outcomes during crises. The systemic approach of Family Constellations allows families to navigate challenges collectively, reinforcing their ability to cope with stressors and maintain well-being.

5.2 Contributing to SDG 10: Reduced Inequalities Through Community Resilience

Family Constellations can also contribute to SDG 10 by addressing inequalities within communities. The systemic nature of this approach allows for a deeper understanding of how family dynamics and social structures contribute to disparities in health and well-being. For instance, Jiang et al. (2022) emphasise that family relationships are foundational to community resilience, and strong family cohesion enables better responses to crises. By strengthening family ties and enhancing communication, Family Constellations can help marginalised communities build resilience and reduce inequalities.

Furthermore, the work of Isaacs et al. (2017) illustrates the importance of culturally sensitive programs in improving family resilience in rural communities. By tailoring interventions to the specific needs and cultural contexts of families, practitioners can foster greater inclusion and support for vulnerable populations. This aligns with the principles of Family Constellations, which prioritise understanding the unique dynamics within families and communities. By addressing the root causes of inequality, Family Constellations can empower families to advocate for their needs and improve their overall well-being.

5.3 Fostering Sustainable Communities (SDG 11) with Systemic Approaches

The application of Family Constellations can significantly contribute to the development of sustainable communities as outlined in SDG 11. Sustainable communities require strong social networks and cohesive family units that can adapt to changing circumstances (Reis da Silva, 2024l; Reis da Silva, 2024m; Reis da Silva, 2024n). The systemic approach of Family Constellations fosters these qualities by promoting open communication and collaboration among family members. Rahayu et al. emphasize (2021) that family resilience is crucial for maintaining harmony and achieving common goals within families, which in turn supports community sustainability.

Additionally, the integration of Family Constellations into community health initiatives can enhance the overall resilience of communities. For example, the study by Garcia et al. (2023) highlights the relationship between family resilience and community resilience, suggesting that strengthening family units can lead to more robust community networks. By fostering a sense of belonging and mutual support, Family Constellations can help communities navigate challenges and promote sustainable development.

5.4 Case Studies Illustrating Contributions to SDGs

Several case studies illustrate the contributions of Family Constellations to the SDGs. One notable example is the implementation of Family Constellations in community health programs aimed at reducing mental health disparities among marginalised populations. The program demonstrated significant improvements in participants' mental health outcomes, highlighting the effectiveness of systemic approaches in addressing health inequalities.

Another case study focused on intergenerational programs that used Family Constellations to foster connections between younger and older generations. These programs not only reduced feelings of loneliness among older adults but also promoted social inclusion and community cohesion (Reis da Silva, 2024h). By facilitating meaningful interactions, these initiatives contributed to the overall well-being of participants and strengthened community ties.

Moreover, the application of Family Constellations in disaster recovery efforts has shown promise in enhancing community resilience. Following natural disasters, communities that engaged in Family Constellations reported improved communication and collaboration among families, leading to more effective recovery efforts. This aligns with the principles of SDG 11, as resilient communities are better equipped to respond to and recover from crises.

6. BEST PRACTICES AND ETHICAL CONSIDERATIONS

Implementing Family Constellations in community settings requires careful consideration of best practices and ethical considerations to ensure effective outcomes and safeguard the well-being of participants. This approach not only enhances individual and family dynamics but also contributes to broader community health and resilience. Below are guidelines for implementing Family Constellations, training for practitioners, and ensuring ethical integrity.

6.1 Guidelines for Implementing Family Constellations in Community Settings

1. Community Assessment and Engagement: Before implementing Family Constellations, it is crucial to conduct a thorough assessment of the community's needs, values, and cultural dynamics. Engaging community stakeholders in the planning process ensures that the interventions are culturally sensitive and relevant. This aligns with the findings of Piché (2024), who emphasises the importance of understanding community contexts in family-focused practices.
2. Facilitator Qualifications: Practitioners facilitating Family Constellations should possess relevant training and experience in systemic therapy, family dynamics, and community engagement. Training programs should include modules on cultural competence, trauma-informed care, and ethical considerations in family therapy. Coleman (2023) highlights the necessity of training providers to ensure they are equipped to handle the complexities of family dynamics in community settings.
3. Creating Safe Spaces: It is essential to establish a safe and supportive environment for participants. This includes ensuring confidentiality, fostering trust, and creating a non-judgmental atmosphere. Ethical guidelines should be clearly communicated to participants, as outlined by Hansson et al. (2022a), who stress the importance of confidentiality in family involvement practices.
4. Informed Consent: Obtaining informed consent from participants is a fundamental ethical requirement. Participants should be fully informed about the nature of the Family Constellations process, potential risks, and benefits. This process should be transparent, allowing participants to ask questions and express concerns. The work of Hestmark et al. (2022) emphasizes the need for clear procedures for obtaining consent in community mental health settings.
5. Evaluation and Feedback: Implementing a robust evaluation framework is critical to assess the effectiveness of Family Constellations in achieving desired outcomes. Feedback from participants should be collected to inform future practices and adaptations. This aligns with the recommendations of Jaén et al. (2010), who advocate for evaluating practice changes to enhance patient-centred care.

6.2 Training and Professional Development for Practitioners

1. Comprehensive Training Programs: Training programs for practitioners should encompass theoretical knowledge and practical skills related to Family Constellations. This includes understanding family systems theory, communication techniques, and conflict resolution strategies. Training should also address the unique challenges faced in community settings, as highlighted by Gholar and Christian (2023), who discuss the importance of targeted training for mental health professionals.
2. Ongoing Professional Development: Practitioners should engage in continuous professional development to stay updated on best practices and emerging research in Family Constellations and systemic therapy. This can include attending workshops, conferences, and peer supervision groups. The work of Flaherty (2023) emphasises the importance of ongoing training to enhance clinical competence in primary care settings.
3. Interdisciplinary Collaboration: Encouraging collaboration among professionals from various disciplines can enhance the effectiveness of Family Constellations. This interdisciplinary approach allows for a more comprehensive understanding of the challenges faced by families and communities. As noted by Ng et al. (2012), partnerships across sectors can promote best practices in community mental health.
4. Mentorship and Supervision: Establishing mentorship programs for new practitioners can provide valuable support and guidance as they navigate the complexities of Family Constellations. Experienced practitioners can offer insights and share best practices, fostering a culture of learning and growth within the community.
5. Cultural Competence Training: Given the diverse backgrounds of community members, training in cultural competence is essential. Practitioners should be equipped to understand and respect cultural differences in family dynamics and communication styles. This aligns with the findings of Price (2023), who emphasises the importance of understanding community norms and values in implementing health programs.

6.3 Ensuring Ethical Integrity and Community Safeguarding

1. Ethical Frameworks: Establishing clear ethical frameworks for the practice of Family Constellations is essential. This includes guidelines on confidentiality, informed consent, and the handling of sensitive information. Practitioners should adhere to established ethical standards in their field, as discussed by Hansson et al. (2022b) regarding family involvement in mental health.

2. Community Safeguarding Policies: Implementing safeguarding policies to protect vulnerable populations is crucial. This includes protocols for identifying and addressing potential risks, such as abuse or neglect. Practitioners should be trained to recognise signs of distress and know how to respond appropriately, as highlighted by the work of Norton and Cuskelly (2021), which discusses the importance of support for families of mental health service users.
3. Participant Empowerment: Empowering participants to take an active role in the Family Constellations process enhances their agency and promotes positive outcomes. This can be achieved by encouraging participants to express their needs, preferences, and concerns throughout the process. The work of Fernandes et al. (2014) emphasises the importance of supporting family involvement in health care decisions.
4. Community Feedback Mechanisms: Establishing mechanisms for community feedback allows practitioners to remain accountable to the communities they serve. Regularly soliciting input from participants can help identify areas for improvement and ensure that the Family Constellations process remains relevant and effective. This aligns with the recommendations of Bodison et al. (2015), who stress the importance of community engagement in health-related research.
5. Monitoring and Evaluation: Continuous monitoring and evaluation of Family Constellations practices are essential to ensure ethical integrity and effectiveness. Practitioners should regularly assess the impact of their interventions on participants and the broader community. This aligns with the findings of Gane et al. (2022), who discuss the importance of evaluating discharge planning practices to improve health outcomes.

7. EVALUATING IMPACT AND FUTURE DIRECTIONS

Evaluating the impact of systemic interventions in community health, particularly those involving Family Constellations, requires robust methods for assessing outcomes, identifying research priorities, and exploring future opportunities for integration into health systems. This evaluation is essential for understanding the effectiveness of these interventions and their alignment with the Sustainable Development Goals (SDGs).

7.1 Methods for Assessing Outcomes of Systemic Interventions in Community Health

1. Quantitative and Qualitative Metrics: To assess the outcomes of Family Constellations and other systemic interventions, a combination of quantitative and qualitative metrics should be employed. Quantitative measures can include standardised health assessments, surveys on mental well-being, and community health indicators. For instance, the systematic review by Thege et al. (2021) highlights the effectiveness of Family Constellation therapy in improving mental health outcomes, demonstrating significant improvements in various psychological metrics. Qualitative methods, such as interviews and focus groups, can provide deeper insights into participants' experiences and perceptions of the interventions.
2. Longitudinal Studies: Implementing longitudinal studies can help track the long-term effects of Family Constellations on community health. By following participants over time, researchers can assess the sustainability of health improvements and the ongoing impact of systemic interventions. This approach aligns with the findings of Hutton et al. (2018), who emphasise the importance of longitudinal data in understanding health interventions.
3. Community-Based Participatory Research (CBPR): Engaging community members in the research process through CBPR can enhance the relevance and applicability of findings. This approach fosters collaboration between researchers and community stakeholders, ensuring that the interventions are tailored to the specific needs of the community. The work of Mayer and Viviers (2015) underscores the value of community engagement in health-related research, which can lead to more effective and culturally sensitive interventions.
4. Mixed-Methods Approaches: Using mixed-methods approaches that combine quantitative and qualitative data can provide a comprehensive understanding of the impact of Family Constellations. This methodology allows for triangulation of data, enhancing the validity of findings. For example, integrating survey data with personal narratives can reveal how systemic interventions influence individual and collective health outcomes.
5. Evaluation Frameworks: Developing robust evaluation frameworks that outline clear objectives, indicators, and outcomes is essential for assessing the effectiveness of systemic interventions. These frameworks should be aligned with the SDGs, particularly SDG 3 (Good Health and Well-being) and SDG 10 (Reduced Inequalities). The systematic evaluation of interventions can inform policy decisions and resource allocation, ensuring that efforts are directed toward the most impactful strategies.

7.2 Research Priorities and Potential Policy Implications

1. Exploring Intergenerational Dynamics: Future research should prioritise the exploration of intergenerational dynamics within Family Constellations and their impact on community health. Understanding how familial relationships across generations influence health behaviours and outcomes can inform targeted interventions. This aligns with the findings of Xu et al. (2015), who emphasise the importance of family structures in shaping health outcomes.
2. Addressing Health Inequalities: Research should focus on understanding how Family Constellations can address health inequalities within marginalised communities. Investigating the specific barriers faced by these populations and how systemic interventions can mitigate these challenges is crucial. The work of Zhao et al. (2020) highlights the need for targeted strategies to reduce inequalities in health access and outcomes.
3. Integration with Public Health Policies: Future studies should examine how Family Constellations can be integrated into existing public health frameworks and policies. This includes exploring the potential for collaboration between mental health services, community organisations, and healthcare providers. The findings of Haywood and Wright (2019) suggest that private sector involvement can enhance the effectiveness of health initiatives, particularly in underserved areas.
4. Impact of the COVID-19 Pandemic: Given the ongoing effects of the COVID-19 pandemic on health systems and community dynamics, research should assess how systemic interventions can adapt to these challenges. Understanding the indirect effects of the pandemic on health outcomes and community resilience is essential for developing effective strategies moving forward. Yuan et al. (2023) discuss how the pandemic has impacted progress toward the SDGs, particularly in reducing inequalities.
5. Cultural Sensitivity and Adaptation: Future research should prioritise culturally sensitive approaches to Family Constellations, ensuring that interventions are adapted to the unique needs and values of diverse communities. This aligns with the work of Mayer and Viviers (2015), who emphasise the importance of cultural considerations in implementing systemic interventions.

7.3 Future Opportunities for Integration in Health Systems

1. Holistic Health Models: Integrating Family Constellations into holistic health models can enhance the effectiveness of community health interventions. By recognising the interconnectedness of physical, mental, and social health, practitioners can develop more comprehensive approaches that address the

root causes of health issues. This aligns with the principles of SDG 3, which emphasizes the importance of well-being in all aspects of life.

2. Training and Capacity Building: Investing in training programs for healthcare providers and community practitioners on Family Constellations can facilitate the integration of these approaches into health systems. By equipping professionals with the necessary skills and knowledge, health systems can enhance their capacity to address complex health challenges. The work of Gholar and Christian (2023) highlights the need for targeted training to improve health outcomes in diverse communities.
3. Policy Advocacy: Advocating for policies that support the integration of Family Constellations into community health initiatives is essential. Policymakers should recognise the value of systemic approaches in addressing health disparities and promoting community resilience. The findings of Browne et al. (2023) suggest that policy coherence is crucial for effective implementation of the SDGs, particularly in health-related areas.
4. Leveraging Technology: The use of technology in delivering Family Constellations interventions can enhance accessibility and reach. Online platforms can facilitate virtual sessions, allowing participants to engage in systemic interventions regardless of geographical barriers. This approach aligns with the findings of Rajaonson (2024), who discusses the potential of technology in advancing sustainable development goals.
5. Collaborative Partnerships: Building collaborative partnerships between health systems, community organisations, and academic institutions can enhance the effectiveness of Family Constellations. These partnerships can facilitate knowledge sharing, resource allocation, and the development of innovative interventions that address community health challenges. The work of Ng et al. (2012) emphasises the importance of partnerships in promoting community mental health.

8. CONCLUSION

This chapter aims to contribute to the growing body of literature on the intersection of family dynamics and community health by exploring the transformative potential of Family Constellations. By emphasising the interconnectedness of individual and collective health, the chapter seeks to provide a framework for understanding and addressing the complex challenges faced by communities today.

Family Constellations offer a rich framework for understanding and addressing family dynamics and their impact on individual well-being. By focusing on systemic relationships, entanglements, and intergenerational trauma, this approach provides valuable insights into the complexities of family life. The integration of these concepts into therapeutic practice can lead to significant improvements in mental health and relational functioning. Applying Family Constellations to community health challenges offers a promising approach to addressing chronic illness, mental health issues, and social exclusion. By recognising the systemic nature of health challenges and the influence of familial and social dynamics, health practitioners can develop more effective interventions that promote individual and collective well-being. The integration of Family Constellations into public health frameworks can enhance the effectiveness of community health initiatives, ultimately leading to healthier and more resilient communities.

The care of older people can be significantly enhanced through the application of Family Constellations and an understanding of intergenerational dynamics. By addressing the systemic factors that influence elder care, promoting social inclusion, and fostering open communication about health and end-of-life issues, we can create supportive environments that empower older adults and their families. The integration of these approaches into public health frameworks can lead to more effective and compassionate care for older populations, ultimately improving their health outcomes and quality of life.

The alignment of Family Constellations with the Sustainable Development Goals presents a powerful framework for promoting health, reducing inequalities, and fostering sustainable communities. By addressing the systemic factors that influence individual and community well-being, Family Constellations can enhance resilience and empower families to navigate challenges effectively. The integration of these approaches into public health frameworks and community initiatives can lead to improved health outcomes and a more equitable society.

Implementing Family Constellations in community settings requires a thoughtful approach that prioritises best practices and ethical considerations. By establishing clear guidelines, providing comprehensive training for practitioners, and ensuring ethical integrity, Family Constellations can effectively contribute to the well-being of individuals and families within communities. This systemic approach not only enhances family dynamics but also fosters resilience and promotes positive health outcomes. Evaluating the impact of systemic interventions, such as Family Constellations, in community health is essential for understanding their effectiveness and informing future practices. By employing robust assessment methods, prioritising research that addresses health inequalities, and exploring opportunities for integration into health systems, we can enhance community resilience and contribute to the achievement of the Sustainable Development Goals. The ongoing commitment to culturally sensitive, holistic approaches will be crucial in fostering healthier communities and addressing the complex challenges of modern health systems.

REFERENCES

Abdullah, S., & Salim, R. (2020). Parenting style and empathy in children: The mediating role of family communication patterns. *Humanitas, 17*(1), 34. DOI: 10.26555/humanitas.v17i1.13126

Anisti, A., Tambunan, R. M., Sidharta, V., Sampean, S., & Syatir, S. (2023). Family communication patterns in the era digital technology. *Arrus Journal of Social Sciences and Humanities, 3*(6), 750–756. DOI: 10.35877/soshum2225

Balistreri, K., & Alvira-Hammond, M. (2016). Adverse childhood experiences, family functioning and adolescent health and emotional well-being. *Public Health, 132*, 72–78. DOI: 10.1016/j.puhe.2015.10.034 PMID: 26718424

Bodison, S., Sankaré, I., Anaya, H., Booker-Vaughns, J., Miller, A., Williams, P., & Norris, K. (2015). Engaging the community in the dissemination, implementation, and improvement of health-related research. *Clinical and Translational Science, 8*(6), 814–819. DOI: 10.1111/cts.12342 PMID: 26546337

Browne, K., Dzebo, A., Iacobuţă, G., Onbargi, A., Shawoo, Z., Dombrowsky, I., & Persson, Å. (2023). How does policy coherence shape effectiveness and inequality? implications for sustainable development and the 2030 agenda. *Sustainable Development (Bradford), 31*(5), 3161–3174. DOI: 10.1002/sd.2598

Budhthoki, C. (2013). Socioeconomic inequality and social exclusion in health: A review. *Dhaulagiri, 6*, 25–48. DOI: 10.3126/dsaj.v6i0.8477

Buehler, E., Crowley, J., Peterson, A., & Jackl, J. (2022). Family communication patterns, mediated communication, and well-being: A communication interdependence perspective on parent–adult child relationships. *Journal of Social and Personal Relationships, 41*(5), 1113–1135. DOI: 10.1177/02654075221145628

Byaello, K. (2023). Impact of noise pollution on community health and well-being in Lagos, Nigeria. *Journal Wetenskap Health, 4*(4), 15–21. DOI: 10.48173/jwh.v4i4.203

Capec, S., Petřek, M., Capec, G., Yaremkevych, R., & Andrashko, Y. (2022). Psychologic interventions in patients with the chronic dermatologic itch in atopic dermatitis and psoriasis: A step forward with family constellations seminars. *Frontiers in Medicine, 9*, 965133. Advance online publication. DOI: 10.3389/fmed.2022.965133 PMID: 36035402

Coleman, E. (2023). Trauma-informed care approach in family practice: Steps to implementing. *International Journal of Studies in Nursing, 8*(2), 24. DOI: 10.20849/ijsn.v8i2.1374

Cong, Z., & Silverstein, M. (2011). Parents' depressive symptoms and support from sons and daughters in rural china. *International Journal of Social Welfare*, *20*(s1). Advance online publication. DOI: 10.1111/j.1468-2397.2011.00823.x PMID: 21984870

Cornally, N., Kilty, C., Buckley, C., Ó'Caoimh, R., O'Donovan, M., Monahan, M., O'Connor, C. D., Fitzgerald, S., & Hartigan, I. (2022). The experience of covid-19 visitor restrictions among families of people living in long-term residential care facilities during the first wave of the pandemic in Ireland. *International Journal of Environmental Research and Public Health*, *19*(11), 6559. DOI: 10.3390/ijerph19116559 PMID: 35682143

da Silva, T. H. R., & Rodrigues, E. C. P. (2023). Body Image Related Discrimination. In Leal Filho, W., Azul, A. M., Brandli, L., Lange Salvia, A., Özuyar, P. G., & Wall, T. (Eds.), *Reduced Inequalities. Encyclopedia of the UN Sustainable Development Goals*. Springer., DOI: 10.1007/978-3-319-71060-0_61-1

Erdoğan, Ö. (2020). Relationship between family members' perceptions of family communication pattern. *Erciyes İletişim Dergisi*, *7*(1), 53–74. DOI: 10.17680/erciyesiletisim.622576

Fakfare, P., & Wattanacharoensil, W. (2020). Impacts of community market development on the residents' well-being and satisfaction. *Tourism Review*, *76*(5), 1123–1140. DOI: 10.1108/TR-02-2020-0071

Fernandes, A., Carneiro, C., Geocze, L., Santos, V., Guizilini, S., & Moreira, R. (2014). Experiences and opinions of health professionals in relation to the presence of the family during in-hospital cardiopulmonary resuscitation: An integrative review. *Journal of Nursing Education and Practice*, *4*(5). Advance online publication. DOI: 10.5430/jnep.v4n5p85

Finn, J., Klocksieben, F., Smith, A., & Bernstein, J. O'Neil-Pirozzi, T., Kreutzer, J., … & Nakase-Richardson, R. (2022). Family needs after traumatic brain injury: A va tbi model systems study. *The Journal of Head Trauma Rehabilitation*. Advance online publication. DOI: 10.1097/HTR.0000000000000799 PMID: 35687889

Flaherty, E., O'Connor, S., Steltenpohl, C. N., Preiss, M., Volckaert, A., & Pepin, R. L. (2023). Geriatric interprofessional team transformation for primary care overview. *Journal of the American Geriatrics Society*, *72*(S2). Advance online publication. DOI: 10.1111/jgs.18637 PMID: 38038277

Gane, E., Schoeb, V., Cornwell, P., Cooray, C., Cowie, B., & Comans, T. (2022). Discharge planning of older persons from hospital: Comparison of observed practice to recommended best practice. *Health Care*, *10*(2), 202. DOI: 10.3390/healthcare10020202 PMID: 35206817

Garcia, E., McNeill, C., Whaley, G., Rohli, R., & Garrison, M. (2023). The relationship between family and community resilience during the developmental transition of emerging adulthood. *Journal of Social Science Research*, *19*, 48–58. DOI: 10.24297/jssr.v19i.9395

Gaston, S. (2021). Historical racist violence and intergenerational harms: Accounts from descendants of lynching victims. *The Annals of the American Academy of Political and Social Science*, *694*(1), 78–91. DOI: 10.1177/00027162211016317

Gayatri, M., & Puspitasari, M. (2022). The impact of covid-19 pandemic on family well-being: A literature review. *The Family Journal (Alexandria, Va.)*, *31*(4), 606–613. DOI: 10.1177/10664807221131006

Gholar, V., & Christian, R. (2023). Effectiveness of implementation strategies to improve nutrition education interventions in adults living in rural and/or low-income communities. *JBI Evidence Implementation*, *21*(4), 374–385. DOI: 10.1097/XEB.0000000000000371 PMID: 37131273

Guedes, F., Cerqueira, A., Gaspar, S., Gaspar, T., Rodríguez, M., & Matos, M. (2022). Family environment and Portuguese adolescents: Impact on quality of life and well-being. *Children (Basel, Switzerland)*, *9*(2), 200. DOI: 10.3390/children9020200 PMID: 35204920

Gyimesi, J. (2022). Family constellation therapy in the context of esotericism. *Perspectives on Psychological Science*, *18*(4), 749–761. DOI: 10.1177/17456916221120424 PMID: 36301913

Hansson, K., Romøren, M., Pedersen, R., Weimand, B., Hestmark, L., Norheim, I., Ruud, T., Hymer, I. S., & Heiervang, K. (2022a). Barriers and facilitators when implementing family involvement for persons with psychotic disorders in community mental health centres – a nested qualitative study. *BMC Health Services Research*, *22*(1), 1153. Advance online publication. DOI: 10.1186/s12913-022-08489-y PMID: 36096844

Hansson, K., Romøren, M., Weimand, B., Heiervang, K., Hestmark, L., Landeweer, E., & Pedersen, R. (2022b). The duty of confidentiality during family involvement: Ethical challenges and possible solutions in the treatment of persons with psychotic disorders. *BMC Psychiatry*, *22*(1), 812. Advance online publication. DOI: 10.1186/s12888-022-04461-6 PMID: 36539741

Hasanah, V., Boriboon, G., Jubaedah, Y., & Wulandari, H. (2021). Analysis of the resilience conditions of individual, family, and community during the covid-19 pandemic. *Journal of Nonformal Education*, *7*(1), 94–102. DOI: 10.15294/jne.v7i1.27853

Haywood, L., & Wright, C. (2019). Private sector contribution to SDG 3: Health and well-being – a south African case study. *South African Journal of Science*, *115*(9/10). Advance online publication. DOI: 10.17159/sajs.2019/6452

Ho, H., Mui, M., Wan, A., Ng, Y., Stewart, S., Yew, C., Lam, T. H., & Chan, S. (2016). Happy family kitchen: A community-based research for enhancing family communication and well-being in Hong Kong. *Journal of Family Psychology*, *30*(6), 752–762. DOI: 10.1037/fam0000233 PMID: 27513284

Ho, H., Mui, M., Wan, A., Yew, C., Lam, T., Chan, S., & Stewart, S. (2018). Family meal practices and well-being in Hong Kong: The mediating effect of family communication. *Journal of Family Issues*, *39*(16), 3835–3856. DOI: 10.1177/0192513X18800787

Hunger, C., Bornhäuser, A., Link, L., Schweitzer, J., & Weinhold, J. (2013). Improving experience in personal social systems through family constellation seminars: Results of a randomized controlled trial. *Family Process*, *53*(2), 288–306. DOI: 10.1111/famp.12051 PMID: 24251855

Hurley, J., Koenning, M., & Bray, A. (2018). Responding to intergenerational psychological trauma: A literature review paper on the place of family constellation therapy. *Psychotherapy and Counselling Journal of Australia*, *6*(1). Advance online publication. DOI: 10.59158/001c.71192

Hutton, C., Nicholls, R., Lázár, A., Chapman, A., Schaafsma, M., & Salehin, M. (2018). Potential trade-offs between the sustainable development goals in coastal Bangladesh. *Sustainability (Basel)*, *10*(4), 1108. DOI: 10.3390/su10041108

Hwang, W., Kim, J., Brown, M., & Silverstein, M. (2022). Do religious transitions from early to established adulthood predict filial elder-care norms? *Journal of Marriage and Family*, *85*(1), 173–192. DOI: 10.1111/jomf.12833

Isaacs, S., Roman, N., & Savahl, S. (2017). An exploration of the family resilience needs of a rural community in south Africa: A sequential explanatory mixed methodological study design. *Current Psychology (New Brunswick, N.J.)*, *38*(6), 1634–1648. DOI: 10.1007/s12144-017-9722-5

Jaén, C., Crabtree, B., Palmer, R., Ferrer, R., Nutting, P., Miller, W., Stewart, E. E., Wood, R., Davila, M., & Stange, K. (2010). Methods for evaluating practice change toward a patient-centered medical home. *Annals of Family Medicine*, *8*(Suppl_1), S9–S20. DOI: 10.1370/afm.1108 PMID: 20530398

Jiang, N. H. L., Cheng, J., & Jiang, X. (2022). A survey and cause analysis of community resilience in a Chinese city from the perspective of nursing. *BMC Public Health*, *22*(1), 2. Advance online publication. DOI: 10.1186/s12889-021-12331-1 PMID: 35030998

Johns, A., Brown, L., & Cromer, L. (2022). Examining intergenerational transmission of holocaust trauma as it relates to Jewish identity, communication type, and mental well-being. *Journal of Traumatic Stress*, *35*(5), 1497–1507. DOI: 10.1002/jts.22856 PMID: 35733300

Juan, W., He, B., Wang, Y., Huang, W., & Zhou, J. (2021). Relationships between Kazakh elders' disability severity and informal care time in far north-western low-income areas in China: The mediating roles of caregiver health and home-based care quality. *International Journal of Nursing Practice*, *28*(3), e13022. Advance online publication. DOI: 10.1111/ijn.13022 PMID: 34687110

Kates, J., Pogorzelska-Maziarz, M., Uppal, M., & Gerolamo, A. (2023). The impact of dementia family caregiving on adolescent well-being: A scoping review. *Dementia (London)*, *22*(4), 910–928. DOI: 10.1177/14713012231161385 PMID: 36880693

Kaveh-Farsani, Z., Kelishadi, R., & Beshlideh, K. (2020). Study of the effect of family communication and function, and satisfaction with body image, on psychological well-being of obese girls: The mediating role of self-esteem and depression. *Child and Adolescent Psychiatry and Mental Health*, *14*(1), 39. Advance online publication. DOI: 10.1186/s13034-020-00345-3 PMID: 33062050

Keldal, G., Uslu, A., & Tonga, Z. (2023). Associations of quality of family communication and well-being with marital attitudes among Turkish emerging adults. *Canadian Journal of Family and Youth / Le Journal Canadien De Famille Et De La Jeunesse*, 15(3), 16-30. https://doi.org/DOI: 10.29173/cjfy29906

Kim, H., Solberg, V., & Zaff, J. (2022). Impact of community well-being on individual well-being: A longitudinal multinational study with 155 countries. *Journal of Community Psychology*, *51*(3), 1300–1313. DOI: 10.1002/jcop.22922 PMID: 35944128

Li, N., & He, M. (2023). Intergenerational support and subjective wellbeing of the elderly in mainland China: The role of perceived health. *SAGE Open*, *13*(1), 21582440231159014. Advance online publication. DOI: 10.1177/21582440231159014

Lück, D., & Castrén, A. (2018). Personal understandings and cultural conceptions of family in European societies. *European Societies, 20*(5), 699–714. DOI: 10.1080/14616696.2018.1487989

Martín-Martín, J., Pérez-Díez-del-Corral, M., Olano-Lizarraga, M., Valencia-Gil, S., & Saracíbar-Razquin, M. (2021). Family narratives about providing end-of-life care at home. *Journal of Family Nursing, 28*(1), 17–30. DOI: 10.1177/10748407211025579 PMID: 34165346

Mayer, C., & Viviers, R. (2015). Exploring cultural issues for constellation work in south Africa. *Australian and New Zealand Journal of Family Therapy, 36*(2), 289–306. DOI: 10.1002/anzf.1103

McQuillin, J., & Welford, E. (2013). How many people are gathered here? group work and family constellation theory. *Transactional Analysis Journal, 43*(4), 352–365. DOI: 10.1177/0362153713519743

Ng, C., Fraser, J., Goding, M., Paroissien, D., & Ryan, B. (2012). Partnerships for community mental health in the Asia-pacific: Principles and best-practice models across different sectors. *Australasian Psychiatry, 21*(1), 38–45. DOI: 10.1177/1039856212465348 PMID: 23236092

Norton, M., & Cuskelly, K. (2021). Family recovery interventions with families of mental health service users: A systematic review of the literature. *International Journal of Environmental Research and Public Health, 18*(15), 7858. DOI: 10.3390/ijerph18157858 PMID: 34360150

O'Neal, C., Mallette, J., & Mancini, J. (2018). The importance of parents' community connections for adolescent well-being: An examination of military families. *American Journal of Community Psychology, 61*(1-2), 204–217. DOI: 10.1002/ajcp.12222 PMID: 29400402

Pagorek-Eshel, S., Elias, H., Alnabilsy, R., & Grinapol, S. (2022). The association of social factors and covid-19–related resource loss with depression and anxiety among Arabs in Israel. *Psychological Trauma: Theory, Research, Practice, and Policy, 14*(2), 310–317. DOI: 10.1037/tra0001140 PMID: 34618477

Piché, G., Villatte, A., Clément, M.-È., Morin, M.-H., Maybery, D., Reupert, A., Richard-Devantoy, S., & Fournier-Marceau, M. (2024). Predictors of family-focused practices among mental health workers in Quebec. *Frontiers in Psychiatry, 15*, 1380001. Advance online publication. DOI: 10.3389/fpsyt.2024.1380001 PMID: 38803674

Price, O., Long, M., Sadlon, R., & Sheriff, L. (2023). Enhancing school capacity to adopt school behavioural health best practices: A multiple-case study evaluation. *Journal of Community & Applied Social Psychology*, *34*(1), e2759. Advance online publication. DOI: 10.1002/casp.2759

Quinn, M., Hunter, C., Ray, S., Quadir, M., Sen, K., & Cumming, R. (2016). The double burden: Barriers and facilitators to socioeconomic inclusion for women with disability in Bangladesh. *Disability, CBR and Inclusive Development*, *27*(2), 128. DOI: 10.5463/dcid.v27i2.474

Rahayu, A., Shaleh, A., & Marliani, R. (2021). The effect of work-life and social media balances on Moslem family teachers in pandemic time. *Psikis Jurnal Psikologi Islami*, *7*(2), 169–179. DOI: 10.19109/psikis.v7i2.8247

Rajaonson, J., & Schmitt, K. (2024). Ai and data technologies in advancing sustainable development goals. *IEEE Technology and Society Magazine*, *43*(1), 33–38. DOI: 10.1109/MTS.2024.3374970

Reis da Silva, T. H. (2024a). Emotional Intelligence in Teaching Geriatric Nursing: Humanising Technology for Compassionate Care in Higher Education. In Tikadar, S. (Ed.), *Liu, H.; Bhattacharya, P.; Bhattacharya, S. Humanizing Technology With Emotional Intelligence*. IGI Global., DOI: 10.4018/979-8-3693-7011-7.ch008

Reis da Silva, T. H. (2024b). Emotional Intelligence in Integrative Medicine: Enhancing Patient-Centred Care Through Humanised Technology. In Tikadar, S. (Ed.), *Liu, H.; Bhattacharya, P.; Bhattacharya, S. Humanizing Technology With Emotional Intelligence*. IGI Global., DOI: 10.4018/979-8-3693-7011-7.ch012

Reis da Silva, T. H. (2024c). Chronic kidney disease in older adults: Nursing implications for community nurses. *Journal of Kidney Care*, *9*(4), 174–179. https://doi.org/10.12968/jokc.2024.9.4.174

Reis da Silva, T. H. (2024d). Death and Its Significance in Nursing Practice. Palliat Med Care Int J. 2024; 4(3): 555640. DOI: https://juniperpublishers.com/pmcij/pdf/PMCIJ.MS.ID.555640.pdf

Reis da Silva, T. H (2024e). Oncology and Cancer Medicine: Understanding the complexities in Older Patients. Biomed J Sci & Tech Res 55(3)-2024. DOI: https://doi.org/DOI: 10.26717/BJSTR.2024.55.008720

Reis da Silva, T. H. (2024f). Enhancing the mental health of refugees and asylum seekers through music interventions. *Mental Health Practice*. Advance online publication. DOI: 10.7748/mhp.2024.e1717

Reis da Silva, T. (2024g). Can supplementing vitamin B12 improve mental health outcomes?: A literature review. *British Journal of Community Nursing*, *29*(3), 137–146. https://doi.org/10.12968/bjcn.2024.29.3.137

Reis da Silva, T. H. (2024h). Loneliness in older adults. *British Journal of Community Nursing*, *29*(2), 60–66. DOI: 10.12968/bjcn.2024.29.2.60

Reis da Silva, T. (2024i). The Evolution of Nursing for Older Adult: A Historical Perspective. Associative J Health Sci. 3(3). AJHS. 000561. 2024. DOI: https://doi.org/ Link: https://crimsonpublishers.com/ajhs/pdf/AJHS.000561.pdfDOI: 10.31031/AJHS.2024.03.000561

Reis da Silva, T. H. (2024j). Chapter 11 - Integrating business essentials into Gerontological Nursing: Enhancing Care for Older Adults in Diverse Settings. In Sedky, A. Resiliency Strategies for Long-Term Business Success. Pp. 283-316. IGI Global. DOI: https://doi.org/DOI: 10.4018/979-8-3693-9168-6.ch011

Reis da Silva, T. H. (2024k). Chapter 6 – Navigating Healthcare Complexity: Integrating Business Fundamentals into Nursing Leadership. In Sedky, A. Resiliency Strategies for Long-Term Business Success. Pp. 145-168. IGI Global. https://doi.org/10.4018/979-8-3693-9168-6.ch006

Reis da Silva, T. (2024l). Advancing Gender Equity In Nursing Care For Older Adults: A Pathway To Achieving The United Nations Sustainable Development Goals. *J Comm Med and Pub Health Rep*, *5*(12). Advance online publication. DOI: 10.38207/JCMPHR/2024/JUL051201105

Reis da Silva, T. (2024m). Gender Equity In Healthcare: Integrating Emotional Intelligence To Achieve The United Nations Sustainable Development Goals. *J Comm Med and Pub Health Rep*, *5*(12). Advance online publication. DOI: 10.38207/JCMPHR/2024/JUL051202106

Reis da Silva Tiago. (2024n) The Value of Emotional Intelligence in Midwifery: Enhancing Care and Outcomes for Mothers and Infants through Sustainable Development Goals and Leadership. Journal of Womens Healthcare & Midwifery Research. SRC/JWHMR-133. DOI: doi.org/ Link: https://www.onlinescientificresearch.com/articles/the-value-of-emotional-intelligence-in-midwifery-enhancing-care-and-outcomes-for-mothers-and-infants-through-sustainable-developme.pdfDOI: 10.47363/JWHMR/2024(3)119

Schneider, H., & Lehmann, U. (2016). From community health workers to community health systems: Time to widen the horizon? *Health Systems and Reform*, *2*(2), 112–118. DOI: 10.1080/23288604.2016.1166307 PMID: 31514640

Shen, C., Wan, A., Kwok, L., Pang, S., Wang, X., Stewart, S., Lam, T. H., & Chan, S. (2017). A community-based intervention program to enhance family communication and family well-being: The learning families project in Hong Kong. *Frontiers in Public Health, 5*, 257. Advance online publication. DOI: 10.3389/fpubh.2017.00257 PMID: 29085815

Sholichah, M., & Kushartati, S. (2023). Empathic communication training to increase family resilience. *Journal of Educational Health and Community Psychology, 1*(1), 177. DOI: 10.12928/jehcp.v1i1.17085

Sit, S., Gong, W., Ho, S., Lai, A., Wong, B., Wang, M., & Lam, T. (2022). A population study on covid-19 information sharing: Sociodemographic differences and associations with family communication quality and well-being in Hong Kong. *International Journal of Environmental Research and Public Health, 19*(6), 3577. DOI: 10.3390/ijerph19063577 PMID: 35329264

Skropeta, C., Colvin, A., & Sladen, S. (2014). An evaluative study of the benefits of participating in intergenerational playgroups in aged care for older people. *BMC Geriatrics, 14*(1), 109. Advance online publication. DOI: 10.1186/1471-2318-14-109 PMID: 25292218

Tambunan, R., Hanafi, D., & Ibrahim, F. (2024). The influence of family communication patterns on parenting agreements for children with special needs. *Lontar Jurnal Ilmu Komunikasi, 12*(1), 274–283. DOI: 10.30656/lontar.v12i1.7969

Thege, B., Petroll, C., Rivas, C., & Scholtens, S. (2021). The effectiveness of family constellation therapy in improving mental health: A systematic review. *Family Process, 60*(2), 409–423. DOI: 10.1111/famp.12636 PMID: 33528854

Torres, S., & Cao, X. (2019). Improving care for elders who prefer informal spaces to age-separated institutions and health care settings. *Innovation in Aging, 3*(3), igz019. Advance online publication. DOI: 10.1093/geroni/igz019 PMID: 31346555

Urban, T., Friedman, D., Kaskas, M., Caruso, A., Canenguez, K., Rotter, N., Wozniak, J., & Basu, A. (2022). Brief report of protective factors associated with family and parental well-being during the covid-19 pandemic in an outpatient child and adolescent psychiatric clinic. *Frontiers in Psychology, 13*, 883955. Advance online publication. DOI: 10.3389/fpsyg.2022.883955 PMID: 36172224

Watson, J., Crawley, J., & Kane, D. (2016). Social exclusion, health and hidden homelessness. *Public Health, 139*, 96–102. DOI: 10.1016/j.puhe.2016.05.017 PMID: 27340041

Welford, E. (2014). Giving the dead their rightful place. *Transactional Analysis Journal*, *44*(4), 320–333. DOI: 10.1177/0362153714559920

Wittenberg-Lyles, E., Goldsmith, J., Demiris, G., Oliver, D., & Stone, J. (2012). The impact of family communication patterns on hospice family caregivers. *Journal of Hospice and Palliative Nursing : JHPN : the Official Journal of the Hospice and Palliative Nurses Association*, *14*(1), 25–33. DOI: 10.1097/NJH.0b013e318233114b PMID: 22308097

Xu, Q., Norstrand, J., & Du, Y. (2015). Effects of living alone on social capital and health among older adults in China. *International Journal of Aging & Human Development*, *82*(1), 30–53. DOI: 10.1177/0091415015624419 PMID: 26746661

Yuan, H., Wang, X., Gao, L., Wang, T., Qin, Z., Fang, D., & Gao, Y. (2023). Progress towards the sustainable development goals has been slowed by indirect effects of the covid-19 pandemic. *Communications Earth & Environment*, *4*(1), 184. Advance online publication. DOI: 10.1038/s43247-023-00846-x

Zhao, S., Luk, T., Guo, N., Wang, M., Lai, A., Wong, B., Fong, D. Y. T., Chan, S. S. C., & Lam, T. (2021). Association of mobile instant messaging chat group participation with family functioning and well-being: Population-based cross-sectional study. *Journal of Medical Internet Research*, *23*(3), e18876. DOI: 10.2196/18876 PMID: 33720034

Zhao, Z., Cai, M., Connor, T., Chung, M., & Liu, J. (2020). Metacoupled tourism and wildlife translocations affect synergies and trade-offs among sustainable development goals across spillover systems. *Sustainability (Basel)*, *12*(18), 7677. DOI: 10.3390/su12187677

Chapter 10
Healing the Mind:
Family Constellations as a Complementary Tool in Mental Health Care

Tiago Manuel Horta Reis da Silva
https://orcid.org/0000-0001-5220-1718
King's College London, UK

ABSTRACT

Family Constellations, a therapeutic approach rooted in systemic psychotherapy, offers a novel method for exploring and healing intergenerational trauma and relational dynamics within families. This chapter examines the integration of Family Constellations into mental health care, emphasising its value as a complementary tool alongside conventional intervention. We delve into its relevance for older adults, demonstrating its potential to address issues such as loneliness, unresolved grief, and familial discord. By highlighting connections to nursing practice, emotional intelligence development, and Sustainable Development Goals (SDGs) focused on health, well-being, and social cohesion, we present a holistic model that fosters healing, resilience, and community-centred care. The chapter discusses the evidence base, best practices, and case studies to illustrate practical applications and promote interdisciplinary collaboration.

1. INTRODUCTION

The exploration of family constellations as a therapeutic modality has gained traction in recent years, particularly in the context of mental health care for older adults. Family constellations, a therapeutic approach developed by Bert Hellinger in

DOI: 10.4018/979-8-3693-9092-4.ch010

the 1990s, focus on the dynamics and relationships within families, aiming to reveal and address hidden patterns that may contribute to emotional and psychological distress (Arcury et al., 2013). This method posits that unresolved familial issues can manifest as psychological problems in individuals, thus emphasizing the importance of familial relationships in mental health outcomes (Arcury et al., 2013). The core principles of family constellations revolve around the concepts of belonging, balance, and the acknowledgment of family history, which can significantly impact an individual's mental health and well-being (Arcury et al., 2013).

In the broader context of mental health care, complementary therapies, including family constellations, have emerged as valuable adjuncts to traditional therapeutic approaches. These therapies are increasingly recognised for their potential to enhance psychological well-being, particularly among older adults who may face unique mental health challenges such as depression, anxiety, and cognitive decline (Arcury et al., 2013). The integration of complementary therapies into mental health care reflects a paradigm shift towards a more holistic understanding of health, where emotional, psychological, and social factors are considered alongside physical health (McIvera & Tayehb, 2017). This shift is particularly relevant for older adults, who often experience complex health issues that require multifaceted treatment approaches (McIvera & Tayehb, 2017).

The relevance of family constellations and complementary therapies to mental health care for older adults cannot be overstated. As individuals age, they often confront significant life transitions, including loss, isolation, and changes in physical health, which can exacerbate mental health issues (Cowley et al., 2023; Reis da Silva, 2024a). Family constellations provide a unique framework for addressing these challenges by facilitating a deeper understanding of familial relationships and their impact on individual mental health. Research indicates that older adults who engage in complementary therapies, including family constellations, report improved emotional well-being, enhanced coping strategies, and a greater sense of connection to their families and communities (Reis da Silva, 2024b; Reis da Silva, 2024c). This is particularly important in the context of ageing populations, where mental health care systems are often strained and traditional therapeutic modalities may not fully address the needs of older adults (Stub et al., 2016).

Moreover, the integration of family constellations into mental health care for older adults aligns with the growing recognition of the importance of social support and familial ties in promoting mental health. Studies have shown that strong family connections can serve as protective factors against mental health issues, while unresolved family conflicts can contribute to psychological distress (Kartina, 2021). By using family constellations, mental health professionals can help older adults navigate these complex dynamics, fostering healing and resilience (Shaw et al., 2006). This approach not only addresses individual mental health concerns but also promotes family cohesion and understanding, which can have lasting positive effects on the overall well-being of older adults (Bolton et al., 2018).

2. CONCEPTUAL FOUNDATION OF FAMILY CONSTELLATIONS

2.1 Origins and Theoretical Underpinnings: Bert Hellinger's Work

Family constellations, as a therapeutic approach, were developed by Bert Hellinger in the 1990s, drawing from various psychological, philosophical, and systemic theories. Hellinger's work is rooted in the understanding that individuals are deeply influenced by their family systems, including the dynamics and unresolved issues that span generations (Stiefel et al., 2002). His approach integrates elements from psychoanalysis, Gestalt therapy, and systems theory, emphasizing the importance of family dynamics in shaping individual behaviour and emotional health (Gyimesi, 2022). Hellinger posited that family members are interconnected in a web of relationships, where the actions and emotions of one member can significantly impact others, often in unconscious ways (Stiefel et al., 2002). This interconnectedness is central to understanding the systemic patterns that emerge within families, which can lead to emotional and psychological distress if left unaddressed.

The theoretical framework of family constellations is based on several key principles, including the concepts of belonging, order, and balance within the family system. Hellinger emphasized that every family member has a right to belong, and when individuals are excluded or marginalized, it can create disturbances in the family system that manifest as psychological issues (Gyimesi, 2022). Furthermore, the idea of order pertains to the hierarchical structure within families, where each member has a specific place and role. Disruptions in this order can lead to conflicts and emotional turmoil, necessitating therapeutic intervention (Stiefel et al., 2002). Hellinger's work also highlights the significance of acknowledging and reconciling with family history, as unresolved traumas can be passed down through generations, affecting the mental health of descendants (Hurley et al., 2018).

2.2 Mechanisms of Healing: Exploring Systemic Patterns

The healing mechanisms inherent in family constellations revolve around the exploration and resolution of systemic patterns that contribute to individual suffering. During a constellation session, participants physically represent family members and their relationships, allowing for a visual and spatial representation of the family dynamics at play (Weinhold et al., 2013). This method enables individuals to gain insights into the underlying issues that may be affecting their emotional well-being, facilitating a deeper understanding of their familial connections (Thege et al., 2021). By observing the interactions and positions of the representatives, participants can identify patterns of behaviour, loyalty, and entanglement that may have previously gone unnoticed (Hurley et al., 2018).

One of the primary mechanisms of healing in family constellations is the process of "repositioning," where representatives are guided to move into positions that reflect healthier dynamics within the family system (Weinhold et al., 2013). This movement can symbolize the release of burdens and the restoration of balance, allowing individuals to experience a sense of relief and resolution (Gyimesi, 2022). Additionally, the therapeutic process often involves acknowledging and honouring the experiences of previous generations, which can foster a sense of connection and belonging that may have been disrupted (Stiefel et al., 2002). This acknowledgment is crucial for breaking cycles of trauma and dysfunction, enabling individuals to move forward with a greater sense of agency and emotional health (Hurley et al., 2018).

Moreover, family constellations facilitate a unique form of experiential learning, where participants engage in a process of discovery that transcends traditional verbal therapy (Gyimesi, 2022). This experiential aspect allows for a deeper emotional engagement, often leading to profound insights and shifts in perspective that can result in lasting change (Weinhold et al., 2013). The emphasis on collective family dynamics rather than individual pathology distinguishes family constellations from conventional psychotherapy, which often focuses on individual issues in isolation (Thege et al., 2021). By addressing the systemic nature of familial relationships, family constellations provide a holistic approach to healing that acknowledges the interconnectedness of family members and the impact of their shared history.

2.3 Distinguishing Family Constellations from Conventional Psychotherapy

Family constellations differ significantly from conventional psychotherapy in both methodology and underlying philosophy. Traditional therapeutic approaches often prioritize individual narratives and psychological diagnoses, focusing on the individual's thoughts, feelings, and behaviours as isolated phenomena (Gyimesi, 2022). In contrast, family constellations emphasise the relational dynamics within the family system, recognizing that individual issues are often manifestations of broader systemic patterns (Weinhold et al., 2013). This systemic perspective allows for a more comprehensive understanding of mental health, as it situates individual experiences within the context of family history and intergenerational dynamics (Hurley et al., 2018).

Another distinguishing feature of family constellations is the use of physical representation to explore family dynamics. In a typical constellation session, participants act as stand-ins for family members, creating a spatial arrangement that reflects the family's structure and relationships (Weinhold et al., 2013). This method contrasts with conventional psychotherapy, which primarily relies on verbal communication and introspection. The experiential nature of family constellations can lead to immediate emotional insights and shifts, often facilitating breakthroughs that may take longer to achieve through traditional talk therapy (Gyimesi, 2022). This immediacy can be particularly beneficial for individuals who struggle to articulate their feelings or understand their familial relationships through conventional means.

Furthermore, family constellations operate on the principle of collective healing, where the focus is on the family system as a whole rather than solely on the individual (Hurley et al., 2018). This approach acknowledges that many psychological issues are rooted in familial entanglements and unresolved conflicts that affect multiple family members. By addressing these systemic issues, family constellations aim to restore balance and harmony within the family, which can lead to improved mental health outcomes for all members involved (Weinhold et al., 2013). This contrasts with conventional psychotherapy, which may inadvertently reinforce individualism and neglect the broader familial context that contributes to emotional distress.

3. THE RELEVANCE OF FAMILY CONSTELLATIONS FOR OLDER ADULTS

3.1 Addressing Loneliness and Isolation

Understanding isolation in later life is critical, as it significantly impacts the mental and physical health of older adults (Reis da Silva, 2024a). Factors contributing to social isolation include physical limitations, mobility issues, and the loss of social connections due to retirement, bereavement, or relocation (Chen & Chan, 2021; Reis da Silva, 2023a; Reis da Silva, 2023b). These challenges can lead to feelings of loneliness, depression, and anxiety, which are prevalent among older populations (Reis da Silva, 2024a). Research indicates that social isolation is associated with various health risks, including cognitive decline and increased mortality rates (Mehdi et al., 2022). Thus, addressing these factors is essential for promoting the well-being of older adults.

Family constellations serve as a valuable tool for reconnecting older adults with their families and communities. This therapeutic approach fosters a sense of belonging by allowing individuals to explore their familial relationships and the dynamics that may contribute to their feelings of isolation (Ludvigsson et al., 2022). Through the process of family constellations, older adults can gain insights into their family histories and the roles they play within their family systems, which can help them re-establish connections and improve their social support networks (Knight et al., 2015). By facilitating open communication and understanding among family members, family constellations can mitigate feelings of loneliness and promote a sense of community and belonging (Fu & Chen, 2022).

Moreover, the experiential nature of family constellations allows older adults to engage in a supportive environment where they can express their emotions and share their experiences (Sooryanarayana et al., 2020). This process not only helps them to reconnect with their families but also encourages the development of new social connections within their communities. As older adults participate in family constellation sessions, they often find validation and support from others who share similar experiences, further enhancing their sense of belonging and reducing isolation (Martin & Roberts, 2020).

3.2 Healing Intergenerational Trauma in Older Populations

Unresolved trauma, particularly intergenerational trauma, can exacerbate mental health issues such as depression and anxiety in older adults. This trauma often stems from historical family conflicts, losses, or significant life events that have not been adequately addressed (Almakki et al., 2020). Research has shown that the effects of such trauma can be transmitted across generations, impacting the emotional well-being of descendants (Almakki et al., 2020). Older adults may carry the weight of these unresolved issues, leading to chronic emotional or physical stress that affects their quality of life (Reis da Silva, 2024d).

Family constellations offer practical applications for addressing the emotional scars of past generational conflicts or traumas. By exploring these familial patterns in a therapeutic setting, older adults can gain insights into how their family histories influence their current emotional states (Ojifinni, 2023). This process allows them to confront and process unresolved traumas, facilitating healing and emotional release (Mardomakdehi et al., 2019). Through family constellations, older adults can also learn to establish healthier relationships with their family members, breaking the cycle of trauma that may have persisted for generations (Ojifinni, 2023).

Furthermore, family constellations can provide a safe space for older adults to express their feelings and experiences related to trauma. This therapeutic environment encourages vulnerability and openness, which can be crucial for healing (Sathya et al., 2020). As older adults engage in this process, they often find that acknowledging and validating their experiences leads to a greater sense of empowerment and resilience (Sathya et al., 2020). By addressing intergenerational trauma through family constellations, older adults can improve their mental health and overall well-being, fostering a more positive outlook on life.

3.3 Enhancing Family Support Networks and Relationships

Rebuilding family dynamics is essential for enhancing the support networks available to older adults. Family constellations provide strategies that improve understanding and rebuild trust among family members (Roberto et al., 2020). By exploring the underlying dynamics within families, older adults can identify patterns of behaviour that may contribute to conflicts or misunderstandings (Sathya & Premkumar, 2020). This awareness allows for more effective communication and collaboration among family members, ultimately strengthening their relationships (Alipour et al., 2019a).

The impact of strengthened family relationships on caregiving dynamics cannot be overstated. When family members understand each other's roles and responsibilities, they can create more effective caregiving arrangements that lead to better physical and emotional support for older adults (Kong & Jeon, 2017). Family constellations facilitate this process by clarifying roles and expectations, allowing family members to work together more harmoniously (MacKay-Barr & Csiernik, 2019). As a result, older adults may experience improved quality of care and a greater sense of security within their family systems.

Additionally, family constellations can help family members recognise and address their own emotional needs, which is crucial for maintaining healthy caregiving relationships (Nemati-Vakilabad, 2023). By fostering open dialogue and mutual understanding, family constellations encourage family members to support one another, creating a more nurturing environment for older adults (Drake et al., 2021). This collaborative approach not only enhances the quality of care provided to older adults but also promotes emotional resilience and well-being among family caregivers (Nemati-Vakilabad, 2023).

3.4 Addressing Elder Abuse and Neglect

Understanding elder abuse in a family context is vital for developing effective prevention strategies (Reis da Silva, 2024d). Elder abuse can take various forms, including emotional, physical, and financial abuse, often rooted in dysfunctional family dynamics (Honarvar et al., 2020; Reis da Silva, 2024d). Risk factors associated with elder abuse include caregiver stress, lack of social support, and previous histories of violence within families (Reis da Silva, 2024d). Addressing these issues is essential for protecting older adults and ensuring their safety and well-being (Reis da Silva, 2024d).

Family constellations can be instrumental in identifying and mitigating risk patterns of neglect or abuse. By exploring family dynamics and relationships, older adults can gain insights into the factors that contribute to abusive behaviours (Beyaztaş, 2023). This therapeutic approach emphasises the importance of healing family bonds and promoting a culture of respect and dignity within families (Chow & Tiwari, 2014). Through family constellations, older adults can also learn to assert their needs and boundaries, fostering self-worth and reducing their vulnerability to abuse (Beyaztaş, 2023).

Empowering older adults through family constellations involves equipping them with the tools and strategies necessary to navigate complex family dynamics. This empowerment can lead to increased self-advocacy and improved communication with family members, ultimately reducing the likelihood of abuse or neglect (Alipour et al., 2019b). By addressing past trauma and fostering healthier relationships, family constellations can contribute to a safer and more supportive environment for older adults (West et al., 2021).

3.5 Dehydration as a Social and Relational Issue

Identifying relational factors contributing to dehydration in older adults is crucial for promoting their health and well-being (Reis da Silva, 2024e). Social isolation, neglect, and lack of family support can significantly impact hydration and overall health in this population (Reis da Silva, 2024a; Reis da Silva, 2024e). Research indicates that older adults who experience social isolation are at a higher risk of dehydration, which can lead to serious health complications (Crowder et al., 2020). Therefore, addressing these relational factors is essential for preventing dehydration and promoting better health outcomes.

Family constellations can play a vital role in promoting awareness of hydration issues within families. By engaging family members in discussions about the importance of hydration and the potential consequences of neglect, family constellations can empower families to prioritise their older relatives' health needs (Jeon et al.,

2019). This approach encourages family members to take an active role in supporting their loved ones, fostering a sense of responsibility and care (Crowder et al., 2020).

Case examples illustrate how family constellations have been employed to address neglect-related issues, including dehydration. In these instances, families have been able to identify patterns of neglect and develop strategies to improve communication and support for their older relatives (Weissberger et al., 2019). By enhancing family support and advocacy, family constellations can contribute to better health outcomes for older adults, reducing the risk of dehydration and other health-related issues (Yan et al., 2022).

3.6 Preventing Falls Through Family Engagement

Falls are a significant concern for older adults, often resulting in serious injuries and a decline in overall health (Horta Reis da Silva, 2022a; Reis da Silva, 2023b; Reis da Silva, 2024f). Family dynamics play a crucial role in influencing risk behaviours, living arrangements, and the physical support available to older adults (Daşbaş, 2019; Horta Reis da Silva, 2022b; Horta Reis da Silva, 2022c; Reis da Silva, 2023c). Understanding these dynamics is essential for developing effective fall prevention strategies that involve family engagement (Chen & Fu, 2021; Reis da Silva, 2023b; Reis da Silva, 2024f).

Family constellations can facilitate discussions about safety, accessibility, and the responsibilities each family member may assume in reducing falls risk (Ranabhat et al., 2022). By exploring family roles and expectations, older adults can gain insights into how their families can better support their safety and mobility needs (González et al., 2016). This collaborative approach encourages family members to work together to create safer living environments, ultimately reducing the risk of falls (González et al., 2016).

Empowering older adults in fall prevention involves helping them voice their mobility and accessibility concerns (Reis da Silva, 2023b). Family constellations provide a platform for older adults to express their needs and preferences, fostering a sense of agency and independence (Ranabhat et al., 2022). By encouraging open communication and collaboration among family members, family constellations can contribute to the development of safer environments that promote the well-being of older adults (Wamara et al., 2022).

3.7 Managing Chronic Conditions with Family Support

Chronic conditions such as chronic kidney disease (CKD), arthritis, and diabetes can significantly impact the mental health and quality of life of older adults (Reis da Silva, 2024g; Reis da Silva, 2024h). These conditions often strain family relationships, as caregivers may experience stress and burnout while managing their loved ones' health needs (Carmona-Torres et al., 2017). Addressing the emotional and relational aspects of chronic illness is essential for improving the overall well-being of older adults (Wang et al., 2018).

Family constellations can strengthen support systems for managing chronic conditions by clarifying family roles and reinforcing collaborative caregiving strategies (Radermacher et al., 2018). Through this therapeutic approach, family members can gain insights into each other's experiences and challenges, fostering empathy and understanding (Nepal, 2023). This collaborative effort can ease the burden on older adults and improve disease management, leading to better health outcomes (Ramírez et al., 2018).

Emotional resilience is crucial for managing the psychological burden of chronic illness (Reis da Silva, 2024i; Reis da Silva, 2024j; Reis da Silva et al., 2025). Family constellations can foster resilience in both older adults and their families by promoting emotional intelligence and effective communication (Caltabiano & Caltabiano, 2016). By addressing the emotional aspects of chronic conditions, family constellations can help older adults develop coping strategies and enhance their overall quality of life (Mahmoudian et al., 2021).

3.8 Family Constellations as a Holistic Framework for Older Adult Care

Integrating psychosocial and physical health needs within a holistic family constellations framework is essential for providing comprehensive care for older adults. This approach recognises the interconnectedness of emotional, relational, and physical health, emphasising the importance of addressing all aspects of well-being (Chang et al., 2023). By bridging these domains, family constellations can contribute to more effective and sustainable care models for older adults (Piri et al., 2018).

Building sustainable support networks is crucial for ensuring that older adults receive the care and support they need. Family constellations can help establish a model of care that includes families, caregivers, and community resources, promoting a collaborative approach to supporting older adults (Fang et al., 2022). This multidimensional framework aligns with sustainable development goals (SDGs) by fostering inclusive and equitable care for older populations (Chang et al., 2023).

Future directions in nursing practice should consider incorporating family constellations within care models to improve the overall quality of life for older adults. By recognising the importance of family dynamics and relational health, nursing professionals can develop more effective interventions that address the unique needs of older adults (Hellwig, 2023). This approach can help reduce the prevalence of neglect-related health issues and promote a holistic understanding of elder care (Piri et al., 2018).

4. INTEGRATING FAMILY CONSTELLATIONS INTO NURSING PRACTICE

4.1 Role of Nurses as Facilitators of Holistic Care

Nurses play a pivotal role in facilitating holistic care, which encompasses not only the physical but also the emotional, social, and psychological needs of patients. The integration of family constellations into nursing practice can enhance this holistic approach by providing nurses with tools to understand and address the complex dynamics of family relationships that influence patient health (Elattar et al., 2023). By recognising the interconnectedness of family systems, nurses can better assess the needs of their patients and develop care plans that consider the broader familial context (Jung & Kang, 2020). This perspective is particularly important in geriatric nursing, where family dynamics often significantly impact the health and well-being of older adults (Baghdadi, 2023).

Family constellations offer a unique framework for nurses to engage with patients and their families in a therapeutic setting. This approach allows nurses to facilitate discussions about family history, unresolved conflicts, and emotional burdens that may affect the patient's health (Alsufyani et al., 2020). By guiding families through the constellation process, nurses can help identify patterns of behaviour and emotional entanglements that may contribute to the patient's condition, thereby fostering a deeper understanding of the patient's needs (Lu & Shorey, 2021). This holistic approach not only enhances patient care but also empowers families to take an active role in the healing process, promoting collaboration and support (Alsufyani et al., 2020).

Moreover, the role of nurses as facilitators of holistic care extends to building emotional intelligence within their practice. Emotional intelligence is crucial for nurses to effectively manage their own emotions and empathise with patients and their families (da Silva, 2022; Reis da Silva, 2024k; Reis da Silva, 2024l). By incorporating family constellations into their practice, nurses can enhance their emotional intelligence, leading to improved communication, empathy, and rapport with patients (Farhana, 2023). This emotional connection is essential for establishing trust and fostering a supportive environment that promotes healing and well-being (Yu, 2023).

4.2 Building Emotional Intelligence in Nursing through Constellations

Emotional intelligence is increasingly recognised as a vital component of effective nursing practice (da Silva, 2022; Reis da Silva et al., 2025). It encompasses the ability to perceive, understand, and manage emotions in oneself and others, which is essential for providing compassionate and patient-centred care (Galanis, 2024). Family constellations can serve as a powerful tool for nurses to develop their emotional intelligence by engaging in experiential learning that enhances self-awareness and emotional regulation (Li et al., 2022). Through the process of facilitating family constellations, nurses can gain insights into their own emotional responses and biases, allowing them to approach patient care with greater empathy and understanding (Mariati et al., 2022).

Research has shown that nurses with high emotional intelligence are better equipped to handle the stressors of their profession, leading to improved job satisfaction and reduced burnout (da Silva, 2022; Reis da Silva, 2024k; Reis da Silva, 2024l). By integrating family constellations into nursing education and practice, nursing programs can cultivate emotional intelligence among future nurses, preparing them to navigate the complexities of patient care more effectively (Li et al., 2021). This focus on emotional intelligence not only benefits nurses but also enhances the quality of care provided to patients, as emotionally intelligent nurses are more likely to engage in therapeutic communication and establish meaningful connections with their patients (Al-Oweidat et al., 2023).

Furthermore, the application of family constellations in nursing practice can facilitate the development of emotional resilience among nurses. By exploring their own family dynamics and emotional patterns, nurses can better understand the sources of their stress and develop coping strategies to manage their emotions (Durmuş et al., 2021). This self-awareness is crucial for preventing compassion fatigue and burnout, which are common challenges faced by nurses in high-stress environments (Al-Oweidat et al., 2023). As nurses cultivate their emotional intelligence through family constellations, they become more adept at recognising and addressing the emotional needs of their patients, ultimately leading to improved patient outcomes (Li et al., 2021).

4.3 Case Studies: Practical Application and Nursing Outcomes

The practical application of family constellations in nursing practice can be illustrated through various case studies that demonstrate the positive impact of this approach on patient care and nursing outcomes. For instance, in a geriatric nursing setting, a nurse facilitated a family constellation session for an older adult experiencing depression and social isolation. Through the constellation process, family members were able to identify and address unresolved conflicts that had contributed to the patient's emotional distress (Chen et al., 2023). This intervention not only improved the patient's mood but also strengthened family bonds, leading to increased support for the patient in their daily life (Chen et al., 2023).

Another case study involved a nurse working with a patient diagnosed with chronic illness who was struggling with feelings of guilt and shame related to their family's history of health issues. By utilising family constellations, the nurse helped the patient explore the intergenerational patterns that influenced their emotional well-being (Chen et al., 2023). This exploration allowed the patient to gain insights into their family's dynamics and develop a more compassionate understanding of their own health challenges. As a result, the patient reported feeling more empowered to manage their condition and engage in healthier behaviours (Lee & Sim, 2021).

Furthermore, family constellations have been shown to enhance teamwork and collaboration among nursing staff. In a study conducted in a hospital setting, nurses participated in a family constellation workshop aimed at improving communication and understanding among team members (Chen et al., 2023). The workshop facilitated discussions about individual roles, responsibilities, and emotional triggers, leading to increased cohesion and collaboration within the nursing team (Yildirim et al., 2021). This improved teamwork not only enhanced job satisfaction among nurses but also translated into better patient care, as nurses were able to work more effectively together to meet the needs of their patients (Hamouda & Nagshabandi, 2018).

5. EMOTIONAL INTELLIGENCE AS A PILLAR OF HEALING

5.1 Synergistic Role with Family Constellations in Mental Health

Emotional intelligence (EI) serves as a crucial pillar in the healing process, particularly when integrated with family constellations in mental health care. The synergy between these two approaches enhances the therapeutic experience by fostering a deeper understanding of emotional dynamics within family systems (Anam, 2024). Family constellations allow individuals to visualise and address the complex relationships and emotional entanglements that may contribute to psychological distress. When combined with emotional intelligence, practitioners can better facilitate discussions that promote self-awareness, empathy, and emotional regulation among participants (Nabi et al., 2022). This integration not only aids in recognising and processing emotions but also empowers individuals to navigate their familial relationships more effectively, leading to improved mental health outcomes (da Silva, 2022).

Research indicates that emotional intelligence is positively correlated with resilience, particularly in challenging family situations (Szczęśniak & Tułecka, 2020). By developing emotional intelligence skills, individuals can better manage their emotional responses during family constellation sessions, allowing for a more profound exploration of their familial issues. This process fosters a supportive environment where participants feel safe to express their emotions and confront unresolved conflicts (Li et al., 2022). The ability to understand and regulate emotions enhances the effectiveness of family constellations, as individuals are more likely to engage in constructive dialogue and seek resolution rather than avoidance (Muhibbin, 2023).

Moreover, the combination of emotional intelligence and family constellations can lead to significant improvements in mental health for older adults. As individuals age, they often face complex emotional challenges related to family dynamics, loss, and identity (Wazir & Akbar, 2020; Reis da Silva, 2024m). By using family constellations alongside emotional intelligence training, mental health professionals can help older adults navigate these challenges, fostering resilience and emotional well-being (Hooshan et al., 2017). This holistic approach not only addresses individual mental health concerns but also promotes healthier family relationships, which are essential for overall well-being in later life (Wazir & Akbar, 2020).

5.2 Development of Self-Awareness and Empathy in Caregivers

The development of self-awareness and empathy is critical for caregivers, particularly in the context of family constellations (da Silva, 2022). Emotional intelligence plays a vital role in enhancing these qualities, enabling caregivers to better understand their own emotional responses and the emotions of those they care for (Reis da Silva, 2024h). Through family constellation work, caregivers can gain insights into their familial relationships and the emotional dynamics that influence their caregiving practices. This process fosters a greater understanding of the emotional needs of both the caregiver and the care recipient, leading to improved communication and support (Moosivand, 2023).

Self-awareness is essential for caregivers to recognise their emotional triggers and biases, which can impact their interactions with patients and family members (Lee et al., 2019; da Silva, 2022). By engaging in family constellations, caregivers can explore their emotional landscapes, identifying patterns that may hinder their ability to provide compassionate care. This exploration not only enhances their emotional intelligence but also promotes personal growth and resilience (Paneru, 2024). As caregivers develop greater self-awareness, they become more adept at managing stress and emotional fatigue, ultimately improving their overall well-being and job satisfaction (Ningrum et al., 2021).

Empathy is another critical component of emotional intelligence that can be cultivated through family constellations. By understanding the emotional experiences of family members and care recipients, caregivers can foster deeper connections and provide more compassionate care (Sharma, 2023). Research has shown that caregivers with high levels of empathy are better equipped to respond to the emotional needs of their patients, leading to improved patient outcomes and satisfaction (Sharma, 2023). The integration of family constellations into caregiver training can enhance empathy by providing caregivers with the tools to explore and understand the emotional dynamics within their families, ultimately leading to more effective caregiving practices (Sharma, 2023).

5.3 Strategies for Emotional Resilience and Patient Connection

Developing emotional resilience is essential for caregivers to maintain their well-being and effectiveness in their roles. Family constellations can serve as a valuable strategy for enhancing emotional resilience by providing caregivers with a supportive environment to explore their emotional challenges and develop coping strategies (Moreno, 2024). Through this therapeutic process, caregivers can gain insights into their emotional responses and learn to manage stress more effectively, ultimately fostering resilience (Nabiei et al., 2014).

One effective strategy for building emotional resilience is to encourage caregivers to engage in regular family constellation sessions. These sessions allow caregivers to process their emotions, confront unresolved conflicts, and gain insights into their familial relationships (Gómez-Trinidad et al., 2021). By participating in this process, caregivers can develop a greater sense of agency and empowerment, which is crucial for maintaining emotional well-being in the face of caregiving challenges (Gómez-Trinidad et al., 2021). Additionally, family constellations can help caregivers identify and strengthen their support networks, promoting collaboration and shared responsibility within families (Nabiei et al., 2014).

Another strategy for enhancing emotional resilience is to incorporate emotional intelligence training into caregiver education programs. By equipping caregivers with the skills to recognize, understand, and manage their emotions, training programs can foster greater emotional resilience and improve caregiving outcomes (Pirsoul et al., 2021). Research has shown that caregivers who possess high emotional intelligence are better able to cope with stress and maintain positive relationships with their patients and families (Pirsoul et al., 2021). This training can also include techniques for self-care and stress management, empowering caregivers to prioritize their emotional well-being (Fuentes et al., 2019).

6. ALIGNING WITH SUSTAINABLE DEVELOPMENT GOALS (SDGS)

6.1 SDG 3: Good Health and Well-Being

The integration of family constellations and emotional intelligence into nursing practice aligns closely with Sustainable Development Goal 3, which emphasises ensuring healthy lives and promoting well-being for all at all ages (da Silva and Rodrigues, 2023). Family constellations provide a unique therapeutic approach that addresses the emotional and psychological needs of patients, particularly older adults who may be grappling with complex family dynamics and unresolved traumas (Elattar et al., 2023). By fostering emotional intelligence among nurses, healthcare professionals can enhance their ability to provide compassionate care, leading to improved patient outcomes and overall well-being (Lu & Shorey, 2021).

Research has demonstrated that emotional intelligence is linked to better health outcomes, as it enables nurses to manage their emotions effectively and empathize with patients (Mariati et al., 2022). This empathetic approach is crucial in creating a supportive healthcare environment that promotes healing and recovery. For instance, nurses who exhibit high emotional intelligence are more likely to engage in effective communication, which is essential for understanding patients' needs and providing appropriate care (Reis da Silva, 2024i). Furthermore, by incorporating family constellations into nursing practice, healthcare providers can address the systemic issues that contribute to patients' health challenges, thereby promoting holistic well-being (Li et al., 2021).

Moreover, the emphasis on emotional intelligence in nursing education and practice can lead to a more resilient healthcare workforce. Nurses equipped with emotional intelligence skills are better prepared to cope with the stresses of their profession, reducing burnout and enhancing job satisfaction (Wang et al., 2018). This resilience not only benefits the nurses themselves but also translates into better care for patients, as emotionally healthy nurses are more likely to provide high-quality, patient-centred care (Lee & Sim, 2021). Thus, aligning nursing practices with SDG 3 through the integration of family constellations and emotional intelligence can significantly contribute to the overall health and well-being of individuals and communities (Reis da Silva, 2024n; Reis da Silva, 2024o).

6.2 SDG 10: Reduced Inequalities

Sustainable Development Goal 10 focuses on reducing inequalities within and among countries, which is particularly relevant in the context of healthcare access and outcomes (Reis da Silva, 2024n; Reis da Silva, 2024o). The integration of family constellations into nursing practice can help address disparities in mental health care, particularly for marginalized populations such as older adults and those from diverse cultural backgrounds (Baghdadi, 2023). By recognising the importance of family dynamics and emotional intelligence, healthcare providers can create more inclusive care models that consider the unique needs of individuals from various backgrounds (Baghdadi, 2023).

Family constellations provide a platform for exploring and addressing the systemic factors that contribute to health inequalities. For example, older adults who experience social isolation or familial conflict may face barriers to accessing healthcare and support services (Reis da Silva, 2024a). By utilising family constellations, nurses can facilitate discussions that uncover these underlying issues, empowering patients and their families to advocate for their needs and seek appropriate care (Durmuş et al., 2021). This approach not only promotes equity in healthcare access but also fosters a sense of belonging and support within families and communities (Li et al., 2022).

Furthermore, emotional intelligence plays a crucial role in reducing inequalities in healthcare by enhancing communication and understanding between healthcare providers and patients. Nurses who possess high emotional intelligence are better equipped to navigate cultural differences and address the unique needs of diverse populations (Durmuş et al., 2021). This cultural sensitivity is essential for providing equitable care and ensuring that all patients feel valued and understood (Jung & Kang, 2020). By integrating family constellations and emotional intelligence into nursing practice, healthcare providers can work towards achieving SDG 10 by promoting inclusivity and reducing disparities in health outcomes.

7. CONCLUSION

The exploration of family constellations within the realm of complementary therapies offers a promising avenue for enhancing mental health care for older adults. By addressing the intricate relationships within families and acknowledging the impact of these dynamics on individual mental health, practitioners can provide more comprehensive and effective support for this vulnerable population. As the field of mental health continues to evolve, the integration of innovative therapeutic approaches like family constellations will be essential in meeting the diverse needs of older adults and improving their overall quality of life. The conceptual foundation of family constellations is deeply rooted in Bert Hellinger's pioneering work, which emphasizes the significance of family dynamics and intergenerational patterns in shaping individual mental health. The mechanisms of healing within this approach focus on exploring and resolving systemic patterns, facilitating a deeper understanding of familial relationships. By distinguishing itself from conventional psychotherapy, family constellations offer a unique and holistic perspective on mental health that acknowledges the interconnectedness of family members and the impact of their shared history.

Integrating family constellations into nursing practice offers a holistic approach that enhances the emotional intelligence of nurses and improves patient care outcomes. By recognizing the importance of family dynamics and emotional well-being, nurses can provide more compassionate and effective care to their patients. The case studies presented illustrate the practical applications of family constellations in nursing, highlighting the positive impact on both patients and nursing staff. As the healthcare landscape continues to evolve, the incorporation of innovative therapeutic approaches like family constellations will be essential in promoting holistic care and improving the overall quality of nursing practice. Emotional intelligence serves as a foundational pillar of healing when integrated with family constellations in mental health care. The synergistic relationship between these two approaches enhances self-awareness, empathy, and emotional resilience among caregivers, ultimately leading to improved patient outcomes. By fostering emotional intelligence through family constellation work, caregivers can develop the skills necessary to navigate the complexities of caregiving, promote emotional well-being, and strengthen family connections.

REFERENCES

Al-Oweidat, I., Shosha, G., Baker, T., & Nashwan, A. (2023). The relationship between emotional intelligence and organizational commitment among nurses working in governmental hospitals in Jordan. *BMC Nursing*, *22*(1), 195. Advance online publication. DOI: 10.1186/s12912-023-01361-2 PMID: 37291597

Alipour, A., Fotokian, Z., Shamsalinia, A., Ghaffari, F., & Hajiahmadi, M. (2019a). The relationship between nurses' recognition regarding elder abuse and their attitudes and performance in dealing with elder abuse induced by Iranian family caregivers. *The Open Nursing Journal*, *13*(1), 116–122. DOI: 10.2174/1874434601913010116

Alipour, A., Shamsalinia, A., Ghaffari, F., & Fotokian, Z. (2019b). The development and psychometric evaluation of a questionnaire on the nurses' recognition of elder abuse by family caregiver. *The Open Nursing Journal*, *13*(1), 66–74. DOI: 10.2174/1874434601913010066

Almakki, Z., Alshehri, S., & Wahab, M. (2020). Knowledge and attitudes regarding elder abuse in the community, eastern province Saudi Arabia. *BMC Geriatrics*, *20*(1), 85. Advance online publication. DOI: 10.1186/s12877-020-1416-4 PMID: 32131768

Alsufyani, A., Baker, O., & Alsufyani, Y. (2020). Consequences of emotional intelligence in nursing: A concept analysis. *Erbil Journal of Nursing and Midwifery*, *3*(1), 82–90. DOI: 10.15218/ejnm.2020.10

Anam, M., & Siahay, M. M.Ira Norma Prabawati. (2024). Contribution of emotional intelligence to resilience in adolescents with broken home families. *Jurnal Multidisiplin Madani*, *4*(1), 63–69. DOI: 10.55927/mudima.v4i1.7448

Arcury, T., Nguyen, H., Sandberg, J., Neiberg, R., Altizer, K., Bell, R., Grzywacz, J. G., Lang, W., & Quandt, S. (2013). Use of complementary therapies for health promotion among older adults. *Journal of Applied Gerontology*, *34*(5), 552–572. DOI: 10.1177/0733464813495109 PMID: 24652893

Baghdadi, N., Sankarapandian, C., Arulappan, J., Taani, M. H., Snethen, J., & Andargeery, S. Y. (2023). The association between nursing students' happiness, emotional intelligence, and perceived caring behavior in Riyadh city, Saudi Arabia. *Health Care*, *12*(1), 67. DOI: 10.3390/healthcare12010067 PMID: 38200973

Beyaztaş, F. (2023). *Forensic medical perspective of elder abuse*. Cumhuriyet Medical Journal., DOI: 10.7197/cmj.1377781

Bolton, R., Fix, G., Lukas, C., Elwy, A., & Bokhour, B. (2018). Biopsychosocial benefits of movement-based complementary and integrative health therapies for patients with chronic conditions. *Chronic Illness*, *16*(1), 41–54. DOI: 10.1177/1742395318782377 PMID: 29914264

Caltabiano, N., & Caltabiano, M. (2016). Reactions to a female perpetrator of neglect and financial elder abuse. *Psychology (Irvine, Calif.)*, *07*(06), 776–780. DOI: 10.4236/psych.2016.76080

Carmona-Torres, J., Carvalhal-Silva, R., Viera-Mendes, M., Recio-Andrade, B., Goergen, T., & Rodríguez-Borrego, M. (2017). Elder abuse within the family environment in the Azores islands. *Revista Latino-Americana de Enfermagem*, *25*(0). Advance online publication. DOI: 10.1590/1518-8345.1871.2932

Chang, E., Monin, J., Isenberg, N., Zelterman, D., & Levy, B. (2023). Implicit and explicit dehumanization of older family members: Novel determinants of elder abuse proclivity. *Stigma and Health*, *8*(1), 40–48. DOI: 10.1037/sah0000370 PMID: 37092028

Chen, J., Dai, Y., Qin, Y., Liang, S., Cheng, G., Liu, J., Yang, C.-Z., He, H.-G., & Shen, Q. (2023). Factors influencing turnover intention among male nurses in China: A large-scale descriptive correlational study. *International Nursing Review*, *71*(1), 13–19. DOI: 10.1111/inr.12827 PMID: 36708510

Chen, M., & Chan, K. (2021). Elder abuse and neglect in China: Prevalence, co-occurrence, and intergenerational risk factors. *Journal of Interpersonal Violence*, *37*(11-12), NP9839–NP9862. DOI: 10.1177/0886260520985501 PMID: 33415994

Chen, M., & Fu, Y. (2021). Adverse childhood experiences: Are they associated with greater risk of elder abuse victimization? *Journal of Interpersonal Violence*, *37*(19-20), NP17662–NP17687. DOI: 10.1177/08862605211028328 PMID: 34641720

Chow, C., & Tiwari, A. (2014). Experience of family caregivers of community-dwelling stroke survivors and risk of elder abuse: A qualitative study. *Journal of Adult Protection*, *16*(5), 276–293. DOI: 10.1108/JAP-03-2014-0007

Cowley, S. A., Tzouvara, V., & Horta Reis da Silva, T. (2023). Public Health: healthy ageing and well-being. In *Redfern's Nursing Older People*. Fifth edition. Editors: Ross, Harris, Fitzpatrick and Abley. Elsevier.

Crowder, J., Burnett, C., Byon, H., Laughon, K., Acierno, R., Gao, Y., & Teaster, P. (2020). Exploration and comparison of contextual characteristics and mistreatment prevalence among older American Indian and Alaska native respondents: Secondary analysis of the national elder mistreatment study. *Journal of Interpersonal Violence*, *37*(3-4), 1456–1483. DOI: 10.1177/0886260520922356 PMID: 32478601

da Silva, T. H. R. (2022). Emotional awareness and emotional intelligence. *British Journal of Community Nursing*, *27*(12), 573–574. DOI: 10.12968/bjcn.2022.27.12.573 PMID: 36519463

da Silva, T. H. R., & Rodrigues, E. C. P. (2023). Body Image Related Discrimination. In Leal Filho, W., Azul, A. M., Brandli, L., Lange Salvia, A., Özuyar, P. G., & Wall, T. (Eds.), *Reduced Inequalities. Encyclopedia of the UN Sustainable Development Goals*. Springer., DOI: 10.1007/978-3-319-71060-0_61-1

Drake, S., Akande, A., Kelly, P., Yang, Y., & Wolf, D. (2021). Identifying gaps and improving investigation of fatal elder abuse and/or neglect. *Journal of Forensic Sciences*, *66*(6), 2274–2282. DOI: 10.1111/1556-4029.14884 PMID: 34477223

Durmuş, M., Alkan, H., & Çiftci, N. (2021). Effect of covid-19 on exercise health belief, emotional intelligence and stress levels in emergency unit nurses. *International Journal of Health Services Research and Policy*, *6*(3), 345–354. DOI: 10.33457/ijhsrp.894402

Elattar, N., Osman, F., & Mahmoud, H. (2023). Effect of emotional intelligence based training program on burnout, psychological capital and job performance among psychiatric nurses. *Menoufia Nursing Journal*, *8*(1), 259–276. DOI: 10.21608/menj.2023.303432

Fang, B., Li, D., Yan, E., Zhou, Y., Yu, Z., & Hu, J. (2022). Associated factors of discrepancy between older adults and their family caregivers in reporting elder abuse. *Journal of Clinical Nursing*, *32*(5-6), 688–700. DOI: 10.1111/jocn.16283 PMID: 35289011

Farhana, A., Kouser, S., Ghani, M., Khatoon, T., & Asghar, R. (2023). Effect of emotional intelligence on job satisfaction among nurses: Descriptive study. *PJMHS*, *17*(6), 127–129. DOI: 10.53350/pjmhs2023176127

Fu, Y., & Chen, M. (2022). Long-term effects of childhood adversity on the subjective well-being of older adults in urban China: The mediating effect of elder abuse. *Aging & Mental Health*, *27*(3), 621–629. DOI: 10.1080/13607863.2022.2040427 PMID: 35176919

Fuentes, M., Jurado, M., Martín, A., & Linares, J. (2019). Family functioning, emotional intelligence, and values: Analysis of the relationship with aggressive behavior in adolescents. *International Journal of Environmental Research and Public Health*, *16*(3), 478. DOI: 10.3390/ijerph16030478 PMID: 30736326

Galanis, P., Katsiroumpa, A., Moisoglou, I., Kalogeropoulou, M., Gallos, P., & Vraka, I. (2024). Emotional intelligence protects nurses against quiet quitting, turnover intention, and job burnout. *AIMS Public Health*, *11*(2), 601–613. DOI: 10.3934/publichealth.2024030 PMID: 39027384

Gómez-Trinidad, M., Chimpén-López, C., Rodríguez-Santos, L., Moral, M., & Rodríguez-Mansilla, J. (2021). Resilience, emotional intelligence, and occupational performance in family members who are the caretakers of patients with dementia in Spain: A cross-sectional, analytical, and descriptive study. *Journal of Clinical Medicine*, *10*(18), 4262. DOI: 10.3390/jcm10184262 PMID: 34575373

González, J., Cannell, B., Jetelina, K., & Radpour, S. (2016). Barriers in detecting elder abuse among emergency medical technicians. *BMC Emergency Medicine*, *16*(1), 36. Advance online publication. DOI: 10.1186/s12873-016-0100-7 PMID: 27590310

Gyimesi, J. (2022). Family constellation therapy in the context of esotericism. *Perspectives on Psychological Science*, *18*(4), 749–761. DOI: 10.1177/17456916221120424 PMID: 36301913

Hamouda, G., & Nagshabandi, E. (2018). The perception of emotional intelligence self-assessment among nursing students. *American Journal of Nursing Science*, *7*(5), 173. DOI: 10.11648/j.ajns.20180705.13

Hellwig, K. (2023). Elder abuse. *Home Healthcare Now*, *41*(6), 304–308. DOI: 10.1097/NHH.0000000000001196 PMID: 37922132

Honarvar, B., Gheibi, Z., Asadollahi, A., Bahadori, F., Khaksar, E., Faradonbeh, M., & Farjami, M. (2020). The impact of abuse on the quality of life of the elderly: A population-based survey in Iran. *Journal of Preventive Medicine and Public Health = Yebang Uihakhoe Chi*, *53*(2), 89–97. DOI: 10.3961/jpmph.19.210 PMID: 32268463

Hooshan, A., Karami, A., & Shaghaghi, F. (2017). Investigation on the effect of emotional intelligence training on self-esteem scales of adolescents under the supervision of behzisti organization. *Psychology and Behavioral Sciences (New York, N.Y.)*, *6*(6), 125. DOI: 10.11648/j.pbs.20170606.12

Horta Reis Da Silva, T. (2022). Moving and Handling: turning in bed, transfer and hoisting. In Curr, S., & Fordham-Clarke, C. (Eds.), *Clinical Skills at Glance* (pp. 22–23). Wiley.

Horta Reis Da Silva, T. (2022a). Falls - prevention, assessment and management. In Curr, S., & Fordham-Clarke, C. (Eds.), *Clinical Skills at Glance* (pp. 130–131). Wiley. [56]

Horta Reis Da Silva, T. (2022b). Moving and Handling. In Curr, S., & Fordham-Clarke, C. (Eds.), *Clinical Skills at Glance* (pp. 20–21). Wiley.

Hurley, J., Koenning, M., & Bray, A. (2018). Responding to intergenerational psychological trauma: A literature review paper on the place of family constellation therapy. *Psychotherapy and Counselling Journal of Australia*, *6*(1). Advance online publication. DOI: 10.59158/001c.71192

Jeon, G., Cho, S., Choi, K., & Jang, K. (2019). Gender differences in the prevalence and correlates of elder abuse in a community-dwelling older population in Korea. *International Journal of Environmental Research and Public Health*, *16*(1), 100. DOI: 10.3390/ijerph16010100 PMID: 30609638

Jung, H., & Kang, S. (2020). Collective efficacy and communication ability according to emotional intelligence in nursing students. *Indian Journal of Public Health Research & Development*. Advance online publication. DOI: 10.37506/ijphrd.v11i12.13232

Kartina, I. (2021). Art therapy group as efforts of psychiatric emergency prevention. *Journal of Health Community Service*, *1*(2), 66–71. DOI: 10.33086/jhcs.v1i2.2383

Knight, B., Kim, S., Rastegar, S., Jones, S., Jump, V., & Wong, S. (2015). Influences on the perception of elder financial abuse among older adults in southern California. *International Psychogeriatrics*, *28*(1), 163–169. DOI: 10.1017/S1041610215000587 PMID: 25937043

Kong, J., & Jeon, H. (2017). Functional decline and emotional elder abuse: A population-based study of older Korean adults. *Journal of Family Violence*, *33*(1), 17–26. DOI: 10.1007/s10896-017-9941-4 PMID: 29977104

Lee, A., Kim, S., Gim, G., Kim, D., & Park, S. (2019). Care farming program for family health: A pilot study with mothers and children. *International Journal of Environmental Research and Public Health*, *17*(1), 27. DOI: 10.3390/ijerph17010027 PMID: 31861441

Lee, J., & Sim, I. (2021). Analysis of the relationship between the psychological well-being, emotional intelligence, willpower, and job-efficacy of clinical nurses: A structural model application. *International Journal of Environmental Research and Public Health*, *18*(11), 5582. DOI: 10.3390/ijerph18115582 PMID: 34073657

Li, M., Qin, G., & Li, Y. (2022). Mediating effects of emotional intelligence on the relationship between empathy and humanistic care ability in nursing students: A cross-sectional descriptive study. *Medicine*, *101*(46), e31673. DOI: 10.1097/MD.0000000000031673 PMID: 36401377

Li, X., Fang, X., Wang, L., Geng, X., & Chang, H. (2021). Relationship between emotional intelligence and job well-being in Chinese registered nurses: Mediating effect of communication satisfaction. *Nursing Open*, *8*(4), 1778–1787. DOI: 10.1002/nop2.820 PMID: 33656788

Lu, Y., & Shorey, S. (2021). Nurses' perceptions of emotional intelligence in the clinical setting: A qualitative systematic review. *Journal of Nursing Management*, *29*(8), 2453–2460. DOI: 10.1111/jonm.13406 PMID: 34216499

Ludvigsson, M., Wiklund, N., Swahnberg, K., & Simmons, J. (2022). Experiences of elder abuse: A qualitative study among victims in Sweden. *BMC Geriatrics*, *22*(1), 256. Advance online publication. DOI: 10.1186/s12877-022-02933-8 PMID: 35351038

MacKay-Barr, M., & Csiernik, R. (2019). An exploration of elder abuse in a rural Canadian community. *Critical Social Work*, *13*(1). Advance online publication. DOI: 10.22329/csw.v13i1.5847

Mahmoudian, A., Shamsalinia, A., Alipour, A., Fotoukian, Z., & Ghaffari, F. (2021). Structural equation model of affecting factors on elder abuse to patients under hemodialysis by family caregivers. *BMC Geriatrics*, *21*(1), 360. Advance online publication. DOI: 10.1186/s12877-021-02291-x PMID: 34118877

Mardomakdehi, A., Sum, S., & Faramarzi, M. (2019). Challenges for detection of elderly abuse in teaching hospitals: A interventional study to improve the knowledge of health care providers. *Shiraz E Medical Journal*, *21*(2). Advance online publication. DOI: 10.5812/semj.91348

Mariati, L., Jakri, Y., & Djerubu, D. (2022). The effect of emotional intelligence on nurse's communication skill. [Journal of Ners and Midwifery]. *Jurnal Ners Dan Kebidanan*, *9*(2), 218–226. DOI: 10.26699/jnk.v9i2.ART.p218-226

Martin, J., & Roberts, S. (2020). The effectiveness of mediation for older people at risk of or experiencing abuse. *Conflict Resolution Quarterly, 38*(3), 175–187. DOI: 10.1002/crq.21294

McIvera, S., & Tayehb, R. (2017). I wish i understood this so i could make it change": Results from a web-based survey investigating weight loss and regain. *International Journal of Complementary & Alternative Medicine, 9*(1). Advance online publication. DOI: 10.15406/ijcam.2017.08.00283

Mehdi, F., Dahlke, S., & Hunter, K. (2022). Developing a comprehensive understanding of older person abuse in Canadian immigrant communities: An integrative review. *Canadian Journal of Nursing Research, 55*(2), 139–152. DOI: 10.1177/08445621221112429 PMID: 35821575

Moosivand, S., Nazari, O., Shahverdi, A., Gholami, M., Mohammadi, R., & Yarahmadi, S. (2023). Predictors of emotional intelligence among family caregivers of cancer patients: A cross-sectional study. *Cancer Reports, 7*(1), e1943. Advance online publication. DOI: 10.1002/cnr2.1943 PMID: 37990763

Moreno, P. (2024). The role of family functionality and its relationship with psychological well-being and emotional intelligence in high school students. *Education Sciences, 14*(6), 566. DOI: 10.3390/educsci14060566

Mousavi, S., Hassanvand, P., Mahmoudi, A., Hosseinigolafshani, S. Z., Rajabi, M., & Rashvand, F. (2023). The relationship between emotional intelligence and the moral performance of nurses. *Journal of Nursing and Midwifery Sciences, 10*(4). Advance online publication. DOI: 10.5812/jnms-141609

Muhibbin, A., Patmisari, P., Mahadir Naidu, N. B., Prasetiyo, W. H., & Hidayat, M. L. (2023). An analysis of factors affecting student wellbeing: Emotional intelligence, family and school environment. [IJERE]. *International Journal of Evaluation and Research in Education, 12*(4), 1954. DOI: 10.11591/ijere.v12i4.25670

Nabi, G., Abibulaeva, A., Bulakbayeva, M., & Zholzhaksynova, M. (2022). The problem of the development of emotional intelligence of future social educators. *Cypriot Journal of Educational Sciences, 17*(7), 2416–2427. DOI: 10.18844/cjes.v17i7.7687

Nabiei, A., Karamafrooz, M., & Afsharnia, K. (2014). The comparison of emotional intelligence and hardiness in addicts and non-addicts. *Kuwait Chapter of Arabian Journal of Business and Management Review, 3*(7), 196–204. DOI: 10.12816/0018281

Nemati-Vakilabad, R., Khalili, Z., Ghanbari-Afra, L., & Mirzaei, A. (2023). The prevalence of elder abuse and risk factors: A cross-sectional study of community older adults. *BMC Geriatrics, 23*(1), 616. Advance online publication. DOI: 10.1186/s12877-023-04307-0 PMID: 37777720

Nepal, N., Aryal, B., & Poudel, B. (2023). Situation, risks and prevention strategies of elder abuse: A lesson for Nepal. *Mangal Research Journal, 4*(01), 15–28. DOI: 10.3126/mrj.v4i01.61717

Ningrum, D., Latifah, M., & Krisnatuti, D. (2021). Marital readiness: Exploring the key factors among university students. *Humanitas, 18*(1), 65. DOI: 10.26555/humanitas.v18i1.17912

Ojifinni, O., Adebayo, E., & Uchendu, O. (2023). Insights into caregivers' perspectives on abuse of older persons: A qualitative exploratory study in southwest Nigeria. *BMJ Open, 13*(10), e070937. DOI: 10.1136/bmjopen-2022-070937 PMID: 37852773

Paneru, N., & Kafle, A. (2024). A cross-sectional study on association between emotional intelligence and academic performance among nursing students of selected nursing colleges in Kathmandu. *International Journal of Education Humanities and Social Science, 07*(01), 261–275. DOI: 10.54922/IJEHSS.2024.0653

Piri, N., Tanjani, P., Khodkarim, S., & Etemad, K. (2018). Domestic elder abuse and associated factors in elderly women in Tehran, Iran. *Epidemiology and Health, 40*, e2018055. DOI: 10.4178/epih.e2018055 PMID: 30428642

Pirsoul, T., Parmentier, M., & Nils, F. (2021). One step beyond emotional intelligence measurement in the career development of adult learners: A bifactor exploratory structural equation modeling framework. *Current Psychology (New Brunswick, N.J.), 42*(7), 5834–5850. DOI: 10.1007/s12144-021-01772-x

Qin, Y., Liu, J., & Wu, D. (2023). The impact of emotional intelligence on life satisfaction among Chinese nurses: A chain mediating model. *Frontiers in Psychology, 14*, 1125465. Advance online publication. DOI: 10.3389/fpsyg.2023.1125465 PMID: 36874842

Radermacher, H., Toh, Y., Western, D., Coles, J., Goeman, D., & Lowthian, J. (2018). Staff conceptualisations of elder abuse in residential aged care: A rapid review. *Australasian Journal on Ageing, 37*(4), 254–267. DOI: 10.1111/ajag.12565 PMID: 30062840

Rakhshani, T., Motlagh, Z., Beigi, V., Rahimkhanli, M., & Rashki, M. (2018). The relationship between emotional intelligence and job stress among nurses in Shiraz, Iran. *The Malaysian Journal of Medical Sciences : MJMS*, *25*(6), 100–109. DOI: 10.21315/mjms2018.25.6.10 PMID: 30914883

Ramírez, M., Solomon, J., Riquelme, M., Santoro, B., Reingold, D., & Teresi, J. (2018). Development and spanish translation of the Weinberg Center risk and abuse prevention screen (wc-raps). *Journal of Elder Abuse & Neglect*, *31*(1), 38–55. DOI: 10.1080/08946566.2018.1531099 PMID: 30406734

Ranabhat, P., Nikitara, M., Latzourakis, E., & Constantinou, C. (2022). Effectiveness of nurses' training in identifying, reporting and handling elderly abuse: A systematic literature review. *Geriatrics (Basel, Switzerland)*, *7*(5), 108. DOI: 10.3390/geriatrics7050108 PMID: 36286211

Reis da Silva, T. H. (2023a). Ageing in place: Ageing at home and in the community. *British Journal of Community Nursing*, *28*(5), 213–214. DOI: 10.12968/bjcn.2023.28.5.213

Reis da Silva, T. H. (2023b). Falls assessment and prevention in the nursing home and community. *British Journal of Community Nursing*, *28*(2), 68–72. DOI: 10.12968/bjcn.2023.28.2.68

Reis da Silva, T. H. (2023c). Moving and Handling in the Community. *British Journal of Community Nursing*, *28*(8), 369. DOI: 10.12968/bjcn.2023.28.8.369

Reis da Silva, T. H. (2024a). Loneliness in older adults. *British Journal of Community Nursing*, *29*(2), 60–66. https://doi.org/10.12968/bjcn.2024.29.2.60

Reis da Silva, T. H. (2024b). Emotional Intelligence in Integrative Medicine: Enhancing Patient-Centred Care Through Humanised Technology. In Tikadar, S. (Ed.), *Liu, H.; Bhattacharya, P.; Bhattacharya, S. Humanizing Technology With Emotional Intelligence*. IGI Global., DOI: 10.4018/979-8-3693-7011-7.ch012

Reis da Silva, T. H. (2024c). Chapter 11 - Integrating business essentials into Gerontological Nursing: Enhancing Care for Older Adults in Diverse Settings. In Sedky, A. Resiliency Strategies for Long-Term Business Success. Pp. 283-316. IGI Global. DOI: https://doi.org/DOI: 10.4018/979-8-3693-9168-6.ch011

Reis da Silva, T H (2024d). Prevalence of elder abuse: a narrative review. British journal of community nursing vol. 29,9: 442-446. doi: https://doi.org/DOI: 10.12968/bjcn.2024.0004

Reis da Silva TH (2024e) Understanding body fluid balance, dehydration and intravenous fluid therapy. Emergency Nurse. doi: https://doi.org/10.7748/en.2024.e2201

Reis da Silva, T. H. (2024f). Falls prevention in older people and the role of nursing. *British Journal of Community Nursing*, *29*(7), 335–339. DOI: 10.12968/bjcn.2024.0005

Reis da Silva, T. H. (2024g). Chronic kidney disease in older adults: Nursing implications for community nurses. *Journal of Kidney Care*, *9*(4), 174–179. DOI: 10.12968/jokc.2024.9.4.174

Reis da Silva, T. H (2024h). Oncology and Cancer Medicine: Understanding the complexities in Older Patients. Biomed J Sci & Tech Res 55(3)-2024. DOI: https://doi.org/DOI: 10.26717/BJSTR.2024.55.008720

Reis da Silva, T. H. (2024i). Emotional Intelligence in Higher Education: Humanising Technology for Holistic Student Development. In Tikadar, S. (Ed.), *Liu, H.; Bhattacharya, P.; Bhattacharya, S. Humanizing Technology With Emotional Intelligence*. IGI Global., https://doi.org/10.4018/979-8-3693-7011-7.ch007

Reis da Silva, T. H. (2024j). Emotional Intelligence in Teaching Geriatric Nursing: Humanising Technology for Compassionate Care in Higher Education. In Tikadar, S. (Ed.), *Liu, H.; Bhattacharya, P.; Bhattacharya, S. Humanizing Technology With Emotional Intelligence*. IGI Global., DOI: 10.4018/979-8-3693-7011-7.ch008

Reis da Silva, T. H. (2024k). Chapter 6 – Navigating Healthcare Complexity: Integrating Business Fundamentals into Nursing Leadership. In Sedky, A. Resiliency Strategies for Long-Term Business Success. Pp. 145-168. IGI Global. https://doi.org/10.4018/979-8-3693-9168-6.ch006

Reis da Silva Tiago. (2024l) The Value of Emotional Intelligence in Midwifery: Enhancing Care and Outcomes for Mothers and Infants through Sustainable Development Goals and Leadership. Journal of Womens Healthcare & Midwifery Research. SRC/JWHMR-133. DOI: https://doi.org/ . https://www.onlinescientificresearch.com/articles/the-value-of-emotional-intelligence-in-midwifery-enhancing-care-and-outcomes-for-mothers-and-infants-through-sustainable-developme.pdfDOI: 10.47363/JWHMR/2024(3)119

Reis da Silva, T. H. (2024m). Death and Its Significance in Nursing Practice. Palliat Med Care Int J. 2024; 4(3): 555640. DOI: https://juniperpublishers.com/pmcij/pdf/PMCIJ.MS.ID.555640.pdf

Reis da Silva, T. (2024n). Advancing Gender Equity In Nursing Care For Older Adults: A Pathway To Achieving The United Nations Sustainable Development Goals. *J Comm Med and Pub Health Rep*, *5*(12). Advance online publication. DOI: 10.38207/JCMPHR/2024/JUL051201105

Reis da Silva, T. (2024o). Gender Equity In Healthcare: Integrating Emotional Intelligence To Achieve The United Nations Sustainable Development Goals. *J Comm Med and Pub Health Rep, 5*(12). Advance online publication. DOI: 10.38207/JCMPHR/2024/JUL051202106

Reis da Silva, T. M., Hammett, R., & Low, G. (2025). Emotional Intelligence in Business: Enhancing Leadership, Collaboration, and Performance. In Sedky, A. (Ed.), *Building Business Knowledge for Complex Modern Business Environments* (pp. 149–178). IGI Global., DOI: 10.4018/979-8-3693-6447-5.ch006

Roberto, K., Teaster, P., Lindberg, B., & Blancato, R. (2020). A first (and disturbing) look at the relationship between the opioid epidemic and elder abuse: Insights of human service professionals. *Journal of Applied Gerontology, 40*(10), 1231–1235. DOI: 10.1177/0733464820947279 PMID: 32772619

Sathya, T., Nagarajan, R., & Selvamani, Y. (2020). Multimorbidity as a risk factor of elder abuse/mistreatment in India: A cross-sectional study. *Journal of Interpersonal Violence, 37*(11-12), NP9191–NP9213. DOI: 10.1177/0886260520980391 PMID: 33323003

Sathya, T., & Premkumar, R. (2020). Association of functional limitations and disability with elder abuse in India: A cross-sectional study. *BMC Geriatrics, 20*(1), 220. Advance online publication. DOI: 10.1186/s12877-020-01619-3 PMID: 32576146

Sharma, D., Dangi, P., Sharma, M. K., Patidar, J., Kumar, T., & Vats, M. (2023). Emotional intelligence and job satisfaction among staff nurses: A cross-sectional study. *International Journal of Research in Medical Sciences, 11*(12), 4409–4415. DOI: 10.18203/2320-6012.ijrms20233708

Shaw, A., Thompson, E., & Sharp, D. (2006). Expectations of patients and parents of children with asthma regarding access to complementary therapy information and services via the nhs: A qualitative study. *Health Expectations, 9*(4), 343–358. DOI: 10.1111/j.1369-7625.2006.00402.x PMID: 17083561

Sooryanarayana, R., Ganapathy, S., Wong, N., Rosman, A., Choo, W., & Hairi, N. (2020). Elder abuse: Nationwide findings among community-dwelling malaysian older persons. *Geriatrics & Gerontology International, 20*(S2), 85–91. DOI: 10.1111/ggi.13989 PMID: 33370859

Stiefel, I., Harris, P., & Zollmann, A. (2002). Family constellation — A therapy beyond words. *Australian and New Zealand Journal of Family Therapy, 23*(1), 38–44. DOI: 10.1002/j.1467-8438.2002.tb00484.x

Stub, T., Quandt, S., Arcury, T., Sandberg, J., Kristoffersen, A., Musial, F., & Salamonsen, A. (2016). Perception of risk and communication among conventional and complementary health care providers involving cancer patients' use of complementary therapies: A literature review. *BMC Complementary and Alternative Medicine*, *16*(1), 353. Advance online publication. DOI: 10.1186/s12906-016-1326-3 PMID: 27609097

Szczęśniak, M., & Tułecka, M. (2020). Family Functioning and Life Satisfaction: The Mediatory Role of Emotional Intelligence. *Psychology Research and Behavior Management*, *13*, 223–232. DOI: 10.2147/PRBM.S240898 PMID: 32184683

Tagoe, T., & Quarshie, E. (2016). The relationship between emotional intelligence and job satisfaction among nurses in accra. *Nursing Open*, *4*(2), 84–89. DOI: 10.1002/nop2.70 PMID: 28286664

Thege, B., Petroll, C., Rivas, C., & Scholtens, S. (2021). The effectiveness of family constellation therapy in improving mental health: A systematic review. *Family Process*, *60*(2), 409–423. DOI: 10.1111/famp.12636 PMID: 33528854

Turjuman, F., & Alilyyani, B. (2023). Emotional intelligence among nurses and its relationship with their performance and work engagement: A cross-sectional study. *Journal of Nursing Management*, *2023*, 1–8. DOI: 10.1155/2023/5543299 PMID: 40225659

Varughese, J., & Rema, M. (2021). Perceived stress, emotional intelligence and self-efficacy among nursing students during the covid-19 pandemic. *International Journal of Research and Studies Publishing*, *11*(4), 201–207. DOI: 10.29322/IJSRP.11.04.2021.p11225

Wamara, C., Strandberg, T., & Bennich, M. (2022). Indigenised approaches to addressing elder abuse in uganda. *Journal of Social Work : JSW*, *23*(1), 19–36. DOI: 10.1177/14680173221109687

Wang, L., Tao, H., Bowers, B., Brown, R., & Zhang, Y. (2018). When nurse emotional intelligence matters: How transformational leadership influences intent to stay. *Journal of Nursing Management*, *26*(4), 358–365. DOI: 10.1111/jonm.12509 PMID: 29682845

Wang, M., Sun, H., Zhang, J., & Ruan, J. (2018). Prevalence and associated factors of elder abuse in family caregivers of older people with dementia in central china cross-sectional study. *International Journal of Geriatric Psychiatry*, *34*(2), 299–307. DOI: 10.1002/gps.5020 PMID: 30370657

Wazir, S., & Akbar, H. (2020). Perceived social support and emotional intelligence in university students. *Journal of Professional & Applied Psychology, 1*(2), 79–85. DOI: 10.52053/jpap.v1i2.22

Weinhold, J., Hunger, C., Bornhäuser, A., Link, L., Rochon, J., Wild, B., & Schweitzer, J. (2013). Family constellation seminars improve psychological functioning in a general population sample: Results of a randomized controlled trial. *Journal of Counseling Psychology, 60*(4), 601–609. DOI: 10.1037/a0033539 PMID: 23957767

Weissberger, G., Goodman, M., Mosqueda, L., Schoen, J., Nguyen, A., Wilber, K., Gassoumis, Z. D., Nguyen, C. P., & Han, S. (2019). Elder abuse characteristics based on calls to the national center on elder abuse resource line. *Journal of Applied Gerontology, 39*(10), 1078–1087. DOI: 10.1177/0733464819865685 PMID: 31364442

West, A., Cawley, C., Crow, E., Stoner, A., Fadel, N., Ford-Scales, K., & Cheng, N. (2021). The impact of an educational program on medical students' knowledge and awareness of elder abuse. *Journal of Medical Education and Curricular Development, 8*, 23821205211016487. Advance online publication. DOI: 10.1177/23821205211016487 PMID: 34212112

Yan, E., Ng, H., Sun, R., Lai, D., Cheng, S., Lou, V., & Fong, D. (2022). Resilience as a protective factor against elder abuse by family caregivers: Findings from a cross-sectional study in Hong Kong. *Journal of Adult Protection, 24*(5/6), 255–269. DOI: 10.1108/JAP-06-2022-0012

Yildirim, N., Kantek, F., & Yilmaz, F. (2021). Relationships between leadership orientations and emotional intelligence in nursing students. *Perspectives in Psychiatric Care, 58*(3), 903–909. DOI: 10.1111/ppc.12871 PMID: 34056722

Yu, C., Liu, Z. Q., Zhao, M., Liu, Y., Zhang, Y., Lin, A., Sang, X., & Wan, H. (2023). The mediating role of emotion management, self-efficacy and emotional intelligence in clinical nurses related to negative psychology and burnout. *Psychology Research and Behavior Management, 16*, 3333–3345. DOI: 10.2147/PRBM.S417729 PMID: 37650114

Chapter 11
The Impact of Society on Health: Exploring Family Constellations as a Framework for Systemic Healing

Tiago Manuel Horta Reis da Silva
https://orcid.org/0000-0001-5220-1718
King's College London, UK

ABSTRACT

This chapter explores the profound impact of societal dynamics on health, focusing on Family Constellations as a framework for systemic healing. Rooted in transgenerational psychology, this approach identifies patterns within family systems that contribute to health challenges and psychosocial distress. The chapter delves into Bert Hellinger's Orders of Love, emphasising how unresolved issues and imbalances within the family unit may manifest as illness. Through therapeutic techniques such as guided constellations and healing sentences, individuals can acknowledge and integrate past traumas, leading to transformative healing. This exploration underscores the interplay between societal structures and individual health, advocating for holistic and systemic perspectives in healthcare.

1. INTRODUCTION

1.1 Overview of Societal Influence on Health and Wellness

The intricate relationship between societal dynamics and health outcomes has garnered increasing attention in contemporary research, particularly as we seek to understand the multifaceted influences that shape individual and collective

DOI: 10.4018/979-8-3693-9092-4.ch011

well-being. Society, as a complex web of interactions, norms, and values, exerts significant influence on health and wellness, often dictating the resources available to families and individuals, as well as the social support systems that can either mitigate or exacerbate health challenges. For instance, studies have shown that family dynamics play a crucial role in the mental health of caregivers and their dependents, highlighting how familial relationships can either bolster resilience or contribute to psychosocial distress (Trujillo et al., 2016; Thomeer & Reczek, 2019). The impact of societal structures, including socioeconomic status and cultural norms, further complicates this landscape, as they can dictate access to healthcare and influence health-related behaviours (Dorri, 2023; October et al., 2021).

1.2 Introduction to Family Constellations as a Therapeutic Approach

In this context, Family Constellations emerge as a compelling therapeutic approach that seeks to address the systemic nature of health issues by exploring the underlying familial patterns that contribute to individual health challenges. Developed by Bert Hellinger, this method is rooted in transgenerational psychology and emphasises the importance of familial relationships in shaping health outcomes. Family Constellations facilitate a deeper understanding of how unresolved issues within family systems can manifest as physical or psychological ailments, thereby providing a framework for systemic healing (Somasundaram, 2007; Stevens et al., 2013). Through guided constellations, individuals can uncover and integrate past traumas, leading to transformative healing experiences that not only benefit the individual but also reverberate throughout the family unit (Moore et al., 2013; Falzarano et al., 2022).

1.3 Historical and Theoretical Underpinnings of Systemic Healing

The historical and theoretical underpinnings of systemic healing through Family Constellations are grounded in a rich tapestry of psychological theories and practices. The Orders of Love, as articulated by Hellinger, elucidate the fundamental principles governing familial relationships, such as belonging, order, and balance. These principles underscore the notion that disruptions in familial harmony can lead to various health issues, both physical and mental (Nickerson et al., 2011; Chatterji et al., 2011). Moreover, the therapeutic techniques employed within Family Constellations, including healing sentences and guided imagery, are designed to foster a sense of connection and understanding among family members, thereby promoting healing at both the individual and systemic levels (Yu et al., 2021). This chapter will delve into these themes, exploring the profound impact of societal dynamics on health, the therapeutic potential of Family Constellations, and the historical context that informs this innovative approach to systemic healing.

2. THEORETICAL FOUNDATIONS OF FAMILY CONSTELLATIONS

The theoretical foundations of Family Constellations, developed by Bert Hellinger, are rooted in a synthesis of various psychological and philosophical principles that emphasise the interconnectedness of family systems and their impact on individual health. Hellinger's work emerged in the late 20th century, drawing from diverse influences, including systemic family therapy, existential phenomenology, and the ancestral reverence practices of the South African Zulu culture. This multifaceted approach allows for a nuanced understanding of how familial relationships and unresolved issues can manifest as psychological and physical ailments in individuals. The Family Constellation method posits that individuals are not isolated entities but rather part of a larger familial system, where dynamics and traumas can reverberate across generations (Cohen, 2006; Welford, 2014).

2.1 Origin and Evolution of Family Constellations by Bert Hellinger

The evolution of Family Constellations as a therapeutic modality reflects a growing recognition of the importance of systemic structures in understanding health and well-being. Hellinger's framework introduces the concept of "Orders of Love," which delineates the fundamental laws governing familial relationships, such as belonging, order, and balance. These orders suggest that disruptions within the family system—such as exclusion, entanglement, or unresolved grief — can lead to significant psychosocial distress and health issues. The therapeutic process involves participants representing family members in a spatial arrangement, allowing for the visualisation of relational dynamics and the identification of hidden patterns that may contribute to individual suffering (Welford, 2014). This experiential approach facilitates a deeper understanding of the systemic nature of health, emphasizing the need for holistic interventions that address both individual and familial needs.

2.2 Relationship Between Systemic Structures and Individual Health

The relationship between systemic structures and individual health is further illuminated through the lens of transgenerational transmission of trauma. Research indicates that unresolved traumas can be passed down through generations, affecting the psychological and physical health of descendants. This phenomenon is often referred to as "intergenerational trauma," where the experiences of one generation—such as war, loss, or systemic oppression — can profoundly influence the emotional and behavioural patterns of subsequent generations (Lombana, 2021; McQuillin & Welford, 2013). Family Constellations provide a therapeutic framework for addressing these inherited traumas, enabling individuals to acknowledge and integrate the experiences of their ancestors. By doing so, participants can break the cycle of trauma, fostering healing not only for themselves but also for their family lineage (Welford, 2014; Gyimesi, 2022).

2.3 Overview of Transgenerational Transmission of Trauma

Transgenerational transmission of trauma refers to how trauma experienced by one generation can affect subsequent generations, manifesting as psychological distress, behavioural patterns, or even physical health issues. Understanding this process is crucial for therapeutic interventions such as Family Constellations, which explore and address these inherited impacts.

2.3.1 Mechanisms of Transmission

Psychological Mechanisms: Trauma can shape how individuals perceive and interact with the world, influencing their parenting and emotional availability. Traumatized parents may exhibit symptoms like anxiety or PTSD, affecting their children's emotional development. Research has shown children of traumatized parents are more susceptible to mood and anxiety disorders due to internalised behaviours and emotional responses (Hurley et al., 2018).

Biological Mechanisms: Epigenetic studies have revealed that trauma can cause gene expression changes passed to future generations. Such biological transmissions may include altered stress response systems or changes in brain structures that predispose descendants to anxiety and depression. Examples include modified cortisol levels and impacts on emotional regulation (Hurley et al., 2018).

Social Mechanisms: Family dynamics, cultural narratives, and societal attitudes also contribute to trauma's transmission. Family silence or avoidance about trauma perpetuates intergenerational cycles, and societal stigma can further isolate individuals, discouraging open discussion or help-seeking behaviour (Hurley et al., 2018).

2.3.2 Impact on Individual Health

Psychological Health: Transgenerational trauma significantly raises the risk of mental health disorders in descendants, such as anxiety and depression. Children of parents with PTSD, for instance, are more likely to develop similar disorders, reflecting the burden of inherited trauma. Feelings of guilt, shame, and inadequacy can exacerbate mental health issues (Hurley et al., 2018).

Physical Health: The impact of inherited trauma extends to physical health. Chronic stress from transgenerational trauma increases risks for cardiovascular diseases, autoimmune disorders, and other chronic conditions due to heightened inflammation and altered physiological markers (Hurley et al., 2018).

Behavioural Patterns: Inherited trauma often leads to maladaptive behaviours, such as substance abuse or self-harm, as coping mechanisms. These behaviours reflect unresolved trauma or learned responses to stress within family dynamics (Hurley et al., 2018).

3. ORDERS OF LOVE IN FAMILY CONSTELLATIONS

3.1 Explanation of Orders of Love: Belonging, Hierarchy, and Balance

The concept of "Orders of Love," as articulated by Bert Hellinger, serves as a foundational element in the therapeutic approach known as Family Constellations. This framework posits that healthy family dynamics are governed by three primary principles: belonging, hierarchy, and balance. Each of these orders plays a crucial role in maintaining the integrity of family systems and ensuring the well-being of their members.

Belonging refers to the fundamental human need to be part of a family or group. Hellinger emphasizes that every family member has an inherent right to belong, regardless of their actions or circumstances (Hellinger, 2001). When individuals are excluded from the family system—whether due to death, estrangement, or other reasons—it creates a disturbance that can lead to emotional and psychological distress for those left behind. This exclusion can manifest in various ways, including feelings of guilt, shame, or unworthiness, which can ultimately affect one's health and relationships. For instance, if a family member who committed a crime is rejected or disowned, a descendant may unconsciously represent this person and face challenges such as addiction or depression. Including this member back into the family system through acknowledgment can restore balance and harmony (Hellinger, 2001; Thege et al., 2021; Hurley et al., 2018).

Hierarchy pertains to the natural order within family systems, where each member has a specific role and position. This order is often based on generational lines, with parents holding authority over children (Hellinger, 1998). When this hierarchy is disrupted—such as when children take on parental roles or when parents fail to fulfil their responsibilities—it can lead to confusion and dysfunction within the family. Such disruptions can result in significant emotional turmoil, as individuals struggle to navigate their roles and responsibilities (Hellinger, 1998; Lund et al., 2019). By recognising and restoring the proper roles, the systemic burden is lifted, and the child can return to their rightful place (Hellinger, 1998; Lund et al., 2019).

Balance involves the equitable exchange of giving and receiving within family relationships. Healthy family dynamics require that love, support, and resources flow freely among members. When there is an imbalance—such as one member consistently giving without receiving, or another taking without giving—it can create resentment and conflict. This imbalance can lead to emotional distress and health issues, as individuals may feel undervalued or overwhelmed by their responsibilities (Thege et al., 2021; Hurley et al., 2018).

3.2 Impact of Violations of These Orders on Individual Health

The violation of the Orders of Love can have profound implications for individual health, both psychologically and physically. When family members experience exclusion, hierarchical disruptions, or imbalances in giving and receiving, the consequences can manifest in various health-related issues (Thege et al., 2021). For instance, individuals who feel excluded from their family system may experience feelings of isolation, depression, or anxiety. This emotional distress can lead to physical health problems, such as chronic stress, which has been linked to a range of health conditions, including cardiovascular disease and weakened immune function. The psychological burden of feeling unworthy or unloved can also contribute to unhealthy coping mechanisms, such as substance abuse or self-harm, further exacerbating health issues (Thege et al., 2021; Hurley et al., 2018).

Disruptions in hierarchy can lead to role confusion, particularly in families where children assume parental responsibilities. This role reversal can create significant stress for young individuals, who may struggle to balance their own developmental needs with the demands placed upon them. Research has shown that children in such situations often experience heightened levels of anxiety and depression, which can persist into adulthood (Lund et al., 2019). Furthermore, these individuals may carry unresolved issues related to their family dynamics, leading to difficulties in forming healthy relationships in their adult lives (Lund et al., 2019).

Imbalances in giving and receiving can also have detrimental effects on health. For example, caregivers who consistently prioritise the needs of others over their own may experience burnout, leading to physical and emotional exhaustion. This phenomenon is particularly evident in families dealing with chronic illness or disability, where the caregiver's health may deteriorate as they neglect their own needs in favour of their loved ones. The resulting stress can contribute to a range of health issues, including anxiety disorders, depression, and physical ailments (Thege et al., 2021; Lund et al., 2019).

Overall, the impact of violations of the *Orders of Love* underscores the importance of addressing family dynamics in therapeutic settings. By recognising and rectifying these violations, individuals can begin to heal and restore balance within their family systems, ultimately improving their overall health and well-being.

3.3 Case Examples Illustrating Disruptions and Resolutions

To illustrate the impact of the Orders of Love and the potential for resolution through Family Constellations, several case examples can be examined. These examples highlight the ways in which violations of the orders can manifest in individual health challenges and how therapeutic interventions can facilitate healing.

Case Example 1: Exclusion and Its Effects

In a Family Constellation session, a participant named Sarah presented with chronic anxiety and feelings of inadequacy. Through the constellation process, it was revealed that Sarah's father had been estranged from the family for many years, leading to her feeling excluded from her family lineage. This exclusion created a deep sense of unworthiness, which manifested as anxiety and self-doubt.

During the session, representatives for Sarah's family members were positioned in a way that visually represented the family dynamics. As the facilitator guided the process, Sarah was able to express her feelings of exclusion and acknowledge her father's absence. By recognising the impact of this exclusion, Sarah was able to find a sense of closure and acceptance. The session concluded with a healing sentence that allowed her to integrate her father's absence into her life narrative, fostering a sense of belonging and reducing her anxiety (Thege et al., 2021; Hurley et al., 2018).

Case Example 2: Hierarchical Disruption

Another participant, John, sought help for feelings of anger and resentment towards his parents. During the constellation, it became clear that John had taken on a parental role for his younger siblings after their mother became ill. This disruption of the natural hierarchy created significant stress for John, who felt overwhelmed by the responsibilities placed upon him.

Through the constellation process, John was able to express his feelings of frustration and recognise the impact of this role reversal on his emotional well-being. The facilitator guided John in re-establishing the appropriate hierarchy within the family system, allowing him to reclaim his position as a child rather than a caregiver. This shift enabled John to release his anger and resentment, leading to a sense of relief and improved emotional health (Lund et al., 2019).

Case Example 3: Imbalance in Giving and Receiving

In a third case, a participant named Lisa presented with chronic fatigue and feelings of being undervalued. During the constellation, it was revealed that Lisa had been the primary caregiver for her elderly parents, often neglecting her own needs in the process. This imbalance in giving and receiving had led to her physical exhaustion and emotional distress.

Through the constellation process, Lisa was able to articulate her feelings of being overwhelmed and unappreciated. The facilitator helped her to visualise a more balanced exchange within the family system, allowing Lisa to express her needs and desires. By acknowledging her own worth and the importance of self-care, Lisa was able to restore balance in her relationships, leading to a significant improvement in her overall health and well-being (Thege et al., 2021; Lund et al., 2019).

These case examples illustrate the profound impact of the Orders of Love on individual health and the potential for healing through Family Constellations. By addressing violations of belonging, hierarchy, and balance, individuals can begin to restore harmony within their family systems, ultimately leading to improved emotional and physical health.

4. SYSTEMIC HEALING AND HEALTH

4.1 Mechanisms by Which Systemic Healing Influences Physical and Mental Health

Systemic healing, particularly as it pertains to Family Constellations, operates on the premise that individual health is deeply intertwined with familial and societal dynamics. This interconnectedness is facilitated through various mechanisms that influence both physical and mental health.

1. Emotional Release and Processing: One of the primary mechanisms of systemic healing is the emotional release that occurs during Family Constellation sessions. Participants often confront and process deep-seated emotions related to family traumas, unresolved conflicts, and historical grievances (Jafari, 2023). This emotional catharsis can lead to significant psychological relief, reducing symptoms of anxiety, depression, and stress-related disorders. Research has shown that emotional processing is crucial for mental health recovery, as it allows individuals to integrate past experiences and move towards healing (Jafari, 2023).
2. Reestablishing Family Dynamics: Systemic healing also involves reestablishing healthy family dynamics. By visualising family relationships through constellation work, participants can identify and address imbalances, exclusions, or disruptions in familial roles (Jafari, 2023). Restoring these dynamics can lead to improved communication, enhanced emotional support, and a greater sense of belonging within the family unit. Such improvements can have a direct impact on individual health, as supportive family environments are linked to better mental health outcomes and resilience against stress (Asadi, 2023).
3. Mind-Body Connection: The mind-body connection is another critical aspect of systemic healing. The emotional and psychological experiences processed during Family Constellations can manifest physically, influencing bodily health. For instance, unresolved emotional issues may lead to chronic pain, fatigue, or other physical ailments. By addressing these emotional roots, individuals often experience relief from physical symptoms, highlighting the importance of holistic approaches in healthcare that consider both mental and physical health (Ram et al., 2017).
4. Cognitive Restructuring: Systemic healing can facilitate cognitive restructuring, where individuals reframe their understanding of family dynamics and their own roles within these systems. This cognitive shift can lead to improved self-esteem, greater self-efficacy, and a more positive outlook on life. Cognitive-behavioural theories support the idea that changing one's thought patterns can

lead to changes in emotional and physical health, reinforcing the benefits of systemic healing practices (Jafari, 2023).

5. Social Support Networks: Finally, systemic healing fosters the development of social support networks. Participants in Family Constellation sessions often find solidarity and understanding among others who share similar experiences. This sense of community can enhance feelings of connectedness and reduce isolation, which are crucial for mental health. Studies have shown that strong social support networks are associated with lower levels of stress and better overall health outcomes (Asadi, 2023).

4.2 Integration of Body-Mind Connections Within Constellations Therapy

The integration of body-mind connections within Family Constellations therapy is a fundamental aspect of its effectiveness. This approach recognises that emotional and psychological issues are often reflected in physical symptoms, and vice versa.

1. Somatic Awareness: Family Constellations encourage participants to develop somatic awareness, which involves tuning into bodily sensations and recognising how emotions manifest physically. For example, participants may notice tension in their shoulders or a tightness in their chest when discussing family issues. This awareness allows individuals to connect emotional experiences with physical sensations, facilitating a deeper understanding of their health challenges (Jafari, 2023).
2. Embodied Representation: During constellation sessions, representatives for family members often embody the emotions and dynamics of those individuals. This embodied representation allows participants to experience the physicality of their family dynamics, leading to insights that may not be accessible through verbal processing alone. By engaging with these embodied experiences, participants can release pent-up emotions and foster healing (Ram et al., 2017).
3. Healing Through Movement: Movement is another critical component of integrating body-mind connections in Family Constellations. Participants may be guided to move in specific ways that reflect their emotional states or family dynamics. This movement can facilitate the release of stored emotions and promote a sense of liberation and healing. Research has shown that movement therapies can enhance emotional processing and contribute to overall well-being (Jafari, 2023).
4. Mindfulness Practices: Mindfulness practices are often incorporated into Family Constellations to enhance the connection between body and mind. Participants may be encouraged to practice mindfulness techniques, such as deep breathing

or meditation, during the constellation process. These practices can help individuals remain present and grounded, facilitating a more profound emotional experience and promoting healing (Ram et al., 2017).

5. Holistic Health Outcomes: The integration of body-mind connections within Family Constellations ultimately leads to holistic health outcomes. By addressing both emotional and physical aspects of health, individuals can experience improvements in mental health, physical well-being, and overall life satisfaction. This holistic approach aligns with contemporary understandings of health, which emphasise the interconnectedness of mind, body, and spirit (Asadi, 2023).

4.3 The Role of Societal Norms and Cultural Influences on Family Dynamics

Societal norms and cultural influences play a significant role in shaping family dynamics and, consequently, individual health outcomes. Understanding these influences is crucial for effective systemic healing.

1. Cultural Expectations: Different cultures have varying expectations regarding family roles, responsibilities, and behaviours. These cultural norms can dictate how family members interact, communicate, and support one another. For instance, collectivist cultures may emphasise familial loyalty and interdependence, while individualistic cultures may prioritise personal autonomy. These cultural expectations can significantly impact mental health, as individuals may feel pressure to conform to societal norms that do not align with their personal experiences (Jafari, 2023).
2. Stigma and Mental Health: Societal stigma surrounding mental health issues can also influence family dynamics. In cultures where mental illness is viewed negatively, families may be reluctant to discuss or seek help for psychological issues. This silence can perpetuate cycles of trauma and distress, affecting the overall health of family members. Conversely, cultures that promote open dialogue about mental health may foster supportive environments that encourage healing and resilience (Asadi, 2023).
3. Intergenerational Transmission of Values: Cultural values and beliefs are often transmitted across generations, shaping family dynamics and individual behaviours. For example, families may pass down beliefs about health, illness, and coping strategies, influencing how members respond to challenges. Understanding these intergenerational transmissions can help individuals recognise patterns that may be detrimental to their health and facilitate change (Jafari, 2023).

4. Socioeconomic Factors: Societal norms related to socioeconomic status can also impact family dynamics. Families facing economic hardship may experience increased stress and conflict, affecting their overall health. Additionally, access to healthcare and resources can vary significantly based on socioeconomic status, further complicating the relationship between family dynamics and health outcomes (Asadi, 2023).
5. Cultural Sensitivity in Therapy: Finally, recognising the role of societal norms and cultural influences is essential for effective therapeutic practices, including Family Constellations. Culturally sensitive approaches that acknowledge and respect diverse family structures and values can enhance the effectiveness of systemic healing. By considering cultural contexts, therapists can better address the unique challenges faced by individuals and families, promoting more meaningful and lasting healing (Jafari, 2023).

5. THERAPEUTIC TECHNIQUES IN FAMILY CONSTELLATIONS

5.1 Structure and Process of a Typical Family Constellations Session

A Family Constellations session is a therapeutic approach that allows individuals to explore and resolve familial issues through a visual and experiential process. The structure of a typical session involves several key components that facilitate the exploration of family dynamics and the healing of emotional wounds (figure 1).

Figure 1. Structure of Family Constellations

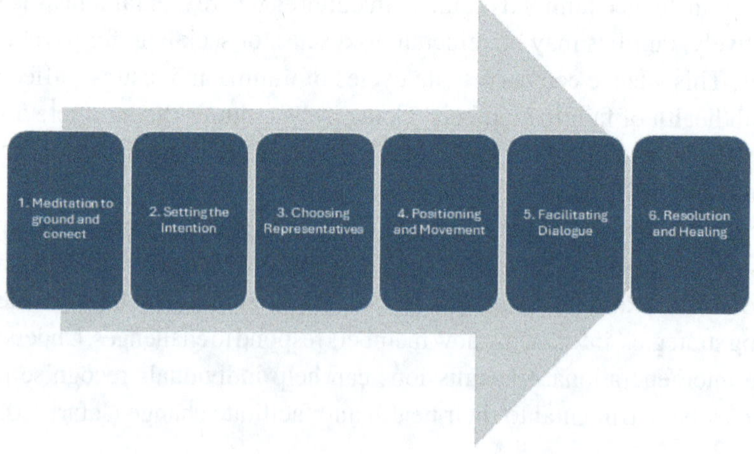

1. Connect with the "void". Mindfulness.

Relaxation exercise. Example:

This meditation is designed to prepare participants for a Family Constellation focused on the *Order of Love*, fostering a deeper connection with their ancestors and bringing awareness to any unresolved dynamics. The practice centres on creating a space of stillness, honouring the ancestors, and opening to systemic healing.

1. Finding a Comfortable Position (2-3 minutes)

"Begin by finding a comfortable seated position. Place your feet flat on the ground if you are sitting in a chair or cross your legs if seated on the floor. Rest your hands gently on your lap. Allow your spine to be straight but relaxed, as if a string is pulling gently upward through the top of your head. Close your eyes if that feels safe and comfortable. Take a deep breath in through your nose… and slowly release it through your mouth. Let your body soften with each breath."

2. Grounding and Centring (2-3 minutes)

"Now, bring your attention to the soles of your feet. Imagine roots growing from the base of your feet, extending deep into the earth. Feel yourself anchored and supported by the ground beneath you. Fill that the roots are in the centre of the Earth and being fed by a golden liquid. That golden liquid flows through the roots all way up, the roots, the feet, the legs, the torso, the arms, the neck, the head. Each breath helps you feel more connected, nourished, stable, and safe. Allow any tension or worries to release into the earth, knowing you are held and grounded."

3. Inviting the Presence of Ancestors (4-5 minutes)

"Shift your focus to your heart centre. Feel the gentle rhythm of your heartbeat. With each breath, imagine a warm light expanding from your heart, connecting you to the generations before you. As you breathe in, invite the presence of your ancestors—known and unknown, near and distant. Allow them to gather around you in a circle of love and support. Sense their presence, acknowledging their struggles, their joys, their lives."

"Whisper inwardly: 'I welcome you, my ancestors. I see you. I honour you. I am grateful for the life you have given me.' Take a few moments to simply be in this circle of connection, feeling any emotions or sensations that arise without judgment."

4. Honouring the Order of Love (4-5 minutes)

"Visualise yourself standing in a long line of your ancestors. Each person represents a generation that came before you. Notice how you stand in your rightful place in this lineage. Feel the strength of the generations that came before you, and recognise that you, too, belong to this sacred order. Whisper inwardly: 'I acknowledge each of you. I respect the order that life has given. I honour your place, and I accept mine.'"

"If there are any moments of disconnection, take a deep breath and offer a silent recognition to those who may have been forgotten or excluded. Imagine light and love flowing through the line, restoring balance, acknowledgment, and harmony."

5. Setting an Intention for the Constellation (3-4 minutes)

"Take a moment to reflect on what you hope to heal or uncover during the Family Constellation. State your intention silently: 'I open myself to healing, to restoring balance, and to honouring the love that flows through my family.' Allow this intention to anchor in your heart."

6. Closing the Meditation (2-3 minutes)

"Gradually bring your awareness back to the present moment. Feel the ground beneath you and your breath moving in and out. When you are ready, gently open your eyes, carrying this connection and intention with you into the constellation."

Closing Reflection

"May this meditation help you honour the Orders of Love, bringing healing, balance, and connection to your family system."

2. Setting the Intention: At the beginning of the session, the facilitator invites participants to set a clear intention regarding the issue they wish to explore. This intention may relate to a specific family member, a recurring family pattern, or a personal challenge. Participants are encouraged to articulate their concerns and the desired outcomes of the session, fostering a sense of purpose and focus (Thege et al., 2021; Weinhold et al., 2013).
3. Choosing Representatives: The facilitator then guides the participant in selecting representatives from the group to embody family members or significant figures related to the issue at hand. These representatives are typically chosen based on their intuitive resonance with the roles they will play. This selection process is crucial, as it allows for the emergence of authentic dynamics within the family system (Hurley et al., 2018).

4. Positioning and Movement: Once the representatives are chosen, they are positioned in the space according to the participant's perception of their family dynamics. The facilitator observes the arrangement and may prompt representatives to express their feelings, sensations, and insights related to their positions. This process often reveals hidden dynamics, unresolved conflicts, and emotional entanglements within the family system (Hurley et al., 2018).
5. Facilitating Dialogue: The facilitator encourages dialogue among the representatives, allowing them to communicate their experiences and emotions. This dialogue can lead to the revelation of underlying issues and patterns that may have been previously unacknowledged. The facilitator plays a vital role in guiding this process, ensuring that it remains respectful and constructive (Thege et al., 2021; Weinhold et al., 2013).
6. Resolution and Healing: As the session progresses, the facilitator may introduce healing sentences or phrases that representatives can use to express acknowledgment, forgiveness, or reconciliation. These sentences serve to honour the family system and facilitate emotional release. The session typically concludes with a reflection on the insights gained and the emotional shifts experienced by the participants (Hurley et al., 2018).

5.2 Healing Sentences: Definition, Purpose, and Examples

Healing sentences are a core component of Family Constellations therapy, serving as a powerful tool for emotional healing and reconciliation within family systems. These sentences are carefully crafted phrases that express acknowledgment, acceptance, and love, often directed towards family members or ancestors.

1. Definition: Healing sentences are succinct statements that encapsulate the essence of a participant's emotional experience and the dynamics at play within their family system. They are designed to honour the past, acknowledge pain, and promote healing by fostering a sense of connection and understanding (Hurley et al., 2018).
2. Purpose: The primary purpose of healing sentences is to facilitate emotional release and resolution. By articulating feelings of love, acceptance, and forgiveness, participants can begin to heal emotional wounds and restore balance within their family systems. Healing sentences also serve to acknowledge the complexities of family relationships, allowing individuals to move beyond blame and resentment (Hurley et al., 2018).
3. Examples: Healing sentences can take various forms, depending on the specific dynamics being addressed. Some common examples include:

- "I honour you and the pain you have carried; I release you from my burden."
- "I see you, and I acknowledge your struggles; I choose to love you as you are."
- "I forgive you for the past, and I embrace the love that connects us."
- "I accept my place in this family, and I release the need to carry the pain of others."
- "I recognise the sacrifices made by my ancestors, and I choose to honour their legacy with love."

These sentences are often spoken aloud during the constellation process, allowing participants to internalise their meanings and experience the emotional shifts that accompany them. By using healing sentences, individuals can foster a sense of closure and connection, paving the way for personal and familial healing (Hurley et al., 2018).

5.3 Case Vignettes Demonstrating the Therapeutic Impact of Healing Sentences

To illustrate the therapeutic impact of healing sentences within Family Constellations, several case vignettes can be examined. These examples highlight how healing sentences can facilitate emotional release, promote understanding, and foster reconciliation within family systems.

Case Vignette 1: Acknowledging Parental Struggles

In a Family Constellation session, a participant named Maria sought to address her feelings of resentment towards her mother, who had struggled with mental health issues throughout Maria's childhood. During the constellation, Maria chose representatives to embody herself, her mother, and her grandmother. As the session unfolded, it became clear that generational trauma and unresolved emotional pain were influencing their dynamics.

As part of the resolution process, the facilitator guided Maria to articulate a healing sentence directed towards her mother: "I see your struggles, and I honour the pain you have carried; I choose to love you as you are." Upon expressing this sentence, Maria experienced a profound emotional release, allowing her to let go of long-held resentment and embrace compassion for her mother's struggles. This shift not only improved Maria's emotional well-being but also fostered a sense of connection with her family (Hurley et al., 2018).

Case Vignette 2: Releasing Familial Burdens

Another participant, David, attended a session to explore his feelings of guilt related to his father's early death. David had always felt responsible for his father's struggles and believed he had failed to support him adequately. During the constellation, David positioned representatives to represent himself, his father, and his father's deceased parents.

As the session progressed, David was guided to express a healing sentence: "I release you from my burden, and I honour the love we shared." This statement allowed David to acknowledge his father's pain while simultaneously releasing the guilt he had carried for years. The emotional weight lifted, and David reported feeling a newfound sense of freedom and acceptance regarding his father's legacy (Hurley et al., 2018).

Case Vignette 3: Embracing Ancestral Legacy

In a third case, a participant named Lisa sought to explore her feelings of inadequacy stemming from her family's history of academic achievement. During the constellation, it became evident that Lisa felt overshadowed by her family's expectations and accomplishments. The facilitator encouraged Lisa to express a healing sentence directed towards her ancestors: "I honour your achievements, and I choose to create my own path."

Upon articulating this sentence, Lisa experienced a significant emotional shift. She felt empowered to embrace her unique journey and release the pressure to conform to her family's expectations. This newfound sense of agency allowed Lisa to pursue her passions without the weight of comparison, leading to improved mental health and self-esteem (Hurley et al., 2018).

These case vignettes demonstrate the profound therapeutic impact of healing sentences within Family Constellations. By articulating these statements, participants can facilitate emotional release, promote understanding, and foster reconciliation, ultimately leading to transformative healing within their family systems.

6. CHALLENGES AND LIMITATIONS IN FAMILY CONSTELLATIONS

6.1 Ethical Considerations and Cultural Adaptation of Family Constellations

Family Constellations therapy, while offering insights into familial dynamics and emotional healing, raises several ethical considerations, particularly concerning cultural adaptation. The practice originated in a specific cultural context and may not universally apply to all cultural backgrounds. Therefore, it is crucial for practitioners to be aware of the cultural nuances that influence family structures, values, and healing practices.

1. Cultural Sensitivity: Practitioners must approach Family Constellations with cultural humility, recognising that family dynamics and healing processes can vary significantly across cultures. For instance, collectivist cultures may prioritise family unity and interdependence, while individualistic cultures may emphasise personal autonomy. A lack of cultural sensitivity can lead to misunderstandings and may inadvertently reinforce harmful stereotypes or biases (Lombana, 2021; Karodia et al., 2015).
2. Informed Consent: Ethical practice in Family Constellations requires obtaining informed consent from participants. This involves ensuring that individuals understand the nature of the therapy, the potential emotional risks involved, and the cultural implications of the process. Practitioners should provide clear explanations and allow participants to ask questions, fostering an environment of trust and respect (Lombana, 2021; Karodia et al., 2015).
3. Power Dynamics: The facilitator's role in Family Constellations can create power dynamics that may affect participants' experiences. It is essential for facilitators to be aware of their influence and to create a safe space where all voices are heard. This is particularly important in culturally diverse settings, where participants may have varying degrees of comfort in expressing their emotions and experiences (Loa, 2018).
4. Integration of Traditional Healing Practices: In some cultures, traditional healing practices may coexist with Family Constellations. Practitioners should be open to integrating these practices into their work, recognising the value of holistic approaches to healing. This integration can enhance the therapeutic experience and promote culturally relevant care (Aubel et al., 2021).
5. Evaluation of Outcomes: Ethical considerations also extend to the evaluation of outcomes in Family Constellations. Practitioners should be transparent about the effectiveness of the therapy and be open to feedback from participants. This

ongoing evaluation can help refine the practice and ensure that it meets the needs of diverse populations (Young et al., 2016).

6.2 Limitations in Empirical Validation and Integration Within Mainstream Healthcare

While Family Constellations have gained popularity as a therapeutic approach, there are notable limitations in empirical validation and integration within mainstream healthcare systems.

1. Lack of Rigorous Research: One of the primary challenges facing Family Constellations is the limited empirical research supporting its efficacy. Although some studies suggest positive outcomes, the overall quality and quantity of evidence remain low. A systematic review indicated that while Family Constellation therapy may provide mental health benefits, more rigorous research is needed to establish its effectiveness and to understand the mechanisms underlying its impact (O'Hara, 2022; Sanchez, 2018).
2. Integration Challenges: The integration of Family Constellations into mainstream healthcare poses challenges, particularly within conventional medical frameworks that prioritize evidence-based practices. Many healthcare professionals may be unfamiliar with systemic approaches and may view them as unscientific or lacking in empirical support. This scepticism can hinder the acceptance and implementation of Family Constellations in clinical settings (Bunik et al., 2014; Høgmo, 2023).
3. Training and Standardisation: The lack of standardised training programs for Family Constellations practitioners can lead to variability in practice quality. Without a consistent framework for training and certification, the effectiveness of the therapy may be inconsistent, further complicating its integration into mainstream healthcare (Grumbach, 2023).
4. Cultural Barriers: The cultural origins of Family Constellations may create barriers to its acceptance in diverse populations. Practitioners must navigate cultural differences and be prepared to adapt their approaches to meet the needs of various communities. This adaptability is essential for fostering trust and engagement among participants (Lombana, 2021; Aubel et al., 2021).
5. Perception of Alternative Therapies: The perception of Family Constellations as an alternative therapy may limit its acceptance among healthcare providers and patients. Many individuals may prefer conventional medical treatments, viewing alternative therapies as secondary or less credible. This perception can impede the collaborative integration of Family Constellations into holistic healthcare models (DuBose et al., 2016; Kodeeswaran et al., 2020).

6.3 Criticisms of Systemic Approaches and Addressing Misconceptions

Despite the potential benefits of Family Constellations and systemic approaches, there are several criticisms and misconceptions that practitioners must address.

1. Reductionism: Critics argue that systemic approaches, including Family Constellations, may oversimplify complex individual issues by attributing them solely to family dynamics. This reductionist perspective can overlook other contributing factors, such as biological, psychological, and environmental influences. It is essential for practitioners to maintain a holistic view that considers the interplay of various factors affecting an individual's health (Shahrajabian et al., 2019; Lovallo, 2013).
2. Overemphasis on Family Dynamics: Some critics contend that Family Constellations may place excessive emphasis on family dynamics at the expense of individual agency. While family systems undoubtedly influence individual behaviour and mental health, it is crucial to recognise that individuals also possess the capacity for personal growth and change independent of their family backgrounds (Glas, 2017; Haycock et al., 2014).
3. Misunderstanding of the Process: There are misconceptions surrounding the Family Constellations process, particularly regarding its effectiveness and the nature of the therapy. Some individuals may view it as a quick fix for deep-seated issues, leading to unrealistic expectations. Practitioners must clarify the therapeutic process, emphasising that healing is often a gradual journey that requires ongoing effort and reflection (Prime, 2023; Bethell, 2023).
4. Cultural Appropriation: The adaptation of Family Constellations in different cultural contexts raises concerns about cultural appropriation. Practitioners must be mindful of the cultural origins of the therapy and approach its application with respect and sensitivity. This involves understanding the cultural significance of family dynamics and healing practices within specific communities (Lombana, 2021; Aubel et al., 2021).
5. Need for Continued Dialogue: Addressing criticisms and misconceptions requires ongoing dialogue among practitioners, researchers, and communities. By fostering open conversations about the strengths and limitations of Family Constellations, practitioners can promote a more nuanced understanding of the therapy and its role within the broader landscape of mental health care (Josiah et al., 2023; Luchies et al., 2019).

7. INTEGRATING SYSTEMIC HEALING IN HEALTHCARE PRACTICE

7.1 Practical Applications for Healthcare Professionals

Integrating systemic healing into healthcare practice involves applying the principles of Family Constellations and systemic approaches to enhance patient care and overall health outcomes. Healthcare professionals can adopt various practical applications to incorporate systemic healing into their daily practice.

1. Holistic Assessment: Healthcare professionals can begin by conducting holistic assessments that consider not only the physical symptoms of patients but also their emotional, psychological, and social contexts. This approach encourages practitioners to explore family dynamics, cultural backgrounds, and personal histories that may influence a patient's health. By understanding the broader context of a patient's life, healthcare providers can develop more effective and personalized treatment plans (Arāja, 2022).
2. Facilitating Family Involvement: Encouraging family involvement in the treatment process can enhance the effectiveness of care. Healthcare professionals can invite family members to participate in consultations, discussions, and decision-making processes. This inclusion fosters a supportive environment where family dynamics can be addressed, and emotional support can be provided. It also allows healthcare providers to gain insights into the patient's family history and the potential impact of familial relationships on health (Dermody et al., 2022).
3. Training in Systemic Approaches: Healthcare professionals can benefit from training in systemic approaches, including Family Constellations. Workshops and continuing education programs can equip practitioners with the skills to recognise and address systemic issues within their practice. This training can enhance their ability to facilitate conversations about family dynamics and emotional health, ultimately leading to better patient outcomes (Arora et al., 2018).
4. Creating Supportive Environments: Healthcare settings can be designed to promote systemic healing by creating supportive environments that encourage open communication and emotional expression. This may involve redesigning waiting areas, consultation rooms, and treatment spaces to foster a sense of safety and comfort. Additionally, incorporating elements such as art, nature, and community engagement can enhance the healing atmosphere (Barson et al., 2018).

5. Using Healing Sentences: Healthcare professionals can incorporate healing sentences into their practice as a means of promoting emotional healing. These sentences can be used in therapeutic conversations with patients, allowing them to express feelings of acknowledgment, acceptance, and forgiveness. By facilitating this emotional release, healthcare providers can help patients address unresolved issues and promote overall well-being (Leaman et al., 2017).

7.2 Strategies for Fostering Systemic Awareness in Patient Care

Fostering systemic awareness in patient care requires intentional strategies that encourage healthcare professionals to consider the interconnectedness of family dynamics, societal influences, and individual health.

1. Interdisciplinary Collaboration: Encouraging collaboration among healthcare professionals from various disciplines can enhance systemic awareness. By working together, practitioners can share insights and perspectives on how family dynamics and societal factors influence health. This interdisciplinary approach promotes a more comprehensive understanding of patient care, allowing for more effective interventions (Seo et al., 2018).
2. Patient Education: Educating patients about the importance of family dynamics and systemic factors in their health can empower them to take an active role in their care. Healthcare professionals can provide resources, workshops, and discussions that highlight the interconnectedness of emotional, psychological, and physical health. This education can help patients recognise the impact of their family histories and relationships on their well-being (Nguyen et al., 2020).
3. Reflective Practice: Encouraging healthcare professionals to engage in reflective practice can enhance their systemic awareness. By regularly reflecting on their interactions with patients and considering the broader context of care, practitioners can identify patterns and dynamics that may influence health outcomes (Reis da Silva, 2024a). This self-awareness can lead to more empathetic and effective patient care (Burnhope et al., 2020; da Silva, 2022; Reis da Silva, 2024b).
4. Community Engagement: Engaging with the community can provide healthcare professionals with valuable insights into the social determinants of health that affect their patients. By participating in community events, outreach programs, and support groups, practitioners can better understand the challenges faced by patients and their families. This engagement fosters a sense of connection and allows healthcare providers to tailor their approaches to meet the unique needs of the community (Antoñanzas et al., 2017).

5. Feedback Mechanisms: Implementing feedback mechanisms within healthcare settings can facilitate ongoing learning and improvement. Encouraging patients and families to share their experiences and perspectives can provide valuable insights into the effectiveness of care and highlight areas for improvement. This feedback can inform systemic changes that enhance patient care and promote healing (Omary et al., 2011).

7.3 Benefits of Interdisciplinary Approaches in Systemic Healing

Interdisciplinary approaches in systemic healing offer numerous benefits that can enhance patient care and improve health outcomes.

1. Comprehensive Care: Interdisciplinary collaboration allows healthcare professionals to address the multifaceted nature of health. By integrating insights from various disciplines, practitioners can develop comprehensive care plans that consider physical, emotional, and social factors. This holistic approach promotes better health outcomes and enhances the overall patient experience (Johannessen & Steihaug, 2013).
2. Enhanced Communication: Collaboration among healthcare professionals fosters improved communication and information sharing. This enhanced communication can lead to more coordinated care, reducing the risk of fragmented services and ensuring that all aspects of a patient's health are addressed. Effective communication also promotes a shared understanding of patient needs and goals (Manyazewal et al., 2016).
3. Increased Innovation: Interdisciplinary approaches encourage creativity and innovation in problem-solving. By bringing together diverse perspectives and expertise, healthcare teams can develop novel solutions to complex health challenges. This innovation can lead to the implementation of new practices and interventions that enhance patient care (Raheem, 2020).
4. Improved Patient Outcomes: Research has shown that interdisciplinary collaboration can lead to improved patient outcomes, including higher satisfaction rates, better adherence to treatment plans, and reduced hospital readmissions. By addressing the interconnectedness of health factors, interdisciplinary teams can provide more effective and personalized care (Obu & Aggrey-Bluwey, 2021).
5. Empowerment of Patients and Families: Interdisciplinary approaches empower patients and families by involving them in the decision-making process. By recognising the importance of family dynamics and social contexts, healthcare professionals can create a more inclusive environment that values the input and

experiences of patients and their families. This empowerment fosters a sense of ownership over health and well-being (Svarts, 2017).

8. CONCLUSION

The integration of systemic perspectives into healthcare practice highlights the profound impact of societal dynamics on health. By recognising the interconnectedness of family systems, cultural influences, and individual well-being, healthcare professionals can adopt a more holistic approach to patient care. This systemic awareness not only enhances the understanding of health issues but also fosters compassionate and effective interventions that address the root causes of distress.

8.1 Summarising the Societal Impact on Health Through Systemic Perspectives

Societal factors play a critical role in shaping health outcomes, as they influence family dynamics, access to resources, and individual behaviours. The systemic perspective emphasizes that health is not merely the absence of disease but a complex interplay of biological, psychological, social, and environmental factors. By acknowledging these interconnections, healthcare providers can better understand the challenges faced by their patients and develop more effective treatment strategies. For instance, recognizing the impact of familial relationships on mental health can lead to interventions that involve family members in the healing process, thereby enhancing support systems and improving overall health outcomes (Bangcola, 2021).

8.2 Future Directions for Research and Clinical Integration of Family Constellations

As the field of Family Constellations continues to evolve, there is a pressing need for further research to validate its efficacy and explore its integration into mainstream healthcare. Future studies should focus on rigorous empirical evaluations of Family Constellations, examining its impact on various health conditions and patient populations. Additionally, research should investigate the mechanisms underlying the therapeutic effects of systemic healing, providing insights into how these approaches can be effectively implemented in clinical settings (Ohta, 2023).

Moreover, interdisciplinary collaboration is essential for the successful integration of Family Constellations into healthcare. By fostering partnerships between mental health professionals, medical practitioners, and community organisations, a more comprehensive approach to patient care can be developed. This collaboration can facilitate the sharing of knowledge and resources, ultimately leading to improved health outcomes for individuals and families (Bangcola, 2021).

8.3 Call to Action for Holistic and Compassionate Healthcare Models

The need for holistic and compassionate healthcare models has never been more urgent. As healthcare systems face increasing pressures from chronic diseases, mental health challenges, and social determinants of health, it is imperative to adopt approaches that prioritize the well-being of the whole person. Healthcare professionals are encouraged to embrace systemic perspectives, integrating Family Constellations and other holistic practices into their work.

This call to action involves not only adopting new therapeutic techniques but also advocating for policy changes that support holistic care. By promoting awareness of the importance of family dynamics and societal influences on health, healthcare providers can contribute to a more compassionate and effective healthcare system. Ultimately, the goal is to create an environment where individuals feel supported, understood, and empowered to take charge of their health and well-being (Bangcola, 2021).

REFERENCES

Antoñanzas, F., Terkola, R., Overton, P., Shalet, N., & Postma, M. (2017). Defining and measuring the affordability of new medicines: A systematic review. *PharmacoEconomics, 35*(8), 777–791. DOI: 10.1007/s40273-017-0514-4 PMID: 28477220

Arāja, D. (2022). Resilience and complex adaptive systems:a perspective on healthcare. *Journal of Business and Management, 20*, 23–35. DOI: 10.32025/JBM22006

Arora, S., Bergland, A., Straiton, M., Rechel, B., & Debesay, J. (2018). Older migrants' access to healthcare: A thematic synthesis. *International Journal of Migration, Health and Social Care, 14*(4), 425–438. DOI: 10.1108/IJMHSC-05-2018-0032

Asadi, K. (2023). The role of family in shaping financial literacy and economic behavior. *JPRFC*, 22-29. https://doi.org/DOI: 10.61838/kman.jprfc.1.3.4

Aubel, J., Sl, M., & Cunningham, K. (2021). Introduction: A family systems approach to promote maternal, child and adolescent nutrition. *Maternal and Child Nutrition, 17*(S1), e13228. Advance online publication. DOI: 10.1111/mcn.13228 PMID: 34241950

Bangcola, A. (2021). The development of spiritual nursing care theory using deductive axiomatic approach. *Belitung Nursing Journal, 7*(3), 163–170. DOI: 10.33546/bnj.1456 PMID: 37469349

Barson, S., Gauld, R., Gray, J., Henriks, G., Krause, C., Lachman, P., Maher, L., Massoud, M. R., Mathias, L., Wagner, M., & Villa, L. (2018). What initiatives do healthcare leaders agree are needed for healthcare system improvement? results of a modified-Delphi study. *Journal of Health Organization and Management, 32*(8), 1002–1012. DOI: 10.1108/JHOM-08-2017-0216 PMID: 30468416

Bethell, C., Wells, N., Bergman, D., Reuland, C., Stumbo, S. P., Gombojav, N., & Simpson, L. A. (2023). Scaling family voices and engagement to measure and improve systems performance and whole child health: Progress and lessons from the child and adolescent health measurement initiative. *Maternal and Child Health Journal.* Advance online publication. DOI: 10.1007/s10995-023-03755-9 PMID: 37624473

Bunik, M., Dunn, D., Watkins, L., & Talmi, A. (2014). Trifecta approach to breastfeeding. *Journal of Human Lactation, 30*(2), 143–147. DOI: 10.1177/0890334414523333 PMID: 24595703

Burnhope, E., Waring, M., Guilder, A., Malhotra, B., Cardoso, J., Razavi, R., & Carr-White, G. (2020). A systematic approach towards implementing value-based health care in heart failure: Understandings from retrospective analysis methods in south London. *Health Services Management Research*, *35*(1), 37–47. DOI: 10.1177/0951484820971442 PMID: 33256480

Chatterji, P., Lahiri, K., & Song, J. (2011). The dynamics of income-related health inequality among us children. SSRN *Electronic Journal*. https://doi.org/DOI: 10.2139/ssrn.1927813

Cohen, D. (2006). "Family Constellations": An innovative systemic phenomenological group process from Germany. *The Family Journal (Alexandria, Va.)*, *14*(3), 226–233. DOI: 10.1177/1066480706287279

da Silva, T. H. R. (2022). Emotional awareness and emotional intelligence. *British Journal of Community Nursing*, *27*(12), 573–574. DOI: 10.12968/bjcn.2022.27.12.573 PMID: 36519463

Dermody, S., Bhambhani, C., Swiecicki, P., Brenner, J., & Tewari, M. (2022). Transrenal cell-free tumor DNA for urine-based liquid biopsy of cancer. *Frontiers in Genetics*, *13*, 879108. Advance online publication. DOI: 10.3389/fgene.2022.879108 PMID: 35571046

Dorri, A., Stone, A. L., Heffington, B. I., Njowo, P. J., Rivera, G., Schnarrs, P. W., & Salcido, R.Jr. (2023). "we're not gonna talk about this, it didn't happen. you're confused": Adverse communication in family responses to mental health, childhood sexual assault, and LGBTQ identities. *Society and Mental Health*, *14*(1), 39–55. DOI: 10.1177/21568693231170901

DuBose, J., MacAllister, L., Hadi, K., & Sakallaris, B. (2016). Exploring the concept of healing spaces. *HERD*, *11*(1), 43–56. DOI: 10.1177/1937586716680567 PMID: 29514569

Falzarano, F., Cimarolli, V., & Siedlecki, K. (2022). Staying in the loop: Quality of family-paid caregiver communication and influences on resident mental health in long-term care. *Journal of the American Geriatrics Society*, *71*(4), 1209–1219. DOI: 10.1111/jgs.18184 PMID: 36514200

Glas, G. (2017). Public and institutional aspects of professional responsibility in medicine and psychiatry. *Philosophia Reformata*, *82*(2), 146–166. DOI: 10.1163/23528230-08202005

Grumbach, K. (2023). Forging a social movement to dismantle entrenched power and liberate primary care as a common good. *Annals of Family Medicine, 21*(2), 180–184. DOI: 10.1370/afm.2950 PMID: 36973058

Gyimesi, J. (2022). Family constellation therapy in the context of esotericism. *Perspectives on Psychological Science, 18*(4), 749–761. DOI: 10.1177/17456916221120424 PMID: 36301913

Haycock, C., Curry, D., & Sevilla, X. (2014). Philanthropy and service excellence. *Nursing Administration Quarterly, 38*(4), 348–355. DOI: 10.1097/NAQ.0000000000000061 PMID: 25208155

Hellinger, B. (1998). *Acknowledging What Is: Conversations with Bert Hellinger*. Zeig, Tucker & Theisen.

Hellinger, B. (2001). *Love's Hidden Symmetry: What Makes Love Work in Relationships.* Zeig, Tucker & Theisen.

Henize, A., Beck, A., Klein, M., Adams, M., & Kahn, R. (2015). A road map to address the social determinants of health through community collaboration. *Pediatrics, 136*(4), e993–e1001. DOI: 10.1542/peds.2015-0549 PMID: 26391941

Høgmo, B., Alstveit, M., & Bondas, T. (2023). Being a "warrior" to care for the new family: A meta-ethnography of nurses' perspectives on municipal postnatal healthcare. *Global Qualitative Nursing Research, 10*, 23333936231218843. Advance online publication. DOI: 10.1177/23333936231218843 PMID: 38149124

Hunger, C., Bornhäuser, A., Link, L., Schweitzer, J., & Weinhold, J. (2013). Improving experience in personal social systems through family constellation seminars: Results of a randomized controlled trial. *Family Process, 53*(2), 288–306. DOI: 10.1111/famp.12051 PMID: 24251855

Hurley, J., Koenning, M., & Bray, A. (2018). Responding to intergenerational psychological trauma: A literature review paper on the place of family constellation therapy. *Psychotherapy and Counselling Journal of Australia, 6*(1). Advance online publication. DOI: 10.59158/001c.71192

Jafari, Z. (2023). Understanding family functioning: the influence of cultural marginalization and social competence. *JPRFC*, 4-10. https://doi.org/DOI: 10.61838/kman.jprfc.1.4.2

Johannessen, A., & Steihaug, S. (2013). The significance of professional roles in collaboration on patients' transitions from hospital to home via an intermediate unit. *Scandinavian Journal of Caring Sciences, 28*(2), 364–372. DOI: 10.1111/scs.12066 PMID: 23879767

Josiah, N., Shoola, H., Rodney, T., Arscott, J., Ndzi, M., Bush, A., Wilson, P. R., Jacques, K., Baptiste, D.-L., & Starks, S. (2023). Addressing systemic racism and intergenerational transmission of anxiety using Bowenian family therapy with African American populations: A discursive paper. *Journal of Advanced Nursing*, *79*(5), 1714–1723. DOI: 10.1111/jan.15610 PMID: 36825628

Karodia, A., Naranjee, N., & Bikitsha, M. (2015). An evaluation of a holistic approach to managing the integration of the traditional healer into the western biomedical practice: A study of patients of the Khayelitsha medical practice in the western cape province (South Africa). *Academic Journal of Research in Economics and Management*, *2*(9), 1–31. DOI: 10.12816/0017363

Kodeeswaran, J., Campaigne, M., & Benoit, A. (2020). Indigenous women from the sixties scoop healing through the full moon ceremony and storytelling at Winona's place. *University of Toronto Journal of Public Health*, *1*(1). Advance online publication. DOI: 10.33137/utjph.v1i1.33835

Leaman, J., Richards, A., Emslie, L., & O'Moore, É. (2017). Improving health in prisons – from evidence to policy to implementation – experiences from the UK. *International Journal of Prisoner Health*, *13*(3/4), 139–167. DOI: 10.1108/IJPH-09-2016-0056 PMID: 28914122

Loa, R. (2018). Facilitators and barriers to self-management of tuberculosis patients: A qualitative study. *International Journal of Integrated Care*, *18*(s2), 285. DOI: 10.5334/ijic.s2285

Lombana, Y. (2021). Possibilities and challenges in providing psychotherapeutic interventions to meet the needs of the latinx population in the United States. *Genealogy*, *5*(1), 12. DOI: 10.3390/genealogy5010012

Lovallo, W. (2013). Early life adversity reduces stress reactivity and enhances impulsive behavior: Implications for health behaviors. *International Journal of Psychophysiology*, *90*(1), 8–16. DOI: 10.1016/j.ijpsycho.2012.10.006 PMID: 23085387

Luchies, L., Barbour, B., & Anderson, B. (2019). Children's healing center involvement reduces social isolation and loneliness among immunocompromised children and their family members. *American Journal of Recreation Therapy*, *18*(3), 37–47. DOI: 10.5055/ajrt.2019.0194

Lund, I., Handal, M., Bukten, A., Torvik, F., Ystrøm, E., & Andreas, J. (2019). Association of constellations of parental risk with children's subsequent anxiety and depression. *JAMA Pediatrics*, *173*(3), 251. DOI: 10.1001/jamapediatrics.2018.4360 PMID: 30615089

Manyazewal, T., Oosthuizen, M., & Matlakala, M. (2016). Proposing evidence-based strategies to strengthen implementation of healthcare reform in resource-limited settings: A summative analysis. *BMJ Open*, *6*(9), e012582. DOI: 10.1136/bmjopen-2016-012582 PMID: 27650769

Mayer, C., & Viviers, A. (2015). Constellation work principles, resonance phenomena, and shamanism in south Africa. *South African Journal of Psychology. Suid-Afrikaanse Tydskrif vir Sielkunde*, *46*(1), 130–145. DOI: 10.1177/0081246315591339

McQuillin, J., & Welford, E. (2013). How many people are gathered here? group work and family constellation theory. *Transactional Analysis Journal*, *43*(4), 352–365. DOI: 10.1177/0362153713519743

Moore, S., Hackworth, N., Hamilton, V., Northam, E., & Cameron, F. (2013). Adolescents with type 1 diabetes: Parental perceptions of child health and family functioning and their relationship to adolescent metabolic control. *Health and Quality of Life Outcomes*, *11*(1), 50. Advance online publication. DOI: 10.1186/1477-7525-11-50 PMID: 23521786

Nguyen, N., Subhan, F., Williams, K., & Chan, C. (2020). Barriers and mitigating strategies to healthcare access in indigenous communities of Canada: A narrative review. *Health Care*, *8*(2), 112. DOI: 10.3390/healthcare8020112 PMID: 32357396

Nickerson, A., Bryant, R., Brooks, R., Steel, Z., Silove, D., & Chen, J. (2011). The familial influence of loss and trauma on refugee mental health: A multilevel path analysis. *Journal of Traumatic Stress*, *24*(1), 25–33. DOI: 10.1002/jts.20608 PMID: 21268119

O'Hara, N. (2022). Eliciting health care preferences with discrete choice experiments. *JAMA Network Open*, *5*(4), e228794. DOI: 10.1001/jamanetworkopen.2022.8794 PMID: 35467737

Obu, R. and Aggrey-Bluwey, L. (2021). A case study of complementary alternative medicines in primary healthcare in Ghana. *Journal of Complementary and Alternative Medical Research*, 23-33. https://doi.org/DOI: 10.9734/jocamr/2021/v15i130256

October, K., Petersen, L., Adebiyi, B., Rich, E., & Roman, N. (2021). Covid-19 daily realities for families: A south African sample. *International Journal of Environmental Research and Public Health*, *19*(1), 221. DOI: 10.3390/ijerph19010221 PMID: 35010480

Ohta, R., & Sano, C. (2023). Integrating clinical and socio-environmental approaches in managing rheumatoid arthritis with social determinants of health: A case study of an elderly patient in rural Japan. *Cureus*. Advance online publication. DOI: 10.7759/cureus.50915 PMID: 38249275

Omary, Z., Mtenzi, F., Wu, B., & O'Driscoll, C. (2011). Ubiquitous healthcare information system: Assessment of its impacts to patient's information. *International Journal for Information Security Research*, *1*(3), 71–77. DOI: 10.20533/ijisr.2042.4639.2011.0009

Power, J., Goodyear, M., Maybery, D., Reupert, A., O'Hanlon, B., Cuff, R., & Perlesz, A. (2015). Family resilience in families where a parent has a mental illness. *Journal of Social Work : JSW*, *16*(1), 66–82. DOI: 10.1177/1468017314568081

Prime, H., Walsh, F., & Masten, A. S. (2023). Building family resilience in the wake of a global pandemic: Looking back to prepare for the future. *Canadian Psychology*, *64*(3), 200–211. DOI: 10.1037/cap0000366

Raheem, Y. (2020). Prevention in healthcare practice: An issue with rising importance. *Al-Kindy College Medical Journal*, *15*(2), 1–3. DOI: 10.47723/kcmj.v15i2.150

Ram, D., Whipple, C., & Jason, L. (2017). Family dynamics may influence an individual's substance use abstinence self-efficacy. *Journal of Addiction and Preventive Medicine*, *02*(01). Advance online publication. DOI: 10.19104/japm.2016.106 PMID: 28868520

Reis da Silva, T. H. (2024a). Emotional Intelligence in Integrative Medicine: Enhancing Patient-Centred Care Through Humanised Technology. In Tikadar, S. (Ed.), *Liu, H.; Bhattacharya, P.; Bhattacharya, S. Humanizing Technology With Emotional Intelligence*. IGI Global., DOI: 10.4018/979-8-3693-7011-7.ch012

Reis da Silva Tiago. (2024b) The Value of Emotional Intelligence in Midwifery: Enhancing Care and Outcomes for Mothers and Infants through Sustainable Development Goals and Leadership. Journal of Womens Healthcare & Midwifery Research. SRC/JWHMR-133. DOI: DOI: 10.47363/JWHMR/2024(3)119

Sanchez, A. (2018). An examination of the folk healing practice of curanderismo in the hispanic community. *Journal of Community Health Nursing*, *35*(3), 148–161. DOI: 10.1080/07370016.2018.1475801 PMID: 30024284

Seo, J., Kim, W., Hewner, S., & Dickerson, S. (2018). Lived experience of health seeking and healthcare utilization among Korean immigrant women living in suburban communities. *Asian/Pacific Island Nursing Journal*, *3*(1), 8–20. DOI: 10.31372/20180301.1086

Shahrajabian, M., Sun, W., & Cheng, Q. (2019). The influence of traditional iranian and chinese medicine on western and Islamic countries. *Asian Journal of Medical and Biological Research, 5*(2), 94–99. DOI: 10.3329/ajmbr.v5i2.42490

Somasundaram, D. (2007). Collective trauma in northern sri lanka: A qualitative psychosocial-ecological study. *International Journal of Mental Health Systems, 1*(1), 5. DOI: 10.1186/1752-4458-1-5 PMID: 18271989

Stevens, L., Perrin, P., Hubbard, R., Sosa, D., Jove, I., & Arango-Lasprilla, J. (2013). Using multiple views of family dynamics to predict the mental health of individuals with tbi and their caregivers in Mexico. *NeuroRehabilitation, 33*(2), 273–283. DOI: 10.3233/NRE-130955 PMID: 23949065

Svarts, A. (2017). Healthcare managers' perception of economies of scale. *Journal of Health Organization and Management, 31*(3), 317–330. DOI: 10.1108/JHOM-01-2017-0006 PMID: 28686128

Thege, B., Petroll, C., Rivas, C., & Scholtens, S. (2021). The effectiveness of family constellation therapy in improving mental health: A systematic review. *Family Process, 60*(2), 409–423. DOI: 10.1111/famp.12636 PMID: 33528854

Thomeer, M., & Reczek, C. (2019). Intergenerational coresidential patterns by young adult's and their mother's mental health and substance use. *Journal of Family Issues, 41*(9), 1498–1524. DOI: 10.1177/0192513X19894348 PMID: 33293753

Trujillo, M., Perrin, P., Panyavin, I., Peralta, S., Stolfi, M., Morelli, E., & Arango-Lasprilla, J. (2016). Mediation of family dynamics, personal strengths, and mental health in dementia caregivers. *Journal of Latina/o Psychology, 4*(1), 1–17. DOI: 10.1037/lat0000046

Weinhold, J., Hunger, C., Bornhäuser, A., Link, L., Rochon, J., Wild, B., & Schweitzer, J. (2013). Family constellation seminars improve psychological functioning in a general population sample: Results of a randomized controlled trial. *Journal of Counseling Psychology, 60*(4), 601–609. DOI: 10.1037/a0033539 PMID: 23957767

Welford, E. (2014). Giving the dead their rightful place. *Transactional Analysis Journal, 44*(4), 320–333. DOI: 10.1177/0362153714559920

Young, C., Tong, A., Gunasekera, H., Sherriff, S., Kalucy, D., Fernando, P., & Craig, J. (2016). Health professional and community perspectives on reducing barriers to accessing specialist health care in metropolitan aboriginal communities: A semi-structured interview study. *Journal of Paediatrics and Child Health, 53*(3), 277–282. DOI: 10.1111/jpc.13374 PMID: 27748557

Yu, W., Jia, C., Sun, S., Liu, P., Ouyang, L., & Ji-ze, H. (2021). The reciprocal associations between caregiver burden, and mental health in primary caregivers of cancer patients: A longitudinal study. *Psycho-Oncology*, *30*(6), 892–900. DOI: 10.1002/pon.5667 PMID: 33686757

Chapter 12
TB Patients' Perception of the 5Ss Approach in their Community Engagement Activities

S. Srinivasan
https://orcid.org/0009-0002-0179-9849
Department of Humanities and Social Sciences, Graphic Era University, Dehradun, India

R. Vallipriya
https://orcid.org/0009-0008-6692-603X
Department of Physical Science, Institute of Education, (B.ED College), Trichy, India

Ajay Kumar Singh
https://orcid.org/0000-0003-0429-0925
Department of Humanities and Social Sciences, Graphic Era Deemed to be University, Dehradun, India

ABSTRACT

The study examines TB patients' perceptions of the 5Ss approach (Self, Society, State, System, and Spiritual aspects) and its role in reducing stigma, enhancing self-care, and improving treatment outcomes. It highlights the importance of healthcare system support and the 5Ss in creating a TB-free society and improving patient well-being. Research design used for the study is descriptive research with quantitative analysis, using a self-structured survey. Sampling adopted purposive sampling of 75 TB patients from five TB units in Trichy District, Tamil Nadu, covering urban, rural, and semi-urban settings. The demographic details included age, gender, and treatment

DOI: 10.4018/979-8-3693-9092-4.ch012

stage. Themes provide Self-responsibility, societal attitudes, state support, healthcare experience, and spiritual beliefs. Ethical committee approval ensured participant anonymity and confidentiality. Analysis of the result through SPSS software was used to identify patterns and correlations in 5Ss perceptions.

INTRODUCTION

Tuberculosis (TB) remains one of the major public health challenges globally, particularly in low- and middle-income countries. The healthcare impact is limited by access issues in TB disease (Harries et al., 2020). Despite advances in TB diagnosis, treatment, and public health efforts globally, especially in underdeveloped countries, TB remains a significant health challenge (Walzl et al., 2018). TB affects millions of people every year, increasing morbidity and mortality rates in the country (Daley, 2019). The study emphasizes not only medical aspects but also includes community health engagement activities focused on improving TB patients' outcomes, successful treatment, and better interventions. The various aspects involved in community engagement, such as family, society, the healthcare system, self-efficacy, the state, and spirituality, can help prevent TB disease (Artawan Eka Putra et al., 2023).

The qualitative research study aims to understand the multifaceted dimensions to improve the lives of TB patients and achieve better treatment outcomes. It explores in-depth awareness of TB patients regarding the causes, symptoms, transmission, and treatment of TB. The importance of the study on TB patients, their illness, and effective TB control can support overcoming their fear, stigma, delays in diagnosis, and delays in healthcare services, thereby promoting health-seeking behavior (Ayalew et al., 2020; Onyango et al., 2021).

The 5Ss involve TB patient care and support for the well-being of TB patients. TB patients' knowledge, attitude, and behavior, along with their life experiences, can enhance the healthcare system (Chinenye, 2015). Support, as well as spiritual beliefs in traditional systems, can improve the lives of TB patients. The factors involved in TB patients' lives and treatment adherence support successful treatment and outcomes (Shasha, 2013). The study addresses TB patients' perceptions of using the 5Ss strategy and involves community engagement. Understanding that TB patients can involve the 5Ss approach—self, society, state, system, and spirituality—can enhance effective TB management by addressing patients' barriers and challenges. The study addresses the role of effective healthcare providers, medical emphasis, and policymakers in developing targeted interventions, responding to policy-making, and improving the quality of life for TB patients. The research highlights TB patient care and services with the support of various aspects of the 5Ss to improve successful treatment for TB patients.

GENERAL PERSPECTIVE FOR TB INFECTION DISEASES

In the past 20 years, there has been an increasing trend globally in the spread of infectious diseases caused by bacteria and other microorganisms. This is evident in many ways in America and other such countries, as reported in newspapers, media, and various advertisements (Tomes 2010). It is evident that the public is anxious about infectious diseases such as AIDS and TB due to recent outbreaks. It is evident that the public is anxious about infectious diseases such as AIDS and TB due to recent outbreaks. The increasing number of TB cases has drawn worldwide attention, starting from the period of 1993, as per WHO records, when it was declared a global emergency for TB disease. WHO conducted 16 focus group discussions among TB patients and non-TB participants about their beliefs regarding TB disease in Vietnam.

The study results provided a comprehensive outcome, highlighting the dangerous nature of TB among the general public. It is a contagious disease caused by micro-organisms. A significant number of respondents believed that TB is hereditary and can be transmitted from older to younger family members through blood relations. Additionally, they perceived that men are affected due to heavy physical work, while women are more affected by mental causes such as excessive thinking and worrying. Furthermore, smoking habits and lung issues caused by microorganisms transmitted through respiratory-related diseases were noted as factors in Vietnam. There are three main reasons affecting TB: a long delay in diagnosis, an increased level of stigma, and isolation of TB patients and their families, which are the primary factors impacting TB patients (Kimmel, 2003).

Beliefs Related to Coping Strategies of Those Suffering From TB

The existing review studies focused on patient perception as a core aspect of the study, with clinical assessments determining the quality of life in patients with end-stage renal disease. The quality of life among patients is influenced by their perceptions of symptoms, spiritual beliefs, and psychosocial factors related to ethnicity. The study outcome found that symptoms of pain are related to psychological and spiritual factors among patients, which are connected to the quality of life in end-stage renal disease (Kimmel et al., 2003).

The past study emphasizes the religious beliefs and practices of Taiwanese parents whose children are affected by pediatric cancer. The religious beliefs include worshiping at a temple, where people can pray and draw the 'chien.' In the temple, people cast lots for their fate, seeking fortune, and explaining the meaning of the lots as part of divination. Their traditional beliefs and ritual aspects include 'Fu' water, which is believed to cure diseases. People believe in Taoist priests for the blessed water, and they write on a piece of paper with magic words to cure and change a child's name when conducting temple ceremonies. It can be performed to diminish the harmful effects of childhood diseases This kind of beliefs and practices without the knowledge of healthcare professionals and practitioners. It can be observed in the poor relationship between parents and health professionals. The author argues that it can be considered for families and caregivers to interconnect with religious and cultural aspects, which can help improve and establish holistic nursing practices (Yeh, 2001).

The author illustrated in the study that many patients are involved with therapists, and it is considerable to seek alternative medicine and products that might not have been subjected to testing or proven to be efficacious, which may pose a danger. The study provides valuable insights, such as people's beliefs about their social and cultural aspects and psychological factors, including the illusion that ineffective therapy can work and the factors that actually influence its effectiveness. Social and cultural reasons lead them to believe in the superiority of natural products and their dislike for scientific biomedicine. There are psychological reasons that include patients' demands, wishful thinking, errors in judgment, and the determination of their beliefs. The ineffective therapy can involve the natural course or cyclical nature of the disease, the placebo effect, misdiagnosis, or spontaneous remission. The study highlights that when someone becomes too sick, it can provide false promises to cure their health, beguiling them (Beyerstein, 2001).

The study examines the causes of infertility and treatment-seeking behavior for infertility, as well as the consequences of childlessness among the Muslim population in Dhaka, Bangladesh. It can provide insight into the causes of infertility, which are believed to be caused by evil spirits or physiological problems in women, and it can affect men with psychosexual and physiological problems. They prefer herbalists and traditional practitioners for the treatment of women. Men, on the other hand, consider remarriage as an option, followed by the advice of herbalists or traditional practitioners (Papreen, 2000).

The study provides a comprehensive understanding of TB patients' perceptions of the 5Ss Approach in the community, which includes self, society, state, system, and spiritual aspects. It examines the levels of stigma among TB patients at the individual, family, and community levels, including self-stigmatization. Additionally, it explores system support, such as the role of healthcare workers and providers, in enhancing the health and well-being of TB patients for improved treatment outcomes. How the 5Ss approach plays a vital role in supporting better treatment, enhancing TB patients' successful outcomes, and contributing to a TB-free society. The study provides TB patients' perceptions and knowledge to emphasize the need for future and further research studies. It can address the standardization process in the healthcare system, gaining traction to demonstrate a positive impact on TB patient care and safety. This approach also helps reduce stigma levels, improves patients' self-care, and benefits society as a whole.

THE 5SS APPROACH INVOLVES PATIENTS' PERCEPTIONS

The 5Ss are self, society, state, system, and spiritual aspects. The impact of the 5Ss on patients affected by disease can later influence their recovery, particularly regarding the self (Faherty, 1996). They recover by themselves, but it takes time to resolve their problems. After that, they may face societal issues, including stigma and isolation within their family and community, hindering their ability to adapt to the situation. The state provides valuable awareness to the community to protect the affected population and provide care and support. The system can adopt strong policies and provide valuable advocacy for the affected community (Hargreaves et al., 2011). It can resolve patients' safe care and support, and the system can improve. Spiritual beliefs can vary according to the area, and people believe in improving the spiritual aspects of their lives and the entire treatment course (Bryant-Davis & Wong, 2013). This can improve treatment outcomes, lead to successful treatment, and decrease TB, a communicable disease. It can also strengthen the effort for TB-free nations.

The core aspects of the study mainly emphasize patients' perceptions when they are affected by diseases (Lawn et al., 2006). They believe in the 5Ss approach, which includes the aspects of self, society, state, system, and spiritual beliefs. The study mainly focuses on patients' perceptions and community engagement activities aimed at rectifying the patients' diseases in their sociocultural aspects, while they continue to follow their own traditional practices and beliefs.

The Real Issues in TB Management

1. **Self:** Compliance with the medication, self care for taking the medicine on time and timely reaching out for medical assistance to prevent any complications. This can also be labelled as Self Empowerment for which the client and caregivers need to work as a team.
2. **Society:** Society, Family providing support to the client and reassurance. This can be called as the Societal Empowerment of Client. Society, Family, Friends and Environment empowers the client to cope and manage the disease.

3. **System:** Ensuring the availability of medical professionals for client clinical management and those of any complications. This could be labelled as the System Empowerment for the client. His Faith on the caregiver and healthcare professional empowers client to deal with the condition.
4. **State:** Ensuring the availability of management regimes by the Pharma companies and providing special centers providing targeted care. The State laws, policies, rules and regulations empowers the client to feel secure and have faith to look towards the State led system and institutions to be able to manage the disease.
5. **Spirituality:** The client history taking to elucidate his Faith or belief in Self/ higher supreme, his ability to understand the meaning of spirituality and that of life its importance and influence on self for better compliance and betterment, interventions needed to keep the client on track; his community where he lives and availability of any community support groups for his rehabilitation and reintegration and Attention of the care givers and health professionals. This is called the "FICA" model; and can facilitate the client rehabilitation.

So the inputs of 5Ss' are geared towards the quality outcome for the client, family and community; empowering client and having an impact towards disease prevention, reducing prevalence and managing the client for reducing morbidity and mortality (Qidwai, 2024).

BACKGROUND OF THE STUDY

The background of the study highlights that TB continues to be a leading communicable and highly contagious disease globally, affecting millions of people, especially in areas with high poverty rates and limited healthcare resources. As per WHO reports, the TB incidence rate in recent years indicates that the disease remains a major public health concern, especially in Asia and Africa. The stigma associated with TB, combined with socio-economic problems and gaps in the healthcare system, can hinder real-time diagnosis and the provision of effective treatment, exacerbating the burden of the disease.

Community engagement provides stronger support in the fight against TB. It is an effective approach to reduce stigma. Effective community engagement can help reduce stigma, enhance TB treatment, and provide health awareness about TB symptoms, causes of TB, the TB burden in India, adverse drug reactions (ADRs), and various government schemes and support for affected TB patients. Identification of new TB patients gets general public incentive support. TB patients have focused on medical support and broader aspects, such as social, cultural, and spiritual factors, which influence their behavior and treatment outcomes. The study can address various gaps, especially in the 5Ss approach to continue the self, society, stature, system, and spiritual aspects. It can provide patients with effective treatment and community engagement support to enhance TB patients' wellness services.

Self: It can focus on individual knowledge regarding health, basic TB awareness, self-care, and health hygiene as part of personal responsibility among TB patients, enabling them to manage their health conditions in a systematic way.

Society: It can identify the patients' societal norms, their cultural beliefs, and family and community attitudes toward TB. It can often play a vital role in improving TB patients' experiences by encouraging willingness and seeking help at the societal level.

State: The state can involve government policies and health-related activities and programs. It can address the public health strategic plan to ensure equitable access to TB care, with the state government providing necessary policies to strengthen the TB patient community and ensure equitable TB care services.

System: The system aims to provide a better healthcare infrastructure, increase the number and efficiency of healthcare providers, and strengthen support services to enhance effective diagnosis, treatment, and follow-up adherence for TB patients.

Spirituality: Spirituality can encompass TB patients' experiences when they are affected by the disease. They may increase their spiritual beliefs, sometimes blaming God, and at other times involving themselves more deeply in spiritual practices. It can provide emotional support and motivation for resilience among TB patients, playing a pivotal role in coping with challenges and the disease.

The focus of the study is to explore TB patients' perceptions, particularly through the 5Ss approach, which involves community engagement activities.It can enlighten cultural sensitivity in interventions addressing physical, psychological, and psycho social aspects, allowing TB patients to ventilate their feelings. This can improve the overall quality of life and treatment outcomes.

Definition: TB Patients' Perception of the 5Ss Approach

TB patients, their perception, and the 5Ss approaches—self, society, state, system, and spiritual beliefs—help to understand their attitudes and experiences. In this regard, these five dimensions can play a significant role in their health journey after TB, including prevention, care, and recovery. The TB patients' self-awareness, confidence level, and willingness to take responsibility for their health are crucial to adhering to the treatment. Society influences and improves the social support system and community norms for TB patients, which can include addressing stigma and fostering empathy. The state government initiates various policies and programs to enable access and affordability, aiming to improve the quality of TB care. The system ensures the effectiveness and reliability needed to provide a patient-centered approach, enhancing the healthcare system and addressing the needs of TB patients. Spiritual beliefs can impact patients' faith, cultural values, and spiritual practices, serving as coping mechanisms and fostering resilience to improve health-seeking behaviors. TB patients' perception of the balance and interaction of these elements fosters support for the environment, TB recovery, and their well-being.

LITERATURE REVIEW

The author explores how the WHO clearly indicates the International Standards for Tuberculosis Care (ISTC).TB is a global health problem, and SDG Goal 3, which indicates good health and well-being, highlights the need to improve medical facilities and strengthen community engagement to eliminate TB disease (Srinivasan et al., 2023). The existing review provides an overview of the 5Ss as a global patient safety approach initiated by the World Health Organization (WHO). It aims to develop and implement Standard Operating Protocols (SOPs) for the global community to achieve measurable and significant progress in sustaining the reduction of safety-related challenges (Leotsakos et al., 2014). The study effectively implements the 5Ss to innovate the patient care process in hospitals within the country and provides services through healthcare workers.

This approach aims to adopt behavior and situational analysis to improve the standard of care for TB patients (Leotsakos et al., 2014). Patient-centric care plays an important role in TB management by increasing treatment, care, and support services through health professionals, community health workers, and health visitors, who provide successful treatment support for TB patients (Srinivasan, 2025).The existing review provides a comprehensive understanding of the additional support needed for TB patients to improve their health. NGOs and corporate can also get involved to support TB patients' health and well-being in the community (Srinivasan & Praba Lama, 2025). The study highlights that TB patients have comorbidity issues, are unable to access healthcare facilities, do not receive proper information, and are unaware of TB education. They may be dependent on others in society or their family members and face stigma-related problems. The study emphasizes these issues (Srinivasan et al., 2023).

Table 1. Relevant literature review of the study

Sl. No	Author(s), year of publication	Target country of Study	Methodology adopted for the study	Objective of the Study	Finding of the study
1	(Davis et al., 2018)	Kenya	Review based study	The objective of the study on community engagement is to assess the various barriers to quality care and services in healthcare concerns.	The outcome of the study aims to improve healthcare delivery by enhancing the role of community health workers and utilizing mHealth technology to access clinics and enhance community engagement for quality care and services.
2	(Munang et al., 2016)	UK	Observational cohort study	The core aspect of the study is the social network among the disease-affected community.	The study findings for the affected immunodeficiency virus indicate that patients may face social risk factors related to drug resistance, which are associated with health impacts on affected individuals.
3	(Pratiwi et al., 2021)	Indonesia	Cross sectional study	The main aim of the study is to examine anxiety and spiritual activity during the recovery of TB patients.	The result of the study shows an association between anxiety and motivation in TB patients' recovery, with a p-value of 0.000 and an r-value of -0.436.
4	(Datiko et al., 2020)	Ethiopia	Mixed methods	The objective of the study is to examine healthcare and insufficient health-seeking behavior among affected people, considering their socioeconomic level and stigma level.	The result of the study shows the knowledge level of TB, with an AOR of 0.62 and a 95% CI of 0.49-0.78. The stigma score and fear of job loss affect nearly 32.5% of patients, while isolation impacts nearly 15.3%, and 9.3% report feelings related to the disclosure of their TB status.
5	(Chang et al., 2004)	Review study	A Systematic Review	Quality of life among TB patients and their perception.	TB can impose a greater financial burden, as patients face high health expenses. It affects both developed and underdeveloped countries, and their families and communities may ostracize the patients.

continued on following page

Table 1. Continued

Sl. No	Author(s), year of publication	Target country of Study	Methodology adopted for the study	Objective of the Study	Finding of the study
6	(Saleem & Majeed, 2023)	Pakistan	Survey Method	The aim of the study is to examine the association between spiritual beliefs and self-management skills in determining the depression and anxiety levels of TB-affected people.	The results indicate a significant positive correlation between spiritual aspects and self-management ($r = .42, p < .001$). There is a negative relationship between spiritual aspects and depression levels ($r = -0.25, p < .01$) as well as anxiety levels ($r = -0.27, p < .01$). Self-management shows a negative association with both depression and anxiety.
7	(McDade, 2013)	African American and Haitian populations	Mixed Method	Spirituality and TB Medication Adherence**: The study emphasizes TB patients' medication and treatment adherence in the context of spirituality.**	The findings of the study aim to provide improved educational interventions to support TB treatment, prevent its transmission, and reduce mortality.
8	(Hansel et al., 2004)	US	Focus Group Discussion	The study investigates the psychological health, spiritual, and physical roles of TB patients. It emphasizes social stigma, isolation, the burden of their lives, sexual dysfunction, job loss, and increased fear in the lives of those affected by TB.	The findings of the study indicate the impact of sexual dysfunction on their lives and highlight increased spirituality as a way to improve their life perspective. Therapy plays a vital role during TB treatment and helps enhance the long-term quality of life.

continued on following page

Table 1. Continued

Sl. No	Author(s), year of publication	Target country of Study	Methodology adopted for the study	Objective of the Study	Finding of the study
9	(Tseng et al., 2019)	South Africa	The study adopted a qualitative method, including observation, FGD, and interviews.	The study mainly emphasizes the role of field workers and community health workers in integrating patient care and improving the health system.	The outcome of the study emphasizes that, under thorough supervision, effective implementation by community healthcare workers includes daily assistance and updating to provide comprehensive reports. This can enhance community engagement activities involving family members and clinic staff to ensure patient care and support. However, the results indicate lower trust from clients.
10	(Kanamori et al., 2016)	Senegal	Quasi Experimental Study	The aim of the study is to assess the impact of the 5Ss intervention on providing effective support for client satisfaction and improving the experience of patients and caretakers at health facilities.	The outcome of the study shows a significant effect of the 5Ss intervention, represented by a 0.19-point increase in intervention outcomes when the treatment duration is 6 to 8 months, with a p-value of 0.002. The regression values indicate an increase of 0.44 ($p = 0.002$), 0.14 ($p = 0.002$), 0.06 ($p = 0.019$), and 0.17 ($p = 0.044$). These increases suggest that healthcare workers and professionals effectively communicate instructions regarding illness and cases, leading to overall patient satisfaction.
11	(Nakhaei et al., 2020)	Iran	Correlational Study	The study provides a comprehensive understanding of patient mindfulness and their spiritual experiences as coping strategies to improve the quality of life for patients affected by TB.	The outcome of the study addresses the relationship between mindfulness and quality of life. It improves the variable for prediction by nearly 38%, with spiritual experiences contributing nearly 27%. It also focuses on coping strategies, which account for approximately 5.2% of the variance in quality of life.

continued on following page

Table 1. Continued

Sl. No	Author(s), year of publication	Target country of Study	Methodology adopted for the study	Objective of the Study	Finding of the study
12	(Davtyan et al., 2019)	Republic of Armenia	Cross-Sectional study through telephone survey	The core aspects of the study address TB patients' satisfaction with TB services, considering demographic and health aspects, the treatment received, and their overall satisfaction.	The outcome of the study shows that a total of 386 respondents, with nearly 76.4% being men and the remaining women, fall into an age group with a mean of 45.5 years, which is nearly 0.7 years. About 8.9% of them are affected by Adverse Drug Reaction (ADR) complications. The TB patients' non-adherence rate is nearly 9%. The majority, nearly 93%, are receiving full-fledged TB services and are satisfied. The TB services focus on TB treatment, non-adherence, and addressing drug-resistant TB, especially among those with higher education.
13	(Loa, 2018)	Philippines	Qualitative study conducted case study	The objective of the study is to examine the barriers TB patients face in self-management and receiving treatment at health facilities.	The outcome of the study shows that TB patients' self-management, family support, and healthcare workers, along with spirituality aspects such as physical and emotional support, are impacted by stigma and dissatisfaction with the healthcare system.

continued on following page

Table 1. Continued

Sl. No	Author(s), year of publication	Target country of Study	Methodology adopted for the study	Objective of the Study	Finding of the study
14	Ozturk & Hisar, (2014)	Turkey	Descriptive study	The aim of the study is to examine TB patients' diagnosis and treatment, focusing on the stigma and barriers they face.	The result of the study shows that the stigma level affects nearly half of the patients, with 53.4% reporting a high level of stigma. The patient scale represents values of nearly 29.9 and 6.3, with the lowest values related to family and friends' relationships, at nearly 11.3 and 3.8, respectively.
15	(Adaji, 2013)	Nigeria	Survey Method Cross-Sectional Study	The objective of the study is to examine healthcare workers' role in supporting TB patients' treatment adherence and the significant barriers they face.	The overall findings of the study provide a comprehensive understanding of the various factors involved in treatment adherence and healthcare workers' roles. They can help resolve the barriers TB patients face and improve treatment adherence during the treatment process. The study overall provides better outcomes for TB patients and improved TB management.

Figure 1. 5Ss approach for the TB patients perception

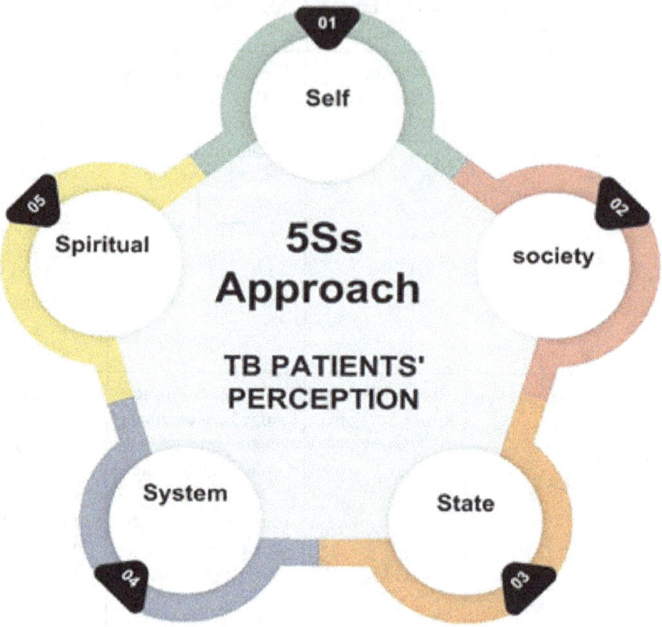

Figure 1 provides TB patients' perceptions regarding the aspects of the **5Ss approach**. The figure addresses a comprehensive understanding of TB patients, including their knowledge, attitudes, and behaviors when affected by TB. It starts from the onset of symptoms and diagnosis. After being identified as TB positive, patients begin to adapt to their situation, reflecting on their self-realization and understanding their circumstances.

They consider society's perception, including the views of family members, life partners, and neighbors, as well as their relationships within the community. TB patients, after being affected by TB, may worry about their health, experience a decline in mental health, and be unable to work at their jobs.The 5Ss can play a vital role in improving TB patients' self, society, system, state, and spirituality. They can address the problem and provide better solutions through community engagement activities.

TB patients are emotionally affected by their mental health; they may prefer to engage in spiritual activities, such as regular visits to the temple or prayer, which can improve their emotional well-being and increase self-efficacy.TB patients who are able to recover from TB can receive successful treatment in order to address the condition.

RESEARCH QUESTIONS

1. What is the current status and socio-economic condition of the TB patients?
2. How do TB patients' perceptions involve the 5Ss approach (Self, Society, State, System, Beliefs)?
3. What are the main factors impacting the 5Ss approach?
4. How is the 5Ss approach correlated with the first state (Self) and age correlation?
5. How are society and location correlated?
6. How is the state and TB patients' gender correlation accessed?
7. How is the system and type of TB affected by correlations?
8. What are the beliefs and marital status correlations?
9. How is the influence of TB patients affected by the type of TB and 5Ss approach correlations?
10. What are the factors involved in the 5Ss approach in the Correlations Matrix?

Objective of the Study

- To know the demographic details of the TB patients.
- To access the 5Ss—Self, Society, System, State, and Spiritual— for TB patients' perceptions.

Figure 2. Selected TU

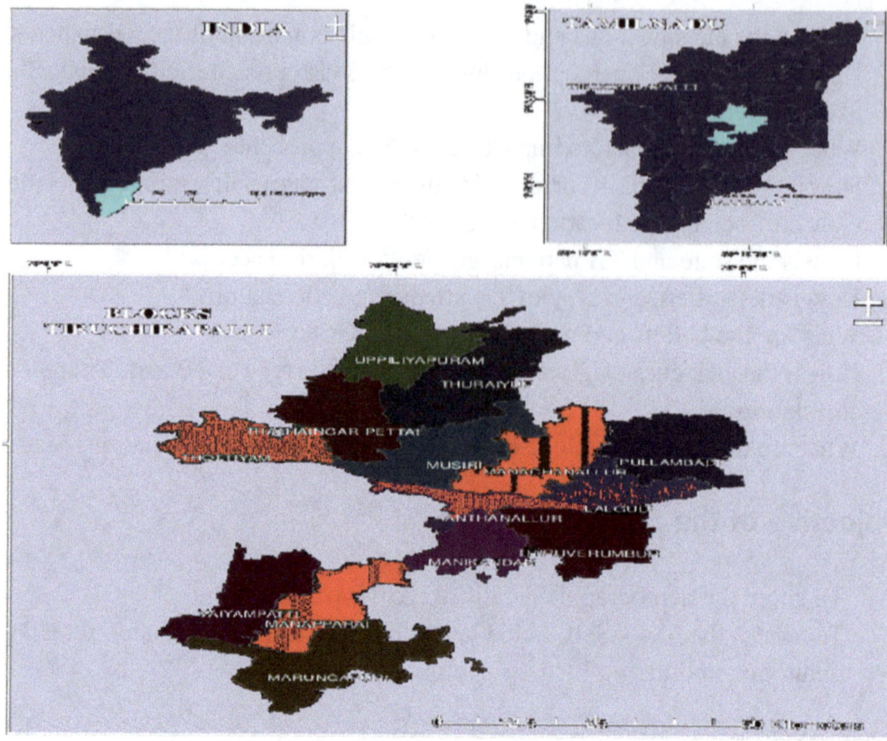

Five TUs were selected in Trichy District: Andhanallur, Lalgudi, Manachanallur, Manaparai, and Thotiyam. Fifteen TB patients were selected from each TU to assess the 5Ss of TB patients' perceptions: Self, Society, State, System, and Spiritual aspects.

Methodology of the Study

The methodology of the study can include TB patients' perceptions to improve the 5Ss components, such as Self, Society, State, System, and Spiritual. It can improve community engagement activities to provide the following outline.

Research Design

The study adopted a descriptive research design and utilized quantitative techniques to analyze patient perceptions. The quantitative tools and techniques used include a self-structured survey questionnaire, which can gather information from TB patients and measure their perceptions of the 5Ss.The study used purposive sampling with a total sample size of 75 TB patients, selected from five TB units: Lalgudi, Manaprai, Manachanallur, Srirangam, and Thotiyam. Fifteen TB patients were covered in each unit in Trichy District, Tamil Nadu, India. The study focused on purposive sampling, including various TB communities and addressing the socio-economic background across different geographical locations: urban, rural, and semi-urban. This study includes demographic factors such as age, gender, and treatment stage.The study emphasizes the following five themes: TB patients' self-responsibility, societal attitudes, state support, healthcare system experience, and spiritual beliefs. Ethical considerations for TB patients concern all the patients, with approval from the ethical committees to maintain anonymity and confidentiality for the participants. The result analysis for the study used SPSS software to provide descriptive statistics of TB patients' 5Ss perceptions and identify correlations in the significant patterns of the 5Ss.

Study Population

Inclusion Criteria: The inclusion criteria focus only on diagnosed TB patients who are on treatment, as well as those who have completed treatment, including both pulmonary and extra-pulmonary TB patients. The study includes only TB patients who have undergone community engagement activities. This study focused on adults above 18 years old.

Exclusion Criteria: The exclusion criteria include patients who are not interested, do not provide consent, or are not willing to respond or participate. This excludes patients with severe health conditions to prevent interviews, and other comorbid diseases are excluded from the study.

RESULT AND DISCUSSION

Table 2. Demographic details

Demographic Details	Options	Frequency	%	Mean	SD	Range
Age	19 to 30	6	8	2.693	0.804	3
	31 to 45	21	28			
	46 to 60	38	50.7			
	> 60	10	13.3			
	Total	75	100			

continued on following page

Table 2. Continued

Demographic Details	Options	Frequency	%	Mean	SD	Range
Gender	Male	64	85.3	1.146	0.356	1
	Female	11	14.7			
	Total	75	100			
Education	Illiterate	21	28	2.16	0.93	3
	Primary	27	36			
	Secondary	21	28			
	Graduate or above	6	8			
	Total	75	100			
Employment Status	Employed	16	21.3	2.066	0.703	2
	Unemployed	38	50.7			
	Self-employed	21	28			
	Total	75	100			
Marital Status	Single	13	17.3	1.826	0.381	1
	Married	62	82.7			
	Total	75	100			
Living Area	Rural	26	34.7	1.906	0.774	2
	Urban	30	40			
	Semi-urban	19	25.3			
	Total	75	100			
Name of the TU	Lalgudi	15	20	3	1.423	4
	Manaparai	15	20			
	Anthanallur	15	20			
	Thotiyam	15	20			
	Manachanallur	15	20			
	Total	75	100			
Type of TB	Pulmonary TB	43	57.3	1.426	0.497	1
	Extra Pulmonary TB	32	42.7			
	Total	75	100			
Part of Body TB Infected	Lungs	58	77.3	1.4133	0.790	2
	Brain	3	4			
	Other parts of body	14	18.7			
	Total	75	100			

continued on following page

Table 2. Continued

Demographic Details	Options	Frequency	%	Mean	SD	Range
Type of Diagnosis TB	Sputum test	56	74.7	1.28	0.508	2
	X-ray	17	22.7			
	CT Scan	2	2.7			
	Total	75	100			
Advance Test for TB	CBNAAT	48	64	1.36	0.483	1
	TrueNat	27	36			
	Total	75	100			

The age distribution indicates that the majority of respondents fall in the age group of 46 to 60 years, accounting for 50.7%, while nearly 28% of the TB patients are in the age group of 31 to 45 years. The majority of them are male, accounting for 85.3%, while 14.7% of them are TB-affected females. The mean value is 1.146, and the standard deviation (SD) is 0.356, indicating a skewed gender distribution towards males. The educational level of the respondents shows that the majority, 36% of TB patients, have primary education, while 28% of them are illiterate. Nearly 8% of the TB patients are graduates, and very few have advanced education in the group. The mean value is 2.16, and the standard deviation (SD) reflects the diversity in educational attainment. Nearly half of the age group, 50.7%, are unemployed, 28% are self-employed, and 21.3% highlight the economic challenges faced by many TB patients. The mean value is 2.066, and the standard deviation (SD) is 0.703, which indicates a tendency towards unemployment.

In terms of marital status, the majority, 82.7%, are married, while 17.3% are not married. The mean value is 1.826, and the standard deviation (SD) is 0.381, indicating a high prevalence of marital stability. TB patients from TU units in Lalgudi, Manapparai, Anthanallur, Thottiyam, and Manachanallur each contribute equally, with 20% of the patients coming from each location. The mean value is 3, and the standard deviation (SD) is 1.423, indicating the distribution of patients across the TU. Pulmonary TB is more prevalent, with nearly 57.3% of patients having pulmonary TB and 42.7% having extra-pulmonary TB. The mean value is 1.426, and the standard deviation (SD) is 0.497. Part-body TB infection shows that 77.3% of the patients are affected in the lungs, 18.7% have infections in other parts of the body, and 4% are affected by brain TB. The mean value is 1.413, and the standard deviation (SD) is 0.790, showing that lung TB is the dominant type.

In terms of the type of diagnosis, nearly 74.7% of patients are diagnosed through sputum tests, which is the most common diagnostic method. 22.7% are diagnosed through X-ray tests, and CT scans are rarely used, with only 2.7% identified through this method. The mean value is 1.28, and the standard deviation (SD) is 0.508, indicating that the sputum test is the primary diagnostic tool. The advancement of TB tests shows that nearly 64% of patients are commonly tested using the CBNAAT test, while 36% are tested with the TrueNat test for advanced testing. The mean value is 1.36, and the standard deviation (SD) is 0.483, indicating a preference for the CBNAAT test among the patients.

Figure 3. Area living TB patients

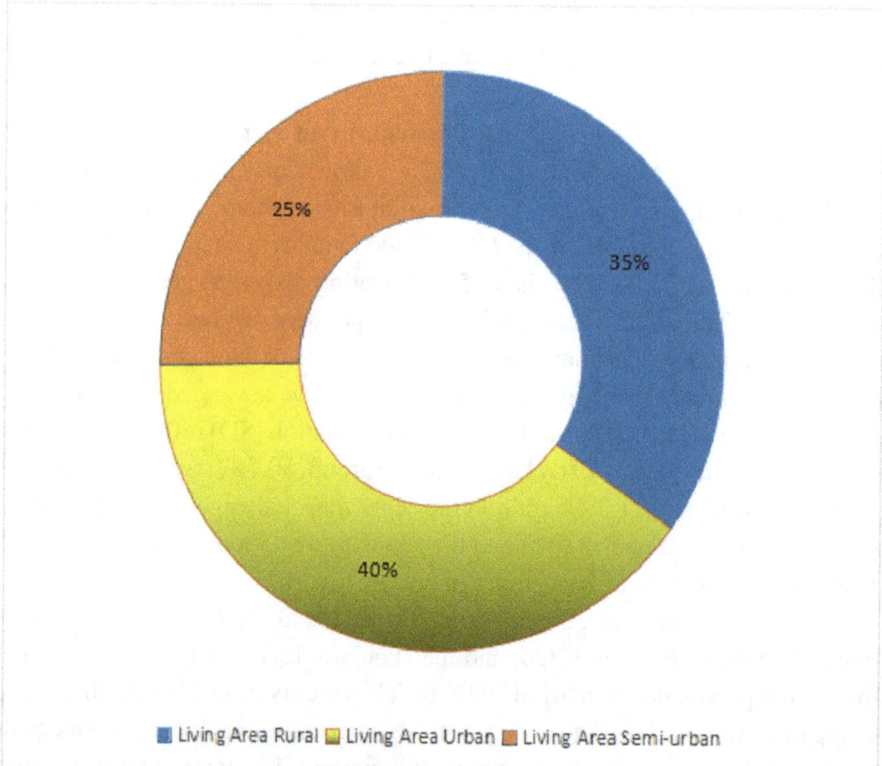

TB patients' living areas show that nearly 40% reside in urban areas, 34.7% in rural areas, and 25.3% live in semi-urban areas.

Table 3. TB patients' perception of the 5Ss approach

5Ss Dimensions	Options	Frequency	%	SE
Self				
Aware TB Symptoms before Diagnosis	Not at all aware	28	37.3	0.884
	Somewhat aware	30	40	
	Fully aware	17	22.7	
	Total	75	100	
Feel Confident in Managing Treatment Plan (medication adherence, lifestyle changes)	Strongly disagree	15	20	0.138
	Disagree	22	29.3	
	Neutral	21	28	
	Agree	11	14.7	
	Strongly agree	6	8	
	Total	75	100	
Experienced Stigma Affecting Self-Esteem After Diagnosis	Yes	25	33.3	0.548
	No	50	66.7	
	Total	75	100	
Society				
Family Support during the TB Treatment Journey	Not supportive	15	20	0.892
	Somewhat supportive	26	34.7	
	Very supportive	34	45.3	
	Total	75	100	
Faced Stigma or Discrimination from the community After Diagnosed with TB	Yes	26	34.7	0.553
	No	49	65.3	
	Total	75	100	
Community Awareness Programs TB effective	Strongly disagree	8	10.7	0.134
	Disagree	4	5.3	
	Neutral	13	17.3	
	Agree	37	49.3	
	Strongly agree	13	17.3	
	Total	75	100	
State				
Aware Gvernment-provide support for TB Patients (e.g., free medication, nutritional support)	Yes	39	52	0.058
	No	36	48	
	Total	75	100	

continued on following page

Table 3. Continued

5Ss Dimensions	Options	Frequency	%	SE
Self				
Government Programs During Treatment Supported	Yes	47	62.7	0.056
	No	28	37.3	
	Total	75	100	
Satisfied with Government's Efforts Providing TB-Related Support	Very dissatisfied	3	4	0.121
	Dissatisfied	7	9.3	
	Neutral	22	29.3	
	Very satisfied	27	36	
	Very satisfied	16	21.3	
	Total	75	100	
System				
Accessible is healthcare for TB treatment	Very inaccessible	6	8	0.147
	Somewhat inaccessible	18	24	
	Neutral	18	24	
	Accessible	16	21.3	
	Very accessible	17	22.7	
	Total	75	100	
Healthcare Workers (doctors, nurses, etc.) treating you with respect and compassion	Strongly disagree	7	9.3	0.136
	Disagree	14	18.7	
	Neutral	24	32	
	Agree	19	25.3	
	Strongly agree	11	14.7	
	Total	75	100	
Healthcare System TB patient supportive	Very poor	7	9.3	0.130
	Poor	14	18.7	
	Average	21	28	
	Good	26	34.7	
	Excellent	7	9.3	
	Total	75	100	
Spiritual				
Spiritual or Religious Practices to Cope with TB Diagnosis	Yes	35	46.7	0.0579
	No	40	53.3	
	Total	75	100	

continued on following page

Table 3. Continued

5Ss Dimensions	Options	Frequency	%	SE
Self				
Spirituality/Religion to provide emotional strength during treatment	Not important	21	28	0.1
	Somewhat important	14	18.7	
	Very important	40	53.3	
	Total	75	100	
Support from faith-based organizations or spiritual leaders in community	Yes	55	73.3	0.514
	No	20	26.7	
	Total	75	100	
5Ss Approach				
5Ss do you feel has the greatest impact on recovery and engagement	Self	23	30.7	0.186
	Society	17	22.7	
	State	8	10.7	
	System	7	9.3	
	Spiritual Approach	20	26.7	
	Total	75	100	

Self: The table clearly illustrates the improvement in self-awareness of TB symptoms before diagnosis. Nearly 40% of patients are aware, while 37.3% are not aware, reflecting the need for better awareness of symptoms and the conduction of awareness campaigns. 22.7% of the people are fully aware, which indicates that they have realized the self-detection of TB symptoms. Confidence in managing the treatment plan: The majority of TB patients, 49.3%, strongly disagreed with their ability to manage the treatment plan, indicating a need for enhanced counseling and educational programs. The majority, 33.3%, experienced stigma, while 66.7% did not face any stigma.

Society: The majority, 45.3%, feel that their family was very supportive during treatment, while 20% feel no support from their family, which had a negative impact on their recovery. Thirty-four point seven percent (34.7%) of them face stigma and discrimination from their community, revealing social barriers in TB management. The majority of the respondents, 66.6%, strongly agree that community awareness programs are an effective suggestion to improve valuable initiatives that reduce stigma and increase knowledge.

State: The state government provides support, with nearly 52% of people aware of government-related services, while 48% are not aware of such services. The effective government programs are available and believed to have a positive impact.

Nearly 62.7% of them experienced the positive effects of state interventions during treatment. Nearly 36% were very satisfied, while 13.3% of the people were dissatisfied with the government's TB-related initiatives.

System: The majority, 44%, of the respondents find healthcare for TB treatment very accessible, while 32% find it somewhat inaccessible. This highlights the potential barriers to healthcare delivery. Forty percent (40%) of them feel that healthcare workers treat them with respect, 28% are neutral, and 28% have mixed experiences with healthcare providers. The majority, 44%, of the TB patients find the healthcare system good to excellent, while nearly 28% rate it as average, and 28% experience it as poor to very poor, indicating a need for improvement.

Spiritual: The majority of TB patients, 46.7%, engage in spiritual and religious practices to cope with TB, which play a role in their spiritual and emotional resilience. Fifty-three point three percent (53.3%) consider spirituality very important for emotional strength, while nearly 28% consider it not important. This reflects the diversity of coping mechanisms. The majority, 73.3%, of the affected people believe faith-based organizations play a significant role in community-based care.

This analysis aims to improve TB patients' self-confidence, reduce societal stigma, enhance healthcare accessibility, and strengthen the spiritual aspect to positively affect TB care strategies.

Figure 4. 5Ss TB patients perceptions

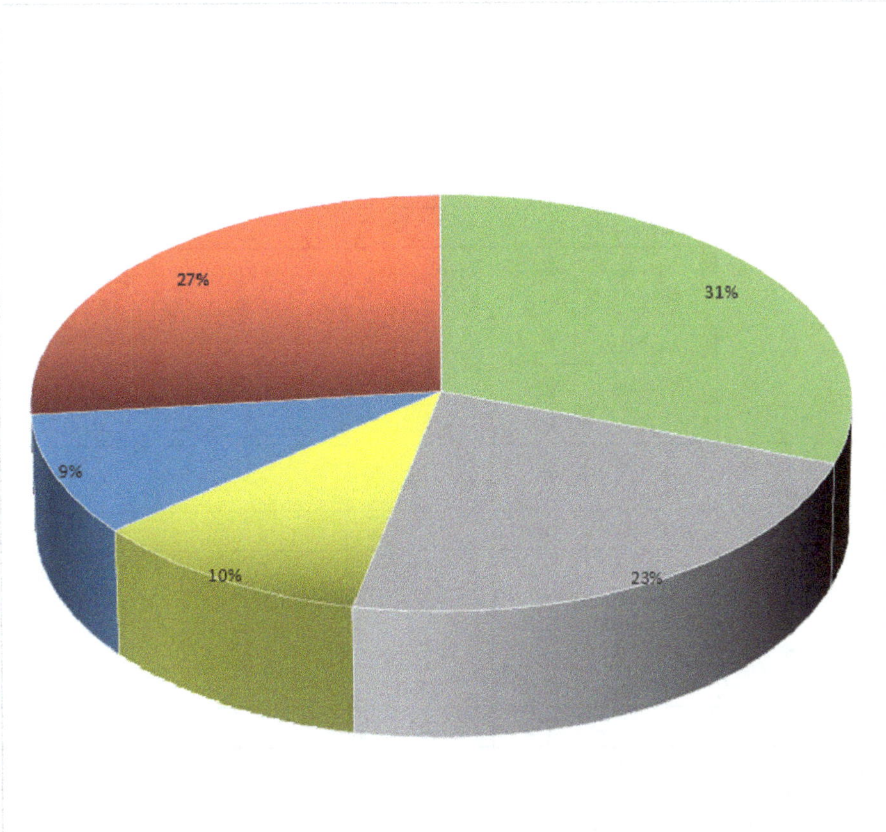

5Ss Approach Impact: Nearly 31% highly perceive self-dimensions, followed by 27% for spiritual and 23% for society. The state, with 11%, and the system, with 10%, were perceived as having less impact, suggesting the need for greater focus on improvement. This reflects that faith-based support for TB patients is effective in community awareness, with positive perceptions of spirituality making a significant contribution to the patients.

Table 4. Self and age correlations

Self and Age Correlation		Age	Aware TB Symptoms before Diagnosis	Feel Confident in Managing Treatment Plan (medication adherence, lifestyle changes)	Experienced Stigma Affecting Self-Esteem After Diagnosis
Age	Pearson Correlation	1			
	Sig. (2-tailed)				
	Sum of Squares and Cross-products	47.947			
	Covariance	0.648			
	N	75			
AwareTBSymptoms before Diagnosis	Pearson Correlation	.321**	1		
	Sig. (2-tailed)	0.005			
	Sum of Squares and Cross-products	14.627	43.387		
	Covariance	0.198	0.586		
	N	75	75		
Feel Confident in Managing Treatment Plan (medication adherence, lifestyle changes)	Pearson Correlation	.591**	0.07	1	
	Sig. (2-tailed)	0	0.55		
	Sum of Squares and Cross-products	42.107	4.747	105.787	
	Covariance	0.569	0.064	1.43	
	N	75	75	75	
Experienced Stigma Affecting Self-Esteem After Diagnosis	Pearson Correlation	.295*	0.012	.365**	1
	Sig. (2-tailed)	0.01	0.916	0.001	
	Sum of Squares and Cross-products	8.333	0.333	15.333	16.667
	Covariance	0.113	0.005	0.207	0.225
	N	75	75	75	75

**. Correlation is significant at the 0.01 level (2-tailed).

*. Correlation is significant at the 0.05 level (2-tailed).

The table provides the correlation between age and awareness of TB symptoms before the TB diagnosis. The summary of the table on age and awareness of TB symptoms before diagnosis shows a Pearson value of 0.321 (p-value of 0.005). There is a moderate positive correlation, with older individuals tending to be more aware of TB symptoms. The significance value is reliable at the 0.01 level. The Pearson correlation value between age and confidence in managing the treatment plan is 0.591 ($p<0.001$). There is a strong positive correlation, with older patients being more confident in managing treatment, including medication and adherence to lifestyle changes. The significance of these findings is robust. Age and experienced stigma affect self-esteem. The Pearson correlation is nearly 0.295 (p-value = 0.01). There is a moderate positive correlation for older individuals, who slightly experience stigma and its impact on self-esteem. The significance level is reliable at 0.05.

The awareness of TB symptoms and confidence in managing treatment have a Pearson correlation value of 0.07 (p-value = 0.55). It is mentioned that there is a weak, non-significant correlation, indicating no substantial relationship. The awareness of TB symptoms and experienced stigma have a Pearson correlation value of 0.012 (p-value = 0.916), indicating a very weak and non-significant correlation. It does not influence the stigma level. Confidence in managing treatment is affected by experienced stigma. The Pearson correlation is 0.365 (p-value = 0.001), indicating a moderate positive correlation between the patient's confidence level and the reported stigma, which affects self-esteem. The overall performance of age significantly influences TB awareness and treatment confidence, as well as experiences with stigma. The TB symptoms show a moderate rate of correlation with age, but they do not impact TB treatment confidence or stigma experiences. The level of treatment confidence improves with age and stigma, suggesting that older adults and confident patients may experience increased stigma more frequently. Specific age interventions should focus on enhancing treatment confidence to reduce stigma, particularly for older patients.

Table 5. Location and society correlations

Location and Society		Location	Family Support during the TB Treatment Journey	Faced Stigma or Discrimination from the community After Diagnosed with TB	Community Awareness Programs TB effective
Location	Pearson Correlation	1			
	Sig. (2-tailed)				
	Sum of Squares and Cross-products	44.347			
	Covariance	0.599			
	N	75			
Family Support during the TB Treatment Journey	Pearson Correlation	-0.005	1		
	Sig. (2-tailed)	0.965			
	Sum of Squares and Cross-products	-0.227	44.187		
	Covariance	-0.003	0.597		
	N	75	75		
Faced Stigma or Discrimination from the community After Diagnosed with TB	Pearson Correlation	0.021	0.167	1	
	Sig. (2-tailed)	0.859	0.151		
	Sum of Squares and Cross-products	0.573	4.587	16.987	
	Covariance	0.008	0.062	0.23	
	N	75	75	75	

continued on following page

Table 5. Continued

Location and Society		Location	Family Support during the TB Treatment Journey	Faced Stigma or Discrimination from the community After Diagnosed with TB	Community Awareness Programs TB effective
Community Awareness Programs TB effective	Pearson Correlation	.705**	.257*	.240*	1
	Sig. (2-tailed)	0	0.026	0.038	
	Sum of Squares and Cross-products	47.013	17.107	9.907	100.347
	Covariance	0.635	0.231	0.134	1.356
	N	75	75	75	75

**. Correlation is significant at the 0.01 level (2-tailed).

*. Correlation is significant at the 0.05 level (2-tailed).

The correlation analysis for the location and family support during TB treatment shows a Pearson correlation value of -0.005 (p-value = 0.965). There is no significant relationship for the location; it does not affect their family support. The area and facing stigma for TB patients and the level of discrimination faced: the Pearson correlation value is 0.021 (p value = 0.859). There is no significant relationship between stigma and discrimination in their living place; it is not dependent. The area of living and the provision of community awareness programs were effective. The Pearson correlation value is 0.705 ($p < 0.001$). There is a strong positive correlation, which provides the effective impact of community awareness programs. The family support and community awareness program are effective. The Pearson correlation value is 0.257 (p-value = 0.026). It is a moderate positive correlation, and it involves strong family support, which provides a better perception of the program's effectiveness. Face stigma and community awareness program effectiveness: The Pearson correlation value is 0.240 (p-value = 0.038). The moderate positive value significantly correlates the stigma and community awareness program as perceived effective.

The living location of TB patients determines the effectiveness of the community awareness program, highlighting the need for location-specific strategic approaches. Family support engages the perception and awareness of related issues. The stigma has a moderate effect, and the suggested efforts for awareness can help mitigate the stigma. The effective community awareness program leverages family and social support to improve TB patients' health, well-being, and successful treatment.

Table 6. Gender and state correlation

Gender and State Correlation		Gender	Aware Government-provide support for TB Patients (e.g., free medication, nutritional support)	Government Programs During Treatment Supported	Satisfied with Government's Efforts Providing TB-Related Support
Gender	Pearson Correlation	1			
	Sig. (2-tailed)				
	N	75			
Aware Government-provide support for TB Patients (e.g., free medication, nutritional support)	Pearson Correlation	-.247*	1		
	Sig. (2-tailed)	0.032			
	N	75	75		
Government Programs During Treatment Supported	Pearson Correlation	0.148	-0.079	1	
	Sig. (2-tailed)	0.207	0.498		
	N	75	75	75	75
Satisfied with Government's Efforts Providing TB-Related Support	Pearson Correlation	0.081	0.126	0.075	1
	Sig. (2-tailed)	0.488	0.282	0.525	
	N	75	75	75	75

*. Correlation is significant at the 0.05 level (2-tailed).

The table provides the relationship between gender and state to understand the correlation between gender and the benefits of various awareness programs and government support for TB patients. The correlation coefficient is -0.247 and the p-value is 0.032. The negative correlation indicates that females and males are less aware of the government's TB support. The gender and government program during the treatment correlation coefficient value is 0.148, and the p-value is 0.207. There is no significant relationship between gender and the government program during the treatment. The gender and satisfaction level for the government initiatives have a correlation coefficient value of 0.081 and a p-value of ($p = 0.488$). There is no significance for gender and satisfaction level. The awareness of government support initiatives during the treatment for TB patients shows no association between government initiatives and TB treatment, with a correlation value of (-0.079, p =

0.498). The satisfaction level of government efforts shows no positive correlation (0.126, p = 0.282). The table provides the negative correlation between gender and the government awareness program; there are disparities, indicating the need for targeted interventions in the study.

Table 7. System and type of TB correlations

System and Type of TB Correlations		Type of TB	Accessible is healthcare for TB treatment	Healthcare Workers (doctors, nurses, etc.) treating you with respect and compassion	Healthcare System TB patient supportive
Type of TB	**Pearson Correlation**	1	.499**	.264*	0.19
	Sig. (2-tailed)		0	0.022	0.103
	N	75	75	75	75
Accessible healthcare for TB treatment	**Pearson Correlation**	.499**	1	.454**	.449**
	Sig. (2-tailed)	0		0	0
	N	75	75	75	75
Healthcare Workers treating you with respect and compassion	**Pearson Correlation**	.264*	.454**	1	0.04
	Sig. (2-tailed)	0.022	0		0.734
	N	75	75	75	75
Healthcare System TB patient supportive	**Pearson Correlation**	0.19	.449**	0.04	1
	Sig. (2-tailed)	0.103	0	0.734	
	N	75	75	75	75

**. Correlation is significant at the 0.01 level (2-tailed).
*. Correlation is significant at the 0.05 level (2-tailed).

It provides information on the type of TB and accessibility to healthcare. The correlation coefficient is 0.499, and the p-value is (p = 0.000). The moderate positive correlation influences the type of TB and significantly affects healthcare accessibility. The type of TB and respect for healthcare workers have a correlation coefficient of 0.264 and a p-value of 0.022. There is a weak positive correlation, and it affects the perception of respect and compassion for healthcare workers. There is a correlation coefficient of 0.190 between the type of TB and healthcare system supportiveness, with a p-value of 0.103. No significant relationship was observed. The healthcare accessibility and other variables, including respect for healthcare workers, show a moderate positive correlation (0.454, p = 0.000). Better accessibility enhances the perceived respect. The healthcare system's supportiveness shows a moderate positive correlation (0.449, p = 0.000). It improves accessibility and correlates with a higher perception of supportiveness. The respect for healthcare workers and healthcare system supportiveness, with a correlation coefficient of 0.040 (p = 0.734), shows no association between respect and the influence of system supportiveness. The type of TB provides a significant impact on accessibility and respect; it does not strongly influence the perception of system support. Healthcare accessibility provides a strong correlation and can impact the respect for support perception, indicating its pivotal role in patient experiences.

Table 8. Beliefs and marital status of correlations

Correlations		**Marital status**	**Spiritual or Religious Practices to Cope with TB Diagnosis**	**Spirituality/Religion to provide emotional strength during treatment**	**Support from faith-based organizations or spiritual leaders in community**
Marital status	Pearson Correlation	1	0.137	0.012	0.117
	Sig. (2-tailed)		0.243	0.919	0.318
	N	75	75	75	75
Spiritual or Religious Practices to Cope with TB Diagnosis	Pearson Correlation	0.137	1	0.058	.322**
	Sig. (2-tailed)	0.243		0.623	0.005
	N	75	75	75	75
Spirituality/Religion to provide emotional strength during treatment	Pearson Correlation	0.012	0.058	1	-0.142
	Sig. (2-tailed)	0.919	0.623		0.225
	N	75	75	75	75
Support from faith-based organizations or spiritual leaders in community	Pearson Correlation	0.117	.322**	-0.142	1
	Sig. (2-tailed)	0.318	0.005	0.225	
	N	75	75	75	75

**. Correlation is significant at the 0.01 level (2-tailed).

Spiritual practices and faith-based support have a correlation coefficient of 0.322 (p = 0.005). There is a moderate positive correlation, which engages spiritual and religious practices to cope with TB, and it is likely to support faith-based organizations. There is no significant relationship between marital status and spiritual variables; it does not influence spiritual practices and emotional strength related to religion and faith-based organizations. There is no significant relationship between emotional strength and faith-based support. Faith-based support for TB patients can engage in spiritual practices to strengthen the role. There are factors involving cultural and economic influences on spiritual coping mechanisms, and marital status does not play a significant role.

Table 9. Type of TB and 5Ss approach correlations

Correlations		Type of TB	5Ss do you feel has the greatest impact on recovery and engagement
Type of TB	**Pearson Correlation**	1	-0.154
	Sig. (2-tailed)		0.186
	N	75	75
5Ss Impact on recovery and engagement	**Pearson Correlation**	-0.154	1
	Sig. (2-tailed)	0.186	
	N	75	75

The correlation between the type of TB patients and the whole 5S approach, such as self, society, state, system, and spiritual beliefs, shows no significant relationship for the variables. The correlation coefficient value is -0.154, and the p-value is ($p = 0.186$). There is an association between the correlation of the type of TB, but it does not strongly influence the perceptions of the effectiveness of the 5S approach for TB recovery engagement. The larger sample provides additional variables to explore potential trends. It can investigate the patient experience with the 5S approach to involve the nuances of their perceived impact.

Table 10. Correlation matrix

Correlation	Feel Confident in Managing Treatment Plan	Stigma Affecting Self-Esteem After Diagnosis	Family Support during the TB Treatment	Stigma or Discrimination from the community After Diagnosed with TB	Community Awareness Programs TB effective	Aware Government-provide support for TB Patients	Government Programs During Treatment Supported	Satisfied with Government's Efforts TB related	Accessible is healthcare for TB treatment	Healthcare Workers treating respect	Healthcare System TB patient supportive	Spiritual or Religious Practices to Cope with TB Diagnosis	Spirituality/Religion emotional strength during treatment	Support from faith-based organizations or spiritual	5Ss impact on recovery and engagement
Feel Confident in Managing Treatment Plan	1														
Stigma Affecting Self-Esteem After Diagnosis	0.365	1													
Family Support during the TB Treatment	0.078	0.012	1												
Stigma or Discrimination from the community After Diagnosed with TB	0.046	0.02	0.167	1											
Community Awareness Programs TB effective	0.375	0.13	0.257	0.24	1										
Aware Government-provide support for TB Patients	0.156	0	0.065	0.195	0.308	1									
Government Programs During Treatment Supported	-0.259	-0.039	-0.327	0.157	-0.12	-0.079	1								
Satisfied with Government's Efforts TB related	0.127	0.172	0.155	0.347	0.68	0.126	0.075	1							
Accessible is healthcare for TB treatment	0.661	0.305	-0.247	0.219	0.523	0.135	0.12	0.46	1						
Healthcare Workers treating respect	0.326	0.177	-0.064	0.299	0.271	0.177	0.357	0.175	0.454	1					
Healthcare System TB patient supportive	0.608	0.328	0.263	0.154	0.063	0.149	-0.086	0.167	0.449	0.04	1				
Spiritual or Religious Practices to Cope with TB Diagnosis	-0.08	0.132	-0.039	-0.007	0.186	-0.011	0.114	0.191	0.007	0.139	-0.057	1			
Spirituality/Religion emotional strength during treatment	0.433	0.24	0.064	-0.013	0.667	0.274	-0.226	0.285	0.364	-0.017	0.151	0.058	1		
Support from faith-based organizations or spiritual	0.171	0.107	0.233	0.186	-0.09	-0.036	0.033	0.05	-0.008	0.065	0.291	0.322	-0.142	1	
5Ss impact on recovery and engagement	0.104	-0.129	0.25	-0.045	0.526	-0.072	-0.104	0.285	0.054	-0.08	-0.085	0.042	0.26	-0.051	1

The limitation of the study is that it provides valuable understanding for TB patients regarding their perception with the help of the 5Ss approach through community engagement activities. It addresses their problems and helps them cope with the situations. The study can focus on the effects on TB patients and provide generalizability for the findings. The perception of TB patients can be effective for understanding their socio-cultural aspects, including age, gender, and socioeconomic conditions. The research can emphasize that TB patients can gain a holistic understanding through community engagement activities, supporting TB patients and leading to better treatment outcomes, TB care, and services received. The limitation of the study is to address TB patients' knowledge and the importance of their perceptions in community engagement activities. It can focus on future research to enhance a better understanding of how the 5Ss approach can improve TB care for patients, leading to better outcomes and treatment adherence.

Outcome of the Study

The outcome of the study explores TB patients' perceptions and the integration of the 5Ss approach, focusing on self, society, state, system, and spirituality in relation to community engagement activities. The study provides valuable insights into how various dimensions influence patient experiences and treatment outcomes. The outcome for TB patients and their perceptions of the 5Ss—Self, Society, State, System, and Spiritual—can engage community-based activities. It can highlight the multifaceted nature of TB care and recovery for the following outcomes. It is focused on the 5Ss—Self, Society, State, System, and Spiritual. For the Self, it can perceive the role of adhering to TB treatment, which is critical to recovery, and it can facilitate lifestyle adjustments. Self-awareness for TB patients can lead to self-realization. It can enhance health, reduce stigma, improve counseling, and provide emerging positive outcomes for the patients. The Society responds with community support to reduce stigma and improve patient engagement. The positive change in patients' social perception can strengthen the community, likely contributing to better treatment adherence and providing advocacy for the role of patients. The State's role is to improve policies and programs to support TB patients.

The government can ensure treatment adherence support, nutritional support, and financial support, which can enhance patient well-being. The state government and central government should initiate the NTEP's role to address the gaps and provide support for the rural and peripheral affected population to ensure the delivery of services. The healthcare system should provide better delivery and efficiency in offering diagnostic support, treatment services, and counseling, which can improve patient perceptions. Timeliness and accessibility in providing compassionate care by healthcare workers can improve trust and engagement. The patients' spiritual and emotional support can include faith-based initiatives to help them with coping strategies and reduce the psychological burden of TB.TB patients might express gratitude for the holistic approaches that improve their social and emotional well-being, contributing to physical recovery. The outcome provides various dimensions to influence TB patients and strengthen

SELF EMPOWER FOR TB PATIENTS AND IMPROVE THEIR SELF EFFICACY

TB patients face various experiences, and improving their self-confidence is crucial. Community engagement activities involve sharing their stories and increasing awareness, which can enhance their self-esteem. The stigma level for TB patients is high, as they face societal judgment during their experience and TB life journey. This can lead to feelings of isolation and an increase in stigma. Self-improvement through positive feelings in their lives can help alleviate symptoms of depression and anxiety associated with TB patients.

Society Perception and Improve the Social Support for the TB Patients

To increase social support for TB patients during their treatment, the 5Ss approach is emphasized for social recovery's patients receive emotional, moral, and financial support. The level of social stigma for TB patients is reduced there result of the study highlights the need for empathy towards TB patients to foster a supportive environment positive support from society and family. The community awareness emphasizes reducing stigma through education in the general community. This leads to a better understanding of the disease in society and can help prevent it in the future.

Strengthen the Government Polity and Improve the Advocacy Level

The government provides better knowledge about the schemes and welfare programs for TB patients and offers various assistance and support, which can help TB patients gain better opportunities. Many government state-level schemes, such as the Ullavar Kapitu Thitam in Tamil Nadu, are provided for affected TB patients. However, these schemes do not reach all TB patients, especially those in rural areas, who are unable to avail themselves of the benefits. Even then, it is not easy to access; there are many procedures to follow in order to receive the benefits. The government assistance scheme provides nutritional support for a better and healthier life for

TB patients. Many TB patients receive the NPY scheme, which offers Rs. 500 per month from the Indian Central Government through Direct Benefit Transfer (DBT). This support is beneficial until the completion of their treatment. A patient-centered care approach provides community-based interventions at the societal level. The government initiates more schemes and provides greater support for TB patients, enhancing the TB policy and improving the healthcare delivery system.

System Strengthening and Provide the Healthcare Infrastructure

The 5Ss approach helps improve the healthcare system for TB patients by providing regular, on-time treatment and services with the support of healthcare workers. The regular, on-time treatment and services with the support of healthcare workers are essential. The study enhances TB patients' follow-up and promotes treatment adherence to the regimens. The study emphasizes the role of community health workers in bridging the gap between the patient and the health facility. The healthcare workers monitor TB patients on a regular and rotational basis, providing drugs, counseling, nutritional support, and linking them to government policy schemes.

Spiritual Support for the TB Patients and Improve the Resilience level

Many TB patients, after being affected by the disease, experience an increase in their spiritual level, which helps improve their peace and resilience during the treatment period. They can involve spiritual aspects by joining a prayer team, making regular visits to the temple, and believing in God. This can improve their emotional level, mental health, and overall well-being. The spiritual aspects of TB patients include their beliefs in spiritual activities, which can increase their coping mechanism levels. The positive aspects of their life improve their mental health and motivation, helping them complete the treatment and successfully finish the TB treatment course. The spiritual support they receive provides more energy and mental peace, reduces negative feelings, and allows them to share their experiences. This helps reduce isolation and uplifts their family members.

FUTURE IMPLICATIONS FOR FURTHER RESEARCH

The further implications of the study for TB patients' perceptions and their involvement in the 5Ss approach can include the self, society, state, system, and spiritual aspects in community engagement activities. There are various aspects to add for the research, which can help understand and implement this approach.

TB Patients' Health Outcomes Impacted by the 5Ss Approach

This study can provide a better understanding of TB patients' perceptions and can involve future research to directly assess the impact of the 5Ss approach in addressing health outcomes such as treatment adherence, health improvement, and enhancing the quality of life. Longitudinal studies can address patient care, track the patient's treatment journey, and support recovery through the 5Ss factors.

Healthcare Settings Can Expand Their Diverse Population

Future studies can apply the 5Ss in different geographical locations to identify different types of populations, including marginalized communities, especially those living in peripheral areas.The study can provide the better understand to identified the TB patients their culture, economic, healthcare and provide the better and comprehensive understand for the applicability for the situation.

Getting Involved With Community Stakeholder Aspects as a Healthcare Provider

Further, the study can focus, especially on healthcare providers, to involve and support TB patients and their family members. To understand their challenges and opportunities in implementing the 5Ss approach to enhance the holistic view of the community and provide feasible and sustainable solutions in the cultural aspects of the study.

The 5S Framework Based on Intervention

The study will focus on future-specific interventions for the 5Ss approach in community-based interventions, especially spiritual health education. Government policy can strengthen the healthcare system to improve societal support, which can impact TB treatment adherence and TB patients' satisfaction.

Enhancing the Digital Health Solution

Digital health technologies can involve mobile health and telemedicine opportunities, providing an IVR system that can be more useful for TB patients and integrated with the 5Ss approach. Future research can provide a digital solution platform that enhances self-management, the healthcare system, community support, and spiritual engagement, particularly in resource-limited settings.

TB Patients' Psycho-Social and Cultural Engagement in the Community

The research study provides a deeper understanding of the psychosocial aspects of TB patients and engages with the 5Ss approach. It can address the barriers faced by TB patients, including their stigma, fear, and facilitate this through community engagement activities.

CONCLUSION

The conclusion provides valuable information on the 5Ss approach in order to improve TB patients' self-efficacy, society's viewpoint on TB patients, system strengthening, and state policies. It also emphasizes the improvement of spiritual beliefs among TB patients, which can address their quality of life and well-being, and contribute to better lives within the community. The 5Ss can enhance TB patients' well-being through community engagement activities, reduce stigma, and decrease isolation within the family and community. Healthcare workers provide comprehensive support for TB patients.

It can emphasize the cultural aspects of TB patients, help overcome stigma, and ensure that healthcare provides better policies for vulnerable populations. The 5Ss can address a comprehensive understanding of TB patients' health and wellness through community engagement activities. The implication of the study is to improve healthcare providers, community health workers, policymakers, and researchers. The study can address the patient-centered care approach by integrating the 5Ss components. The study can place more emphasis on interventions for TB patients' treatment experience. The future research study should address the 5Ss approach as a component of TB treatment outcomes and further validate these components to expand their application to diverse healthcare settings. Spiritual beliefs can address emotional support for TB patients, foster coping mechanisms, and enhance resilience services for TB patients.

The final conclusion of the study addresses the 5Ss approach in the TB patients' pathway to improve their lifestyle during treatment and meet the multifaceted needs of TB patients. It supports TB patients' self-management, community involvement, and their effective strategy to improve the healthcare system. An effective healthcare system can reduce barriers among TB patients, improve policies and advocacy, address spiritual well-being, emphasize TB management, and enhance the advancement of quality of life, which is affected by individuals. It can fight against TB by continuing the 5Ss approach to provide effective support for a holistic approach and increase healthcare services for TB patients at a global level.

REFERENCES

Adaji, T. M. (2013). Use of National Guidelines in the Treatment of Severe Malaria: A Retrospective Study of Severe Malaria Management in Under 5s in Benue State. DOI: 10.21522/TIJPH.2013.12.02.Art018

Adeoye, B. D., Michael, T. O., & Agbana, R. D. (2024). Insights, beliefs, and myths surrounding tuberculosis among pulmonary patients with delayed healthcare access in a high-burden TB state in Nigeria–a qualitative inquiry. *Frontiers in Sociology*, *9*, 1378586. DOI: 10.3389/fsoc.2024.1378586 PMID: 38765220

Artawan Eka Putra, I. W. G., Purnama Dewi, N. P. E., Probandari, A. N., Notobroto, H. B., & Wahyuni, C. (2023). The implementation of comprehensive health education to improve household contacts' participation in early detection of tuberculosis. *Health Education & Behavior*, *50*(1), 136–143. DOI: 10.1177/1090198121 1001829 PMID: 33829894

Ayalew, Y. E., Yehualashet, F. A., Bogale, W. A., & Gobeza, M. B. (2020). Delay for tuberculosis treatment and its predictors among adult tuberculosis patients at Debremarkos town public health facilities, north West Ethiopia. *Tuberculosis Research and Treatment*, *2020*, 1–8. DOI: 10.1155/2020/1901890 PMID: 33014464

Beyerstein, B. L. (2001). Alternative medicine and common errors of reasoning. *Academic Medicine*, *76*(3), 230–237. https://journals.lww.com/academicmedicine/abstract/2001/03000/alternative_medicine_and_common_errors_of.9.aspx. DOI: 10.1097/00001888-200103000-00009 PMID: 11242572

Bryant-Davis, T., & Wong, E. C. (2013). Faith to move mountains: religious coping, spirituality, and interpersonal trauma recovery. *American Psychologist*, *68*(8), 675. sDOI: 10.1037/a0034380

Chang, B., Wu, A. W., Hansel, N. N., & Diette, G. B. (2004). Quality of life in tuberculosis: A review of the English language literature. *Quality of Life Research: An International Journal of Quality of Life Aspects of Treatment, Care and Rehabilitation*, *13*(10), 1633–1642. DOI: 10.1007/s11136-004-0374-1 PMID: 15651535

Chinenye, N. M. (2015). Evaluation of knowledge, attitude and practices of TB diagnosed patients in Rwanda towards TB infection. Case of TB diagnosed patients in Kigali urban and rural health facilities. *International Journal of Scientific and Research Publications*, *5*(8), 1–19. https://citeseerx.ist.psu.edu/document?repid=rep1&type=pdf&doi=2cf8f36a79ece1d6b04b50debeab7e272a721a59#page=478

Daley, C. L. (2019). The global fight against tuberculosis. *Thoracic Surgery Clinics, 29*(1, s1), 19–25. https://www.thoracic.theclinics.com/article/S1547-4127(18)30137-3/abstract. DOI: 10.1016/j.thorsurg.2018.09.010 PMID: 30454918

Datiko, D. G., Jerene, D., & Suarez, P. (2020). Stigma matters in ending tuberculosis: Nationwide survey of stigma in Ethiopia. *BMC Public Health, 20*(1), 190. DOI: 10.1186/s12889-019-7915-6 PMID: 32028914

Davis, E. C., Arana, E. T., Creel, J. S., Ibarra, S. C., Lechuga, J., Norman, R. A., Parks, H. R., Qasim, A., Watkins, D. Y., & Kash, B. A. (2018). The role of community engagement in building sustainable health-care delivery interventions for Kenya. *European Journal of Training and Development, 42*(1/2), 35–47. DOI: 10.1108/EJTD-06-2016-0042

Davtyan, K., Aghabekyan, S., Davtyan, H., Hayrapetyan, A., & Aslanyan, G. (2019). Quality of care provided to tuberculosis patients in Armenia: How satisfied are the patients?. *The Journal of Infection in Developing Countries, 13*(05.1), 028S-034S. DOI: 10.3855/jidc.10873

Faherty, K. M. (1996). *Self care discipline's impact on well-being, pain and functional status*. Yeshiva University.

Hansel, N. N., Wu, A. W., Chang, B., & Diette, G. B. (2004). Quality of life in tuberculosis: Patient and provider perspectives. *Quality of Life Research: An International Journal of Quality of Life Aspects of Treatment, Care and Rehabilitation, 13*(3), 639–652. DOI: 10.1023/B:QURE.0000021317.12945.f0 PMID: 15130027

Hargreaves, J. R., Boccia, D., Evans, C. A., Adato, M., Petticrew, M., & Porter, J. D. (2011). The social determinants of tuberculosis: From evidence to action. *American Journal of Public Health, 101*(4), 654–662. DOI: 10.2105/AJPH.2010.199505 PMID: 21330583

Harries, A. D., Kumar, A. M., Satyanarayana, S., Takarinda, K. C., Timire, C., & Dlodlo, R. A. (2020). Treatment for latent tuberculosis infection in low-and middle-income countries: Progress and challenges with implementation and scale-up. *Expert Review of Respiratory Medicine, 14*(2), 195–208. DOI: 10.1080/17476348.2020.1694907 PMID: 31760848

Kanamori, S., Castro, M. C., Sow, S., Matsuno, R., Cissokho, A., & Jimba, M. (2016). Impact of the Japanese 5S management method on patients' and caretakers' satisfaction: A quasi-experimental study in Senegal. *Global Health Action, 9*(1), 32852. DOI: 10.3402/gha.v9.32852 PMID: 27900932

Kanamori, S., Castro, M. C., Sow, S., Matsuno, R., Cissokho, A., & Jimba, M. (2016). Impact of the Japanese 5S management method on patients' and caretakers' satisfaction: A quasi-experimental study in Senegal. *Global Health Action*, *9*(1), 32852. DOI: 10.3402/gha.v9.32852 PMID: 27900932

Kimmel, P. L., Emont, S. L., Newmann, J. M., Danko, H., & Moss, A. H. (2003). ESRD patient quality of life: Symptoms, spiritual beliefs, psychosocial factors, and ethnicity. *American Journal of Kidney Diseases*, *42*(4), 713–721. DOI: 10.1016/S0272-6386(03)00907-7 PMID: 14520621

Kimmel, P. L., Emont, S. L., Newmann, J. M., Danko, H., & Moss, A. H. (2003). ESRD patient quality of life: Symptoms, spiritual beliefs, psychosocial factors, and ethnicity. *American Journal of Kidney Diseases*, *42*(4), 713–721. DOI: 10.1016/S0272-6386(03)00907-7 PMID: 14520621

Lawn, S. D., Myer, L., Bekker, L. G., & Wood, R. (2006). Burden of tuberculosis in an antiretroviral treatment programme in sub-Saharan Africa: Impact on treatment outcomes and implications for tuberculosis control. *AIDS (London, England)*, *20*(12), 1605–1612. DOI: 10.1097/01.aids.0000238406.93249.cd PMID: 16868441

Leotsakos, A., Zheng, H., Croteau, R., Loeb, J. M., Sherman, H., Hoffman, C., Morganstein, L., O'Leary, D., Bruneau, C., Lee, P., Duguid, M., Thomeczek, C., Schrieck-De Loos, E., & Munier, B. (2014). Standardization in patient safety: The WHO High 5s project. *International Journal for Quality in Health Care : Journal of the International Society for Quality in Health Care*, *26*(2), 109–116. DOI: 10.1093/intqhc/mzu010 PMID: 24713313

Loa, R. F. (2018). Facilitators and Barriers to Self-Management of Tuberculosis Patients: A Qualitative Study. *International Journal of Integrated Care*, *18*(s2), 285. DOI: 10.5334/ijic.s2285

Long, N. H., Johansson, E., Diwan, V. K., & Winkvist, A. (1999). Different tuberculosis in men and women: Beliefs from focus groups in Vietnam. *Social Science & Medicine*, *49*(6), 815–822. DOI: 10.1016/S0277-9536(99)00171-9 PMID: 10459892

McDade, R. (2013). A mixed method study of spirituality and the influence on TB medication adherence. https://digitalcommons.fiu.edu/cgi/viewcontent.cgi?article=1260&context=sferc

Min, J., Chung, C., Jung, S. S., Park, H. K., Lee, S. S., & Lee, K. M. (2019). Understanding illness perception in pulmonary tuberculosis patients: One step towards patient-centered care. *PLoS One*, *14*(6), e0218106. DOI: 10.1371/journal.pone.0218106 PMID: 31188871

Munang, M. L., Browne, C., Evans, J. T., Smith, E. G., Hawkey, P. M., Welch, S. B., Kaur, H., & Dedicoat, M. J. (2016). Programmatic utility of tuberculosis cluster investigation using a social network approach in Birmingham, United Kingdom. *The International Journal of Tuberculosis and Lung Disease : the Official Journal of the International Union against Tuberculosis and Lung Disease*, *20*(10), 1300–1305. DOI: 10.5588/ijtld.16.0161 PMID: 27725038

Nakhaei, S., Amiri Majd, M., Mohammadi Arya, A., & Shirazi, M. (2020). The role of mindfulness, spiritual experiences, and coping strategies in anticipation of the quality of life of patients with tuberculosis. *Journal of Research and Health*, *10*(3), 143–150. https://jrh.gmu.ac.ir/browse.php?a_id=1402&sid=1&slc_lang=en. DOI: 10.32598/JRH.10.3.1402.1

Ojiezeh, T. I., Ogundipe, O. O., & Adefosoye, V. A. (2015). A retrospective study on incidence of pulmonary tuberculosis and human immunodeficiency virus co-infection among patients attending National Tuberculosis and leprosy control Programme, Owo centre. *The Pan African Medical Journal*, *20*, 5643. DOI: 10.11604/pamj.2015.20.345.5643

Onyango, P. A., Ter Goon, D., & Rala, N. M. D. (2021). Knowledge, attitudes and health-seeking behaviour among patients with tuberculosis: A cross-sectional study. *The Open Public Health Journal*, *13*(1), 739–747. DOI: 10.2174/1874944502013010739

Ozturk, F. O., & Hisar, F. (2014). Stigmatisation of tuberculosis patients. *International Journal of Community Medicine and Public Health*, *1*(1), 37. DOI: 10.5455/2394-6040.ijcmph20141108

Papreen, N., Sharma, A., Sabin, K., Begum, L., Ahsan, S. K., & Baqui, A. H. (2000). Living with infertility: experiences among urban slum populations in Bangladesh. *Reproductive health matters, 8*(15), 33-44. doi: s10.1016/S0968-8080(00)90004-1

Pratiwi, I. N., Hidayati, L., Alviani, N. I., & McKenna, L. (2021). The correlation between anxiety levels and spiritual activities with motivation to recover in pulmonary tuberculosis. *Enfermeria Clinica*, *31*, 535–539. DOI: 10.1016/j.enfcli.2020.10.037

Qidwai, M. A. (2024). The 5Ss' Approach for Managing Health of Client, Family and Community. *National Journal*, *9*(4), 232. DOI: 10.21089/njhs.94.0231

Saleem, S., & Majeed, S. (2023). *Spiritual Intelligence*. Self-Management Skills, Depression and Anxiety in Patients with Tuberculosis., DOI: 10.57232/jiimc.june23.629

Shasha, A. C. N. (2013). *Patient experiences and perceptions of non-compliance with TB treatment* (Doctoral dissertation, Stellenbosch: Stellenbosch University). https://scholar.sun.ac.za/items/03a5c605-d130-4b14-afd1-b6d10c6ba125

Srinivasan, M. S., Lama, P., Tyagi, N., Yadav, K., Naval, M. N., & Swati, M. Elderly TB patients in India: Situation Analysis. *Tuijin Jishu/Journal of Propulsion Technology, 44*(6), 2023.doi:DOI: 10.52783/tjjpt.v44.i6.3140

Srinivasan, S. (2025). Patient-Centric Care in Tuberculosis Management: Addressing Challenges and Improving Health Outcomes. In *Convergence of Population Health Management, Pharmacogenomics, and Patient-Centered Care* (pp. 265-282). IGI Global. DOI: DOI: 10.4018/979-8-3693-3260-3.ch012

Srinivasan, S., & Praba Lama (2025). Patient-Centered Care for TB Patients: An Effective Approach to Corporate Social Responsibility. In Corporate Social Responsibility in Health and Social Care (pp. 183-218).IGI Global. DOI:DOI: 10.4018/979-8-3693-5991-4.ch008

Srinivasan, S., Prabha Lama, D. K., & Udhayakumar, P. Situation of Elderly Person with TB: A Comparative Study of Countries in the SAARC Region. doi:.DOI: 10.36713/epra2013

Tomes, N. (2000). The making of a germ panic, then and now. *American Journal of Public Health, 90*(2), 191–198. DOI: 10.2105/AJPH.90.2.191 PMID: 10667179

Tseng, Y. H., Griffiths, F., De Kadt, J., Nxumalo, N., Rwafa, T., Malatji, H., & Goudge, J. (2019). Integrating community health workers into the formal health system to improve performance: A qualitative study on the role of on-site supervision in the South African programme. *BMJ Open, 9*(2), e022186. DOI: 10.1136/bmjopen-2018-022186 PMID: 30819698

Walzl, G., McNerney, R., du Plessis, N., Bates, M., McHugh, T. D., Chegou, N. N., & Zumla, A. (2018). Tuberculosis: Advances and challenges in development of new diagnostics and biomarkers. *The Lancet. Infectious Diseases, 18*(7), e199–e210. https://www.thelancet.com/journals/laninf/article/PIIS1473-3099(18)30111-7/abstract. DOI: 10.1016/S1473-3099(18)30111-7 PMID: 29580818

Yeh, C. H. (2001). Religious beliefs and practices of Taiwanese parents of pediatric patients with cancer. *Cancer Nursing, 24*(6), 476–482. https://journals.lww.com/cancernursingonline/abstract/2001/12000/religious_beliefs_and_practices_of_taiwanese.9.aspx. DOI: 10.1097/00002820-200112000-00009 PMID: 11762510

Chapter 13
The Role of the State in Health Management, a Comprehensive Analysis: State and Health Management

Muhammad Farooq Umer
https://orcid.org/0000-0001-7779-1929
King Faisal University, Hofuf, Saudi Arabia

ABSTRACT

The state plays a pivotal role in health management by integrating individual, societal, systemic, and cultural dimensions into cohesive frameworks for public health governance. This chapter explores the evolving responsibilities of the state in health policy formulation, disease control, resource allocation, and collaboration with international health organizations. Anchored in the innovative 5S framework—Self, Society, State, System, and Spirituality—it highlights the intricate interplay between personal health responsibility, community initiatives, systemic healthcare delivery, and the influence of cultural beliefs. The analysis underscores the necessity of aligning health policies with social determinants to enhance equity and resilience. By emphasizing evidence-based approaches and interdisciplinary collaboration, this chapter offers insights into overcoming contemporary health challenges and fostering sustainable public health outcomes.

DOI: 10.4018/979-8-3693-9092-4.ch013

1. INTRODUCTION TO THE ROLE OF THE STATE IN HEALTH MANAGEMENT

The state plays a major role in shaping the health of both individuals and communities. The advent of a modern public health system that improved health standards in Europe and world was the result of state intervention. The state's role in health management changed much over time. In modern times, the concept of health management has evolved and now it includes decision-making, development of health policy, planning, organization, and financial implementation of managing care, as it is comprehensive in nature. Governance is first described as a constructive link between statutory and organizational principles for the functioning of sovereign states, captured in Hobbesian terms, which was later characterized as 'the art and science of policy environment. (Andrews, 2008)

This development is similar between the two waves, but healthcare settings post-democratic governance are quite different, especially after the de-institutionalization of control and delinking of people from their previously established social structures as a result of global changes in the pattern of government, politics, economy, ideology, and society. Health policy and its implementation must be made in the light of national and global contexts. The performance of any healthcare system depends upon the management and strategies adopted by the policymakers to ensure its success. Government policies based on the principles of equity and social justice are of prime importance. Policies that respond to social determinants have an important role in improving population health. Public health researchers are increasingly calling for public health and healthcare solutions to be predominant in health policy. Far from the controversial debate about whether healthcare policies are important in improving health outcomes, the policy guidance provides an opportunity for policymakers to recognize the dominant pattern of healthcare in health policy and its impact on policy objectives. The challenge is to explain public health research in the field of healthcare policy that appeals to policymakers. (Sigal & Bakumenko, 2020)

2. THE 5S APPROACH IN HEALTH MANAGEMENT

We chose to discuss in this chapter the 5S approach as a comprehensive framework on health, for it represents the five interconnected dimensions of health and well-being: self, society, state, system, and spirituality. Let us break this down. First, the understanding of 'self' throws light on the significance of personal role and responsibility in an individual's health maintenance. 'Society' questions the status quo of how communities would run into crises and disorders, compromising human well-being, highlighting the significance of local health initiatives. This approach articulates the significance of positive well-being primarily at the local level. The 'state' underlines the responsibility of the government to maintain the ecosystem of services and systems associated with healthcare. Case studies shall help us make this conceptual and bring in the flavor of practicality to this dimension.

Furthermore, the 'system' emphasizes how infrastructure or systems are significant for the availability of healthcare services to the people. Case replication through stories aims to throw light on this dimension. 'Spirituality' is included as a dimension, realizing and practically acknowledging the belief system regarding health in different cultures. While analyzing this approach, we opine that as people accept ideologies, they tend to initiate specific lifestyle adjustments according to their values and philosophies. In the same vein, the authorities of different nations will be inclined to evolve health policies and strategies in their respective countries consistent with the cultural and spiritual beliefs. These may be interlinked with other dimensions: policymakers would include a good impact on the spiritual dimension in the healthcare arrangements of the state; local health initiatives would also be influenced by spiritual beliefs and thus on the prototype of care available in these initiatives. (Rassool, 2021)

2.1. Self: Individual Responsibility in Health

An important aspect of health and the health management discussion, which largely underlies other sections, is the concept of an individual's self. Historically, the self is synonymous with responsibility and culpability, as well as being autonomous. Regarding health, it is widely recognized that individuals can directly affect the state of their health. Through personal choices and behaviors, such as diet, exercise, and smoking and drinking habits, individuals can increase or decrease their health opportunities and outcomes. In this way, health responsibility arises, depicting individuals as responsible for whatever state of health they enjoy.

Denying individuals' ability to affect their health outcomes necessarily devalues their self, treating them as objects of compelling forces and undermining personhood, as this strips autonomy from individuals. As our theme revolves around health management, some views forward that boiling health resolution down to "what do you want?" obscures the operative functions behind it. Here, democratizing information about the array of complex health determinants ought to serve as educative and empowering for individuals, thus allowing them maximum power over their personal health. Once informed, people can bear the responsibility to manage their state of health accordingly. As such, health, as part of the self-formation access, is acquired through acquiring information and can only be valuable through an informed and hence autonomous agreement. Again, education and knowledge step to the fore, this time in relation to health management. Therefore, those who espouse the principle are also duty bearers as potential allies to individuals doing Socratic teaching. As noted above, currently many individuals do abdicate health management, express little interest, and often rely on self-doctoring (of variable quality with the potential to make them even less health enhancing). This is endorsed in giving some space to individualism, highlighting that some aspects we desire remain private and beyond government remit, as we should have the freedom to consciously disregard and do harm to ourselves. However, we may create resistances to bad lifestyle habits and foster different governmental approaches emphasizing proactive duties. Similarly, psychological and social factors need to be addressed, especially to improve powerfully on public health. Therefore, the promotion of individualism, with a duty to take responsibility for the impact of one's choices on one's own and potentially others' health, could be a key advancement in our strategic response to COVID and pandemics of the future. We must nurture this resurgence of interest in individual action. Moreover, the case was made that proponents of health nationalism should extend their trajectory to include those already in need. Further, there appears to be growing demand from the public for a more individualistic approach. In engaging with individuals, it is of huge importance to use positive messages and encourage social learning to enable behavior change, which ultimately becomes a stable norm. In this way, individuals specifically or populations of society develop a self-perpetuating drive to be more economically and environmentally minded in particular and to develop their well-being. In conclusion, the state has an outsized role to play in health management, as well as in financing. This in turn can itself improve the quality of democracy. And whilst normative accounts articulating when and why states should devolve health management towards an individual level are often met with resistance, an important prescription has emerged inferring that public health management should at least nurture individual responsibility and autonomy, no matter to what extent the power is actually distributed. .(Beaglehole, Bonita, Horton, Adams, & McKee, 2004)

2.2. Society: Community Health Initiatives

Health is promoted not only at the individual level; the community can also play a significant role in public health outcomes. Community initiatives often engage in developing programs and interventions that serve to promote good health and its associated behaviors. Because of the essential role of many village members in community initiatives, such efforts can also focus on reducing individual risk for primary prevention and treatment-focused strategies for secondary and tertiary prevention. Initiatives may include village volunteers to serve as mediators and community health educators, religious-centers-initiated (e.g., church-initiated and mosque-initiated) health fairs, or disease-awareness programs. Implementing this strategy involves cooperation between village members, local support groups, and professionals who coordinate targeted health activities. Health initiatives for the community are successful on a small scale. Research has shown that grassroots health initiatives can help promote good health through hand washing, swimming safety training, and immunization awareness. Testimonials are the key to successful grassroots health programs.

2.2.1. Examples/Case Report

Socio-Ecologic Initiatives. Healthy People 2010 social ecology emphasizes brain activity as a community health center. Groups that share our social factors influence individual and group health. Access to basic resources such as shelter, school, and health care reinforces income, strengthens social ties, and makes the environment enjoyable in terms of safety. Unfortunately, organizations serving minorities face some real barriers to maintaining a healthy focus. Sometimes disadvantaged socio-economic areas improve the social situation and encourage a positive attitude. Socioeconomic disparities can affect, but ultimately impact individual communities. Lower income, education, and children limit access to healthy foods, healthy living conditions, and safe outdoor activities. In children, traditionally high-income, well-educated children are advised on nutrition. Addressing health also needs to respond to cultural champions in more diverse groups. Understanding and respecting socio-economic factors play an important role in mental health prevention activities. Parents who value mental health messages and health workers should rethink our approach to using social networks for child health advocacy. Internet-based social networks offer an opportunity to improve access to and acceptance of health messages by parents. Overall, health promotion activities include community parents, children, schools, professionals, and policymakers. Everyone can play a collective role in this effort. All the actors will go public, "Support children who are healthy, educated, and thoughtful." The public plays an important role in ensuring the health of society. People must always report their groups and support their causes. In the end, healthy people are one of the major goals of the group, and this is accomplished by the participation of the whole community. All community members need to work together to meet certain health promotion goals. For example, a city where everyone has access to effective health care, environmentally friendly water, and clean water with few instances of violence and injury when introduced to healthy foods. (Henderson & Armah, 2010)(Henderson & Armah, 2010)

2.3. State: Government's Role in Health Management

Government, at various levels, formulates public policies and frameworks to guide the delivery of health and social services across individual countries. These frameworks mainly lay down in terms of policy priorities, objectives, targets, and intended strategies to deliver healthcare services and safeguard the public's health. These policies are generally outcomes of political or public participation. The policy pillars of relevant frameworks generally revolve around improving population health status, improving access to, and choice of, consumer services of high quality, strengthening primary, secondary, and tertiary health care services, and prioritizing specific population groups like the aged, the disadvantaged, or those with specific health care needs. Government also has a role in being the main provider and/or funder of health care through: Health and health-related budgets targeted to health services; A broader range of social policies, for example, policies that promote access to housing, education, social justice; and supportive economic policies and/or safety nets. Health care systems are responsive to the health status of the population.

2.3.1. Examples/Case Report

Governments also have a role in monitoring the health of the populations and evaluating the outcomes of policy implementation across public, private, and non-profit based programs and services. Governments collaborate with stakeholders from across and outside of the health sector to establish and/or respond to current policies and plan with short, medium, and long-term timeframes. Additionally, monitoring the results of these approaches on the health status of the population is another government responsibility. Several challenges are encountered, and these include the notion that health is not a theoretically objective issue, but influenced by social, government, and private sectors, populations, and bureaucracy. Advocacy groups and community control and response loops also influence the direction and financing of health agencies. Furthermore, government actions can result in controversial issues such as fiscal tightening policies and market deregulation, which impact the population's health status. Moreover, health care quality and safety can be influenced through the introduction of regulation at numerous levels. Finally, overall health expenditure levels at national levels are dependent on factors such as national gross domestic product, tax, national debt levels, and other competing areas, and government and/or other drivers in terms of supply, clinical, and demand issues. (Cuckler et al., 2018)

2.4. System: Healthcare Infrastructure and Delivery

Hospitals and hospital-based services are the lynchpin of any healthcare system. Hospital infrastructure largely defines the delivery system in many parts of the country. India had a total of 8.7 lakh hospital beds distributed widely across the country via government, private, and charitable hospitals. Infrastructure needs for hospitals depend upon the patient flow in hospitals from various segments such as curative, preventive, referral, and the population that it caters to. Nearly three-fourths of outpatient and inpatient care is received in the public sector, while approximately 15% of India's hospitals are facilities serving rural areas. 97% of the combined hospitals in both rural and urban areas are working on the allopathic system of medicine. Moreover, 89% of the hospitals serve as inpatient service providers. Various tiers of public care comprise (in decreasing order of magnitude): community health centers, district hospitals, sub-district hospitals, and primary health centers.

2.4.1. Examples/Case Report

The healthcare system comprises (a) hospitals, including various facilities under it such as district hospitals, sub-district hospitals, and community health centers for providing secondary care, and primary health centers to ensure primary care; (b) various clinics providing specialized healthcare services; and (c) supporting facilities such as blood banks, diagnostic centers, rehabilitation centers, and outreach units. In the modern era of medicine, information and communication technology plays a vital role in the effective delivery of healthcare services. Telemedicine has been introduced all over the country. Hospitals are getting connected with various clinics in order to deliver quality healthcare services. All this calls for the management of healthcare expenses and financial resources. Controlling the finance in healthcare is challenging as the people's perception of healthcare has changed to a more or less "consumerism" approach. Unfortunately, healthcare is not only a marketable commodity, but it is also a public good. The management of resources should be compatible with the socio-economic status of the people in the related area. It is quite complex and needs to maintain a balance between supply and demand. (Raghav, 2017)

2.5. Spirituality: Cultural and Belief Systems Impact on Health

Prominent researchers have long bolstered the idea that "people's ways of perceiving and understanding the body, health, illness, curing, healing, and dying are central to how they respond to them." These authors suggest that cultural belief systems that stress the relationship between the fully integrated mind–body–spirit can impact "how people behave, whether they seek medical care, follow doctors' orders, participate in rehabilitation and exercise programs, and engage in preventive health practices," and that religion, an institutional embodiment of spirituality, and mosque-visiting; churchgoing and likes are assumed to "lead to improved emotional health." Spiritual health is the focus of the second of three approaches to health care delivery in the sociology of health and illness, the synthesis focus.

From the perspective of health disparities, the cultural reluctance of some populations to seek care far removed from a reciprocal mind–body–spirit relationship must be factored into a holistic health care model.

2.5.1. Examples/Case Report

For example, a study on cancer and spirituality illustrates that despite the growth of anti-Touhid movements, "Islamic beliefs and instructions still directly influence the formation of belief systems related to psycho-oncology, health promotion, and therapy in Islamic societies." Similarly, "in general, spiritual beliefs hold for all of Islam, affecting all situations and decisions among humans." Likewise, patients cannot be asked to ignore deeply ingrained cultural connections between cancer and health without a quarrel "since, within their culturally immersed societies, to be struck with the disease is to be seen as internally filthy, to have one's soul marked by sin or possessed by spirits, and to reek of moral and spiritual stench." And although some anger towards doctors exists, sufferers can also be encouraged to alleviate their cancers through Islamically banned deadening practices such as "divorce," which could be construed as a negative site of drift because "the approach of trying to beat glumness through divorcement cuts against normative beliefs about spiritual and cultural health and the notion of 'good life.'" Thus, spirituality and cultural beliefs are linked to natural healing protocols and "inextricably tied" to conceptions of God because "conceptions of the holy as encompassing spirituality work on the sick directly." Overall, the relationships with God of our patients, and others, necessitate that the sociology of health and medicine never fall out of touch with sociology and cultural anthropology of religion. Failure to do so will have confounding effects on medical services and population health. Aware of this dichotomy, many shared decision-aid programs strive to ensure that all participants receive the same basic information in "as spiritually neutral a format as possible." This will only work if all chronic disease participants share a belief in equally neutral definitions of life courage, health, quality of life, etc. In short, "physicians need to be sure that choices made are based on the desires of the patient or the party representing them, and not from the need to follow God's precepts." Only when traditional disease protocols meet this standard can society assure the health, independence, resilience, and discrete health given in each individual's relative spiritual/ideological and physical locations. In a modern, population-driven disease management system, this approach is more important than ever, requiring all disease programs that deal with spirits or spirituality to meet these standards. (Fitch & Bartlett, 2018)

3. TEN ESSENTIAL PUBLIC HEALTH SERVICES

Assessment is performed regularly to monitor status and identify community health problems. Policies that support individual and community health efforts are created through policy development. Effective communication strategies are devised to make various determinants of health known to individuals and the public. Community engagement involves members of the community in activities that address health problems. The capacity of the individual organizations to support individuals and communities in achieving better health is developed through workforce development. Legal and regulatory support is in place to protect and assure the public's health. Research for new insights and innovative solutions to health problems is conducted. In advanced world, state health agencies were early in developing a vision for their service delivery system, but they are reforming public health around the Essential Services framework, using the Ten Essential Public Health Services to set performance standards, provide targets for improvement, accredit local health departments, and define the content of the core functions for the public health system. Additional uses of the Essential Services framework include developing a core knowledge database that includes models, literature reviews, and original papers relevant to the Ten Essential Public Health Services. Practicing the Essential Services of Public Health fosters stakeholder buy-in to initiatives for improvement. The Modern Standards and Services in Public Health emphasize the importance of research that standardizes measurement criteria, establishes relevant reference groups, and is based on a comprehensive understanding of the service environment. (Ng & Colombani, 2015)(Rajapakshe, 2024)

3.1. Assessment

Assessment is the public health service that systematically collects, assembles, analyzes, and makes available information on the health needs of the community and the factors related to these needs. The objective of this assessment is to determine the health status and health needs of the population, to identify and collect data on any existing population groups, and to identify available services for the population of interest. Moreover, it determines the core measures or most important needs of the constituent area. The top recorded core measures after analysis of findings are access to care, communicable diseases and immunizations, healthy behaviors, maternal and child health, mental health and substance abuse, non-communicable diseases, bullying in schools, community resources access and evaluation, elderly care, and disaster health.

The information collected through assessments serves to raise public and professional awareness regarding important issues and to introduce a necessary alternative of wellness and illness prevention as primary, secondary, and tertiary studies of health problems from the viewpoint of wellness. (Anderson & Shinn, 2023)

3.2. Policy Development

Policies are the rules, standards, and guidelines by which public, community, and partner organizational actions are regulated. They, therefore, have a profound impact on the health of a population. The best policies are those based on accurate data derived through the use of comprehensive assessments of health trends and problems. It is best to enforce measures to counteract emerging trends. It is also true that health policies have the greatest impact when they benefit the most people. Inclusive health policies create a benefit for everyone in society; they provide equity in health. There are several frameworks for developing policies that reduce disparities and create equity. Once these policies are in place, evaluative policies assure that the policies are accomplishing their purpose. The changes in the frame of government change laws and regulations necessary to implement the changes. The enforcement bodies then make sure that the changes take place. The government represents most of the funding for health care, and to turn our negative, sickness-based system around, we must reverse the chronic diseases. The strategies expressed can reduce the amount of money it would require to identify and treat the proportion of our populations with ongoing disease and disability. Critical to the success of policy development is the ongoing assessment process. Without data, organizations and agencies drive blind. Regular policy updates are also essential. With a focus on operations, policies can move us forward efficiently and effectively. Evaluations play an essential part in ensuring policy development is fostering improved health outcomes. (Musa et al., 2023)

3.3. Communication

Communication is a critical part of effective public health. Clear and accurate information needs to be shared quickly and in a way that is accessible and understandable. Such information should include the goals of a public health program or intervention, the risks, a logical explanation for action, how it will be implemented, and what supporting measures are in place.

Health literacy is a priority for improving every citizen's capacity to understand and use health information to take actions that prevent illness and improve health. However, many people have low levels of health literacy, while some have no health literacy. Not all people understand or respond to health messages in the same way, so public health messages need to consider and address those differences when disseminating information. One example of this is the rise in vaccine hesitancy leading to increasing levels of non-vaccination among the western world. Health organizations are working to explore factors linked to vaccine uptake, which considers how best to frame communication messages to specific groups. A report identified that countries which have focused on health literacy had begun to generate interest and gather data in order to understand individuals at risk of poor health literacy. Improving health literacy will ensure that people have the knowledge, confidence, and access to care and support that they need and are entitled to – so they can play an active role in maintaining a healthy lifestyle. (Parnell, McCulloch, Mieres, & Edwards, 2014)

3.4. Community Engagement

Community participation has become an important part of public health practices. When the community has an active role in the decision-making process, public health programs are more successful, and the interventions developed are more appropriate for the community culture. Strategies that facilitate the participation and collaboration of communities in public health and local programs can help any program be more effective. Meaningful engagement can lay the groundwork for improved public health program and policy implementation.

Understanding community dynamics is an important first step in developing meaningful community engagement. Communities are most productive when they possess a strong network of people who have trusting, respectful relationships. Partnerships developed with central figures in the community usually have a positive influence on the effectiveness of health programs. The people in the community who have leadership roles influence the larger community in a variety of ways. Community leaders can be recognized in a variety of ways, such as their position, the roles they have with organizations, the formal and informal influence they have within the community, their length of residency in the community, and their involvement in other community activities. Successful community engagement requires significant community input to design a program that works given social, cultural, environmental, and economic factors. People are often the most important feature of an organizational investment. (Hudson, Gilbert, & Goodman, 2023)

3.5. Workforce Development

Workforce development has been identified as one of the key foundations on which a people-centered integrated care framework should be built. It also highlights how skill mix evolves over time to accommodate new or rising health threats. The primary task of the next phase of public health is to prepare the health professionals to meet the health challenges of the twenty-first century. This new vision called for a range of specific initiatives across the spectrum of public health training and development to create a public health workforce competent to tackle the range of health challenges expected to be faced by the population in the years ahead.

The comprehensive set of competencies required for twenty-first century public health practice will be quite different from those required last century. Public health teams need, and increasingly utilize, a diverse skill set range in their day-to-day work. Interdisciplinary working makes the best use of multi-skilled and experienced team members to provide high-quality and efficient services to the public. It was identified that, as a result of the increasing emphasis on continuous professional development, employers should be noting the positive impact that such interventions have on the work and management functions, rather than merely measuring outcomes. The need for leadership across the workforce in public health practice is highlighted as being important to foster an environment where workforce members are encouraged and supported to continue to innovate and improve their efficiency. (Yeager, Wisniewski, Chapple-McGruder, Castrucci, & Gould, 2018)

3.6. Legal and Regulatory Support

State and local laws and regulations provide the foundation upon which public health operates and protects communities. These legal authorities establish standards in health and provide the basis for sanctioning those who violate these standards. Public health is charged with protecting the public; therefore, public health actions often involve regulation to assure those objectives. Public health refers to the organized efforts of society to ensure the conditions necessary for people to be healthy. Legal authorities and regulations are needed to implement these societal efforts to assure health. Lack of strong legal support for public health has complicated the successful pursuit of public health goals.

For example, three legal frameworks underpin public health operations in the United States: the Constitution, statutory authority, and regulatory authority. These frameworks give the power to act at the federal, state, and local levels to promote, protect, and assure the health of the public. The federal agency provides a set of regulatory guidelines and principles for public health. To be effective, healthcare providers must comply with the laws related to public health. In areas in which state and federal laws conflict, federal law supersedes state law. On the other hand, the conduct of some federal agencies is constrained by state law. Public health officials and providers should be alert to situations in which the conduct of a federal agency has not been authorized by the state or may be in conflict with state law. In an emergency, the federal government has emergency powers to assume some of these functions for a limited period of time in separate locations. In some states, an over-reliance on federal health codes might create significant barriers to the improvement of local health outcomes and might have significant health consequences. (Fowler, Hill, Levin, & Obradovich, 2020)

3.7. Access to Healthcare Services

Access to essential health services has long been an issue of significant concern to public health professionals. Certain subgroups of the populations have consistently faced barriers in accessing healthcare, including, the population living below the poverty level, and undocumented sections. The determinants of the ability to access healthcare include social, economic, policy, and systemic factors. Geographical location, race and ethnicity, income, gender, and age influence the extent to which people can access quality healthcare services. Additionally, it is not simply health insurance coverage or the ability to pay that contributes to inequitable care, but also socioeconomic status, patient treatment preferences, cultural beliefs, and health literacy. Furthermore, one of the most basic elements of healthcare access is whether or not a patient can physically get into the healthcare facility for an appointment. Because of this, access to healthcare focuses on whether or not one can actually physically travel to a healthcare facility, afford the care, and obtain personal help with healthcare needs.

While having health insurance and the ability to pay for healthcare are essential to access, other key factors that impact access include getting a single appointment to take care of multiple issues and having sufficient time to cover preventive and routine care at an appointment. Moreover, transportation is a critical variable, as non-walkable transportation might limit access to healthcare. Similarly, those who can pay for health insurance may find that the state of healthcare availability impacts the number of providers who accept the healthcare coverage; the more different portals to care there are, the lesser the likelihood that the patient can be seen as a patient right away. Understanding and enhancing access is essential for public health goals related to health system performance and safe, equitable, and timely care. (Fitts et al., 2021)

3.8. Quality Improvement

Quality improvement as a factor in public health service delivery is foundational. There is a wealth of literature on the development of quality frameworks and methodologies. The development of frameworks has arisen from various sources such as evidence-based research, the development of tools, and strategies for implementation. There is a great deal of research around quality improvement initiatives that have led to an increase in patient safety, health outcomes, patient satisfaction, and service delivery cost savings. A standard that has gained much acceptance is that of continuous quality improvement, whose focus is paramount in improving patient safety.

Continuous quality initiatives for improvement have been utilized in several settings to improve organizational performance and the delivery of healthcare. Several cultural factors that are barriers to change and therefore quality management within healthcare include fear of change, poor staff development, inadequate resources, a personally selected career approach, poor staff relations, and outdated management styles. The area of workforce training and development can overcome some of these barriers. Case studies have demonstrated the effectiveness of that quality management approach. There is much in the literature and in the way the quality framework is proposed that is transferable to public health. Public health has similar goals to clinical healthcare, which is to improve the quality of life, care, service, programs, or systems. As such, it too must be efficient and effective. Public health should not be just a collection of programs, but rather public health activity should be designed as a comprehensive, unified, and bold strategy with a purpose, goal, and vision directed at improving and protecting the health and well-being of the community. Public health should not be tied to the deficit theory of suffering it has traditionally been mired in. Public health activities should seek the greatest public health good. Population health is the more successful theory that public health should be following. Public health can have a significant impact on the overall development of community well-being. (Ng & Colombani, 2015)

3.9. Emergency Preparedness

The ability of agencies in public health and health care to prepare for and respond to public health emergencies, such as natural disasters, acts of terrorism, and pandemics, is one of the most critical tasks facing the field. The development of strategies and tools to enhance preparedness and response has drawn the attention of policymakers at the state and federal levels, as well as public health officials, health researchers, and the general public. It is well accepted among all stakeholders that public health emergencies pose a significant and unique challenge to the public health infrastructure, impacting the relationships between communities, the health sector, and governments. Perhaps most critically, public health emergencies require the close cooperation of public health agencies and other essential health partners in the preparedness and response efforts. The fundamental components in planning and responding to public health emergencies are preparedness, recognition, response, and recovery. Incorporating these steps into emergency response activities, collaboration with local communities and other emergency preparedness agencies is key. Health departments regularly carry out training and drills to ensure the readiness of their staff and emergency systems. In a public health emergency, effective information and warning notification to the public and health care organizations is imperative. In addition, because public health emergencies can have both short- and long-term effects on a population, specific data is needed to identify and verify the emergency, define the impact, and aid in the resolution. Research such as risk assessment and disease surveillance can offer guidance to health departments with their response. (Chen, Zi-lin, & Luo, 2022)

3.10. Research

Research is an important foundation; all public health practices must be informed by research. For this to happen, we need to undertake different kinds of research related to public health. A lot of the work may be epidemiological, linking health status with particular health determinants within populations. This helps to build a picture of the health of a community. Other kinds of research that are important to public health are evaluations of programs or policies that come under public health. We need to provide evidence that policies or programs directed towards people's health can work, or should we be doing something different.

Changing policy and programs takes resources and can be challenging, so decisions should be based on the best evidence possible. The role of research or knowledge creation and utilization becomes very important. Over the last ten years or so, there has been a big push for all public health initiatives to be based on evidence. This means that research has led to producing evidence that is utilized by those who develop the programs. This has also led to increased funding for research studies in public health and partnerships between academic institutions and public health agencies to foster research collaboration, which has been positive. However, doing this kind of research is not without its challenges.

There are many ethical implications surrounding public health research and many debates about what is an acceptable way to gain access to and use community-level data that is not available to the public. It is important for the findings of such a range of research undertaken to assist in health system management to be translated from academic papers into practical usage, which can occur through the development of guidelines or via the publication of Best Practice Data through the appraisal of evidence for clinical and public health. Both of these recommendations, based on reviews of the literature, provide a way to assess a range of evidence and turn it into best practice. This concept is taken from the work known as evidence-based healthcare and is relevant to any organization that is trying to improve systems and practices. (Nantsupawat et al., 2023)

4. STATE POLICIES AND DISEASE CONTROL

The role of the state in controlling diseases and protecting general health goes beyond the performance of health services and the implementation of single interventions, as its actions include the definition of guidelines and regulations necessary to control the risks associated with multiple determinants. These determinants include water and air, work organization, urban planning, among others. The purpose of any public health policy is to reduce health-damaging behaviors and exposures, such as poor nutrition, smoking, chemical exposure, among others, and to protect the population from specific risks. The more effective and accessible health services are, the more these services will reach the more vulnerable population.

Policies to control diseases are fundamental to promote the health of populations. The state is responsible for the epidemiological surveillance to monitor the diseases that may affect its population and to organize the resources related to the control and prevention of diseases. The more efficient a policy is, the greater the possibility of not being observed, while the greater effectiveness of a program, a health policy, for example, does not need to use its services, since compliance often coincides with its greater effects in terms of health. With this compatibility, we are aware of the relevance of efforts to protect health. Vaccination policies are a good example of the importance of state action in the control of diseases through the definition of vaccination strategies, aiming at increased vaccine coverage. Resource allocation in health is critical if states are to define and implement policies for the control of diseases.

Decisions about funding for the installation and operation of preventive programs, encompassing a broad spectrum of preventive actions, should be based on evidence collected through cost-effectiveness studies. Only in this way will it be feasible to allocate funds so as not to compromise the continuity of activities of certain prevention programs. It is not possible to think that all resources in the area are intended for a single program, for example, the policy of maternal and child health, taking into account systemic needs. In some cases, and particularly, the control of certain diseases may not only be implemented at the regional level of the federal government, but may also need to develop strategies in conjunction with other states. (Fielding, Teutsch, & Breslow, 2010)

4.1. Epidemiological Surveillance

In the field of health, a key tool is the use of epidemiological surveillance. In the public health sphere, epidemiological surveillance systems function as health status monitors. Identifying trends as well as shifts from norms, such as outbreaks associated with disease or isolated cases, has a direct and strong relationship with public health and the activities in which employees are engaged. Surveillance, in its various forms, such as passive case finding, syndromic, routine, and event-based, aids in the early detection of infectious and communicable diseases and public health emergencies, as well as following up with those who may have been exposed, offering prophylactic and curative services, and tackling other environmental health-related inquiries as well.

Without the possibilities and opportunities that have been provided by data collection methods, powerful computer surveillance systems, and the use of Information and Communications Technologies, the early warning system that surveillance systems allow would be hampered. This, in turn, has its effect on reducing the level of response and affects both operations and, to a limited extent, the capacity to meet future targets. It is possible to suggest that a relationship also exists between the existence of surveillance systems and timely public health response. Effective community-based public health and the epidemiological surveillance sector require close collaboration and partnership among the key players in health. Epidemiology is the basic science of public health, as it allows public health workers to work in partnership, as well as enabling them to understand the dynamics of public health problems. Some of the main problems in public health are economic challenges, while there is also a preference for communicable diseases over non-communicable or environmental diseases identified with health gain. (Sigal & Bakumenko, 2020)

4.2. Preventive Measures and Vaccination Policies

Interventions aimed at promoting health and preventing disease are the foundation of the entire health policy. One of the most fundamental preventive measures consists of the vaccination of infants to prevent otherwise frequent or reputedly severe childhood diseases. The burden attributable to infectious diseases remains high, and the difficulties in containing some epidemic outbreaks, mostly due to international travel, migration, and displacement, underline the importance of preventive strategies in public health management, especially concerning infectious diseases. The importance of vaccine coverage is correlated to the phenomenon of community immunity or herd immunity, which, by impeding the spread of a pathogen in large groups of people, can reduce the risk of microorganism circulation. The lack of adequate coverage with the necessary vaccinations involves a higher likelihood of outbreaks. Since vaccination is one of the policies that can prevent infectious diseases, the child immunization plan is crucial.

The solutions proposed through this child vaccination plan adopt evidence-based criteria and indicate a scientific framework that provides examples of vaccination schedules for the prevention of infectious diseases from the first days of life to adolescence. Nowadays, the main issue across vaccination policies is hesitancy, which, however, can have different roots, from levels of access problems to levels of belief, concern, and/or values conflict. Moreover, equity often remains one of the most challenging objectives also in the field of vaccine coverage, especially when groups and individuals have different degrees of reaching a national immunization program. The main role for health professionals and new communication tools and strategies is addressed to guarantee the role of vaccines in society. Strong scientific evidence correlates vaccination strategies and public actions in global health and pandemic spread. (Vaccination and trust (2017)

4.3. Healthcare Resource Allocation

Healthcare resource allocation is a crucial part of public health, as it determines the distribution of resources and their strategic contribution to different health outcomes. One of the principles of public health is to spend money to maximize the chances that the population is healthy. Factors that affect how resources are distributed include the cost-effectiveness of the benefits produced by the resource, the needs of the population, and what other services are available. It is therefore important to consider the distribution of health service staff and financing at all levels of government when allocating resources. Additionally, it is important to consider the extent of need identified as a result of other programs, whether they are prevention, early intervention, or treatment programs.

The concept of allocating resources relies on achieving health equity. Health equity is a multifaceted idea, but at its core means equal access to health care, and in particular, primary health care. The local and federal governments have policies concerning the way health care is to be delivered in their states, which, in part, determines the allocation of resources. How services are to be distributed to address ill health and how to prevent future ill health are therefore steered by the policies of the state.

Most public health policies are concerned with preventing disease and injury, controlling the spread of disease when prevention fails, and preventing death and suffering by offering an appropriate level of treatment. To maximize the effect of these services, resource allocation mechanisms assess the underlying cause of need, determine what changes in inputs are needed, analyze how these services can deliver these inputs, and what budget implications that would have. Other factors that influence resource allocation are what other interventions are available, what need reduction they achieve, at what cost, and how to phase in these measures. Careful consideration needs to be given to strategic resource distribution to ensure that: The total resources available in the region are used to maximize the health status of the population; The entire public health service is structured to have appropriate placement and skill mix to service local health needs in an efficient, accessible, and equitable manner. The public health service will not duplicate health care services, and the bundling of municipal services with other services delivers some sort of economy of scale. (FENG, 2020)

4.4. Collaboration with International Health Organizations

Almost all health systems find it necessary to collaborate with international health organizations for the following reasons: no country is immune from the health problems of its neighbors; and collaborative international efforts to eradicate or reduce diseases have been quite successful in the past, such as the eradication of smallpox or the elimination of polio in the Western Hemisphere. Diseases do not respect national or state borders, thereby disrupting world economies and affecting everyone's health.

However, there are some challenges to international collaboration and cooperation in the area of health: differences in priority, disparities in resources, lack of international funding, and different time frames. Sharing knowledge and building capacity to enhance health systems in developing countries are other areas where different countries' health systems need to collaborate. Two great successes of international cooperation are the eradication of smallpox and the elimination of polio from the Western Hemisphere and an effort at promoting health and related laws resulted in some of the lowest rates for death and disease from communicable and non-communicable diseases in Europe. (Chang et al., 2018)

5. CHALLENGES AND FUTURE DIRECTIONS

Health is shaped primarily by the circumstances in which people are born, live, work, and age. The resources that fund expanded entitlements for all services are limited and restrict access to a wide variety of preferred services and key prevention programs, especially for vulnerable populations and when elected officials direct state action. Developments in infectious diseases, violence and injury control, tobacco control, bioterrorism and other public health emergencies, and preparedness, in general, have challenged the division between the public health and healthcare systems, the governance arrangements for public health programs and departments, and the strength of the public health infrastructure. One future area of work is to better demonstrate the interconnectedness of public health with other policy domains by providing a more detailed understanding of how the Ten Essential Services can help improve health in other sectors. Preparing people to respond to new or increased health concerns that have local and global consequences responds to the needs of communities by increasing their healthy functioning, supporting peaceful and prosperous social environments, and building meaningful options tailored to their preferences. Technological advances are important factors supporting state practice, with progress in epidemiology, data management, communications, and tools to assist individuals in self-management, self-determined living, and home care.

5.1. Current Challenges in Public Health

The immediate and rapid onslaught of the COVID-19 pandemic and related significant health, social, and economic policy changes has, over the past few years, highlighted that public health is very much a current concern. While recent global health crises may be rare, the contemporary strains placed on public health infrastructure, health system preparedness, as well as clinical, public health, and social responses to an international pandemic have underscored the ongoing challenges facing health management and policy today. A variety of multidimensional, longer-term workforce, funding, and resource constraints continue to threaten population as well as individual health. These include uneven service coverage, increasing antibiotic resistance, new health threats, growing chronic illness with complex etiologies and solutions, a growing number of interrelated determinants that influence health, the negative impacts of climate change and environmental degradation on health, and the social and financial impacts of ill health and healthcare. Approaching health responses at a juncture in time that is also marked by misinformation and a troubling erosion of public trust in health expertise and health services more generally has only exacerbated the struggle that public health at all levels has had in recent history. In order to develop a robust and effective response to these contemporary and near-future public health challenges, a comprehensive, multilevel strategy is vital. This will involve not only a coordinated workforce, surveillance, healthcare, and public health system approach, but also a focus on policymaking, community participation, and the exploration of innovative solutions to ensure that a more resilient public health system is able to manage inevitable future challenges. Work to achieve these goals should not only take place in times of crisis or when the pace of healthcare policy development and infrastructure change increases, but should be at the forefront of health policy, often at the state level, but also at the community, national, and international level. In the formulation of this framework, however, the critical fact that capacity in this area is often termed the responsibility of the state should not be underestimated. At the same time, however, those in all sectors of the system – healthcare, public health, and beyond – have a responsibility to prepare together and are mutually accountable for their collective and individual contribution to a coordinated, effective, and prepared response.

6. CONCLUSION

The role of the state in health management is both foundational and transformative, encompassing the governance of healthcare delivery, the promotion of public health policies, and the integration of community and individual health initiatives. This chapter illustrates the critical need for state-led frameworks that address complex health challenges through inclusive and equitable strategies. By incorporating the innovative 5S framework, the analysis underscores the importance of holistic approaches to health management, which consider the interplay of self, society, systems, and spirituality. The evolving landscape of public health requires the state to embrace adaptive policies that address emerging health threats, leverage technological advancements, and foster resilience within communities. As global health systems face unprecedented challenges, the state's role in ensuring accessible, effective, and culturally sensitive healthcare services remains paramount.

6.1. Implications for Practice and Future Research

This chapter provides a robust foundation for practitioners and policymakers to enhance the design and implementation of public health initiatives. The integration of the 5S framework into health management strategies offers a comprehensive lens for addressing diverse health determinants. Practically, it highlights the need for proactive policies that prioritize health equity, resource optimization, and interdisciplinary collaboration. Future research should explore the operationalization of the 5S framework across diverse socio-political contexts, with a focus on evaluating its impact on health outcomes and system resilience. Additionally, further studies should investigate the integration of spiritual and cultural dimensions into global health strategies, fostering a deeper understanding of how these elements influence healthcare access and behaviors. Such efforts will pave the way for innovative, inclusive, and sustainable approaches to contemporary public health challenges.

ACKNOWLEDGMENT

This chapter was written with the assistance from Dr. Minhaj A. Qidwai, who is the editor of the book "Enhancing Client, Family and Community Health" and his 5Ss approach of Self, Society, State, Systems and Spirituality".

Funding:

The Deanship of Scientific Research, Vice Presidency supported this research for Graduate Studies and Scientific Research, King Faisal University, Saudi Arabia. [Project Number: KFU251552].

REFERENCES

Anderson, L. M., & Shinn, C. (2023, February). Please provide me with the text you want me to extract the title from. I need the actual text to be able to identify the title. Retrieved January 11, 2025, from https://stacks.cdc.gov/view/cdc/20707

Andrews, M. (2008, November 15). The Good Governance Agenda: Beyond Indicators without Theory. Oxford Development Studies. Taylor & Francis. Retrieved January 2025, from DOI: 10.1080/13600810802455120

Beaglehole, R., Bonita, R., Horton, R., Adams, O., & McKee, M. (2004, June 1). Public health in the new era: improving health through collective action. The Lancet. Elsevier BV. Retrieved December 2024, from DOI: 10.1016/S0140-6736(04)16461-1

Chang, A. Y., Riumalló-Herl, C., Perales, N., Clark, S., Clark, A., Constenla, D., Garske, T., Jackson, M. L., Jean, K., Jit, M., Jones, E. O., Li, X., Suraratdecha, C., Bullock, O., Johnson, H., Brenzel, L., & Verguet, S. (2018, February 1). The Equity Impact Vaccines May Have On Averting Deaths And Medical Impoverishment In Developing Countries. *Health Affairs (Project Hope)*, *37*(2), 316–324. Advance online publication. Retrieved December 2024, from. DOI: 10.1377/hlthaff.2017.0861 PMID: 29401021

Chen, H., Zi-lin, L., & Luo, F. (2022, January 6). Establishment, Analysis, and Application of the Information Transmission and Response Model for Students of Vocational Colleges under Public Health Emergencies. Journal of Healthcare Engineering. Hindawi Publishing Corporation. Retrieved December 2024, from DOI: 10.1155/2022/6701364

Cuckler, G. A., Sisko, A. M., Poisal, J. A., Keehan, S. P., Smith, S. D., Madison, A. J., Wolfe, C. J., et al. (2018, February 14). National Health Expenditure Projections, 2017–26: Despite Uncertainty, Fundamentals Primarily Drive Spending Growth. Health Affairs. Project HOPE. Retrieved January 2025, from DOI: 10.1377/hlthaff.2017.1655

Feng, J. (2020, August 19). Research on the Efficiency of Local Government Medical and Health Resources Allocation under Market Economy System. DEStech Transactions on Social Science Education and Human Science. Destech Publications. Retrieved January 2025, from DOI: 10.12783/dtssehs/ecemi2020/34716

Fielding, J. E., Teutsch, S. M., & Breslow, L. (2010, June 1). A Framework for Public Health in the United States. Public health reviews. Springer Science+Business Media. Retrieved January 2025, from DOI: 10.1007/BF03391597

Fitch, M. I., & Bartlett, R. (2018, October 24). Patient Perspectives about Spirituality and Spiritual Care. Asia-Pacific Journal of Oncology Nursing. Medknow. Retrieved December 2024, from DOI: 10.4103/apjon.apjon_62_18

Fitts, M. S., Humphreys, J., Dunbar, T., Bourke, L., Mulholland, K., Guthridge, S., Zhao, Y., et al. (2021, August 1). Understanding and responding to the cost and health impact of short-term health staffing in remote and rural Aboriginal and Torres Strait Islander community-controlled health services: a mixed methods study protocol. BMJ Open. BMJ. Retrieved December 2024, from DOI: 10.1136/bmjopen-2020-043902

Fowler, J. H., Hill, S. J., Levin, R., & Obradovich, N. (2020, January 1). The effect of stay-at-home orders on COVID-19 cases and fatalities in the United States. arXiv (Cornell University). Cornell University. Retrieved December 2024, from https://arxiv.org/abs/2004.06098 DOI: 10.1101/2020.04.13.20063628

Henderson, B. R., & Armah, N. (2010, March 1). Making the case for community-based wellness programs. National Civic Review. Wiley. Retrieved January 2025, from DOI: 10.1002/ncr.20006

Hudson, D., Gilbert, K. L., & Goodman, M. S. (2023, February 7). Promoting Authentic Academic—Community Engagement to Advance Health Equity. International Journal of Environmental Research and Public Health. Multidisciplinary Digital Publishing Institute. Retrieved December 2024, from DOI: 10.3390/ijerph20042874

Musa, S. M., Haruna, U. A., Manirambona, E., Eshun, G., Ahmad, D. M., Dada, D. A., Gololo, A. A., et al. (2023, August 29). Paucity of Health Data in Africa: An Obstacle to Digital Health Implementation and Evidence-Based Practice. Public health reviews. Springer Science+Business Media. Retrieved January 2025, from DOI: 10.3389/phrs.2023.1605821

Nantsupawat, A., Wichaikhum, O., Abhicharttibutra, K., Udkunta, K., Poghosyan, L., & Shorey, S. (2023, June 19). Factors influencing evidence-based practice among undergraduate nursing students: A cross-sectional analysis. International Journal of Nursing Sciences. Elsevier BV. Retrieved December 2024, from DOI: 10.1016/j.ijnss.2023.06.002

Ng, E., & Colombani, P. de. (2015, November 17). Framework for Selecting Best Practices in Public Health: A Systematic Literature Review. Deleted Journal. Retrieved December 2024, from DOI: 10.4081/jphr.2015.577

Parnell, T. A., McCulloch, E., Mieres, J. H., & Edwards, F. (2014, January 28). Health Literacy as an Essential Component to Achieving Excellent Patient Outcomes. *NAM Perspectives*, *4*(1). Advance online publication. Retrieved December 2024, from. DOI: 10.31478/201401b

Raghav, S. (2017, August 10). “Hr as Strategic Partner: Manpower- Engines of Change in Health Sector Reforms and Human Resource.” JOJ Nursing & Health Care. Retrieved December 2024, from DOI: 10.19080/JOJNHC.2017.03.555603

Rajapakshe, W. (2024). Fundamentals of Performance Management. Advances in logistics, operations, and management science book series (p. 1). Routledge. Retrieved January 2025, from DOI: 10.4018/979-8-3693-4387-6.ch001

Rassool, G. H. (2021, October 19). Re-Examining the Anatomy of Islamic Psychotherapy and Counselling: Envisioned and Enacted Practices. Islamic Guidance and Counseling Journal. Institut Agama Islam Ma’arif NU (IAIMNU) Metro Lampung. Retrieved December 2024, from DOI: 10.25217/igcj.v4i2.1840

Sigal, A. V., & Bakumenko, M. (2020, January 1). The Level of the Country’s Health Care as an Indicator of its Economic Development. Advances in economics, business and management research/Advances in Economics, Business and Management Research. Atlantis Press. Retrieved January 2025, from DOI: 10.2991/aebmr.k.200312.151

Yeager, V. A., Wisniewski, J., Chapple-McGruder, T., Castrucci, B. C., & Gould, E. (2018, June 21). Public Health Workforce Self-Identified Training Needs by Jurisdiction and Job Type. Journal of Public Health Management and Practice. Lippincott Williams & Wilkins. Retrieved January 2025, from DOI: 10.1097/PHH.0000000000000830

Chapter 14

Community Health Nursing Practice in Pakistan

Tazeen Saeed Ali
https://orcid.org/0000-0002-8896-8766
Aga Khan University, Karachi, Pakistan

Saleema Gulzar
https://orcid.org/0000-0001-7245-9214
Aga Khan University, Karachi, Pakistan

Samina Subzali Vertejee
https://orcid.org/0000-0001-9080-4560
Aga Khan University, Karachi, Pakistan

Rozina Karmaliani
https://orcid.org/0000-0002-9565-5514
Aga Khan University, Karachi, Pakistan

ABSTRACT

A CHN plays a vital role in community health and development through community participation to promote empowerment and build sustainability. The central concepts which are necessary for this process include community participation, monitoring and evaluation, epidemiological surveillance, community empowerment, sustainability, development of the community-based organization and the community health management health teams, voluntarism, motivation, capacity building, health promotion and disease prevention, curative services, and other developmental activities. A CHN trains individuals to raise their voices for the benefit of the community and to plan, implement, and evaluate interventions. The CHN should provide the theory

DOI: 10.4018/979-8-3693-9092-4.ch014

and practice in training.

OBJECTIVES

This chapter will enhance the reader's understanding of the following:

- Disease burden in Pakistan and the global strategies to address these issues at present.
- Challenges of practicing community health nursing; and
- Role and practice of community health nursing in addressing the issue using the PHC approach.

The changing demography and triple burdens of diseases are the key elements that demand a specialized cadre to envisage and respond to health's social, political, economic and biological contexts. Pakistan is the sixth most populous country in the world, with a population growth rate of 2.0 per cent in 2012-2013. The challenges facing Pakistan and other developing countries in overcoming the burden of disease include natural and artificial disasters and political crises (United Nations Development Programme [UNDP], n.d.). These challenges are further amplified by scarce Human Resources for Health (HRH) due to brain drain and poorly trained health service providers.

The Alma Ata Declaration of 1978 outlined primary health care as a strategy to assist people in addressing their individual health and societal development issues. Together with the eight health-related Millennium Development Goals (MDGs) agreed upon by 189 countries in 2000, there is a direction to overcome health disparities. Yet, there is a long way to go (Commonwealth Foundation, 2013). Accordingly, community health practice refers to the art of disease prevention and health promotion interventions to improve a community's quality of life. It is a key component of achieving these goals (Bennett, 1979). A key component of community health practice is the deployment of nurses with proper academic preparedness to help address health and development issues.

A community health nurse (CHN) is a human resource component of a health system that includes lady health visitors, midwives and physicians. A CHN can play an important role in addressing the health and developmental needs of the community by applying nursing and scientific knowledge to enhance the quality of their health services. The CHN practices in the community and provides primary, secondary, and tertiary care in various settings (i.e. homes, schools, health clinics, and workplaces) (Stanhope & Lancaster, 2008). Through continued follow-up and community participation, a CHN can be instrumental in improving health and developmental indicators by applying public health concepts with an individual touch.

Finnish CHNs are trained in preventive medicine and health promotion and play a key role in addressing health issues and reducing infant and maternal mortality rates through their work at the front lines (Siivola & Martikanen, 1990). Their holistic perspective while addressing community health needs is key to their success. During training, CHNs are equipped with the required competencies and skills to understand the interaction between individuals, families, and the community (including social determinants of health) through public health and primary healthcare lenses. Emphasis is placed on the ability of a CHN to adapt to different working conditions for service provision, ensuring access and affordability at the point of care (Meadows, 2009).

The Intervention Wheel Model was originally introduced in 1998 by the Minnesota Department of Health, Section of Public Nursing. This model guides CHNs as a population-based practice. Its approach includes three practice levels (i.e. system, community, and individual/family) and 17 public health interventions. Each intervention and practice level contributes to improving population health. It includes surveillance, disease investigation, outreach, case finding, screening, delegated function, referral, follow-up, case management, counselling, consultation, collaboration, coalition building, community organizing, advocacy, social marketing, policy development & enforcement, and health teaching. (Minnesota Department of Health, n.d.)

This chapter highlights how the CHN practice uses different competencies and provides culturally sensitive care. This chapter is written mainly based on personal experience as a CHN. The two main concepts discussed in this chapter are practice site selection and community participation. Both of these are equally important in managing the community's health and development, and the success of one of these concepts is interconnected with the enhancement of the other. Both concepts include the concepts of voluntarism, motivation, capacity building, health promotion, disease prevention, and curative services through an integrated primary healthcare approach. It also includes other social developmental activities (i.e. poverty eradication, improving literacy).

SITE SELECTION

The first step involves the site selection, it comprises the identification of both the stakeholders and the development of a mutual agenda at the community level. These factors are then used to work on mutual agenda at the community levels such as participation, monitoring, epidemiological surveillance and evaluation, community empowerment, and sustainability.

The CHN and other team members will explore different communities to implement the PHC prototype. There are two ways through which communities can be identified during the project planning stage: either (1) the service provider is approached directly by a community to facilitate their health and developmental needs, or (2) the service provider surveys the various ways in identifying an appropriate community after concept mapping:

1. The focus for the mapping project is identified.
2. Community stakeholders (i.e., traditional birth attendants, elders, religious leaders, and community-based non-political organizations) are identified.
3. Meetings are conducted to sort out the logistics of the project. During this step, the CHN will also discuss the purpose and benefits of community health nursing for the community.
4. The CHN will conduct initial brainstorming sessions with active community members and stakeholders to discuss the relative importance of the project and the feasibility of working together. Community stakeholders are actively involved in the interpretation of the resulting maps.
5. In the utilization phase, the maps results and purposes of the PHC are the main focus, where each stakeholder generates their statements. Then after negotiations, CHN would develop a final purpose statement so that future collaboration with the stakeholders is well-defined regarding contributions to human and financial resource sharing. (Trochim & Kane, 2005) Each entity offers diversity in perspective. Their particular knowledge and skills enhance the community's efforts to address critical needs and solve problems. A stakeholder facilitates or undermines strategic efforts to improve community health. (Stanhope & Lancaster, 2008)
6. In the next stage, the CHN formalizes a community-based organization (CBO) to formally work for the community's health and development in a non-political capacity. A CBO is a nonprofit organization that operates within the civil society of a single local community; it is a subset of the broader category of nonprofits. They are often run voluntarily and are self-funded (University of Michigan School of Public Health, n.d.).

Once the CBO has been established, the CHN conducts a baseline survey. This assessment is necessary to understand the existing formal and informal infrastructure, the communication networks, and the local culture and traditions (Stanhope & Lancaster, 2008). To build a trustworthy relationship with the community from the onset, the data collectors and survey supervisors for the baseline assessment must be hired from the community. This also helps to develop capacity. On completion of this assessment, the CHN presents the findings to the CBO (including data collectors), stakeholders, and any interested members of the community. This builds awareness among the community of baseline health and development indicators and assesses the impact of morbidities and mortality on community life. The CHN then conducts seminars and workshops to prioritize the long list of activities and conduct qualitative in-depth interviews to understand the community's priorities. The primary objective of the CBO is that the CHN conduct assessments in collaboration with the community.

COMMUNITY PARTICIPATION

Successful entry into the community can be defined as gaining "community participation" (10). Studies have documented that community engagement improves health indicators, resulting in empowerment and sustainability (Minkler & Wallerstein, n.d.; Tindana et al., 2007). Community participation (CP) ensures resource development, volunteerism, operational planning and implementation, and monitoring and evaluation of community interventions (Zakus & Lysack, 1998). Through CP, holistic and cost-effective interventions are achieved. There is no correct way to achieve CP, as success will vary based on the characteristics of each community. However, some common elements of active participation can be seen almost in all communities: equal involvement of any community individual, group, or organization that is instrumental for community progress (Bhuyan, 2004); Furthermore, having open and transparent processes resulting in real actions and results.

During site selection and before physical infrastructure development, awareness, sensitization, and capability building can be initiated through workshops, seminars, or training courses for stakeholders. This will facilitate the ability of the community to contribute to effective health planning in the presence or absence of CHNs. The empowerment of the community to raise their voice for their community's health needs, the ability to take action and be recognized for their work (Drury & Reicher, 2009; Laverack, 2006), and the ability to resolve conflicts of interest are key components of CP.

DEVELOPMENT OF COMMUNITY HEALTH MANAGEMENT TEAM/ORGANIZATION

A Community Health Management Team (CHMT) must be developed to work independently to generate a budget, develop a plan and implementation strategy, and independently evaluate community-based activities. The intended outcome is to establish a sense of ownership amongst the stakeholders in order to incorporate sustainability into community initiatives. Formulating the CHMT requires several steps:

1. They are conducting "sensitization and awareness" sessions, conducting the aforementioned baseline assessment with the help of community activists and stakeholders to develop the list of health and developmental needs. During this process, a CHN will face two kinds of people: community stakeholders (already working for their communities) and those who were inspired by the sensitization sessions and are willing to work with this team.
2. After quantitative and qualitative assessment, results are shared with community members, and efforts are made to identify more problems and some of the root causes.
3. The CHN takes the time to get to know the community and its stakeholders, including religious leaders, activists, and community groups. The CHN also seeks to understand the roles and responsibilities of all relevant levels of Government. During this time, the CHN will look at the patterns of morbidity and mortality indicators, risk factors, and existing healthcare practices.
4. Involving more partners as allies in tackling the community's health issues (Roussos & Fawcett, 2000) while keeping in mind that the CHN is not yet forming an organization but is laying the foundation for the CHMT. For this reason, the CHN should engage the CBO at every step. The CHN will consider the need for more members to achieve outcomes effectively through budgeting, proposal & report writing, and management of human resources. It is necessary to have members who are writers, educators, strong public speakers, managers, and those familiar with government or nonprofit organizational structures.
5. Organizational inventory is conducted for the CHN to understand existing resources and the gaps that must be filled for the CHMT to be effective once established. If the community needs more capacity, the CHN will have to build it up.
6. The specifics of the initial meeting (i.e. date, time, location, agenda, hospitality responsibilities) are determined, and the CBO is mobilized to become the CHMT. An organizational structure must now be created; therefore, important

matters must be considered: Will the CHMT have a board? If so, what will the board structure be? In order to successfully do this, bylaws must be established.

7. The organization sets its mandate and determines the strengths and weaknesses of its members. An organizational 'culture' will begin to form, and the CHMT will have its code of ethics and begin strategizing to achieve its goal. The organization should always continue evolving. These early brainstorming sessions are extremely important in transitioning from an informal group of community activists to a registered CHMT. The brain comes into action here: argue, debate, discuss, dispute and contest (Papineau & Kiely, 1996).
8. At this stage, the CHN facilitates the CBO networking with other community organizations to enhance support in implementing health and developmental activities.
9. Tentative and final plans are made. For positive change to occur, groups must have clear written goals and an implementation plan.
10. The process is legitimized. When the CHN has already developed a plan of action with the community group/organization, they need to spell out the management process to which it will adhere in implementing that plan, including financial, supervision and feasibility aspects. The CHN will ensure that this CBO is registered with the Government and become a community Based Management Team (CHMT).
11. The plan is implemented. A well-thought-out plan will reduce uncertainties in the implementation stage. Efforts should be made to stay true to the original plan, mandate, and vision.
12. An evaluation is conducted. With the help of the CHN, the community group should make indicators to evaluate the implementation, make plans to disseminate findings, and take steps for plans.

Throughout this process, the community is involved actively and, by doing so, is empowered and enabled towards autonomy.

VOLUNTEERISM

After the development of the CHMT and the inauguration of the health centre, human resources are necessary. Building on the foundation of community participation, the CHMT should invite volunteers to participate and take ownership of their activities, including acting as an advisor for career-building, training and retention. Retention is a key component of the process, as volunteers play a lead role in the sustainability of any community project. The CHN provides formal training and mentoring with assistance from the CHMT. Volunteers who come with health knowledge can be given a chance to conduct the sessions as master trainers and could be given added responsibilities (i.e., taking attendance and listening to problems and concerns) in order to enhance their leadership skills. Volunteers who clearly understand their goals, events, and time commitment are more motivated in their work. (Lerner et al., 2005) The most active volunteers working with CHN are invited to membership in CHMT. They attend meetings to discuss the community and volunteers' problems. CHN ensures that each volunteer can attend multiple trainings and follow up on the training. The duties are assigned based on the volunteer's interest and career development plan.

In addition to volunteers, parents must also be committed to the mission of the organization when their dependent children are enrolled as volunteers, and clear communication on roles and responsibilities must be outlined.

CAPACITY BUILDING

Capacity building is necessary for the CHMT and volunteers to bring empowerment and sustainability. A CHN, because of academic preparedness, would be able to build the capacity of CHMT for the leadership & management, planning cycle, and developmental program activities with its monitoring and evaluation. Simultaneously volunteers are trained in management and service delivery skills, and CHN creates motivation among volunteers by engaging them in the planning and implementation of CHMT activities. Furthermore, governmental and non-governmental organizations could be the stakeholders to conduct the training.

Similarly, organizations such as Hilal-e-Dahmer could be approached to train community volunteers for vaccination programs, which is a semi-governmental organization. After the community's volunteers are trained, CHMT formal and informal mentorship should be provided for leadership and management skills. After this, their health service delivery-related practice training has to be given so that they can supervise their community volunteers with the help of government officials or with some NGOs.

The CHN conducts close and continuous supervision and feedback for the volunteer's performances. Those who are excellent volunteers would be identified as mentors or master trainers for others.

In more detail, it is discussed in the lower sections that epidemiological surveillance is done to measure morbidities and mortalities. Still, monitoring or evaluating the interventions implemented by trained community volunteers is important. Capacity building is one of the most important strategies for training community members, whether ordinary members, community organization members, or volunteers.

HEALTH PROMOTION AND DISEASE PREVENTION

One of the important roles in health promotion and disease prevention for CHN (she) is to focus on some important areas. The first is the lifestyle and behavioral approaches, from where she identifies the health education needs during her assessment. Health education should be a part of primary prevention; however, secondary and tertiary prevention of diseases are equally essential. Furthermore, it is important to have skill development for the mothers, like how to prepare ORS in case its packets are unavailable. The main focus of CHN should be on the risk groups like the malnourished population.

CHN must also examine sociological issues to improve community health and development. To work in this area, CHN must build partnerships with community and non-governmental organizations. Furthermore, CHN could provide more attention to vulnerable groups like illiterate women, the youngest daughter-in-law and high-risk mothers.

Another important role in health promotion and disease prevention activities is the community's ongoing assessment and community health research. CHN acts like it has a lot of branches; only then will CHN reach every individual through its volunteers, including CHMT, GOs, and NGOs. This would also be a collaborative approach, where her role is extremely critical.

CURATIVE SERVICE

CHN's role in curative services is very important. A CHN could also provide services by conducting a clinic for minor ailments. (Werner et al., 1993) A CHN has prescriptive authority whereby she can prescribe WHO-recommended medications. CHN needs to manage a patient holistically through medication and other preventive, curative and rehabilitative management care and services. A CHN could use an integrated primary health care approach whereby she could invite medical and nursing students, family medicine residents, and doctors to conduct the clinic. Sometimes, students may come to the clinic only when available. In that case, CHN with CHMT could approach the local government to provide a few placements for doctors. For example, in one field site, some specialists visited the health center only once a week. This will also enhance the public-private partnership.

Case study 1:In one of the communities the CHN advocated for specialized doctors to visit the community. The specialty of these doctors includes pulmonology, ophthalmology, in addition a dentist was also placed by the provincial level. By doing so, this enhances the partnership between the public and private sector. Later, in the same community, mortality and morbidity rates were increased. CHN motivated

CHMT to conduct several meetings with the District Health Officer (DHO) and Executive District Health Officer (EDHO) to open one of the government health dispensaries within their community. So, finally, after six months of efforts, the dispensary was inaugurated for service provision.

Then the CHN working alongside community members to monitor health activities such as malnutrition, natal care, post - natal care, immunization, hygiene, water and sanitation etc

DEVELOPMENTAL ACTIVITIES

Since health is the state of physical, sexual, psychological, and social well-being; (Gruskin, Mills, & Tarantola, 2007), it is necessary for the CHN to provide holistic care. Poverty and illiteracy are the two main factors that cause vulnerability towards illness. A CHN demanded the community to educate their children in order to aid them with the struggles they face as a result of unemployment. This was done in effort to lessen prevalence of poverty among community members.

Case study 2: In one of the communities, the Hindus and Muslims lived amongst each other. Due to the misunderstandings and fear, there was reluctance among Hindus to allow their children to attend a school that has Muslim management. This was due to the fear that they might not be accepted and/or enrolled. The Muslim teachers feared that the presence of Hindu children would impact and influence the religious beliefs of their Muslim peers. The CHN and CHMT conducted in - depth assessments, multiple meetings to ensure the enrollment of Hindu children.

Case study 3: A CHN identified that many illiterate adults were interested in being literate; they wanted to change their situation. A CHN, with the help of the CHMT and the government education department, opened a home-based school. CHN encouraged the partners to participate in resource development. As a result, the community gave free premises for school and government departments with schoolteachers and books. Since the education department only promised to give teachers' salaries for a year, CHN ensured that the school should have some fees, which were used as income generation for the teacher's future salary. Later Allama Iqbal's home-based education department was approached to ensure that home-based community students could receive the certification of class five, then an intermediate.

Income Generation: What comes in income generation? Income generation would be the number of activities through which money could be generated. These need to be used for volunteers for their motivation, and the remaining leftovers could be used for running & maintaining program-related things.

Case study 4: The community opened a small volunteer-based lab in which hemoglobin, serum glucose and urine pregnancy tests were tested, but not many people were using the facility. So CHN educated the CHMT to initiate other microfinance activities. CHN identified "Women bank", but the requirement was that only skilled women would receive the loan. CHN contacted the Layree Income Generation Program and facilitated workshops for the community women. These women received the skills of embroidery, detergent making, juice making, candle formation, paintwork, etc. Most of the skilled women received loans. They paid the loan back under the supervision of CHMT.

Provision of water & Sanitation: CHN's responsible for ensuring that all primary health care basic elements are available for the community with the help of CHMT. CHN sensitizes the community for the provision of working towards developmental activities.

Case study 5: When one of the CHMTs decided to work in water and sanitation, CHN facilitated a visit to the water board and sanitation department. CHN used other mediums like media to pressure the Government on the availability of water and sanitation in the community.

Monthly and quarterly meetings should be done with the health team, CHMT and volunteers to discuss what was being done, what was next, what was discussed, and who will be the collaborators.

MONITORING AND EVALUATIONS

The CHN develops input, process, and output indicators to measure the improvement of services. When the services are fully improved, the CHN could call all the community members to reflect on whether the overall services of the community are improving. It is difficult to say if there is an overall impact on morbidity and mortality. Still, based on the evaluation tool, at least CHN could observe changes in input, process and output indicators.

EPIDEMIOLOGICAL SURVEILLANCE

A surveillance system involves identifying and reporting a health event or disease outbreak in the population, which is moved from the periphery to the federal level. There are mainly four kinds of surveillance: active, passive, sentinel, and special. Surveillance and notification of communicable diseases help CHN to understand the importance of data collection on a steady base. (4) A CHN often collects the information once or twice a year or according to needs, for example life threatening diseases . Not only does a CHN needs to conduct small surveys, but it is also important to compare the progress with the baseline survey. Surveillance should be done in 4 parts: the services part, the education part, the management part and the research part.

In the services, she has to know how delivery of the health packages or services is being done with the collaboration of the CHMT, Volunteers, GOs, and NGOs. After conducting the epidemiological surveillance, she has to look at the overall improvement within the community so that the services can be improved according to (input process and output indicators).

CHN'S ROLE IS IMPORTANT IN MANAGEMENT

Case study 7:For this section, here is my suggestion: Through the surveillance conducted in one of the communities, the CHN identified 30% of children as malnourished. These very same children are infected with acute respiratory tract infections as well. The CHN functions as a manager by meeting with community stakeholders and the CHMT with volunteers. Through the community approach the CHN must plans the intervention, who will carry it out, where, who and when it should be implemented and how many partners such as UNICEF will be involved. Moreover, it should be considered from where the budget would be generated. In the results, not only did prevalence decrease, but the incidence rate of acute respiratory tract infections decreased.

If some implementation is there, epidemiological surveillance at both levels should be compared with the baseline and on regular bases. Monitoring and evaluation must be done to see the prevalence and incidence of the disease. It is also imperative that other than epidemiological surveillance, some other small research questions are raised simultaneously, which could be studied by the students or interns; they will be able to see the overall improvement. And above all, impact studies have to be conducted after identifying impact measurement indicators.

EMPOWERMENT

"Empowerment is *willingly* and *knowingly* granting official power to others." (22) or having control of their own lives (Van Hooser, n.d.). This rich definition frames empowerment comprehensively: "Empowered employees exercise their freedom to act within their area of competence to satisfy customer needs. They take responsibility, accept accountability, exercise initiative, and deliver results." (Deb, 2006)

Empowerment can mainly be defined with three elements: voice, action and recognition. In 1999, a National Empowerment Centre conducted a study. After much discussion, they defined empowerment as having several qualities such as having decision-making power, having access to information and resources, having a range of options from which choices to make (not just yes/no, either/or.), developing assertiveness and the realization of the idea that an individual has the capacity to create change (being hopeful) . Empowerment brings in critical thinking, learning the conditioning and seeing things differently. Empowered individuals and groups learn to redefine who we are (speaking in our voice), their relationships to institutionalized power and how to express anger.

Participation in community services has many advantages: the individual doesn't feel alone but a part of a group, understands that people have rights, brings about a change in one's life and one's community, learns skills (e.g., communication) which are defined as important, changes others' perceptions of one's competency and capacity to act, comes out of the closet, undergoes growth and change that is never ending and self-initiated, increases one's positive self-image and overcomes stigma. However, the most important step in empowerment is capacity building (which is the basic element in community participation).

The ideal scenario involves the volunteers running the center. However, there are times where the community needs the space or is unable to provide volunteers. However, the organization should pay the rent for a limited time since it is an important step towards community empowerment and sustainability.

SUSTAINABILITY

As CHNs take the lead in the initiatives and work in collaboration, the sustainability of the initiatives becomes critical. According to evaluative research, the sustainability measures have been divided into four categories: maintaining program activities, continuing to serve substantial numbers of clients, building and sustaining collaborative structures, and maintaining attention to the ideas underlying the projects by disseminating them to others. (Scheirer, Hartling, & Hagerman, 2008) It is necessary to continue the project activities by the CBMT and provide services to the maximum number of community clients. However, there should be a focus on improving the quality for maximum client coverage (Scheirer, 2005). In maintaining the capacity of the health team and healthcare structure, CHN must ensure the partnership with Government and non-government organizations (Alexander et al., 2003). The most important is maintaining attention to the issues addressed by the program. This means a CHN needs to continue advocacy efforts to clarify the concepts of the primary health care program to meet the community's needs (Scheirer, Hartling, & Hagerman, 2008).

Furthermore, there are three degrees of program sustainability: non-routinized activities, routines and standardized routines. It also suggests that measures can be taken to impact the development of programs from the very beginning to make them last. Distinguishing routines and standards identify two levels of action conducive to the sustainability of a program: organizational and state. (Pluye et al., 2005)

When thinking of sustainability programs and primarily through the context of organizational routines places it within the reach of all health promoters. . Further, thinking of sustainability in terms of institutional standards ultimately allows public health practitioners to act on healthy public policies. This conceptualization may help practitioners, decision-makers, and researchers to integrate the future of programs into their concerns, reconcile innovations and routines, and to become more reflexive in their practice. (Pluye, Potvin, & Denis, 2004)

CHALLENGES OF PRACTICING COMMUNITY HEALTH NURSING

The first and foremost challenge is the acceptance of the cadre at a national level, as the cases described above are only practiced in isolated cases in the private sector. As described in chapters two and three, there needs to be a deployment plan and carrier structure for nurses in the public sector. (29) In private, they are hired to serve the community at the rural health centre. The CHNs posted in the urban and rural sectors are primarily assigned to offer center-based services, which leaves a gap in reaching the community to address problems at grass root levels. The scarcity of health human resources, especially nurses, can be one of the key factors in offering outreach services. In addition, the need for a coordination and supervision plan to provide an operational service structure between CHNs, lady health visitors, midwives and lady health workers to offer grass root services. (Upvall et al., 2005) Moreover, continuing education and professional development is another grey area of CHN practice in Pakistan; two main reasons for this include nurses' burnout due to work overload giving hardly any space for continued education and a second lack of opportunities to access continuing education. eLearning could be utilized to provide professional development to PHNs, especially when distance is an issue. In addition, some other challenges identified are lack of infrastructure, sanitary conditions and safety securities, which are also demotivating factors to promote CHN practice. (Gulzar, Shamim, & Khuwaja, n.d.)

Hence the above challenges are eye openers for the stakeholders to view the cadre as the need of the country in the prevailing situation to overcome health disparities. Therefore, serious attention is required on the deployment plan, strengthening the existing CHN workforce and improving working conditions to attract and retain nurses to work as CHNs.

CONCLUSION

A CHN plays a vital role in community health and development through community participation to promote empowerment and build sustainability. The central concepts which are necessary for this process include community participation, monitoring and evaluation, epidemiological surveillance, community empowerment, sustainability, development of the community-based organization and the community health management health teams, voluntarism, motivation, capacity building, health promotion and disease prevention, curative services, and other developmental activities. A CHN trains individuals to raise their voices for the benefit of the community and to plan, implement, and evaluate interventions.

Capacity building is a key component for the CHMT and its volunteers to bring in empowerment and sustainability. The main focus should be leadership & management, planning, program development and monitoring and evaluation competencies for the CHMT. Concurrently, volunteers should be made available for both management and service delivery skills. The CHN should provide the theory and practice in training. It is also the obligation to guarantee that all the major healthcare elements are accessible to the community with the help of the CHMT. Most significantly, a CHN needs to go for her advanced education if she is only baccalaureate-prepared and not master or PhD prepared so that her research and conducting of surveillance competencies are enriched.

REFERENCES

Alexander, J. A., Weiner, B. J., Metzger, M. E., Shortell, S. M., Bazzoli, G. J., Hasnain-Wynia, R., Sofaer, S., & Conrad, D. A. (2003). Sustainability of collaborative capacity in community health partnerships. *Medical Care Research and Review : MCRR, 60*(4, suppl), 130S–160S. DOI: 10.1177/1077558703259069 PMID: 14687432

Bennett, F. J. (1979). Primary health care and developing countries. *Social Science & Medicine. Part A, Medical Sociology, 13*, 505–514. DOI: 10.1016/0271-7123(79)90092-0 PMID: 472779

Bhuyan, K. K. (2004). Health promotion through self-care and community participation: Elements of a proposed programme in the developing countries. *BMC Public Health, 4*(1), 11. DOI: 10.1186/1471-2458-4-11 PMID: 15086956

Commonwealth Foundation. (2013). *National report.*

Deb, T. (2006). Strategic approach to human resource management. Atlantic Publishers & Distributors.

Drury, J., & Reicher, S. (2009). Collective psychological empowerment as a model of social change: Researching crowds and power. *The Journal of Social Issues, 65*(4), 707–725. DOI: 10.1111/j.1540-4560.2009.01622.x

Gruskin, S., Mills, E. J., & Tarantola, D. (2007). History, principles, and practice of health and human rights. *Lancet, 370*(9585), 449–455. DOI: 10.1016/S0140-6736(07)61200-8 PMID: 17679022

Gulzar, S. A., Shamim, M. S., & Khuwaja, A. K. (2010). Promoting motivation towards community health care: A qualitative study from nurses in Pakistan. *JPMA. The Journal of the Pakistan Medical Association, 60*(6), 501–504. PMID: 20527656

Laverack, G. (2006). Improving health outcomes through community empowerment: A review of the literature. *Journal of Health, Population and Nutrition, 24*(1), 113–120. PMID: 16796158

Lerner, R. M., Lerner, J. V., Almerigi, J. B., Theokas, C., Phelps, E., Gestsdottir, S., Naudeau, S., Jelicic, H., Alberts, A., Ma, L., Smith, L. M., Bobek, D. L., Richman-Raphael, D., Simpson, I., Christiansen, E. D. D., & von Eye, A. (2005). Positive youth development, participation in community youth development programs, and community contributions of fifth-grade adolescents: Findings from the first wave of the 4-H Study of Positive Youth Development. *The Journal of Early Adolescence, 25*(1), 17–71. DOI: 10.1177/0272431604272461

Meadows, P. (2009). Community health nursing. AJN. *The American Journal of Nursing, 109*(10), 19. DOI: 10.1097/01.NAJ.0000343102.62178.80 PMID: 21753458

Minkler, M., & Wallerstein, N. (Eds.). (2008). *Community-based participatory research for health: From process to outcomes* (2nd ed.). Jossey-Bass.

Minnesota Department of Health. (n.d.). Public health nursing resources. https://www.health.state.mn.us/divs/chs/phn/resources.html

Nonnecke, B., Andrews, D., & Preece, J. (2006). Non-public and public online community participation: Needs, attitudes and behaviour. *Electronic Commerce Research, 6*(1), 7–20. DOI: 10.1007/s10660-006-5985-x

Papineau, D., & Kiely, M. C. (1996). Participatory evaluation in a community organization: Fostering stakeholder empowerment and utilization. *Evaluation and Program Planning, 19*(1), 79–93. DOI: 10.1016/0149-7189(95)00041-0

Pluye, P., Potvin, L., & Denis, J.-L. (2004). Making public health programs last: Conceptualizing sustainability. *Evaluation and Program Planning, 27*(2), 121–133. DOI: 10.1016/j.evalprogplan.2004.01.001

Pluye, P., Potvin, L., Denis, J.-L., Pelletier, J., & Mannoni, C. (2005). Program sustainability begins with the first events. *Evaluation and Program Planning, 28*(2), 123–137. DOI: 10.1016/j.evalprogplan.2004.10.003

Roussos, S. T., & Fawcett, S. B. (2000). A review of collaborative partnerships as a strategy for improving community health. *Annual Review of Public Health, 21*(1), 369–402. DOI: 10.1146/annurev.publhealth.21.1.369 PMID: 10884958

Scheirer, M. A. (2005). Is sustainability possible? A review and commentary on empirical studies of program sustainability. *The American Journal of Evaluation, 26*(3), 320–347. DOI: 10.1177/1098214005278752

Scheirer, M. A., Hartling, G., & Hagerman, D. (2008). Defining sustainability outcomes of health programs: Illustrations from an online survey. *Evaluation and Program Planning, 31*(4), 335–346. DOI: 10.1016/j.evalprogplan.2008.08.004 PMID: 18835642

Siivola, U., & Martikainen, T. (Eds.). (1990). The public health nurse—Is the linchpin of primary health care. In World Health Forum.

Stanhope, M., & Lancaster, J. (2008). *Public health nursing* (7th ed.). Mosby Elsevier.

Tindana, P. O., Singh, J. A., Tracy, C. S., Upshur, R. E. G., Daar, A. S., Singer, P. A., Frohlich, J., & Lavery, J. V. (2007). Grand challenges in global health: Community engagement in research in developing countries. *PLoS Medicine*, *4*(9), e273. DOI: 10.1371/journal.pmed.0040273 PMID: 17850178

Trochim, W., & Kane, M. (2005). Concept mapping: An introduction to structured conceptualization in health care. *International Journal for Quality in Health Care : Journal of the International Society for Quality in Health Care*, *17*(3), 187–191. DOI: 10.1093/intqhc/mzi038 PMID: 15872026

United Nations Development Programme. (n.d.). Country info: Pakistan. https://www.pk.undp.org/content/pakistan/en/home/countryinfo

University of Michigan School of Public Health. (n.d.). What is public health nursing? https://www.sph.umich.edu/ncbon/whatis.html

Upvall, M. J., Karmaliani, R., Pirani, F., Gul, R., & Khalid, F. (2005). Developing nursing leaders through graduate education in Pakistan. *International Journal of Nursing Education Scholarship*, *1*(1). Advance online publication. DOI: 10.2202/1548-923X.1079 PMID: 16646893

Van Hooser, P. (n.d.). Leaders ought to know. http://www.leadersoughttoknow.com/tag/phil-van-hooser/page/2/

Werner, D., Thuman, C., Maxwell, J., Pearson, A., & Cary, F. (1993). *Where there is no doctor: A village health care handbook for Africa*. Macmillan.

Zakus, J. D. L., & Lysack, C. L. (1998). Revisiting community participation. *Health Policy and Planning*, *13*(1), 1–12. DOI: 10.1093/heapol/13.1.1 PMID: 10178181

Chapter 15
Community Health Nursing Education in Pakistan

Samina Subzali Vertejee
https://orcid.org/0000-0001-9080-4560
Aga Khan University, Karachi, Pakistan

Saleema Gulzar
https://orcid.org/0000-0001-7245-9214
Aga Khan University, Karachi, Pakistan

Tazeen Saeed Ali
https://orcid.org/0000-0002-8896-8766
Aga Khan University, Pakistan

Rozina Karmaliani
https://orcid.org/0000-0002-9565-5514
Aga Khan University, Pakistan

ABSTRACT

Health is an equilibrium of biological, physical, social and spiritual factors; the access to health should be socially, culturally and economically viable to ensure the complete state of wellbeing. Having said this community health nursing (CHN) practice at grass root level should also be in congruence to offer culturally sensitive, affordable, available and accessible care to people it serves. However, this is dependent on the quality of education a nurse acquire to work with multidisciplinary team within the community settings. In consideration to this, the development of CHN has been a great journey. The role got recognized at national level especially in undergraduate nursing curriculum. The thoughtful inclusion of the course in cur-

DOI: 10.4018/979-8-3693-9092-4.ch015

riculum helped preparing nurses to understand the concept of working with people at grass root level; to empower people for their own health decision.

INTRODUCTION

Community Health Nursing (CHN) practice focuses on culturally sensitive care that is affordable, available, and accessible to the people it serves. The care is focused on social determinants of health, including the environment, age, economic status, etc., that impact the lives of the communities (Thornton & Persaud, 2018). Hence, the quality of services provided is subject to the quality of education (Schofield et al., 2018). Therefore, CHN teaching engages educators as mentors to maximize student's learning and serves as facilitators for improving the community's health and well-being (Schofield et al., 2018). This chapter will discuss the development of CHN as a core component in the nursing curriculum at a national level in Pakistan. It will further delineate CHN education in a local context with the application of the planning cycle as a framework to teach the community as a partner concept to undergraduate nursing students. The chapter will also discuss how classroom teaching on CHN and the Primary Health Care (PHC) approach is integrated into clinical settings for hands-on practice. Moreover, this chapter will also highlight some challenges encountered in preparing future CHNs and recognizing their role in the healthcare system. In addition, the chapter also discusses the dual role of CHN educators which includes preparing future workforce for primary healthcare settings while participating in community-led activities to facilitate the health and developmental needs of the community.

COMMUNITY HEALTH NURSING IN THE LOCAL CONTEXT

CHN as a core component with hands-on practice in the nursing curriculum was first introduced by Aga Khan University School of Nursing and Midwifery (AKUSONAM) Pakistan in the 1980s with the inception of its first batch of diploma in nursing program. This was the time when no other institution taught CHN as a core subject. Over the time, CHN was adopted as a core course by all schools of nursing throughout Pakistan in undergraduate and graduate nursing programs under the regulation of the Pakistan Nursing Council (Mohammad et al., 2019) and the Higher Education Commission of Pakistan. It covers approximately 21% nursing curriculum (Mohammad et al., 2019; Harnar et al., 1993). The concepts are taught on the built-on model of learning, whereby at the undergraduate degree level, the final-year student nurses are taught the concept of "community as a partner". The process is discussed later in this chapter. Student nurses integrate and demonstrate leadership roles and conduct evidence-based community projects in the community clinical settings. This helps them assume the role of a CHN working with the communities on health and developmental issues. Later at a graduate level, they can establish a deeper understanding of the concepts and develop skills in the scholarship of teaching, research, and service.

The faculty plays a pivotal role in preparing future CHNs; they enable nursing students to respond to the needs of the population by applying health promotion and disease prevention strategies using the primary healthcare approach. The faculty also assists students in integrating the learned concepts into practice. It is, therefore, important that the nurse educator be knowledgeable and competent enough to help students put the learned concepts into practice in a real setting. It is also important to ascertain that the nursing curriculum should focus on transformative learning; it prepares students beyond gaining knowledge to be reflective learners and develop critical thinking skills (Thornton & Persaud, 2018; Sabato et al., 2018). Moreover, Gerber suggested that for the students to be able to work successfully with the community, they are required to integrate learned concepts into practice with the ability to demonstrate critical thinking skills (Gerber, 2012).

Hence, faculty competencies and the ability of curriculum to promote students' community clinical learning are the key determinants that ensure students practice health promotion, disease prevention, and health maintenance with community participation and empowerment to adopt community as a partner concept mentioned earlier. The process encompasses the basic elements of community partnership and is ensured through networking, collaboration, and resource mobilization to ensure sustainable initiatives (Gulzar et al., 2012; Kulbok et al., 2012)

The role of a faculty is to ensure the delivery of content for knowledge and skill development through establishing a culture of trust, mutual understanding, and autonomy for nursing students to clarify the concepts and build contextual meaning to the new knowledge. Furthermore, research findings also focus on the faculty's insight into their attitude and behaviors that impact students learning (Gill Meeley, 2021). It is noted that the CHN faculty facilitates student learning by using various teaching-learning strategies to generate new knowledge. Callen & Joyce used Carper's theory of way of knowing (Callen et al., 2013) to generate understanding and knowledge development among the learners. According to Carper's theory, a nurse's action while working with the community depends on four things: empirical, ethical, aesthetic, and self-knowledge. Application of Carper's theory of knowledge development in community settings for students has been observed to be essential. The "empirical" knowing, is the use of factual information deemed important to demonstrate evidence-based practice (Callen et al., 2013; Carper, 1978). This is best applied with the use of community assessment tools to collect and analyze data for evidence-based initiatives. The second knowing is the "personal knowledge" which determines the importance of empathy while working with clients. For instance, appropriate dietary rehabilitation for a financially constrained family is needed. This realization helps the student to work out the best strategy for the client to suit the situation. Thirdly, "ethical knowing" is cognizant of moral values and beliefs to determine the plan of care and its acceptability. While dealing with people, CHN students encounter cultural, religious, and ethnic diversity. The role of the CHN faculty is to facilitate student's understanding and be sensitive to diversity for success and adaptability. Ethical knowledge development may be best described by CHN students respecting individual values and beliefs and maintaining confidentially. The last knowledge development is "aesthetic knowing," which helps to understand the client as a whole or as a subsystem of a larger picture. Understanding this knowledge will again help students to plan need-based care; this also encompasses understanding the clients' surroundings while planning the care for its acceptability. The high morbidity and mortality rate due to diarrheal diseases in a community may be due to several other factors forming the web of causation and not only the disease process.

Each of the four knowing by Barbra Carper is interdependent and is not mutually exclusive, and the teaching of one knowing does not justify the rejection of the other. Chinn and Kramer (2011) added that the fifth, knowing "emancipatory," refers to the unfair social circumstances that impact the health of the population, such as universal access to health for all without any discrimination (Chinn & Kramer, 2015). All five ways of knowing can be incorporated while teaching community health courses to student nurses. Furthermore, based on the above-mentioned theories of knowledge development, clinical support, and supervision are implicitly important in guiding and giving constructive feedback to students for effective contributions in community settings.

COMMUNITY CLINICAL PLACEMENT FOR UNDERGRADUATE CHN STUDENTS

Exposing CHN students to the community clinical setting is an opportunity to tie theory to practice and acquire acquaintances in the practical setting to develop an understanding of the nurse's role outside hospital boundaries. It helps CHN students develop the knowledge, attitudes, and skills necessary for practicing community health nursing beyond the hospital settings for health promotion and disease prevention. A hands-on nursing practice attained through clinical courses prepares student nurses to incorporate theory into practice. This is witnessed by the CHN's actions, which are governed by the knowledge and skills acquired during the nursing training program. Therefore, it is a key consideration in nursing education to prepare nurses to address the changing trends of the healthcare system. As discussed earlier in this chapter, hands-on practice is an essential component for mastery of the skill. In this learning process, student-faculty interaction takes place for two major reasons: knowledge and skill development, as well as familiarizing student nurses with the values of nursing as a profession (Thomas et al., 2018). Therefore, alongside the delivery of community health nursing content in classroom settings, student nurses are exposed to urban and rural community settings for the application of learned concepts. The link between theory and practice also facilitates experiential learning amongst the CHN students. Meaningful experiences take place during clinical practices, which further transform them into professional nurses (Thomas et al., 2018).

When enrolled in the CHN course, students are assigned to pre-selected areas for hands-on practice in community settings. Several factors are taken into consideration while selecting community clinical placements. These include the availability of structured primary health care centers for coordination and collaboration to address the health needs of the community. Secondly, to ensure the best use of student's time within the community, traveling time and distance to and from the academic institution is also considered. Thirdly, most significantly, the safety/security of the practicum placement is the key component in the selection criteria. These ensure productivity to benefit the community and maximize student learning (Harwood et al., 2009).

Theory and practice both go hand in hand to ensure a high level of learner cognitive engagement. In years one and three of the undergraduate nursing program, student nurses are expected to work with individuals and families respectively on health and developmental issues (Thomas et al., 2018). While in the fourth year of the undergraduate nursing program, students are given thorough exposure to the "community as a partner." At this stage, students are taken through the entire process of project planning by using the "Planning Cycle" as a tool to address the health/developmental needs of the community. The group of student nurses is directly supervised and facilitated by a CHN clinical faculty member. During the facilitation process, "community as a partner" by Anderson & McFarlane (2011) is used to promote students' learning of community health nursing concepts. Students are familiarized with key concepts of community participation and the application of the planning cycle to identify and work on need-based issues with the community as partners. Each student is also given a caseload of at least five families to learn individualized care at the community level. The objective is to orient students to the role of a CHN in addressing the health or development issues of a community. However, the reciprocity community also benefits from the expert knowledge of CHN faculty and students. To achieve reciprocity, the CHN faculty role is very crucial in mentoring the CHN students. Several elements are considered while mentoring students to pursue community as a partner. Amongst them, community participation, local resource mobilization, project sustainability, and exit strategy are key components.

Facilitating the students on community clinical placement, they are walked through the process of stakeholder mapping and mobilizing. The purpose of this exercise is to establish a common platform to work on common goals and objectives. The stakeholder mapping and organizing them into an organized group is deemed essential for ownership and continuity of the project. The details of the concepts are presented later in this chapter under a community partnership model. After stakeholder identification and collaboration, numerous tools are utilized as a framework to proceed further working in the community. For instance, it is followed by community assessment to assess community demography and identify the prevailing health and developmental issues, and potential available resources such as money, material, and manpower. Additionally, possible or potential risk factors present in the community are also examined to determine the level of difficulties that may be encountered while working with communities. Several methods are used for data collection, including observations and interviewing community members through household surveys, windshield surveys, and drawing of eco-maps. While household surveys assist in collecting information from individuals within the community, windshield surveys, and eco-maps help identify the community's association with the surrounding environment and resources as mentioned earlier. These also help in resource mapping and utilization and provide information on facilities and services, whether available, scarce, or not available. Moreover, these also suggest the time distance to access the facility.

Case study: Community Assessment Process In the past, private universities in Pakistan used several assessment tools to gather data and identify community needs, which were collected in three stages. This process was very tedious and time-consuming for the students. On several occasions, not only students but also community members verbalized the issue of the waste of time in repeated visits for assessment purposes. Therefore, a group of faculty members, along with the students, worked out a comprehensive assessment tool to collect data from the community only once. The modified tool focused on the relevancy of the data, yet it is an in-depth tool that assists students in collecting all-inclusive information during one visit. In isolated cases, this requires repeat visits to reconfirm the information provided by the client/community member. The new tool not only saved time but also gained community confidence by reducing the number of visits to collect data repeatedly, which was, at times, frustrating and time-consuming for the community. Since the students' visits last for a duration of three to four months, it also allowed the students' time to be productively used in other components of the planning cycle.

Students are taught to draw community eco-maps, which are used as tools to understand individual associations with the environment and the accessibility of the services. Students are also taught how to assess and analyze individual and family assessments to understand and develop insight into health and developmental patterns that prevail within the community. It also prepares CHN students to plan culturally sensitive care necessary to address the health or developmental issues of the community. The data is then aggregated to generate meaning and presented in tabular forms, graphs, and bars. The data, along with the problem list, is then shared with the community members to identify priority problems in the community. While setting the priority, four key elements are taken into consideration: the prevalence of the issue within the community, the seriousness of the issue, the manageability to address the issue, and the community's concern to address the issue. The priority-setting exercise is the first reality shock for the students when they come across community stakeholders and leaders as a group to contribute by sharing their diverse ideas. Students experience moderating the group discussion and helping them to draw a consensus. This is a lifetime learning process when they are facilitated by the faculty and learn to address diverse groups of people with multiple reasoning to prioritize issues based on their understanding and preferences.

It is, therefore, mandatory to prepare students to manage such community meetings where people of various mindsets, age groups, and, in some cases, diverse backgrounds may be gathered and have their way of dealing with issues. Community clinical faculty plays a significant role, especially for these reasons, including enhancing students' learning, establishing community rapport, and prioritizing and identifying the problem to be addressed. It is therefore also advisable to give mock drills for priority setting exercises by creating a community setting environment. This is done after the vigorous analysis of the data in hand, which students performed under faculty supervision. This mock event gives students the courage to handle the varied sizes of groups in the community with respect and dignity and, at the same time, meet the goal of prioritizing the issue. An example of a Priority-setting Exercise is given below. Problem identification and priority setting are followed by budgeting and planning the project/s to address the problem at hand. As mentioned earlier, planning and budgeting require local resource mobilization.

It has been observed that in several cases where local resources, including money, material, and manpower, were utilized, the interest level was higher. The local resource contributions give ownership of the task and also ensure sustainability. At each stage, student nurses are emphasized to keep community stakeholders involved for two basic reasons mentioned earlier, including community ownership and sustainability of the interventions. Student CHNs are also emphasized to have a well-planned exit strategy for the continuity of the project and smooth phase-out of the community by handing over the projects to the local stakeholders.

TEACHING COMMUNITY PARTICIPATION AS A GOVERNANCE MODEL

CHN students, while under training, learn several processes; amongst them is the governance model. This is particularly emphasized to ensure that the student nurses learn to empower the community to take ownership and be self-reliant for their health. Student nurses need to appreciate that people in the community have a wealth of knowledge; therefore, it is important to involve them in program planning and execution. Likewise, community ownership and sustainability of community projects are highly dependent on acknowledging community contributions and participation, whether active or passive. It shapes the future directions with minimum support from outside resources. It also promotes joint decision-making, appropriate resource mobilization, and allocation process. In other words, community participation is the key concept for the prosperity of the community, where each member shares responsibilities and plays a role in achieving the expected outcome. If the projects are dependent on outside support of money, material, and manpower, they may have short-lived support. Hence, the community returns to square one of the developmental projects with the lapse of the project-driven resources from outside the community.

The teaching of CHN focuses on the belief that the community is a partner from the beginning of the project; it ensures sustainability. The concept is even more important in facilitating community health nursing practicum experiences. In Pakistan, students visit the community setting for a fixed duration, and on completion of the course period and meeting learning objectives, they phase out. This period usually lasts for three to four months. Therefore, it is even more important for CHN faculty to place more emphasis on community participation to ensure the continuity of student activities in the communities.

The key objectives of community participation also lie in capacity building; students are facilitated to practice equipping the community with the knowledge and skills necessary for health maintenance and health promotion. Students are facilitated to learn community empowerment as an active process that helps communities to have control of their own health development and quality of life. To achieve the objective of understanding the concepts of community participation and community empowerment, student nurses are walked through the entire process of stakeholder mapping and collaboration. This includes stakeholder identification, coordination with them, and agreement on common goals. Under the governance model, the role of community stakeholders as gatekeepers is significantly emphasized, and they are considered authorized people to allow students to enter the community.

The stakeholders are the entry point in working with the communities, and they are the ultimate people responsible for sustaining the initiatives for a longer period. They carry the capacity to influence the community to either withdraw or participate in the initiatives, whether active or passive. However, working with these stakeholders may be slow but steady. This prevails because of the diversity of agendas between the community and the outside resources. Establishing common grounds for understanding the problems is tedious and time-consuming. This also leads to disappointments and a lack of interest in the CHN to rather withdraw and put the efforts elsewhere. However, this develops student's insight into the real challenges of the community.

CHALLENGES OF COMMUNITY PARTNERSHIP

The significant role of community partnership is discussed in detail earlier; however, challenges may be encountered while ensuring this governance model. Several challenges a community health team encounters need to be highlighted while teaching the concepts to CHN students. Amongst the challenges, the most significant is the lack of academic preparedness opportunities available for CHN faculty necessary to facilitate teaching of CHN concepts. Additionally, poor involvement in community ownership and results in a waste of time and other resources. On the contrary, even having academically sound CHN faculty, the chances of poor community participation and involvement do exist. Therefore, student CHN has to take into consideration the challenges of initiating the process of community participation. It is again imperative to highlight to the CHN student to understand what could be the reasons for poor participation and ensure that they are avoided. Several reasons include poor capacity building of community members, poor control and decision-making powers of the community members, diverse goals due to pre-existing conflicts within the community and lack of consensus, and marginalizing individuals and groups.

In addition to the above there are other challenges in the application of the governance model these include the high expectations of the partners may also result in failures. The expectations must be discussed to avoid any disappointments and failure to meet the goals.

POTENTIAL BENEFITS

Though several challenges have been highlighted about the teaching practice of CHN concepts in the local context, there have been benefits associated with it for all the partners. Since the community health nursing practice is the core of community health, it is important to consider addressing and overcoming the issues to achieve greater benefits for all partners involved. The key partners involved are communities, academic institutions, government, and nongovernment organizations. The academic institutions in this scenario are significant partners in initiating the reciprocal relationship by providing resources to the community while ensuring students' learning at the same time.

Reciprocal Effects on the Community

Though not much data is available on the impact of reciprocity on the community, some literature does suggest the benefits of gaining access to experts from academic institutions. The literature also suggests that the higher the commitment, the better the engagement between the partners. Pakistan, being a developing country, is yet faced with greater health challenges, especially those that can be addressed through a primary health care approach. Hence, due to poor health infrastructure and a lack of public and private initiatives to address the needs of the community, students can be a great resource to the community through a win-win situation. Undergraduate CHN students at an advanced level practice community as clients; this is an opportunity for the communities to overcome the shortage of human resources for health. The expert knowledge of the university faculty accompanying the students reaching the doorstep of the community can be an asset to the community, especially for resource mobilization and networking.

Reciprocal Effects on GOs and NGOs

CHN faculty and students establish networking between the community and the organization (both government and non-government organizations) to mobilize the resources. These efforts lead to gaining the trust of external agencies which also aim to work in collaboration with credible academic institutions. While this results in resource mobilization and networking to benefit the community, at the same time, the organizations can achieve their desired targets.

Reciprocal Effects on Academic Institution

Eventually, CHN students are also able to meet CHN clinical objectives and learn the entire process of project planning and management simultaneously community priority issues are also addressed. In doing so academic institutions are able to maximize students' contextual learning transforming their attitudes toward working in a community setting and developing a sense of social responsibility amongst the students. The coordinated efforts between the partners resulted in reaching the Millennium developmental goals.

CHALLENGES OF TEACHING CHN

The changing demography requires a shift of the health care system's focus from tertiary care to primary care approach. The focus of care is the prevention of diseases and health promotion. Much has been done to achieve the objective, yet serious attention is needed from the public and private sectors. Harner, Marshal, Burns, & Karmaliani report significant challenges for community health nursing education in Pakistan, with a scarce number of nurses in service and education. Not much is documented, but there have been initiatives to overcome the challenge; however, there is still a great need to prepare role models in community settings.

One of the most significant challenges experienced over the years of teaching CHN to nursing students is the lack of trust and support from the communities. Several factors are associated with this, including the lack of continuity of student projects. As mentioned earlier, students spend a fairly short time within the community for the clinical experience; after they phase out, the next group enters the community almost after a year; during this gap, there isn't a structured mechanism to monitor and follow up on students' initiatives. The lack of coordination and follow-up between the academia and the communities leads to mistrust and poor cooperation from community stakeholders.

Secondly, the lack of practice settings also leads to utilizing the same site for several groups of students; this increases the saturation levels within the community. In such a scenario, a high level of poor community cooperation increases faculty and student frustrations and results in demotivation amongst them. This lack of motivation can be additional to the pre-existing attitudes of students considering the course as least important. A study confirms the lack of community-oriented attitude and non-serious behavior of students who undergo CHN courses before starting a complex course. Study results in Iran by Ildarabadi, Moonaghi, Heydari, & Taghipour also reveal the lack of interest by nursing students due to the set future direction of being expected to work in secondary or tertiary care settings. Although the nursing students took a keen interest, they verbalized the lack of avenues to practice CHN and the cultural restriction of being bound to work within the hospital setting.

According to Gulzar et al. few challenges have been highlighted by study participants, including poor infrastructure, poor sanitary conditions, financial constrain hindering health promotion activities, and lack of orientation towards community health. In addition, not getting the deserved status and due recognition by society was an added de-motivating factor. In addition to that, the lack of teaching placement to expose CHN students to understanding the local context of public health concepts and the lack of a deployment plan are also contributing challenges to teaching CHN. Furthermore, continuing education and professional development of the academic cadre is almost non-existent within the country. Although international universities offer various courses both online and face-to-face, economically, the opportunity to avail of them is not possible. The situation favors the lack of updated knowledge in the field of public health, which results in compromised quality of CHN education.

The consultation findings of the Canadian Association of Schools of Nursing's (CASN) task force also affirm the challenges that impact the integration of learned concepts into practice. The task force categorized these challenges into external and internal challenges. The external challenges included a lack of practice placements for students, fewer trained preceptors, and valuing of curative services at the individual level. On the other hand, the internal challenges were the lack of trained faculty to deliver the content effectively and the unclear academic leadership structure that impacted the quality of CHN education.

RECOMMENDATION

The lack of poorly structured clinical placement for CHN clinical exposure is one of the challenges mentioned earlier in this chapter, which may account for compromised hands-on practice. This is further augmented by a lack of support and trust by the community members due to either saturation level or lack of continuity of care. Similar issues have been witnessed in developed countries, such as a lack of clinical placement, and trained clinical faculty to facilitate CHN clinical learning. To address the challenges, some of the strategic interventions include academic preparedness of Human Resource for Health (HRH) and well-trained academic people to prepare HRH. A study was carried out to explore the effectiveness of clinical settings that are not traditional. The study termed it as "Innovative Clinical Placement (ICP)". Though the model was a new initiative and faced some challenges, according to survey results, those challenges were not as strong as those of compromised student learning through the ICP model (14). The overall study results revealed much greater satisfaction than in a traditional clinical setting. ICPs helped students understand the concepts learned in community health more effectively and offered a chance to learn community development.

While Pakistan is also faced with the challenge of community clinical placement and ensuring that students learn CHN concepts, ICP could be an answer to the issue. In our context, ICP can reduce safety and security threats to students as they will be placed within proximity to their homes. While the student is a local person from the community, the strategy could also promote acceptance of the community interventions and maximize reciprocal relationships as well as the student's contextual learning and transformation into a future CHN. Students represent the community and will return to the same community after completion of the undergraduate nursing program, which may serve as a resource that will eliminate the issue of lack of follow-up and monitoring project activities. In addition, it also will ensure the sustainability of the project. Due to the increased number of student population, administratively, it will reduce some of the logistics costs for transporting students to the clinical area. In such circumstances, a faculty member will have to visit the student's placement as opposed to the entire group of students visiting the community clinical placements regularly, resulting in financial constraints.

REFERENCES

Anderson, B., & McFarlane, C. (2011). Assemblage and geography. *Area*, *43*(2), 124–127. DOI: 10.1111/j.1475-4762.2011.01004.x

Callen, B., Smith, C. M., Joyce, B., Lutz, J., Brown-Schott, N., & Block, D. (2013). Teaching/learning strategies for the essentials of baccalaureate nursing education for entry-level community/public health nursing. *Public Health Nursing (Boston, Mass.)*, *30*(6), 537–547. DOI: 10.1111/phn.12033 PMID: 24579713

Carper, B. A. (1978). Fundamental patterns of knowing in nursing. *Advances in Nursing Science*, *1*(1), 13–24. DOI: 10.1097/00012272-197810000-00004 PMID: 110216

Chinn, P. L., & Kramer, M. K. (2015). *Knowledge development in nursing: Theory and process* (9th ed.). Mosby Elsevier.

Gerber, L. (2012). Community health nursing: A partnership of care. *The American Journal of Nursing*, *112*(1), 19–20. DOI: 10.1097/01.NAJ.0000410170.06154.bb PMID: 22207538

Gill Meeley, N. (2021). Undergraduate student nurses' experiences of their community placements. *Nurse Education Today*, *106*, 105054. DOI: 10.1016/j.nedt.2021.105054 PMID: 34329964

Gulzar, S. A., Faheem, Z. A., & Somani, R. K. (2012). Role of community health nurse in earthquake affected areas. *JPMA. The Journal of the Pakistan Medical Association*, *62*(10), 1083. PMID: 23866452

Harnar, R., Burns, J., Marshall, P., & Karmaliani, R. (1993). Community-based nursing education in Pakistan. *Journal of Continuing Education in Nursing*, *25*(3), 130–132. DOI: 10.3928/0022-0124-19940501-11 PMID: 7797690

Harwood, C. H., Reimer-Kirkham, S., Sawatzky, R., Terblanche, L., & Van Hofwegen, L. (2009). Innovation in community clinical placements: A Canadian survey. *International Journal of Nursing Education Scholarship*, *6*(1), 28. Advance online publication. DOI: 10.2202/1548-923X.1860 PMID: 19799562

Kulbok, P. A., Thatcher, E., Park, E., & Meszaros, P. S. (2012). Evolving public health nursing roles: Focus on community participatory health promotion and prevention. *Online Journal of Issues in Nursing*, *17*(2). Advance online publication. DOI: 10.3912/OJIN.Vol17No02Man01 PMID: 22686109

Mohammad, Y. J., Vertejee, S., Gulzar, S., Shehzad, S., & Sachwani, S. (2019, September). Community health nursing clinical teaching models practiced in undergraduate nursing program at a private university in Pakistan. *JPMA. The Journal of the Pakistan Medical Association*. PMID: 31511708

Sabato, E., Owens, J., Mauro, A., Findley, P., Lamba, S., & Fenesy, K. (2018). Integrating social determinants of health into dental curricula: An interprofessional approach. *Journal of Dental Education*, *82*(3), 237–245. DOI: 10.21815/JDE.018.022 PMID: 29496801

Schofield, R., Chircop, A., Baker, C., Duncan, S., & Wotton, D. (2018). Entry-to-practice public health nursing competencies: A Delphi method and knowledge translation strategy. *Nurse Education Today*, *65*, 102–107. DOI: 10.1016/j.nedt.2018.03.001 PMID: 29547810

Thomas, L. J., Revell, S. H., & Ryan, M. (2018). Promoting resilience among nursing students in clinical education. *Nurse Education in Practice*, *28*, 231–234. Advance online publication. DOI: 10.1016/j.nepr.2017.10.001 PMID: 29128734

Thornton, M., & Persaud, S. (2018, September). Preparing today's nurses: Social determinants of health and nursing education. *Online Journal of Issues in Nursing*, *23*(3), 9. https://search.ebscohost.com/login.aspx?direct=true&AuthType=sso&db=ccm&AN=132181879&site=ehost-live. DOI: 10.3912/OJIN.Vol23No03Man05

Mohammad, T. K., Venkat, S., [illegible], S., Shelham, S., [illegible] (20[illegible], September). Community health nursing [illegible] [illegible]

[illegible]

Chapter 16

Spirituality for Medical Curriculum and Health Care Providers:

The Role of Spirituality in Undergraduate Medical Curriculum

Asif Ahmed
https://orcid.org/0009-0003-3421-8729
Baqai Medical University, Karachi, Pakistan

ABSTRACT

Considering the limitations of current treatment plans and the rising need for a more holistic approach to health, mixing spirituality into the medical curriculum is indispensable. Standardizing the integration of Energy or Spiritual Diagnostics with Therapeutic Programs Like Guided Consciousness Liberation Program (GCLP) can meaningfully improve health outcomes. By including Spiritual Healing Techniques, Future Healthcare Providers can better address the root causes of illnesses, promote comprehensive healing, and improve the quality of life for their patients.

CURRENT MEDICAL UNDERSTANDING

The main philosophy behind this chapter is to understand the hidden concepts of realities related to spirituality and to shelf this knowledge and understandings for better health care outcomes. Of course everything that is a part of modern curriculum would facilitate growing medical minds towards certain types of un-

DOI: 10.4018/979-8-3693-9092-4.ch016

derstanding regarding philosophy related to life, health and diseases. This chapter clearly articulates about current health situation, powers related to current medical regimes and finally the lacuna present in practicing medical system. Moreover this narrative is particularly directed towards space and value of spirituality in health care services and importance of integration of spirituality in medical curriculum.

As a fundamental matter of facts The World Health Organization (WHO) articulates that *Heart Disease, Cancer, Chronic Respiratory Diseases & Diabetes* are the *Foremost Causes of Death Globally*, accounting for 71% of all Deaths Each Year (World Health Organization, 2023; World Health Organization, n.d.-a; World Health Organization, n.d.-b; World Health Organization, 2021) In this context the most common etiological factors are related with various factors that commonly includes;

1. **Biological Factors** Like Pathogen & Genetic Mutations
2. **Behavioural Factors** like *Lifestyles, Emotions & Habits etc.*
3. **Environnemental Factor** Like *Pollution, Climate Change, Social Pressures etc.*
4. **Socioeconomic Factor** like *Poverty, Education etc.*
5. **Psychosocial Factors:***Stress, Mental Health & Social Support Systems*

Majorly to combat against the disastrous and horrific medical challenges, at present the current medical resources are focused towards *Traditional Molecular Medicine (TMM)* that employs *four Methods to Lever Cellular Imbalances*, that includes *pharmaceutical agents, Surgery & Allied Tools, Counselling & Psychological Support & finally Physiotherapy& Physical Therapy Techniques (Bustin & Jellinger, 2023).* In depth if a medical practice is scrutinized, it is quite obvious that, the treatment strategies that are in practical is the part medical curriculum and medical management algorithms has many gaps such as,

Infectious Diseases are being by Antibiotics, antivirals, anti-parasitics, and vaccines; but evident that antibiotic resistance, access to vaccines, and healthcare infrastructure issues. Similarly in case of *Non-Communicable Diseases (NCDs),* Lifestyle changes, pharmacological interventions (e.g., antihypertensives, insulin), and surgical procedures are mainstay, and on the same time the *Limitations of this approach are* Chronic nature of diseases, side effects of medications, lack of curative treatments, and high costs. As far as Mental & Behavioral Disorders are concerning Traditional Molecular Medicinal approach includes Psychotherapy, pharmacotherapy (e.g., antidepressants, antipsychotics), and community support programs. The common pitfalls in these modalities are Stigma, treatment accessibility, and the need for long-term management. Further Nutritional Disorders has got significant space in the disease load and Treatment are based Dietary modifications, supplements, and public health interventions and Limitations are access to nutritious food, economic constraints, and cultural factors (Shah, Roy, & Flari, 2024; NCD Alliance, n.d.; Médecins Sans Frontières, 2024). On the other side, it's imperative to expand the treatment horizon towards new direction to focus for Better Health Care We Need to integrated several stakeholders as human health manages like *Lifestyles Management, Emotions Regulation, Habits Maintenance, Climate Change Control, Social Pressures Management & Socioeconomic Factor like Poverty Control, Psychosocial Factors: Stress, Mental Health Management and most importantly includes the value of Spiritual Care.*

Integrated Molecules, Energy & Spirit: Given the Current Global Disease Load, Human Disorders Classification, Etiological Factors, Disease Morbidity - Mortality, & present treatment plans limitations, there is a growing acknowledgement of the need for Integrated Medicine. Integrated Medicine, also known as Integrative or Holistic Medicine, syndicates Conventional Medical Treatments with Complementary & Alternative Therapies to address the *Physical, Emotional, Mental, Social & Spiritual a*spects of health (World Health Organization, 2023; World Health Organization, n.d.-a; University of Notre Dame, n.d.; Micozzi, 2018; Barnes, Bloom, & Nahin, 2008; Berman & Straus, 2004; Coulter et al., 2013).

It's the time to enforce new medical strategies that may expand human thinking in the direction to improve treatment outcome. In this respect it is fundamental to commence a process of Conventional Molecular Medicine with Energy Medicine. As human life is the integrated outcome of molecules (Physical Component) & Energy (Spirit as a Metaphysical Component). We need to see life with different angle as understanding of life would modify the treatment modalities in desirable direction that would be focused towards better clinical outcomes (Rubik, Muehsam, Hammerschlag, & Jain, 2015; Ross, 2019).

What is Life, is the basic question that may open a new direction of research and would be helpful in the direction of right treatment, the life may be viewed in multiple shades like, A Biological Process, Challenges & Problems, Success & Failures, Needs & Goals, Health & Disease (Quora, n.d.). Further to evaluate the value of spirituality, it is prudent to evaluate the core factors related to human existence. *Human Existence is erected on following 4 pillars*;*Divine Order, Spirit, Psyche, Physical Body.* The most critical discussion should remain directed towards the basic understanding of spirit all matters related to this. Spirit can be considered as a specialized type of Energy. Spirit is a multi-layered term often used to mention to the non-physical essence of a person or entity. Presently there is no unified definition of Spirit. Commonly the explanation of spirit is made under different titles. It can include a range of meanings, including; (SSRN, n.d.; Emerald Insight, n.d.; Ryff, 2021).

1. *Vital Force*: The inherent life force that animates living beings, frequently considered the breath of life or the animating principle.
2. *Soul:* The immaterial part of a person that is stared as immortal, transcending the physical body and frequently related with *Consciousness, Self-Awareness & Identity.*
3. *Emotional Essence*: The core of one's emotional and psychological being, reflecting their *True Nature, Character and Passions.*
4. *Supernatural Entity*: An immaterial being or presence, frequently measured to have supernatural,
5. *Inner Drive*: The inner motivation or enthusiasm that drives persons to act, persist, and pursue their dreams and goals.

What is Psyche: Another matter of discussion is the establishment of Spirit that what the basic different present between Spirit & Psyche is. As a matter of fact, if we analyze the literature the text related with subject psyche is more developed as compared to information related to spirit. Hence it is much desirable to discuss the psyche in details first and whatever that is not cover under the term psyche may be considered as under the heading of spirit. As popularly known that word Psyche has its origins in ancient Greek and is frequently used in contemporary contexts to mention to the human mind, surrounding both conscious and unconscious processes. It represents the entirety of the human mind, including its behaviors, thoughts and emotions. Common Psyche Features & attributes are; (Winther, n.d.; Study.com, n.d.; Álvarez, 2017).

a. *Conscious Mind*: The part of the psyche that contains *Awareness and Rational Thought Processes.* It comprises everything we are presently aware of, like thoughts, feelings and perceptions.
b. *Unconscious Mind*: The part of the psyche that lies external of conscious awareness. It comprises *Suppressed Desires, Memories, Feelings, As Well As Deep-Seated Motivations and Instincts.* The unconscious mind meaningfully effects *experiences and behavior.*
c. *Ego:* Frequently mentioned as the organized part of the psyche that arbitrates between the person's *Interior Desires and The External World.* It includes aspects of *Reality Testing, Self-Identity, and Decision-Making Functions.*
d. *Id:* The id is the primal part of the psyche that covers *Elementary Instincts and Drives,* like sexual desire and aggression. It functions on the *Pleasure Principle* and thus always work for seeking instant gratification.
e. *Superego:* The part of the psyche that *Internalizes Societal Values and Norms,* acting as a *Moral Conscience.* It strives for perfection and judges our actions, leading to feelings of pride or guilt.

f. *Cognitive Processes*: The mental activities involved in *acquiring understanding and knowledge including reasoning, perception, memory, and decision-making*.
g. *Emotional Processes*: The *Emotional Responses and Feelings* that are part of the psyche, influencing how we react to dissimilar situations and experiences. The psyche is a multifaceted and lively entity, playing a vital role in shaping our Thoughts, Behaviors,

Now human life, health and diseases are many interlinked variables that importantly includes, Molecules, Physical Body, Energy, Emotion, Thoughts, Feelings, Consciousness, Spirit & finally Divine Order. Although these diversified variables are interconnected but the exact boundaries are still beyond human understanding. The value of Spirit in this context may be considered as a pivotal factor in life dynamics and kinetics, spirit is Life – Life is Energy – Spirit is Energy- No Energy – Death- No Spirit means Death. Essentially Human physical body is Electro-Chemical in Nature All the Molecules are packets of Energy (Langevin, 2024; Gautam et al., 2024). All Types of inner cellular metabolism Needs Energy & Produces Energy. It is important to understand that spirit as a specialized type of energy works in the physical corpus that synergies with;

Cellular Bioenergy: Cellular Bioenergy is related to the energy generated and used by cells to perform their functions. This energy is chiefly stored in the form of ATP, which is shaped through cellular respiration, including Glycolysis, Citric Acid Cycle & Oxidative Phosphorylation. Energy medicine tools often focus in objectives to effect bioenergy by enhancing cellular energy production, enhancing metabolic functions, and indorsing overall energy balance within the body.

Body Energy System: The *Body Energy System* denotes to the system of biological processes that generate & regulate essential energy for cellular functions. This system comprises numerous metabolic pathways, energy storing mechanisms, and the conversion of nutrients into usable energy, frequently in the form of *Adenosine Triphosphate* (ATP). The integration of *Conventional Molecular Medicine with Energy Medicine* signifies an evolving border in healthcare that aims to offer an additional holistic and actual approach to treatment. *Conventional Molecular Medicine* emphases on diagnosing and treating diseases at the molecular and cellular levels, often using *Pharmaceuticals & Surgical Interventions.* In difference, *Energy Medicine* includes a variety of therapies that include the use of energy fields to *Promote Healing.*

Electron Transport Chain: The electron transport chain (ETC) is a sequence of protein complexes positioned in the inner mitochondrial membrane. It plays a vital role in cellular respiration by moving electrons from electron donors (NADH and FADH2) to electron acceptors (oxygen) through redox reactions. This process makes a *Proton Gradient* across the mitochondrial membrane, which energies the synthesis of ATP via ATP synthase. The ETC is important to energy production and is a crucial connection between *Molecular Medicine & Energy Medicine*, as disruptions in this chain can lead to numerous diseases.

Mitochondria are often mentioned to as the dynamos of the cell because they are the chief site of ATP production through oxidative phosphorylation. Each cell contains hundreds to thousands of mitochondria, which produce the energy required for numerous cellular processes. Disfunction in mitochondrial function can lead to a variety of metabolic and degenerative diseases, highlighting the rank of these organelles in *Conventional & Energy Medicine* (Wallace, 2005; National Center for Complementary and Integrative Health, n.d.; Micozzi, 2018; Boon, Verhoef, O'Hara, & Findlay, 2004; Dossey, 1995; Puchalski & Ferrell, 2009).

Scientific Link between Spirit, Body Molecules & Body Energy: An important scientific connection between body molecules and body energy lies in the important processes that withstand life at the cellular level. This connection is chiefly mediated by the body's energy systems, including the; Electron Transport Chain, Cellular Bioenergy and Role of Mitochondria. Therefore, it's equally imperative to understand the most fundament life Energy that is Spirit. This is Universal Finding that all the Cellular Energies get shut down call, when some special type of event happens at the time of Death, that is exit of Spirit leads to cessation of all Molecular Energy System. Therefore, one must appreciate a true value & impact Spirit in human System & must integrated Spirit Related in health care.

Integrated Medicine – Rationale: The healthcare backdrop is experiencing a noteworthy revolution, driven by a rising demand for Holistic & Patient-Centred Care (WHO). This change reproduces Newer Research-based Recognition *of the limits of inherent in conventional healthcare models* that mainly focus on treating physical symptoms. *This Everchanging Dynamics in Healthcare* provides a new nexus of *Paradigm Shift*, towards Integrative Medicine that includes newer tools, therapies aimed to minimize physical health loss by managing; Emotions, *Thinking, Feeling, Perception, Revival of Natural Eating, Recovery of Good Sleep, Re-Establishment of Burn out Relations, Restoration of Natural Bio-Resonance Healthy Frequencies & special addition of shelf for Spirituality*. This Expanded version in health care would be desirable value addition in medical curriculum as well in clinical practice. As literature is pointing that these meta-physical variables like Emotions, *Thinking, Feeling & Spirituality are linked health care issues*

The Spirituality & Medical Curriculum: Human existence is fundamentally supported by four pillars: the *Physical, Psyche, Spirit & Divine Order*. These pillars are entangled, creating a multifaceted interplay between our touchable & immaterial selves. In this context, health cannot be viewed exclusively through a *Physical Lens*. In its place, it must incorporate both the Physical Dimension, as exemplified by the presence of molecules, and the Metaphysical Dimension, represented by the spirit, which can be considered a specialized form of energy.

The medical scenery is rapidly developing, wrestling with a crowd of challenges posed by the growing global disease load, varied etiological factors, and the High Morbidity & Mortality Rates linked with various conditions. Traditional Treatment Plans, while effective to a certain extent, frequently fall short in addressing the multifaceted and multi-layered nature of human health. This has led to a growing acknowledgement of the need for Integrated Medicine, which combines conventional medical practices with alternative therapies to holistically address the physical, emotional, mental, social, and spiritual aspects of health. Now with backdrop and plethora of research work, one can appreciate that inclusion of space for spirituality in health care system would be positive inclusion. Moreover it's a high time to consider that standard research must do in direction of impact and effects of spirituality in healthcare management algorithms

The Asif Intelligent Healing Theory (AIHT): In this backdrop the author has already proposed a Spiritual Healing that may provide wide scale primordial platform for further progress in the direction of Spiritual Integration in Healthcare System & Medical Curriculum. According to the Asif Intelligent Healing Theory (AIHT), health is deeply dependent on the complicated connections between molecules and energy. This theory postulates that the *Physical & Metaphysical Health Components*, that are interlinked, suggesting that any imbalance in one dimension unavoidably affects the other. AIHT underlines the rank of understanding and mixing these dimensions to achieve ideal health outcomes.

Spirituality As Metaphysical Life Variable: The *Health Metaphysical Dimension* includes the spirit, plays a vital role in overall well-being. Spirituality, in this context, is not just a religious or philosophical concept but a serious aspect of human health that effects physical, emotional, and mental states. The *Guided Consciousness Liberation Program (GCLP),* for instance, is a *Spiritual Therapeutic Approach* that aims to balance energy, detoxify emotions and importantly nurtures a bottomless connection with the *Divine Order*. By addressing spiritual inequities, application GCLP methods helps in reaching a holistic state of health.

Integrating Spirituality into Medical Curriculum: Considering the limitations of current treatment plans and the rising need for a more holistic approach to health, mixing spirituality into the medical curriculum is indispensable. Standardizing the integration of *Energy or Spiritual Diagnostics with Therapeutic Programs like GCLP* can meaningfully improve health outcomes. By including *Spiritual Healing Techniques, Future Healthcare Providers* can *better address the root causes of illnesses, promote comprehensive healing, and improve the quality of life for their patients.*

Emotional & Spiritual Detox by Guided Consciousness Liberation Program (GCLP): A holistic approach for cleansing and revitalizing Emotional & Spiritual Health.

GCLP Emotional Detox

Purpose: To release negative emotions such as anger, fear, and resentment etc. for restoration of inner balance

Techniques: Seven Intelligent Healing Corridors practices & emotional release exercises.

Benefits: Increased emotional resilience, clarity & inner peace.

GCLP Spiritual Detox:

Purpose: To clear spiritual blockages & enhance the connection with the Divine Order.

Techniques: 14 Spiritual Skills

Benefits: Deepened sense of purpose, alignment with spiritual values, and enhanced spiritual awareness.

7 GCLP Core Spiritual Values: Spirit is Specialized & Enigmatic type of Energy System, that can be identified on the basis of 7 core values, as follows; two Major Divisions of Human Existence (Physical & Metaphysical), The Four Major pillars of Human Existence (Physical Body, Psyche, Spirit & Divine Order), Harmonious interplay of Physical Structure and Metaphysical Factors, Truth, Reality, Purity & Divine Alignment (Harvard Health Publishing, n.d.; Goleman, 1995; Koenig, McCullough, & Larson, 2001; Puchalski, Vitillo, Hull, & Reller, 2014). GCLP provides desirable algorithm for Medical Curriculum & Adjunctive tool for Health Care. AIHT hypothesize that emotions are stationed in Psyche but the content, control & regulation are related with spiritual pacing. GCLP as spirituality healing tool kit provides practical methodology and skills required for manipulation of content, control & regulation are related to emotions. In other words, GCLP facilitates Emotional Detox. In GCLP, three pillars of Emotions are address through series of techniques & skills related to fundamental formation of emotions that is *Truth, Reality, Purity & Value of Divine Alignment.*

Truth: The Influence of Truth on Human Life and Health: The concept of truth is operative in various aspects of human life, manipulating not only our ethical and moral frameworks but also our psychological and physiological well-being. *Philosophers, Psychologists & Medical Researchers* have long discovered the multi-layered influences of truth on human health, highlighting that living in arrangement with truth can lead to holistic well-being (Rogers, 1961; Ford, n.d.; Holt-Lunstad, Smith, & Layton, 2010; Bodhi, 1999; Gebagi, 2024).

Reality: The Value of Reality in Human Health and Life: Reality, often labeled as the state of things as they *Actually Exist*, plays a critical role in shaping human health and life. Understanding and accepting reality can lead to healthier mental and physical health, better-quality decision-making, and improved overall well-being (Beck, 2011; Sapolsky, 2004; Frankl, 2006; Mack et al., 2012).

Purity: The Value of Purity in Health and Life: Purity, often related with integrity, cleanliness & moral uprightness, holds important value in both health and life. The concept of purity includes physical, mental, emotional, and spiritual dimensions, each causative to overall well-being. *Spiritual Purity* is frequently related with living in alignment with one's values and beliefs, and maintaining honesty and moral uprightness. In many spiritual traditions, purity is seen as a path to achieving spiritual illumination and inner peace. Practices such as prayer, contemplation, and ethical living are highlighted to cultivate spiritual purity. According to Emmons and McCullough (2003), *Spiritual Practices* are linked to greater life satisfaction and overall well-being (Goyal et al., 2014; Emmons & McCullough, 2003; Holt-Lunstad, Smith, & Layton, 2010).

The Value of Divine Alignment in Health & Life often referred to as living in agreement with a higher spiritual order or purpose, is a concept comprised by Spiritual Traditions This alignment includes understanding and adhering to principles believed to be set forth by a higher power, which can deeply *Influence Health & Overall Life Satisfaction* (Holt-Lunstad, Smith, & Layton, 2010; Buettner, 2012; Koenig, McCullough, & Larson, 2001; Toussaint et al., 2012; Lim & Putnam, 2010; Pargament, 1997; Curlin et al., 2007).

Spirituality in Undergraduate Medical Curriculum: Integrating spirituality into the undergraduate medical curriculum is progressively recognized as vital for holistic medical education. This addition helps upcoming physicians understand and address the spiritual requirements of their patients, helping comprehensive patient care and refining health outcomes. Following are important key roles of spirituality that would enhance quality of undergraduate medical curriculum focused on Holistic Patient Care, Improving Patient Outcomes as Studies have shown that considering spiritual needs can improve patient outcomes, predominantly in chronic and incurable illnesses (Koenig, 2012; Lucchetti et al., 2011; Puchalski et al., 2014; Anandarajah & Hight, 2001; Koenig, McCullough, & Larson, 2001; Pargament & Lomax, 2013; King & Bushwick, 1994; Sulmasy, 2009; Lee & Newberg, 2005; Puchalski, 2006; Koenig, 2008; Rasinski et al., 2011).

SUGGESTED SPIRITUALITY COURSE FOR MEDICAL CURRICULUM

This curriculum goals to provide medical students with a complete understanding of spirituality's role in health care, making them to offer empathetic, holistic care to their upcoming patients.

Course Title: Integrating Spirituality into Health Care

Course Description: This course provides medical students with an;

1. Understanding of the role of spirituality in health care
2. It aims to equip future physicians with the skills to address the spiritual needs of their patients, enhancing holistic patient care
3. Improving patient outcomes, and nurturing compassionate, empathetic medical practice.

Course Objectives

1. Understand the spirituality concept & meaning in health care.
2. Recognize the spirituality impact on patient over all well-being and cumulative health outcomes.
3. Develop skills for showing spiritual valuations and mixing spiritual care into clinical practice.
4. Improve communication skills to efficiently deliberate spiritual subjects with patients.
5. Nurture ethical decision-making and empathetic care through the addition of spirituality.
6. Promote self-care and stress management methods for medical students and specialists through spiritual practices.

Course Structure

- **Duration:** One semester (16 weeks)
- **Format:***Lectures, Workshops, Seminars, Clinical Rotations, & Reflective Practice*
- *Credits: 3*

  Week 1-2: Introduction to Spirituality in Health Care
  Week 3-4: Spirituality and Patient Outcomes
  Week 5-6: Spiritual Assessments
  Week 7-8: Communication Skills and Spirituality

Week 9-10: Interdisciplinary Approach to Spiritual Care
Week 11-12: Ethical and Cultural Considerations
Week 13-14: Self-Care and Stress Management for Medical Professionals
Week 15: Clinical Rotations and Practical Applications
Week 16: Course Review and Final Assessment

Assessment Methods

- Participation in class discussions and workshops
- Role-playing exercises and practical assessments
- Written assignments and reflective essays
- Final written and practical exams

REFERENCES

Ahmed, A. (n.d.). Divine harmony & restoring inner balance: A guided exploration with encouragement for conscious wisdom, spiritual healing and self-regulation. https://www.amazon.com/dp/B0CPWK1YY4?ref_=pe_93986420_774957520

Alliance, N. C. D. (n.d.). Antimicrobial resistance: Putting infectious and non-communicable disease treatment at risk. https://ncdalliance.org/news-events/news/antimicrobial-resistance-putting-infectious-and-noncommunicable-disease-treatment-at-risk

Álvarez, M. P. (2017). Psychology as a science of subject and comportment, beyond the mind and behavior. *Integrative Psychological & Behavioral Science*, *52*(1), 25–51. DOI: 10.1007/s12124-017-9408-4 PMID: 29063995

Anandarajah, G., & Hight, E. (2001). Spirituality and medical practice: Using the HOPE questions as a practical tool for spiritual assessment. *American Family Physician*, *63*(1), 81–88. PMID: 11195773

Barnes, P. M., Bloom, B., & Nahin, R. L. (2008). Complementary and alternative medicine use among adults and children: United States, 2007. *National Health Statistics Reports*, (12), 1–23. PMID: 19361005

Beck, J. S. (2011). *Cognitive behavior therapy: Basics and beyond*. Guilford Press.

Berman, B. M., & Straus, S. E. (2004). Implementing a research agenda for complementary and alternative medicine. *Annual Review of Medicine*, *55*(1), 239–254. DOI: 10.1146/annurev.med.55.091902.103657 PMID: 14746520

Bodhi, B. (1999). *The noble eightfold path: The way to the end of suffering*. Buddhist Publication Society.

Boon, H., Verhoef, M., O'Hara, D., & Findlay, B. (2004). From parallel practice to integrative health care: A conceptual framework. *BMC Health Services Research*, *4*(1), 15. DOI: 10.1186/1472-6963-4-15 PMID: 15230977

Bettner, D. (2012). *The Blue Zones: Lessons for living longer from the people who've lived the longest*. National Geographic Society.

Bustin, S. A., & Jellinger, K. A. (2023). Advances in molecular medicine: Unravelling disease complexity and pioneering precision healthcare. *International Journal of Molecular Sciences*, *24*(18), 14168. DOI: 10.3390/ijms241814168 PMID: 37762471

Coulter, I., Herman, P. M., & Nataraj, S. (2013). Economic analysis of complementary, alternative, and integrative medicine: Considerations raised by an expert panel. *BMC Complementary and Alternative Medicine*, *13*(1), 191. DOI: 10.1186/1472-6882-13-191 PMID: 23885789

Curlin, F. A., Lawrence, R. E., Odell, S., Chin, M. H., Lantos, J. D., Koenig, H. G., & Meador, K. G. (2007). Religion, spirituality, and medicine: Psychiatrists' and other physicians' differing observations, interpretations, and clinical approaches. *The American Journal of Psychiatry*, *164*(12), 1825–1831. DOI: 10.1176/appi.ajp.2007.06122088 PMID: 18056237

Dossey, L. (1995). Healing words: The power of prayer and the practice of medicine. https://www.amazon.com/Healing-Words-Prayer-Practice-Medicine/dp/0062502522

Emerald Insight. (n.d.). https://www.emerald.com/insight/content/doi/10.1108/jwam-08-2020-0038/full/html

Emmons, R. A., & McCullough, M. E. (2003). Counting blessings versus burdens: An experimental investigation of gratitude and subjective well-being in daily life. *Journal of Personality and Social Psychology*, *84*(2), 377–389. DOI: 10.1037/0022-3514.84.2.377 PMID: 12585811

Ford, C. V. (n.d.). Lies! Lies!! Lies!!!: The psychology of deceit (1st ed.). https://www.amazon.com/Lies-Psychology-Deceit/dp/0880489979

Frankl, V. E. (2006). *Man's search for meaning*. Beacon Press.

Gautam, A., Jain, A., Chaudhary, J., Gautam, M., Gaur, M., & Grover, S. (2024). Concept of mental health and mental well-being, its determinants and coping strategies. *Indian Journal of Psychiatry*, *66*(Suppl 2), S231–S244. DOI: 10.4103/indianjpsychiatry.indianjpsychiatry_707_23 PMID: 38445271

Gebagi, R. (2024). Inner mastery guided journal. https://www.amazon.com/Inner-Mastery-Guided-Journal-Gebagi/dp/B0DNRYCXDG

Goleman, D. (1995). Emotional intelligence. Bantam Books. How stress affects your health. https://www.apa.org/topics/stress/health

Goyal, M., Singh, S., Sibinga, E. M., Gould, N. F., Rowland-Seymour, A., Sharma, R., Berger, Z., Sleicher, D., Maron, D. D., Shihab, H. M., Ranasinghe, P. D., Linn, S., Saha, S., Bass, E. B., & Haythornthwaite, J. A. (2014). Meditation programs for psychological stress and well-being: A systematic review and meta-analysis. *JAMA Internal Medicine*, *174*(3), 357–368. DOI: 10.1001/jamainternmed.2013.13018 PMID: 24395196

Harvard Health Publishing. (n.d.). Mind & mood. Retrieved from https://www.health.harvard.edu/topics/mind-and-mood

Holt-Lunstad, J., Smith, T. B., & Layton, J. B. (2010). Social relationships and mortality risk: A meta-analytic review. *PLoS Medicine*, *7*(7), e1000316. DOI: 10.1371/journal.pmed.1000316 PMID: 20668659

Holt-Lunstad, J., Smith, T. B., & Layton, J. B. (2010). Social relationships and mortality risk: A meta-analytic review. *PLoS Medicine*, *7*(7), e1000316. DOI: 10.1371/journal.pmed.1000316 PMID: 20668659

King, D. E., & Bushwick, B. (1994). Beliefs and attitudes of hospital inpatients about faith healing and prayer. *The Journal of Family Practice*, *39*(4), 349–352. PMID: 7931113

Koenig, H. G. (2008). Concerns about measuring "spirituality" in research. *The Journal of Nervous and Mental Disease*, *196*(5), 349–355. DOI: 10.1097/NMD.0b013e31816ff796 PMID: 18477877

Koenig, H. G. (2012). Religion, spirituality, and health: The research and clinical implications. *ISRN Psychiatry*, *278730*, 1–33. Advance online publication. DOI: 10.5402/2012/278730 PMID: 23762764

Koenig, H. G., McCullough, M. E., & Larson, D. B. (2001). *Handbook of religion and health.* Oxford University Press., DOI: 10.1093/acprof:oso/9780195118667.001.0001

Koenig, H. G., McCullough, M. E., & Larson, D. B. (2001). *Handbook of religion and health.* Oxford University Press., DOI: 10.1093/acprof:oso/9780195118667.001.0001

Koenig, H. G., McCullough, M. E., & Larson, D. B. (2001). *Handbook of religion and health.* Oxford University Press. DOI: 10.1093/acprof:oso/9780195118667.001.0001

Langevin, H. M. (2024). Health and well-being: Distinct and intertwined concepts. *Medical Care*, *62*(12, Suppl 1), S13–S14. DOI: 10.1097/MLR.0000000000002061 PMID: 39514486

Lee, B. Y., & Newberg, A. B. (2005). Religion and health: A review and critical analysis. *Zygon*, *40*(2), 443–468. DOI: 10.1111/j.1467-9744.2005.00674.x

Lim, C., & Putnam, R. D. (2010). Religion, social networks, and life satisfaction. *American Sociological Review*, *75*(6), 914–933. DOI: 10.1177/0003122410386686

Lucchetti, G., Granero Lucchetti, A. L., & Koenig, H. G. (2011). Religion, spirituality, and cardiovascular disease: Research, clinical implications, and opportunities in Brazil. *Brazilian Journal of Cardiovascular Surgery*, *26*(3), 430–437. DOI: 10.1590/S0102-76382011000300020

Mack, J. W., Cronin, A., Taback, N., Huskamp, H. A., Keating, N. L., Malin, J. L., Earle, C. C., & Weeks, J. C. (2012). End-of-life care discussions among patients with advanced cancer: A cohort study. *Annals of Internal Medicine, 156*(3), 204–210. DOI: 10.7326/0003-4819-156-3-201202070-00008 PMID: 22312140

Médecins Sans Frontières. (2024). *Clinical guidelines - Diagnosis and treatment manual* (ISBN 978-2-37585-264-4).

Micozzi, M. S. (2018). *Fundamentals of complementary, alternative, and integrative medicine*. Elsevier Health Sciences.
Micozzi, M. S. (2018). *Fundamentals of complementary, alternative, and integrative medicine*. Elsevier Health Sciences.
National Center for Complementary and Integrative Health. (n.d.). Complementary, alternative, or integrative health: What's in a name? https://www.nccih.nih.gov/health/complementary-alternative-or-integrative-health-whats-in-a-name

Pargament, K. I. (1997). *The psychology of religion and coping: Theory, research, practice*. Guilford Press.

Pargament, K. I., & Lomax, J. W. (2013). Understanding and addressing religion among people with mental illness. *World Psychiatry; Official Journal of the World Psychiatric Association (WPA), 12*(1), 26–32. DOI: 10.1002/wps.20005 PMID: 23471791

Puchalski, C. M. (2006). The role of spirituality in health care. *Proceedings - Baylor University. Medical Center, 14*(4), 352–357. DOI: 10.1080/08998280.2001.11927788 PMID: 16369646

Puchalski, C. M., & Ferrell, B. (2009). Making health care whole: Integrating spirituality into patient care. https://www.amazon.com/Making-Health-Care-Whole-Spirituality/dp/159947350

Puchalski, C. M., Vitillo, R., Hull, S. K., & Reller, N. (2014). Improving the spiritual dimension of whole person care: Reaching national and international consensus. *Journal of Palliative Medicine, 17*(6), 642–656. DOI: 10.1089/jpm.2014.9427 PMID: 24842136
Puchalski, C. M., Vitillo, R., Hull, S. K., & Reller, N. (2014). Improving the spiritual dimension of whole person care: Reaching national and international consensus. *Journal of Palliative Medicine, 17*(6), 642–656. DOI: 10.1089/jpm.2014.9427 PMID: 24842136

Quora. (n.d.). What real-life or everyday problem, issue, or question does your research hope to address? https://www.quora.com/What-real-life-or-everyday-problem-issue-or-question-does-your-research-hope-to-address

Rasinski, K. A., Kalad, Y. G., Yoon, J. D., & Curlin, F. A. (2011). An assessment of US physicians' training in religion, spirituality, and medicine. *Medical Teacher*, *33*(11), 944–945. DOI: 10.3109/0142159X.2011.588976 PMID: 22022906

Rogers, C. R. (1961). *On becoming a person: A therapist's view of psychotherapy*. Houghton Mifflin Harcourt.

Ross, C. L. (2019). Energy medicine: Current status and future perspectives. *Global Advances in Health and Medicine : Improving Healthcare Outcomes Worldwide*, *8*, 2164956119831221. DOI: 10.1177/2164956119831221 PMID: 30834177

Rubik, B., Muehsam, D., Hammerschlag, R., & Jain, S. (2015). Biofield science and healing: History, terminology, and concepts. *Global Advances in Health and Medicine : Improving Healthcare Outcomes Worldwide*, *4*(1_suppl, Suppl), 8–14. DOI: 10.7453/gahmj.2015.038.suppl PMID: 26665037

Ryff, C. D. (2021). Spirituality and well-being: Theory, science, and the nature connection. *Religions*, *12*(11), 914. DOI: 10.3390/rel12110914 PMID: 34881052

Sapolsky, R. M. (2004). *Why Zebras Don't Get Ulcers: The Acclaimed Guide to Stress, Stress-Related Diseases, and Coping*. Holt Paperbacks.

Shah, M. H., Roy, S., & Flari, E. (2024). The critical need for disaster medicine in modern medical education. *Disaster Medicine and Public Health Preparedness*, *18*, e80. DOI: 10.1017/dmp.2024.56 PMID: 38682546

SSRN. (n.d.). https://papers.ssrn.com/sol3/papers.cfm?abstract_id=5007588

Study.com. (n.d.). Human psyche: Definition, lesson & quiz. https://study.com/academy/lesson/human-psyche-definition-lesson-quiz.html

Sulmasy, D. P. (2009). Spirituality, religion, and clinical care. *Chest*, *135*(6), 1634–1642. DOI: 10.1378/chest.08-2241 PMID: 19497898

Toussaint, L., Williams, D. R., Musick, M. A., & Everson-Rose, S. A. (2012). The association of forgiveness and 12-month prevalence of major depressive episodes in a nationally representative sample of US adults. *Journal of Health Psychology*, *17*(7), 1010–1018. DOI: 10.1177/1359105311433905

University of Notre Dame. (n.d.). Notre Dame makes $68 million commitment to fighting mental health crisis; scalable solutions could become national model. https://news.nd.edu/news/notre-dame-makes-68-million-commitment-to-fighting-mental-health-crisis-scalable-solutions-could-become-national-model/?gad_source=1&gclid=CjwKCAjw_Na1BhAlEiwAM-dm7NmtxbPsCjY4paVxzLYPo58RXGMLE9R39ycVtpil-5525aQXfBYneRoC_00QAvD_BwE

Wallace, D. C. (2005). A mitochondrial paradigm of metabolic and degenerative diseases, aging, and cancer: A dawn for evolutionary medicine. *Annual Review of Genetics*, *39*(1), 359–407. DOI: 10.1146/annurev.genet.39.110304.095751 PMID: 16285865

Winther, M. (n.d.). Spirit and psyche – complementary paradigms. https://www.academia.edu/13052952/Spirit_and_Psyche_Complementary_Paradigms

World Health Organization. (2021). *Global expenditure on health: Public spending on the rise?*https://www.who.int/publications/i/item/9789240041219

World Health Organization. (2023, September 16). *Noncommunicable diseases*. https://www.who.int/news-room/fact-sheets/detail/noncommunicable-diseases

World Health Organization. (2023, September 16). *Noncommunicable diseases*. https://www.who.int/news-room/fact-sheets/detail/noncommunicable-diseases

World Health Organization. (n.d.). Disease burden, 2000–2021: *Global health estimates: Leading causes of DALYs*. https://www.who.int/data/gho/data/themes/mortality-and-global-health-estimates/global-health-estimates-leading-causes-of-dalys

World Health Organization. (n.d.). *Infectious diseases*. https://www.emro.who.int/health-topics/infectious-diseases/index.html

World Health Organization. (n.d.). Disease burden, 2000–2021: *Global health estimates: Leading causes of DALYs*. https://www.who.int/data/gho/data/themes/mortality-and-global-health-estimates/global-health-estimates-leading-causes-of-dalys

World Health Organization. (n.d.). Disease burden, 2000–2021: *Global health estimates: Leading causes of DALYs*. https://www.who.int/data/gho/data/themes/mortality-and-global-health-estimates/global-health-estimates-leading-causes-of-dalys

ADDITIONAL READING

Anderson, M. C., & Green, C. (2001). Suppressing unwanted memories by executive control. *Nature*, *410*(6826), 366–369. DOI: 10.1038/35066572 PMID: 11268212

Baum, A. (n.d.). The handbook of stress science: Biology, psychology, and health. https://www.amazon.com/s?k=9780826117717&i=stripbooks&linkCode=q

Curlin, F. A., Lawrence, R. E., Odell, S., Chin, M. H., Lantos, J. D., Koenig, H. G., & Meador, K. G. (2007). Religion, spirituality, and medicine: Psychiatrists' and other physicians' differing observations, interpretations, and clinical approaches. *The American Journal of Psychiatry*, *164*(12), 1825–1831. DOI: 10.1176/appi.ajp.2007.06122088 PMID: 18056237

Ernst, E. (2000). The role of complementary and alternative medicine. *BMJ (Clinical Research Ed.)*, *321*(7269), 1133–1135. DOI: 10.1136/bmj.321.7269.1133 PMID: 11061738

Ghaedi, F.. (2017). Usage and its determinant factors among outpatients in southeast of Iran. *Journal of Evidence-Based Complementary & Alternative Medicine*, *22*(2), 210–215. DOI: 10.1177/2156587215621462 PMID: 26666436

Gross, J. J. (2002). *Emotion regulation: Affective, cognitive, and social consequences*. Cambridge University Press., DOI: 10.1017/CBO9780511809374

Hughes, E. F. (2001). Overview of complementary, alternative, and integrative medicine. *Clinical Obstetrics and Gynecology*, *44*(4), 774–779. DOI: 10.1097/00003081-200112000-00015 PMID: 11600858

Lim, C., & Putnam, R. D. (2010). Religion, social networks, and life satisfaction. *American Sociological Review*, *75*(6), 914–933. DOI: 10.1177/0003122410386686

Maslach, C., & Leiter, M. P. (2016). Understanding the burnout experience: Recent research and its implications for psychiatry. *World Psychiatry; Official Journal of the World Psychiatric Association (WPA)*, *15*(2), 103–111. DOI: 10.1002/wps.20311 PMID: 27265691

Muresan, D., Voidăzan, S., Salcudean, A., Bodo, C., & Grecu, I. (2022). Bioresonance, an alternative therapy for mild and moderate depression. *Experimental and Therapeutic Medicine*, *23*(4), 264. DOI: 10.3892/etm.2022.11190 PMID: 35251330

Neisser, U. (1976). Cognition and reality: Principles and implications of cognitive psychology. https://www.amazon.com/Cognition-Reality-Principles-Implications-Psychology/dp/0716704773

Ostermann, T., Langhorst, J., & Beer, A.-M. (2013). The effects of integrative in-patient treatment on patients' quality of life: A meta-analysis. *Evidence-Based Complementary and Alternative Medicine : eCAM, 2013*, 416510. Advance online publication. DOI: 10.1155/2013/416510 PMID: 23431339

Pargament, K. I. (1997). *The psychology of religion and coping: Theory, research, practice*. Guilford Press.

Toussaint, L., Williams, D. R., Musick, M. A., & Everson-Rose, S. A. (2012). The association of forgiveness and 12-month prevalence of major depressive episodes in a nationally representative sample of US adults. *Journal of Health Psychology, 17*(7), 1010–1018. DOI: 10.1177/1359105311432491

Walker, M. (2017). Why we sleep: Unlocking the power of sleep and dreams. https://www.amazon.com/Why-We-Sleep-Unlocking-Dreams/dp/1501144316

Willett, W. C. (n.d.). *Eat, drink, and be healthy: The Harvard Medical School guide to healthy eating*. Harvard University Press.

Chapter 17
Humanistic Medicine as a Spiritual Driver for Improving the Quality of Work Life of Healthcare Providers and Managing Improved Health Outcomes

Arfa Masihuddin
https://orcid.org/0009-0006-4697-6318
Rufayda, Karachi, Pakistan

Zoella Ali Shaikh
https://orcid.org/0009-0004-2362-0517
Ziauddin University, Pakistan

Ahsana Nazish
https://orcid.org/0000-0002-9778-4811
Pakistan Kidney and Liver Institute and Research Centre (PKLI and RC), Lahore, Pakistan

ABSTRACT

This chapter explores the principles and implementation of humanistic medicine as a spiritual driver for improving the quality of work life of healthcare providers and managing improved health outcomes. The focus is on integrating the specific

DOI: 10.4018/979-8-3693-9092-4.ch017

attributes of spirituality, like mindfulness, introspection, gratitude, and appreciation, with humanistic medicine's emphasis on its features of empathy, compassion, and holistic care. The goal is to explore how this strategy can improve the quality of work life of healthcare providers, helping them to rediscover their passion and enabling them to provide care that is humanistic and person-centered to improve patient experiences and outcomes. This approach also acts as a spiritual and emotional driver for addressing physician burnout and job satisfaction. The chapter also discusses implementation strategies for humanistic medicine. While discussing the challenges of such an approach to health management, the chapter also advocates policies prioritizing and balancing person-centered care and healthcare provider well-being.

INTRODUCTION

The progressive achievement of universal health coverage necessitates that health services are not only available and accessible but also provided to the population in a manner that is acceptable, compassionate, respectful, and culturally sensitive, ensuring quality care. Humanistic medicine represents a transformative approach to healthcare, prioritizing empathy, compassion, and the holistic delivery of these health services (Sessanna et al., 2011). As modern healthcare systems increasingly rely on technological advancements and efficiency, the spirit of personal connection and patient-centered care often disappears (Kogan et al., 2015). Humanistic medicine aims to bridge this gap by addressing the unique physical, emotional, social, and spiritual needs of each patient (Balbale et al., 2014). This approach explores the principles and implementation of humanistic medicine as a spiritual driver for improving the quality of work life of healthcare providers and managing improved health outcomes (Greene et al., 2012). The focus is on integrating the specific attributes of spirituality, like mindfulness, introspection, gratitude, and appreciation, with humanistic medicine's emphasis on its features of empathy, compassion, and holistic care, and ways to integrate it into LMICs (Doram et al., 2017). This integration is particularly relevant in low- and middle-income countries (LMICs), where the challenges of healthcare delivery necessitate innovative strategies that prioritize both patient and provider well-being (Zaidi et al., 2021).

Rooted in the philosophical movement of Renaissance humanism, humanistic medicine has a rich historical background that believes in the importance of viewing patients as whole persons (Thibault, 2019). The moral tenets of the Hippocratic Oath, which prioritize patient welfare and ethical standards, also laid the foundation for modern humanistic medicine reinforcing the commitment to compassionate care and respect for patient dignity.

In today's healthcare landscape, the need for humanistic medicine is more urgent than ever. Technological advancements, while beneficial, often lead to depersonalization in patient care, where individuals are seen as mere cases rather than unique beings. This lack of empathy contributes to physician burnout, diminished job satisfaction, and a decline in the quality of patient care. By reintroducing empathy and person-centered practices, humanistic medicine addresses these challenges, promoting a more compassionate and effective healthcare environment.

Moreover, the principles of humanistic medicine align closely with human rights, promoting dignity, autonomy, and non-discrimination (He et al., 2021). In lower- and middle-income countries (LMICs), where healthcare challenges such as resource limitations and high patient volumes are prevalent, humanistic medicine offers a pathway to improve patient outcomes and satisfaction (Ma et al., 2023). This chapter suggests the adaptation of successful models from high-income countries to LMICs, emphasizing the role of global collaborations and initiatives in advancing humanistic care (Wagner et al., 2011).

The competencies of health workers are crucial in delivering humanistic medicine; however, their behavior is also shaped by the policy and governance environment in which they operate, requiring actions that enable health workers to optimize their roles and fulfill their responsibilities (Lowery, 2011). Through comprehensive medical education and continuous professional development, healthcare providers can be equipped with the skills necessary to deliver compassionate, patient-centered care (Lowery, 2010). This integration of humanistic principles into healthcare policies and organizational practices is essential for creating a balanced approach that honors technological advancements as well as the irreplaceable human touch (Fundytus et al., 2021). The chapter sheds light on all the above aspects to signify the urgent need for instituting humanistic medicine into the health service delivery model of LMICs in hopes of achieving optimum health outcomes.

WHAT IS HUMANISTIC MEDICINE?

Definition and Core Principles of Humanistic Medicine

The term "humanistic medicine" focuses on an approach to healthcare that emphasizes the compassionate and empathetic treatment of patients as individuals with unique needs, including their physical, emotional, social, and spiritual dimensions Marshman (2024). At its core, humanistic medicine seeks to view patients holistically, not as mere cases or diseases but as complete beings with complex personal experiences (Miles, 2013). Empathy allows healthcare providers to understand patients' feelings and perspectives, fostering a deeper connection and trust (Lavoie-

Tremblay, 2024). Compassion involves acting to alleviate patients' suffering, while spirituality offers another important layer of support, addressing patients' need for meaning, peace, and comfort in the face of illness (Jaiswal et al., 2019). Spiritual care respects and nurtures the beliefs, values, and cultural backgrounds of patients, supporting them in their spiritual journey, which may involve religious faith, personal beliefs, or existential questions around their illnesses (Rambiritch et al., 2021). By including spiritual care alongside empathy and compassion, humanistic medicine becomes a truly holistic practice in lower-middle-income countries where religion and faith are deeply ingrained in society, enhancing the healing process, providing emotional resilience, and contributing to a more comprehensive therapeutic relationship (Hirpa et al., 2020).

Characterized by the aforementioned qualities, humanistic medicine defines the physician's genuine care for the patient and their responsiveness to the individual's values and concerns while respecting and addressing their psychological, social, and spiritual needs holistically (Saasouh, 2024). Its mission is to deliver care that is scientific, compassionate, and ethical (Stagno et al., 2016). Modern healthcare systems are now facing challenges in matching rising demands compared to limited healthcare budgets, whereas healthcare professionals are experiencing increased levels of pressure, exhaustion, and burnout (Kekeghe, 2021). Numerous patient stories expressing dissatisfaction due to physician burnout have highlighted gaps in current approaches to patient care and medical education (Croker et al., 2018). Humanistic medicine is a response to this growing crisis, aiming to restore the fundamental values of empathy, patient-centered care, and spirituality within the healthcare profession, recognizing that healthcare should care for the soul as well as the body and mind (October et al., 2016).

A study analyzing physicians seen as 'highly humanistic' revealed that they intuitively responded to various challenges by recognizing patients in distress, providing comfort, sharing their own experiences through compassionate actions, and including their respective faiths while counseling them (Tavares et al., 2020). This contrasts with the notable lack of empathy and spiritual awareness observed among medical students, educators, and residents, which contributes to high rates of burnout, emotional exhaustion, and a decreased sense of accomplishment (Kato et al., 2021). Humanistic medicine emphasizes fostering a respectful and compassionate relationship between physicians, healthcare team members, and patients, thereby addressing these critical gaps and enhancing the overall quality of care (Cypher & Axman, 2022).

Historical Background and Evolution of Humanistic Medicine

The philosophical movement of humanism began during the Renaissance, leading to the influential theory that human interests, values, and dignity drive the art, literature, and creativity of that era (Hulail, 2018). Humanism has consistently been a fundamental aspect of medicine throughout history, tracing back to the 5th century BC with the Hippocratic Oath, which emphasizes prioritizing patients' needs while adhering to ethical standards (Hulail, 2018). By the Renaissance, physicians were expected to be knowledgeable in both the sciences and the humanities, and many medieval physicians, such as Avicenna and Maimonides, were well-versed in these subjects (Hulail, 2018).

The first conference on humanism in medicine was held in 1993 at the University of Chicago, advocating for humanistic principles as a foundation for medical decision-making (Wu et al., 2017). During the 1960s and 1970s, humanities disciplines began to re-enter the curricula of many medical schools, starting with the establishment of the first Department of Humanities at Pennsylvania State College of Medicine around 1967 (Nelson et al., 2013).

Humanistic medicine has evolved significantly over the centuries, influenced by physicians, researchers, and philosophers. The effort to renew the connection between medicine and humanism became prominent in the last decades of the 20th century, driven by the desire to 'humanize' medicine in response to perceived 'dehumanizing' forces that were believed to divert medicine from its historical roots (Hulail, 2018). With the integration of humanistic medicine into undergraduate curricula, new scholarships in the arts, literature, and philosophy are being developed, leading to cross-disciplinary departments that emphasize the social relations of medicine and science (Wu et al., 2017). As Sir William Osler famously stated, "It is much more important to know what sort of person has a disease than to know what sort of disease a certain person has" (Horowitz et al., 2003).

Key Components: Honesty, Empathy, Compassion, Altruism, Patient Centered Care, And Holistic Treatment Approaches

Humanistic medicine targets three core issues: defining the goal of medicine, defining the conditions that make the goal possible, and identifying the important values necessary to achieve that goal. It aims to provide healthcare with honesty, empathy, compassion, altruism, and respect for patients and their families' physical, emotional, social, and spiritual needs through a holistic approach. By adopting a humanistic attitude that embraces spirituality, physicians can provide care that respects and responds to the entire person—body, mind, and spirit. Spirituality thus becomes a core component of the humanistic approach. It can be said that developing the attributes of empathy and compassion is deeply linked to an individual's spirituality. While spirituality can be defined as the quality of being concerned with the human spirit or soul as opposed to material or physical things, its attributes of mindfulness, introspection, gratitude and appreciation nurture a more empathetic and compassionate approach to life. Hence, investing in their spirituality can push healthcare providers to be more humanistic in the care they provide to their patients and their professional conduct. This will not only improve patient satisfaction scores but also give better health outcomes and improve the quality of work life of healthcare providers. Clinicians who exhibit greater empathy towards their patients often experience higher levels of job satisfaction, which in turn leads to fewer instances of burnout, and eventually, malpractice and patient dissatisfaction. It will also help providers recognize that healing is not merely about treating physical symptoms but also about addressing the deeper, often existential, concerns that patients may have, and calling on to their faith to reaffirm their will-power to heal.

ROLE OF SPIRITUALITY IN PRACTICING AND DELIVERING HUMANISTIC MEDICINE

For healthcare providers, engaging in spiritual care can also enhance empathy, reduce burnout, and provide a sense of fulfillment as they witness the positive impact of addressing both the material and immaterial aspects of health. Practices like mindfulness, introspection, gratitude, and appreciation are some ways of nurturing spirituality.

Mindfulness is being fully present and aware of the moment without wandering thoughts. E.g., by being fully present in the moment while examining or counseling a patient rather than getting distracted by the pending tasks, clinicians will be able to offer them more undivided attention, truly listening and engaging without distraction. This approach will allow providers to be more calm and open, nurturing a deeper connection with their patients by being more attuned to their emotional and psychological needs.

Introspection promotes self-awareness and reflection on one's own thoughts, judgements, feelings, and biases. By regularly introspecting about their roles as healthcare providers and colleagues, they will get the chance to self-evaluate and understand their own emotional responses, motivations, and limitations. This can help them manage personal biases or emotional triggers, allowing for more empathetic responses to patients' circumstances, and also examine their own performance and hence, be more conscious in their conduct, reinforcing compassionate behavior in clinical settings.

By developing an appreciation and gratitude for their profession - for being able to help so many people lead better lives, they can also shift their perspective from the negative aspects of the job, such as stress and fatigue, to positive aspects like meaningful patient interactions and the privilege of caring for others. Healthcare providers who consciously practice gratitude are more likely to have an optimistic outlook and an increased sense of purpose in their work. Gratitude also promotes resilience, reducing burnout and, therefore, improving their ability to empathize with patients by recognizing the value in each patient encounter.

Spirituality can also enhance the practice and delivery of humanistic medicine by addressing the deeper existential needs of patients alongside their physical, emotional, and social well-being, especially in lower-middle-income countries. In humanistic medicine, spirituality encourages the healthcare provider to see beyond the immediate illness, recognizing also the significance of the patient's spiritual beliefs in coping with suffering, illness, and healing. This practice respects the diverse spiritual backgrounds of patients, offering comfort, meaning, and solace during difficult times. People in the developing world tend to have strong religious values and beliefs that have an impact on their life choices. E.g. some religions do not allow for euthanasia or organ donation. An understanding of these factors can have a significant impact on delivering person-centered care, by considering the patients' preferences, and therefore, offering management plans that respect them. This may lead to increased compliance and better patient outcomes, thereby, improving healthcare service delivery.

Using spirituality as a stepping stone towards developing a humanistic approach towards patient care not only fosters deeper patient-provider relationships but also nurtures an environment that is compassionate, dignified, and responsive to the whole person and also their families, catering to the needs of the community at large, improving both the quality of work life of healthcare providers and health outcomes.

THE NEED FOR HUMANISTIC MEDICINE IN MODERN MEDICINE

The Impact Of Technological Advancements On Health Outcomes

The need for humanistic medicine continues to grow as increasing dependence on scientific research and technology such as electronic health records, artificial intelligence, and telemedicine, while beneficial for efficiency and accuracy, can overshadow the moral and spiritual aspects of patient care leading to its dehumanization. This overemphasis on technological solutions can depersonalize the healing relationship between doctors and patients, reducing individuals to data points. This in turn, weakens the healing relationship between doctors and patients, resulting in the erosion of trust between patients and healthcare providers, and a decline in the standard of care and an increase in lawsuits against healthcare practitioners.

Challenges In Maintaining Human Touch In An Increasingly Digital And Automated Healthcare Environment

Despite the vast advances in technology, there is no replacement for the human touch in healthcare, particularly the spiritual connection that nurtures healing. While technology can streamline processes and improve diagnostic accuracy, it cannot replace the deep interpersonal connections between humans that builds trust and satisfaction among both staff and patients. The absence of personal interactions can make patients feel isolated and ignored, while healthcare providers may experience burnout and emotional exhaustion as their work becomes more focused on data management rather than human connection. These interactions, then, contribute to a positive work environment by boosting job satisfaction and loyalty among healthcare professionals. When doctors realize that they care for all patients equally, even in difficult situations, they become more resistant to burnout and resilient in the face of challenges. To bring about significant and meaningful differences, efforts do not need to be labor- or time-intensive. Even 40 seconds of compassion—less than the time taken to log into medical software—can bring about this change.

Spiritual care plays a vital role in countering this depersonalization by nurturing a deeper, more meaningful connection between providers and patients. Addressing both their own and a patient's spiritual needs—whether through prayer, meditation, or simply engaging in conversations about life's purpose—can restore a sense of dignity and individuality to the care process.

For example, even in a busy hospital setting dominated by technology, taking a moment to discuss a patient's spiritual concerns or offering to connect them with spiritual support services can build a trust that supersedes the transactional nature of modern healthcare. Such moments foster a healing environment where patients feel truly cared for as whole beings—physically, emotionally, and spiritually.

Evidence-Based Benefits Of Humanistic Approaches On Health Outcomes And Patient Satisfaction

Dr. Thomas Lee, a renowned leader in the field of patient experience advancement, famously quoted in 2016, *"Physician burnout and patient experience: flip sides of the same coin."* This insight reflects the growing evidence showing that humanistic care, which includes attending to the spiritual needs of patients, enhances both patient satisfaction and physician well-being. Studies have established that exposure to and investment in humanistic study makes doctors better clinicians. It helps them understand their patients as whole people within the context of their lives and trains them to think critically. Furthermore, humanistic study can be a sustaining resource for physicians to maintain their resilience, life balance, and well-being.

An empathetic physician fosters increased levels of respect, trust, and mutual understanding in the doctor-patient relationship. This improved communication encourages patients to cooperate and volunteer more precise information, leading to successful treatment while reducing the hazards of occupational burnout. Furthermore, it collectively helps restore patients' trust in the healthcare system.

In the post-COVID world, where healthcare delivery has become more dependent on digital platforms, the inclusion of spiritual care into humanistic medicine can bridge the emotional and personal gaps left by technology. It can reintroduce the warmth and humanity that patients yearn for, even when interactions are through screens or automated systems.

Need for Humanistic Medicine in Lower-and-Middle Income countries (LMIC'S) and Pakistan

Unique Healthcare Challenges In LMICs, Including Resource Limitations, High Patient Volume And Strong Spiritual Beliefs

The lack of motivation, resource shortages, and instability among healthcare providers hinder the quality of care in low- and middle-income countries. With rising cases of communicable diseases, non-communicable diseases, and road traffic accidents, these regions face a growing triple burden, leading to a health workforce that is overworked and mentally and physically exhausted. If these rapidly declining circumstances are not addressed promptly, they may have a detrimental impact on an already strained healthcare system and economic state.

In many LMICs, spiritual beliefs and practices play a significant role in how individuals cope with illness and suffering. By incorporating spiritual care into humanistic medical practice, healthcare providers can foster a sense of hope and meaning for patients, encouraging them to adhere to treatment and engage more fully in their recovery. This approach can also help address the root causes of patient dissatisfaction and mistrust, which often stem from a perceived lack of compassion and connection.

The American Society of Clinical Oncology has identified culturally appropriate patient-centered care as a way to enhance and strengthen patient involvement in their care. For example, African Americans often report minimal communication with providers and a higher level of unmet needs. In contrast, patients who share the same race as their providers report less discrimination and a more participatory attitude during visits. These insights highlight the importance of culturally sensitive approaches to healthcare to improve health outcomes through better patient-provider relationships.

GLOBAL EFFORTS TO PROMOTE HUMANISTIC MEDICINE

Overview of International Initiatives And Organizations Advocating For Humanistic Medicine

Global efforts to reinstate humanism in medicine are underway through various programs, courses, and certifications in humanism, including those offered by the Arnold P. Gold Foundation and various courses offered as part of the curriculum at the Ohio State University College of Medicine, Stanford University, and NYU Lagone Health, to name a few. These programs are designed to teach future healthcare professionals the importance of holistic care, including spiritual aspects, through courses on the humanities, communication skills, and ethics.

International Initiatives Integrating Spirituality Into Healthcare

One notable example is the World Health Organization's (WHO) palliative care programs, which emphasize spiritual care as a core component. Palliative care, focused on improving the quality of life for patients with life-threatening illnesses, recognizes that spiritual well-being is essential for holistic treatment. Many WHO-endorsed programs train healthcare providers to address patients' spiritual needs, ensuring that care is not only physically and emotionally supportive but also spiritually fulfilling. These programs can be adapted for low- and middle-income countries where spiritual beliefs often play a crucial role in patients' perceptions of illness and recovery.

Another global example is the National Health Service (NHS) in the United Kingdom, which has implemented spiritual care services across hospitals. These services offer spiritual counseling and pastoral support to patients of all faiths, or those seeking meaning and comfort during illness as part of routine healthcare, acknowledging the deep impact that spirituality can have on a patient's experience of illness, particularly in end-of-life care. Such models can be adapted in LMICs to bridge gaps in patient care, especially in regions where spiritual beliefs significantly influence health decisions.

Successful Models And Practices From High- Income Countries That Can Be Adapted To Enhance Humanistic Care

The General Medical Council in the United Kingdom underlined the importance of medical humanities through its report called 'Tomorrows Doctor'. This report consisted of a proposed curriculum formed through interdisciplinary subjects like philosophy, law, history, the arts, and communication skills. The council advised the integration of this curriculum into undergraduate medical education to help promote skills and legal issues that are relevant to the clinical practices and rights of patients. If these similar aspects of humanities and humanism can be taught to medical students through lectures, training in interpersonal skills, and role modeling, it could become a successful practice for many countries to adapt in light of enhancing humanistic care. Along with that, multiple assessment tools can be used revolving around humanistic attitudes and behaviors among medical students. Amongst these methods are observation, history-taking, and objective structured clinical examinations (OSCE's). These methods help assess the perceptions of students. Medical educators must remember that humanism comes under the umbrella of an interdisciplinary subject that is then intermingled with the basic biomedical sciences.

The National Institute for Integrative Medicine (NIIM) in Australia has also developed successful models that integrate spirituality into healthcare. The institute promotes holistic approaches to healing that combine conventional medicine with spiritual practices like meditation, prayer, and spiritual counseling.

Collaboration Between Global Health Entities And Lmic's To Enhance Humanistic And Spiritual Care

The lack of motivation, shortages, and instability associated with healthcare providers hinder the quality of care in low- and middle-income countries. The health care burden in these countries has recently increased as they are now faced with rising cases of not only communicable diseases but also non-communicable ones and road traffic accidents, consequently putting them under a triple burden. These rapidly declining circumstances, if not addressed timely, may have a detrimental impact on an already underutilized healthcare system and economic state. Thus, humanistic medicine, through compassionate communication and empathy, helps patients stick to the advice and care options that are provided by their healthcare workers, leading to better health outcomes.

The Gold Humanism Honor Society, founded by Arnold P. Gold, is a community of medical students, physicians, and other leaders who have been recognized for their work in compassion care. The society reinforces and supports the human connection in healthcare, which is essential for the health of patients and clinicians.

The Arnold P. Gold Foundation reported that humanism is characterized by a respectful and compassionate relationship between healthcare providers and their patients, reflecting respect for health care members to value the cultural and ethnic backgrounds of others.

The CUGH Global Health Humanities Working Group seeks to explore global health through diverse humanities perspectives in an effort to highlight dimensions of the human experience that are neglected in current global health activities and also help LMICs enhance their expertise in humanistic care.

HOW CAN HUMANISTIC MEDICINE BE PRACTICED IN LMICS?

Since its inception, the impactful practice and implementation of humanistic medicine have struggled to remain consistent. This is especially true for lower-middle-income countries that face unique healthcare challenges, including resource constraints, high patient volumes, and socio-cultural barriers, making the integration of humanistic medicine both necessary and challenging. Hence, there is a dire need to design human-centered, sustainable, and cost-effective pathways to include humanistic medicine in our policies and health systems.

The following are some strategies suggesting how humanistic medicine can be incorporated into existing healthcare systems.

Role of Education And Training For Healthcare Providers

Education and training are critical for equipping healthcare providers with the skills and knowledge needed to practice humanistic medicine. Medical schools and training institutions in LMICs should revise their curricula to include courses on medical ethics, communication skills, emotional intelligence, and cultural competence. These courses should emphasize the importance of empathy, compassion, and patient-centered care in healthcare delivery, preparing future healthcare providers to deliver compassionate and holistic care.

The courses alone are ineffective unless complimented by experiential learning opportunities that are particularly effective in fostering humanistic skills. Medical and nursing students can benefit from hands-on training, such as patient interactions, role-playing exercises, and community service activities, which allow them to practice and refine their communication and empathy skills in real-world settings. Studies have shown that such experiential learning can significantly enhance students' ability to deliver compassionate care.

Continuing education programs for practicing healthcare providers are also essential. Workshops, seminars, and online courses focused on refreshing how to practice humanistic medicine can help professionals stay updated on best practices and reinforce the importance of patient-centered care. For instance, a study found that healthcare providers who participated in empathy training programs reported improved patient satisfaction and better clinical outcomes. Additionally, mentoring programs where experienced practitioners guide younger colleagues can facilitate the passing down of humanistic values and practices.

In most countries, integrating the basis of medical humanity into current medical school syllabuses allows undergraduates to continue building their scientific concepts while simultaneously incorporating the idea of empathy and sensitivity in their day-to-day care towards their future patients. The importance of humanism can be taught through training programs and role modeling to help physicians develop interpersonal skills in communication with their patients. Recently, small standardized teaching groups, hospital rounds, and assistance learning experiences all contributed to learning methods for humanism. Different role models in different settings are followed by their students to emulate their clinical experience, showcasing humanistic characteristics. This method has been approved for encouraging acts of humanism in medical students.

Humanistic Health Service Delivery

Integrating humanistic medicine into existing healthcare systems in LMICs requires a multifaceted approach that addresses systemic, cultural, and practical challenges. One effective strategy is to incorporate humanistic principles into the healthcare service delivery model and operational management. This can be achieved by establishing patient-centered care protocols that prioritize empathy and holistic treatment approaches. This approach requires healthcare providers to actively listen to patients, conduct thorough patient histories, including psychosocial factors, respect their choices, and involve them in decision-making processes. Studies have shown that patient-centered care improves patient satisfaction, adherence to treatment, and overall health outcomes.

Effective and compassionate communication is another critical component of humanistic health service delivery. Training programs should focus on developing both verbal and non-verbal communication skills. Techniques such as active listening, open-ended questioning, and empathy expressions are essential for building rapport and trust with patients. When healthcare providers practice active listening, patients feel heard and valued. The clear, honest, and respectful exchanges that then follow between healthcare providers and patients enable providers to explain medical conditions, treatment options, and management plans in a way that patients can understand and follow, leading to improved patient outcomes. This builds patient trust and engagement, leading to better health outcomes.

Additionally, fostering a humanistic organizational culture that delivers, values, and rewards humanistic care requires a multifaceted approach. This may include implementing interdisciplinary team approaches to provide holistic and coordinated care, encouraging open communication and mutual respect among healthcare providers and patients, creating recognition programs that highlight and reward compassionate care practices, and promoting work environments that support the well-being of healthcare providers, thereby reducing burnout and enhancing their ability to deliver empathetic care.

Another critical strategy involves enhancing the infrastructure to support humanistic care. This includes creating environments that facilitate better patient-provider interactions. For example, redesigning hospital spaces to be more welcoming and less intimidating can help alleviate patient anxiety and foster a more compassionate atmosphere where patients come in with a positive attitude.

Measuring patient satisfaction is an important aspect of humanistic health service delivery and can be measured through satisfaction surveys and feedback mechanisms. This information can be used to identify areas for improvement and ensure that healthcare services meet patients' needs and expectations.

Role of Leadership And Governance In Humanistic Operation Management

Operational management in humanistic health services involves embedding humanistic principles into every aspect of healthcare delivery. This can be achieved by developing protocols and policies that prioritize and appreciate patient-centered care, empathy, and compassion. The role of humanistic leadership and governance is indispensable here. Leading by example, they must embody the humanistic values that they advocate for, creating a culture that prioritizes humanistic care. This includes providing training and resources for staff to develop humanistic skills, recognizing and rewarding exemplary patient-centered practices, ensuring that organizational policies support humanistic approaches, and treating their team with respect, compassion, and appreciation. For instance, sending out appreciative messages and thanking the team for their work when disbursing salaries can boost their morale, promote a healthy workplace environment, and lead to greater levels of job satisfaction that could positively influence their patient care. However, this appreciation must be genuine and heartfelt. Small, cost-effective gestures can go a long way in ensuring a humanistic work environment.

Policy Recommendations To Support Humanistic Practices

Public health views individuals in their economic, social, and cultural environments to better understand health determinants and health inequalities, promoting prevention and not reducing patients to their biological bodies (a "biopsychosocial" approach) that also encourages the clinicians to be able to recognize all aspects of the patient and be cognizant of their emotional and spiritual needs along with the physical ones, therefore delivering a humanistic model of care. This demonstrates how humanistic health policies and collective work can be more impactful than training individual clinicians working in a flawed system that promotes an anti-humanistic approach. To be available and efficient for all, this approach ought not to be restricted to individual practitioners, as demonstrated by the French cancer plans and supportive care. The need is to not only focus on the patient-physician relationship but also on the environment and conditions of that relationship, i.e., the health system and its regulatory knobs (administrative, legal, financial, etc.).

A foundational strategy is the development of a robust policy framework by governments and healthcare authorities to develop and implement policies that not only promote patient-centered care and prioritize the holistic well-being of patients but also safeguard the well-being of healthcare providers. This requires recognizing the complex interplay among expectations, human rights, individual action, and systemic conditions. The resulting policies can, hence, include guidelines for humanistic practices, ensuring that they are focused on individual health workers and patients and are incorporated into standard operating procedures in hospitals and clinics, including the overall health system governance. Hence, an integrated approach can help mitigate the drivers of mistreatment, improve the humanistic policy environment and raise community awareness about patient rights. Globally, there is also an emerging move towards operationalizing a human rights approach to address this issue at all three levels.

Policies should also address the well-being of healthcare providers, recognizing that their ability to deliver compassionate care is influenced by their own mental and physical health. Implementing policies that promote work-life balance, provide mental health support, regularly acknowledge and appreciate the workforce, offer lucrative incentives, and encourage continuous professional development, including skills like dealing with burnout, setbacks, and building emotional intelligence, can help healthcare providers maintain their well-being and deliver high-quality care. The World Health Organization (WHO), for example, has highlighted the importance of supportive work environments in enhancing healthcare provider well-being and patient care quality.

Furthermore, policies should encourage the involvement of community health workers (CHWs) in the healthcare system. CHWs can play a crucial role in promoting humanistic medicine by providing culturally sensitive care and supporting patients in navigating the healthcare system. Governments should develop policies that provide training, certification, and adequate compensation for CHWs, ensuring their sustainability and effectiveness.

Use of Community Health Workers And Local Resources To Promote Humanistic Medicine

Community health workers (CHWs) are invaluable assets in promoting humanistic medicine in LMICs. CHWs often come from the communities they serve and understand the cultural and social contexts of their patients. Similarly, leveraging local resources and community networks is another effective strategy. This makes them uniquely positioned to provide patient-centered care that is both effective and culturally sensitive. They can help patients navigate the healthcare system, encourage healthy behaviors, provide health education, and offer emotional and social support to patients and their families. This makes them uniquely positioned to provide patient-centered care that is both effective and culturally sensitive.

Training CHWs in the humanistic principles of empathy, communication skills, and patient-centered care, enabling them to deliver compassionate and holistic care to patients, is essential for maximizing their impact. For example, a study in rural India found that CHWs trained in humanistic care principles significantly improved patient satisfaction and adherence to treatment plans.

Incorporating community feedback into healthcare planning and delivery is also crucial. Establishing patient advisory boards that include representatives from diverse backgrounds can help healthcare providers understand the needs and preferences of the community. This approach ensures that healthcare services are tailored to the specific cultural and social contexts of the population, enhancing the effectiveness and acceptance of humanistic medicine.

Promoting Humanistic Medicine Through Digital Outreach

While tackling the necessary organizational factors and the policy regulations that are needed is important, a top-down approach may not be feasible in an overburdened system where healthcare providers are already struggling with limited resources. Individual-level efforts may be more effective in catalyzing the adoption and conscious practice of humanistic medicine. It is more feasible to use the tools that are widely available, easily used, and have been proven to be effective. Social media is one such tool. It has been endorsed as a major influencer towards building a sense of community, promoting certain attitudes, fostering discussions, shaping people's perceptions, actions, and behaviors, and raising awareness for public health outreach campaigns.

This can be achieved by providing a unified platform for a conversation starter, raising awareness of and emphasizing the importance of practicing humanistic medicine to offer quality healthcare, and through training sessions and support groups to simultaneously strengthen the health workforce. Online social media communities moderated by medical professionals who identify as enthusiasts of the humanistic cause may prove to be a cost-effective method to do so. Hence, social media can be used as a powerful tool to raise awareness and influence people's attitudes, and its use to promote humanistic medicine is a feasible and sustainable option for the busy healthcare workforce.

ROLE OF GOVERNMENT AND NON-GOVERNMENTAL ORGANIZATIONS IN THE PRACTICE AND IMPLEMENTATION OF HUMANISTIC MEDICINE IN LMICS

The practice and implementation of humanistic medicine in LMICs require the collaborative efforts of governments and NGOs. Governments play a crucial role in developing supportive policies and frameworks that prioritize patient-centered care and the well-being of healthcare providers. NGOs contribute by providing training, advocating for policy changes, and engaging with communities to promote humanistic practices. Together, their cumulative impact can be more effective in yielding long-term results.

Government Policies And Frameworks Supporting Humanistic Medicine

Governments in LMICs hold significant responsibility for fostering an environment where humanistic medicine can thrive. Policy development is a key area where governments can influence the practice of humanistic medicine by creating frameworks that prioritize patient-centered care and the holistic well-being of both patients and providers.

One of the fundamental steps is to integrate humanistic principles into national health policies. These policies should outline the importance of empathy, compassion, and comprehensive care. For example, governments can mandate the inclusion of humanistic care training in medical and nursing curricula to ensure that healthcare providers are equipped with the skills necessary to deliver compassionate and patient-centered care from the outset of their careers.

Governments can also implement regulations that promote humanistic leadership and management styles in healthcare organizations and work-life balance for healthcare providers. Recognizing the high levels of stress and burnout in the medical profession, policies that offer mental health support, flexible working hours, and opportunities for professional development can enhance the ability of healthcare providers to deliver humanistic care. Similarly, operational efficiency and organizational management should be formulated according to the specific needs of the health workforce, offering them an environment that empowers them and respects their needs. The World Health Organization (WHO) also emphasizes the importance of creating supportive work environments to improve healthcare provider well-being and patient care quality.

Furthermore, governments can invest in healthcare infrastructure that supports humanistic practices. This includes developing facilities that allow for private consultations, adequate patient rest areas, and spaces that promote patient-provider interactions. Financial incentives, such as subsidies or grants, can be provided to healthcare institutions that adopt humanistic care models.

Contributions of Non-Governmental Organizations In Promoting Humanistic Practices

NGOs play a pivotal role in advancing humanistic medicine, particularly in resource-constrained settings of LMICs. These organizations often have the flexibility and innovative capacity to implement programs that directly address the needs of the communities they serve.

NGOs can contribute to humanistic medicine by providing training and resources to healthcare providers. Many NGOs operate training programs that emphasize the importance of empathy, communication skills, and cultural competence. For instance, the international organization Médecins Sans Frontières (MSF) offers training that focuses on delivering compassionate care in crisis situations, highlighting the importance of understanding and addressing patients' emotional and psychological needs alongside their medical conditions.

Additionally, NGOs can serve as advocates for policy changes by engaging with government bodies and other stakeholders. By presenting evidence-based research and success stories, NGOs can influence policy decisions that support humanistic medicine. Organizations such as Partners in Health (PIH) have been instrumental in advocating for healthcare models that prioritize patient-centered care and have successfully influenced health policies in several LMICs.

NGOs also play a crucial role in community engagement and education. They can work directly with communities to raise awareness about the importance of humanistic care and empower patients to advocate for their needs. Health education programs conducted by NGOs can inform patients about their rights and the benefits of holistic and empathetic healthcare.

PATIENT PERSPECTIVES ON HUMANISTIC CARE AND ITS IMPACT ON HEALTH OUTCOMES

Understanding Patient Experiences And Expectations Of Humanistic Care

Patients in LMICs face numerous challenges, including limited access to healthcare, economic constraints, and cultural barriers. These factors influence their healthcare experiences and shape their expectations of care.

Patients expect healthcare providers to not only address their medical needs but also to show empathy, respect, and understanding. Studies have shown that patients value healthcare providers who take the time to listen to their concerns, explain treatment options clearly, and involve them in decision-making processes. In LMICs, where healthcare resources are often scarce, the quality of the patient-provider relationship becomes even more significant.

In Rwanda, for example, patients reported high levels of satisfaction with community health workers who provided empathetic and culturally sensitive care. These workers, who are often from the same communities as the patients, understand local customs and languages, making patients feel more comfortable and understood. Similarly, in India, the ASHA program has improved patient experiences by ensuring that healthcare workers are approachable and responsive to the needs of the community.

Impact of Humanistic Practices On Patient Satisfaction And Health Outcomes

Humanistic practices have been shown to significantly impact patient satisfaction and health outcomes. When patients feel respected and valued, they are more likely to trust their healthcare providers, adhere to treatment plans, and engage in preventive health behaviors.

A study conducted in Kenya's AMPATH program found that patients who received holistic care, including social and psychological support, reported higher levels of satisfaction and better health outcomes compared to those who received standard medical care devoid of these attributes. The program's emphasis on understanding patients' broader life contexts and addressing their comprehensive needs resulted in improved adherence to treatment and reduced rates of hospital readmission.

In Bangladesh, the BRAC health program has demonstrated that humanistic care can lead to significant improvements in maternal and child health outcomes, with patients receiving care from BRAC health workers reporting feeling more supported and confident in managing their health.

Humanistic practices also positively influence mental health outcomes. In a study conducted in rural India, patients who received empathetic care from healthcare providers reported lower levels of anxiety and depression compared to those who received impersonal care. The study highlighted the importance of empathy and communication in improving mental health outcomes, particularly in resource-limited settings where formal mental health services may be lacking.

LEVERAGING AI AND TECHNOLOGY IN HUMANISTIC MEDICINE

Potential of AI to Support Humanistic Practices Through Personalized Care And Decision Support

Artificial intelligence has the potential to significantly enhance humanistic practices in healthcare by providing personalized care and robust decision-support. Personalized care, a cornerstone of humanistic medicine, involves tailoring medical treatment to the individual characteristics of each patient. AI systems can analyze vast amounts of data, including genetic information, medical history, and lifestyle factors, to develop personalized treatment plans that address the unique needs of each patient. For instance, AI algorithms can identify patterns and predict disease outcomes with high accuracy, enabling healthcare providers to offer proactive and preventive care. This not only improves health outcomes but also enhances the patient experience by demonstrating a deep understanding of their individual health needs. AI-driven predictive analytics can help clinicians anticipate complications and intervene early, which is particularly valuable in LMICs where resources are limited and early intervention can prevent costly and resource-intensive treatments.

Moreover, AI can support decision-making processes by providing evidence-based recommendations. Clinical decision support systems (CDSS) powered by AI can analyze patient data in real-time, offering suggestions for diagnosis, treatment options, and care management. This ensures that healthcare providers have access to the latest medical knowledge and can make informed decisions that align with the best interests of their patients. For example, AI-based CDSS can assist in diagnosing complex conditions by cross-referencing symptoms with vast medical databases, thereby reducing diagnostic errors and ensuring patients receive appropriate and timely care.

Balancing Technology Use With Maintaining A Human Touch In Healthcare

While the benefits of AI in healthcare are important, it is necessary to balance technology use with maintaining a human touch. The empathy, compassion, and patient-provider relationship in humanistic medicine cannot be entirely replaced by technology. The challenge lies in integrating AI in a way that complements and enhances these humanistic values rather than undermining them.

Healthcare providers must remain vigilant in ensuring that AI tools are used to augment their interactions with patients rather than replace them. For instance, AI can handle routine tasks and data analysis, freeing up healthcare providers to spend more time engaging with patients. This approach allows them to focus on building rapport, understanding patient concerns, and offering emotional support, all of which are essential components of humanistic care.

Training healthcare professionals to effectively use AI tools while maintaining a compassionate and empathetic approach is also critical. Medical education should emphasize the importance of communication skills and empathy, ensuring that future healthcare providers are equipped to deliver humanistic care in a technologically advanced environment. For example, incorporating AI literacy into medical curricula can help providers understand the strengths and limitations of AI, enabling them to use these tools judiciously and effectively.

However, ethical considerations must be considered to ensure that AI applications do not compromise patient autonomy or privacy. Transparent and accountable AI systems will be needed to maintain patient trust and uphold the ethical principles of humanistic medicine. Developing guidelines and regulatory frameworks that govern the use of AI in healthcare can help protect against potential ethical pitfalls and ensure that AI applications align with the values of humanistic care.

Examples of AI Applications That Enhance Rather Than Replace Human Interactions

Several AI applications have proven their potential to enhance human interactions in healthcare, reinforcing the principles of humanistic medicine. One such example is the use of AI in telemedicine. AI-powered chatbots and virtual assistants can conduct initial patient assessments, triage cases, and provide health information. These tools can improve access to care, especially in remote or underserved areas, while ensuring that patients receive personalized attention.

CHALLENGES AND ETHICAL CONSIDERATIONS

Barriers to Implementing Humanistic Medicine in LMICs

Funding Constraints

One of the main barriers to implementing humanistic medicine in LMICs is the lack of adequate funding. Healthcare systems in these countries often operate on limited budgets, which are primarily allocated to addressing immediate and pressing health concerns, such as infectious diseases, maternal and child health, and emergency care. As a result, there is little room for investing in the development and maintenance of humanistic care practices, which require additional resources for training, patient-centered infrastructure, and supportive technologies.

Training and Education Deficits

Another significant barrier is the lack of training and education in humanistic medicine. While healthcare providers in LMICs receive training that focuses heavily on clinical and technical skills, there is limited emphasis on communication, empathy, and patient-centered care. This gap in training results in healthcare professionals who may be technically proficient but lack the skills necessary to deliver compassionate and holistic care.

Inadequate infrastructure

The infrastructure necessary to support humanistic medicine is often underdeveloped in LMICs. Healthcare facilities may be overcrowded, understaffed, and lacking in essential resources such as private consultation rooms, patient support services, and adequate medical supplies. These conditions make it challenging to provide care that is respectful of patients' privacy, dignity, and individual needs.

Potential Solutions And Innovations To Overcome These Challenges

Strategic Allocation Of Resources

Addressing the funding barrier requires strategic allocation of resources and innovative financing solutions. Governments and international organizations can prioritize funding for humanistic care initiatives, recognizing that compassionate care can improve health outcomes and patient satisfaction, which in turn can enhance the efficiency and effectiveness of healthcare systems. Public-private partnerships and philanthropic contributions can also provide additional funding streams to support humanistic medicine programs.

Enhancing Training And Education

Improving training and education in humanistic medicine involves comprehensive training in communication, emotional intelligence, empathy, and patient-centered care. Continuous professional development programs can ensure that healthcare providers stay updated on the latest humanistic care practices.

Infrastructure Development

Investing in infrastructure includes building or renovating healthcare facilities to ensure they have the necessary spaces and resources to provide patient-centered care. Simple innovations, such as creating private consultation rooms and patient waiting areas that are comfortable and dignified, can significantly enhance the patient experience. Additionally, leveraging mobile health (mHealth) technologies can extend the reach of humanistic care to remote and underserved areas.

Ethical Principles Governing Humanistic Medicine

Respect for Autonomy

Respecting patient autonomy involves recognizing and honoring patients' rights to make informed decisions about their own health and treatment. Healthcare providers must ensure that patients are fully informed about their conditions and treatment options, and support them in making choices that align with their values and preferences.

Beneficence and Non-Maleficence

The principles of beneficence and non-maleficence mandate healthcare providers to act in the best interests of their patients and to do no harm. In the context of humanistic medicine, this means providing care that is not only addressing patients' physical health needs but is also supporting their emotional, psychological, and social well-being, employing a holistic approach to care that considers the whole person, rather than just their medical condition.

Justice and Equity

Justice and equity, as important elements of upholding human rights, are crucial ethical principles in the practice of humanistic medicine, particularly in LMICs where resources are often scarce. Healthcare providers must strive to ensure that all patients receive fair and equitable access to care, regardless of their socioeconomic status, gender, ethnicity, or geographical location. This entails advocating for policies and practices that reduce health disparities and promote social justice.

FUTURE DIRECTIONS

Future Research Areas And Opportunities For Advancing Humanistic Medicine Globally

Evidence-Based Approaches To Humanistic Medicine

Future research must focus on developing and validating evidence-based approaches to humanistic medicine. This involves conducting rigorous studies to evaluate the effectiveness of various humanistic interventions that include a spiritual component on health outcomes. For instance, randomized controlled trials (RCTs) and longitudinal studies can provide robust evidence on the impact of empathy training, patient-centered communication, and holistic care approaches on patient satisfaction, adherence to treatment, and overall health outcomes.

Additionally, research should explore the mechanisms through which humanistic practices influence health outcomes. Understanding these mechanisms can help refine and optimize interventions. For example, studies could investigate the role of leadership, governance, and organizational factors in humanistic healthcare service delivery in promoting positive health behaviors and improving clinical outcomes.

Integrating Technology And Humanistic Care

As technology continues to transform healthcare, research should explore how to integrate technological advancements with humanistic care. This includes studying the use of artificial intelligence (AI), telemedicine, and electronic health records (EHRs) to enhance patient-centered care. For example, AI-driven decision support systems can provide personalized treatment recommendations while maintaining the human touch in patient interactions.

Research should also investigate the ethical implications of using technology in humanistic medicine. Ensuring that technology enhances rather than detracts from the patient-provider relationship is crucial. Studies could explore best practices for maintaining empathy and compassion in virtual consultations and how to design user-friendly digital tools that support patient engagement and autonomy.

Culturally Competent Care

Given the global diversity of patient populations, future research must prioritize culturally competent care within the framework of humanistic medicine. This involves developing and testing interventions tailored to the cultural and spiritual contexts of different communities. For instance, research could examine the effectiveness of culturally adapted empathy training programs for healthcare providers working in diverse settings.

Furthermore, studies should also explore how cultural and spiritual beliefs and practices influence patients' perceptions of humanistic care. Cross-cultural comparative studies can provide valuable insights guiding the design of interventions that respect and incorporate patients' cultural values and preferences, enabling humanistic medicine to be effectively practiced in different cultural contexts.

Training and Education In Humanistic Medicine

Advancing humanistic medicine requires a strong focus on training and education for healthcare providers. Future research should investigate the most effective methods for teaching humanistic principles and skills to medical students and practicing clinicians. This includes evaluating the impact of spiritual experiential learning, role-playing, and reflective practice on developing empathy, compassion, and patient-centered communication.

Additionally, research should explore how to sustain and reinforce humanistic values throughout healthcare providers' careers. Longitudinal studies could examine the long-term effects of humanistic training programs on professional behavior and patient care. Identifying the key factors that contribute to the retention of humanistic values in clinical practice is essential for developing sustainable educational interventions.

Policy and System-Level Interventions

Future research should also focus on policy and system-level interventions to promote humanistic medicine. This includes studying the impact of healthcare policies, organizational culture, and leadership on the practice of humanistic care. For example, research could investigate how policies that prioritize patient-centered care and incentivize compassionate practices influence healthcare providers' behavior and patient outcomes, and the role of spirituality in practicing humanistic traits.

Furthermore, studies should explore the role of healthcare organizations in fostering a culture of humanistic care. This involves examining the effectiveness of interventions such as team-based care models, interdisciplinary collaboration, and supportive work environments in promoting empathy and compassion among healthcare providers.

Addressing Burnout And Promoting Well-Being

Healthcare provider burnout is a significant barrier to the practice of humanistic medicine. Future research should investigate strategies that include a spiritual component, to address burnout and promote the well-being of healthcare providers. This includes studying the impact of interventions such as psychotherapy, cognitive behavioral therapy, mindfulness training, gratitude, resilience-building programs, and work-life balance initiatives on reducing burnout and enhancing providers' ability to deliver compassionate care.

Additionally, research should explore the relationship between provider well-being and patient outcomes. Understanding how healthcare providers' emotional and psychological health influences their ability to practice humanistic care can inform the development of holistic interventions that support both provider and patient well-being.

Patient and Community Engagement

Engaging patients and communities in the research and practice of humanistic medicine is a major component of the successful and continued implementation of humanistic medicine. Future research should explore methods for involving patients and communities in the design, implementation, and evaluation of humanistic interventions. This includes studying the role of addressing the spiritual needs of patients. The impact of patient advisory councils, community health worker programs, and participatory action research on improving patient-centered care must also be investigated.

Furthermore, understanding patients' perspectives and preferences is essential for developing interventions that truly meet their needs, and hence, research should investigate how to empower patients to actively participate in their own care. This can be achieved by studying the effectiveness of interventions that promote patient education, shared decision-making, and self-management in enhancing patient engagement and satisfaction.

Global Collaboration And Knowledge Exchange

Advancing humanistic medicine globally requires collaboration and knowledge exchange among researchers, healthcare providers, policymakers, and communities. Future research should investigate the best practices for fostering international collaboration and sharing knowledge and resources between organizations that are already working towards the same goal. This includes studying the impact of global health initiatives, international partnerships, and cross-cultural exchanges on promoting humanistic care. Focusing on ways to adapt successful humanistic interventions from high-income countries to LMICs will help in identifying the key elements of these interventions that can be tailored to different contexts, which is essential for scaling up humanistic practices globally. Similarly, comparative studies can provide valuable insights into the factors that contribute to the success of humanistic care initiatives in various settings.

Economic Evaluations Of Humanistic Medicine And Mobilization Of Pharmaceutical Industry

Economic evaluations of humanistic medicine are essential for demonstrating its value and securing funding and support for its implementation. Future research should focus on conducting cost-effectiveness analyses and return-on-investment studies to quantify the economic benefits of humanistic care. This includes examining the impact of humanistic interventions on healthcare costs, patient outcomes, and productivity. Research should explore the economic implications of integrating humanistic medicine into existing healthcare systems to understand the costs and benefits of different implementation strategies. This will enable policymakers and healthcare organizations to make evidence-based decisions about investing in humanistic care while also advocating for the inclusion of humanistic medicine in health policy agendas.

Moreover, through the mobilization of the pharmaceutical industry through targeted campaigns and endorsements, they can play an important role in advocating for and implementing the practice and culture of humanistic medicine.

Ethical and Legal Considerations

Studying the ethical dilemmas that arise in providing compassionate care in resource-constrained settings and developing frameworks for addressing these dilemmas will go a long way toward ensuring its sustainability. For example, research could explore the ethical implications of prioritizing patient-centered care in contexts where resources are limited and how to balance competing ethical principles.

Furthermore, studies should investigate the legal frameworks that support or hinder the practice of humanistic medicine. This involves examining the impact of healthcare regulations, professional codes of conduct, and patient rights legislation on the delivery of compassionate care.

Advancing humanistic medicine globally requires a multifaceted approach that encompasses evidence-based research, technological integration, culturally competent care, training and education, policy and system-level interventions, addressing burnout, patient and community engagement, global collaboration, economic evaluations, and ethical and legal considerations. By focusing on these future research areas and opportunities, the healthcare community can develop and implement effective strategies to promote empathy, compassion, and patient-centered care worldwide.

As healthcare systems continue to evolve, it is essential to prioritize humanistic medicine as a fundamental component of quality care. By investing in research and innovation, fostering collaboration and knowledge exchange, and addressing ethical and legal challenges, we can create a global healthcare system that truly values and practices humanistic medicine. This will ultimately lead to improved health outcomes, enhanced patient satisfaction, and a more compassionate and equitable healthcare system for all.

CONCLUSION

Healthcare leaders, healthcare providers, policy makers, researchers, educators, technologists, community health workers can together work towards the seamless integration of humanistic medicine into our health systems.

Healthcare Leaders

Champion the principles of humanistic medicine with its spiritual components within their organizations.

Foster an environment that prioritizes patient-centered care and supports the well-being of healthcare providers.

Encourage open communication, teamwork, and the continuous improvement of care practices. Lead by example, demonstrating a commitment to empathy, respect, and ethical practice.

Healthcare Providers

Cultivate a culture of compassion and empathy in clinical practice.

Engage in continuous professional development focused on humanistic medicine.

Engage in personal development focused on their spirituality as means to be more humanistic.

Collaboration among healthcare teams is essential to ensure holistic care for patients.

Policymakers

Develop and implement policies that prioritize patient-centered care and support humanistic practices.

Encourage the integration of humanistic principles in medical education and healthcare systems. Promote funding for research and initiatives aimed at enhancing humanistic medicine.

Researchers

Encourage further research on the impact of humanistic medicine on patient outcomes, healthcare provider well-being, and healthcare systems.

Explore innovative solutions and best practices from different regions to address common challenges.

Foster global collaboration to promote the implementation of humanistic medicine in diverse healthcare settings.

Educators

Integrate humanistic medicine into medical and healthcare education curricula.

Provide training that emphasizes the importance of empathy, ethical considerations, and patient-centered care.

Facilitate interdisciplinary learning experiences to foster a holistic understanding of patient needs.

Technologists

Design and develop AI and technology solutions that enhance, rather than replace, human interactions in healthcare.

Ensure transparency in AI algorithms, data usage, and privacy policies.

Collaborate with healthcare professionals to create tools that support personalized and compassionate care.

Community Health Workers

Leverage local knowledge and resources to promote patient-centered care in underserved areas. Engage with patients to understand their unique needs and provide culturally sensitive care. Serve as a bridge between healthcare providers and communities to enhance trust and communication.

SUMMARY

In this chapter, we have explored the practice and implementation of humanistic medicine as a spiritual driver for improving the quality of work life of healthcare providers and health outcomes. We began by defining humanistic medicine, linking the role of spirituality in enhancing the ability of healthcare providers to practice humanistic medicine. We explored strategies for integrating humanistic practices into existing healthcare systems, including LMICs, and the importance of education and training for healthcare providers. Policy recommendations, the contributions of community health workers and local resources, and the importance of healthcare leaders in providing an organizational culture that promotes the delivery of humanistic medicine were also discussed. The potential of AI and technology to support humanistic practices was also explored, highlighting the importance of maintaining a human touch in healthcare. We identified common challenges and unique solutions across different LMICs. Finally, we addressed the barriers, ethical considerations, and proposed future directions for promoting humanistic medicine globally.

REFERENCES

Abbott, R., Hui, K., Mandel, J., Goldstein, M., Winegarden, B., Glaser, D., ... & Brunton, L. (2011). Medical student attitudes toward complementary, alternative and integrative medicine. Evidence-Based Complementary and Alternative Medicine, 2011(1). DOI: 10.1093/ecam/nep195

Acosta, L., & Ely, E. W. (2023). Holistic care in healthy aging: Caring for the wholly and holy human. *Aging Cell*, *23*(1), e14021. Advance online publication. DOI: 10.1111/acel.14021 PMID: 37873723

Adeniji, A., Osibanjo, A., Iruonagbe, T., Olawande, T., Ibidunni, A., & Olokundun, M. (2019). From job satisfaction to organizational commitment: The mediating influence of perceived treatment of diversity among nigeria's public healthcare employees. *Open Access Macedonian Journal of Medical Sciences*, *7*(12), 2031–2035. DOI: 10.3889/oamjms.2019.346 PMID: 31406550

Ahmed, Z., Bhinder, K., Amna, T., Tahir, M., Mehmood, Q., Tabassum, M., & Yousaf, Z. (2022). Knowledge, attitude, and practice of artificial intelligence among doctors and medical students in pakistan: A cross-sectional online survey. *Annals of Medicine and Surgery (London)*, *76*. Advance online publication. DOI: 10.1016/j.amsu.2022.103493 PMID: 35308436

Akologo, A., Abuosi, A., & Anaba, E. (2019). A cross-sectional survey on patient safety culture among healthcare providers in the upper east region of ghana. *PLoS One*, *14*(8), e0221208. DOI: 10.1371/journal.pone.0221208 PMID: 31430303

Alenezi, N. K., Alyami, A. H., Alrehaili, B. O., Arruhaily, A. A., Alenazi, N. K., & Radman Al-Dubai, S. A.ALEnezi. (2022). Prevalence and associated factors of burnout among saudi resident doctors: A multicenter cross-sectional study. *Alpha Psychiatry*, *23*(4), 173–183. DOI: 10.5152/alphapsychiatry.2022.21361 PMID: 36425745

Aloisio, L., Gifford, W., McGilton, K., Lalonde, M., Estabrooks, C., & Squires, J. (2018). Individual and organizational predictors of allied healthcare providers' job satisfaction in residential long-term care. *BMC Health Services Research*, *18*(1), 491. Advance online publication. DOI: 10.1186/s12913-018-3307-3 PMID: 29940949

Alvarez, A., Pagani, M., & Meucci, P. (2012). The clinical application of the biopsychosocial model in mental health. *American Journal of Physical Medicine & Rehabilitation*, *91*(13), S173–S180. DOI: 10.1097/PHM.0b013e31823d54be PMID: 22193327

Amedior, N. (2023). Ethical implications of artificial intelligence in the healthcare sector. *Advances in Multidisciplinary & Scientific Research Journal Publication, 36*, 1–12. DOI: 10.22624/AIMS/ACCRABESPOKE2023P1

Ariesmansyah, A., Arisanti, I., & Rahmawati, R. (2024). The effect of employee support policy effectiveness, collaborative leadership, and work rewards on organizational innovation in the manufacturing industry in west java. *West Science Social and Humanities Studies, 2*(04), 599–609. DOI: 10.58812/wsshs.v2i04.791

Austin, P., Macdonald, J., & MacLeod, R. (2018). Measuring spirituality and religiosity in clinical settings: A scoping review of available instruments. *Religions, 9*(3), 70. DOI: 10.3390/rel9030070

Bacha, K., Hanley, T., & Winter, L. A. (2020). 'Like a human being, I was an equal, I wasn't just a patient': Service users' perspectives on their experiences of relationships with staff in mental health services. *Psychology and Psychotherapy: Theory, Research and Practice, 93*(2), 367–386. DOI: 10.1111/papt.12218 PMID: 30720230

Balbale, S., Morris, M. A., & LaVela, S. L. (2014). Using photovoice to explore patient perceptions of patient-centered care in the veterans affairs health care system. The Patient - Patient-Centered Outcomes Research, 7(2), 187-195. DOI: 10.1007/s40271-014-0044-5

Balbale, S., Morris, M. A., & LaVela, S. L. (2014). Using photovoice to explore patient perceptions of patient-centered care in the veterans affairs health care system. The Patient - Patient-Centered Outcomes Research, 7(2), 187-195. DOI: 10.1007/s40271-014-0044-5

Barnett, J., Vasileiou, K., Djemil, F., Brooks, L., & Young, T. (2011). Understanding innovators' experiences of barriers and facilitators in implementation and diffusion of healthcare service innovations: A qualitative study. *BMC Health Services Research, 11*(1), 342. Advance online publication. DOI: 10.1186/1472-6963-11-342 PMID: 22176739

Beacham, A., King, A., & Nash, B. (2023). Psychologists' role in addressing healthcare provider burnout and well-being. *Journal of Health Service Psychology, 49*(2), 63–75. DOI: 10.1007/s42843-023-00083-y

Bergmo, T. S. (2015). How to measure costs and benefits of ehealth interventions: An overview of methods and frameworks. *Journal of Medical Internet Research, 17*(11), e254. DOI: 10.2196/jmir.4521 PMID: 26552360

Biller-Andorno, N., Ferrario, A., Jöbges, S., Krones, T., Massini, F., Barth, P., & Krauthammer, M. (2021). Ai support for ethical decision-making around resuscitation: Proceed with care. *Journal of Medical Ethics*, *48*(3), 175–183. DOI: 10.1136/medethics-2020-106786 PMID: 33687916

Bodenheimer, T., & Sinsky, C. (2014). From triple to quadruple aim: Care of the patient requires care of the provider. *Annals of Family Medicine*, *12*(6), 573–576. DOI: 10.1370/afm.1713 PMID: 25384822

Braithwaite, J., Herkes, J., Ludlow, K., Testa, L., & Lamprell, G. (2017). Association between organisational and workplace cultures, and patient outcomes: Systematic review. *BMJ Open*, *7*(11), e017708. DOI: 10.1136/bmjopen-2017-017708 PMID: 29122796

Bramley, L., & Matiti, M. (2014). How does it really feel to be in my shoes? patients' experiences of compassion within nursing care and their perceptions of developing compassionate nurses. *Journal of Clinical Nursing*, *23*(19-20), 2790–2799. DOI: 10.1111/jocn.12537 PMID: 24479676

Brighton, L., Miller, S., Farquhar, M., Booth, S., Yi, D., Gao, W., Bajwah, S., Man, W. D.-C., Higginson, I. J., & Maddocks, M. (2018). Holistic services for people with advanced disease and chronic breathlessness: A systematic review and meta-analysis. *Thorax*, *74*(3), 270–281. DOI: 10.1136/thoraxjnl-2018-211589 PMID: 30498004

Bringmann, H., Michalsen, A., Jeitler, M., Kessler, C., Brinkhaus, B., Brunnhuber, S., & Sedlmeier, P. (2022). Meditation-based lifestyle modification in mild to moderate depression—A randomized controlled trial. *Depression and Anxiety*, *39*(5), 363–375. DOI: 10.1002/da.23249 PMID: 35312137

Cajander, Å., Lárusdóttir, M., & Hedström, G. (2020). The effects of automation of a patient-centric service in primary care on the work engagement and exhaustion of nurses. *Quality and User Experience*, *5*(1), 9. Advance online publication. DOI: 10.1007/s41233-020-00038-x

Carrington, A. (2014). Expanding the debate. *Qualitative Research Journal*, *14*(2), 179–196. DOI: 10.1108/QRJ-08-2013-0049

Carvalho, D. (2024). Access from healthcare professionals to evidence-based pharmacotherapy in allergy management. Current Opinion in Allergy &Amp. *Clinical Immunology (Orlando, Fla.)*, *24*(4), 274–279. DOI: 10.1097/ACI.0000000000000989 PMID: 38640143

Cassim, S., Chepulis, L., Keenan, R., Kidd, J., Firth, M., & Lawrenson, R. (2019). Patient and carer perceived barriers to early presentation and diagnosis of lung cancer: A systematic review. *BMC Cancer, 19*(1), 25. Advance online publication. DOI: 10.1186/s12885-018-5169-9 PMID: 30621616

Castagno, S., & Khalifa, M. (2020). Perceptions of artificial intelligence among healthcare staff: A qualitative survey study. *Frontiers in Artificial Intelligence, 3*, 578983. Advance online publication. DOI: 10.3389/frai.2020.578983 PMID: 33733219

Chamane, N., Kuupiel, D., & Mashamba-Thompson, T. (2019). Experiential learning for primary healthcare workers in low- and middle-income countries: A scoping review protocol. *Systematic Reviews, 8*(1), 123. Advance online publication. DOI: 10.1186/s13643-019-1040-6 PMID: 31109377

Chaudru, S., Müllenheim, P., Faucheur, A., Kaladji, A., Jaquinandi, V., & Mahé, G. (2016). Training to perform ankle-brachial index: Systematic review and perspectives to improve teaching and learning. *European Journal of Vascular and Endovascular Surgery, 51*(2), 240–247. DOI: 10.1016/j.ejvs.2015.09.005 PMID: 26602321

Chen, L., Jiang, W., & Zhao, R. (2022). Application effect of kolb's experiential learning theory in clinical nursing teaching of traditional chinese medicine. *Digital Health, 8*, 205520762211383. DOI: 10.1177/20552076221138313 PMID: 36406155

Chou, C., Kellom, K., & Shea, J. (2014). Attitudes and habits of highly humanistic physicians. *Academic Medicine, 89*(9), 1252–1258. DOI: 10.1097/ACM.0000000000000405 PMID: 25006710

Chou, C., Kellom, K., & Shea, J. (2014). Attitudes and habits of highly humanistic physicians. *Academic Medicine, 89*(9), 1252–1258. DOI: 10.1097/ACM.0000000000000405 PMID: 25006710

Chou, C., Kellom, K., & Shea, J. (2014). Attitudes and habits of highly humanistic physicians. *Academic Medicine, 89*(9), 1252–1258. DOI: 10.1097/ACM.0000000000000405 PMID: 25006710

Clyne, B., Fitzgerald, C., Quinlan, A., Hardy, C., Galvin, R., Fahey, T., & Smith, S. M. (2016). Interventions to address potentially inappropriate prescribing in community-dwelling older adults: A systematic review of randomized controlled trials. *Journal of the American Geriatrics Society, 64*(6), 1210–1222. DOI: 10.1111/jgs.14133 PMID: 27321600

Coffey, A., Saab, M., Landers, M., Cornally, N., Hegarty, J., Drennan, J., Lunn, C., & Savage, E. (2019). The impact of compassionate care education on nurses: A mixed-method systematic review. *Journal of Advanced Nursing*, *75*(11), 2340–2351. DOI: 10.1111/jan.14088 PMID: 31162701

Coimbra, L., & Noakes, A. (2021). A systematic review into healthcare professionals' attitudes towards self-harm in children and young people and its impact on care provision. *Journal of Child Health Care*, *26*(2), 290–306. DOI: 10.1177/13674935211014405 PMID: 33929264

Cox, R., Kendall, M., Molineux, M., Miller, E., & Tanner, B. (2022). Refining a capability development framework for building successful consumer and staff partnerships in healthcare quality improvement: A coproduced edelphi study. *Health Expectations*, *25*(4), 1563–1579. DOI: 10.1111/hex.13499 PMID: 35472122

Croker, A., Brown, L., Little, A., Squires, K., & Crowley, E. (2018). Developing and maintaining collaborative practice: Exploring perspectives from dietetics and speech pathology about 'what works well'. *Nutrition & Dietetics: the Journal of the Dietitians Association of Australia*, *76*(1), 28–37. DOI: 10.1111/1747-0080.12506 PMID: 30585376

Cypher, M., & Axman, L. (2022). Determinants of location of death: A secondary analysis utilizing multinomial logistic regression. *The American Journal of Hospice & Palliative Care*, *39*(12), 1397–1402. DOI: 10.1177/10499091221077883 PMID: 35232266

Davydov, G. (2023). Revolutionizing healthcare delivery: The transformative impact of telemedicine in the post-pandemic era. *Journal for International Medical Graduates*, *2*(1). Advance online publication. DOI: 10.56570/jimgs.v2i1.90

Díaz, O., Guidi, G., Ivashchenko, O., Colgan, N., & Zanca, F. (2021). Artificial intelligence in the medical physics community: An international survey. *Physica Medica*, *81*, 141–146. DOI: 10.1016/j.ejmp.2020.11.037 PMID: 33453506

Domagała, A., Bała, M., Storman, D., Peña-Sánchez, J., Świerz, M., Kaczmarczyk, M., & Storman, M. (2018). Factors associated with satisfaction of hospital physicians: A systematic review on european data. *International Journal of Environmental Research and Public Health*, *15*(11), 2546. DOI: 10.3390/ijerph15112546 PMID: 30428606

Donnou, C., Chaudru, S., Stivalet, O., Paul, E., Charasson, M., Selli, J., & Jaquinandi, V. (2017). How to become proficient in performance of the resting ankle–brachial index: Results of the first randomized controlled trial. *Vascular Medicine*, *23*(2), 109–113. DOI: 10.1177/1358863X17740993 PMID: 29125051

Doram, K., Chadwick, W., Bokovoy, J., Profit, J., Sexton, J. D., & Sexton, J. B. (2017). Got spirit? the spiritual climate scale, psychometric properties, benchmarking data and future directions. *BMC Health Services Research, 17*(1), 132. Advance online publication. DOI: 10.1186/s12913-017-2050-5 PMID: 28189142

Doyle, C., Lennox, L., & Bell, D. (2013). A systematic review of evidence on the links between patient experience and clinical safety and effectiveness. *BMJ Open, 3*(1), e001570. DOI: 10.1136/bmjopen-2012-001570 PMID: 23293244

Dyrbye, L., Shanafelt, T., Sinsky, C., Cipriano, P., Bhatt, J., Ommaya, A., West, C. P., & Meyers, D. (2017). Burnout among health care professionals: A call to explore and address this underrecognized threat to safe, high-quality care. *NAM Perspectives, 7*(7). Advance online publication. DOI: 10.31478/201707b

Elliott, R. (2002). The effectiveness of humanistic therapies: A meta-analysis.

Evangelista, C., Lopes, M., Costa, S., Batista, P., Batista, J., & Oliveira, A. (2016). Cuidados paliativos e espiritualidade: Revisao integrativa da literatura. *Revista Brasileira de Enfermagem, 69*(3), 591–601. DOI: 10.1590/0034-7167.2016690324i PMID: 27355311

Faryal, , & Irum Naqvi, . (2023). The relationship between job satisfaction and job performance: A study on frontline healthcare workers. *Annals of Social Sciences and Perspective, 4*(1), 171–183. DOI: 10.52700/assap.v4i1.255

Foster, S., & Foster, A. (2019). The impact of workplace spirituality on work-based learners. *Journal of Work-Applied Management, 11*(1), 63–75. DOI: 10.1108/JWAM-06-2019-0015

Frost, K., Edelhäuser, F., Hofmann, M., Tauschel, D., & Lutz, G. (2019). History and development of medical studies at the university of witten/herdecke – an example of “continuous reform”. DOI: 10.3205/zma001269

Frost, K., Edelhäuser, F., Hofmann, M., Tauschel, D., & Lutz, G. (2019). History and development of medical studies at the university of witten/herdecke – an example of “continuous reform”. *GMS Journal for Medical Education, 36*(5), Doc61. DOI: 10.3205/zma001269 PMID: 31815171

Fundytus, A., Sengar, M., Lombe, D., Hopman, W. M., Jalink, M., Gyawali, B., Trapani, D., Roitberg, F., De Vries, E. G. E., Moja, L., Ilbawi, A., Sullivan, R., & Booth, C. M. (2021). Access to cancer medicines deemed essential by oncologists in 82 countries: An international, cross-sectional survey. *The Lancet. Oncology, 22*(10), 1367–1377. DOI: 10.1016/S1470-2045(21)00463-0 PMID: 34560006

Fundytus, A., Sengar, M., Lombe, D., Hopman, W. M., Jalink, M., Gyawali, B., Trapani, D., Roitberg, F., De Vries, E. G. E., Moja, L., Ilbawi, A., Sullivan, R., & Booth, C. M. (2021). Access to cancer medicines deemed essential by oncologists in 82 countries: An international, cross-sectional survey. *The Lancet. Oncology*, *22*(10), 1367–1377. DOI: 10.1016/S1470-2045(21)00463-0 PMID: 34560006

Ganguli, A., Clewell, J., & Shillington, A. (2016). The impact of patient support programs on adherence, clinical, humanistic, and economic patient outcomes: A targeted systematic review. *Patient Preference and Adherence*, *711*, 711. Advance online publication. DOI: 10.2147/PPA.S101175 PMID: 27175071

García-Navarro, E., Medina-Ortega, A., & Navarro, S. (2021). Spirituality in patients at the end of life—Is it necessary? a qualitative approach to the protagonists. *International Journal of Environmental Research and Public Health*, *19*(1), 227. DOI: 10.3390/ijerph19010227 PMID: 35010487

Gijsberts, M., Liefbroer, A., Otten, R., & Olsman, E. (2019). Spiritual care in palliative care: A systematic review of the recent european literature. *Medical Science*, *7*(2), 25. DOI: 10.3390/medsci7020025 PMID: 30736416

Gijsberts, M., Liefbroer, A., Otten, R., & Olsman, E. (2019). Spiritual care in palliative care: A systematic review of the recent european literature. *Medical Science*, *7*(2), 25. DOI: 10.3390/medsci7020025 PMID: 30736416

Golparvar, M., & Parsakia, K. (2023). Building resilience: Psychological approaches to prevent burnout in health professionals. *KMAN Counsel and Psych Nexus*, *1*(1), 159–166. DOI: 10.61838/kman.psynexus.1.1.18

Greene, S. M., Tuzzio, L., & Cherkin, D. (2012). A framework for making patient-centered care front and center. *The Permanente Journal*, *16*(3), 49–53. DOI: 10.7812/TPP/12-025 PMID: 23012599

Griffith, D. (2016). Biopsychosocial approaches to men's health disparities research and policy. *Behavioral Medicine (Washington, D.C.)*, *42*(3), 211–215. DOI: 10.1080/08964289.2016.1194158 PMID: 27337626

Guo, J., & Li, B. (2018). The application of medical artificial intelligence technology in rural areas of developing countries. *Health Equity*, *2*(1), 174–181. DOI: 10.1089/heq.2018.0037 PMID: 30283865

Guo, R., Berkshire, S. D., Fulton, L. V., & Hermanson, P. M. (2017). Use of evidence-based management in healthcare administration decision-making. *Leadership in Health Services*, *30*(3), 330–342. DOI: 10.1108/LHS-07-2016-0033 PMID: 28693398

Gupta, K., Anand, T., Kaur, G., Thapliyal, S., & Lal, P. (2022). Job satisfaction among medical officers working in delhi. *Journal of Family Medicine and Primary Care, 11*(1), 155–161. DOI: 10.4103/jfmpc.jfmpc_268_21 PMID: 35309650

Gyedu, A., Abantanga, F., Boakye, G., Gupta, S., Otupiri, E., Agbeko, A., Kushner, A., & Stewart, B. (2016). Barriers to essential surgical care experienced by women in the two northernmost regions of ghana: A cross-sectional survey. *BMC Women's Health, 16*(1), 27. Advance online publication. DOI: 10.1186/s12905-016-0308-4 PMID: 27230890

Haileamlak, A. (2018). Editorial: The triple challenges of low and middle-income countries. *Ethiopian Journal of Health Sciences, 28*(1), 1. DOI: 10.4314/ejhs.v28i1.1 PMID: 29622901

Haileamlak, A. (2018). Editorial: The triple challenges of low and middle-income countries. *Ethiopian Journal of Health Sciences, 28*(1), 1. DOI: 10.4314/ejhs.v28i1.1 PMID: 29622901

Han, E., Yeo, S., Kim, M., Lee, Y., Park, K., & Roh, H. (2019). Medical education trends for future physicians in the era of advanced technology and artificial intelligence: An integrative review. *BMC Medical Education, 19*(1), 460. Advance online publication. DOI: 10.1186/s12909-019-1891-5 PMID: 31829208

Hanley, T., Winter, L., & Burrell, K. (2019). Supporting emotional well-being in schools in the context of austerity: An ecologically informed humanistic perspective. *The British Journal of Educational Psychology, 90*(1), 1–18. DOI: 10.1111/bjep.12275 PMID: 30912121

Harhash, D., Ahmed, M., & Elshereif, H. (2020). Healthcare organizational culture: A concept analysis. *Menoufia Nursing Journal, 5*(1), 55–63. DOI: 10.21608/menj.2020.123846

Harhash, D., Shrief, H., & Ahmed, M. (2021). The relationship between healthcare organizational culture and nurses' empowerment. *International Journal of Studies in Nursing, 6*(4), 87. DOI: 10.20849/ijsn.v6i4.975

Hassen, N., Lofters, A., Michael, S., Mall, A., Pinto, A., & Rackal, J. (2021). Implementing anti-racism interventions in healthcare settings: A scoping review. *International Journal of Environmental Research and Public Health, 18*(6), 2993. DOI: 10.3390/ijerph18062993 PMID: 33803942

Haveri, S., Nm, S., & Nath, A. (2016). Attitude of medical students towards learning communication skills. *International Journal of Community Medicine and Public Health, 157-160*, 157–160. Advance online publication. DOI: 10.18203/2394-6040.ijcmph20151553

He, Z., Gan, L., Li, X., Shao, X., Zuo, L., Gao, J., & Chen, H. (2021). The implementation of patient-centered humanistic care for covid-19 closely contacted hemodialysis patients under the hospital-based group medical quarantine: A brief research report. *Frontiers in Psychology*, *12*, 553234. Advance online publication. DOI: 10.3389/fpsyg.2021.553234 PMID: 34690846

Hirpa, M., Woreta, T., Addis, H., & Kebede, S. (2020). What matters to patients? a timely question for value-based care. *PLoS One*, *15*(7), e0227845. DOI: 10.1371/journal.pone.0227845 PMID: 32644993

Holzinger, A., Langs, G., Denk, H., Zatloukal, K., & Müller, H. (2019). Causability and explainability of artificial intelligence in medicine. *Wiley Interdisciplinary Reviews. Data Mining and Knowledge Discovery*, *9*(4), e1312. Advance online publication. DOI: 10.1002/widm.1312 PMID: 32089788

Horowitz, C., Suchman, A., Branch, W.Jr, & Frankel, R. (2003). What do doctors find meaningful about their work? *Annals of Internal Medicine*, *138*(9), 772–775. DOI: 10.7326/0003-4819-138-9-200305060-00028 PMID: 12729445

Huang, Q. (2023). Role of narrative education in cultivating humanistic care and empathy in nursing students. DOI: 10.21203/rs.3.rs-3284130/v1

Hulail, M. (2018). Humanism in medical practice: What, why and how? *Hospice and Palliative Medicine International Journal*, *2*(6). Advance online publication. DOI: 10.15406/hpmij.2018.02.00119

Hung, M., Zhang, W., Chen, W., Bounsanga, J., Cheng, C., Franklin, J. D., Crum, A. B., Voss, M. W., & Hon, S. D. (2015). Patient-reported outcomes and total health care expenditure in prediction of patient satisfaction: Results from a national study. *JMIR Public Health and Surveillance*, *1*(2), e4360. DOI: 10.2196/publichealth.4360 PMID: 27227131

İbrahimoğlu, Ö., Mersin, S., & Çağlar, M. (2020). The turkish adaptation of the compassionate communication scale: A validity and reliability study. *Perspectives in Psychiatric Care*, *57*(1), 43–49. DOI: 10.1111/ppc.12522 PMID: 32314364

Ikeda, K., Tasaka, A., Kasubuchi, K., Jono, Y., & Matsuda, J. (2022). Work beliefs and experiential learning among proficient physical therapists in japan: Developing a method to support belief formation. *Journal of Physical Therapy Science*, *34*(4), 262–268. DOI: 10.1589/jpts.34.262 PMID: 35400828

Jaiswal, C., Anderson, K., & Haesler, E. (2019). A self-report of the healer's art by junior doctors: Does the course have a lasting influence on personal experience of humanism, self-nurturing skills and medical counterculture? *BMC Medical Education*, *19*(1), 443. Advance online publication. DOI: 10.1186/s12909-019-1877-3 PMID: 31783846

Jha, N., Shankar, P., Al-Betar, M., Mukhia, R., Hada, K., & Palaian, S. (2022). Undergraduate medical students' and interns' knowledge and perception of artificial intelligence in medicine. *Advances in Medical Education and Practice*, *13*, 927–937. DOI: 10.2147/AMEP.S368519 PMID: 36039185

Jiang, K., Tian, L., Yan, C., Li, Y., Fang, H., Sun, P., & Liu, M. (2019). A cross-sectional survey on patient safety culture in secondary hospitals of northeast china. *PLoS One*, *14*(3), e0213055. DOI: 10.1371/journal.pone.0213055 PMID: 30893337

Jones, D. (2014). A complete medical education includes the arts and humanities. *The Virtual Mentor*, *16*(8), 636–641. DOI: 10.1001/virtualmentor.2014.16.08.msoc1-1408 PMID: 25140687

Kato, K., Tomita, M., Kato, M., Goto, T., & Nishizono, K. (2021). Prospective cohort study on the incidence and risk factors of emergency home visits among japanese home care patients. *Journal of General and Family Medicine*, *22*(6), 334–340. DOI: 10.1002/jgf2.461 PMID: 34754711

Kaye, D. R., Richardson, C. R., Ye, Z., Herrel, L. A., Ellimoottil, C., & Miller, D. C. (2017). Association between patient satisfaction and short-term outcomes after major cancer surgery. *Annals of Surgical Oncology*, *24*(12), 3486–3493. DOI: 10.1245/s10434-017-6049-2 PMID: 28819930

Kekeghe, S. (2021). Dramatic art, medical ethics and rehabilitation: Patient-centred therapeutic relationship in omobowale's <i>the president's physician</i>. *International Journal of Literature and Arts*, *9*(4), 177. DOI: 10.11648/j.ijla.20210904.16

Kelly, E., Hyer, M., Payne, N., & Pawlik, T. (2020). A mixed-methods approach to understanding the role of religion and spirituality in healthcare provider well-being. *Psychology of Religion and Spirituality*, *12*(4), 487–493. DOI: 10.1037/rel0000297

Kennedy, G. D., Tevis, S. E., & Kent, K. C. (2014). Is there a relationship between patient satisfaction and favorable outcomes? *Annals of Surgery*, *260*(4), 592–600. DOI: 10.1097/SLA.0000000000000932 PMID: 25203875

Kerry, R., Young, K. J., Evans, D. W., Lee, E., Georgopoulos, V., Meakins, A., McCarthy, C., Cook, C., Ridehalgh, C., Vogel, S., Banton, A., Bergström, C., Mazzieri, A. M., Mourad, F., & Hutting, N. (2024). A modern way to teach and practice manual therapy. *Chiropractic & Manual Therapies*, *32*(1), 17. Advance online publication. DOI: 10.1186/s12998-024-00537-0 PMID: 38773515

Khademi, M., Mohammadi, E., & Vanaki, Z. (2016). A grounded theory of humanistic nursing in acute care work environments. *Nursing Ethics*, *24*(8), 908–921. DOI: 10.1177/0969733016638140 PMID: 27009740

Kim, J., Kim, J., Shen, E., & Yoon, J. (2022). Sustaining the intrinsic motivations of the "good physician": A content analysis of medical students' and physicians' responses from two national surveys. *Southern Medical Journal*, *115*(10), 727–733. DOI: 10.14423/SMJ.0000000000001450 PMID: 36191907

Klop, H., Veer, A., Dongen, S., Francké, A., Rietjens, J., & Onwuteaka-Philipsen, B. (2018). Palliative care for homeless people: A systematic review of the concerns, care needs and preferences, and the barriers and facilitators for providing palliative care. *BMC Palliative Care*, *17*(1), 67. Advance online publication. DOI: 10.1186/s12904-018-0320-6 PMID: 29690870

Kogan, A. C., Wilber, K. H., & Mosqueda, L. (2015). Person-centered care for older adults with chronic conditions and functional impairment: A systematic literature review. *Journal of the American Geriatrics Society*, *64*(1). Advance online publication. DOI: 10.1111/jgs.13873 PMID: 26626408

Koon, V. (2024). Unveiling the impact of corporate humanistic responsibility on sustainable employee well-being: Exploring perceived support and shared experiences. Business Strategy &Amp. *Business Strategy & Development*, *7*(2), e381. Advance online publication. DOI: 10.1002/bsd2.381

Koper, I., Pasman, H., Schweitzer, B., Kuin, A., & Onwuteaka-Philipsen, B. (2019). Spiritual care at the end of life in the primary care setting: Experiences from spiritual caregivers - a mixed methods study. *BMC Palliative Care*, *18*(1), 98. Advance online publication. DOI: 10.1186/s12904-019-0484-8 PMID: 31706355

Koponen, J., Pyörälä, E., & Isotalus, P. (2012). Comparing three experiential learning methods and their effect on medical students' attitudes to learning communication skills. *Medical Teacher*, *34*(3), e198–e207. DOI: 10.3109/0142159X.2012.642828 PMID: 22364477

Koponen, J., Pyörälä, E., & Isotalus, P. (2014). Communication skills for medical students. *Simulation & Gaming*, *45*(2), 235–254. DOI: 10.1177/1046878114538915

Kutac, J., Osipov, R., & Childress, A. (2015). Innovation through tradition: Rediscovering the "humanist" in the medical humanities. *The Journal of Medical Humanities*, *37*(4), 371–387. DOI: 10.1007/s10912-015-9364-2 PMID: 26561349

Lavoie-Tremblay, M., Boies, K., Clausen, C., Frechette, J., Manning, K., Gelsomini, C., Cyr, G., Lavigne, G., Gottlieb, B., & Gottlieb, L. N. (2024). Evaluation of the effectiveness of a strengths-based nursing and healthcare leadership program aimed at building leadership capacity: A concurrent mixed-methods study. *International Journal of Nursing Studies Advances*, *6*, 100184. DOI: 10.1016/j.ijnsa.2024.100184 PMID: 38746801

Lawati, M., Dennis, S., Short, S., & Abdulhadi, N. (2018). Patient safety and safety culture in primary health care: A systematic review. *BMC Family Practice*, *19*(1), 104. Advance online publication. DOI: 10.1186/s12875-018-0793-7 PMID: 29960590

Lee, J., Slack, M., Martin, J., Ehrman, C., & Chisholm-Burns, M. (2013). Geriatric patient care by u.s. pharmacists in healthcare teams: Systematic review and meta-analyses. *Journal of the American Geriatrics Society*, *61*(7), 1119–1127. DOI: 10.1111/jgs.12323 PMID: 23796001

Lee, W., Harris, C., Mortensen, K., Long, L., & Sugimoto-Matsuda, J. (2016). Enhancing student perspectives of humanism in medicine: Reflections from the kalaupapa service learning project. *BMC Medical Education*, *16*(1), 137. Advance online publication. DOI: 10.1186/s12909-016-0664-7 PMID: 27159976

Létourneau, D., Goudreau, J., & Cara, C. (2020). Facilitating and hindering experiences to the development of humanistic caring in the academic and clinical settings: An interpretive phenomenological study with nursing students and nurses. *International Journal of Nursing Education Scholarship*, *17*(1), 20190036. Advance online publication. DOI: 10.1515/ijnes-2019-0036 PMID: 32710718

Létourneau, D., Goudreau, J., & Cara, C. (2020). Facilitating and hindering experiences to the development of humanistic caring in the academic and clinical settings: An interpretive phenomenological study with nursing students and nurses. *International Journal of Nursing Education Scholarship*, *17*(1), 20190036. Advance online publication. DOI: 10.1515/ijnes-2019-0036 PMID: 32710718

Lev, N. (2024). Strategic healthcare workforce planning in light of healthcare inequalities: a comparative analysis of workforce planning policy in israel and comparable oecd countries. DOI: 10.20944/preprints202406.0066.v1

Liang, M., Liang, J., Xu, J., Chen, Q., & Lu, Q. (2024). Experience of multidisciplinary medical teams on humanistic palliative care in oncology wards: A descriptive qualitative study in southern china. *BMJ Open*, *14*(2), e074628. DOI: 10.1136/bmjopen-2023-074628 PMID: 38413159

Liang, M., Liang, J., Xu, J., Chen, Q., & Lu, Q. (2024). Experience of multidisciplinary medical teams on humanistic palliative care in oncology wards: A descriptive qualitative study in southern china. *BMJ Open*, *14*(2), e074628. DOI: 10.1136/bmjopen-2023-074628 PMID: 38413159

Liang, M., Liang, J., Xu, J., Chen, Q., & Lu, Q. (2024). Experience of multidisciplinary medical teams on humanistic palliative care in oncology wards: A descriptive qualitative study in southern china. *BMJ Open*, *14*(2), e074628. DOI: 10.1136/bmjopen-2023-074628 PMID: 38413159

Liao, L., Zhang, F., Zhang, Y., Guan, C., Xu, G., Yuan, C., Yang, X., Huang, L., Wang, W., He, X., Xu, J., & Liu, Y. (2023). Nurse managers' perceptions and experiences of caring behavior for clinical nurses: A multicenter survey. *BMC Nursing*, *22*(1), 383. Advance online publication. DOI: 10.1186/s12912-023-01541-0 PMID: 37845648

Liikanen, E., & Lehto, L. (2013). Training of nurses in point-of-care testing: A systematic review of the literature. *Journal of Clinical Nursing*, *22*(15-16), 2244–2252. DOI: 10.1111/jocn.12235 PMID: 23679832

Lin, Y., & Lin, C. (2010). Factors predicting patients' perception of privacy and satisfaction for emergency care. *Emergency Medicine Journal : EMJ*, *28*(7), 604–608. DOI: 10.1136/emj.2010.093807 PMID: 20660898

Lina, M., Qin, G., & Yang, L. (2022). Mediating effects of emotional intelligence on the relationship between empathy and humanistic care ability in nursing students: A cross-sectional descriptive study. *Medicine*, *101*(46), e31673. DOI: 10.1097/MD.0000000000031673 PMID: 36401377

Liu, Y., Zhang, F., Guan, C., Song, B., Zhang, H., Fu, M., Wang, F., Tang, C., Chen, H., Guo, Q., Fan, L., Hou, X., Wang, H., Wu, B., Shan, G., Zhang, H., Yu, F., Lou, X., Xie, H., & Guo, S. (2023). Patient satisfaction with humanistic nursing in chinese secondary and tertiary public hospitals: A cross-sectional survey. *Frontiers in Public Health*, *11*, 1163351. Advance online publication. DOI: 10.3389/fpubh.2023.1163351 PMID: 37711237

Liu, Y., Zhang, F., Guan, C., Song, B., Zhang, H., Fu, M., Wang, F., Tang, C., Chen, H., Guo, Q., Fan, L., Hou, X., Wang, H., Wu, B., Shan, G., Zhang, H., Yu, F., Lou, X., Xie, H., & Guo, S. (2023). Patient satisfaction with humanistic nursing in chinese secondary and tertiary public hospitals: A cross-sectional survey. *Frontiers in Public Health, 11*, 1163351. Advance online publication. DOI: 10.3389/fpubh.2023.1163351 PMID: 37711237

Liu, Y., Zhang, F., Guan, C., Song, B., Zhang, H., Fu, M., Wang, F., Tang, C., Chen, H., Guo, Q., Fan, L., Hou, X., Wang, H., Wu, B., Shan, G., Zhang, H., Yu, F., Lou, X., Xie, H., & Guo, S. (2023). Patient satisfaction with humanistic nursing in Chinese secondary and tertiary public hospitals: A cross-sectional survey. *Frontiers in Public Health, 11*, 1163351. DOI: 10.3389/fpubh.2023.1163351 PMID: 37711237

Lowery, B. (2010). Interagency collaboration: A strategy for obesity policy success. *Bariatric Nursing and Surgical Patient Care, 5*(4), 331–334. DOI: 10.1089/bar.2010.9989

Lowery, B. (2011). The future of nursing report: Policy implications for nursing. *Bariatric Nursing and Surgical Patient Care, 6*(1), 49–51. DOI: 10.1089/bar.2011.9980

Lu, D., Dresden, S., McCloskey, C., Branzetti, J., & Gisondi, M. (2015). Impact of burnout on self-reported patient care among emergency physicians. *The Western Journal of Emergency Medicine, 16*(7), 996–1001. DOI: 10.5811/westjem.2015.9.27945 PMID: 26759643

Lucchetti, G., Lucchetti, A., Espinha, D., Oliveira, L., Leite, J., & Koenig, H. (2012). Spirituality and health in the curricula of medical schools in brazil. *BMC Medical Education, 12*(1), 78. Advance online publication. DOI: 10.1186/1472-6920-12-78 PMID: 22900476

Lucchetti, G., Oliveira, L., Koenig, H., Leite, J., & Lucchetti, A. (2013). Medical students, spirituality and religiosity-results from the multicenter study sbrame. *BMC Medical Education, 13*(1), 162. Advance online publication. DOI: 10.1186/1472-6920-13-162 PMID: 24314327

Ma, F., Zhu, Y., Liu, Y., & Lu, L. (2023). Association analysis of nursing humanistic care demands and psychological distress in cancer surgery patients: a cross-sectional study. DOI: 10.21203/rs.3.rs-1878362/v2

Mahendradhata, Y., Souares, A., Phalkey, R., & Sauerborn, R. (2014). Optimizing patient-centeredness in the transitions of healthcare systems in low- and middle-income countries. *BMC Health Services Research, 14*(1), 386. Advance online publication. DOI: 10.1186/1472-6963-14-386 PMID: 25212684

Mahendradhata, Y., Souares, A., Phalkey, R., & Sauerborn, R. (2014). Optimizing patient-centeredness in the transitions of healthcare systems in low- and middle-income countries. *BMC Health Services Research*, *14*(1), 386. Advance online publication. DOI: 10.1186/1472-6963-14-386 PMID: 25212684

Marshman, C., Allen, J., Ling, D., & Brand, G. (2024). 'it's very values driven': A qualitative systematic review of the meaning of compassion according to healthcare professionals. *Journal of Clinical Nursing*, *33*(5), 1647–1665. DOI: 10.1111/jocn.16998 PMID: 38240044

Marterre, B., Hinshaw, D., & Shinall, M. (2023). Spirituality in surgery-a double-edged scalpel. *The American Surgeon*, *89*(5), 1347–1351. DOI: 10.1177/00031348231157805 PMID: 36786501

Mazur, B. (2024). Organizational culture in enterprises applying the humanistic and economic paradigm of management.. DOI: 10.5772/intechopen.113155

McDowell, L., & South, R. (2017). Christians' perceptions of receiving spiritual care in the bible belt of the united states: A qualitative study of care provided in the healthcare setting. *Religions*, *8*(7), 127. DOI: 10.3390/rel8070127

McSherry, W., & Jamieson, S. (2013). The qualitative findings from an online survey investigating nurses' perceptions of spirituality and spiritual care. *Journal of Clinical Nursing*, *22*(21-22), 3170–3182. DOI: 10.1111/jocn.12411 PMID: 24118520

Miles, A. (2013). Science, humanism, judgement, ethics: Person-centered medicine as an emergent model of modern clinical practice / наука, гуманизм, преценка, этика, пациент. гуманизм в медицина - новая модель в современн ой клинической практике. *Folia Medica*, *55*(1), 5–24. DOI: 10.2478/folmed-2013-0001 PMID: 23905483

1. Miles, A. (2013). Science, humanism, judgement, ethics: Person-centered medicine as an emergent model of modern clinical practice / наука, гуманизм, преценка, этика, пациент. гуманизм в медицина - новая модель в современн ой клинической практике. *Folia Medica*, *55*(1), 5–24. DOI: 10.2478/folmed-2013-0001 PMID: 23905483

Mitchell, C., Epstein-Peterson, Z., Bandini, J., Amobi, A., Cahill, J., Enzinger, A., Noveroske, S., Peteet, J., Balboni, T., & Balboni, M. (2016). Developing a medical school curriculum for psychological, moral, and spiritual wellness: Student and faculty perspectives. *Journal of Pain and Symptom Management*, *52*(5), 727–736. DOI: 10.1016/j.jpainsymman.2016.05.018 PMID: 27693904

Mohamad, F., & Abiddin, N. Z. (2024). Enhancing employee well-being and productivity in evolving work environments. *Academic Journal of Interdisciplinary Studies*, *13*(3), 289. DOI: 10.36941/ajis-2024-0081

Monteith, S., Glenn, T., Geddes, J., Whybrow, P., Achtyes, E., & Bauer, M. (2022). Expectations for artificial intelligence (ai) in psychiatry. *Current Psychiatry Reports*, *24*(11), 709–721. DOI: 10.1007/s11920-022-01378-5 PMID: 36214931

Mostafa, A., Hoque, R., Mostafa, M., Rana, M., & Mostafa, F. (2014). Empathy in undergraduate medical students of bangladesh: Psychometric analysis and differences by gender, academic year, and specialty preferences. *ISRN Psychiatry*, *2014*, 1–7. DOI: 10.1155/2014/375439 PMID: 25006522

Mustika, R., & Soemantri, D. (2020). Unveiling the hurdles in cultivating humanistic physicians in the clinical setting: An exploratory study. *The Malaysian Journal of Medical Sciences : MJMS*, *27*(3), 117–124. DOI: 10.21315/mjms2020.27.3.12 PMID: 32684812

Mustika, R., & Soemantri, D. (2020). Unveiling the hurdles in cultivating humanistic physicians in the clinical setting: An exploratory study. *The Malaysian Journal of Medical Sciences : MJMS*, *27*(3), 117–124. DOI: 10.21315/mjms2020.27.3.12 PMID: 32684812

Nazir, M., Wayenberg, E., & Qureshi, S. (2023). Exploring the role of policy actors in the implementation of social distancing: A case of covid-19 in pakistan. *Public Administration and Policy*, *26*(1), 93–106. DOI: 10.1108/PAP-04-2022-0033

Nelson, L., Maramaldi, P., Kinnunen, T., & Kalenderian, E. (2013). Early performance in a humanistic medicine course as a predictor of dental students' later clinical performance. *Journal of Dental Education*, *77*(8), 1006–1012. DOI: 10.1002/j.0022-0337.2013.77.8.tb05569.x PMID: 23929570

Nelson, L. P., Maramaldi, P., Kinnunen, T., & Kalenderian, E. (2013). Early performance in a humanistic medicine course as a predictor of dental students' later clinical performance. *Journal of Dental Education*, *77*(8), 1006–1012. DOI: 10.1002/j.0022-0337.2013.77.8.tb05569.x PMID: 23929570

October, T., Hinds, P., Wang, J., Dizon, Z., Cheng, Y., & Roter, D. (2016). Parent satisfaction with communication is associated with physician's patient-centered communication patterns during family conferences*. *Pediatric Critical Care Medicine*, *17*(6), 490–497. DOI: 10.1097/PCC.0000000000000719 PMID: 27058750

Oduoye, M., Fatima, E., Muzammil, M. A., Dave, T., Irfan, H., Fariha, F. N. U., Marbell, A., Ubechu, S. C., Scott, G. Y., & Elebesunu, E. E. (2024). Impacts of the advancement in artificial intelligence on laboratory medicine in low- and middle-income countries: Challenges and recommendations—a literature review. *Health Science Reports*, *7*(1), e1794. Advance online publication. DOI: 10.1002/hsr2.1794 PMID: 38186931

Olin, S., Williams, N., Pollock, M., Armusewicz, K., Kutash, K., Glisson, C., & Hoagwood, K. (2013). Quality indicators for family support services and their relationship to organizational social context. *Administration and Policy in Mental Health*, *41*(1), 43–54. DOI: 10.1007/s10488-013-0499-z PMID: 23709286

Olorunsogo, T. (2024). Ethical considerations in ai-enhanced medical decision support systems: A review. *World Journal of Advanced Engineering Technology and Sciences*, *11*(1), 329–336. DOI: 10.30574/wjaets.2024.11.1.0061

Ordons, A. (2018). How clinicians integrate humanism in their clinical workplace—'just trying to put myself in their human being shoes'. *Perspectives on Medical Education*, *7*(5), 318–324. DOI: 10.1007/S40037-018-0455-4 PMID: 30298438

Ozdemir, C., & Kaplan, A. (2024). Examining nurses' humanistic behaviour ability and empathy levels in clinical practice: A descriptive and exploratory study. *Journal of Clinical Nursing*, *33*(8), 3115–3127. DOI: 10.1111/jocn.16992 PMID: 38234293

Ozdemir, C., & Kaplan, A. (2024). Examining nurses' humanistic behaviour ability and empathy levels in clinical practice: A descriptive and exploratory study. *Journal of Clinical Nursing*, *33*(8), 3115–3127. DOI: 10.1111/jocn.16992 PMID: 38234293

Öztürk, A., & Kaçan, H. (2021). Compassionate communication levels of nursing students: Predictive role of empathic skills and nursing communication course. *Perspectives in Psychiatric Care*, *58*(1), 248–255. DOI: 10.1111/ppc.12954 PMID: 34601733

Paal, P., Helo, Y., & Frick, E. (2015). Spiritual care training provided to healthcare professionals: A systematic review. *The Journal of Pastoral Care & Counseling*, *69*(1), 19–30. DOI: 10.1177/1542305015572955 PMID: 26162203

Parvathavarthine, C., Krishna, M., Janaki, C., Sophia, M., & Chandar, S. (2022). Awareness about the future of artificial intelligence in healthcare among medical students in kancheepuram district, tamil nadu. *International Journal of Health Sciences*, •••, 5697–5705. DOI: 10.53730/ijhs.v6nS8.13571

Pawirosumarto, S., Sarjana, P., & Gunawan, R. (2017). The effect of work environment, leadership style, and organizational culture towards job satisfaction and its implication towards employee performance in parador hotels and resorts, indonesia. *International Journal of Law and Management*, *59*(6), 1337–1358. DOI: 10.1108/IJLMA-10-2016-0085

Pentland, D., Forsyth, K., Maciver, D., Walsh, M., Murray, R., Irvine, L., & Sikora, S. (2011). Key characteristics of knowledge transfer and exchange in healthcare: Integrative literature review. *Journal of Advanced Nursing*, *67*(7), 1408–1425. DOI: 10.1111/j.1365-2648.2011.05631.x PMID: 21466576

Pentland, D., Forsyth, K., Maciver, D., Walsh, M., Murray, R., Irvine, L., & Sikora, S. (2011). Key characteristics of knowledge transfer and exchange in healthcare: Integrative literature review. *Journal of Advanced Nursing*, *67*(7), 1408–1425. DOI: 10.1111/j.1365-2648.2011.05631.x PMID: 21466576

Perrin, P. (2012). Humanistic psychology's social justice philosophy. *Journal of Humanistic Psychology*, *53*(1), 52–69. DOI: 10.1177/0022167812447133

Perry, H., Zulliger, R., & Rogers, M. (2014). Community health workers in low-, middle-, and high-income countries: An overview of their history, recent evolution, and current effectiveness. *Annual Review of Public Health*, *35*(1), 399–421. DOI: 10.1146/annurev-publhealth-032013-182354 PMID: 24387091

Peter, A., & Aighobahi, J. (2019). Assessment of the implementation of tuberculosis and diabetes care in health systems: a situational analysis in western nigeria for consideration. DOI: 10.21203/rs.2.12294/v1

Petersen, I., Rensburg, A., Kigozi, F., Semrau, M., Hanlon, C., Abdulmalik, J., & Thornicroft, G. (2019). Scaling up integrated primary mental health in six low- and middle-income countries: Obstacles, synergies and implications for systems reform. *BJPsych Open*, *5*(5), e69. Advance online publication. DOI: 10.1192/bjo.2019.7 PMID: 31530322

Puchalski, C., Blatt, B., Kогaн, M., & Butler, A. (2014). Spirituality and health. *Academic Medicine*, *89*(1), 10–16. DOI: 10.1097/ACM.0000000000000083 PMID: 24280839

Raja, S., Hasnain, M., Vadakumchery, T., Hamad, J., Shah, R., & Hoersch, M. (2015). Identifying elements of patient-centered care in underserved populations: A qualitative study of patient perspectives. *PLoS One*, *10*(5), e0126708. DOI: 10.1371/journal.pone.0126708 PMID: 25993110

Rambiritch, V., Vermeulen, M., Bell, H., Knox, P., Nedelcu, E., Al-Riyami, A., & Berg, K. (2021). Transfusion medicine and blood banking education and training for blood establishment laboratory staff: A review of selected countries in africa. *Transfusion*, *61*(6), 1955–1965. DOI: 10.1111/trf.16372 PMID: 33738810

Rathod, S., Pinninti, N., Irfan, M., Gorczynski, P., Rathod, P., Gega, L., & Naeem, F. (2017). Mental health service provision in low- and middle-income countries. *Health Services Insights*, *10*, 1178632917694350. Advance online publication. DOI: 10.1177/1178632917694350 PMID: 28469456

Rêgo, F., & Nunes, R. (2016). The interface between psychology and spirituality in palliative care. *Journal of Health Psychology*, *24*(3), 279–287. DOI: 10.1177/1359105316664138 PMID: 27531369

Rider, E., Gilligan, M., Osterberg, L., Litzelman, D., Plews-Ogan, M., Weil, A., Dunne, D. W., Hafler, J. P., May, N. B., Derse, A. R., Frankel, R. M., & Branch, W.Jr. (2018). Healthcare at the crossroads: The need to shape an organizational culture of humanistic teaching and practice. *Journal of General Internal Medicine*, *33*(7), 1092–1099. DOI: 10.1007/s11606-018-4470-2 PMID: 29740787

Rider, E. A., Gilligan, M. A., Osterberg, L., Litzelman, D. K., Plews-Ogan, M., Weil, A., Dunne, D. W., Hafler, J. P., May, N. B., Derse, A. R., Frankel, R. M., & Branch, W. T.Jr. (2018). Healthcare at the crossroads: The need to shape an organizational culture of humanistic teaching and practice. *Journal of General Internal Medicine*, *33*(7), 1092–1099. DOI: 10.1007/s11606-018-4470-2 PMID: 29740787

Roosen, I., Salway, S., & Osei-Kwasi, H. A. (2021). Transnational social networks, health, and care: A systematic narrative literature review. *International Journal for Equity in Health*, *20*(1), 138. Advance online publication. DOI: 10.1186/s12939-021-01467-6 PMID: 34118934

Rosenthal, E., Brownstein, J., Rush, C., Hirsch, G., Willaert, A., Scott, J., Holderby, L. R., & Fox, D. (2010). Community health workers: Part of the solution. *Health Affairs*, *29*(7), 1338–1342. DOI: 10.1377/hlthaff.2010.0081 PMID: 20606185

Ruelas, E., Gómez-Dantés, O., Leatherman, S., Fortune, T., & Gay-Molina, J. (2012). Strengthening the quality agenda in health care in low- and middle-income countries: Questions to consider. *International Journal for Quality in Health Care : Journal of the International Society for Quality in Health Care*, *24*(6), 553–557. DOI: 10.1093/intqhc/mzs061 PMID: 23074183

Saasouh, W., Ghanem, K., Al-Saidi, N., LeQuia, L., McKelvey, G., & Jaffar, M. (2024). Patient-centered perspectives on perioperative care. *Frontiers in Anesthesiology*, *3*, 1267127. Advance online publication. DOI: 10.3389/fanes.2024.1267127

Sarkar, S., Verma, R., & Singh, S. (2022). Faculty and students' perceptions on experiential learning based anatomy dissection hall sessions for medical undergraduates. *Advances in Medical Education and Practice*, *13*, 543–554. DOI: 10.2147/AMEP.S359140 PMID: 35651479

Scammon, D. L., Tabler, J., Brunisholz, K. D., Gren, L. H., Kim, J., Tomoaia-Cotisel, A., Day, J., Farrell, T. W., Waitzman, N. J., & Magill, M. K. (2014). Organizational culture associated with provider satisfaction. *Journal of the American Board of Family Medicine : JABFM*, *27*(2), 219–228. DOI: 10.3122/jabfm.2014.02.120338 PMID: 24610184

Schaaf, J., Sedlmayr, M., Schaefer, J., & Storf, H. (2020). Diagnosis of rare diseases: A scoping review of clinical decision support systems. *Orphanet Journal of Rare Diseases*, *15*(1), 263. Advance online publication. DOI: 10.1186/s13023-020-01536-z PMID: 32972444

Scheepers, R., Boerebach, B., Arah, O., Heineman, M., & Lombarts, K. (2015). A systematic review of the impact of physicians' occupational well-being on the quality of patient care. *International Journal of Behavioral Medicine*, *22*(6), 683–698. DOI: 10.1007/s12529-015-9473-3 PMID: 25733349

Seddigh, R., Azarnik, S., Memaryan, N., & Hadi, F. (2020). Spirituality as a sociocultural determinant of health in the context of medical curriculum: A call for action. *Medical Journal of the Islamic Republic of Iran*. Advance online publication. DOI: 10.47176/mjiri.34.6 PMID: 32284930

Sessanna, L., Finnell, D. S., Underhill, M. L., Chang, Y. P., & Peng, H. L. (2011). Measures assessing spirituality as more than religiosity: A methodological review of nursing and health-related literature. *Journal of Advanced Nursing*, *67*(8), 1677–1694. DOI: 10.1111/j.1365-2648.2010.05596.x PMID: 21371082

Shapiro, J., Coulehan, J., Wear, D., & Montello, M. (2009). Medical humanities and their discontents: Definitions, critiques, and implications. *Academic Medicine*, *84*(2), 192–198. DOI: 10.1097/ACM.0b013e3181938bca PMID: 19174663

Sharmake, A. (2024). Healthcare disparities among socioeconomic groups. *IJHSS*, *2*(5), 50–63. DOI: 10.47941/ijhss.1889

Shen, Q. and Tang, L. (2021). Analysis on clinical effects of humanistic nursing care on chronic pelvic inflammatory disease. ijps, 83. DOI: 10.36468/pharmaceutical-sciences.spl.222

Shinners, L., Aggar, C., Grace, S., & Smith, S. (2019). Exploring healthcare professionals' understanding and experiences of artificial intelligence technology use in the delivery of healthcare: An integrative review. *Health Informatics Journal, 26*(2), 1225–1236. DOI: 10.1177/1460458219874641 PMID: 31566454

Shinners, L., Aggar, C., Grace, S., & Smith, S. (2019). Exploring healthcare professionals' understanding and experiences of artificial intelligence technology use in the delivery of healthcare: An integrative review. *Health Informatics Journal, 26*(2), 1225–1236. DOI: 10.1177/1460458219874641 PMID: 31566454

Shinners, L., Aggar, C., Stephens, A., & Grace, S. (2023). Healthcare professionals' experiences and perceptions of artificial intelligence in regional and rural health districts in australia. *The Australian Journal of Rural Health, 31*(6), 1203–1213. DOI: 10.1111/ajr.13045 PMID: 37795659

Shojaei, H., Lakha, S., Lyon, A., Halabecki, M., Donaghy, M., & Mailis, A. (2022). Evolution of a chronic pain management program in a northwestern ontario community: From structural elements to practical application. *BMC Health Services Research, 22*(1), 1355. Advance online publication. DOI: 10.1186/s12913-022-08766-w PMID: 36380300

Shyamala, K., Kulkarni, V., Shenoy, V., & Khatri, B. (2022). Impact of communication skills training in postgraduate medical education. *National Journal of Community Medicine, 13*(06), 359–363. DOI: 10.55489/njcm.13062022403

Simha, S., Noble, S., & Chaturvedi, S. (2013). Spiritual concerns in hindu cancer patients undergoing palliative care: A qualitative study. *Indian Journal of Palliative Care, 19*(2), 99. DOI: 10.4103/0973-1075.116716 PMID: 24049350

Sinclair, S., Norris, J., McConnell, S., Chochinov, H., Hack, T., Hagen, N., McClement, S., & Bouchal, S. (2016). Compassion: A scoping review of the healthcare literature. *BMC Palliative Care, 15*(1), 6. Advance online publication. DOI: 10.1186/s12904-016-0080-0 PMID: 26786417

Sinha, R., Roy, A., Kumar, N., & Mondal, H. (2023). Applicability of chatgpt in assisting to solve higher order problems in pathology. *Cureus*. Advance online publication. DOI: 10.7759/cureus.35237 PMID: 36968864

Sit, C., Srinivasan, R., Amlani, A., Muthuswamy, K., Azam, A., Monzon, L., & Poon, D. (2020). Attitudes and perceptions of uk medical students towards artificial intelligence and radiology: A multicentre survey. *Insights Into Imaging, 11*(1), 14. Advance online publication. DOI: 10.1186/s13244-019-0830-7 PMID: 32025951

Soler, O., & Barreto, J. (2019). Community-level pharmaceutical interventions to reduce the risks of polypharmacy in the elderly: Overview of systematic reviews and economic evaluations. *Frontiers in Pharmacology*, *10*, 302. Advance online publication. DOI: 10.3389/fphar.2019.00302 PMID: 31001117

Sony, M., Antony, J., & McDermott, O. (2022). The impact of medical cyber–physical systems on healthcare service delivery. *The TQM Journal*, *34*(7), 73–93. DOI: 10.1108/TQM-01-2022-0005

Stagno, S., Crapanzano, K., & Schwartz, A. (2016). Keeping the patient at the center: Teaching about elements of patient-centered care. *MedEdPORTAL: the Journal of Teaching and Learning Resources*, 10500. Advance online publication. DOI: 10.15766/mep_2374-8265.10500 PMID: 30984842

Suhaimi, A., Ibrahim, N., Tan, K., Silim, U., Moore, G., Ryan, B., & Castle, D. J. (2020). Effectiveness of a culturally adapted biopsychosocial intervention (pohon sihat) in improving self-efficacy in patients with diabetes attending primary health-care clinics in putrajaya, malaysia: Study protocol of a randomised controlled trial. *BMJ Open*, *10*(2), e033920. DOI: 10.1136/bmjopen-2019-033920 PMID: 32066607

Sullivan, B., Esmaili, B., & Cunningham, C. (2017). Barriers to initiating tuberculosis treatment in sub-saharan africa: A systematic review focused on children and youth. *Global Health Action*, *10*(1), 1290317. Advance online publication. DOI: 10.1080/16549716.2017.1290317 PMID: 28598771

Tanaka, K., & Son, D. (2019). Experiential learning for junior residents as a part of community-based medical education in japan. *Education for Primary Care*, *30*(5), 282–288. DOI: 10.1080/14739879.2019.1625288 PMID: 31185822

Taskiran, N.TAŞKIRAN. (2023). Effect of artificial intelligence course in nursing on students' medical artificial intelligence readiness. *Nurse Educator*, *48*(5), E147–E152. DOI: 10.1097/NNE.0000000000001446 PMID: 37133231

Tavares, L., Enns, S., Ayres, J., & Tempski, P. (2020). Humanism in the narratives of first-year medical students. DOI: 10.21203/rs.2.24827/v2

Taverna, M., Berberat, P., Sattel, H., & Frick, E. (2019). A Survey on the Integration of Spiritual Care in Medical Schools from the German-Speaking Faculties. *Advances in Medical Education and Practice*, *10*, 1009–1019. DOI: 10.2147/AMEP.S224679 PMID: 31839718

Thibault, G. (2019). Humanism in medicine: What does it mean and why is it more important than ever? *Academic Medicine*, *94*(8), 1074–1077. DOI: 10.1097/ACM.0000000000002796 PMID: 31135401

Thibault, G. E. (2019). Humanism in medicine: What does it mean and why is it more important than ever? *Academic Medicine*, *94*(8), 1074–1077. DOI: 10.1097/ACM.0000000000002796 PMID: 31135401

Tierney, S., Seers, K., Tutton, E., & Reeve, J. (2017). Enabling the flow of compassionate care: A grounded theory study. *BMC Health Services Research*, *17*(1), 174. Advance online publication. DOI: 10.1186/s12913-017-2120-8 PMID: 28253874

Tran, B., Vu, G., Ha, G., Vuong, Q., H , M., Vuong, T., La, V.-P., Ho, M.-T., Nghiem, K.-C. P., Nguyen, H. L. T., Latkin, C. A., Tam, W. W. S., Cheung, N.-M., Nguyen, H.-K. T., Ho, C. S. H., & Ho, R. (2019). Global evolution of research in artificial intelligence in health and medicine: A bibliometric study. *Journal of Clinical Medicine*, *8*(3), 360. DOI: 10.3390/jcm8030360 PMID: 30875745

Turabián, J. (2022). The biopsychosocial approach gives relevance to general medicine as a tool of public health. *Medpress Public Health and Epidemiolog*, *1*(1). Advance online publication. DOI: 10.33582/mpphe.2022.202210006

Umene-Nakano, W., Kato, T. A., Kikuchi, S., Tateno, M., Fujisawa, D., Hoshuyama, T., & Nakamura, J. (2013). Nationwide survey of work environment, work-life balance and burnout among psychiatrists in japan. *PLoS One*, *8*(2), e55189. DOI: 10.1371/journal.pone.0055189 PMID: 23418435

2. Üstgörül, S., & Popescu, C. (2023). What is the mediating role of communication skills and sexual satisfaction between job and life satisfaction of healthcare employees? *Behavioral Sciences (Basel, Switzerland)*, *13*(5), 368. DOI: 10.3390/bs13050368 PMID: 37232605

2. Visconti, R. M., & Morea, D. (2019). Big data for the sustainability of healthcare project financing. *Sustainability (Basel)*, *11*(13), 3748. DOI: 10.3390/su11133748

Wagner, A. K., Graves, A. J., Reiss, S. K., LeCates, R. F., Zhang, F., & Ross-Degnan, D. (2011). Access to care and medicines, burden of health care expenditures, and risk protection: Results from the world health survey. *Health Policy (Amsterdam)*, *100*(2-3), 151–158. DOI: 10.1016/j.healthpol.2010.08.004 PMID: 20828854

Wang, S., Wang, X., Liu, X., Zhao, C., & Duan, J. (2023). Moderating effects of humanistic care and socioeconomic status on the relationship among pain intensity, psychological factors, and psychological function in adults with cancer pain from a province of china: A cross-sectional study. *Frontiers in Psychiatry*, *14*, 928727. Advance online publication. DOI: 10.3389/fpsyt.2023.928727 PMID: 37082761

Wang, Z., Wang, Z., Liang, X., Zhao, H., Li, X., Zhang, S.; & Pang, X. (2021). Spiritual care needs and their associated influencing factors among elderly patients with moderate-to-severe chronic heart failure in china: A cross-sectional study. *Palliative & Supportive Care*, *20*(2), 264–274. DOI: 10.1017/S1478951521001279 PMID: 35574915

Wang, Z., Xie, L., Liang, Z., Fan, J., Fan, L., Deng, J., & Xu, X. (2022). Perceived stress and humanistic care ability among chinese healthcare workers: The chain mediating role of social support and life satisfaction. *Frontiers in Psychology*, *13*, 1029265. Advance online publication. DOI: 10.3389/fpsyg.2022.1029265 PMID: 36438328

Wang, Z., Xie, L., Liang, Z., Fan, J., Fan, L., Deng, J., & Xu, X. (2022). Perceived stress and humanistic care ability among chinese healthcare workers: The chain mediating role of social support and life satisfaction. *Frontiers in Psychology*, *13*, 1029265. Advance online publication. DOI: 10.3389/fpsyg.2022.1029265 PMID: 36438328

Wasir, R., Irawati, S., Makady, A., Postma, M. J., Goettsch, W., Feenstra, T., & Buskens, E. (2019). The implementation of hta in medicine pricing and reimbursement policies in indonesia: Insights from multiple stakeholders. *PLoS One*, *14*(11), e0225626. DOI: 10.1371/journal.pone.0225626 PMID: 31774854

Watkins, L., & Colgate, R. (2016). Improving healthcare for people with intellectual disabilities: The development of an evidence-based teaching programme. *Advances in Mental Health and Intellectual Disabilities*, *10*(6), 333–341. DOI: 10.1108/AMHID-07-2016-0009

Wenham, J., Best, M., & Ac, D. (2021). Systematic review of medical education on spirituality. *Internal Medicine Journal*, *51*(11), 1781–1790. DOI: 10.1111/imj.15421 PMID: 34142417

Westerbeek, L., Bruijn, G., Weert, H., Abu-Hanna, A., Medlock, S., & Weert, J. (2022). General practitioners' needs and wishes for clinical decision support systems: A focus group study. *International Journal of Medical Informatics*, *168*, 104901. DOI: 10.1016/j.ijmedinf.2022.104901 PMID: 36279654

Wu, F., Song, Z., Wen, Z., & Xiao, Y. (2017). Medical humanities play an important role in improving the doctor-patient relationship. *Bioscience Trends*, *11*(2), 134–137. DOI: 10.5582/bst.2017.01087 PMID: 28458332

Wye, L., Brangan, E., Cameron, A. M., Gabbay, J., Klein, J. H., & Pope, C. (2015). Evidence based policy making and the 'art' of commissioning – how english health-care commissioners access and use information and academic research in 'real life' decision-making: An empirical qualitative study. *BMC Health Services Research*, *15*(1), 430. Advance online publication. DOI: 10.1186/s12913-015-1091-x PMID: 26416368

Xu, M., Choi, J., Capasso, A., & DiClemente, R. (2024). Improving hpv vaccination uptake among adolescents in low resource settings: Sociocultural and socioeconomic barriers and facilitators. *Adolescent Health, Medicine and Therapeutics*, *15*, 73–82. DOI: 10.2147/AHMT.S394119 PMID: 39100520

Xu, T., Wang, Y., Wang, R., Lamb, K., Ren, D., Gui-zhi, D., & Yue, P. (2020). Predictors of caring ability and its dimensions among nurses in china: A cross-sectional study. *Scandinavian Journal of Caring Sciences*, *35*(4), 1226–1239. DOI: 10.1111/scs.12941 PMID: 33615516

Zaidi, W. H., Mohydin, M., Ahmad, S. A., Asghar, M., Hashmi, N., Umair, M., & Butt, A. N. (2021). Evaluation of patient and family-centered care; a survey of neonatal and paediatric intensive care units. *Pakistan Journal of Medical & Health Sciences*, *15*(11), 2882–2885. DOI: 10.53350/pjmhs2115112882

Zhang, J., & Tian, Y. (2024). Final-year nursing students' perceptions of humanistic education in nursing: A cross-sectional descriptive study. *BMC Medical Education*, *24*(1), 392. Advance online publication. DOI: 10.1186/s12909-024-05377-3 PMID: 38594668

Zhang, Y. (2022). Application research of humanistic care and situational integration in nursing of schizophrenia in recovery period. Contrast Media & Molecular Imaging, 2022(1). DOI: 10.1155/2022/4705107

Zhong, X., Liu, X., & Sheng, Y. (2021). The effect of the humanistic care teaching model on nurse patient conflict and nurse turnover intention in a pediatric outpatient department: Results of a randomized trial. *Translational Pediatrics*, *10*(8), 2016–2023. DOI: 10.21037/tp-21-214 PMID: 34584871

Zhou, P., Bundorf, M., Chang, J., Huang, J., & Xue, D. (2011). Organizational culture and its relationship with hospital performance in public hospitals in china. *Health Services Research*, *46*(6pt2), 2139–2160. DOI: 10.1111/j.1475-6773.2011.01336.x PMID: 22092228

Zhu, Y., Liu, G., Shen, Y., Wang, J., Lu, M., & Wang, J. (2022). Humanistic nursing care for patients in low-resourced clinical settings from students' perspectives: A participatory qualitative study. *International Journal of Environmental Research and Public Health, 19*(19), 12656. DOI: 10.3390/ijerph191912656 PMID: 36231956

Zikusooka, M., Elci, Ö., & Özdemir, H. (2021). Job satisfaction among syrian healthcare workers in refugee health centres. *Human Resources for Health, 19*(1), 1. DOI: 10.1186/s12960-021-00685-x PMID: 34775958

Compilation of References

Abbott, R., Hui, K., Mandel, J., Goldstein, M., Winegarden, B., Glaser, D., ... & Brunton, L. (2011). Medical student attitudes toward complementary, alternative and integrative medicine. Evidence-Based Complementary and Alternative Medicine, 2011(1). DOI: 10.1093/ecam/nep195

Abdullah, S., & Salim, R. (2020). Parenting style and empathy in children: The mediating role of family communication patterns. *Humanitas, 17*(1), 34. DOI: 10.26555/humanitas.v17i1.13126

Accreditation Canada. (2021). Overview of healthcare accreditation.

Acosta, L., & Ely, E. W. (2023). Holistic care in healthy aging: Caring for the wholly and holy human. *Aging Cell, 23*(1), e14021. Advance online publication. DOI: 10.1111/acel.14021 PMID: 37873723

Adaji, T. M. (2013). Use of National Guidelines in the Treatment of Severe Malaria: A Retrospective Study of Severe Malaria Management in Under 5s in Benue State. DOI: 10.21522/TIJPH.2013.12.02.Art018

Adeniji, A., Osibanjo, A., Iruonagbe, T., Olawande, T., Ibidunni, A., & Olokundun, M. (2019). From job satisfaction to organizational commitment: The mediating influence of perceived treatment of diversity among nigeria's public healthcare employees. *Open Access Macedonian Journal of Medical Sciences, 7*(12), 2031–2035. DOI: 10.3889/oamjms.2019.346 PMID: 31406550

Adeoye, B. D., Michael, T. O., & Agbana, R. D. (2024). Insights, beliefs, and myths surrounding tuberculosis among pulmonary patients with delayed healthcare access in a high-burden TB state in Nigeria–a qualitative inquiry. *Frontiers in Sociology, 9*, 1378586. DOI: 10.3389/fsoc.2024.1378586 PMID: 38765220

Agirreazkuenaga, L. (2019). Embedding sustainable development goals in education. teachers' perspective about education for sustainability in the Basque autonomous community. *Sustainability (Basel), 11*(5), 1496. DOI: 10.3390/su11051496

Ahirwar, R., & Khan, N. (2022). *Smart Wireless Nanosensor Systems for Human Healthcare*. CRC Press. DOI: 10.1201/9781003093534-15

Ahmad, I., & Alqurashi, F. (2024, December). Early cancer detection using deep learning and medical imaging: A survey. *Critical Reviews in Oncology/Hematology*, *204*, 104528. DOI: 10.1016/j.critrevonc.2024.104528 PMID: 39413940

Ahmed, A. (n.d.). Divine harmony & restoring inner balance: A guided exploration with encouragement for conscious wisdom, spiritual healing and self-regulation. https://www.amazon.com/dp/B0CPWK1YY4?ref_=pe_93986420_774957520

Ahmed, Z., Bhinder, K., Amna, T., Tahir, M., Mehmood, Q., Tabassum, M., & Yousaf, Z. (2022). Knowledge, attitude, and practice of artificial intelligence among doctors and medical students in pakistan: A cross-sectional online survey. *Annals of Medicine and Surgery (London)*, *76*. Advance online publication. DOI: 10.1016/j.amsu.2022.103493 PMID: 35308436

Akologo, A., Abuosi, A., & Anaba, E. (2019). A cross-sectional survey on patient safety culture among healthcare providers in the upper east region of ghana. *PLoS One*, *14*(8), e0221208. DOI: 10.1371/journal.pone.0221208 PMID: 31430303

Akoria, O. (2016). Establishing in-hospital geriatrics services in Africa: Insights from the university of Benin teaching hospital geriatrics project. *Annals of African Medicine*, *15*(3), 145. DOI: 10.4103/1596-3519.188896 PMID: 27549420

Alderwick, H., Hutchings, A., Briggs, A., & Mays, N. (2021). The impacts of collaboration between local health care and non-health care organizations and factors shaping how they work: A systematic review of reviews. *BMC Public Health*. Retrieved from springer.com

Aldred, H., Gott, M., & Gariballa, S. (2005). Advanced heart failure: Impact on older patients and informal carers. *Journal of Advanced Nursing*, *49*(2), 116–124. DOI: 10.1111/j.1365-2648.2004.03271.x PMID: 15641944

Alenezi, N. K., Alyami, A. H., Alrehaili, B. O., Arruhaily, A. A., Alenazi, N. K., & Radman Al-Dubai, S. A.ALEnezi. (2022). Prevalence and associated factors of burnout among saudi resident doctors: A multicenter cross-sectional study. *Alpha Psychiatry*, *23*(4), 173–183. DOI: 10.5152/alphapsychiatry.2022.21361 PMID: 36425745

Alexander, J. A., Weiner, B. J., Metzger, M. E., Shortell, S. M., Bazzoli, G. J., Hasnain-Wynia, R., Sofaer, S., & Conrad, D. A. (2003). Sustainability of collaborative capacity in community health partnerships. *Medical Care Research and Review : MCRR, 60*(4, suppl), 130S–160S. DOI: 10.1177/1077558703259069 PMID: 14687432

Alipour, A., Fotokian, Z., Shamsalinia, A., Ghaffari, F., & Hajiahmadi, M. (2019a). The relationship between nurses' recognition regarding elder abuse and their attitudes and performance in dealing with elder abuse induced by Iranian family caregivers. *The Open Nursing Journal, 13*(1), 116–122. DOI: 10.2174/1874434601913010116

Alipour, A., Shamsalinia, A., Ghaffari, F., & Fotokian, Z. (2019b). The development and psychometric evaluation of a questionnaire on the nurses' recognition of elder abuse by family caregiver. *The Open Nursing Journal, 13*(1), 66–74. DOI: 10.2174/1874434601913010066

Alliance, N. C. D. (n.d.). Antimicrobial resistance: Putting infectious and non-communicable disease treatment at risk. https://ncdalliance.org/news-events/news/antimicrobial-resistance-putting-infectious-and-noncommunicable-disease-treatment-at-risk

Almakki, Z., Alshehri, S., & Wahab, M. (2020). Knowledge and attitudes regarding elder abuse in the community, eastern province Saudi Arabia. *BMC Geriatrics, 20*(1), 85. Advance online publication. DOI: 10.1186/s12877-020-1416-4 PMID: 32131768

Aloisio, L., Gifford, W., McGilton, K., Lalonde, M., Estabrooks, C., & Squires, J. (2018). Individual and organizational predictors of allied healthcare providers' job satisfaction in residential long-term care. *BMC Health Services Research, 18*(1), 491. Advance online publication. DOI: 10.1186/s12913-018-3307-3 PMID: 29940949

Al-Oweidat, I., Shosha, G., Baker, T., & Nashwan, A. (2023). The relationship between emotional intelligence and organizational commitment among nurses working in governmental hospitals in Jordan. *BMC Nursing, 22*(1), 195. Advance online publication. DOI: 10.1186/s12912-023-01361-2 PMID: 37291597

Alpay, L., Van Der Boog, P., & Dumaij, A. (2011). An empowerment-based approach to developing innovative e-health tools for self-management. *Health Informatics Journal, 17*(4), 247–255. DOI: 10.1177/1460458211420089 PMID: 22193825

Alsufyani, A., Baker, O., & Alsufyani, Y. (2020). Consequences of emotional intelligence in nursing: A concept analysis. *Erbil Journal of Nursing and Midwifery, 3*(1), 82–90. DOI: 10.15218/ejnm.2020.10

Alvarez, A., Pagani, M., & Meucci, P. (2012). The clinical application of the biopsychosocial model in mental health. *American Journal of Physical Medicine & Rehabilitation, 91*(13), S173–S180. DOI: 10.1097/PHM.0b013e31823d54be PMID: 22193327

Álvarez, M. P. (2017). Psychology as a science of subject and comportment, beyond the mind and behavior. *Integrative Psychological & Behavioral Science, 52*(1), 25–51. DOI: 10.1007/s12124-017-9408-4 PMID: 29063995

Al-Wathinani, A., Barten, D. G., Alsahli, H., Alhamid, A., Alghamdi, W., Alqahtani, W., Alghamdi, R., Aljuaid, M., Albaqami, N. A., & Goniewicz, K. (2023). The right to refuse: Understanding healthcare providers' perspectives on patient autonomy in emergency care. *Health Care, 11*(12), 1756. DOI: 10.3390/healthcare11121756 PMID: 37372874

Amedior, N. (2023). Ethical implications of artificial intelligence in the healthcare sector. *Advances in Multidisciplinary & Scientific Research Journal Publication, 36*, 1–12. DOI: 10.22624/AIMS/ACCRABESPOKE2023P1

American Association for Cancer Research. (2023). *Screening for early detection.* In *AACR Cancer Progress Report 2023*. Retrieved November 7, 2024, from https://cancerprogressreport.aacr.org/progress/cpr23-contents/cpr23-screening-for-early-detection/

Amor, R. E., Nakhleh, M. K., Barash, O., & Haick, H. (2019, June). Breath analysis of cancer in the present and the future. *European Respiratory Review : an Official Journal of the European Respiratory Society, 28*(152), 190002. Advance online publication. DOI: 10.1183/16000617.0002-2019 PMID: 31243094

Anam, M., & Siahay, M. M.Ira Norma Prabawati. (2024). Contribution of emotional intelligence to resilience in adolescents with broken home families. *Jurnal Multidisiplin Madani, 4*(1), 63–69. DOI: 10.55927/mudima.v4i1.7448

Anandarajah, G., & Hight, E. (2001). Spirituality and medical practice: Using the HOPE questions as a practical tool for spiritual assessment. *American Family Physician, 63*(1), 81–88. PMID: 11195773

Anderson, L. M., & Shinn, C. (2023, February). Please provide me with the text you want me to extract the title from. I need the actual text to be able to identify the title. Retrieved January 11, 2025, from https://stacks.cdc.gov/view/cdc/20707

Anderson, B., & McFarlane, C. (2011). Assemblage and geography. *Area, 43*(2), 124–127. DOI: 10.1111/j.1475-4762.2011.01004.x

Andrews, M. (2008, November 15). The Good Governance Agenda: Beyond Indicators without Theory. Oxford Development Studies. Taylor & Francis. Retrieved January 2025, from DOI: 10.1080/13600810802455120

Anisman, H., & Kusnecov, A. W. (2022, January). Cancer therapies: Caveats, concerns, and momentum. In *Cancer* (pp. 401–430). DOI: 10.1016/B978-0-323-91904-3.00001-X

Anisti, A., Tambunan, R. M., Sidharta, V., Sampean, S., & Syatir, S. (2023). Family communication patterns in the era digital technology. *Arrus Journal of Social Sciences and Humanities*, *3*(6), 750–756. DOI: 10.35877/soshum2225

Antoñanzas, F., Terkola, R., Overton, P., Shalet, N., & Postma, M. (2017). Defining and measuring the affordability of new medicines: A systematic review. *PharmacoEconomics*, *35*(8), 777–791. DOI: 10.1007/s40273-017-0514-4 PMID: 28477220

Arāja, D. (2022). Resilience and complex adaptive systems:a perspective on healthcare. *Journal of Business and Management*, *20*, 23–35. DOI: 10.32025/JBM22006

Arcury, T., Nguyen, H., Sandberg, J., Neiberg, R., Altizer, K., Bell, R., Grzywacz, J. G., Lang, W., & Quandt, S. (2013). Use of complementary therapies for health promotion among older adults. *Journal of Applied Gerontology*, *34*(5), 552–572. DOI: 10.1177/0733464813495109 PMID: 24652893

Ariesmansyah, A., Arisanti, I., & Rahmawati, R. (2024). The effect of employee support policy effectiveness, collaborative leadership, and work rewards on organizational innovation in the manufacturing industry in west java. *West Science Social and Humanities Studies*, *2*(04), 599–609. DOI: 10.58812/wsshs.v2i04.791

Arora, M. K., Lal, S., Singh, B., & Olyaee, M. (2024). Through an Energy Lens: Examining SDGs From a Policy Perspective. In Riswandi, B., Singh, B., Kaunert, C., & Vig, K. (Eds.), *AI Applications for Clean Energy and Sustainability* (pp. 320–343). IGI Global., DOI: 10.4018/979-8-3693-6567-0.ch016

Arora, S., Bergland, A., Straiton, M., Rechel, B., & Debesay, J. (2018). Older migrants' access to healthcare: A thematic synthesis. *International Journal of Migration, Health and Social Care*, *14*(4), 425–438. DOI: 10.1108/IJMHSC-05-2018-0032

Artawan Eka Putra, I. W. G., Purnama Dewi, N. P. E., Probandari, A. N., Notobroto, H. B., & Wahyuni, C. (2023). The implementation of comprehensive health education to improve household contacts' participation in early detection of tuberculosis. *Health Education & Behavior*, *50*(1), 136–143. DOI: 10.1177/10901981211001829 PMID: 33829894

Asadi, K. (2023). The role of family in shaping financial literacy and economic behavior. *JPRFC*, 22-29. https://doi.org/DOI: 10.61838/kman.jprfc.1.3.4

Aubel, J., Sl, M., & Cunningham, K. (2021). Introduction: A family systems approach to promote maternal, child and adolescent nutrition. *Maternal and Child Nutrition*, *17*(S1), e13228. Advance online publication. DOI: 10.1111/mcn.13228 PMID: 34241950

Austin, P., Macdonald, J., & MacLeod, R. (2018). Measuring spirituality and religiosity in clinical settings: A scoping review of available instruments. *Religions*, *9*(3), 70. DOI: 10.3390/rel9030070

Avula, H., Dittborn, M., & Brierley, J. (2021). 'who ya gonna call …?' ethical and legal dilemmas in specialist children centres and district general hospitals. *Clinical Ethics*, *17*(4), 415–424. DOI: 10.1177/14777509211036649

Ayalew, Y. E., Yehualashet, F. A., Bogale, W. A., & Gobeza, M. B. (2020). Delay for tuberculosis treatment and its predictors among adult tuberculosis patients at Debremarkos town public health facilities, north West Ethiopia. *Tuberculosis Research and Treatment*, *2020*, 1–8. DOI: 10.1155/2020/1901890 PMID: 33014464

Bacha, K., Hanley, T., & Winter, L. A. (2020). 'Like a human being, I was an equal, I wasn't just a patient': Service users' perspectives on their experiences of relationships with staff in mental health services. *Psychology and Psychotherapy: Theory, Research and Practice*, *93*(2), 367–386. DOI: 10.1111/papt.12218 PMID: 30720230

Baghdadi, N., Sankarapandian, C., Arulappan, J., Taani, M. H., Snethen, J., & Andargeery, S. Y. (2023). The association between nursing students' happiness, emotional intelligence, and perceived caring behavior in Riyadh city, Saudi Arabia. *Health Care*, *12*(1), 67. DOI: 10.3390/healthcare12010067 PMID: 38200973

Balbale, S., Morris, M. A., & LaVela, S. L. (2014). Using photovoice to explore patient perceptions of patient-centered care in the veterans affairs health care system. The Patient - Patient-Centered Outcomes Research, 7(2), 187-195. DOI: 10.1007/s40271-014-0044-5

Balistreri, K., & Alvira-Hammond, M. (2016). Adverse childhood experiences, family functioning and adolescent health and emotional well-being. *Public Health*, *132*, 72–78. DOI: 10.1016/j.puhe.2015.10.034 PMID: 26718424

Banerjee, A., Chakraborty, C., & Rathi, M.Sr. (2020). Medical imaging, artificial intelligence, internet of things, wearable devices in terahertz healthcare technologies. In *Terahertz biomedical and healthcare technologies* (pp. 145–165). Elsevier. DOI: 10.1016/B978-0-12-818556-8.00008-2

Bangcola, A. (2021). The development of spiritual nursing care theory using deductive axiomatic approach. *Belitung Nursing Journal*, *7*(3), 163–170. DOI: 10.33546/bnj.1456 PMID: 37469349

Bannasch, P., & van Kaick, G. (1992). What does 'early' stand for in cancer diagnosis? *Cancer Diagnosis*, *1–2*, 1–2. Advance online publication. DOI: 10.1007/978-3-642-76899-6_1

Barnes, P. M., Bloom, B., & Nahin, R. L. (2008). Complementary and alternative medicine use among adults and children: United States, 2007. *National Health Statistics Reports*, (12), 1–23. PMID: 19361005

Barnes, R., & Zvarikova, K. (2021). Artificial intelligence-enabled wearable medical devices, clinical and diagnostic decision support systems, and Internet of Things-based healthcare applications in COVID-19 prevention, screening, and treatment. *American Journal of Medical Research (New York, N.Y.)*, *8*(2), 9–22. DOI: 10.22381/ajmr8220211

Barnett, J., Vasileiou, K., Djemil, F., Brooks, L., & Young, T. (2011). Understanding innovators' experiences of barriers and facilitators in implementation and diffusion of healthcare service innovations: A qualitative study. *BMC Health Services Research*, *11*(1), 342. Advance online publication. DOI: 10.1186/1472-6963-11-342 PMID: 22176739

Barson, S., Gauld, R., Gray, J., Henriks, G., Krause, C., Lachman, P., Maher, L., Massoud, M. R., Mathias, L., Wagner, M., & Villa, L. (2018). What initiatives do healthcare leaders agree are needed for healthcare system improvement? results of a modified-Delphi study. *Journal of Health Organization and Management*, *32*(8), 1002–1012. DOI: 10.1108/JHOM-08-2017-0216 PMID: 30468416

Bast, R. C.Jr, & Srivastava, S. (2020, December). The National Cancer Institute Early Detection Research Network: Two decades of progress. *Cancer Epidemiology, Biomarkers & Prevention*, *29*(12), 2396–2400. DOI: 10.1158/1055-9965.EPI-20-1158 PMID: 33262198

Batko, K., & Ślęzak, A. (2022). The use of Big Data Analytics in healthcare. *Journal of Big Data*. Retrieved from springer.com

Beacham, A., King, A., & Nash, B. (2023). Psychologists' role in addressing healthcare provider burnout and well-being. *Journal of Health Service Psychology*, *49*(2), 63–75. DOI: 10.1007/s42843-023-00083-y

Beaglehole, R., Bonita, R., Horton, R., Adams, O., & McKee, M. (2004, June 1). Public health in the new era: improving health through collective action. The Lancet. Elsevier BV. Retrieved December 2024, from DOI: 10.1016/S0140-6736(04)16461-1

Beck, J. S. (2011). *Cognitive behavior therapy: Basics and beyond*. Guilford Press.

Bell, J., Dziekan, G., Pollack, C., & Mahachai, V. (2016). Self-Care in the Twenty First Century: A Vital Role for the Pharmacist. *Advances in Therapy*, *33*(10), 1691–1703. DOI: 10.1007/s12325-016-0395-5 PMID: 27535290

Benmira, S., & Agboola, M. (2021). Evolution of leadership theory. *BMJ Leader*. Retrieved from bmj.com

Bennett, F. J. (1979). Primary health care and developing countries. *Social Science & Medicine. Part A, Medical Sociology*, *13*, 505–514. DOI: 10.1016/0271-7123(79)90092-0 PMID: 472779

Bergmo, T. S. (2015). How to measure costs and benefits of ehealth interventions: An overview of methods and frameworks. *Journal of Medical Internet Research*, *17*(11), e254. DOI: 10.2196/jmir.4521 PMID: 26552360

Berman, B. M., & Straus, S. E. (2004). Implementing a research agenda for complementary and alternative medicine. *Annual Review of Medicine*, *55*(1), 239–254. DOI: 10.1146/annurev.med.55.091902.103657 PMID: 14746520

Berwick, D. M. (2009). What 'patient-centered' ought to mean—Confessions of an extremist. *Health Affairs*, *28*(4, Supplement 1), w555–w565. DOI: 10.1377/hlthaff.28.4.w555 PMID: 19454528

Bethell, C., Wells, N., Bergman, D., Reuland, C., Stumbo, S. P., Gombojav, N., & Simpson, L. A. (2023). Scaling family voices and engagement to measure and improve systems performance and whole child health: Progress and lessons from the child and adolescent health measurement initiative. *Maternal and Child Health Journal*. Advance online publication. DOI: 10.1007/s10995-023-03755-9 PMID: 37624473

Bettner, D. (2012). *The Blue Zones: Lessons for living longer from the people who've lived the longest*. National Geographic Society.

Beyaztaş, F. (2023). *Forensic medical perspective of elder abuse*. Cumhuriyet Medical Journal., DOI: 10.7197/cmj.1377781

Beyerstein, B. L. (2001). Alternative medicine and common errors of reasoning. *Academic Medicine*, *76*(3), 230–237. https://journals.lww.com/academicmedicine/abstract/2001/03000/alternative_medicine_and_common_errors_of.9.aspx. DOI: 10.1097/00001888-200103000-00009 PMID: 11242572

Bhattarai, S., Adhikari, A., Rayamajhee, B., Dhungana, J., Singh, R., Koirala, S., & Shakya, D. (2022). Participatory approach to develop evidence-based clinical ethics guidelines for the care of covid-19 patients: A mixed method study from Nepal. *Frontiers in Public Health, 10*, 873881. Advance online publication. DOI: 10.3389/fpubh.2022.873881 PMID: 35832276

Bhuyan, K. K. (2004). Health promotion through self-care and community participation: Elements of a proposed programme in the developing countries. *BMC Public Health, 4*(1), 11. DOI: 10.1186/1471-2458-4-11 PMID: 15086956

Bigaignon-Cantineau, J., Gonzalez, M., Broessel, N., Denu, B., Hamzaoui, H., & Cantineau, A. (2005). Occupational health nurses' contribution to health care workers' health. *Scandinavian Journal of Work, Environment & Health*, (Supplements, 1), 54–57.

Biller-Andorno, N., Ferrario, A., Jöbges, S., Krones, T., Massini, F., Barth, P., & Krauthammer, M. (2021). Ai support for ethical decision-making around resuscitation: Proceed with care. *Journal of Medical Ethics, 48*(3), 175–183. DOI: 10.1136/medethics-2020-106786 PMID: 33687916

Blackler, L., Scharf, A., Matsoukas, K., Colletti, M., & Voigt, L. (2021). Call to action: Empowering patients and families to initiate clinical ethics consultations. *Journal of Medical Ethics, 49*(4), 240–243. DOI: 10.1136/medethics-2021-107426 PMID: 34732393

Bodenheimer, T., & Sinsky, C. (2014). From triple to quadruple aim: Care of the patient requires care of the provider. *Annals of Family Medicine, 12*(6), 573–576. DOI: 10.1370/afm.1713 PMID: 25384822

Bodhi, B. (1999). *The noble eightfold path: The way to the end of suffering*. Buddhist Publication Society.

Bodison, S., Sankaré, I., Anaya, H., Booker-Vaughns, J., Miller, A., Williams, P., & Norris, K. (2015). Engaging the community in the dissemination, implementation, and improvement of health-related research. *Clinical and Translational Science, 8*(6), 814–819. DOI: 10.1111/cts.12342 PMID: 26546337

Bolden, R., Gosling, J., & Hawkins, B. (2023). Exploring leadership: Individual, organizational, and societal perspectives. Retrieved from academia.edu

Bolton, R., Fix, G., Lukas, C., Elwy, A., & Bokhour, B. (2018). Biopsychosocial benefits of movement-based complementary and integrative health therapies for patients with chronic conditions. *Chronic Illness, 16*(1), 41–54. DOI: 10.1177/1742395318782377 PMID: 29914264

Boon, H., Verhoef, M., O'Hara, D., & Findlay, B. (2004). From parallel practice to integrative health care: A conceptual framework. *BMC Health Services Research, 4*(1), 15. DOI: 10.1186/1472-6963-4-15 PMID: 15230977

Braithwaite, J., Herkes, J., Ludlow, K., Testa, L., & Lamprell, G. (2017). Association between organisational and workplace cultures, and patient outcomes: Systematic review. *BMJ Open, 7*(11), e017708. DOI: 10.1136/bmjopen-2017-017708 PMID: 29122796

Bramley, L., & Matiti, M. (2014). How does it really feel to be in my shoes? patients' experiences of compassion within nursing care and their perceptions of developing compassionate nurses. *Journal of Clinical Nursing, 23*(19-20), 2790–2799. DOI: 10.1111/jocn.12537 PMID: 24479676

Breslin, J., MacRae, S., Bell, J., & Сингер, П. (2005). Top 10 health care ethics challenges facing the public: Views of Toronto bioethicists. *BMC Medical Ethics, 6*(1), 5. Advance online publication. DOI: 10.1186/1472-6939-6-5 PMID: 15978136

Brighton, L., Miller, S., Farquhar, M., Booth, S., Yi, D., Gao, W., Bajwah, S., Man, W. D.-C., Higginson, I. J., & Maddocks, M. (2018). Holistic services for people with advanced disease and chronic breathlessness: A systematic review and meta-analysis. *Thorax, 74*(3), 270–281. DOI: 10.1136/thoraxjnl-2018-211589 PMID: 30498004

Bringmann, H., Michalsen, A., Jeitler, M., Kessler, C., Brinkhaus, B., Brunnhuber, S., & Sedlmeier, P. (2022). Meditation-based lifestyle modification in mild to moderate depression—A randomized controlled trial. *Depression and Anxiety, 39*(5), 363–375. DOI: 10.1002/da.23249 PMID: 35312137

Bronikowski, M., Bronikowska, M., & Glapa, A. (2016). Do they need goals or support? A report from a goal-setting intervention using physical activity monitors in youth. *International Journal of Environmental Research and Public Health, 13*(9), 914. DOI: 10.3390/ijerph13090914 PMID: 27649219

Broome, M. E. (2025). *Transformational leadership in nursing: From expert clinician to influential leader*. Retrieved from. [HTML]

Browne, K., Dzebo, A., Iacobuţă, G., Onbargi, A., Shawoo, Z., Dombrowsky, I., & Persson, Å. (2023). How does policy coherence shape effectiveness and inequality? implications for sustainable development and the 2030 agenda. *Sustainable Development (Bradford), 31*(5), 3161–3174. DOI: 10.1002/sd.2598

Bryant-Davis, T., & Wong, E. C. (2013). Faith to move mountains: religious coping, spirituality, and interpersonal trauma recovery. *American Psychologist, 68*(8), 675. sDOI: 10.1037/a0034380

Bryce, C., Ring, P., Ashby, S., & Wardman, J. K. (2022). Resilience in the face of uncertainty: Early lessons from the COVID-19 pandemic. *COVID, 19*, •••. city.ac.uk

Budhthoki, C. (2013). Socioeconomic inequality and social exclusion in health: A review. *Dhaulagiri, 6*, 25–48. DOI: 10.3126/dsaj.v6i0.8477

Buehler, E., Crowley, J., Peterson, A., & Jackl, J. (2022). Family communication patterns, mediated communication, and well-being: A communication interdependence perspective on parent–adult child relationships. *Journal of Social and Personal Relationships, 41*(5), 1113–1135. DOI: 10.1177/02654075221145628

Buhr, G., Dixon, C., Dillard, J., Nickolopoulos, E., Bowlby, L., Canupp, H., Matters, L., Konrad, T., Previll, L., Heflin, M., & McConnell, E. (2019). Geriatric resource teams: Equipping primary care practices to meet the complex care needs of older adults. *Geriatrics (Basel, Switzerland), 4*(4), 59. DOI: 10.3390/geriatrics4040059 PMID: 31640232

Bunik, M., Dunn, D., Watkins, L., & Talmi, A. (2014). Trifecta approach to breastfeeding. *Journal of Human Lactation, 30*(2), 143–147. DOI: 10.1177/0890334414523333 PMID: 24595703

Burnhope, E., Waring, M., Guilder, A., Malhotra, B., Cardoso, J., Razavi, R., & Carr-White, G. (2020). A systematic approach towards implementing value-based health care in heart failure: Understandings from retrospective analysis methods in south London. *Health Services Management Research, 35*(1), 37–47. DOI: 10.1177/0951484820971442 PMID: 33256480

Bustin, S. A., & Jellinger, K. A. (2023). Advances in molecular medicine: Unravelling disease complexity and pioneering precision healthcare. *International Journal of Molecular Sciences, 24*(18), 14168. DOI: 10.3390/ijms241814168 PMID: 37762471

Byaello, K. (2023). Impact of noise pollution on community health and well-being in Lagos, Nigeria. *Journal Wetenskap Health, 4*(4), 15–21. DOI: 10.48173/jwh.v4i4.203

Cajander, Å., Lárusdóttir, M., & Hedström, G. (2020). The effects of automation of a patient-centric service in primary care on the work engagement and exhaustion of nurses. *Quality and User Experience, 5*(1), 9. Advance online publication. DOI: 10.1007/s41233-020-00038-x

Callen, B., Smith, C. M., Joyce, B., Lutz, J., Brown-Schott, N., & Block, D. (2013). Teaching/learning strategies for the essentials of baccalaureate nursing education for entry-level community/public health nursing. *Public Health Nursing (Boston, Mass.), 30*(6), 537–547. DOI: 10.1111/phn.12033 PMID: 24579713

Caltabiano, N., & Caltabiano, M. (2016). Reactions to a female perpetrator of neglect and financial elder abuse. *Psychology (Irvine, Calif.), 07*(06), 776–780. DOI: 10.4236/psych.2016.76080

Camerini, L., Schulz, P. J., & Nakamoto, K. (2012). Differential effects of health knowledge and health empowerment over patients' self-management and health outcomes: A cross-sectional evaluation. *Patient Education and Counseling, 89*(2), 337–344. DOI: 10.1016/j.pec.2012.08.005 PMID: 22959333

Cancer Council Australia. (n.d.). *Types of cancer*. Retrieved November 9, 2024, from https://www.cancer.org.au/cancer-information/types-of-cancer

Cancer Imaging Program. (n.d.). *CT scans*. Retrieved November 14, 2024, from https://imaging.cancer.gov/imaging_basics/cancer_imaging/ct_scans.htm

Capec, S., Petřek, M., Capec, G., Yaremkevych, R., & Andrashko, Y. (2022). Psychologic interventions in patients with the chronic dermatologic itch in atopic dermatitis and psoriasis: A step forward with family constellations seminars. *Frontiers in Medicine, 9*, 965133. Advance online publication. DOI: 10.3389/fmed.2022.965133 PMID: 36035402

Cappelli, E., Zaghini, F., Fiorini, J., & Sili, A. (2024). Healthcare-associated infections and nursing leadership: A systematic review. *Journal of Infection Prevention*. Advance online publication. DOI: 10.1177/17571774241287467 PMID: 39544633

Carden, J., Jones, R. J., & Passmore, J. (2022). Defining Self-Awareness in the Context of Adult Development: A Systematic Literature Review. *Journal of Management Education, 46*(1), 140–177. DOI: 10.1177/1052562921990065

Care Quality Commission. (2023). Safety and quality norms.

Carmona-Torres, J., Carvalhal-Silva, R., Viera-Mendes, M., Recio-Andrade, B., Goergen, T., & Rodríguez-Borrego, M. (2017). Elder abuse within the family environment in the Azores islands. *Revista Latino-Americana de Enfermagem, 25*(0). Advance online publication. DOI: 10.1590/1518-8345.1871.2932

Carper, B. A. (1978). Fundamental patterns of knowing in nursing. *Advances in Nursing Science, 1*(1), 13–24. DOI: 10.1097/00012272-197810000-00004 PMID: 110216

Carrington, A. (2014). Expanding the debate. *Qualitative Research Journal, 14*(2), 179–196. DOI: 10.1108/QRJ-08-2013-0049

Carvalho, D. (2024). Access from healthcare professionals to evidence-based pharmacotherapy in allergy management. Current Opinion in Allergy &Amp. *Clinical Immunology (Orlando, Fla.)*, *24*(4), 274–279. DOI: 10.1097/ACI.0000000000000989 PMID: 38640143

Cassim, S., Chepulis, L., Keenan, R., Kidd, J., Firth, M., & Lawrenson, R. (2019). Patient and carer perceived barriers to early presentation and diagnosis of lung cancer: A systematic review. *BMC Cancer*, *19*(1), 25. Advance online publication. DOI: 10.1186/s12885-018-5169-9 PMID: 30621616

Castagno, S., & Khalifa, M. (2020). Perceptions of artificial intelligence among healthcare staff: A qualitative survey study. *Frontiers in Artificial Intelligence*, *3*, 578983. Advance online publication. DOI: 10.3389/frai.2020.578983 PMID: 33733219

Chamane, N., Kuupiel, D., & Mashamba-Thompson, T. (2019). Experiential learning for primary healthcare workers in low- and middle-income countries: A scoping review protocol. *Systematic Reviews*, *8*(1), 123. Advance online publication. DOI: 10.1186/s13643-019-1040-6 PMID: 31109377

Chandra, M., Kumar, K., Thakur, P., Chattopadhyaya, S., Alam, F., & Kumar, S. (2022). Digital technologies, healthcare and COVID-19: Insights from developing and emerging nations. [Retrieved from springer.com]. *Health and Technology*, *12*(2), 547–568. DOI: 10.1007/s12553-022-00650-1 PMID: 35284203

Chang, D., Chang, X., He, Y., & Tan, K. J. K. (2022). The determinants of COVID-19 morbidity and mortality across countries. *Scientific Reports*. Retrieved from nature.com

Chang, A. Y., Riumalló-Herl, C., Perales, N., Clark, S., Clark, A., Constenla, D., Garske, T., Jackson, M. L., Jean, K., Jit, M., Jones, E. O., Li, X., Suraratdecha, C., Bullock, O., Johnson, H., Brenzel, L., & Verguet, S. (2018, February 1). The Equity Impact Vaccines May Have On Averting Deaths And Medical Impoverishment In Developing Countries. *Health Affairs (Project Hope)*, *37*(2), 316–324. Advance online publication. Retrieved December 2024, from. DOI: 10.1377/hlthaff.2017.0861 PMID: 29401021

Chang, B., Wu, A. W., Hansel, N. N., & Diette, G. B. (2004). Quality of life in tuberculosis: A review of the English language literature. *Quality of Life Research: An International Journal of Quality of Life Aspects of Treatment, Care and Rehabilitation*, *13*(10), 1633–1642. DOI: 10.1007/s11136-004-0374-1 PMID: 15651535

Chang, E., Monin, J., Isenberg, N., Zelterman, D., & Levy, B. (2023). Implicit and explicit dehumanization of older family members: Novel determinants of elder abuse proclivity. *Stigma and Health*, *8*(1), 40–48. DOI: 10.1037/sah0000370 PMID: 37092028

Chatterji, P., Lahiri, K., & Song, J. (2011). The dynamics of income-related health inequality among us children. SSRN *Electronic Journal*. https://doi.org/DOI: 10.2139/ssrn.1927813

Chatzipanagiotou, P., & Katsarou, E. (2023). Crisis management, school leadership in disruptive times, and the recovery of schools in the post-COVID-19 era: A systematic literature review. *Education Sciences*. Retrieved from mdpi.com

Chaudru, S., Müllenheim, P., Faucheur, A., Kaladji, A., Jaquinandi, V., & Mahé, G. (2016). Training to perform ankle-brachial index: Systematic review and perspectives to improve teaching and learning. *European Journal of Vascular and Endovascular Surgery*, *51*(2), 240–247. DOI: 10.1016/j.ejvs.2015.09.005 PMID: 26602321

Chelliah, R., Wei, S., Daliri, E. B. M., Rubab, M., Elahi, F., Yeon, S. J., Jo, K., Yan, P., Liu, S., & Oh, D. H. (2021). Development of nanosensors based intelligent packaging systems: Food quality and medicine. *Nanomaterials (Basel, Switzerland)*, *11*(6), 1515. DOI: 10.3390/nano11061515 PMID: 34201071

Chen, H., Zi-lin, L., & Luo, F. (2022, January 6). Establishment, Analysis, and Application of the Information Transmission and Response Model for Students of Vocational Colleges under Public Health Emergencies. Journal of Healthcare Engineering. Hindawi Publishing Corporation. Retrieved December 2024, from DOI: 10.1155/2022/6701364

Chen, J., Dai, Y., Qin, Y., Liang, S., Cheng, G., Liu, J., Yang, C.-Z., He, H.-G., & Shen, Q. (2023). Factors influencing turnover intention among male nurses in China: A large-scale descriptive correlational study. *International Nursing Review*, *71*(1), 13–19. DOI: 10.1111/inr.12827 PMID: 36708510

Chen, L., Jiang, W., & Zhao, R. (2022). Application effect of kolb's experiential learning theory in clinical nursing teaching of traditional chinese medicine. *Digital Health*, *8*, 205520762211383. DOI: 10.1177/20552076221138313 PMID: 36406155

Chen, M., & Chan, K. (2021). Elder abuse and neglect in China: Prevalence, co-occurrence, and intergenerational risk factors. *Journal of Interpersonal Violence*, *37*(11-12), NP9839–NP9862. DOI: 10.1177/0886260520985501 PMID: 33415994

Chen, M., & Fu, Y. (2021). Adverse childhood experiences: Are they associated with greater risk of elder abuse victimization? *Journal of Interpersonal Violence*, *37*(19-20), NP17662–NP17687. DOI: 10.1177/08862605211028328 PMID: 34641720

Chen, Y., Chang, L., Liu, C., Ho, Y., Weng, S., & Tsai, T. (2018). The Roles of Social Support and Health Literacy in Self-Management Among Patients With Chronic Kidney Disease. *Journal of Nursing Scholarship*, *50*(3), 265–275. DOI: 10.1111/jnu.12377 PMID: 29569423

Chinenye, N. M. (2015). Evaluation of knowledge, attitude and practices of TB diagnosed patients in Rwanda towards TB infection. Case of TB diagnosed patients in Kigali urban and rural health facilities. *International Journal of Scientific and Research Publications*, *5*(8), 1–19. https://citeseerx.ist.psu.edu/document?repid=rep1&type=pdf&doi=2cf8f36a79ece1d6b04b50debeab7e272a721a59#page=478

Chinn, P. L., & Kramer, M. K. (2015). *Knowledge development in nursing: Theory and process* (9th ed.). Mosby Elsevier.

Chou, C., Kellom, K., & Shea, J. (2014). Attitudes and habits of highly humanistic physicians. *Academic Medicine*, *89*(9), 1252–1258. DOI: 10.1097/ACM.0000000000000405 PMID: 25006710

Chow, C., & Tiwari, A. (2014). Experience of family caregivers of community-dwelling stroke survivors and risk of elder abuse: A qualitative study. *Journal of Adult Protection*, *16*(5), 276–293. DOI: 10.1108/JAP-03-2014-0007

Chron. (n.d.). Role & duties of a home care nurse. https://work.chron.com/role-duties-home-care-nurse-13396.html

Clyne, B., Fitzgerald, C., Quinlan, A., Hardy, C., Galvin, R., Fahey, T., & Smith, S. M. (2016). Interventions to address potentially inappropriate prescribing in community-dwelling older adults: A systematic review of randomized controlled trials. *Journal of the American Geriatrics Society*, *64*(6), 1210–1222. DOI: 10.1111/jgs.14133 PMID: 27321600

Coffey, A., Saab, M., Landers, M., Cornally, N., Hegarty, J., Drennan, J., Lunn, C., & Savage, E. (2019). The impact of compassionate care education on nurses: A mixed-method systematic review. *Journal of Advanced Nursing*, *75*(11), 2340–2351. DOI: 10.1111/jan.14088 PMID: 31162701

Cohen, D. (2006). "Family constellations": An innovative systemic phenomenological group process from Germany. *The Family Journal (Alexandria, Va.)*, *14*(3), 226–233. DOI: 10.1177/1066480706287279

Coimbra, L., & Noakes, A. (2021). A systematic review into healthcare professionals' attitudes towards self-harm in children and young people and its impact on care provision. *Journal of Child Health Care*, *26*(2), 290–306. DOI: 10.1177/13674935211014405 PMID: 33929264

Coleman, E. (2023). Trauma-informed care approach in family practice: Steps to implementing. *International Journal of Studies in Nursing*, *8*(2), 24. DOI: 10.20849/ijsn.v8i2.1374

Commonwealth Foundation. (2013). *National report.*

Cong, Z., & Silverstein, M. (2011). Parents' depressive symptoms and support from sons and daughters in rural china. *International Journal of Social Welfare*, *20*(s1). Advance online publication. DOI: 10.1111/j.1468-2397.2011.00823.x PMID: 21984870

Connal, S., Cameron, J. M., Sala, A., Brennan, P. M., Palmer, D. S., Palmer, J. D., Perlow, H., & Baker, M. J. (2023, December). Liquid biopsies: The future of cancer early detection. *Journal of Translational Medicine*, *21*(1), 1–18. DOI: 10.1186/s12967-023-03960-8 PMID: 36774504

Cornally, N., Kilty, C., Buckley, C., Ó'Caoimh, R., O'Donovan, M., Monahan, M., O'Connor, C. D., Fitzgerald, S., & Hartigan, I. (2022). The experience of covid-19 visitor restrictions among families of people living in long-term residential care facilities during the first wave of the pandemic in Ireland. *International Journal of Environmental Research and Public Health*, *19*(11), 6559. DOI: 10.3390/ijerph19116559 PMID: 35682143

Coulter, I., Herman, P. M., & Nataraj, S. (2013). Economic analysis of complementary, alternative, and integrative medicine: Considerations raised by an expert panel. *BMC Complementary and Alternative Medicine*, *13*(1), 191. DOI: 10.1186/1472-6882-13-191 PMID: 23885789

Cowley, S. A., Tzouvara, V., & Horta Reis da Silva, T. (2023). Public Health: healthy ageing and well-being. In *Redfern's Nursing Older People*. Fifth edition. Editors: Ross, Harris, Fitzpatrick and Abley. Elsevier.

Cox, D. (2020). A guide to establishing ethics committees in behavioral health settings. *Behavior Analysis in Practice*, *13*(4), 939–949. DOI: 10.1007/s40617-020-00455-6 PMID: 33269203

Cox, R., Kendall, M., Molineux, M., Miller, E., & Tanner, B. (2022). Refining a capability development framework for building successful consumer and staff partnerships in healthcare quality improvement: A coproduced edelphi study. *Health Expectations*, *25*(4), 1563–1579. DOI: 10.1111/hex.13499 PMID: 35472122

Cramm, J. M., Hartgerink, J. M., Steyerberg, E. W., Bakker, T. J., Mackenbach, J. P., & Nieboer, A. P. (2013). Understanding older patients' self-management abilities: Functional loss, self-management, and well-being. *Quality of Life Research: An International Journal of Quality of Life Aspects of Treatment, Care and Rehabilitation*, *22*(1), 85–92. DOI: 10.1007/s11136-012-0131-9 PMID: 22350532

Croker, A., Brown, L., Little, A., Squires, K., & Crowley, E. (2018). Developing and maintaining collaborative practice: Exploring perspectives from dietetics and speech pathology about 'what works well'. *Nutrition & Dietetics: the Journal of the Dietitians Association of Australia*, *76*(1), 28–37. DOI: 10.1111/1747-0080.12506 PMID: 30585376

Crowder, J., Burnett, C., Byon, H., Laughon, K., Acierno, R., Gao, Y., & Teaster, P. (2020). Exploration and comparison of contextual characteristics and mistreatment prevalence among older American Indian and Alaska native respondents: Secondary analysis of the national elder mistreatment study. *Journal of Interpersonal Violence*, *37*(3-4), 1456–1483. DOI: 10.1177/0886260520922356 PMID: 32478601

Cuckler, G. A., Sisko, A. M., Poisal, J. A., Keehan, S. P., Smith, S. D., Madison, A. J., Wolfe, C. J., et al. (2018, February 14). National Health Expenditure Projections, 2017–26: Despite Uncertainty, Fundamentals Primarily Drive Spending Growth. Health Affairs. Project HOPE. Retrieved January 2025, from DOI: 10.1377/hlthaff.2017.1655

Curlin, F. A., Lawrence, R. E., Odell, S., Chin, M. H., Lantos, J. D., Koenig, H. G., & Meador, K. G. (2007). Religion, spirituality, and medicine: Psychiatrists' and other physicians' differing observations, interpretations, and clinical approaches. *The American Journal of Psychiatry*, *164*(12), 1825–1831. DOI: 10.1176/appi.ajp.2007.06122088 PMID: 18056237

Cypher, M., & Axman, L. (2022). Determinants of location of death: A secondary analysis utilizing multinomial logistic regression. *The American Journal of Hospice & Palliative Care*, *39*(12), 1397–1402. DOI: 10.1177/10499091221077883 PMID: 35232266

da Silva, T. H. R. (2022). Emotional awareness and emotional intelligence. *British Journal of Community Nursing*, *27*(12), 573–574. DOI: 10.12968/bjcn.2022.27.12.573 PMID: 36519463 da Silva, T. H. R., & Rodrigues, E. C. P. (2023). Body Image Related Discrimination. In Leal Filho, W., Azul, A. M., Brandli, L., Lange Salvia, A., Özuyar, P. G., & Wall, T. (Eds.), *Reduced Inequalities. Encyclopedia of the UN Sustainable Development Goals*. Springer., DOI: 10.1007/978-3-319-71060-0_61-1

Daley, C. L. (2019). The global fight against tuberculosis. *Thoracic Surgery Clinics, 29*(1, s1), 19–25. https://www.thoracic.theclinics.com/article/S1547-4127(18)30137-3/abstract. DOI: 10.1016/j.thorsurg.2018.09.010 PMID: 30454918

Dariah, A., Salleh, M., Yahaia, M., & Mafruhat, A. (2019). Integrating dimensions of sustainable development goals (SDGs) within Umranic framework. *Journal of Sustainable Development, 12*(6), 82. DOI: 10.5539/jsd.v12n6p82

Darling-Hammond, L., Cobb, V., & Bullmaster, M. (2021). Professional Development Schools as Contexts for Teacher Learning and Leadership. In *Organizational Learning in Schools* (pp. 149–175). Taylor & Francis. DOI: 10.1201/9781003077459-9

Datiko, D. G., Jerene, D., & Suarez, P. (2020). Stigma matters in ending tuberculosis: Nationwide survey of stigma in Ethiopia. *BMC Public Health, 20*(1), 190. DOI: 10.1186/s12889-019-7915-6 PMID: 32028914

Davis, E. C., Arana, E. T., Creel, J. S., Ibarra, S. C., Lechuga, J., Norman, R. A., Parks, H. R., Qasim, A., Watkins, D. Y., & Kash, B. A. (2018). The role of community engagement in building sustainable health-care delivery interventions for Kenya. *European Journal of Training and Development, 42*(1/2), 35–47. DOI: 10.1108/EJTD-06-2016-0042

Davtyan, K., Aghabekyan, S., Davtyan, H., Hayrapetyan, A., & Aslanyan, G. (2019). Quality of care provided to tuberculosis patients in Armenia: How satisfied are the patients?. *The Journal of Infection in Developing Countries, 13*(05.1), 028S-034S. DOI: 10.3855/jidc.10873

Davydov, G. (2023). Revolutionizing healthcare delivery: The transformative impact of telemedicine in the post-pandemic era. *Journal for International Medical Graduates, 2*(1). Advance online publication. DOI: 10.56570/jimgs.v2i1.90

Deb, T. (2006). Strategic approach to human resource management. Atlantic Publishers & Distributors.

DeCamp, M., Alasmar, A., Fischer, S., & Kutner, J. (2022). Meeting ethical challenges with authenticity when engaging patients and families in end-of-life and palliative care research: A qualitative study. *BMC Palliative Care, 21*(1), 74. Advance online publication. DOI: 10.1186/s12904-022-00964-x PMID: 35578262

Dermody, S., Bhambhani, C., Swiecicki, P., Brenner, J., & Tewari, M. (2022). Transrenal cell-free tumor DNA for urine-based liquid biopsy of cancer. *Frontiers in Genetics, 13*, 879108. Advance online publication. DOI: 10.3389/fgene.2022.879108 PMID: 35571046

Desai, D., & Shende, P. (2021). Integration of Internet of Things with Quantum Dots: A State-of-the-art of Medicine. *Current Pharmaceutical Design, 27*(17), 2068–2075. DOI: 10.2174/1381612827666210222113740 PMID: 33618640

Di Trani, M., Mariani, R., Ferri, R., De Berardinis, D., & Frigo, M. G. (2021). From resilience to burnout in healthcare workers during the COVID-19 emergency: The role of the ability to tolerate uncertainty. [Retrieved from frontiersin.org]. *Frontiers in Psychology, 12*, 646435. DOI: 10.3389/fpsyg.2021.646435 PMID: 33935905

Díaz, O., Guidi, G., Ivashchenko, O., Colgan, N., & Zanca, F. (2021). Artificial intelligence in the medical physics community: An international survey. *Physica Medica, 81*, 141–146. DOI: 10.1016/j.ejmp.2020.11.037 PMID: 33453506

Dineen-Griffin, S., Garcia-Cardenas, V., Williams, K., & Benrimoj, S. I. (2019). Helping patients help themselves: A systematic review of self-management support strategies in primary health care practice. *PLoS One, 14*(8), e0220116. DOI: 10.1371/journal.pone.0220116 PMID: 31369582

Dobie, S. (2007). Reflections on a well-traveled path: Self-awareness, mindful practice, and relationship-centered care as foundations for medical education. *Academic Medicine, 82*(4), 422–427. DOI: 10.1097/01.ACM.0000259374.52323.62 PMID: 17414201

Domagała, A., Bała, M., Storman, D., Peña-Sánchez, J., Świerz, M., Kaczmarczyk, M., & Storman, M. (2018). Factors associated with satisfaction of hospital physicians: A systematic review on european data. *International Journal of Environmental Research and Public Health, 15*(11), 2546. DOI: 10.3390/ijerph15112546 PMID: 30428606

Donabedian, A. (1988). The standard of treatment: How might one measure it? *Journal of Medicine, 260*(12), 1743–1748.

Donnou, C., Chaudru, S., Stivalet, O., Paul, E., Charasson, M., Selli, J., & Jaquinandi, V. (2017). How to become proficient in performance of the resting ankle–brachial index: Results of the first randomized controlled trial. *Vascular Medicine, 23*(2), 109–113. DOI: 10.1177/1358863X17740993 PMID: 29125051

Doram, K., Chadwick, W., Bokovoy, J., Profit, J., Sexton, J. D., & Sexton, J. B. (2017). Got spirit? the spiritual climate scale, psychometric properties, benchmarking data and future directions. *BMC Health Services Research*, *17*(1), 132. Advance online publication. DOI: 10.1186/s12913-017-2050-5 PMID: 28189142

Dorri, A., Stone, A. L., Heffington, B. I., Njowo, P. J., Rivera, G., Schnarrs, P. W., & Salcido, R.Jr. (2023). "we're not gonna talk about this, it didn't happen. you're confused": Adverse communication in family responses to mental health, childhood sexual assault, and LGBTQ identities. *Society and Mental Health*, *14*(1), 39–55. DOI: 10.1177/21568693231170901

Dossey, L. (1995). Healing words: The power of prayer and the practice of medicine. https://www.amazon.com/Healing-Words-Prayer-Practice-Medicine/dp/0062502522

Doyle, C., Lennox, L., & Bell, D. (2013). A systematic review of evidence on the links between patient experience and clinical safety and effectiveness. *BMJ Open*, *3*(1), e001570. DOI: 10.1136/bmjopen-2012-001570 PMID: 23293244

Drake, S., Akande, A., Kelly, P., Yang, Y., & Wolf, D. (2021). Identifying gaps and improving investigation of fatal elder abuse and/or neglect. *Journal of Forensic Sciences*, *66*(6), 2274–2282. DOI: 10.1111/1556-4029.14884 PMID: 34477223

Drewett, G., Gibney, G., & Ko, D. (2021). Practical ethical challenges and moral distress among staff in a hospital covid-19 screening service. *Internal Medicine Journal*, *51*(9), 1513–1516. DOI: 10.1111/imj.15471 PMID: 34541765

Drury, J., & Reicher, S. (2009). Collective psychological empowerment as a model of social change: Researching crowds and power. *The Journal of Social Issues*, *65*(4), 707–725. DOI: 10.1111/j.1540-4560.2009.01622.x

DuBose, J., MacAllister, L., Hadi, K., & Sakallaris, B. (2016). Exploring the concept of healing spaces. *HERD*, *11*(1), 43–56. DOI: 10.1177/1937586716680567 PMID: 29514569

Durmuş, M., Alkan, H., & Çiftci, N. (2021). Effect of covid-19 on exercise health belief, emotional intelligence and stress levels in emergency unit nurses. *International Journal of Health Services Research and Policy*, *6*(3), 345–354. DOI: 10.33457/ijhsrp.894402

Du, S., & Yuan, C. (2010). Evaluation of patient self-management outcomes in health care: A systematic review. *International Nursing Review*, *57*(2), 159–167. DOI: 10.1111/j.1466-7657.2009.00794.x PMID: 20579149

Dyrbye, L., Shanafelt, T., Sinsky, C., Cipriano, P., Bhatt, J., Ommaya, A., West, C. P., & Meyers, D. (2017). Burnout among health care professionals: A call to explore and address this underrecognized threat to safe, high-quality care. *NAM Perspectives*, *7*(7). Advance online publication. DOI: 10.31478/201707b

Elattar, N., Osman, F., & Mahmoud, H. (2023). Effect of emotional intelligence based training program on burnout, psychological capital and job performance among psychiatric nurses. *Menoufia Nursing Journal*, *8*(1), 259–276. DOI: 10.21608/menj.2023.303432

Elliott, R. (2002). The effectiveness of humanistic therapies: A meta-analysis.

Emerald Insight. (n.d.). https://www.emerald.com/insight/content/doi/10.1108/jwam-08-2020-0038/full/html

Emmons, R. A., & McCullough, M. E. (2003). Counting blessings versus burdens: An experimental investigation of gratitude and subjective well-being in daily life. *Journal of Personality and Social Psychology*, *84*(2), 377–389. DOI: 10.1037/0022-3514.84.2.377 PMID: 12585811

Erdoğan, Ö. (2020). Relationship between family members' perceptions of family communication pattern. *Erciyes İletişim Dergisi*, *7*(1), 53–74. DOI: 10.17680/erciyesiletisim.622576

Evangelista, C., Lopes, M., Costa, S., Batista, P., Batista, J., & Oliveira, A. (2016). Cuidados paliativos e espiritualidade: Revisao integrativa da literatura. *Revista Brasileira de Enfermagem*, *69*(3), 591–601. DOI: 10.1590/0034-7167.2016690324i PMID: 27355311

Faherty, K. M. (1996). *Self care discipline's impact on well-being, pain and functional status*. Yeshiva University.

Fakfare, P., & Wattanacharoensil, W. (2020). Impacts of community market development on the residents' well-being and satisfaction. *Tourism Review*, *76*(5), 1123–1140. DOI: 10.1108/TR-02-2020-0071

Falko, N., & Zhukov, O. (2023). Transition from hierarchy to adhocratic organizational culture in a Ukrainian university: From survival to successful development in the conditions of war. [Retrieved from]. *Problems and Perspectives in Management*, *21*(2), 15–22. DOI: 10.21511/ppm.21(2-si).2023.03

Falzarano, F., Cimarolli, V., & Siedlecki, K. (2022). Staying in the loop: Quality of family-paid caregiver communication and influences on resident mental health in long-term care. *Journal of the American Geriatrics Society*, *71*(4), 1209–1219. DOI: 10.1111/jgs.18184 PMID: 36514200

Fang, B., Li, D., Yan, E., Zhou, Y., Yu, Z., & Hu, J. (2022). Associated factors of discrepancy between older adults and their family caregivers in reporting elder abuse. *Journal of Clinical Nursing*, *32*(5-6), 688–700. DOI: 10.1111/jocn.16283 PMID: 35289011

Farhana, A., Kouser, S., Ghani, M., Khatoon, T., & Asghar, R. (2023). Effect of emotional intelligence on job satisfaction among nurses: Descriptive study. *PJMHS*, *17*(6), 127–129. DOI: 10.53350/pjmhs2023176127

Faryal, , & Irum Naqvi, . (2023). The relationship between job satisfaction and job performance: A study on frontline healthcare workers. *Annals of Social Sciences and Perspective*, *4*(1), 171–183. DOI: 10.52700/assap.v4i1.255

Feng, J. (2020, August 19). Research on the Efficiency of Local Government Medical and Health Resources Allocation under Market Economy System. DEStech Transactions on Social Science Education and Human Science. Destech Publications. Retrieved January 2025, from DOI: 10.12783/dtssehs/ecemi2020/34716

Fernandes, A., Carneiro, C., Geocze, L., Santos, V., Guizilini, S., & Moreira, R. (2014). Experiences and opinions of health professionals in relation to the presence of the family during in-hospital cardiopulmonary resuscitation: An integrative review. *Journal of Nursing Education and Practice*, *4*(5). Advance online publication. DOI: 10.5430/jnep.v4n5p85

Fielding, J. E., Teutsch, S. M., & Breslow, L. (2010, June 1). A Framework for Public Health in the United States. Public health reviews. Springer Science+Business Media. Retrieved January 2025, from DOI: 10.1007/BF03391597

Filho, W., Simaens, A., Diaz, P., Vasconcelos, C., Fritzens, B., & Mac-Lean, C. (2023). Integrating the sustainable development goals into the strategy of higher education institutions. *International Journal of Sustainable Development and World Ecology*, *30*(5), 564–575. DOI: 10.1080/13504509.2023.2167884

Finn, J., Klocksieben, F., Smith, A., & Bernstein, J. O'Neil-Pirozzi, T., Kreutzer, J., … & Nakase-Richardson, R. (2022). Family needs after traumatic brain injury: A va tbi model systems study. *The Journal of Head Trauma Rehabilitation*. Advance online publication. DOI: 10.1097/HTR.0000000000000799 PMID: 35687889

Fitch, M. I., & Bartlett, R. (2018, October 24). Patient Perspectives about Spirituality and Spiritual Care. Asia-Pacific Journal of Oncology Nursing. Medknow. Retrieved December 2024, from DOI: 10.4103/apjon.apjon_62_18

Fitts, M. S., Humphreys, J., Dunbar, T., Bourke, L., Mulholland, K., Guthridge, S., Zhao, Y., et al. (2021, August 1). Understanding and responding to the cost and health impact of short-term health staffing in remote and rural Aboriginal and Torres Strait Islander community-controlled health services: a mixed methods study protocol. BMJ Open. BMJ. Retrieved December 2024, from DOI: 10.1136/bmjopen-2020-043902

Flaherty, E., O'Connor, S., Steltenpohl, C. N., Preiss, M., Volckaert, A., & Pepin, R. L. (2023). Geriatric interprofessional team transformation for primary care overview. *Journal of the American Geriatrics Society*, *72*(S2). Advance online publication. DOI: 10.1111/jgs.18637 PMID: 38038277

Fonseca, L., Domingues, P., & Dima, A. (2020). Mapping the sustainable development goals relationships. *Sustainability (Basel)*, *12*(8), 3359. DOI: 10.3390/su12083359

Ford, C. V. (n.d.). Lies! Lies!! Lies!!!: The psychology of deceit (1st ed.). https://www.amazon.com/Lies-Psychology-Deceit/dp/0880489979

Foser, S., Maiese, K., Digumarthy, S. R., Puig-Butille, J. A., & Rebhan, C. (2024, January). Looking to the future of early detection in cancer: Liquid biopsies, imaging, and artificial intelligence. *Clinical Chemistry*, *70*(1), 27–32. DOI: 10.1093/clinchem/hvad196 PMID: 38175601

Foster, S., & Foster, A. (2019). The impact of workplace spirituality on work-based learners. *Journal of Work-Applied Management*, *11*(1), 63–75. DOI: 10.1108/JWAM-06-2019-0015

Fowler, J. H., Hill, S. J., Levin, R., & Obradovich, N. (2020, January 1). The effect of stay-at-home orders on COVID-19 cases and fatalities in the United States. arXiv (Cornell University). Cornell University. Retrieved December 2024, from https://arxiv.org/abs/2004.06098 DOI: 10.1101/2020.04.13.20063628

Franklin, K. (2021). Strategies healthcare leaders use to improve patient satisfaction. Retrieved from waldenu.edu

Frankl, V. E. (2006). *Man's search for meaning*. Beacon Press.

Frost, K., Edelhäuser, F., Hofmann, M., Tauschel, D., & Lutz, G. (2019). History and development of medical studies at the university of witten/herdecke – an example of "continuous reform". DOI: 10.3205/zma001269

Fuentes, M., Jurado, M., Martín, A., & Linares, J. (2019). Family functioning, emotional intelligence, and values: Analysis of the relationship with aggressive behavior in adolescents. *International Journal of Environmental Research and Public Health*, *16*(3), 478. DOI: 10.3390/ijerph16030478 PMID: 30736326

Fundytus, A., Sengar, M., Lombe, D., Hopman, W. M., Jalink, M., Gyawali, B., Trapani, D., Roitberg, F., De Vries, E. G. E., Moja, L., Ilbawi, A., Sullivan, R., & Booth, C. M. (2021). Access to cancer medicines deemed essential by oncologists in 82 countries: An international, cross-sectional survey. *The Lancet. Oncology*, *22*(10), 1367–1377. DOI: 10.1016/S1470-2045(21)00463-0 PMID: 34560006

Furler, J., Walker, C., Blackberry, I., Dunning, T., Sulaiman, N., Dunbar, J., Best, J., & Young, D. (2008). The emotional context of self-management in chronic illness: A qualitative study of the role of health professional support in the self-management of type 2 diabetes. *BMC Health Services Research*, *8*(1), 214. DOI: 10.1186/1472-6963-8-214 PMID: 18928555

Fu, Y., & Chen, M. (2022). Long-term effects of childhood adversity on the subjective well-being of older adults in urban China: The mediating effect of elder abuse. *Aging & Mental Health*, *27*(3), 621–629. DOI: 10.1080/13607863.2022.2040427 PMID: 35176919

Galanis, P., Katsiroumpa, A., Moisoglou, I., Kalogeropoulou, M., Gallos, P., & Vraka, I. (2024). Emotional intelligence protects nurses against quiet quitting, turnover intention, and job burnout. *AIMS Public Health*, *11*(2), 601–613. DOI: 10.3934/publichealth.2024030 PMID: 39027384

Gane, E., Schoeb, V., Cornwell, P., Cooray, C., Cowie, B., & Comans, T. (2022). Discharge planning of older persons from hospital: Comparison of observed practice to recommended best practice. *Health Care*, *10*(2), 202. DOI: 10.3390/healthcare10020202 PMID: 35206817

Ganguli, A., Clewell, J., & Shillington, A. (2016). The impact of patient support programs on adherence, clinical, humanistic, and economic patient outcomes: A targeted systematic review. *Patient Preference and Adherence*, *711*, 711. Advance online publication. DOI: 10.2147/PPA.S101175 PMID: 27175071

Gaobotse, G., Mbunge, E., Batani, J., & Muchemwa, B. (2022). Non-invasive smart implants in healthcare: Redefining healthcare services delivery through sensors and emerging digital health technologies. *Sensors International*, *3*, 100156. DOI: 10.1016/j.sintl.2022.100156

Garcia, E., McNeill, C., Whaley, G., Rohli, R., & Garrison, M. (2023). The relationship between family and community resilience during the developmental transition of emerging adulthood. *Journal of Social Science Research*, *19*, 48–58. DOI: 10.24297/jssr.v19i.9395

García-Navarro, E., Medina-Ortega, A., & Navarro, S. (2021). Spirituality in patients at the end of life—Is it necessary? a qualitative approach to the protagonists. *International Journal of Environmental Research and Public Health, 19*(1), 227. DOI: 10.3390/ijerph19010227 PMID: 35010487

Gaston, S. (2021). Historical racist violence and intergenerational harms: Accounts from descendants of lynching victims. *The Annals of the American Academy of Political and Social Science, 694*(1), 78–91. DOI: 10.1177/00027162211016317

Gautam, A., Jain, A., Chaudhary, J., Gautam, M., Gaur, M., & Grover, S. (2024). Concept of mental health and mental well-being, its determinants and coping strategies. *Indian Journal of Psychiatry, 66*(Suppl 2), S231–S244. DOI: 10.4103/indianjpsychiatry.indianjpsychiatry_707_23 PMID: 38445271

Gayatri, M., & Puspitasari, M. (2022). The impact of covid-19 pandemic on family well-being: A literature review. *The Family Journal (Alexandria, Va.), 31*(4), 606–613. DOI: 10.1177/10664807221131006

Gebagi, R. (2024). Inner mastery guided journal. https://www.amazon.com/Inner-Mastery-Guided-Journal-Gebagi/dp/B0DNRYCXDG

Gerber, L. (2012). Community health nursing: A partnership of care. *The American Journal of Nursing, 112*(1), 19–20. DOI: 10.1097/01.NAJ.0000410170.06154.bb PMID: 22207538

Gholar, V., & Christian, R. (2023). Effectiveness of implementation strategies to improve nutrition education interventions in adults living in rural and/or low-income communities. *JBI Evidence Implementation, 21*(4), 374–385. DOI: 10.1097/XEB.0000000000000371 PMID: 37131273

Gijsberts, M., Liefbroer, A., Otten, R., & Olsman, E. (2019). Spiritual care in palliative care: A systematic review of the recent european literature. *Medical Science, 7*(2), 25. DOI: 10.3390/medsci7020025 PMID: 30736416

Gill Meeley, N. (2021). Undergraduate student nurses' experiences of their community placements. *Nurse Education Today, 106*, 105054. DOI: 10.1016/j.nedt.2021.105054 PMID: 34329964

Glas, G. (2017). Public and institutional aspects of professional responsibility in medicine and psychiatry. *Philosophia Reformata, 82*(2), 146–166. DOI: 10.1163/23528230-08202005

Goel, S. S., Goel, A., Kumar, M., & Moltó, G. (2021). A review of Internet of Things: Qualifying technologies and boundless horizon. *Journal of Reliable Intelligent Environments, 7*(1), 23–33. DOI: 10.1007/s40860-020-00127-w

Goldman, D. P., & Smith, J. P. (2002). Can patient self-management help explain the SES health gradient? *Proceedings of the National Academy of Sciences of the United States of America*, *99*(16), 10929–10934. DOI: 10.1073/pnas.162086599 PMID: 12140364

Goleman, D. (1995). Emotional intelligence. Bantam Books. How stress affects your health. https://www.apa.org/topics/stress/health

Golparvar, M., & Parsakia, K. (2023). Building resilience: Psychological approaches to prevent burnout in health professionals. *KMAN Counsel and Psych Nexus*, *1*(1), 159–166. DOI: 10.61838/kman.psynexus.1.1.18

Gómez-Trinidad, M., Chimpén-López, C., Rodríguez-Santos, L., Moral, M., & Rodríguez-Mansilla, J. (2021). Resilience, emotional intelligence, and occupational performance in family members who are the caretakers of patients with dementia in Spain: A cross-sectional, analytical, and descriptive study. *Journal of Clinical Medicine*, *10*(18), 4262. DOI: 10.3390/jcm10184262 PMID: 34575373

González, J., Cannell, B., Jetelina, K., & Radpour, S. (2016). Barriers in detecting elder abuse among emergency medical technicians. *BMC Emergency Medicine*, *16*(1), 36. Advance online publication. DOI: 10.1186/s12873-016-0100-7 PMID: 27590310

Goyal, M., Singh, S., Sibinga, E. M., Gould, N. F., Rowland-Seymour, A., Sharma, R., Berger, Z., Sleicher, D., Maron, D. D., Shihab, H. M., Ranasinghe, P. D., Linn, S., Saha, S., Bass, E. B., & Haythornthwaite, J. A. (2014). Meditation programs for psychological stress and well-being: A systematic review and meta-analysis. *JAMA Internal Medicine*, *174*(3), 357–368. DOI: 10.1001/jamainternmed.2013.13018 PMID: 24395196

Grady, P. A., & Gough, L. L. (2014). Self-Management: A Comprehensive Approach to Management of Chronic Conditions. *American Journal of Public Health*, *104*(8), e25–e31. DOI: 10.2105/AJPH.2014.302041 PMID: 24922170

Greene, S. M., Tuzzio, L., & Cherkin, D. (2012). A framework for making patient-centered care front and center. *The Permanente Journal*, *16*(3), 49–53. DOI: 10.7812/TPP/12-025 PMID: 23012599

Griffith, D. (2016). Biopsychosocial approaches to men's health disparities research and policy. *Behavioral Medicine (Washington, D.C.)*, *42*(3), 211–215. DOI: 10.1080/08964289.2016.1194158 PMID: 27337626

Groenewald, E., Kilag, O. K., Cabuenas, M. C., Camangyan, J., Abapo, J. M., & Abendan, C. F. (2023). The influence of principals' instructional leadership on the professional performance of teachers. *Excellencia: International Multi-disciplinary* [Retrieved from multijournals.org]. *Journal of Education, 1*(6), 433–443.

Grumbach, K. (2023). Forging a social movement to dismantle entrenched power and liberate primary care as a common good. *Annals of Family Medicine, 21*(2), 180–184. DOI: 10.1370/afm.2950 PMID: 36973058

Gruskin, S., Mills, E. J., & Tarantola, D. (2007). History, principles, and practice of health and human rights. *Lancet, 370*(9585), 449–455. DOI: 10.1016/S0140-6736(07)61200-8 PMID: 17679022

Guedes, F., Cerqueira, A., Gaspar, S., Gaspar, T., Rodríguez, M., & Matos, M. (2022). Family environment and Portuguese adolescents: Impact on quality of life and well-being. *Children (Basel, Switzerland), 9*(2), 200. DOI: 10.3390/children9020200 PMID: 35204920

Gulzar, S., & Khoja, S. (2012, May 27). Innovation: Health care at doorstep. Daily Dawn. http://dawn.com/2012/05/27/innovation-healthcare-at-the-doorstep/

Gulzar, S. A., Faheem, Z. A., & Somani, R. K. (2012). Role of community health nurse in earthquake affected areas. *JPMA. The Journal of the Pakistan Medical Association, 62*(10), 1083. PMID: 23866452

Gulzar, S. A., Shamim, M. S., & Khuwaja, A. K. (2010). Promoting motivation towards community health care: A qualitative study from nurses in Pakistan. *JPMA. The Journal of the Pakistan Medical Association, 60*(6), 501. PMID: 20527656

Gulzar, S., Khoja, S., & Sajwani, A. (2013). Experience of nurses with using eHealth in Gilgit-Baltistan, Pakistan: A qualitative study in primary and secondary healthcare. *BMC Nursing, 12*(1), 6. DOI: 10.1186/1472-6955-12-6 PMID: 23452373

Guo, J., & Li, B. (2018). The application of medical artificial intelligence technology in rural areas of developing countries. *Health Equity, 2*(1), 174–181. DOI: 10.1089/heq.2018.0037 PMID: 30283865

Guo, R., Berkshire, S. D., Fulton, L. V., & Hermanson, P. M. (2017). Use of evidence-based management in healthcare administration decision-making. *Leadership in Health Services, 30*(3), 330–342. DOI: 10.1108/LHS-07-2016-0033 PMID: 28693398

Gupta, K., Anand, T., Kaur, G., Thapliyal, S., & Lal, P. (2022). Job satisfaction among medical officers working in delhi. *Journal of Family Medicine and Primary Care, 11*(1), 155–161. DOI: 10.4103/jfmpc.jfmpc_268_21 PMID: 35309650

Gyedu, A., Abantanga, F., Boakye, G., Gupta, S., Otupiri, E., Agbeko, A., Kushner, A., & Stewart, B. (2016). Barriers to essential surgical care experienced by women in the two northernmost regions of ghana: A cross-sectional survey. *BMC Women's Health, 16*(1), 27. Advance online publication. DOI: 10.1186/s12905-016-0308-4 PMID: 27230890

Gyimesi, J. (2022). Family constellation therapy in the context of esotericism. *Perspectives on Psychological Science, 18*(4), 749–761. DOI: 10.1177/17456916221120424 PMID: 36301913

Haddad, E. (2024). Leveraging social media, big data, and smart technologies for intercultural communication and effective leadership: Empirical study at the Ministry of Digital Economy and Entrepreneurship. [Retrieved from growingscience.com]. *International Journal of Data and Network Science, 8*(2), 857–870. DOI: 10.5267/j.ijdns.2023.12.019

Haileamlak, A. (2018). Editorial: The triple challenges of low and middle-income countries. *Ethiopian Journal of Health Sciences, 28*(1), 1. DOI: 10.4314/ejhs.v28i1.1 PMID: 29622901

Hamouda, G., & Nagshabandi, E. (2018). The perception of emotional intelligence self-assessment among nursing students. *American Journal of Nursing Science, 7*(5), 173. DOI: 10.11648/j.ajns.20180705.13

Han, B., Tomer, V., Nguyen, T. A., Farmani, A., & Singh, P. K. (Eds.). (2020). *Nanosensors for smart cities*. Elsevier.

Han, E., Yeo, S., Kim, M., Lee, Y., Park, K., & Roh, H. (2019). Medical education trends for future physicians in the era of advanced technology and artificial intelligence: An integrative review. *BMC Medical Education, 19*(1), 460. Advance online publication. DOI: 10.1186/s12909-019-1891-5 PMID: 31829208

Hanley, T., Winter, L., & Burrell, K. (2019). Supporting emotional well-being in schools in the context of austerity: An ecologically informed humanistic perspective. *The British Journal of Educational Psychology, 90*(1), 1–18. DOI: 10.1111/bjep.12275 PMID: 30912121

Hansel, N. N., Wu, A. W., Chang, B., & Diette, G. B. (2004). Quality of life in tuberculosis: Patient and provider perspectives. *Quality of Life Research: An International Journal of Quality of Life Aspects of Treatment, Care and Rehabilitation, 13*(3), 639–652. DOI: 10.1023/B:QURE.0000021317.12945.f0 PMID: 15130027

Hansson, K., Romøren, M., Pedersen, R., Weimand, B., Hestmark, L., Norheim, I., Ruud, T., Hymer, I. S., & Heiervang, K. (2022a). Barriers and facilitators when implementing family involvement for persons with psychotic disorders in community mental health centres – a nested qualitative study. *BMC Health Services Research*, *22*(1), 1153. Advance online publication. DOI: 10.1186/s12913-022-08489-y PMID: 36096844

Hansson, K., Romøren, M., Weimand, B., Heiervang, K., Hestmark, L., Landeweer, E., & Pedersen, R. (2022b). The duty of confidentiality during family involvement: Ethical challenges and possible solutions in the treatment of persons with psychotic disorders. *BMC Psychiatry*, *22*(1), 812. Advance online publication. DOI: 10.1186/s12888-022-04461-6 PMID: 36539741

Han, X. (2023). A novel assimilated navigation model based on advanced optical systems (AOS), internet of things (IoT) and artificial intelligence (AI). *Optical and Quantum Electronics*, *55*(7), 655. DOI: 10.1007/s11082-023-04947-x

Hargreaves, J. R., Boccia, D., Evans, C. A., Adato, M., Petticrew, M., & Porter, J. D. (2011). The social determinants of tuberculosis: From evidence to action. *American Journal of Public Health*, *101*(4), 654–662. DOI: 10.2105/AJPH.2010.199505 PMID: 21330583

Harhash, D., Ahmed, M., & Elshereif, H. (2020). Healthcare organizational culture: A concept analysis. *Menoufia Nursing Journal*, *5*(1), 55–63. DOI: 10.21608/menj.2020.123846

Harhash, D., Shrief, H., & Ahmed, M. (2021). The relationship between healthcare organizational culture and nurses' empowerment. *International Journal of Studies in Nursing*, *6*(4), 87. DOI: 10.20849/ijsn.v6i4.975

Harnar, R., Burns, J., Marshall, P., & Karmaliani, R. (1993). Community-based nursing education in Pakistan. *Journal of Continuing Education in Nursing*, *25*(3), 130–132. DOI: 10.3928/0022-0124-19940501-11 PMID: 7797690

Harries, A. D., Kumar, A. M., Satyanarayana, S., Takarinda, K. C., Timire, C., & Dlodlo, R. A. (2020). Treatment for latent tuberculosis infection in low-and middle-income countries: Progress and challenges with implementation and scale-up. *Expert Review of Respiratory Medicine*, *14*(2), 195–208. DOI: 10.1080/17476348.2020.1694907 PMID: 31760848

Harvard Health Publishing. (n.d.). Mind & mood. Retrieved from https://www.health.harvard.edu/topics/mind-and-mood

Harwood, C. H., Reimer-Kirkham, S., Sawatzky, R., Terblanche, L., & Van Hofwegen, L. (2009). Innovation in community clinical placements: A Canadian survey. *International Journal of Nursing Education Scholarship*, *6*(1), 28. Advance online publication. DOI: 10.2202/1548-923X.1860 PMID: 19799562

Hasanah, V., Boriboon, G., Jubaedah, Y., & Wulandari, H. (2021). Analysis of the resilience conditions of individual, family, and community during the covid-19 pandemic. *Journal of Nonformal Education*, *7*(1), 94–102. DOI: 10.15294/jne.v7i1.27853

Hassen, N., Lofters, A., Michael, S., Mall, A., Pinto, A., & Rackal, J. (2021). Implementing anti-racism interventions in healthcare settings: A scoping review. *International Journal of Environmental Research and Public Health*, *18*(6), 2993. DOI: 10.3390/ijerph18062993 PMID: 33803942

Haveri, S., Nm, S., & Nath, A. (2016). Attitude of medical students towards learning communication skills. *International Journal of Community Medicine and Public Health*, *157-160*, 157–160. Advance online publication. DOI: 10.18203/2394-6040.ijcmph20151553

Haycock, C., Curry, D., & Sevilla, X. (2014). Philanthropy and service excellence. *Nursing Administration Quarterly*, *38*(4), 348–355. DOI: 10.1097/NAQ.0000000000000061 PMID: 25208155

Haywood, L., & Wright, C. (2019). Private sector contribution to SDG 3: Health and well-being – a south African case study. *South African Journal of Science*, *115*(9/10). Advance online publication. DOI: 10.17159/sajs.2019/6452

He, L., & Eastburn, M. (2022, August). Smart nanosensor networks for body injury detection. In 2022 IEEE International Conference on Smart Internet of Things (SmartIoT) (pp. 15-19). IEEE. DOI: 10.1109/SmartIoT55134.2022.00012

Heijmans, M., Waverijn, G., Rademakers, J., van der Vaart, R., & Rijken, M. (2015). Functional, communicative and critical health literacy of chronic disease patients and their importance for self-management. *Patient Education and Counseling*, *98*(1), 41–48. DOI: 10.1016/j.pec.2014.10.006 PMID: 25455794

Hellinger, B. (1998). *Acknowledging What Is: Conversations with Bert Hellinger*. Zeig, Tucker & Theisen.

Hellinger, B. (2001). *Love's Hidden Symmetry: What Makes Love Work in Relationships*. Zeig, Tucker & Theisen.

Hellwig, K. (2023). Elder abuse. *Home Healthcare Now*, *41*(6), 304–308. DOI: 10.1097/NHH.0000000000001196 PMID: 37922132

Hem, M., Gjerberg, E., Husum, T., & Pedersen, R. (2016). Ethical challenges when using coercion in mental healthcare: A systematic literature review. *Nursing Ethics*, *25*(1), 92–110. DOI: 10.1177/0969733016629770 PMID: 26931767

Hem, M., Molewijk, B., Weimand, B., & Pedersen, R. (2023). Patients with severe mental illness and the ethical challenges related to confidentiality during family involvement: A scoping review. *Frontiers in Public Health*, *10*, 960815. Advance online publication. DOI: 10.3389/fpubh.2022.960815 PMID: 36711422

Hem, M., Pedersen, R., Norvoll, R., & Molewijk, B. (2014). Evaluating clinical ethics support in mental healthcare. *Nursing Ethics*, *22*(4), 452–466. DOI: 10.1177/0969733014539783 PMID: 25091004

Henderson, B. R., & Armah, N. (2010, March 1). Making the case for community-based wellness programs. National Civic Review. Wiley. Retrieved January 2025, from DOI: 10.1002/ncr.20006

Henize, A., Beck, A., Klein, M., Adams, M., & Kahn, R. (2015). A road map to address the social determinants of health through community collaboration. *Pediatrics*, *136*(4), e993–e1001. DOI: 10.1542/peds.2015-0549 PMID: 26391941

He, Z., Gan, L., Li, X., Shao, X., Zuo, L., Gao, J., & Chen, H. (2021). The implementation of patient-centered humanistic care for covid-19 closely contacted hemodialysis patients under the hospital-based group medical quarantine: A brief research report. *Frontiers in Psychology*, *12*, 553234. Advance online publication. DOI: 10.3389/fpsyg.2021.553234 PMID: 34690846

Hirpa, M., Woreta, T., Addis, H., & Kebede, S. (2020). What matters to patients? a timely question for value-based care. *PLoS One*, *15*(7), e0227845. DOI: 10.1371/journal.pone.0227845 PMID: 32644993

Høgmo, B., Alstveit, M., & Bondas, T. (2023). Being a "warrior" to care for the new family: A meta-ethnography of nurses' perspectives on municipal postnatal healthcare. *Global Qualitative Nursing Research*, *10*, 23333936231218843. Advance online publication. DOI: 10.1177/23333936231218843 PMID: 38149124

Ho, H., Mui, M., Wan, A., Ng, Y., Stewart, S., Yew, C., Lam, T. H., & Chan, S. (2016). Happy family kitchen: A community-based research for enhancing family communication and well-being in Hong Kong. *Journal of Family Psychology*, *30*(6), 752–762. DOI: 10.1037/fam0000233 PMID: 27513284

Ho, H., Mui, M., Wan, A., Yew, C., Lam, T., Chan, S., & Stewart, S. (2018). Family meal practices and well-being in Hong Kong: The mediating effect of family communication. *Journal of Family Issues*, *39*(16), 3835–3856. DOI: 10.1177/0192513X18800787

Holman, H., & Lorig, K. (2014). Perceived self-efficacy in self-management of chronic disease. *Self-Efficacy*, 305–324.

Holt-Lunstad, J., Smith, T. B., & Layton, J. B. (2010). Social relationships and mortality risk: A meta-analytic review. *PLoS Medicine*, *7*(7), e1000316. DOI: 10.1371/journal.pmed.1000316 PMID: 20668659

Holzinger, A., Langs, G., Denk, H., Zatloukal, K., & Müller, H. (2019). Causability and explainability of artificial intelligence in medicine. *Wiley Interdisciplinary Reviews. Data Mining and Knowledge Discovery*, *9*(4), e1312. Advance online publication. DOI: 10.1002/widm.1312 PMID: 32089788

Honarvar, B., Gheibi, Z., Asadollahi, A., Bahadori, F., Khaksar, E., Faradonbeh, M., & Farjami, M. (2020). The impact of abuse on the quality of life of the elderly: A population-based survey in Iran. *Journal of Preventive Medicine and Public Health = Yebang Uihakhoe Chi*, *53*(2), 89–97. DOI: 10.3961/jpmph.19.210 PMID: 32268463

Hooshan, A., Karami, A., & Shaghaghi, F. (2017). Investigation on the effect of emotional intelligence training on self-esteem scales of adolescents under the supervision of behzisti organization. *Psychology and Behavioral Sciences (New York, N.Y.)*, *6*(6), 125. DOI: 10.11648/j.pbs.20170606.12

Horowitz, C., Suchman, A., Branch, W.Jr, & Frankel, R. (2003). What do doctors find meaningful about their work? *Annals of Internal Medicine*, *138*(9), 772–775. DOI: 10.7326/0003-4819-138-9-200305060-00028 PMID: 12729445

Horta Reis Da Silva, T. (2022). Moving and Handling: turning in bed, transfer and hoisting. In Curr, S., & Fordham-Clarke, C. (Eds.), *Clinical Skills at Glance* (pp. 22–23). Wiley.

Huang, J., Wu, X., Huang, W., Wu, X., & Wang, S. (2021). Internet of things in health management systems: A review. *International Journal of Communication Systems*, *34*(4), e4683. DOI: 10.1002/dac.4683

Huang, Q. (2023). Role of narrative education in cultivating humanistic care and empathy in nursing students. DOI: 10.21203/rs.3.rs-3284130/v1

Hudson, D., Gilbert, K. L., & Goodman, M. S. (2023, February 7). Promoting Authentic Academic—Community Engagement to Advance Health Equity. International Journal of Environmental Research and Public Health. Multidisciplinary Digital Publishing Institute. Retrieved December 2024, from DOI: 10.3390/ijerph20042874

Hudson, P. (2003). Home-based support for palliative care families: Challenges and recommendations. *The Medical Journal of Australia*, *179*(6), S35. DOI: 10.5694/j.1326-5377.2003.tb05576.x PMID: 12964935

Hulail, M. (2018). Humanism in medical practice: What, why and how? *Hospice and Palliative Medicine International Journal, 2*(6). Advance online publication. DOI: 10.15406/hpmij.2018.02.00119

Hunger, C., Bornhäuser, A., Link, L., Schweitzer, J., & Weinhold, J. (2013). Improving experience in personal social systems through family constellation seminars: Results of a randomized controlled trial. *Family Process, 53*(2), 288–306. DOI: 10.1111/famp.12051 PMID: 24251855

Hung, M., Licari, F. W., Hon, E. S., Lauren, E., Su, S., Birmingham, W. C., Wadsworth, L. L., Lassetter, J. H., Graff, T. C., Harman, W., Carroll, W. B., & Lipsky, M. S. (2021). In an era of uncertainty: Impact of COVID-19 on dental education. [Retrieved from wiley.com]. *Journal of Dental Education, 85*(2), 148–156. DOI: 10.1002/jdd.12404 PMID: 32920890

Hung, M., Zhang, W., Chen, W., Bounsanga, J., Cheng, C., Franklin, J. D., Crum, A. B., Voss, M. W., & Hon, S. D. (2015). Patient-reported outcomes and total health care expenditure in prediction of patient satisfaction: Results from a national study. *JMIR Public Health and Surveillance, 1*(2), e4360. DOI: 10.2196/publichealth.4360 PMID: 27227131

Hurley, D., & Popescu, G. H. (2021). Medical big data and wearable internet of things healthcare systems in remotely monitoring and caring for confirmed or suspected COVID-19 patients. *American Journal of Medical Research (New York, N.Y.), 8*(2), 78–90. DOI: 10.22381/ajmr8220216

Hurley, J., Koenning, M., & Bray, A. (2018). Responding to intergenerational psychological trauma: A literature review paper on the place of family constellation therapy. *Psychotherapy and Counselling Journal of Australia, 6*(1). Advance online publication. DOI: 10.59158/001c.71192

Hutton, C., Nicholls, R., Lázár, A., Chapman, A., Schaafsma, M., & Salehin, M. (2018). Potential trade-offs between the sustainable development goals in coastal Bangladesh. *Sustainability (Basel), 10*(4), 1108. DOI: 10.3390/su10041108

Hwang, W., Kim, J., Brown, M., & Silverstein, M. (2022). Do religious transitions from early to established adulthood predict filial elder-care norms? *Journal of Marriage and Family, 85*(1), 173–192. DOI: 10.1111/jomf.12833

İbrahimoğlu, Ö., Mersin, S., & Çağlar, M. (2020). The turkish adaptation of the compassionate communication scale: A validity and reliability study. *Perspectives in Psychiatric Care, 57*(1), 43–49. DOI: 10.1111/ppc.12522 PMID: 32314364

Ikeda, K., Tasaka, A., Kasubuchi, K., Jono, Y., & Matsuda, J. (2022). Work beliefs and experiential learning among proficient physical therapists in japan: Developing a method to support belief formation. *Journal of Physical Therapy Science*, *34*(4), 262–268. DOI: 10.1589/jpts.34.262 PMID: 35400828

Imamov, M., & Semenikhina, N. (2021). The impact of the digital revolution on the global economy. *Linguistics and Culture Review*. Retrieved from lingcure.org

Ince, F. (2023). Transformational leadership in a diverse and inclusive organizational culture. In *Handbook of Research on Promoting an Inclusive Organizational Culture for Entrepreneurial Sustainability* (pp. 188–201). Retrieved from. [HTML]

Index Mundi. (n.d.). Pakistan – Life expectancy at birth. https://www.indexmundi.com/facts/pakistan/life-expectancy-at-birth

Institute for Healthcare Improvement. (2022). Applied science for healthcare improvement.

Isaacs, S., Roman, N., & Savahl, S. (2017). An exploration of the family resilience needs of a rural community in south Africa: A sequential explanatory mixed methodological study design. *Current Psychology (New Brunswick, N.J.)*, *38*(6), 1634–1648. DOI: 10.1007/s12144-017-9722-5

ISO. (2022). Quality management systems ISO 9001:2015.

Jaén, C., Crabtree, B., Palmer, R., Ferrer, R., Nutting, P., Miller, W., Stewart, E. E., Wood, R., Davila, M., & Stange, K. (2010). Methods for evaluating practice change toward a patient-centered medical home. *Annals of Family Medicine*, *8*(Suppl_1), S9–S20. DOI: 10.1370/afm.1108 PMID: 20530398

Jafari, Z. (2023). Understanding family functioning: the influence of cultural marginalization and social competence. *JPRFC*, 4-10. https://doi.org/DOI: 10.61838/kman.jprfc.1.4.2

Jaiswal, C., Anderson, K., & Haesler, E. (2019). A self-report of the healer's art by junior doctors: Does the course have a lasting influence on personal experience of humanism, self-nurturing skills and medical counterculture? *BMC Medical Education*, *19*(1), 443. Advance online publication. DOI: 10.1186/s12909-019-1877-3 PMID: 31783846

Jarrett, N. J., Payne, S. A., & Wiles, R. A. (1999). Terminally ill patients' and lay carers' perceptions and experiences of community-based services. *Journal of Advanced Nursing*, *29*(2), 476–483. DOI: 10.1046/j.1365-2648.1999.00908.x PMID: 10197949

Jenkins, T. (2022). Wearable medical sensor devices, machine and deep learning algorithms, and internet of things-based healthcare systems in COVID-19 patient screening, diagnosis, monitoring, and treatment. *American Journal of Medical Research (New York, N.Y.)*, *9*(1), 49–64. DOI: 10.22381/ajmr9120224

Jeon, G., Cho, S., Choi, K., & Jang, K. (2019). Gender differences in the prevalence and correlates of elder abuse in a community-dwelling older population in Korea. *International Journal of Environmental Research and Public Health*, *16*(1), 100. DOI: 10.3390/ijerph16010100 PMID: 30609638

Jerab, D., & Mabrouk, T. (2023). The role of leadership in changing organizational culture. Available at *SSRN* 4574324. Retrieved from *ssrn*.com DOI: 10.2139/ssrn.4574324

Jha, N., Shankar, P., Al-Betar, M., Mukhia, R., Hada, K., & Palaian, S. (2022). Undergraduate medical students' and interns' knowledge and perception of artificial intelligence in medicine. *Advances in Medical Education and Practice*, *13*, 927–937. DOI: 10.2147/AMEP.S368519 PMID: 36039185

Jiang, K., Tian, L., Yan, C., Li, Y., Fang, H., Sun, P., & Liu, M. (2019). A cross-sectional survey on patient safety culture in secondary hospitals of northeast china. *PLoS One*, *14*(3), e0213055. DOI: 10.1371/journal.pone.0213055 PMID: 30893337

Jiang, N. H. L., Cheng, J., & Jiang, X. (2022). A survey and cause analysis of community resilience in a Chinese city from the perspective of nursing. *BMC Public Health*, *22*(1), 2. Advance online publication. DOI: 10.1186/s12889-021-12331-1 PMID: 35030998

Johannessen, A., & Steihaug, S. (2013). The significance of professional roles in collaboration on patients' transitions from hospital to home via an intermediate unit. *Scandinavian Journal of Caring Sciences*, *28*(2), 364–372. DOI: 10.1111/scs.12066 PMID: 23879767

Johns, A., Brown, L., & Cromer, L. (2022). Examining intergenerational transmission of holocaust trauma as it relates to Jewish identity, communication type, and mental well-being. *Journal of Traumatic Stress*, *35*(5), 1497–1507. DOI: 10.1002/jts.22856 PMID: 35733300

Joint Commission International. (2022). Hospital JCI accreditation guidelines.

Jones, D. (2014). A complete medical education includes the arts and humanities. *The Virtual Mentor*, *16*(8), 636–641. DOI: 10.1001/virtualmentor.2014.16.08.msoc1-1408 PMID: 25140687

Josiah, N., Shoola, H., Rodney, T., Arscott, J., Ndzi, M., Bush, A., Wilson, P. R., Jacques, K., Baptiste, D.-L., & Starks, S. (2023). Addressing systemic racism and intergenerational transmission of anxiety using Bowenian family therapy with African American populations: A discursive paper. *Journal of Advanced Nursing*, *79*(5), 1714–1723. DOI: 10.1111/jan.15610 PMID: 36825628

Juan, W., He, B., Wang, Y., Huang, W., & Zhou, J. (2021). Relationships between Kazakh elders' disability severity and informal care time in far north-western low-income areas in China: The mediating roles of caregiver health and home-based care quality. *International Journal of Nursing Practice*, *28*(3), e13022. Advance online publication. DOI: 10.1111/ijn.13022 PMID: 34687110

Jung, H., & Kang, S. (2020). Collective efficacy and communication ability according to emotional intelligence in nursing students. *Indian Journal of Public Health Research & Development*. Advance online publication. DOI: 10.37506/ijphrd.v11i12.13232

Juvet, T. M., Corbaz-Kurth, S., Roos, P., Benzakour, L., Cereghetti, S., Moullec, G., Suard, J.-C., Vieux, L., Wozniak, H., Pralong, J. A., & Weissbrodt, R. (2021). Adapting to the unexpected: Problematic work situations and resilience strategies in healthcare institutions during the COVID-19 pandemic's first wave. [Retrieved from sciencedirect.com]. *Safety Science*, *139*, 105277. DOI: 10.1016/j.ssci.2021.105277 PMID: 34720426

Kaluza, A. J., Weber, F., van Dick, R., & Junker, N. M. (2021). When and how health-oriented leadership relates to employee well-being—The role of expectations, self-care, and LMX. [Retrieved from wiley.com]. *Journal of Applied Social Psychology*, *51*(4), 404–424. DOI: 10.1111/jasp.12744

Kamel Boulos, M. N., & Zhang, P. (2021). Digital twins: From personalised medicine to precision public health. *Journal of Personalized Medicine*. Retrieved from mdpi.com

Kanamori, S., Castro, M. C., Sow, S., Matsuno, R., Cissokho, A., & Jimba, M. (2016). Impact of the Japanese 5S management method on patients' and caretakers' satisfaction: A quasi-experimental study in Senegal. *Global Health Action*, *9*(1), 32852. DOI: 10.3402/gha.v9.32852 PMID: 27900932

Karatas, M., Eriskin, L., Deveci, M., Pamucar, D., & Garg, H. (2022). Big Data for Healthcare Industry 4.0: Applications, challenges, and future perspectives. [Retrieved from]. *Expert Systems with Applications*, *200*, 116912. DOI: 10.1016/j.eswa.2022.116912

Karodia, A., Naranjee, N., & Bikitsha, M. (2015). An evaluation of a holistic approach to managing the integration of the traditional healer into the western biomedical practice: A study of patients of the Khayelitsha medical practice in the western cape province (South Africa). *Academic Journal of Research in Economics and Management*, *2*(9), 1–31. DOI: 10.12816/0017363

Kartina, I. (2021). Art therapy group as efforts of psychiatric emergency prevention. *Journal of Health Community Service*, *1*(2), 66–71. DOI: 10.33086/jhcs.v1i2.2383

Kates, J., Pogorzelska-Maziarz, M., Uppal, M., & Gerolamo, A. (2023). The impact of dementia family caregiving on adolescent well-being: A scoping review. *Dementia (London)*, *22*(4), 910–928. DOI: 10.1177/14713012231161385 PMID: 36880693

Kato, K., Tomita, M., Kato, M., Goto, T., & Nishizono, K. (2021). Prospective cohort study on the incidence and risk factors of emergency home visits among japanese home care patients. *Journal of General and Family Medicine*, *22*(6), 334–340. DOI: 10.1002/jgf2.461 PMID: 34754711

Kaveh-Farsani, Z., Kelishadi, R., & Beshlideh, K. (2020). Study of the effect of family communication and function, and satisfaction with body image, on psychological well-being of obese girls: The mediating role of self-esteem and depression. *Child and Adolescent Psychiatry and Mental Health*, *14*(1), 39. Advance online publication. DOI: 10.1186/s13034-020-00345-3 PMID: 33062050

Kaye, D. R., Richardson, C. R., Ye, Z., Herrel, L. A., Ellimoottil, C., & Miller, D. C. (2017). Association between patient satisfaction and short-term outcomes after major cancer surgery. *Annals of Surgical Oncology*, *24*(12), 3486–3493. DOI: 10.1245/s10434-017-6049-2 PMID: 28819930

Kekeghe, S. (2021). Dramatic art, medical ethics and rehabilitation: Patient-centred therapeutic relationship in omobowale's <i>the president's physician</i>. *International Journal of Literature and Arts*, *9*(4), 177. DOI: 10.11648/j.ijla.20210904.16

Keldal, G., Uslu, A., & Tonga, Z. (2023). Associations of quality of family communication and well-being with marital attitudes among Turkish emerging adults. *Canadian Journal of Family and Youth / Le Journal Canadien De Famille Et De La Jeunesse*, 15(3), 16-30. https://doi.org/DOI: 10.29173/cjfy29906

Kelly, E., Hyer, M., Payne, N., & Pawlik, T. (2020). A mixed-methods approach to understanding the role of religion and spirituality in healthcare provider well-being. *Psychology of Religion and Spirituality*, *12*(4), 487–493. DOI: 10.1037/rel0000297

Kendall, E., Catalano, T., Kuipers, P., Posner, N., Buys, N., & Charker, J. (2007). Recovery following stroke: The role of self-management education. *Social Science & Medicine, 64*(3), 735–746. DOI: 10.1016/j.socscimed.2006.09.012 PMID: 17079060

Kennedy, G. D., Tevis, S. E., & Kent, K. C. (2014). Is there a relationship between patient satisfaction and favorable outcomes? *Annals of Surgery, 260*(4), 592–600. DOI: 10.1097/SLA.0000000000000932 PMID: 25203875

Kerry, R., Young, K. J., Evans, D. W., Lee, E., Georgopoulos, V., Meakins, A., McCarthy, C., Cook, C., Ridehalgh, C., Vogel, S., Banton, A., Bergström, C., Mazzieri, A. M., Mourad, F., & Hutting, N. (2024). A modern way to teach and practice manual therapy. *Chiropractic & Manual Therapies, 32*(1), 17. Advance online publication. DOI: 10.1186/s12998-024-00537-0 PMID: 38773515

Khademi, M., Mohammadi, E., & Vanaki, Z. (2016). A grounded theory of humanistic nursing in acute care work environments. *Nursing Ethics, 24*(8), 908–921. DOI: 10.1177/0969733016638140 PMID: 27009740

Khan, T., Civas, M., Cetinkaya, O., Abbasi, N. A., & Akan, O. B. (2020). Nanosensor networks for smart health care. In *Nanosensors for Smart Cities* (pp. 387–403). Elsevier. DOI: 10.1016/B978-0-12-819870-4.00022-0

Khoja, S., Gulzar, S., & Tirmizi, S. (2015). Low cost telehealth network on the roof of the world: Evidences from Pakistan. *Journal of Nursing (Luton, England), 5*(1).

Kilag, O. K. T., & Sasan, J. M. (2023). Unpacking the role of instructional leadership in teacher professional development. [Retrieved from researchsynergypress.com]. *Advanced Qualitative Research, 1*(1), 63–73. DOI: 10.31098/aqr.v1i1.1380

Kim, H., Solberg, V., & Zaff, J. (2022). Impact of community well-being on individual well-being: A longitudinal multinational study with 155 countries. *Journal of Community Psychology, 51*(3), 1300–1313. DOI: 10.1002/jcop.22922 PMID: 35944128

Kim, J., Kim, J., Shen, E., & Yoon, J. (2022). Sustaining the intrinsic motivations of the "good physician": A content analysis of medical students' and physicians' responses from two national surveys. *Southern Medical Journal, 115*(10), 727–733. DOI: 10.14423/SMJ.0000000000001450 PMID: 36191907

Kimmel, P. L., Emont, S. L., Newmann, J. M., Danko, H., & Moss, A. H. (2003). ESRD patient quality of life: Symptoms, spiritual beliefs, psychosocial factors, and ethnicity. *American Journal of Kidney Diseases, 42*(4), 713–721. DOI: 10.1016/S0272-6386(03)00907-7 PMID: 14520621

King, D. E., & Bushwick, B. (1994). Beliefs and attitudes of hospital inpatients about faith healing and prayer. *The Journal of Family Practice*, *39*(4), 349–352. PMID: 7931113

Klop, H., Veer, A., Dongen, S., Francké, A., Rietjens, J., & Onwuteaka-Philipsen, B. (2018). Palliative care for homeless people: A systematic review of the concerns, care needs and preferences, and the barriers and facilitators for providing palliative care. *BMC Palliative Care*, *17*(1), 67. Advance online publication. DOI: 10.1186/s12904-018-0320-6 PMID: 29690870

Knight, B., Kim, S., Rastegar, S., Jones, S., Jump, V., & Wong, S. (2015). Influences on the perception of elder financial abuse among older adults in southern California. *International Psychogeriatrics*, *28*(1), 163–169. DOI: 10.1017/S1041610215000587 PMID: 25937043

Kodeeswaran, J., Campaigne, M., & Benoit, A. (2020). Indigenous women from the sixties scoop healing through the full moon ceremony and storytelling at Winona's place. *University of Toronto Journal of Public Health*, *1*(1). Advance online publication. DOI: 10.33137/utjph.v1i1.33835

Koehrsen, J. (2021). Muslims and climate change: How Islam, Muslim organizations, and religious leaders influence climate change perceptions and mitigation activities. *Wiley Interdisciplinary Reviews: Climate Change*. Retrieved from wiley.com

Koenig, H. G. (2008). Concerns about measuring "spirituality" in research. *The Journal of Nervous and Mental Disease*, *196*(5), 349–355. DOI: 10.1097/NMD.0b013e31816ff796 PMID: 18477877

Koenig, H. G. (2012). Religion, spirituality, and health: The research and clinical implications. *ISRN Psychiatry*, *278730*, 1–33. Advance online publication. DOI: 10.5402/2012/278730 PMID: 23762764

Koenig, H. G., McCullough, M. E., & Larson, D. B. (2001). *Handbook of religion and health*. Oxford University Press., DOI: 10.1093/acprof:oso/9780195118667.001.0001

Kogan, A. C., Wilber, K. H., & Mosqueda, L. (2015). Person-centered care for older adults with chronic conditions and functional impairment: A systematic literature review. *Journal of the American Geriatrics Society*, *64*(1). Advance online publication. DOI: 10.1111/jgs.13873 PMID: 26626408

Kong, J., & Jeon, H. (2017). Functional decline and emotional elder abuse: A population-based study of older Korean adults. *Journal of Family Violence*, *33*(1), 17–26. DOI: 10.1007/s10896-017-9941-4 PMID: 29977104

Koon, V. (2024). Unveiling the impact of corporate humanistic responsibility on sustainable employee well-being: Exploring perceived support and shared experiences. Business Strategy &Amp. *Business Strategy & Development*, *7*(2), e381. Advance online publication. DOI: 10.1002/bsd2.381

Koper, I., Pasman, H., Schweitzer, B., Kuin, A., & Onwuteaka-Philipsen, B. (2019). Spiritual care at the end of life in the primary care setting: Experiences from spiritual caregivers - a mixed methods study. *BMC Palliative Care*, *18*(1), 98. Advance online publication. DOI: 10.1186/s12904-019-0484-8 PMID: 31706355

Koponen, J., Pyörälä, E., & Isotalus, P. (2012). Comparing three experiential learning methods and their effect on medical students' attitudes to learning communication skills. *Medical Teacher*, *34*(3), e198–e207. DOI: 10.3109/0142159X.2012.642828 PMID: 22364477

Koponen, J., Pyörälä, E., & Isotalus, P. (2014). Communication skills for medical students. *Simulation & Gaming*, *45*(2), 235–254. DOI: 10.1177/1046878114538915

Kristanti, M., Kusmaryanto, K., & Effendy, C. (2021). Common ethical dilemmas of family caregivers of palliative patients in Indonesia. *Belitung Nursing Journal*, *7*(3), 246–250. DOI: 10.33546/bnj.1457 PMID: 37469338

Kruk, M. E., Gage, A. D., Arsenault, C., Jordan, K., Leslie, H. H., Roder-DeWan, S., Adeyi, O., Barker, P., Daelmans, B., Doubova, S. V., English, M., García-Elorrio, E., Guanais, F., Gureje, O., Hirschhorn, L. R., Jiang, L., Kelley, E., Lemango, E. T., Liljestrand, J., & Pate, M. (2018). High-quality health systems in the Sustainable Development Goals era: Time for a revolution. *The Lancet. Global Health*, *6*(11), e1196–e1252. DOI: 10.1016/S2214-109X(18)30386-3 PMID: 30196093

Kulbok, P. A., Thatcher, E., Park, E., & Meszaros, P. S. (2012). Evolving public health nursing roles: Focus on community participatory health promotion and prevention. *Online Journal of Issues in Nursing*, *17*(2). Advance online publication. DOI: 10.3912/OJIN.Vol17No02Man01 PMID: 22686109

Kumar, P. M., Khan, L. U., & Hong, C. S. (2022). Notice of Violation of IEEE Publication Principles: Affirmative Fusion Process for Improving Wearable Sensor Data Availability in Artificial Intelligence of Medical Things. IEEE Sensors Journal.

Kumar, S., & Kumari, P. (2021). Flexible Nano Smart sensors. Nanosensors for Smart Manufacturing, 199.

Kumar, P. M., Hong, C. S., Afghah, F., Manogaran, G., Yu, K., Hua, Q., & Gao, J. (2021). Clouds proportionate medical data stream analytics for internet of things-based healthcare systems. *IEEE Journal of Biomedical and Health Informatics*, *26*(3), 973–982. DOI: 10.1109/JBHI.2021.3106387 PMID: 34415841

Kumar, P. M., Khan, L. U., & Hong, C. S. (2022). Affirmative fusion process for improving wearable sensor data availability in artificial intelligence of medical things. *IEEE Sensors Journal*.

Kutac, J., Osipov, R., & Childress, A. (2015). Innovation through tradition: Rediscovering the "humanist" in the medical humanities. *The Journal of Medical Humanities*, *37*(4), 371–387. DOI: 10.1007/s10912-015-9364-2 PMID: 26561349

La Torre, G., D'Andreano, F., Lecce, G., Di Muzio, M., Chiarini, M., & Pulimeno, A. M. (2020). The occupational health nurse and his/her role in the prevention of work-related diseases: Results of an observational study. *Annali d'Igiene*, *32*(1).

Lam, M. B., Figueroa, J. F., Feyman, Y., Reimold, K. E., Orav, E. J., & Jha, A. K. (2018). Association between patient outcomes and accreditation in US hospitals: Observational study. *BMJ (Clinical Research Ed.)*, *363*, k4011. DOI: 10.1136/bmj.k4011 PMID: 30337294

Langevin, H. M. (2024). Health and well-being: Distinct and intertwined concepts. *Medical Care*, *62*(12, Suppl 1), S13–S14. DOI: 10.1097/MLR.0000000000002061 PMID: 39514486

Laverack, G. (2006). Improving health outcomes through community empowerment: A review of the literature. *Journal of Health, Population and Nutrition*, *24*(1), 113–120. PMID: 16796158

Lavoie-Tremblay, M., Boies, K., Clausen, C., Frechette, J., Manning, K., Gelsomini, C., Cyr, G., Lavigne, G., Gottlieb, B., & Gottlieb, L. N. (2024). Evaluation of the effectiveness of a strengths-based nursing and healthcare leadership program aimed at building leadership capacity: A concurrent mixed-methods study. *International Journal of Nursing Studies Advances*, *6*, 100184. DOI: 10.1016/j.ijnsa.2024.100184 PMID: 38746801

Lawati, M., Dennis, S., Short, S., & Abdulhadi, N. (2018). Patient safety and safety culture in primary health care: A systematic review. *BMC Family Practice*, *19*(1), 104. Advance online publication. DOI: 10.1186/s12875-018-0793-7 PMID: 29960590

Lawn, S. D., Myer, L., Bekker, L. G., & Wood, R. (2006). Burden of tuberculosis in an antiretroviral treatment programme in sub-Saharan Africa: Impact on treatment outcomes and implications for tuberculosis control. *AIDS (London, England)*, *20*(12), 1605–1612. DOI: 10.1097/01.aids.0000238406.93249.cd PMID: 16868441

Lazzara, E. H., Salisbury, M., Hughes, A. M., Rogers, J. E., King, H. B., & Salas, E. (2022). The morbidity and mortality conference: Opportunities for enhancing patient safety. [Retrieved from rice.edu]. *Journal of Patient Safety*, *18*(1), e275–e281. DOI: 10.1097/PTS.0000000000000765 PMID: 34951610

Leaman, J., Richards, A., Emslie, L., & O'Moore, É. (2017). Improving health in prisons – from evidence to policy to implementation – experiences from the UK. *International Journal of Prisoner Health*, *13*(3/4), 139–167. DOI: 10.1108/IJPH-09-2016-0056 PMID: 28914122

Lee, A., Kim, S., Gim, G., Kim, D., & Park, S. (2019). Care farming program for family health: A pilot study with mothers and children. *International Journal of Environmental Research and Public Health*, *17*(1), 27. DOI: 10.3390/ijerph17010027 PMID: 31861441

Lee, B. Y., & Newberg, A. B. (2005). Religion and health: A review and critical analysis. *Zygon*, *40*(2), 443–468. DOI: 10.1111/j.1467-9744.2005.00674.x

Lee, G., Pickstone, N., Facultad, J., & Titchener, K. (2017). The future of community nursing: Hospital in the home. *British Journal of Community Nursing*, *22*(4), 174–180. DOI: 10.12968/bjcn.2017.22.4.174 PMID: 28414540

Lee, J., & Sim, I. (2021). Analysis of the relationship between the psychological well-being, emotional intelligence, willpower, and job-efficacy of clinical nurses: A structural model application. *International Journal of Environmental Research and Public Health*, *18*(11), 5582. DOI: 10.3390/ijerph18115582 PMID: 34073657

Lee, J., Slack, M., Martin, J., Ehrman, C., & Chisholm-Burns, M. (2013). Geriatric patient care by u.s. pharmacists in healthcare teams: Systematic review and meta-analyses. *Journal of the American Geriatrics Society*, *61*(7), 1119–1127. DOI: 10.1111/jgs.12323 PMID: 23796001

Lee, W., Harris, C., Mortensen, K., Long, L., & Sugimoto-Matsuda, J. (2016). Enhancing student perspectives of humanism in medicine: Reflections from the kalaupapa service learning project. *BMC Medical Education*, *16*(1), 137. Advance online publication. DOI: 10.1186/s12909-016-0664-7 PMID: 27159976

Leotsakos, A., Zheng, H., Croteau, R., Loeb, J. M., Sherman, H., Hoffman, C., Morganstein, L., O'Leary, D., Bruneau, C., Lee, P., Duguid, M., Thomeczek, C., Schrieck-De Loos, E., & Munier, B. (2014). Standardization in patient safety: The WHO High 5s project. *International Journal for Quality in Health Care : Journal of the International Society for Quality in Health Care*, *26*(2), 109–116. DOI: 10.1093/intqhc/mzu010 PMID: 24713313

Lerner, R. M., Lerner, J. V., Almerigi, J. B., Theokas, C., Phelps, E., Gestsdottir, S., Naudeau, S., Jelicic, H., Alberts, A., Ma, L., Smith, L. M., Bobek, D. L., Richman-Raphael, D., Simpson, I., Christiansen, E. D. D., & von Eye, A. (2005). Positive youth development, participation in community youth development programs, and community contributions of fifth-grade adolescents: Findings from the first wave of the 4-H Study of Positive Youth Development. *The Journal of Early Adolescence*, *25*(1), 17–71. DOI: 10.1177/0272431604272461

Létourneau, D., Goudreau, J., & Cara, C. (2020). Facilitating and hindering experiences to the development of humanistic caring in the academic and clinical settings: An interpretive phenomenological study with nursing students and nurses. *International Journal of Nursing Education Scholarship*, *17*(1), 20190036. Advance online publication. DOI: 10.1515/ijnes-2019-0036 PMID: 32710718

Lev, N. (2024). Strategic healthcare workforce planning in light of healthcare inequalities: a comparative analysis of workforce planning policy in israel and comparable oecd countries. DOI: 10.20944/preprints202406.0066.v1

Liang, M., Liang, J., Xu, J., Chen, Q., & Lu, Q. (2024). Experience of multidisciplinary medical teams on humanistic palliative care in oncology wards: A descriptive qualitative study in southern china. *BMJ Open*, *14*(2), e074628. DOI: 10.1136/bmjopen-2023-074628 PMID: 38413159

Liao, L., Zhang, F., Zhang, Y., Guan, C., Xu, G., Yuan, C., Yang, X., Huang, L., Wang, W., He, X., Xu, J., & Liu, Y. (2023). Nurse managers' perceptions and experiences of caring behavior for clinical nurses: A multicenter survey. *BMC Nursing*, *22*(1), 383. Advance online publication. DOI: 10.1186/s12912-023-01541-0 PMID: 37845648

Li, C., Liu, Y., Xue, D., & Chan, C. W. H. (2020, October). Effects of nurse-led interventions on early detection of cancer: A systematic review and meta-analysis. *International Journal of Nursing Studies*, *110*, 103684. DOI: 10.1016/j.ijnurstu.2020.103684 PMID: 32702568

Liikanen, E., & Lehto, L. (2013). Training of nurses in point-of-care testing: A systematic review of the literature. *Journal of Clinical Nursing*, *22*(15-16), 2244–2252. DOI: 10.1111/jocn.12235 PMID: 23679832

Lillemoen, L., & Pedersen, R. (2012). Ethical challenges and how to develop ethics support in primary health care. *Nursing Ethics*, *20*(1), 96–108. DOI: 10.1177/0969733012452687 PMID: 22918061

Li, M., Qin, G., & Li, Y. (2022). Mediating effects of emotional intelligence on the relationship between empathy and humanistic care ability in nursing students: A cross-sectional descriptive study. *Medicine*, *101*(46), e31673. DOI: 10.1097/MD.0000000000031673 PMID: 36401377

Lim, C., & Putnam, R. D. (2010). Religion, social networks, and life satisfaction. *American Sociological Review*, *75*(6), 914–933. DOI: 10.1177/0003122410386686

Li, N., & He, M. (2023). Intergenerational support and subjective wellbeing of the elderly in mainland China: The role of perceived health. *SAGE Open*, *13*(1), 21582440231159014. Advance online publication. DOI: 10.1177/21582440231159014

Lineberry, M. J., & Ickes, M. J. (2014). The role and impact of nurses in American elementary schools: A systematic review of the research. *The Journal of School Nursing: the Official Publication of the National Association of School Nurses*. Advance online publication. DOI: 10.1177/1059840514540940 PMID: 24972802

Lin, Y., & Lin, C. (2010). Factors predicting patients' perception of privacy and satisfaction for emergency care. *Emergency Medicine Journal : EMJ*, *28*(7), 604–608. DOI: 10.1136/emj.2010.093807 PMID: 20660898

Liu, S., & Willoughby, J. F. (2018). Do Fitness Apps Need Text Reminders? An Experiment Testing Goal-Setting Text Message Reminders to Promote Self-Monitoring. *Journal of Health Communication*, *23*(4), 379–386. DOI: 10.1080/10810730.2018.1455768 PMID: 29601270

Liu, Y., Zhang, F., Guan, C., Song, B., Zhang, H., Fu, M., Wang, F., Tang, C., Chen, H., Guo, Q., Fan, L., Hou, X., Wang, H., Wu, B., Shan, G., Zhang, H., Yu, F., Lou, X., Xie, H., & Guo, S. (2023). Patient satisfaction with humanistic nursing in chinese secondary and tertiary public hospitals: A cross-sectional survey. *Frontiers in Public Health*, *11*, 1163351. Advance online publication. DOI: 10.3389/fpubh.2023.1163351 PMID: 37711237

Li, X., Fang, X., Wang, L., Geng, X., & Chang, H. (2021). Relationship between emotional intelligence and job well-being in Chinese registered nurses: Mediating effect of communication satisfaction. *Nursing Open*, *8*(4), 1778–1787. DOI: 10.1002/nop2.820 PMID: 33656788

Loa, R. (2018). Facilitators and barriers to self-management of tuberculosis patients: A qualitative study. *International Journal of Integrated Care, 18*(s2), 285. DOI: 10.5334/ijic.s2285

Lomas, C. (2009). Is nursing's great challenge care of the elderly? *Nursing Times.*

Lombana, Y. (2021). Possibilities and challenges in providing psychotherapeutic interventions to meet the needs of the Latinx population in the United States. *Genealogy, 5*(1), 12. DOI: 10.3390/genealogy5010012

Long, N. H., Johansson, E., Diwan, V. K., & Winkvist, A. (1999). Different tuberculosis in men and women: Beliefs from focus groups in Vietnam. *Social Science & Medicine, 49*(6), 815–822. DOI: 10.1016/S0277-9536(99)00171-9 PMID: 10459892

Lorig, K. (1993). Self-management of chronic illness: A model for the future. *Generations: Journal of the American Society on Aging, 17*(3), 11–14.

Lorig, K. (1996). Chronic Disease Self-Management: A Model for Tertiary Prevention. *The American Behavioral Scientist, 39*(6), 676–683. DOI: 10.1177/0002764296039006005

Lorig, K. R., & Holman, H. R. (2003). Self-management education: History, definition, outcomes, and mechanisms. *Annals of Behavioral Medicine, 26*(1), 1–7. DOI: 10.1207/S15324796ABM2601_01 PMID: 12867348

Lorig, K. R., Ritter, P., Stewart, A. L., Sobel, D. S., Brown, B. W.Jr, Bandura, A., Gonzalez, V. M., Laurent, D. D., & Holman, H. R. (2001). Chronic disease self-management program: 2-year health status and health care utilization outcomes. *Medical Care, 39*(11), 1217–1223. DOI: 10.1097/00005650-200111000-00008 PMID: 11606875

Lovallo, W. (2013). Early life adversity reduces stress reactivity and enhances impulsive behavior: Implications for health behaviors. *International Journal of Psychophysiology, 90*(1), 8–16. DOI: 10.1016/j.ijpsycho.2012.10.006 PMID: 23085387

Lowery, B. (2010). Interagency collaboration: A strategy for obesity policy success. *Bariatric Nursing and Surgical Patient Care, 5*(4), 331–334. DOI: 10.1089/bar.2010.9989

Lowery, B. (2011). The future of nursing report: Policy implications for nursing. *Bariatric Nursing and Surgical Patient Care, 6*(1), 49–51. DOI: 10.1089/bar.2011.9980

Lucchetti, G., Granero Lucchetti, A. L., & Koenig, H. G. (2011). Religion, spirituality, and cardiovascular disease: Research, clinical implications, and opportunities in Brazil. *Brazilian Journal of Cardiovascular Surgery*, *26*(3), 430–437. DOI: 10.1590/S0102-76382011000300020

Lucchetti, G., Lucchetti, A., Espinha, D., Oliveira, L., Leite, J., & Koenig, H. (2012). Spirituality and health in the curricula of medical schools in brazil. *BMC Medical Education*, *12*(1), 78. Advance online publication. DOI: 10.1186/1472-6920-12-78 PMID: 22900476

Lucchetti, G., Oliveira, L., Koenig, H., Leite, J., & Lucchetti, A. (2013). Medical students, spirituality and religiosity-results from the multicenter study sbrame. *BMC Medical Education*, *13*(1), 162. Advance online publication. DOI: 10.1186/1472-6920-13-162 PMID: 24314327

Luchies, L., Barbour, B., & Anderson, B. (2019). Children's healing center involvement reduces social isolation and loneliness among immunocompromised children and their family members. *American Journal of Recreation Therapy*, *18*(3), 37–47. DOI: 10.5055/ajrt.2019.0194

Lück, D., & Castrén, A. (2018). Personal understandings and cultural conceptions of family in European societies. *European Societies*, *20*(5), 699–714. DOI: 10.1080/14616696.2018.1487989

Lu, D., Dresden, S., McCloskey, C., Branzetti, J., & Gisondi, M. (2015). Impact of burnout on self-reported patient care among emergency physicians. *The Western Journal of Emergency Medicine*, *16*(7), 996–1001. DOI: 10.5811/westjem.2015.9.27945 PMID: 26759643

Ludvigsson, M., Wiklund, N., Swahnberg, K., & Simmons, J. (2022). Experiences of elder abuse: A qualitative study among victims in Sweden. *BMC Geriatrics*, *22*(1), 256. Advance online publication. DOI: 10.1186/s12877-022-02933-8 PMID: 35351038

Lund, I., Handal, M., Bukten, A., Torvik, F., Ystrøm, E., & Andreas, J. (2019). Association of constellations of parental risk with children's subsequent anxiety and depression. *JAMA Pediatrics*, *173*(3), 251. DOI: 10.1001/jamapediatrics.2018.4360 PMID: 30615089

Lu, Y., & Shorey, S. (2021). Nurses' perceptions of emotional intelligence in the clinical setting: A qualitative systematic review. *Journal of Nursing Management*, *29*(8), 2453–2460. DOI: 10.1111/jonm.13406 PMID: 34216499

MacKay-Barr, M., & Csiernik, R. (2019). An exploration of elder abuse in a rural Canadian community. *Critical Social Work, 13*(1). Advance online publication. DOI: 10.22329/csw.v13i1.5847

Mackey, L. M., Doody, C., Werner, E. L., & Fullen, B. (2016). Self-Management Skills in Chronic Disease Management: What Role Does Health Literacy Have? *Medical Decision Making, 36*(6), 741–759. DOI: 10.1177/0272989X16638330 PMID: 27053527

Mack, J. W., Cronin, A., Taback, N., Huskamp, H. A., Keating, N. L., Malin, J. L., Earle, C. C., & Weeks, J. C. (2012). End-of-life care discussions among patients with advanced cancer: A cohort study. *Annals of Internal Medicine, 156*(3), 204–210. DOI: 10.7326/0003-4819-156-3-201202070-00008 PMID: 22312140

Ma, F., Zhu, Y., Liu, Y., & Lu, L. (2023). Association analysis of nursing humanistic care demands and psychological distress in cancer surgery patients: a cross-sectional study. DOI: 10.21203/rs.3.rs-1878362/v2

Magalnick, H., & Mazyck, D. (2008). Role of the school nurse in providing school health services. *Pediatrics, 121*(5), 1052–1056. DOI: 10.1542/peds.2008-0382 PMID: 18450912

Mahendradhata, Y., Souares, A., Phalkey, R., & Sauerborn, R. (2014). Optimizing patient-centeredness in the transitions of healthcare systems in low- and middle-income countries. *BMC Health Services Research, 14*(1), 386. Advance online publication. DOI: 10.1186/1472-6963-14-386 PMID: 25212684

Mahmoudian, A., Shamsalinia, A., Alipour, A., Fotoukian, Z., & Ghaffari, F. (2021). Structural equation model of affecting factors on elder abuse to patients under hemodialysis by family caregivers. *BMC Geriatrics, 21*(1), 360. Advance online publication. DOI: 10.1186/s12877-021-02291-x PMID: 34118877

Majid, M. F. (2020, June 7). *Rethinking health spending. The News (Pakistan).* https://www.thenews.com.pk/tns/detail/668387-rethinking-health-spending

Malik, A., & Kumar, A. (2022). assimilation of blockchain with Internet of Things (IoT) with possible issues and solutions for better connectivity and proper security. In New Trends and Applications in Internet of Things (IoT) and Big Data Analytics (pp. 187-207). Cham: Springer International Publishing.

Malik, P. K., Sharma, R., Singh, R., Gehlot, A., Satapathy, S. C., Alnumay, W. S., Pelusi, D., Ghosh, U., & Nayak, J. (2021). Industrial Internet of Things and its applications in industry 4.0: State of the art. *Computer Communications, 166*, 125–139. DOI: 10.1016/j.comcom.2020.11.016

Manogaran, G., Alazab, M., Song, H., & Kumar, N. (2021). CDP-UA: Cognitive data processing method wearable sensor data uncertainty analysis in the internet of things assisted smart medical healthcare systems. *IEEE Journal of Biomedical and Health Informatics*, *25*(10), 3691–3699. DOI: 10.1109/JBHI.2021.3051288 PMID: 33439849

Manyazewal, T., Oosthuizen, M., & Matlakala, M. (2016). Proposing evidence-based strategies to strengthen implementation of healthcare reform in resource-limited settings: A summative analysis. *BMJ Open*, *6*(9), e012582. DOI: 10.1136/bmjopen-2016-012582 PMID: 27650769

Mardomakdehi, A., Sum, S., & Faramarzi, M. (2019). Challenges for detection of elderly abuse in teaching hospitals: A interventional study to improve the knowledge of health care providers. *Shiraz E Medical Journal*, *21*(2). Advance online publication. DOI: 10.5812/semj.91348

Mariati, L., Jakri, Y., & Djerubu, D. (2022). The effect of emotional intelligence on nurse's communication skill. [Journal of Ners and Midwifery]. *Jurnal Ners Dan Kebidanan*, *9*(2), 218–226. DOI: 10.26699/jnk.v9i2.ART.p218-226

Marshman, C., Allen, J., Ling, D., & Brand, G. (2024). 'it's very values driven': A qualitative systematic review of the meaning of compassion according to healthcare professionals. *Journal of Clinical Nursing*, *33*(5), 1647–1665. DOI: 10.1111/jocn.16998 PMID: 38240044

Marterre, B., Hinshaw, D., & Shinall, M. (2023). Spirituality in surgery-a double-edged scalpel. *The American Surgeon*, *89*(5), 1347–1351. DOI: 10.1177/00031348231157805 PMID: 36786501

Martin, J., & Roberts, S. (2020). The effectiveness of mediation for older people at risk of or experiencing abuse. *Conflict Resolution Quarterly*, *38*(3), 175–187. DOI: 10.1002/crq.21294

Martín-Martín, J., Pérez-Díez-del-Corral, M., Olano-Lizarraga, M., Valencia-Gil, S., & Saracíbar-Razquin, M. (2021). Family narratives about providing end-of-life care at home. *Journal of Family Nursing*, *28*(1), 17–30. DOI: 10.1177/10748407211025579 PMID: 34165346

Materon, E. M., Gómez, F. R., Joshi, N., Dalmaschio, C. J., Carrilho, E., & Oliveira Jr, O. N. (2021). Smart materials for electrochemical flexible nanosensors: advances and applications. Nanosensors for smart manufacturing, 347-371.

Mayer, C., & Viviers, A. (2015). Constellation work principles, resonance phenomena, and shamanism in south Africa. *South African Journal of Psychology. Suid-Afrikaanse Tydskrif vir Sielkunde, 46*(1), 130–145. DOI: 10.1177/0081246315591339

Mayer, C., & Viviers, R. (2015). Exploring cultural issues for constellation work in south Africa. *Australian and New Zealand Journal of Family Therapy, 36*(2), 289–306. DOI: 10.1002/anzf.1103

Mazur, B. (2024). Organizational culture in enterprises applying the humanistic and economic paradigm of management.. DOI: 10.5772/intechopen.113155

McDade, R. (2013). A mixed method study of spirituality and the influence on TB medication adherence. https://digitalcommons.fiu.edu/cgi/viewcontent.cgi?article=1260&context=sferc

McDonald, S. M. (2012). *The effects of a SMART goal setting and self-monitoring intervention on physical activity and fitness in middle school students.* https://ir.library.oregonstate.edu/concern/graduate_thesis_or_dissertations/xd07gw96b

McDonald, S. M., & Trost, S. G. (2015). The effects of a goal setting intervention on aerobic fitness in middle school students. *Journal of Teaching in Physical Education, 34*(4), 576–587. DOI: 10.1123/jtpe.2014-0138

McDowell, L., & South, R. (2017). Christians' perceptions of receiving spiritual care in the bible belt of the united states: A qualitative study of care provided in the healthcare setting. *Religions, 8*(7), 127. DOI: 10.3390/rel8070127

McIvera, S., & Tayehb, R. (2017). I wish i understood this so i could make it change": Results from a web-based survey investigating weight loss and regain. *International Journal of Complementary & Alternative Medicine, 9*(1). Advance online publication. DOI: 10.15406/ijcam.2017.08.00283

McQuillin, J., & Welford, E. (2013). How many people are gathered here? group work and family constellation theory. *Transactional Analysis Journal, 43*(4), 352–365. DOI: 10.1177/0362153713519743

McSherry, W., & Jamieson, S. (2013). The qualitative findings from an online survey investigating nurses' perceptions of spirituality and spiritual care. *Journal of Clinical Nursing, 22*(21-22), 3170–3182. DOI: 10.1111/jocn.12411 PMID: 24118520

Meadows, P. (2009). Community health nursing. AJN. *The American Journal of Nursing, 109*(10), 19. DOI: 10.1097/01.NAJ.0000343102.62178.80 PMID: 21753458

Meara, J. G., Leather, A. J., Hagander, L., Alkire, B. C., Alonso, N., Ameh, E. A., Bickler, S. W., Conteh, L., Dare, A. J., Davies, J., Mérisier, E. D., El-Halabi, S., Farmer, P. E., Gawande, A., Gillies, R., Greenberg, S. L. M., Grimes, C. E., Gruen, R. L., Ismail, E. A., & Yip, W. (2015). Global Surgery 2030: Evidence and solutions for achieving health, welfare, and economic development. *Lancet*, *386*(9993), 569–624. DOI: 10.1016/S0140-6736(15)60160-X PMID: 25924834

Médecins Sans Frontières. (2024). *Clinical guidelines - Diagnosis and treatment manual* (ISBN 978-2-37585-264-4).

Mehdi, F., Dahlke, S., & Hunter, K. (2022). Developing a comprehensive understanding of older person abuse in Canadian immigrant communities: An integrative review. *Canadian Journal of Nursing Research*, *55*(2), 139–152. DOI: 10.1177/08445621221112429 PMID: 35821575

Mejdahl, C., Nielsen, B., Mehlsen, M., Hollesen, M., Pedersen, M., Engkjaer-Trautwein, G., Funch, L. V., & Terkildsen, M. (2022). Covid-19 as moral breakdown: Entangled ethical demands experienced by hospital-based nurses in the early onset of the pandemic. *Nursing Inquiry*, *30*(1), e12508. Advance online publication. DOI: 10.1111/nin.12508 PMID: 35709227

Micozzi, M. S. (2018). *Fundamentals of complementary, alternative, and integrative medicine*. Elsevier Health Sciences.

Miles, A. (2013). Science, humanism, judgement, ethics: Person-centered medicine as an emergent model of modern clinical practice / наука, гуманизм, преценка, этика, пациент. гуманизм в медицина - новая модель в современн ой клинической практике. *Folia Medica*, *55*(1), 5–24. DOI: 10.2478/folmed-2013-0001 PMID: 23905483

Milner, D. A.Jr, & Lennerz, J. K. (2024). Technology and future of multi-cancer early detection. *Life (Chicago, Ill.)*, *14*(7), 833. DOI: 10.3390/life14070833 PMID: 39063587

Min, J., Chung, C., Jung, S. S., Park, H. K., Lee, S. S., & Lee, K. M. (2019). Understanding illness perception in pulmonary tuberculosis patients: One step towards patient-centered care. *PLoS One*, *14*(6), e0218106. DOI: 10.1371/journal.pone.0218106 PMID: 31188871

Minkler, M., & Wallerstein, N. (Eds.). (2008). *Community-based participatory research for health: From process to outcomes* (2nd ed.). Jossey-Bass.

Minnesota Department of Health. (n.d.). Public health nursing resources. https://www.health.state.mn.us/divs/chs/phn/resources.html

Mitchell, C., Epstein-Peterson, Z., Bandini, J., Amobi, A., Cahill, J., Enzinger, A., Noveroske, S., Peteet, J., Balboni, T., & Balboni, M. (2016). Developing a medical school curriculum for psychological, moral, and spiritual wellness: Student and faculty perspectives. *Journal of Pain and Symptom Management*, *52*(5), 727–736. DOI: 10.1016/j.jpainsymman.2016.05.018 PMID: 27693904

Moen, P., Kelly, E., & Huang, R. (2008). Fit inside the work-family black box: An ecology of the life course, cycles of control reframing. *Journal of Occupational and Organizational Psychology*, *81*(3), 411–433. DOI: 10.1348/096317908X315495 PMID: 19809532

Mohamad, F., & Abiddin, N. Z. (2024). Enhancing employee well-being and productivity in evolving work environments. *Academic Journal of Interdisciplinary Studies*, *13*(3), 289. DOI: 10.36941/ajis-2024-0081

Mohammadi, F., Naderi, Z., Nikrouz, L., Oshvandi, K., Masoumi, S. Z., Sabetsarvestani, P., & Bijani, M. (2023). Ethical challenges as perceived by nurses in pediatric oncology units. *Nursing Ethics*, *31*(2-3), 268–280. DOI: 10.1177/09697330231191278 PMID: 37624231

Mohammad, Y. J., Vertejee, S., Gulzar, S., Shehzad, S., & Sachwani, S. (2019, September). Community health nursing clinical teaching models practiced in undergraduate nursing program at a private university in Pakistan. *JPMA. The Journal of the Pakistan Medical Association*. PMID: 31511708

Mohebi, S., Azadbakht, L., Feizi, A., Sharifirad, G., & Kargar, M. (2013). Review the key role of self-efficacy in diabetes care. *Journal of Education and Health Promotion*, *2*(1), 36. DOI: 10.4103/2277-9531.115827 PMID: 24083286

Molewijk, B., Hem, M., & Pedersen, R. (2015). Dealing with ethical challenges: A focus group study with professionals in mental health care. *BMC Medical Ethics*, *16*(1), 4. Advance online publication. DOI: 10.1186/1472-6939-16-4 PMID: 25591923

Monteith, S., Glenn, T., Geddes, J., Whybrow, P., Achtyes, E., & Bauer, M. (2022). Expectations for artificial intelligence (ai) in psychiatry. *Current Psychiatry Reports*, *24*(11), 709–721. DOI: 10.1007/s11920-022-01378-5 PMID: 36214931

Moodley, N., Weidler, E. M., Ochoa, B., Eldredge, R. S., Rakkar, M., Boles, K., & van Leeuwen, K. (2024). Satisfaction with multidisciplinary team structure and function in a pediatric outpatient clinic. [Retrieved from]. *Journal of Pediatric Surgery*, •••, 162103. PMID: 39733606

Moore, S., Hackworth, N., Hamilton, V., Northam, E., & Cameron, F. (2013). Adolescents with type 1 diabetes: Parental perceptions of child health and family functioning and their relationship to adolescent metabolic control. *Health and Quality of Life Outcomes*, *11*(1), 50. Advance online publication. DOI: 10.1186/1477-7525-11-50 PMID: 23521786

Moosivand, S., Nazari, O., Shahverdi, A., Gholami, M., Mohammadi, R., & Yarahmadi, S. (2023). Predictors of emotional intelligence among family caregivers of cancer patients: A cross-sectional study. *Cancer Reports*, *7*(1), e1943. Advance online publication. DOI: 10.1002/cnr2.1943 PMID: 37990763

Moreno, P. (2024). The role of family functionality and its relationship with psychological well-being and emotional intelligence in high school students. *Education Sciences*, *14*(6), 566. DOI: 10.3390/educsci14060566

Mostafa, A., Hoque, R., Mostafa, M., Rana, M., & Mostafa, F. (2014). Empathy in undergraduate medical students of bangladesh: Psychometric analysis and differences by gender, academic year, and specialty preferences. *ISRN Psychiatry*, *2014*, 1–7. DOI: 10.1155/2014/375439 PMID: 25006522

Mousa, M., Boyle, J., Skouteris, H., Mullins, A. K., Currie, G., Riach, K., & Teede, H. J. (2021). Advancing women in healthcare leadership: A systematic review and meta-synthesis of multi-sector evidence on organisational interventions. [Retrieved from thelancet.com]. *EClinicalMedicine*, *39*, 39. DOI: 10.1016/j.eclinm.2021.101084 PMID: 34430838

Mousavi, M., Khodayari-Zarnaq, R., & Hajizadeh, A. (2021). Main challenges in adoption of consultation services of hospital ethics committees: A systematic review of the literature. *Clinical Ethics*, *17*(1), 41–50. DOI: 10.1177/1477750921994278

Mousavi, S., Hassanvand, P., Mahmoudi, A., Hosseinigolafshani, S. Z., Rajabi, M., & Rashvand, F. (2023). The relationship between emotional intelligence and the moral performance of nurses. *Journal of Nursing and Midwifery Sciences*, *10*(4). Advance online publication. DOI: 10.5812/jnms-141609

Muhibbin, A., Patmisari, P., Mahadir Naidu, N. B., Prasetiyo, W. H., & Hidayat, M. L. (2023). An analysis of factors affecting student wellbeing: Emotional intelligence, family and school environment. [IJERE]. *International Journal of Evaluation and Research in Education*, *12*(4), 1954. DOI: 10.11591/ijere.v12i4.25670

Mujawar, M. A., Gohel, H., Bhardwaj, S. K., Srinivasan, S., Hickman, N., & Kaushik, A. (2020). Nano-enabled biosensing systems for intelligent healthcare: Towards COVID-19 management. *Materials Today. Chemistry*, *17*, 100306. DOI: 10.1016/j.mtchem.2020.100306 PMID: 32835155

Munang, M. L., Browne, C., Evans, J. T., Smith, E. G., Hawkey, P. M., Welch, S. B., Kaur, H., & Dedicoat, M. J. (2016). Programmatic utility of tuberculosis cluster investigation using a social network approach in Birmingham, United Kingdom. *The International Journal of Tuberculosis and Lung Disease : the Official Journal of the International Union against Tuberculosis and Lung Disease*, *20*(10), 1300–1305. DOI: 10.5588/ijtld.16.0161 PMID: 27725038

Musa, S. M., Haruna, U. A., Manirambona, E., Eshun, G., Ahmad, D. M., Dada, D. A., Gololo, A. A., et al. (2023, August 29). Paucity of Health Data in Africa: An Obstacle to Digital Health Implementation and Evidence-Based Practice. Public health reviews. Springer Science+Business Media. Retrieved January 2025, from DOI: 10.3389/phrs.2023.1605821

Mustika, R., & Soemantri, D. (2020). Unveiling the hurdles in cultivating humanistic physicians in the clinical setting: An exploratory study. *The Malaysian Journal of Medical Sciences : MJMS*, *27*(3), 117–124. DOI: 10.21315/mjms2020.27.3.12 PMID: 32684812

Nabiei, A., Karamafrooz, M., & Afsharnia, K. (2014). The comparison of emotional intelligence and hardiness in addicts and non-addicts. *Kuwait Chapter of Arabian Journal of Business and Management Review*, *3*(7), 196–204. DOI: 10.12816/0018281

Nabi, G., Abibulaeva, A., Bulakbayeva, M., & Zholzhaksynova, M. (2022). The problem of the development of emotional intelligence of future social educators. *Cypriot Journal of Educational Sciences*, *17*(7), 2416–2427. DOI: 10.18844/cjes.v17i7.7687

Nakhaei, S., Amiri Majd, M., Mohammadi Arya, A., & Shirazi, M. (2020). The role of mindfulness, spiritual experiences, and coping strategies in anticipation of the quality of life of patients with tuberculosis. *Journal of Research and Health*, *10*(3), 143–150. https://jrh.gmu.ac.ir/browse.php?a_id=1402&sid=1&slc_lang=en. DOI: 10.32598/JRH.10.3.1402.1

Nantsupawat, A., Wichaikhum, O., Abhicharttibutra, K., Udkunta, K., Poghosyan, L., & Shorey, S. (2023, June 19). Factors influencing evidence-based practice among undergraduate nursing students: A cross-sectional analysis. International Journal of Nursing Sciences. Elsevier BV. Retrieved December 2024, from DOI: 10.1016/j.ijnss.2023.06.002

National Center for Complementary and Integrative Health. (n.d.). Complementary, alternative, or integrative health: What's in a name? https://www.nccih.nih.gov/health/complementary-alternative-or-integrative-health-whats-in-a-name

National Research Council. (2001, May). *Mammography and beyond.* DOI: 10.17226/10107

Nazir, M., Wayenberg, E., & Qureshi, S. (2023). Exploring the role of policy actors in the implementation of social distancing: A case of covid-19 in pakistan. *Public Administration and Policy*, *26*(1), 93–106. DOI: 10.1108/PAP-04-2022-0033

Nelson, L., Maramaldi, P., Kinnunen, T., & Kalenderian, E. (2013). Early performance in a humanistic medicine course as a predictor of dental students' later clinical performance. *Journal of Dental Education*, *77*(8), 1006–1012. DOI: 10.1002/j.0022-0337.2013.77.8.tb05569.x PMID: 23929570

Nemati-Vakilabad, R., Khalili, Z., Ghanbari-Afra, L., & Mirzaei, A. (2023). The prevalence of elder abuse and risk factors: A cross-sectional study of community older adults. *BMC Geriatrics*, *23*(1), 616. Advance online publication. DOI: 10.1186/s12877-023-04307-0 PMID: 37777720

Nepal, N., Aryal, B., & Poudel, B. (2023). Situation, risks and prevention strategies of elder abuse: A lesson for Nepal. *Mangal Research Journal*, *4*(01), 15–28. DOI: 10.3126/mrj.v4i01.61717

Newsham, I., Sendera, M., Jammula, S. G., & Samarajiwa, S. A. (2024, January). Early detection and diagnosis of cancer with interpretable machine learning to uncover cancer-specific DNA methylation patterns. *Biology Methods and Protocols*, *9*(1), bpae028. Advance online publication. DOI: 10.1093/biomethods/bpae028 PMID: 38903861

Ng, E., & Colombani, P. de. (2015, November 17). Framework for Selecting Best Practices in Public Health: A Systematic Literature Review. Deleted Journal. Retrieved December 2024, from DOI: 10.4081/jphr.2015.577

Ng, C., Fraser, J., Goding, M., Paroissien, D., & Ryan, B. (2012). Partnerships for community mental health in the Asia-pacific: Principles and best-practice models across different sectors. *Australasian Psychiatry*, *21*(1), 38–45. DOI: 10.1177/1039856212465348 PMID: 23236092

Nguyen, N., Subhan, F., Williams, K., & Chan, C. (2020). Barriers and mitigating strategies to healthcare access in indigenous communities of Canada: A narrative review. *Health Care*, *8*(2), 112. DOI: 10.3390/healthcare8020112 PMID: 32357396

Nickerson, A., Bryant, R., Brooks, R., Steel, Z., Silove, D., & Chen, J. (2011). The familial influence of loss and trauma on refugee mental health: A multilevel path analysis. *Journal of Traumatic Stress*, *24*(1), 25–33. DOI: 10.1002/jts.20608 PMID: 21268119

Ningrum, D., Latifah, M., & Krisnatuti, D. (2021). Marital readiness: Exploring the key factors among university students. *Humanitas, 18*(1), 65. DOI: 10.26555/humanitas.v18i1.17912

Nonnecke, B., Andrews, D., & Preece, J. (2006). Non-public and public online community participation: Needs, attitudes and behaviour. *Electronic Commerce Research, 6*(1), 7–20. DOI: 10.1007/s10660-006-5985-x

Normand, M. P. (2008). Increasing physical activity through self-monitoring, goal setting, and feedback. *Behavioral Interventions, 23*(4), 227–236. DOI: 10.1002/bin.267

Norton, M., & Cuskelly, K. (2021). Family recovery interventions with families of mental health service users: A systematic review of the literature. *International Journal of Environmental Research and Public Health, 18*(15), 7858. DOI: 10.3390/ijerph18157858 PMID: 34360150

O'Hara, N. (2022). Eliciting health care preferences with discrete choice experiments. *JAMA Network Open, 5*(4), e228794. DOI: 10.1001/jamanetworkopen.2022.8794 PMID: 35467737

O'Neal, C., Mallette, J., & Mancini, J. (2018). The importance of parents' community connections for adolescent well-being: An examination of military families. *American Journal of Community Psychology, 61*(1-2), 204–217. DOI: 10.1002/ajcp.12222 PMID: 29400402

Obu, R. and Aggrey-Bluwey, L. (2021). A case study of complementary alternative medicines in primary healthcare in Ghana. *Journal of Complementary and Alternative Medical Research*, 23-33. https://doi.org/DOI: 10.9734/jocamr/2021/v15i130256

Occupational Safety and Health Administration. (n.d.). Occupational Health Nursing. https://www.osha.gov/dts/oohn/ohn.html

October, K., Petersen, L., Adebiyi, B., Rich, E., & Roman, N. (2021). Covid-19 daily realities for families: A south African sample. *International Journal of Environmental Research and Public Health, 19*(1), 221. DOI: 10.3390/ijerph19010221 PMID: 35010480

October, T., Hinds, P., Wang, J., Dizon, Z., Cheng, Y., & Roter, D. (2016). Parent satisfaction with communication is associated with physician's patient-centered communication patterns during family conferences*. *Pediatric Critical Care Medicine, 17*(6), 490–497. DOI: 10.1097/PCC.0000000000000719 PMID: 27058750

Oduoye, M., Fatima, E., Muzammil, M. A., Dave, T., Irfan, H., Fariha, F. N. U., Marbell, A., Ubechu, S. C., Scott, G. Y., & Elebesunu, E. E. (2024). Impacts of the advancement in artificial intelligence on laboratory medicine in low- and middle-income countries: Challenges and recommendations—a literature review. *Health Science Reports*, *7*(1), e1794. Advance online publication. DOI: 10.1002/hsr2.1794 PMID: 38186931

Ohta, R., & Sano, C. (2023). Integrating clinical and socio-environmental approaches in managing rheumatoid arthritis with social determinants of health: A case study of an elderly patient in rural Japan. *Cureus*. Advance online publication. DOI: 10.7759/cureus.50915 PMID: 38249275

Ojiezeh, T. I., Ogundipe, O. O., & Adefosoye, V. A. (2015). A retrospective study on incidence of pulmonary tuberculosis and human immunodeficiency virus co-infection among patients attending National Tuberculosis and leprosy control Programme, Owo centre. *The Pan African Medical Journal*, *20*, 5643. DOI: 10.11604/pamj.2015.20.345.5643

Ojifinni, O., Adebayo, E., & Uchendu, O. (2023). Insights into caregivers' perspectives on abuse of older persons: A qualitative exploratory study in southwest Nigeria. *BMJ Open*, *13*(10), e070937. DOI: 10.1136/bmjopen-2022-070937 PMID: 37852773

Olin, S., Williams, N., Pollock, M., Armusewicz, K., Kutash, K., Glisson, C., & Hoagwood, K. (2013). Quality indicators for family support services and their relationship to organizational social context. *Administration and Policy in Mental Health*, *41*(1), 43–54. DOI: 10.1007/s10488-013-0499-z PMID: 23709286

Olorunsogo, T. (2024). Ethical considerations in ai-enhanced medical decision support systems: A review. *World Journal of Advanced Engineering Technology and Sciences*, *11*(1), 329–336. DOI: 10.30574/wjaets.2024.11.1.0061

Omary, Z., Mtenzi, F., Wu, B., & O'Driscoll, C. (2011). Ubiquitous healthcare information system: Assessment of its impacts to patient's information. *International Journal for Information Security Research*, *1*(3), 71–77. DOI: 10.20533/ijisr.2042.4639.2011.0009

Onyango, P. A., Ter Goon, D., & Rala, N. M. D. (2021). Knowledge, attitudes and health-seeking behaviour among patients with tuberculosis: A cross-sectional study. *The Open Public Health Journal*, *13*(1), 739–747. DOI: 10.2174/1874944502013010739

Ordons, A. (2018). How clinicians integrate humanism in their clinical workplace—'just trying to put myself in their human being shoes'. *Perspectives on Medical Education*, *7*(5), 318–324. DOI: 10.1007/S40037-018-0455-4 PMID: 30298438

Oukhatar, A., Bakhouya, M., & El Ouadghiri, D. (2021). Electromagnetic-Based Wireless Nano-Sensors Network: Architectures and Applications. *Journal of Communication, 16*(1), 8–19. DOI: 10.12720/jcm.16.1.8-19

Ownsworth, T. L., McFarland, K., & Young, R. McD. (2002). The investigation of factors underlying deficits in self-awareness and self-regulation. *Brain Injury : [BI], 16*(4), 291–309. DOI: 10.1080/02699050110103986 PMID: 11953001

Ozdemir, C., & Kaplan, A. (2024). Examining nurses' humanistic behaviour ability and empathy levels in clinical practice: A descriptive and exploratory study. *Journal of Clinical Nursing, 33*(8), 3115–3127. DOI: 10.1111/jocn.16992 PMID: 38234293

Öztürk, A., & Kaçan, H. (2021). Compassionate communication levels of nursing students: Predictive role of empathic skills and nursing communication course. *Perspectives in Psychiatric Care, 58*(1), 248–255. DOI: 10.1111/ppc.12954 PMID: 34601733

Ozturk, F. O., & Hisar, F. (2014). Stigmatisation of tuberculosis patients. *International Journal of Community Medicine and Public Health, 1*(1), 37. DOI: 10.5455/2394-6040.ijcmph20141108

Paal, P., Helo, Y., & Frick, E. (2015). Spiritual care training provided to healthcare professionals: A systematic review. *The Journal of Pastoral Care & Counseling, 69*(1), 19–30. DOI: 10.1177/1542305015572955 PMID: 26162203

Page, E. J., Massey, A. S., Prado-Romero, P. N., & Albadawi, S. (2020). The Use of Self-Monitoring and Technology to Increase Physical Activity: A Review of the Literature. *Perspectives on Behavior Science, 43*(3), 501–514. DOI: 10.1007/s40614-020-00260-0 PMID: 33029577

Pagorek-Eshel, S., Elias, H., Alnabilsy, R., & Grinapol, S. (2022). The association of social factors and covid-19–related resource loss with depression and anxiety among Arabs in Israel. *Psychological Trauma: Theory, Research, Practice, and Policy, 14*(2), 310–317. DOI: 10.1037/tra0001140 PMID: 34618477

Pakistan Secretariat, A. S. E. R. (2022, March). ASER-Pakistan 2021. http://aserpakistan.org/document/aser/2021/reports/national/ASER_report_National_2021.pdf

Paneru, N., & Kafle, A. (2024). A cross-sectional study on association between emotional intelligence and academic performance among nursing students of selected nursing colleges in Kathmandu. *International Journal of Education Humanities and Social Science, 07*(01), 261–275. DOI: 10.54922/IJEHSS.2024.0653

Panfilis, L., Tanzi, S., Perin, M., Turola, E., & Artioli, G. (2020). "teach for ethics in palliative care": A mixed-method evaluation of a medical ethics training programme. *BMC Palliative Care*, *19*(1), 149. Advance online publication. DOI: 10.1186/s12904-020-00653-7 PMID: 32977796

Papineau, D., & Kiely, M. C. (1996). Participatory evaluation in a community organization: Fostering stakeholder empowerment and utilization. *Evaluation and Program Planning*, *19*(1), 79–93. DOI: 10.1016/0149-7189(95)00041-0

Papreen, N., Sharma, A., Sabin, K., Begum, L., Ahsan, S. K., & Baqui, A. H. (2000). Living with infertility: experiences among urban slum populations in Bangladesh. *Reproductive health matters, 8*(15), 33-44. doi: s10.1016/S0968-8080(00)90004-1

Pargament, K. I. (1997). *The psychology of religion and coping: Theory, research, practice*. Guilford Press.

Pargament, K. I., & Lomax, J. W. (2013). Understanding and addressing religion among people with mental illness. *World Psychiatry; Official Journal of the World Psychiatric Association (WPA)*, *12*(1), 26–32. DOI: 10.1002/wps.20005 PMID: 23471791

Parnell, T. A., McCulloch, E., Mieres, J. H., & Edwards, F. (2014, January 28). Health Literacy as an Essential Component to Achieving Excellent Patient Outcomes. *NAM Perspectives*, *4*(1). Advance online publication. Retrieved December 2024, from. DOI: 10.31478/201401b

Parvathavarthine, C., Krishna, M., Janaki, C., Sophia, M., & Chandar, S. (2022). Awareness about the future of artificial intelligence in healthcare among medical students in kancheepuram district, tamil nadu. *International Journal of Health Sciences*, •••, 5697–5705. DOI: 10.53730/ijhs.v6nS8.13571

Patel, H. N., Ghodgaonkar, D. K., & Suri, J. S. (2022, December). The role of AI in diagnosis, treatment and monitoring of breast cancer during COVID-19 and ahead. In *Breast Image Reconstruction and Cancer Detection Using Microwave Imaging* (pp. 11-1–11-21). DOI: 10.1088/978-0-7503-2592-9ch11

Patriotis, C., & Srivastava, S. (2023). Early cancer detection: Challenges and opportunities. *Current Cancer Research*, (Part F1235), 619–631. DOI: 10.1007/978-3-031-22903-9_24

Pawirosumarto, S., Sarjana, P., & Gunawan, R. (2017). The effect of work environment, leadership style, and organizational culture towards job satisfaction and its implication towards employee performance in parador hotels and resorts, indonesia. *International Journal of Law and Management*, *59*(6), 1337–1358. DOI: 10.1108/IJLMA-10-2016-0085

Pentland, D., Forsyth, K., Maciver, D., Walsh, M., Murray, R., Irvine, L., & Sikora, S. (2011). Key characteristics of knowledge transfer and exchange in healthcare: Integrative literature review. *Journal of Advanced Nursing*, *67*(7), 1408–1425. DOI: 10.1111/j.1365-2648.2011.05631.x PMID: 21466576

Pepe, M. S., Etzioni, R., Feng, Z., Potter, J. D., Thompson, M. L., Thornquist, M., Winget, M., & Yasui, Y. (2001, July). Phases of biomarker development for early detection of cancer. *Journal of the National Cancer Institute*, *93*(14), 1054–1061. DOI: 10.1093/jnci/93.14.1054 PMID: 11459866

Perrin, P. (2012). Humanistic psychology's social justice philosophy. *Journal of Humanistic Psychology*, *53*(1), 52–69. DOI: 10.1177/0022167812447133

Perry, H., Zulliger, R., & Rogers, M. (2014). Community health workers in low-, middle-, and high-income countries: An overview of their history, recent evolution, and current effectiveness. *Annual Review of Public Health*, *35*(1), 399–421. DOI: 10.1146/annurev-publhealth-032013-182354 PMID: 24387091

Peter, A., & Aighobahi, J. (2019). Assessment of the implementation of tuberculosis and diabetes care in health systems: a situational analysis in western nigeria for consideration. DOI: 10.21203/rs.2.12294/v1

Petersen, I., Rensburg, A., Kigozi, F., Semrau, M., Hanlon, C., Abdulmalik, J., & Thornicroft, G. (2019). Scaling up integrated primary mental health in six low- and middle-income countries: Obstacles, synergies and implications for systems reform. *BJPsych Open*, *5*(5), e69. Advance online publication. DOI: 10.1192/bjo.2019.7 PMID: 31530322

Piché, G., Villatte, A., Clément, M.-È., Morin, M.-H., Maybery, D., Reupert, A., Richard-Devantoy, S., & Fournier-Marceau, M. (2024). Predictors of family-focused practices among mental health workers in Quebec. *Frontiers in Psychiatry*, *15*, 1380001. Advance online publication. DOI: 10.3389/fpsyt.2024.1380001 PMID: 38803674

Piri, N., Tanjani, P., Khodkarim, S., & Etemad, K. (2018). Domestic elder abuse and associated factors in elderly women in Tehran, Iran. *Epidemiology and Health*, *40*, e2018055. DOI: 10.4178/epih.e2018055 PMID: 30428642

Pirsoul, T., Parmentier, M., & Nils, F. (2021). One step beyond emotional intelligence measurement in the career development of adult learners: A bifactor exploratory structural equation modeling framework. *Current Psychology (New Brunswick, N.J.)*, *42*(7), 5834–5850. DOI: 10.1007/s12144-021-01772-x

Pluye, P., Potvin, L., & Denis, J.-L. (2004). Making public health programs last: Conceptualizing sustainability. *Evaluation and Program Planning*, *27*(2), 121–133. DOI: 10.1016/j.evalprogplan.2004.01.001

Pluye, P., Potvin, L., Denis, J.-L., Pelletier, J., & Mannoni, C. (2005). Program sustainability begins with the first events. *Evaluation and Program Planning*, *28*(2), 123–137. DOI: 10.1016/j.evalprogplan.2004.10.003

Pourvakhshoori, N., Norouzi, K., Ahmadi, F., Hosseini, M., & Khankeh, H. (2017). Nursing in disasters: A review of existing models. *International Emergency Nursing*, *31*, 58–63. DOI: 10.1016/j.ienj.2016.06.004 PMID: 27423385

Power, J., Goodyear, M., Maybery, D., Reupert, A., O'Hanlon, B., Cuff, R., & Perlesz, A. (2015). Family resilience in families where a parent has a mental illness. *Journal of Social Work : JSW*, *16*(1), 66–82. DOI: 10.1177/1468017314568081

Powers, J., & Eubank, K. (2018). Geriatrics evaluation and management in the veterans administration—An historical perspective. *Geriatrics (Basel, Switzerland)*, *3*(4), 84. DOI: 10.3390/geriatrics3040084 PMID: 31011119

Pradhan, M. R., Mago, B., & Ateeq, K. (2023). A classification-based sensor data processing method for the internet of things assimilated wearable sensor technology. *Cluster Computing*, *26*(1), 807–822. DOI: 10.1007/s10586-022-03605-3

Pramanik, P. K. D., Solanki, A., Debnath, A., Nayyar, A., El-Sappagh, S., & Kwak, K. S. (2020). Advancing modern healthcare with nanotechnology, nanobiosensors, and internet of nano things: Taxonomies, applications, architecture, and challenges. *IEEE Access : Practical Innovations, Open Solutions*, *8*, 65230–65266. DOI: 10.1109/ACCESS.2020.2984269

Pratiwi, I. N., Hidayati, L., Alviani, N. I., & McKenna, L. (2021). The correlation between anxiety levels and spiritual activities with motivation to recover in pulmonary tuberculosis. *Enfermeria Clinica*, *31*, 535–539. DOI: 10.1016/j.enfcli.2020.10.037

Price, O., Long, M., Sadlon, R., & Sheriff, L. (2023). Enhancing school capacity to adopt school behavioural health best practices: A multiple-case study evaluation. *Journal of Community & Applied Social Psychology*, *34*(1), e2759. Advance online publication. DOI: 10.1002/casp.2759

Prime, H., Walsh, F., & Masten, A. S. (2023). Building family resilience in the wake of a global pandemic: Looking back to prepare for the future. *Canadian Psychology, 64*(3), 200–211. DOI: 10.1037/cap0000366

Puchalski, C. M., & Ferrell, B. (2009). Making health care whole: Integrating spirituality into patient care. https://www.amazon.com/Making-Health-Care-Whole-Spirituality/dp/159947350

Puchalski, C. M. (2006). The role of spirituality in health care. *Proceedings - Baylor University. Medical Center, 14*(4), 352–357. DOI: 10.1080/08998280.2001.11927788 PMID: 16369646

Puchalski, C. M., Vitillo, R., Hull, S. K., & Reller, N. (2014). Improving the spiritual dimension of whole person care: Reaching national and international consensus. *Journal of Palliative Medicine, 17*(6), 642–656. DOI: 10.1089/jpm.2014.9427 PMID: 24842136

Puchalski, C., Blatt, B., Коган, M., & Butler, A. (2014). Spirituality and health. *Academic Medicine, 89*(1), 10–16. DOI: 10.1097/ACM.0000000000000083 PMID: 24280839

Punjab Healthcare Commission. (2021). Minimum service delivery standards.

Qidwai, M. A. (2024). The 5Ss' Approach for Managing Health of Client, Family and Community. *National Journal, 9*(4), 232. DOI: 10.21089/njhs.94.0231

Qin, Y., Liu, J., & Wu, D. (2023). The impact of emotional intelligence on life satisfaction among Chinese nurses: A chain mediating model. *Frontiers in Psychology, 14*, 1125465. Advance online publication. DOI: 10.3389/fpsyg.2023.1125465 PMID: 36874842

Quinn, M., Hunter, C., Ray, S., Quadir, M., Sen, K., & Cumming, R. (2016). The double burden: Barriers and facilitators to socioeconomic inclusion for women with disability in Bangladesh. *Disability, CBR and Inclusive Development, 27*(2), 128. DOI: 10.5463/dcid.v27i2.474

Quora. (n.d.). What real-life or everyday problem, issue, or question does your research hope to address? https://www.quora.com/What-real-life-or-everyday-problem-issue-or-question-does-your-research-hope-to-address

Radermacher, H., Toh, Y., Western, D., Coles, J., Goeman, D., & Lowthian, J. (2018). Staff conceptualisations of elder abuse in residential aged care: A rapid review. *Australasian Journal on Ageing, 37*(4), 254–267. DOI: 10.1111/ajag.12565 PMID: 30062840

Radu, C. (2023). Fostering a positive workplace culture: Impacts on performance and agility. *Human Resource Management—An Update*. Retrieved from intechopen.com

Raghav, S. (2017, August 10). "Hr as Strategic Partner: Manpower- Engines of Change in Health Sector Reforms and Human Resource." JOJ Nursing & Health Care. Retrieved December 2024, from DOI: 10.19080/JOJNHC.2017.03.555603

Rahayu, A., Shaleh, A., & Marliani, R. (2021). The effect of work-life and social media balances on Moslem family teachers in pandemic time. *Psikis Jurnal Psikologi Islami*, *7*(2), 169–179. DOI: 10.19109/psikis.v7i2.8247

Raheem, Y. (2020). Prevention in healthcare practice: An issue with rising importance. *Al-Kindy College Medical Journal*, *15*(2), 1–3. DOI: 10.47723/kcmj.v15i2.150

Rajaonson, J., & Schmitt, K. (2024). Ai and data technologies in advancing sustainable development goals. *IEEE Technology and Society Magazine*, *43*(1), 33–38. DOI: 10.1109/MTS.2024.3374970

Rajapakshe, W. (2024). Fundamentals of Performance Management. Advances in logistics, operations, and management science book series (p. 1). Routledge. Retrieved January 2025, from DOI: 10.4018/979-8-3693-4387-6.ch001

Raja, S., Hasnain, M., Vadakumchery, T., Hamad, J., Shah, R., & Hoersch, M. (2015). Identifying elements of patient-centered care in underserved populations: A qualitative study of patient perspectives. *PLoS One*, *10*(5), e0126708. DOI: 10.1371/journal.pone.0126708 PMID: 25993110

Rakhshani, T., Motlagh, Z., Beigi, V., Rahimkhanli, M., & Rashki, M. (2018). The relationship between emotional intelligence and job stress among nurses in Shiraz, Iran. *The Malaysian Journal of Medical Sciences : MJMS*, *25*(6), 100–109. DOI: 10.21315/mjms2018.25.6.10 PMID: 30914883

Rambiritch, V., Vermeulen, M., Bell, H., Knox, P., Nedelcu, E., Al-Riyami, A., & Berg, K. (2021). Transfusion medicine and blood banking education and training for blood establishment laboratory staff: A review of selected countries in africa. *Transfusion*, *61*(6), 1955–1965. DOI: 10.1111/trf.16372 PMID: 33738810

Ram, D., Whipple, C., & Jason, L. (2017). Family dynamics may influence an individual's substance use abstinence self-efficacy. *Journal of Addiction and Preventive Medicine*, *02*(01). Advance online publication. DOI: 10.19104/japm.2016.106 PMID: 28868520

Ramírez, M., Solomon, J., Riquelme, M., Santoro, B., Reingold, D., & Teresi, J. (2018). Development and spanish translation of the Weinberg Center risk and abuse prevention screen (wc-raps). *Journal of Elder Abuse & Neglect*, *31*(1), 38–55. DOI: 10.1080/08946566.2018.1531099 PMID: 30406734

Ranabhat, P., Nikitara, M., Latzourakis, E., & Constantinou, C. (2022). Effectiveness of nurses' training in identifying, reporting and handling elderly abuse: A systematic literature review. *Geriatrics (Basel, Switzerland)*, *7*(5), 108. DOI: 10.3390/geriatrics7050108 PMID: 36286211

Rani, P. (2022). Nanosensors and their Potential Role in Internet of Medical Things. In *Nanosensors for Futuristic Smart and Intelligent Healthcare Systems* (pp. 293–317). CRC Press. DOI: 10.1201/9781003093534-16

Rasheed, S. P., Younas, A., & Sundus, A. (2019). Self-awareness in nursing: A scoping review. *Journal of Clinical Nursing*, *28*(5–6), 762–774. DOI: 10.1111/jocn.14708 PMID: 30362645

Rasinski, K. A., Kalad, Y. G., Yoon, J. D., & Curlin, F. A. (2011). An assessment of US physicians' training in religion, spirituality, and medicine. *Medical Teacher*, *33*(11), 944–945. DOI: 10.3109/0142159X.2011.588976 PMID: 22022906

Rassool, G. H. (2021, October 19). Re-Examining the Anatomy of Islamic Psychotherapy and Counselling: Envisioned and Enacted Practices. Islamic Guidance and Counseling Journal. Institut Agama Islam Ma'arif NU (IAIMNU) Metro Lampung. Retrieved December 2024, from DOI: 10.25217/igcj.v4i2.1840

Rathod, S., Pinninti, N., Irfan, M., Gorczynski, P., Rathod, P., Gega, L., & Naeem, F. (2017). Mental health service provision in low- and middle-income countries. *Health Services Insights*, *10*, 1178632917694350. Advance online publication. DOI: 10.1177/1178632917694350 PMID: 28469456

Rêgo, F., & Nunes, R. (2016). The interface between psychology and spirituality in palliative care. *Journal of Health Psychology*, *24*(3), 279–287. DOI: 10.1177/1359105316664138 PMID: 27531369

Reis da Silva TH (2024e) Understanding body fluid balance, dehydration and intravenous fluid therapy. Emergency Nurse. doi: https://doi.org/10.7748/en.2024.e2201

Reis da Silva Tiago. (2024n) The Value of Emotional Intelligence in Midwifery: Enhancing Care and Outcomes for Mothers and Infants through Sustainable Development Goals and Leadership. Journal of Womens Healthcare & Midwifery Research. SRC/JWHMR-133. DOI: doi.org/ Link: https://www.onlinescientificresearch.com/articles/the-value-of-emotional-intelligence-in-midwifery-enhancing-care-and-outcomes-for-mothers-and-infants-through-sustainable-developme.pdfDOI: 10.47363/JWHMR/2024(3)119

Reis da Silva, T H (2024d). Prevalence of elder abuse: a narrative review. British journal of community nursing vol. 29,9: 442-446. doi: https://doi.org/DOI: 10.12968/bjcn.2024.0004

Reis da Silva, T H (2024e). Prevalence of elder abuse: a narrative review. British journal of community nursing vol. 29,9 (2024): 442-446. doi: https://doi.org/10.12968/bjcn.2024.0004

Reis da Silva, T. (2024i). The Evolution of Nursing for Older Adult: A Historical Perspective. Associative J Health Sci. 3(3). AJHS. 000561. 2024. DOI: https://doi.org/ Link: https://crimsonpublishers.com/ajhs/pdf/AJHS.000561.pdfDOI: 10.31031/AJHS.2024.03.000561

Reis da Silva, T. H (2024f). Oncology and Cancer Medicine: Understanding the complexities in Older Patients. Biomed J Sci & Tech Res 55(3)-2024. DOI: https://doi.org/DOI: 10.26717/BJSTR.2024.55.008720

Reis da Silva, T. H. (2024d). Death and Its Significance in Nursing Practice. Palliat Med Care Int J. 2024; 4(3): 555640. DOI: https://juniperpublishers.com/pmcij/pdf/PMCIJ.MS.ID.555640.pdf

Reis da Silva, T. H. (2024k). Chapter 6 – Navigating Healthcare Complexity: Integrating Business Fundamentals into Nursing Leadership. In Sedky, A. Resiliency Strategies for Long-Term Business Success. Pp. 145-168. IGI Global. https://doi.org/DOI: 10.4018/979-8-3693-9168-6.ch006

Reis da Silva, T. H. (2024l). Chapter 11 - Integrating business essentials into Gerontological Nursing: Enhancing Care for Older Adults in Diverse Settings. In Sedky, A. Resiliency Strategies for Long-Term Business Success. Pp. 283-316. IGI Global. DOI: https://doi.org/DOI: 10.4018/979-8-3693-9168-6.ch011

Reis da Silva, T. H. (2024m). Death and Its Significance in Nursing Practice. Palliat Med Care Int J. 2024; 4(3): 555640. DOI: https://juniperpublishers.com/pmcij/pdf/PMCIJ.MS.ID.555640.pdf

Reis da Silva. Tiago Horta (2024g). Death and Its Significance in Nursing Practice. Palliat Med Care Int J. 2024; 4(3): 555640. DOI: https://juniperpublishers.com/pmcij/pdf/PMCIJ.MS.ID.555640.pdf

Reis da Silva, T. (2024a). Advancing Gender Equity In Nursing Care For Older Adults: A Pathway To Achieving The United Nations Sustainable Development Goals. *J Comm Med and Pub Health Rep*, *5*(12). Advance online publication. https://doi.org/10.38207/JCMPHR/2024/JUL051201105

Reis da Silva, T. (2024b). Gender Equity In Healthcare: Integrating Emotional Intelligence To Achieve The United Nations Sustainable Development Goals. *J Comm Med and Pub Health Rep*, *5*(12). Advance online publication. DOI: 10.38207/JCMPHR/2024/JUL051202106

Reis da Silva, T. (2024h). Can supplementing vitamin B12 improve mental health outcomes?: A literature review. *British Journal of Community Nursing*, *29*(3), 137–146. DOI: 10.12968/bjcn.2024.29.3.137

Reis da Silva, T. H. (2023a). Falls assessment and prevention in the nursing home and community. *British Journal of Community Nursing*, *28*(2), 68–72. DOI: 10.12968/bjcn.2023.28.2.68

Reis da Silva, T. H. (2023b). Moving and Handling in the Community. *British Journal of Community Nursing*, *28*(8), 369. DOI: 10.12968/bjcn.2023.28.8.369

Reis da Silva, T. H. (2023c). Ageing in place: Ageing at home and in the community. *British Journal of Community Nursing*, *28*(5), 213–214. DOI: 10.12968/bjcn.2023.28.5.213

Reis da Silva, T. H. (2024a). Emotional Intelligence in Teaching Geriatric Nursing: Humanising Technology for Compassionate Care in Higher Education. In Tikadar, S. (Ed.), *Liu, H.; Bhattacharya, P.; Bhattacharya, S. Humanizing Technology With Emotional Intelligence*. IGI Global., DOI: 10.4018/979-8-3693-7011-7.ch008

Reis da Silva, T. H. (2024c). Chronic kidney disease in older adults: Nursing implications for community nurses. *Journal of Kidney Care*, *9*(4), 174–179. https://doi.org/10.12968/jokc.2024.9.4.174

Reis da Silva, T. H. (2024c). Falls prevention in older people and the role of nursing. *British Journal of Community Nursing*, *29*(7), 335–339. DOI: 10.12968/bjcn.2024.0005

Reis da Silva, T. H. (2024d). Loneliness in older adults. *British Journal of Community Nursing*, *29*(2), 60–66. DOI: 10.12968/bjcn.2024.29.2.60

Reis da Silva, T. H. (2024i). Understanding body fluid balance, dehydration and intravenous fluid therapy. *Emergency Nurse*. Advance online publication. DOI: 10.7748/en.2024.e2201

Reis da Silva, T. H. (2024j). Pharmacokinetics in older people: An overview of prescribing practice. *Journal of Prescribing Practice*, *6*(9), 374–381. https://doi.org/10.12968/jprp.2024.6.9.374

Reis da Silva, T. H. (2024m). Enhancing the mental health of refugees and asylum seekers through music interventions. *Mental Health Practice*. Advance online publication. DOI: 10.7748/mhp.2024.e1717

Reis da Silva, T. M., Hammett, R., & Low, G. (2025). Emotional Intelligence in Business: Enhancing Leadership, Collaboration, and Performance. In Sedky, A. (Ed.), *Building Business Knowledge for Complex Modern Business Environments* (pp. 149–178). IGI Global., DOI: 10.4018/979-8-3693-6447-5.ch006

Rezaee, N., Mardani-Hamooleh, M., & Seraji, M. (2020). Nurses' perception of ethical challenges in caring for patients with covid-19: A qualitative analysis. *Journal of Medical Ethics and History of Medicine*. Advance online publication. DOI: 10.18502/jmehm.v13i23.4954 PMID: 34055239

Rhmann, W., & Pandey, B. (2021, October). Early cancer predictions using ensembles of machine learning and deep learning. In *Deep Learning for Personalized Healthcare Services* (pp. 91–114). DOI: 10.1515/9783110708127-005

Richards, K. C., Campenni, C. E., & Muse-Burke, J. L. (2010). Self-care and well-being in mental health professionals: The mediating effects of self-awareness and mindfulness. *Journal of Mental Health Counseling*, *32*(3), 247–264. DOI: 10.17744/mehc.32.3.0n31v88304423806

Rider, E., Gilligan, M., Osterberg, L., Litzelman, D., Plews-Ogan, M., Weil, A., Dunne, D. W., Hafler, J. P., May, N. B., Derse, A. R., Frankel, R. M., & Branch, W.Jr. (2018). Healthcare at the crossroads: The need to shape an organizational culture of humanistic teaching and practice. *Journal of General Internal Medicine*, *33*(7), 1092–1099. DOI: 10.1007/s11606-018-4470-2 PMID: 29740787

Roberson, Q., & Perry, J. L. (2022). Inclusive leadership in thought and action: A thematic analysis. *Group & Organization Management*. Retrieved from umich.edu

Roberto, K., Teaster, P., Lindberg, B., & Blancato, R. (2020). A first (and disturbing) look at the relationship between the opioid epidemic and elder abuse: Insights of human service professionals. *Journal of Applied Gerontology*, *40*(10), 1231–1235. DOI: 10.1177/0733464820947279 PMID: 32772619

Rocca, G., Moylan, K., Crist, B., Volgas, D., Stannard, J., & Mehr, D. (2013). Co-management of geriatric patients with hip fractures. *Geriatric Orthopaedic Surgery & Rehabilitation*, *4*(1), 10–15. DOI: 10.1177/2151458513495238 PMID: 23936734

Rogers, C. R. (1961). *On becoming a person: A therapist's view of psychotherapy*. Houghton Mifflin Harcourt.

Roosen, I., Salway, S., & Osei-Kwasi, H. A. (2021). Transnational social networks, health, and care: A systematic narrative literature review. *International Journal for Equity in Health*, *20*(1), 138. Advance online publication. DOI: 10.1186/s12939-021-01467-6 PMID: 34118934

Rosenthal, E., Brownstein, J., Rush, C., Hirsch, G., Willaert, A., Scott, J., Holderby, L. R., & Fox, D. (2010). Community health workers: Part of the solution. *Health Affairs*, *29*(7), 1338–1342. DOI: 10.1377/hlthaff.2010.0081 PMID: 20606185

Ross, C. L. (2019). Energy medicine: Current status and future perspectives. *Global Advances in Health and Medicine : Improving Healthcare Outcomes Worldwide*, *8*, 2164956119831221. DOI: 10.1177/2164956119831221 PMID: 30834177

Roussos, S. T., & Fawcett, S. B. (2000). A review of collaborative partnerships as a strategy for improving community health. *Annual Review of Public Health*, *21*(1), 369–402. DOI: 10.1146/annurev.publhealth.21.1.369 PMID: 10884958

Rubik, B., Muehsam, D., Hammerschlag, R., & Jain, S. (2015). Biofield science and healing: History, terminology, and concepts. *Global Advances in Health and Medicine : Improving Healthcare Outcomes Worldwide*, *4*(1_suppl, Suppl), 8–14. DOI: 10.7453/gahmj.2015.038.suppl PMID: 26665037

Ruelas, E., Gómez-Dantés, O., Leatherman, S., Fortune, T., & Gay-Molina, J. (2012). Strengthening the quality agenda in health care in low- and middle-income countries: Questions to consider. *International Journal for Quality in Health Care : Journal of the International Society for Quality in Health Care*, *24*(6), 553–557. DOI: 10.1093/intqhc/mzs061 PMID: 23074183

Ryff, C. D. (2021). Spirituality and well-being: Theory, science, and the nature connection. *Religions*, *12*(11), 914. DOI: 10.3390/rel12110914 PMID: 34881052

Saad, J. M., & Prochaska, J. O. (2020). A philosophy of health: Life as reality, health as a universal value. *Palgrave Communications*, *6*(1), 1–11. DOI: 10.1057/s41599-020-0420-9 PMID: 32226633

Saasouh, W., Ghanem, K., Al-Saidi, N., LeQuia, L., McKelvey, G., & Jaffar, M. (2024). Patient-centered perspectives on perioperative care. *Frontiers in Anesthesiology*, *3*, 1267127. Advance online publication. DOI: 10.3389/fanes.2024.1267127

Sabato, E., Owens, J., Mauro, A., Findley, P., Lamba, S., & Fenesy, K. (2018). Integrating social determinants of health into dental curricula: An interprofessional approach. *Journal of Dental Education*, *82*(3), 237–245. DOI: 10.21815/JDE.018.022 PMID: 29496801

Sadler, E., Wolfe, C. D., & McKevitt, C. (2014). Lay and health care professional understandings of self-management: A systematic review and narrative synthesis. *SAGE Open Medicine*, *2*, 2050312114544493. DOI: 10.1177/2050312114544493 PMID: 26770733

Said, N. B., & Chiang, V. C. (2020). The knowledge, skill competencies, and psychological preparedness of nurses for disasters: A systematic review. *International Emergency Nursing*, *48*, 100806. DOI: 10.1016/j.ienj.2019.100806 PMID: 31685363

Saleem, S., & Majeed, S. (2023). *Spiritual Intelligence*. Self-Management Skills, Depression and Anxiety in Patients with Tuberculosis., DOI: 10.57232/jiimc.june23.629

Saltvedt, I., Prestmo, A., Einarsen, E., Johnsen, L., Helbostad, J., & Sletvold, O. (2012). Development and delivery of patient treatment in the Trondheim hip fracture trial. a new geriatric in-hospital pathway for elderly patients with hip fracture. *BMC Research Notes*, *5*(1), 355. Advance online publication. DOI: 10.1186/1756-0500-5-355 PMID: 22800378

Sanchez, A. (2018). An examination of the folk healing practice of curanderismo in the hispanic community. *Journal of Community Health Nursing*, *35*(3), 148–161. DOI: 10.1080/07370016.2018.1475801 PMID: 30024284

Sapolsky, R. M. (2004). *Why Zebras Don't Get Ulcers: The Acclaimed Guide to Stress, Stress-Related Diseases, and Coping*. Holt Paperbacks.

Sarkar, S., Verma, R., & Singh, S. (2022). Faculty and students' perceptions on experiential learning based anatomy dissection hall sessions for medical undergraduates. *Advances in Medical Education and Practice*, *13*, 543–554. DOI: 10.2147/AMEP.S359140 PMID: 35651479

Sathya, T., Nagarajan, R., & Selvamani, Y. (2020). Multimorbidity as a risk factor of elder abuse/mistreatment in India: A cross-sectional study. *Journal of Interpersonal Violence*, *37*(11-12), NP9191–NP9213. DOI: 10.1177/0886260520980391 PMID: 33323003

Sathya, T., & Premkumar, R. (2020). Association of functional limitations and disability with elder abuse in India: A cross-sectional study. *BMC Geriatrics*, *20*(1), 220. Advance online publication. DOI: 10.1186/s12877-020-01619-3 PMID: 32576146

Saunders, P. A., Tractenberg, R. E., Chaterji, R., Amri, H., Harazduk, N., Gordon, J. S., Lumpkin, M., & Haramati, A. (2007). Promoting self-awareness and reflection through an experiential Mind-Body Skills course for first year medical students. *Medical Teacher, 29*(8), 778–784. DOI: 10.1080/01421590701509647 PMID: 17852720

Scammon, D. L., Tabler, J., Brunisholz, K. D., Gren, L. H., Kim, J., Tomoaia-Cotisel, A., Day, J., Farrell, T. W., Waitzman, N. J., & Magill, M. K. (2014). Organizational culture associated with provider satisfaction. *Journal of the American Board of Family Medicine : JABFM, 27*(2), 219–228. DOI: 10.3122/jabfm.2014.02.120338 PMID: 24610184

Schaaf, J., Sedlmayr, M., Schaefer, J., & Storf, H. (2020). Diagnosis of rare diseases: A scoping review of clinical decision support systems. *Orphanet Journal of Rare Diseases, 15*(1), 263. Advance online publication. DOI: 10.1186/s13023-020-01536-z PMID: 32972444

Scheepers, R., Boerebach, B., Arah, O., Heineman, M., & Lombarts, K. (2015). A systematic review of the impact of physicians' occupational well-being on the quality of patient care. *International Journal of Behavioral Medicine, 22*(6), 683–698. DOI: 10.1007/s12529-015-9473-3 PMID: 25733349

Scheirer, M. A. (2005). Is sustainability possible? A review and commentary on empirical studies of program sustainability. *The American Journal of Evaluation, 26*(3), 320–347. DOI: 10.1177/1098214005278752

Scheirer, M. A., Hartling, G., & Hagerman, D. (2008). Defining sustainability outcomes of health programs: Illustrations from an online survey. *Evaluation and Program Planning, 31*(4), 335–346. DOI: 10.1016/j.evalprogplan.2008.08.004 PMID: 18835642

Schneider, H., & Lehmann, U. (2016). From community health workers to community health systems: Time to widen the horizon? *Health Systems and Reform, 2*(2), 112–118. DOI: 10.1080/23288604.2016.1166307 PMID: 31514640

Schneider, N., Steinberg, D., Pahl, D., Steffin, D., & Gangopadhyay, M. (2023). Ethical quandaries at end of life: Navigating real-world case examples as a pediatric psychologist. *Clinical Practice in Pediatric Psychology, 11*(2), 244–251. DOI: 10.1037/cpp0000432

Schofield, G., Dittborn, M., Selman, L., & Huxtable, R. (2021). Defining ethical challenge(s) in healthcare research: A rapid review. *BMC Medical Ethics, 22*(1), 135. Advance online publication. DOI: 10.1186/s12910-021-00700-9 PMID: 34587950

Schofield, R., Chircop, A., Baker, C., Duncan, S., & Wotton, D. (2018). Entry-to-practice public health nursing competencies: A Delphi method and knowledge translation strategy. *Nurse Education Today*, *65*, 102–107. DOI: 10.1016/j.nedt.2018.03.001 PMID: 29547810

Seddigh, R., Azarnik, S., Memaryan, N., & Hadi, F. (2020). Spirituality as a sociocultural determinant of health in the context of medical curriculum: A call for action. *Medical Journal of the Islamic Republic of Iran*. Advance online publication. DOI: 10.47176/mjiri.34.6 PMID: 32284930

Seo, J., Kim, W., Hewner, S., & Dickerson, S. (2018). Lived experience of health seeking and healthcare utilization among Korean immigrant women living in suburban communities. *Asian/Pacific Island Nursing Journal*, *3*(1), 8–20. DOI: 10.31372/20180301.1086

Sessanna, L., Finnell, D. S., Underhill, M. L., Chang, Y. P., & Peng, H. L. (2011). Measures assessing spirituality as more than religiosity: A methodological review of nursing and health-related literature. *Journal of Advanced Nursing*, *67*(8), 1677–1694. DOI: 10.1111/j.1365-2648.2010.05596.x PMID: 21371082

Shah, M. H., Roy, S., & Flari, E. (2024). The critical need for disaster medicine in modern medical education. *Disaster Medicine and Public Health Preparedness*, *18*, e80. DOI: 10.1017/dmp.2024.56 PMID: 38682546

Shahrajabian, M., Sun, W., & Cheng, Q. (2019). The influence of traditional iranian and chinese medicine on western and Islamic countries. *Asian Journal of Medical and Biological Research*, *5*(2), 94–99. DOI: 10.3329/ajmbr.v5i2.42490

Shanafelt, T., Trockel, M., Rodriguez, A., & Logan, D. (2021). Wellness-centered leadership: Equipping healthcare leaders to cultivate physician well-being and professional fulfillment. [Retrieved from lww.com]. *Academic Medicine*, *96*(5), 641–651. DOI: 10.1097/ACM.0000000000003907 PMID: 33394666

Shapiro, J., Coulehan, J., Wear, D., & Montello, M. (2009). Medical humanities and their discontents: Definitions, critiques, and implications. *Academic Medicine*, *84*(2), 192–198. DOI: 10.1097/ACM.0b013e3181938bca PMID: 19174663

Sharma, D., Dangi, P., Sharma, M. K., Patidar, J., Kumar, T., & Vats, M. (2023). Emotional intelligence and job satisfaction among staff nurses: A cross-sectional study. *International Journal of Research in Medical Sciences*, *11*(12), 4409–4415. DOI: 10.18203/2320-6012.ijrms20233708

Sharmake, A. (2024). Healthcare disparities among socioeconomic groups. *IJHSS*, *2*(5), 50–63. DOI: 10.47941/ijhss.1889

Shasha, A. C. N. (2013). *Patient experiences and perceptions of non-compliance with TB treatment* (Doctoral dissertation, Stellenbosch: Stellenbosch University). https://scholar.sun.ac.za/items/03a5c605-d130-4b14-afd1-b6d10c6ba125

Shaw, A., Thompson, E., & Sharp, D. (2006). Expectations of patients and parents of children with asthma regarding access to complementary therapy information and services via the nhs: A qualitative study. *Health Expectations*, *9*(4), 343–358. DOI: 10.1111/j.1369-7625.2006.00402.x PMID: 17083561

Sheikh, A., Anderson, M., Albala, S., Casadei, B., Franklin, B. D., Richards, M., Taylor, D., Tibble, H., & Mossialos, E. (2021). Health information technology and digital innovation for national learning health and care systems. [Retrieved from thelancet.com]. *The Lancet. Digital Health*, *3*(6), e383–e396. DOI: 10.1016/S2589-7500(21)00005-4 PMID: 33967002

Shen, Q. and Tang, L. (2021). Analysis on clinical effects of humanistic nursing care on chronic pelvic inflammatory disease. ijps, 83. DOI: 10.36468/pharmaceutical-sciences.spl.222

Shen, C., Wan, A., Kwok, L., Pang, S., Wang, X., Stewart, S., Lam, T. H., & Chan, S. (2017). A community-based intervention program to enhance family communication and family well-being: The learning families project in Hong Kong. *Frontiers in Public Health*, *5*, 257. Advance online publication. DOI: 10.3389/fpubh.2017.00257 PMID: 29085815

Shinners, L., Aggar, C., Grace, S., & Smith, S. (2019). Exploring healthcare professionals' understanding and experiences of artificial intelligence technology use in the delivery of healthcare: An integrative review. *Health Informatics Journal*, *26*(2), 1225–1236. DOI: 10.1177/1460458219874641 PMID: 31566454

Shinners, L., Aggar, C., Stephens, A., & Grace, S. (2023). Healthcare professionals' experiences and perceptions of artificial intelligence in regional and rural health districts in australia. *The Australian Journal of Rural Health*, *31*(6), 1203–1213. DOI: 10.1111/ajr.13045 PMID: 37795659

Shojaei, H., Lakha, S., Lyon, A., Halabecki, M., Donaghy, M., & Mailis, A. (2022). Evolution of a chronic pain management program in a northwestern ontario community: From structural elements to practical application. *BMC Health Services Research*, *22*(1), 1355. Advance online publication. DOI: 10.1186/s12913-022-08766-w PMID: 36380300

Sholichah, M., & Kushartati, S. (2023). Empathic communication training to increase family resilience. *Journal of Educational Health and Community Psychology*, *1*(1), 177. DOI: 10.12928/jehcp.v1i1.17085

Shrestha, E., Pokharel, R., Rs, M., & Rai, G. (2023). Ethical challenges faced by the healthcare workers to provide health service during covid-19 pandemic. *Journal of Bp Koirala Institute of Health Sciences*, *6*(1), 14–19. DOI: 10.3126/jbpkihs.v6i1.52502

Shyamala, K., Kulkarni, V., Shenoy, V., & Khatri, B. (2022). Impact of communication skills training in postgraduate medical education. *National Journal of Community Medicine*, *13*(06), 359–363. DOI: 10.55489/njcm.13062022403

Sigal, A. V., & Bakumenko, M. (2020, January 1). The Level of the Country's Health Care as an Indicator of its Economic Development. Advances in economics, business and management research/Advances in Economics, Business and Management Research. Atlantis Press. Retrieved January 2025, from DOI: 10.2991/aebmr.k.200312.151

Siivola, U., & Martikainen, T. (Eds.). (1990). The public health nurse—Is the linchpin of primary health care. In World Health Forum.

Simha, S., Noble, S., & Chaturvedi, S. (2013). Spiritual concerns in hindu cancer patients undergoing palliative care: A qualitative study. *Indian Journal of Palliative Care*, *19*(2), 99. DOI: 10.4103/0973-1075.116716 PMID: 24049350

Sinclair, S., Norris, J., McConnell, S., Chochinov, H., Hack, T., Hagen, N., McClement, S., & Bouchal, S. (2016). Compassion: A scoping review of the healthcare literature. *BMC Palliative Care*, *15*(1), 6. Advance online publication. DOI: 10.1186/s12904-016-0080-0 PMID: 26786417

Singh, N., Ogunseitan, O. A., & Tang, Y. (2022). Medical waste: Current challenges and future opportunities for sustainable management. [Retrieved from escholarship.org]. *Critical Reviews in Environmental Science and Technology*, *52*(11), 2000–2022. DOI: 10.1080/10643389.2021.1885325

Sinha, R., Roy, A., Kumar, N., & Mondal, H. (2023). Applicability of chatgpt in assisting to solve higher order problems in pathology. *Cureus*. Advance online publication. DOI: 10.7759/cureus.35237 PMID: 36968864

Sit, C., Srinivasan, R., Amlani, A., Muthuswamy, K., Azam, A., Monzon, L., & Poon, D. (2020). Attitudes and perceptions of uk medical students towards artificial intelligence and radiology: A multicentre survey. *Insights Into Imaging*, *11*(1), 14. Advance online publication. DOI: 10.1186/s13244-019-0830-7 PMID: 32025951

Sit, S., Gong, W., Ho, S., Lai, A., Wong, B., Wang, M., & Lam, T. (2022). A population study on covid-19 information sharing: Sociodemographic differences and associations with family communication quality and well-being in Hong Kong. *International Journal of Environmental Research and Public Health, 19*(6), 3577. DOI: 10.3390/ijerph19063577 PMID: 35329264

Skropeta, C., Colvin, A., & Sladen, S. (2014). An evaluative study of the benefits of participating in intergenerational playgroups in aged care for older people. *BMC Geriatrics, 14*(1), 109. Advance online publication. DOI: 10.1186/1471-2318-14-109 PMID: 25292218

Soler, O., & Barreto, J. (2019). Community-level pharmaceutical interventions to reduce the risks of polypharmacy in the elderly: Overview of systematic reviews and economic evaluations. *Frontiers in Pharmacology, 10*, 302. Advance online publication. DOI: 10.3389/fphar.2019.00302 PMID: 31001117

Somasundaram, D. (2007). Collective trauma in northern sri lanka: A qualitative psychosocial-ecological study. *International Journal of Mental Health Systems, 1*(1), 5. DOI: 10.1186/1752-4458-1-5 PMID: 18271989

Sony, M., Antony, J., & McDermott, O. (2022). The impact of medical cyber–physical systems on healthcare service delivery. *The TQM Journal, 34*(7), 73–93. DOI: 10.1108/TQM-01-2022-0005

Sooryanarayana, R., Ganapathy, S., Wong, N., Rosman, A., Choo, W., & Hairi, N. (2020). Elder abuse: Nationwide findings among community-dwelling malaysian older persons. *Geriatrics & Gerontology International, 20*(S2), 85–91. DOI: 10.1111/ggi.13989 PMID: 33370859

Srinivasan, M. S., Lama, P., Tyagi, N., Yadav, K., Naval, M. N., & Swati, M. Elderly TB patients in India: Situation Analysis. *Tuijin Jishu/Journal of Propulsion Technology, 44*(6), 2023.doi:DOI: 10.52783/tjjpt.v44.i6.3140

Srinivasan, S. (2025). Patient-Centric Care in Tuberculosis Management: Addressing Challenges and Improving Health Outcomes. In *Convergence of Population Health Management, Pharmacogenomics, and Patient-Centered Care* (pp. 265-282). IGI Global. DOI: DOI: 10.4018/979-8-3693-3260-3.ch012

Srinivasan, S., & Praba Lama (2025). Patient-Centered Care for TB Patients: An Effective Approach to Corporate Social Responsibility. In Corporate Social Responsibility in Health and Social Care (pp. 183-218).IGI Global. DOI:DOI: 10.4018/979-8-3693-5991-4.ch008

Srinivasan, S., Prabha Lama, D. K., & Udhayakumar, P. Situation of Elderly Person with TB: A Comparative Study of Countries in the SAARC Region. doi:.DOI: 10.36713/epra2013

SSRN. (n.d.). https://papers.ssrn.com/sol3/papers.cfm?abstract_id=5007588

Stagno, S., Crapanzano, K., & Schwartz, A. (2016). Keeping the patient at the center: Teaching about elements of patient-centered care. *MedEdPORTAL: the Journal of Teaching and Learning Resources*, 10500. Advance online publication. DOI: 10.15766/mep_2374-8265.10500 PMID: 30984842

Stanhope, M., & Lancaster, J. (2008). *Public health nursing* (7th ed.). Mosby Elsevier.

Stanhope, M., & Lancaster, J. (2019). *Public health nursing e-book: Population-centered health care in the community*. Elsevier Health Sciences.

Steffens, N. K., Munt, K. A., van Knippenberg, D., Platow, M. J., & Haslam, S. A. (2021). Advancing the social identity theory of leadership: A meta-analytic review of leader group prototypicality. [Retrieved from sagepub.com]. *Organizational Psychology Review*, *11*(1), 35–72. DOI: 10.1177/2041386620962569

Stevens, L., Perrin, P., Hubbard, R., Sosa, D., Jove, I., & Arango-Lasprilla, J. (2013). Using multiple views of family dynamics to predict the mental health of individuals with tbi and their caregivers in Mexico. *NeuroRehabilitation*, *33*(2), 273–283. DOI: 10.3233/NRE-130955 PMID: 23949065

Stiefel, I., Harris, P., & Zollmann, A. (2002). Family constellation — A therapy beyond words. *Australian and New Zealand Journal of Family Therapy*, *23*(1), 38–44. DOI: 10.1002/j.1467-8438.2002.tb00484.x

Strecher, V. J., McEvoy DeVellis, B., Becker, M. H., & Rosenstock, I. M. (1986). The Role of Self-Efficacy in Achieving Health Behavior Change. *Health Education Quarterly*, *13*(1), 73–92. DOI: 10.1177/109019818601300108 PMID: 3957687

Stub, T., Quandt, S., Arcury, T., Sandberg, J., Kristoffersen, A., Musial, F., & Salamonsen, A. (2016). Perception of risk and communication among conventional and complementary health care providers involving cancer patients' use of complementary therapies: A literature review. *BMC Complementary and Alternative Medicine*, *16*(1), 353. Advance online publication. DOI: 10.1186/s12906-016-1326-3 PMID: 27609097

Study.com. (n.d.). Human psyche: Definition, lesson & quiz. https://study.com/academy/lesson/human-psyche-definition-lesson-quiz.html

Suhaimi, A., Ibrahim, N., Tan, K., Silim, U., Moore, G., Ryan, B., & Castle, D. J. (2020). Effectiveness of a culturally adapted biopsychosocial intervention (pohon sihat) in improving self-efficacy in patients with diabetes attending primary health-care clinics in putrajaya, malaysia: Study protocol of a randomised controlled trial. *BMJ Open*, *10*(2), e033920. DOI: 10.1136/bmjopen-2019-033920 PMID: 32066607

Sullivan, B., Esmaili, B., & Cunningham, C. (2017). Barriers to initiating tuberculosis treatment in sub-saharan africa: A systematic review focused on children and youth. *Global Health Action*, *10*(1), 1290317. Advance online publication. DOI: 10.1080/16549716.2017.1290317 PMID: 28598771

Sulmasy, D. P. (2009). Spirituality, religion, and clinical care. *Chest*, *135*(6), 1634–1642. DOI: 10.1378/chest.08-2241 PMID: 19497898

Suma, D. V. (2021). Wearable IoT based distributed framework for ubiquitous computing. *Journal of Ubiquitous Computing and Communication Technologies*, *3*(1), 23–32. DOI: 10.36548/jucct.2021.1.003

Suvarnabhumi, K., Jorajit, S., Dechpichai, W., & Ativitthayaporn, J. (2022). Expert consensus on core topics of sustainable development online learning module for family physicians: A Delphi study. *BMJ Open*, *12*(12), e061407. DOI: 10.1136/bmjopen-2022-061407 PMID: 36581405

Svarts, A. (2017). Healthcare managers' perception of economies of scale. *Journal of Health Organization and Management*, *31*(3), 317–330. DOI: 10.1108/JHOM-01-2017-0006 PMID: 28686128

Szczęśniak, M., & Tułecka, M. (2020). Family Functioning and Life Satisfaction: The Mediatory Role of Emotional Intelligence. *Psychology Research and Behavior Management*, *13*, 223–232. DOI: 10.2147/PRBM.S240898 PMID: 32184683

Tagoe, T., & Quarshie, E. (2016). The relationship between emotional intelligence and job satisfaction among nurses in accra. *Nursing Open*, *4*(2), 84–89. DOI: 10.1002/nop2.70 PMID: 28286664

Tambunan, R., Hanafi, D., & Ibrahim, F. (2024). The influence of family communication patterns on parenting agreements for children with special needs. *Lontar Jurnal Ilmu Komunikasi*, *12*(1), 274–283. DOI: 10.30656/lontar.v12i1.7969

Tanaka, K., & Son, D. (2019). Experiential learning for junior residents as a part of community-based medical education in japan. *Education for Primary Care*, *30*(5), 282–288. DOI: 10.1080/14739879.2019.1625288 PMID: 31185822

Taskiran, N.TAŞKIRAN. (2023). Effect of artificial intelligence course in nursing on students' medical artificial intelligence readiness. *Nurse Educator*, *48*(5), E147–E152. DOI: 10.1097/NNE.0000000000001446 PMID: 37133231

Tavares, L., Enns, S., Ayres, J., & Tempski, P. (2020). Humanism in the narratives of first-year medical students. DOI: 10.21203/rs.2.24827/v2

Taverna, M., Berberat, P., Sattel, H., & Frick, E. (2019). A Survey on the Integration of Spiritual Care in Medical Schools from the German-Speaking Faculties. *Advances in Medical Education and Practice*, *10*, 1009–1019. DOI: 10.2147/AMEP.S224679 PMID: 31839718

Tenchov, R., Sapra, A. K., Sasso, J., Ralhan, K., Tummala, A., Azoulay, N., & Zhou, Q. A. (2024, March). Biomarkers for early cancer detection: A landscape view of recent advancements, spotlighting pancreatic and liver cancers. *ACS Pharmacology & Translational Science*, *7*(3), 586–613. DOI: 10.1021/acsptsci.3c00346 PMID: 38481702

Thaker, N. G., Dicker, A. P., Loaiza-Bonilla, A., Wallace, A., Kolman, D., Godshalk Ruggles, A., Manda, S., Frank, S. J., Orio, P., & Doria, C. (2024, April). The role of artificial intelligence in early cancer detection: Exploring early clinical applications. *Artificial Intelligence in Precision Oncology*, *1*(2), 91–105. DOI: 10.1089/aipo.2023.0011

Thege, B., Petroll, C., Rivas, C., & Scholtens, S. (2021). The effectiveness of family constellation therapy in improving mental health: A systematic review. *Family Process*, *60*(2), 409–423. DOI: 10.1111/famp.12636 PMID: 33528854

Thibault, G. (2019). Humanism in medicine: What does it mean and why is it more important than ever? *Academic Medicine*, *94*(8), 1074–1077. DOI: 10.1097/ACM.0000000000002796 PMID: 31135401

Thomas, L. J., Revell, S. H., & Ryan, M. (2018). Promoting resilience among nursing students in clinical education. *Nurse Education in Practice*, *28*, 231–234. Advance online publication. DOI: 10.1016/j.nepr.2017.10.001 PMID: 29128734

Thomeer, M., & Reczek, C. (2019). Intergenerational coresidential patterns by young adult's and their mother's mental health and substance use. *Journal of Family Issues*, *41*(9), 1498–1524. DOI: 10.1177/0192513X19894348 PMID: 33293753

Thornton, M., & Persaud, S. (2018, September). Preparing today's nurses: Social determinants of health and nursing education. *Online Journal of Issues in Nursing*, *23*(3), 9. https://search.ebscohost.com/login.aspx?direct=true&AuthType=sso&db=ccm&AN=132181879&site=ehost-live. DOI: 10.3912/OJIN.Vol23No03Man05

Tierney, S., Seers, K., Tutton, E., & Reeve, J. (2017). Enabling the flow of compassionate care: A grounded theory study. *BMC Health Services Research*, *17*(1), 174. Advance online publication. DOI: 10.1186/s12913-017-2120-8 PMID: 28253874

Tindana, P. O., Singh, J. A., Tracy, C. S., Upshur, R. E. G., Daar, A. S., Singer, P. A., Frohlich, J., & Lavery, J. V. (2007). Grand challenges in global health: Community engagement in research in developing countries. *PLoS Medicine*, *4*(9), e273. DOI: 10.1371/journal.pmed.0040273 PMID: 17850178

Toendepi, J. (2021). The catalytic role of authentic leadership in raising collective consciousness in the South African social systems. *Journal of Contemporary Management*. Retrieved from journals.co.za

Tollett, S. M., & Thornby, J. I. (1982). Geriatric and gerontology nursing curricular trends. *The Journal of Nursing Education*, *21*(6), 16–23. DOI: 10.3928/0148-4834-19820601-05 PMID: 6286577

Tomes, N. (2000). The making of a germ panic, then and now. *American Journal of Public Health*, *90*(2), 191–198. DOI: 10.2105/AJPH.90.2.191 PMID: 10667179

Torres, S., & Cao, X. (2019). Improving care for elders who prefer informal spaces to age-separated institutions and health care settings. *Innovation in Aging*, *3*(3), igz019. Advance online publication. DOI: 10.1093/geroni/igz019 PMID: 31346555

Toussaint, L., Williams, D. R., Musick, M. A., & Everson-Rose, S. A. (2012). The association of forgiveness and 12-month prevalence of major depressive episodes in a nationally representative sample of US adults. *Journal of Health Psychology*, *17*(7), 1010–1018. DOI: 10.1177/1359105311433905

Tran, B., Vu, G., Ha, G., Vuong, Q., H , M., Vuong, T., La, V.-P., Ho, M.-T., Nghiem, K.-C. P., Nguyen, H. L. T., Latkin, C. A., Tam, W. W. S., Cheung, N.-M., Nguyen, H.-K. T., Ho, C. S. H., & Ho, R. (2019). Global evolution of research in artificial intelligence in health and medicine: A bibliometric study. *Journal of Clinical Medicine*, *8*(3), 360. DOI: 10.3390/jcm8030360 PMID: 30875745

Trochim, W., & Kane, M. (2005). Concept mapping: An introduction to structured conceptualization in health care. *International Journal for Quality in Health Care : Journal of the International Society for Quality in Health Care*, *17*(3), 187–191. DOI: 10.1093/intqhc/mzi038 PMID: 15872026

Trujillo, M., Perrin, P., Panyavin, I., Peralta, S., Stolfi, M., Morelli, E., & Arango-Lasprilla, J. (2016). Mediation of family dynamics, personal strengths, and mental health in dementia caregivers. *Journal of Latina/o Psychology*, *4*(1), 1–17. DOI: 10.1037/lat0000046

Tseng, Y. H., Griffiths, F., De Kadt, J., Nxumalo, N., Rwafa, T., Malatji, H., & Goudge, J. (2019). Integrating community health workers into the formal health system to improve performance: A qualitative study on the role of on-site supervision in the South African programme. *BMJ Open*, *9*(2), e022186. DOI: 10.1136/bmjopen-2018-022186 PMID: 30819698

Turabián, J. (2022). The biopsychosocial approach gives relevance to general medicine as a tool of public health. *Medpress Public Health and Epidemiolog*, *1*(1). Advance online publication. DOI: 10.33582/mpphe.2022.202210006

Turjuman, F., & Alilyyani, B. (2023). Emotional intelligence among nurses and its relationship with their performance and work engagement: A cross-sectional study. *Journal of Nursing Management*, *2023*, 1–8. DOI: 10.1155/2023/5543299 PMID: 40225659

Udlis, K. A. (2011). Self-management in chronic illness: Concept and dimensional analysis: Self-management in chronic illness: concept and dimensional analysis. *Journal of Nursing and Healthcare of Chronic Illness*, *3*(2), 130–139. DOI: 10.1111/j.1752-9824.2011.01085.x

Udoh, E. E., Hermel, M., Bharmal, M. I., Nayak, A., Patel, S., Butlin, M., & Bhavnani, S. P. (2023). Nanosensor technologies and the digital transformation of healthcare. *Personalized Medicine*, *20*(3), 251–269. DOI: 10.2217/pme-2022-0065 PMID: 37403731

Umene-Nakano, W., Kato, T. A., Kikuchi, S., Tateno, M., Fujisawa, D., Hoshuyama, T., & Nakamura, J. (2013). Nationwide survey of work environment, work-life balance and burnout among psychiatrists in japan. *PLoS One*, *8*(2), e55189. DOI: 10.1371/journal.pone.0055189 PMID: 23418435

United Nations Development Programme. (n.d.). Country info: Pakistan. https://www.pk.undp.org/content/pakistan/en/home/countryinfo

University of Michigan School of Public Health. (n.d.). What is public health nursing? https://www.sph.umich.edu/ncbon/whatis.html

University of Notre Dame. (n.d.). Notre Dame makes $68 million commitment to fighting mental health crisis; scalable solutions could become national model. https://news.nd.edu/news/notre-dame-makes-68-million-commitment-to-fighting-mental-health-crisis-scalable-solutions-could-become-national-model/?gad_source=1&gclid=CjwKCAjw_Na1BhAlEiwAM-dm7NmtxbPsCjY4paVxzLYPo58RXGMLE9R39ycVtpil-5525aQXfBYneRoC_00QAvD_BwE

Upvall, M. J., Karmaliani, R., Pirani, F., Gul, R., & Khalid, F. (2005). Developing nursing leaders through graduate education in Pakistan. *International Journal of Nursing Education Scholarship, 1*(1). Advance online publication. DOI: 10.2202/1548-923X.1079 PMID: 16646893

Urban, T., Friedman, D., Kaskas, M., Caruso, A., Canenguez, K., Rotter, N., Wozniak, J., & Basu, A. (2022). Brief report of protective factors associated with family and parental well-being during the covid-19 pandemic in an outpatient child and adolescent psychiatric clinic. *Frontiers in Psychology, 13*, 883955. Advance online publication. DOI: 10.3389/fpsyg.2022.883955 PMID: 36172224

Urdang, E. (2010). Awareness of Self—A Critical Tool. *Social Work Education, 29*(5), 523–538. DOI: 10.1080/02615470903164950

Vago, D. R., & Silbersweig, D. A. (2012). Self-awareness, self-regulation, and self-transcendence (S-ART): A framework for understanding the neurobiological mechanisms of mindfulness. *Frontiers in Human Neuroscience, 6*, 296. DOI: 10.3389/fnhum.2012.00296 PMID: 23112770

Van Hooser, P. (n.d.). Leaders ought to know. http://www.leadersoughttoknow.com/tag/phil-van-hooser/page/2/

Varughese, J., & Rema, M. (2021). Perceived stress, emotional intelligence and self-efficacy among nursing students during the covid-19 pandemic. *International Journal of Research and Studies Publishing, 11*(4), 201–207. DOI: 10.29322/IJSRP.11.04.2021.p11225

Vassilev, I., Rogers, A., Kennedy, A., & Koetsenruijter, J. (2014). The influence of social networks on self-management support: A metasynthesis. *BMC Public Health, 14*(1), 719. DOI: 10.1186/1471-2458-14-719 PMID: 25023948

Vertejee, S. S., & Karamali, N. N. (2013). Women's health: An achievable goal for public health nursing in Pakistan. *Women's Health.* PMID: 24397102

Vivekananthan, V., Khandelwal, G., Alluri, N. R., & Kim, S. J. (2022). E-Skin for Futuristic Nanosensor Technology for the Healthcare System. In Nanosensors for Futuristic Smart and Intelligent Healthcare Systems (pp. 133-157). CRC Press.

Vu, M., Cruz, A., & Burton, N. (2023). Contributing to the sustainable development goals as normative and instrumental acts: The role of Buddhist religious logics in family SMES. *International Small Business Journal, 42*(2), 246–275. DOI: 10.1177/02662426231182425

Vuong, Q. H., Le, T. T., La, V. P., Nguyen, H. T. T., Ho, M. T., Van Khuc, Q., & Nguyen, M. H. (2022). COVID-19 vaccines production and societal immunization under the serendipity-mindsponge-3D knowledge management theory and conceptual framework. *Humanities and Social Sciences Communications, 9*(1). Retrieved from nature.com

Vuorivirta-Vuoti, E., Kuha, S., & Kanste, O. (2024). Nurse leaders' perceptions of future leadership in hospital settings in the post-pandemic era: A qualitative descriptive study. *Leadership in Health Services*, *37*(5), 33–48. DOI: 10.1108/LHS-05-2023-0032 PMID: 37750849

Wagner, A. K., Graves, A. J., Reiss, S. K., LeCates, R. F., Zhang, F., & Ross-Degnan, D. (2011). Access to care and medicines, burden of health care expenditures, and risk protection: Results from the world health survey. *Health Policy (Amsterdam)*, *100*(2-3), 151–158. DOI: 10.1016/j.healthpol.2010.08.004 PMID: 20828854

Wallace, D. C. (2005). A mitochondrial paradigm of metabolic and degenerative diseases, aging, and cancer: A dawn for evolutionary medicine. *Annual Review of Genetics*, *39*(1), 359–407. DOI: 10.1146/annurev.genet.39.110304.095751 PMID: 16285865

Walzl, G., McNerney, R., du Plessis, N., Bates, M., McHugh, T. D., Chegou, N. N., & Zumla, A. (2018). Tuberculosis: Advances and challenges in development of new diagnostics and biomarkers. *The Lancet. Infectious Diseases*, *18*(7), e199–e210. https://www.thelancet.com/journals/laninf/article/PIIS1473-3099(18)30111-7/abstract. DOI: 10.1016/S1473-3099(18)30111-7 PMID: 29580818

Wamara, C., Strandberg, T., & Bennich, M. (2022). Indigenised approaches to addressing elder abuse in uganda. *Journal of Social Work : JSW*, *23*(1), 19–36. DOI: 10.1177/14680173221109687

Wang, L., Tao, H., Bowers, B., Brown, R., & Zhang, Y. (2018). When nurse emotional intelligence matters: How transformational leadership influences intent to stay. *Journal of Nursing Management*, *26*(4), 358–365. DOI: 10.1111/jonm.12509 PMID: 29682845

Wang, M., Sun, H., Zhang, J., & Ruan, J. (2018). Prevalence and associated factors of elder abuse in family caregivers of older people with dementia in central china cross-sectional study. *International Journal of Geriatric Psychiatry*, *34*(2), 299–307. DOI: 10.1002/gps.5020 PMID: 30370657

Wang, S., Wang, X., Liu, X., Zhao, C., & Duan, J. (2023). Moderating effects of humanistic care and socioeconomic status on the relationship among pain intensity, psychological factors, and psychological function in adults with cancer pain from a province of china: A cross-sectional study. *Frontiers in Psychiatry*, *14*, 928727. Advance online publication. DOI: 10.3389/fpsyt.2023.928727 PMID: 37082761

Wang, Z., Wang, Z., Liang, X., Zhao, H., Li, X., Zhang, S., & Pang, X. (2021). Spiritual care needs and their associated influencing factors among elderly patients with moderate-to-severe chronic heart failure in china: A cross-sectional study. *Palliative & Supportive Care*, *20*(2), 264–274. DOI: 10.1017/S1478951521001279 PMID: 35574915

Wang, Z., Xie, L., Liang, Z., Fan, J., Fan, L., Deng, J., & Xu, X. (2022). Perceived stress and humanistic care ability among chinese healthcare workers: The chain mediating role of social support and life satisfaction. *Frontiers in Psychology*, *13*, 1029265. Advance online publication. DOI: 10.3389/fpsyg.2022.1029265 PMID: 36438328

Wasir, R., Irawati, S., Makady, A., Postma, M. J., Goettsch, W., Feenstra, T., & Buskens, E. (2019). The implementation of hta in medicine pricing and reimbursement policies in indonesia: Insights from multiple stakeholders. *PLoS One*, *14*(11), e0225626. DOI: 10.1371/journal.pone.0225626 PMID: 31774854

Watkins, L., & Colgate, R. (2016). Improving healthcare for people with intellectual disabilities: The development of an evidence-based teaching programme. *Advances in Mental Health and Intellectual Disabilities*, *10*(6), 333–341. DOI: 10.1108/AMHID-07-2016-0009

Watson, J., Crawley, J., & Kane, D. (2016). Social exclusion, health and hidden homelessness. *Public Health*, *139*, 96–102. DOI: 10.1016/j.puhe.2016.05.017 PMID: 27340041

Wazir, S., & Akbar, H. (2020). Perceived social support and emotional intelligence in university students. *Journal of Professional & Applied Psychology*, *1*(2), 79–85. DOI: 10.52053/jpap.v1i2.22

Weinhold, J., Hunger, C., Bornhäuser, A., Link, L., Rochon, J., Wild, B., & Schweitzer, J. (2013). Family constellation seminars improve psychological functioning in a general population sample: Results of a randomized controlled trial. *Journal of Counseling Psychology*, *60*(4), 601–609. DOI: 10.1037/a0033539 PMID: 23957767

Weissberger, G., Goodman, M., Mosqueda, L., Schoen, J., Nguyen, A., Wilber, K., Gassoumis, Z. D., Nguyen, C. P., & Han, S. (2019). Elder abuse characteristics based on calls to the national center on elder abuse resource line. *Journal of Applied Gerontology, 39*(10), 1078–1087. DOI: 10.1177/0733464819865685 PMID: 31364442

Welford, E. (2014). Giving the dead their rightful place. *Transactional Analysis Journal, 44*(4), 320–333. DOI: 10.1177/0362153714559920

Wenham, J., Best, M., & Ac, D. (2021). Systematic review of medical education on spirituality. *Internal Medicine Journal, 51*(11), 1781–1790. DOI: 10.1111/imj.15421 PMID: 34142417

Werner, D., Thuman, C., Maxwell, J., Pearson, A., & Cary, F. (1993). *Where there is no doctor: A village health care handbook for Africa*. Macmillan.

West, A., Cawley, C., Crow, E., Stoner, A., Fadel, N., Ford-Scales, K., & Cheng, N. (2021). The impact of an educational program on medical students' knowledge and awareness of elder abuse. *Journal of Medical Education and Curricular Development, 8*, 23821205211016487. Advance online publication. DOI: 10.1177/23821205211016487 PMID: 34212112

Westerbeek, L., Bruijn, G., Weert, H., Abu-Hanna, A., Medlock, S., & Weert, J. (2022). General practitioners' needs and wishes for clinical decision support systems: A focus group study. *International Journal of Medical Informatics, 168*, 104901. DOI: 10.1016/j.ijmedinf.2022.104901 PMID: 36279654

WHO. (2021). Quality of treatment in LMICs.

Winther, M. (n.d.). Spirit and psyche – complementary paradigms. https://www.academia.edu/13052952/Spirit_and_Psyche_Complementary_Paradigms

Wittenberg-Lyles, E., Goldsmith, J., Demiris, G., Oliver, D., & Stone, J. (2012). The impact of family communication patterns on hospice family caregivers. *Journal of Hospice and Palliative Nursing : JHPN : the Official Journal of the Hospice and Palliative Nurses Association, 14*(1), 25–33. DOI: 10.1097/NJH.0b013e318233114b PMID: 22308097

Woods, S., Beaver, K., & Luker, K. (2000). Users' views of palliative care services: Ethical implications. *Nursing Ethics, 7*(4), 314–326. DOI: 10.1177/096973300000700405 PMID: 11221408

World Health Organization. (2000). *Measuring overall health system performance for 191 countries* (GPE Discussion Paper No. 30). https://www.who.int/healthinfo/paper30.pdf

World Health Organization. (2011). Role of the occupational health nurse in the workplace. https://www.who.int/occupational_health/regions/en/oeheurnursing.pdf?ua=1

World Health Organization. (2021). *Global expenditure on health: Public spending on the rise?*https://www.who.int/publications/i/item/9789240041219

World Health Organization. (2023, September 16). *Noncommunicable diseases.* https://www.who.int/news-room/fact-sheets/detail/noncommunicable-diseases

World Health Organization. (n.d.). *Cancer.* Retrieved November 12, 2024, from https://www.who.int/health-topics/cancer#tab=tab_1

World Health Organization. (n.d.). Disease burden, 2000–2021: *Global health estimates: Leading causes of DALYs.* https://www.who.int/data/gho/data/themes/mortality-and-global-health-estimates/global-health-estimates-leading-causes-of-dalys

World Health Organization. (n.d.). Enhancing the role of community health nursing for universal health coverage.

World Health Organization. (n.d.). *Infectious diseases.* https://www.emro.who.int/health-topics/infectious-diseases/index.html

World Health Organization. (n.d.). *Promoting cancer early diagnosis.* Retrieved November 9, 2024, from https://www.who.int/activities/promoting-cancer-early-diagnosis

Wu, F., Song, Z., Wen, Z., & Xiao, Y. (2017). Medical humanities play an important role in improving the doctor-patient relationship. *Bioscience Trends, 11*(2), 134–137. DOI: 10.5582/bst.2017.01087 PMID: 28458332

Wye, L., Brangan, E., Cameron, A. M., Gabbay, J., Klein, J. H., & Pope, C. (2015). Evidence based policy making and the 'art' of commissioning – how english health-care commissioners access and use information and academic research in 'real life' decision-making: An empirical qualitative study. *BMC Health Services Research, 15*(1), 430. Advance online publication. DOI: 10.1186/s12913-015-1091-x PMID: 26416368

Xie, Z., Liu, K., Or, C., Chen, J., Yan, M., & Wang, H. (2020). An examination of the socio-demographic correlates of patient adherence to self-management behaviors and the mediating roles of health attitudes and self-efficacy among patients with coexisting type 2 diabetes and hypertension. *BMC Public Health, 20*(1), 1227. DOI: 10.1186/s12889-020-09274-4 PMID: 32787809

Xu, M., Choi, J., Capasso, A., & DiClemente, R. (2024). Improving hpv vaccination uptake among adolescents in low resource settings: Sociocultural and socioeconomic barriers and facilitators. *Adolescent Health, Medicine and Therapeutics*, *15*, 73–82. DOI: 10.2147/AHMT.S394119 PMID: 39100520

Xu, Q., Norstrand, J., & Du, Y. (2015). Effects of living alone on social capital and health among older adults in China. *International Journal of Aging & Human Development*, *82*(1), 30–53. DOI: 10.1177/0091415015624419 PMID: 26746661

Xu, T., Wang, Y., Wang, R., Lamb, K., Ren, D., Gui-zhi, D., & Yue, P. (2020). Predictors of caring ability and its dimensions among nurses in china: A cross-sectional study. *Scandinavian Journal of Caring Sciences*, *35*(4), 1226–1239. DOI: 10.1111/scs.12941 PMID: 33615516

Yan, E., Ng, H., Sun, R., Lai, D., Cheng, S., Lou, V., & Fong, D. (2022). Resilience as a protective factor against elder abuse by family caregivers: Findings from a cross-sectional study in Hong Kong. *Journal of Adult Protection*, *24*(5/6), 255–269. DOI: 10.1108/JAP-06-2022-0012

Yeager, V. A., Wisniewski, J., Chapple-McGruder, T., Castrucci, B. C., & Gould, E. (2018, June 21). Public Health Workforce Self-Identified Training Needs by Jurisdiction and Job Type. Journal of Public Health Management and Practice. Lippincott Williams & Wilkins. Retrieved January 2025, from DOI: 10.1097/PHH.0000000000000830

Yeh, C. H. (2001). Religious beliefs and practices of Taiwanese parents of pediatric patients with cancer. *Cancer Nursing*, *24*(6), 476–482. https://journals.lww.com/cancernursingonline/abstract/2001/12000/religious_beliefs_and_practices_of_taiwanese.9.aspx. DOI: 10.1097/00002820-200112000-00009 PMID: 11762510

Yildirim, N., Kantek, F., & Yilmaz, F. (2021). Relationships between leadership orientations and emotional intelligence in nursing students. *Perspectives in Psychiatric Care*, *58*(3), 903–909. DOI: 10.1111/ppc.12871 PMID: 34056722

Young, C., Tong, A., Gunasekera, H., Sherriff, S., Kalucy, D., Fernando, P., & Craig, J. (2016). Health professional and community perspectives on reducing barriers to accessing specialist health care in metropolitan aboriginal communities: A semi-structured interview study. *Journal of Paediatrics and Child Health*, *53*(3), 277–282. DOI: 10.1111/jpc.13374 PMID: 27748557

Yuan, H., Wang, X., Gao, L., Wang, T., Qin, Z., Fang, D., & Gao, Y. (2023). Progress towards the sustainable development goals has been slowed by indirect effects of the covid-19 pandemic. *Communications Earth & Environment*, *4*(1), 184. Advance online publication. DOI: 10.1038/s43247-023-00846-x

Yu, C., Liu, Z. Q., Zhao, M., Liu, Y., Zhang, Y., Lin, A., Sang, X., & Wan, H. (2023). The mediating role of emotion management, self-efficacy and emotional intelligence in clinical nurses related to negative psychology and burnout. *Psychology Research and Behavior Management, 16*, 3333–3345. DOI: 10.2147/PRBM.S417729 PMID: 37650114

Yu, W., Jia, C., Sun, S., Liu, P., Ouyang, L., & Ji-ze, H. (2021). The reciprocal associations between caregiver burden, and mental health in primary caregivers of cancer patients: A longitudinal study. *Psycho-Oncology, 30*(6), 892–900. DOI: 10.1002/pon.5667 PMID: 33686757

Zahedi, F., Kadivar, M., Mojen, L., Asadabadi, M., Tajalli, S., Ilkhani, M., & Larijani, B. (2022). The ethical challenges of palliative care from the perspectives of pediatricians: A qualitative study in Iran. *Frontiers in Pediatrics, 10*, 928476. Advance online publication. DOI: 10.3389/fped.2022.928476 PMID: 36105856

Zaidi, W. H., Mohydin, M., Ahmad, S. A., Asghar, M., Hashmi, N., Umair, M., & Butt, A. N. (2021). Evaluation of patient and family-centered care; a survey of neonatal and paediatric intensive care units. *Pakistan Journal of Medical & Health Sciences, 15*(11), 2882–2885. DOI: 10.53350/pjmhs2115112882

Zakus, J. D. L., & Lysack, C. L. (1998). Revisiting community participation. *Health Policy and Planning, 13*(1), 1–12. DOI: 10.1093/heapol/13.1.1 PMID: 10178181

Zhang, Y. (2022). Application research of humanistic care and situational integration in nursing of schizophrenia in recovery period. Contrast Media & Molecular Imaging, 2022(1). DOI: 10.1155/2022/4705107

Zhang, J., & Tian, Y. (2024). Final-year nursing students' perceptions of humanistic education in nursing: A cross-sectional descriptive study. *BMC Medical Education, 24*(1), 392. Advance online publication. DOI: 10.1186/s12909-024-05377-3 PMID: 38594668

Zhao, S., Luk, T., Guo, N., Wang, M., Lai, A., Wong, B., Fong, D. Y. T., Chan, S. S. C., & Lam, T. (2021). Association of mobile instant messaging chat group participation with family functioning and well-being: Population-based cross-sectional study. *Journal of Medical Internet Research, 23*(3), e18876. DOI: 10.2196/18876 PMID: 33720034

Zhao, Z., Cai, M., Connor, T., Chung, M., & Liu, J. (2020). Metacoupled tourism and wildlife translocations affect synergies and trade-offs among sustainable development goals across spillover systems. *Sustainability (Basel), 12*(18), 7677. DOI: 10.3390/su12187677

Zhong, X., Liu, X., & Sheng, Y. (2021). The effect of the humanistic care teaching model on nurse patient conflict and nurse turnover intention in a pediatric outpatient department: Results of a randomized trial. *Translational Pediatrics*, *10*(8), 2016–2023. DOI: 10.21037/tp-21-214 PMID: 34584871

Zhou, P., Bundorf, M., Chang, J., Huang, J., & Xue, D. (2011). Organizational culture and its relationship with hospital performance in public hospitals in china. *Health Services Research*, *46*(6pt2), 2139–2160. DOI: 10.1111/j.1475-6773.2011.01336.x PMID: 22092228

Zhu, Y., Liu, G., Shen, Y., Wang, J., Lu, M., & Wang, J. (2022). Humanistic nursing care for patients in low-resourced clinical settings from students' perspectives: A participatory qualitative study. *International Journal of Environmental Research and Public Health*, *19*(19), 12656. DOI: 10.3390/ijerph191912656 PMID: 36231956

Zikusooka, M., Elci, Ö., & Özdemir, H. (2021). Job satisfaction among syrian healthcare workers in refugee health centres. *Human Resources for Health*, *19*(1), 1. DOI: 10.1186/s12960-021-00685-x PMID: 34775958

Zimmerman, B. J., & Kitsantas, A. (1996). Self-regulated learning of a motoric skill: The role of goal setting and self-monitoring. *Journal of Applied Sport Psychology*, *8*(1), 60–75. DOI: 10.1080/10413209608406308

About the Contributors

Minhaj A. Qidwai graduated from Dow Medical College-Karachi-Pakistan in 1984. He holds MPH from University of Oklahoma, MBA from University of Hawaii-USA; and Certification in Management Consulting from Canada. Prof. Dr. Qidwai has more than four decades of International Experience in Health Management, Marketing, Research, Human Capacity Building and Academics; in Pakistan, Middle East, and North America. In past, he has collaborated with organizations like CIDA, UNICEF, WHO, OPM, Canadian Cancer Association, Mississauga Board of Trade, and Canada Pakistan Business Council. Prof. Dr. Qidwai was one of the lead persons in establishing the concept of "Ethics Committees" in Research and Quality Circles in Healthcare at Aga Khan University Hospital in Pakistan. He is the pioneer for initiating MBA in Health Management in Pakistan at Institute of Business Management; Health Systems Improvement program at College of Physicians and Surgeons Pakistan and Institute of Business Administration. He is also the founder and former CEO of Sindh Healthcare Commission. Prof. Dr. Qidwai has been associated with academia and research in the areas of Public Health, Pharma Industry, Healthcare Systems Management and Quality Improvement. Currently, he is the Dean of Health and Medical Sciences at Al-Kawthar University Karachi in Pakistan; Faculty Member at American Institute for Healthcare Quality; and CEO of Unet Consultants-Pakistan/Canada. Prof. Dr. Qidwai has been involved in developing academic programs, research, professional and personal development in corporate and healthcare sector. His current focus is mainly on mental health, digital health, health management, and offering mentorship for professional development. He is a reviewer for Higher Education Commission Research Grants and Judge for National Idea Bank. He is passionate for mentoring youth through his Center for Health Innovation and Transformation, nurturing their ideas and startups into an accelerator phase and reality. Prof. Dr. Qidwai is an Honorary Faculty Member at the American Institute of Healthcare Quality, a Member of Population Association of Pakistan, Trustee of SAMEO-UK Based Charity for Healthcare and Director-Pakistan Bridge

Federation. Dr. Qidwai holds dual citizenship of Canada and Pakistan. He is also the pioneer for several philosophies like that of R.E.S.T. (Research, Education, Systems and Training) for curriculum development; G.R.A.S.P. (Governance, Research, Accountability, Sustainability and Profit) Model for Organizational governance; the philosophy of 5Ss' (Self, Society, State, Systems and Spirituality) for Human Wellness Management; and ZERO Error in mental health etc.. Prof. Dr. Qidwai holds a dual citizenship of Canada and Pakistan. He is also an author of Book "A to Z of Healthcare Quality"- Based on his philosophy of 5Ss' (Self, Society, State, Systems and Spirituality) one book published by USA based IGI Global Publications, with title: Intersection of Artificial Intelligence, Human Rights and Health and the 2nd book based on the 5Ss philosophy-Enhancing Client, Family and Community Health is under publication by USA based IGI Global Publication. A 3rd book on the same philosophy titled "Impact of 5Ss on Organizational Culture and the Wellbeing of Healthcare Providers" is being authored.

***

Fozia Asif MBBS, MBA, MHQS(Harvard) Dr. Fozia Asif is a highly accomplished healthcare leader with over two decades of experience, holding an MBBS, an MBA in Healthcare Management, and a Master's in Healthcare Quality and Patient Safety from Harvard University. Her career is distinguished by her commitment to elevating healthcare systems through strategic leadership in patient safety, quality improvement, and risk management. As the Senior Manager at the Center for Patient Safety at Aga Khan University, Dr. Asif leads pivotal initiatives to enhance healthcare quality, drive accreditation processes, and conduct critical root cause analyses. She has successfully guided hospitals in implementing the Joint Commission International Accreditation (JCIA) standards and spearheaded quality improvement projects across multiple healthcare settings. Dr. Asif's contributions extend internationally, where she collaborates with the World Health Organization and participates in forums influencing healthcare policy. As a prolific researcher, her work centers on identifying adverse events in low-resource environments, devising strategies to mitigate patient harm, and fostering

Saurabh Chandra is an accomplished legal scholar and currently serves as an Associate Professor & Assistant Dean at the School of Law, Bennett University, India. With a robust academic foundation, he earned his Bachelor of Arts and Bachelor of Laws (B.A. LL.B.) from the prestigious Aligarh Muslim University (A.M.U.). He further specialized in Business Laws, completing his Master of Laws (LL.M.) at the renowned National Law School of India University (NLSIU), Bangalore. Dr. Chandra's academic journey culminated in a Doctorate in Law (Ph.D.) from the esteemed National Law University (NLU) Delhi. In addition to his impressive legal education from some of India's most prestigious institutions, Dr. Saurabh Chandra also holds a master's degree in Management with specialization in Human Resources in Management and another in Journalism and Mass Communication. With 16 years of teaching experience, he has established himself as an expert in Business and Corporate Laws, with numerous publications to his credit. Dr. Saurabh Chandra is a distinguished expert in Business and Corporate Laws, with a profound understanding of the intricate legal frameworks that govern the business world. His expertise is complemented by a robust portfolio of scholarly publications, which underscores his commitment to advancing knowledge in his field. Throughout his career, Dr. Chandra has consistently produced high-impact research that addresses critical issues in Business and Corporate Law. His publications are widely recognized for their depth of analysis, innovative perspectives, and practical relevance. He has contributed extensively to leading journals, where his work has often set new standards for legal scholarship. His publications not only reflect his scholarly rigor but also his dedication to addressing contemporary challenges faced by businesses and policymakers. By bridging the gap between theoretical insights and real-world applications, Dr. Chandra's work serves as a valuable resource for academics, legal practitioners, and industry professionals alike. Dr. Chandra brings a wealth of experience in Academic Administration, having successfully held various key administrative positions. His diverse qualifications and extensive experience make him a distinguished figure in the academic and legal communities.

Anindita Das is an esteemed Associate Professor and the Head of the Department of Physical Education Pedagogy at Lakshmibai National Institute of Physical Education (LNIPE), Gwalior. With a prolific career, Dr. Das has authored numerous research papers, patents, and books, contributing significantly to the field of physical education. Her work emphasizes innovative teaching methodologies and educational strategies, aimed at fostering excellence in physical education pedagogy. Renowned for her dedication to advancing knowledge and practice in sports education, Dr. Das continues to inspire students and professionals through her leadership, research, and unwavering commitment to academic excellence.

Mohammad Kabir Gawhari, MD I MBA I MSc Health Policy & Management French Medical Institute for Mothers and Children- FMIC Kabul, Kabul Province, Afghanistan Dr Mohammad Kabir Gawhari, French Medical Institute for Mothers and Children (FMIC). FMIC Compound, Behind Kabul Medical University Kabul, Kabul 1001, AF

Saleema Gulzar working as an Associate Professor and Director of Research & Innovation at the Aga Khan University School of Nursing and Midwifery and brings 30 years of experience. She is a well-recognised public health nurse with extensive experience across the South Asian region. In addition, she is serving on an elected board of directors and Joint Secretary at the eHealth Association of Pakistan. She did her PhD at the University of Sydney, Australia, examining adolescents' physical activity levels through a mixed-method approach. She is the first in Pakistan to introduce a comprehensive school health promotion program in Pakistan in which her unique contribution was to develop a school health curriculum framework for the schools till the approval of policy for the position of School Nurse at Aga Khan Education Services, Pakistan. Recently she conducted a research project initiating teleconsultation in the public-school setting, which is sustainable in the local context. She is also an active researcher and author of over 86 publications, including peer-reviewed papers and book chapters, many of which showcase her knowledge and research on Digital Health in various regions of Pakistan, spanning from underdeveloped areas such as Gilgit, Chitral and rural areas of Karachi to Semi-urban areas of Karachi. Her work has contributed to the implementation of the Digital Health project in the Northern Areas of Pakistan. She is known for her exemplary teaching practice and was awarded a scholarship for her research and teaching.

Tiago Horta Reis da Silva is a Lecturer in Nursing Education (AEP) at King's College London, with a range of qualifications including BSc in Nursing, BSc in Traditional Chinese Medicine, MSc in Emotional Intelligence, Counselling and NLP, a Master of Business Administration, and MSc in Traditional Chinese Medicine. He has experience in other Higher Education Institutions and NHS and is a member of the Adult Nursing department, assisting with the running, development, and administration of BSc and MSc programmes. He also assists with teaching other modules' content and assists with interviews and assessment matters for other courses. Tiago is a Senior Fellow in Higher Education, a Fellow of the Royal Society of Medicine, and a Fellow for Faculty Nursing and Midwifery at the Royal College of Southern Ireland.

Vishal Jain is presently working as Professor at Department of Computer Science and Engineering, Sharda School of Engineering and Technology, Sharda University, Greater Noida, U. P., India. Before that, he has worked for several years as an Associate Professor at Bharati Vidyapeeth's Institute of Computer Applications and Management (BVICAM), New Delhi. He has more than 16 years of experience in the academics. He obtained Ph.D (CSE), M.Tech (CSE), MBA (HR), MCA, MCP and CCNA. He is life member of CSI, ISTE and senior member of IEEE. His research areas include information retrieval, semantic web, ontology engineering, data mining, ad hoc networks, and sensor networks. Email(Work): vishal.jain@sharda.ac.in, Personal Email: drvishaljain83@gmail.com

Debajit Karmakar is a dedicated Ph.D. scholar in Physical Education Pedagogy at Lakshmibai National Institute of Physical Education (LNIPE), Gwalior. An accomplished researcher, Mr. Karmakar has authored numerous research papers, patents, and books, contributing significantly to sports education and physical fitness. His work focuses on advancing training methodologies and innovative approaches in physical education, aligning both theory and practice. He brings his passion for sports into his academic pursuits, making impactful contributions to sports science and education. Mr. Karmakar's achievements mark him as a promising figure in physical education and sports science.

Rozina Karmaliani is an Associate Director for the Brain & Mind Institute, overseeing the South and Central Asia region and also Professor at School of Nursing and Midwifery and Community Health Sciences Department at AKU She is the first Pakistani to obtain a Ph.D. in Nursing in 200 from the University of Minnesota. Alongside, she received various national and international research grants and published over 80 peer reviewed articles. Dr Karmaliani's areas of research include women, child and adolescent health, with a special focus on the prevention of gender-based violence, promoting mental health and preventing suicides from a health systems perspective. Currently, she is also developing a community care model for ageing gracefully. She was recognized as one of WHO's Global 100 Nurse and Midwife Leaders in 2020 and received the Women Leaders Award from the Hum Television Network in 2022. Most recently, she became the first nurse from Pakistan and the region to be inducted into the American Academy of Nursing, a prestigious honour as a Fellow of the Academy.

Awesh Khati is a dedicated Ph.D. scholar specializing in Physical Education Pedagogy at the Lakshmibai National Institute of Physical Education (LNIPE), Gwalior. With a strong academic foundation and passion for advancing physical education, he has contributed several research papers in the field. In addition to his scholarly pursuits, Mr. Khati is an accomplished football player, blending theoretical knowledge with practical expertise. His work reflects a commitment to enhancing sports education and promoting holistic physical development, making him a promising figure in the domain of physical education and sports science.

Arfa Masihuddin is the founder of Rufayda - Care for Healthcare, a wellness organization currently in its ideation phase, and committed to supporting healthcare providers worldwide. Rufayda offers hospital management consultancy, mental health counseling, and personal and professional development workshops for healthcare providers. The organization is dedicated to enhancing the organizational efficiency and culture of healthcare institutions, promoting mental well-being, improving quality of life for healthcare providers, and reducing vocational burnout. She is currently working as a Senior Lecturer in the Health and Hospital Management Department at the Institute of Business Management. She is a graduate of Aga Khan University's Master of Health Policy and Management program, where she was awarded the Global Student Award for Excellence in Impact & Innovation, along with the Dolat Noorali Expendable Scholarship. With an MBBS from Ziauddin University, Dr. Masihuddin is passionate about reshaping health systems through a humanistic and patient-centered approach, utilizing innovative tools to drive positive change. In addition to her work in healthcare, Dr. Masihuddin enjoys her side-hustle at Walking Thoughts, an online literary house providing services such as ERAS and university personal statement consultancy, English speaking and writing courses, and IELTS and OET coaching. Her multifaceted career reflects her dedication to both healthcare improvement and educational advancement.

Ahsana Nazish has over 10 years of experience in managing public health projects/ programs. She has been involved in teaching graduate and undergraduate students at one of the most reputed institutions in Pakistan. Currently, she is working as the project director at Pakistan Kidney and Liver Institute and Research Center

Ajay K. Singh is working as an Associate Professor (Research) in the Department of Humanities and Social Science, Graphic Era (Deemed to be University) Dehradun. He has worked as Assistant Professor (Economics) in the School of Liberal Arts & Management, DIT University Dehradun for 6 years. He did Post-Doctorate Research with EDI of India, Ahmedabad, Gujarat (India). He received MPhil (Economics) from DAVV Indore (India), and PhD (Economics) from IIT Indore (India. He has published several research papers in the diversified area such as climate change, agricultural productivity, assessment of food security; estimation of GFSI, development of environmental sustainability index (ESI) and its association with socio-economic indicators; measurement and determinants of entrepreneurship ecosystem, and dimension of sustainable development and its interlinkages with economic development.

Bhupinder Singh working as Professor at Sharda University, India. Also, Honorary Professor in University of South Wales UK and Santo Tomas University Tunja, Colombia. His areas of publications as Smart Healthcare, Medicines, fuzzy logics, artificial intelligence, robotics, machine learning, deep learning, federated learning, IoT, PV Glasses, metaverse and many more. He has 3 books, 139 paper publications, 163 paper presentations in international/national conferences and seminars, participated in more than 40 workshops/FDP's/QIP's, 25 courses from international universities of repute, organized more than 59 events with international and national academicians and industry people's, editor-in-chief and co-editor in journals, developed new courses. He has given talks at international universities, resource person in international conferences such as in Nanyang Technological University Singapore, Tashkent State University of Law Uzbekistan; KIMEP University Kazakhstan, All'ah meh Tabatabi University Iran, the Iranian Association of International Criminal law, Iran and Hague Center for International Law and Investment, The Netherlands, Northumbria University Newcastle UK,

R. Vallipriya has been working in the Department of Physical Sciences at the Institute of Education (Affiliated to Tamilnadu Teacher Education University) as an Assistant Professor. With a wealth of experience, Mrs. R.Vallipriya has accumulated 12 years of extensive teaching. Her scholarly contributions include publishing 7 papers, with 1 peer review in various UGC-CARE, SCOPUS, and peer-reviewed journals.

S. Srinivasan has been working in the Department of Humanities and Social Sciences at Graphic Era (Deemed to be University) as an Assistant Professor. With a wealth of experience, Mr. Srinivasan has accumulated 14 years of extensive teaching and field-level expertise. Prior to his current role, he served in the Ministry of Health and Family Welfare, Government of India, and gained valuable experience. He also contributed as a Guest Faculty at the university level and served for nearly 2 years in the State Government Public Works Department as a Mobilization Training Specialist. In the past year, Mr. S. Srinivasan has enriched his experience by actively participating in a tuberculosis project funded by GFATM and USAID, providing a platform for further exploration of his research and practical field-based knowledge. His scholarly contributions include publishing 30 papers, with 18 more under peer review in various UGC-CARE, SCOPUS, and peer-reviewed journals.

Samina Vertejee is a Public Health Practitioner serving the communities since 1987. She holds a Master in Health Management degree from the University of Wollongong, Australia and is also currently enrolled in PhD (Education) at AeU Malaysia. Over the past three decades, she worked as an educator, and service provider, especially at the grassroots level and a researcher. Hence, her long service is self-explanatory of her commitment to the broader umbrella of public health nursing practice. Under these three pillars, her areas of interest in public health practice include ageing and health and addiction rehabilitation/substance use disorders. For her work in community, she was also an award recipient and was recognized as one of WHO's Global 100 Nurse and Midwife Leaders in 2020 under the category of "Community Heroes". Ms Vertejee also holds voluntary positions in various NGOs related to ageing and health. She was greatly involved in the passing of the "Sind Senior Citizen Welfare Act 2014". The Provincial Council was formulated under this Act and because of her work in ageing, she has also been a member of the Sind Senior Citizen Welfare Council since June 2017-2024.

Index

F

G

H

I

L

M

N

O

P

Q

R

T

W

www.ingramcontent.com/pod-product-compliance
Lightning Source LLC
LaVergne TN
LVHW081319300926
849161LV00008B/1809